STUDYING TEACHING

STUDYING TEACHING

SECOND EDITION

edited by
JAMES RATHS
University of Maryland

JOHN R. PANCELLA
Supervisor of Science
Montgomery County, Maryland

JAMES S. VAN NESS
University of Maryland

PRENTICE-HALL, INC., Englewood Cliffs, N.J.

To LOUIS E. RATHS

Any teacher who chooses to make a difference will make one.—Harold Carter

C-13-858886-4

P-13-858878-3

Library of Congress Catalog Card Number 70-123086

Current Printing (last number):

10 9 8 7 6 5 4 3 2 1

Printed in the United States of America

PRENTICE-HALL INTERNATIONAL, INC., *London*
PRENTICE-HALL OF AUSTRALIA, PTY., LTD., *Sydney*
PRENTICE-HALL OF CANADA, LTD., *Toronto*
PRENTICE-HALL OF INDIA PRIVATE LIMITED, *New Delhi*
PRENTICE-HALL OF JAPAN, INC., *Tokyo*

INTRODUCTION

Methods courses in education have, for many years, been under serious attack both from within institutions of higher learning and from the outside —the lay public, the profession, and various councils, associations, or groups organized for the betterment of American education.

The arguments against methods courses do have some strong points on their side. First, it is indeed true that there are very few generalizations about teaching that have solid empirical support. The relationships between variables in the teaching-learning act are neither highly regular nor completely predictable. While this is true of most areas of study dealing with the human element, it seems especially true of education. Certain techniques may prove effective one day, ineffective the next. At times efforts on a teacher's part can help one-half the class attain the lesson's objectives, but actually hinder the progress of the other half. This complexity is perhaps the most frustrating aspect of teaching. Secondly, many students find methods courses impractical. Sometimes they summarize this feeling by stating that the courses are too theoretical. The sorry fact, which in a sense reflects the first objection, is that there is far too little theory in education. Theory, in part, describes relationships between variables. As noted above, all too few relationships have been identified and tested. Thus, methods courses become impractical when, instead of dealing with relationships between variables supported by data, they proceed with a problems approach leading to solutions on an *ad hoc* basis, rather than in terms of principles of teaching or learning.

If all of the above is in fact true, what is a proper role for methods courses today? Granting the above arguments, the editors of this book of readings make two assumptions about the teaching process. First, we are assuming that the better teachers in our schools are the ones who are rational about the decisions they make in the teaching act. They consider alternatives, weigh possible outcomes, and evaluate their decisions by collecting relevant evidence. From this assumption it follows that methods courses could be most effective in helping prospective teachers identify relevant variables within the teaching-learning process to which they may pay particular attention. In this way, teachers can learn ways to "monitor" their own teaching. Methods courses with this thrust will give students the ability to assess for themselves the kind of job they are doing in the teaching role. Lawrence Kubie suggests of psychiatry students that they must not limit their concern to merely observing themselves in relationship to their subjects. They must use their observations as a basis for introspection. "I always know that a young man has started the long road to becoming a psychiatrist," Kubie states, "when in the presence of a group of his peers he begins to say publicly and without defensiveness and without shame, 'What I said was not so bad, but why did I have to say it that way' or even, 'The way I said it was not so bad, but why did I have to look like that.' Something like this must happen in the process of learning how to become an educator."[1]

Taking its cue from Kubie, this book proposes some ways of helping teachers raise their level of awareness in the teaching act so as to improve their ability to review rationally the decisions they have made and the alternatives they have considered. In short, it is the editors' view that a proper role of methods courses is that of training education students in the various ways by which they may assess their own teaching.

A second assumption is that although there are few generalizations about teaching that are firmly supported by evidence, there are practices and techniques current in teaching that have been deemed successful, if not on factual grounds, at least by the impressions of experience. Are these impressions to be ignored? We think not. A second role of methods courses may be to present techniques and procedures as working hypotheses. The alternatives suggested by experienced teachers and education professors may enlarge the number of choices that beginning teachers may consider and test. Thus, it is appropriate for a methods course to suggest various approaches to planning, testing, carrying out a discussion, etc., that student teachers may ultimately wish to try and to test in their own teaching.

In short, then, this book will attempt to present readings that suggest various methods by which teaching can be examined and described and to offer descriptions of procedures that may serve as a starting point for beginning teachers.

Henry Adams once said, "Teachers affect eternity; they never know

[1] Lawrence S. Kubie, "Research on Protecting Preconscious Functions in Education." Address to the A.S.C.D. Research Institute, Washington, D. C., April, 1960.

where their influence will end." It is our belief that this is true and that the role of the teacher is increasingly important in the world today. It is our fond hope that students using this text will derive greater satisfactions from their teaching as a result of considering the skills and concepts with which it is concerned.

• • •

The editors are greatly indebted to the authors and publishers of the articles which have been included in this book of readings. We are grateful for their generosity in so kindly permitting us to use their contributions.

J.R.
J.R.P.
J.S.V.N.

INTRODUCTION TO THE SECOND EDITION

We are extremely grateful for the comments we have received from colleagues, students, and reviewers concerning the first edition of this text. We have attempted to incorporate many of their ideas into this present edition. While the book's format remains essentially the same, several articles have been added and others deleted to update the materials found in this collection. We hope the changes are improvements.

Again we are greatly indebted to the authors and publishers of the articles which have been included in this book. Also, we would like to acknowledge the efforts of Mrs. Helen Harris, Prentice-Hall, Inc., in working on the manuscript.

College Park, Md.
1970

J.R.
J.R.P.
J.S.V.N.

CONTENTS

CHAPTER SIX

TEACHING FOR THINKING AND VALUING 257

CHAPTER SEVEN

MEETING THE EMOTIONAL NEEDS OF CHILDREN 317

CHAPTER EIGHT

DISCIPLINE 367

WHAT IS TEACHING?

CHAPTER ONE

If we were told that someone was teaching in the room next door, what images would we have of his likely behavior? Is he standing or sitting? Listening or speaking? Asking questions or answering them? Of course, the teaching behavior would vary. As a matter of fact, he may not even be physically present in the room next door and yet consider himself teaching.

The difficulty of defining "teaching" may lead to feelings of inadequacy on the part of some teachers. If a teacher cannot clearly define his task, how can he really feel effective while performing it? The purpose of this section is to suggest ways of identifying teaching behaviors. While some of the selections have titles suggesting that "good" teaching is being compared with "poor" teaching, in a sense the authors are describing teaching acts that may be done well or poorly. It is important to define the acts themselves first before attempting to judge the quality of the performance of those acts. One framework for examining teacher behavior in terms of acts has been advanced by Thomas F. Green.[1] Green suggests that acts of teaching may be considered as those that a teacher carries out in congruence to certain professional rules or principles. Teacher responses, on the other hand, may be seen as rather typical human responses to outside stimuli, *e.g.* fatigue, frustration, or hunger, and so on. Thus, a teaching act is a rational deed performed in accordance with professional principles. One would assume that while other honest educators might disagree upon the efficacy of a given act, on the whole, a teacher would be proud of the acts he has performed during the day. On the other hand, teacher responses are examples of behavior for which a teacher might be embarassed

[1] Thomas F. Green, "Teaching, Acting, and Behaving," *Harvard Educational Review,* XXXIV, No. 4 (1964) 507–9.

—a sharp retort in response to the tenth identical question, an angry glance at a student who delays his lunch hour, and so on. If this framework is adopted, the answer to the question "What is teaching?" may consist of a description of those acts teachers demonstrate that reflect their commitments to a particular philosophy of education. The articles in this section advance alternative behaviors that might be considered as acts. From among the behaviors described here, and from others observed in schools or discussed in other readings, teachers must identify the acts that reflect their own values and demonstrate them in the classrooms.

1. WHAT IS A GOOD TEACHER?

LOUIS E. RATHS

When speaking about a *good teacher* we are probably thinking of many things—the teacher as a person, what he does in the classroom, how he interacts with other members of the faculty. We may also be thinking of him as a representative of the school in the community. We may be thinking of his background of experience and training. This article will concentrate on the most essential things which are expected of all good teachers as they work with children in the classroom.

What do we postulate as the functions of good teaching? This conception of good teaching will be greatly influenced by the culture to which we have been exposed and which we prize; good teaching depends upon one's philosophy of education and upon changing conceptions of what constitutes good teaching. No one pattern of good teaching exists. There are many different patterns—all of which are good.

Writings, conferences, and researches of the past fifty years constitute a base for making some generalized proposals about the functions of teaching, proposals unbiased in that they do not imply goodness or badness of teaching. Judgment of the quality of teaching will follow the collection of data which bear upon these functions. Assuming the following twelve functions to be of great importance in almost every teaching day, we would then want to observe teaching with these twelve points in mind. Our discussions with teachers and those responsible for teacher education programs would revolve around these twelve points. Teachers themselves would be looking at their own work in terms of these same points.

It would be unfortunate if teachers were to be rated by some only in these terms. If these are the deepest

Louis E. Raths, "What Is a Good Teacher?" Childhood Education, XL, No. 9 (May 1964), 451–56. Reprinted by permission of the Association for Childhood Education International, 3615 Wisconsin Avenue, N. W., Washington, D. C., and of the author.

areas of concern the data we collect should be used as a basis for improvement. Teachers themselves will probably want help in one or more of the functions. The points are proposed, not as a rating scale, but as a broad framework for teachers to discover more about themselves in relation to the functions of teaching.

1. Explaining, informing, showing how
2. Initiating, directing, administering
3. Unifying the group
4. Giving security
5. Clarifying attitudes, beliefs, problems
6. Diagnosing learning problems
7. Making curriculum materials
8. Evaluating, recording, reporting
9. Enriching community activities
10. Organizing and arranging classroom
11. Participating in school activities
12. Participating in professional and civic life

Explaining, Informing, Showing How

1. The good teacher is expected to be well informed in the areas in which he teaches. He is expected to be able to communicate information needed for background, enrichment, and motivation, and on many occasions to *explain* relationships to children. The very word "explain" indicates that it isn't a fact to be explained; it is helping children to understand causal relationships; correlations; dependency relations; relationships of opposites, of larger and smaller, of heavier and lighter. In *showing how*, requirements vary for different age and grade levels. For instance, the teacher may be showing children how to put on their boots and jackets or how to mix certain colors. He may be showing them how to handle the number system, how to analyze propaganda, how to draw maps, how to use a book, and how to interview. In addition to clearness and comprehensiveness of the presentation, we expect some effort in getting the children ready for the demonstration. Most important of all, if the object is to show how, we expect the teacher to allow time in the curriculum for the children to practice until they have a certain grasp of the processes—enough so that they can do it at a level of quality which suits the purpose for the grade level at which it is being done. We expect all good teachers to do well at the task of informing, explaining, and showing how.

Initiating, Directing, Administering

2. One function of teaching is largely concerned with initiating, organizing, directing, and making many decisions. From the time he begins the day until he goes home at night the teacher faces decisions which might range from a thoughtful deliberation in making changes in a teaching schedule to a quick decision on sending an ailing child to the nurse's office, or what to do in the absence of a special teacher. His handling of the many unusual situations which turn up in the course of a week is indicative of his ability to recognize and to direct.

It is becoming a much more common practice to include children in much of the planning of the school day. The teacher needs to initiate some of this work, to help get it organized and to direct it. In all these things he helps the children to see alternatives, to see additional resources and to anticipate consequences. Children look to the teacher for decision-making in many situations. There are decisions to give more time on dramatics or science. There are decisions involving the use of consultants, meeting with parents, referring of some children for outside help. Observing teachers gives some clue to their resourcefulness in organizing, managing, and directing.

Unifying the Group

3. At the beginning of each school year the teacher is confronted with a number of children. It is his hope and that of the children that as they live together they will become a unified group. When the children identify with each other and when the teacher's concerns overlap the children's, there is good reason to hope that a group spirit will emerge. When the teacher is fair and just to all he is making a contribution to classroom morale.

Discipline problems begin to be solved as children see that permissiveness is controlled by purposes. Children see that they may do those things which contribute to the agreed-upon purposes and that activities which conflict with those purposes are frowned upon or restricted. When there are some subgroups, most children know what is going on in all of them. A rather wide variety of activities is going on, and children have a sense of participation. Having choices to make, they can frequently choose those in which they have some special skills or abilities to assert. Concentrated attention is relieved occasionally with games or with a dramatic presentation. There is a variety of teaching and learning procedures. Seating is not thought of as a permanent and fixed condition. The teacher is alert to the possibility of cliques and is doing many things to develop the idea of a group. An important task of the teacher is that of developing a group with a group spirit, an identification with common purposes and some common concerns.

Giving Security

4. Many children are in need of a warm, friendly atmosphere. The teacher with love and affection in abundance is creating a climate which makes it easier for these children to learn. Some children are greatly in need of praise and recognition, and one task of the teacher is to differentiate instruction so that all children may have a sense of achievement and accomplishment. Those children who feel a sense of loneliness, isolation, and sometimes rejection need to be helped by teachers to feel that they belong, that they are wanted and needed. Some children are afraid of school, timid on playgrounds, fearful of many things in their lives. With them the teacher diminishes threats, warnings, or unusually heavy penalties and provides support and assurance instead. The teacher tries to help those children plagued by feelings of guilt and shame by showing that all of us make mistakes and that we can profit by them; by indicating that we are all human and that at different times most of us have had these feelings. There are some

children who have little respect for themselves and who feel that they are not worth very much. Here, the teacher asks them for their opinions and sees to it that they assume some responsibilities. Many children have dozens of questions about their relationships to the world and to their inner selves. To the teacher with insight these questions are not irrelevant. And there are some children who have a deep sense of economic insecurity, who wonder if they can count on next week or next month to be as secure as the present week. The classroom teacher brings to children a sense of security in the meeting of these needs. Whenever there are in children cases of aggressiveness, withdrawing, submission, or psychosomatic disturbance, the teacher sees to it that the children's needs for special attention are met promptly.

There is pride in what the pupils are doing, and when they need protection the teacher protects them. In a classroom atmosphere which generates group cooperation rather than competition, children help each other. Because it is not altogether a teacher-dominated room—with all or nearly all questions coming from the teacher and every response going to him—children hold discussions with each other. It matters when a child is absent; it matters that birthdays are observed; it matters that returning to school after holidays is a time for reunion and rejoicing.

Clarifying Attitudes, Beliefs, Problems

5. It is not unreasonable to assume that most of our children are utterly confused by the many social influences surrounding them. Looking at so many different ways of living on TV; listening to many things on radio; reading comics which again introduce new and unusual ideas; moving from one place to another every few years and meeting new people and new teachers; experiencing directly or vicariously the difficulties of a broken family; having few places to play and little opportunity to talk things over with parents who might both be working; living in the aftermath of cruel war and hearing much about possible new wars; being close to and sometimes a participant in racial problems; living under the ominous threat of unemployment; often seeing the glittering array of tempting goods in stores and realizing how little of it his own family has, the child of today must surely be very much confused. He hears nice things from the adults but sees and hears many things which contradict what they tell him.

To help clarify these matters, the teacher creates opportunities for children to state their attitudes, interests, and problems; to talk about their purposes and aspirations; to speak their beliefs and convictions; to indicate what they think might and should be done; to reveal and to share some of the deeper feelings they have; and to tell about the activities in which they are engaging and those in which they would like to share. As deeper expressions of personality come out, the teacher limits questioning and tries to find out how much self-expression means to the children, whether they want help, whether they have thought of alternative action in solving their problems and consequences of actions. He raises questions with the children which only they can answer, for the questions concern the values which children hold. He gives the children opportunities to compare, observe, classify, interpret and puts them in a position to analyze, criticize, and summarize. The teacher helps them to look for assumptions—those things which are taken for granted—and gives them opportunities to imagine and to create. These are problems to be solved and decisions of value to be made. In each specific instance a question or two is asked for the personal reaction of an individual or a small group and the responses are accepted by the teacher. As this is carried on day by day and week by week, the assumption is made that some of the confusion surrounding children is being cleared up. Even more important is the idea that it is possible to clear it up and and children are experiencing a teacher who believes that this is indeed possible. At the same time children are becoming accustomed to saying what they believe, stating what they think; they are becoming adapted to living in a world where people are not all alike, and they are beginning to prize the differences.

Diagnosing Learning Problems

6. In every classroom there are children who are not making the expected progress in their learning, growth, and development. As the teacher lives with these children, it is part of his task to have "hunches" and to suggest to himself possible courses of action. The teacher has to be alert to signs of ill health and sensitive to emotional problems of children. He has to be aware of limits of children's ability as well as of possible negative influences within the room, on the playground, and at home. The teacher faces behavior problems knowing that the behavior represents symptoms, that with the acting out of these symptoms children are asking for help. The naughty boy or girl is asking for help as much as the overshy and exclusively withdrawn. Apathy and flightiness, overconforming and overdissenting—all are taken as signs that the children want help in establishing direction. The impulsive child and the one who is always stuck, the one who seems to get little meaning out of the work, and the one who woolgathers, the one who is loudly assertive, and the one who has little faith in his own ideas are asking for understanding. The prima donna, the rebel without a cause, the unpredictable student, the one who is unrevealing, the one who seeks the exclusive companionship of one other child, the cynic, and the futilitarian all seem to be asking for a more important part in the power structure of the group. The teacher is alert to children who need special help in skills prized by the group. The teacher is grateful to the school with facilities for extra help for children who need more help than the teacher in the crowded school day can give. Surely one of the most important functions of a teacher is to make diagnoses which relate to learning and growth and suggestions which enable children to feel a sense of accomplishment and of identity with their peers.

Making Curriculum Materials

7. All teachers recognize the inadequacy of the available books in meeting the needs of every child in the room. Every teacher is faced

with the necessity of developing curriculum materials to supplement those provided by the local community. The teacher often hectographs or mimeographs materials which seem more appropriate for a particular group. He makes classroom tests; orders movies, slides, and weekly newspapers; makes arrangements for visiting speakers; tries to get display materials of articles which are produced locally or at a great distance. The teacher asks a great many questions which do not appear in the books and makes suggestions for individual study. In a hundred ways he is modifying the curriculum for the needs of his particular group. Curriculum making is an important function of teaching. If a teacher has some practice in this area and some confidence in his ability to work with children in the development of new materials, he is more able to meet the learning needs of all children in the group.

Evaluating, Recording, Reporting

8. All teachers have the task of keeping records and making reports, of recording absences and tardiness. There is the oral report to individual children, sometimes to the whole class about their progress. There are reports to parents, written and oral. Directed toward the plans to make life more productive and zestful for the child, there are reports to go to the administrator and on occasions to other teachers. Reports are necessary which indicate the planning of the schedule and the curriculum, such as a daily log or a projection into the future. In some instances there are anecdotal records to keep track of the behavior of a child, to see if he has decided to change certain of his behaviors. In spring some kind of reporting is usually asked which involves decisions about promotions, retardation, and possible summer work. With respect to most of these things teachers come to their work well prepared, and what they do about this important task is largely dictated by local circumstances.

Enriching Community Activities

9. Most parents believe that a community is better when it has better schools, but the belief has little worth if the school itself is not concerned with the quality of community life. A classroom teacher who identifies himself with the community is sensitive to its problems and how they are solved, its growth and aspirations. The teacher is concerned about playgrounds, libraries, parks, museums, community health, and transportation. As these things are discussed in school, the teacher is able to bring in appropriate illustrations from the community. Parents are frequent visitors and are thought of as colleagues with deep concerns about the education of their children. Community products are exhibited in the school.

There are field trips and visits to local institutions. The hobbies of mothers and fathers are sometimes shared with the children. Newcomers are oriented. Children who are leaving for another school get special attention and ways are sought to help them to a better start in a new location. In meetings with parents as much attention is paid to influential surroundings as to learning problems in the classroom. Harmonious relationships between school and community are a continuing, essential part of school life. When teachers have this concern, daily efforts are made to enrich the community—an important function of teaching.

Arranging and Organizing Classroom

10. It is the task of every teacher with the help of pupils to make the classroom a beautiful, pleasant place in which to live. Appearance and arrangement can make a great impression on a visitor. Ideally, the room seems a wonderfully pleasant place in which to learn: lighting is appropriate; colors are pleasing; equipment and supplies are at hand. The room can be quickly reorganized for a variety of activities. In such a room children feel at home. A room organization which is flexible and adaptable to different purposes brings an additional sense of security to children, who like the classroom better when they have shared in developing plans for its use. Many teachers initiate frequent change in the classroom during the year; for them a room is not fixed for all time in the first month of school. Children's exhibits are changed from time to time. Committees of children have different responsibilities for different tasks in arranging their classroom.

Participating in School Activities

11. In addition to all these classroom matters, there is the obligation of every teacher to participate in school activities, such as committee work, holiday programs to share in, lunchroom duty, bus duties, evening meetings. The teacher who believes that his tasks are fulfilled when he pays attention exclusively to his own classroom soon learns that there is the need to be concerned with the welfare of all children in all grades of the school. His participation in total school life is regarded as one of the important tasks of teaching.

Participating in Professional and Civic Life

12. Every teacher is expected to enter wholly into professional life and to make his contribution to the improvement of the profession. He is expected to belong to professional societies, attend conferences, act in accord with professional ethics, keep up to date in the reading of literature, and make some attempt with his colleagues in the community to share new pertinent research results. In addition, there is the usual expectation of his being a participating citizen in his community.

Those who discharge these responsibilities in an effective manner are making great contributions for good to a troubled world.

2. DESIRABLE BEHAVIORS OF TEACHERS

N. L. GAGE

In a sense, this paper is intended to do for teacher behavior what was done for the behavioral sciences as a whole by Bernard Berelson and Gary Steiner in their *Human Behavior: An Inventory of Scientific Findings.* The spirit of this paper can be better understood by reference to their first chapter, which sets forth the nature and limits of their enterprise. In particular, I must subscribe to their semifacetious caveat that "every finding ought to be preceded by three sets of initials: UCC, OTE, and IOC, standing for 'under certain circumstances,' 'other things equal,' and 'in our culture' " (3:7). I shall elaborate no further on these matters of scope, purpose, and method and shall instead refer the reader to that excellent chapter.

N. L. Gage, "Desirable Behaviors of Teachers," in Teachers for the Disadvantaged, *eds. M. D. Usdan and F. Bertolaet (Chicago, Ill.: Follett Publishing Company, 1966), pp. 4–12. Reprinted with permission from the author and publisher, Follett Educational Corp.*

It is well to note at the outset, however, that the typical behavioral scientist is pessimistic about any attempt to list the positive knowledge derived from research on the behaviors of teachers. The field of research on teaching is widely regarded as barren of such findings. The majority opinion would agree with the only statement in the Berelson-Steiner volume (3:440–441) that deals with the subject of this paper:

> The effect of style of teaching or teachers' characteristics on teacher-student relations or on the number of ideas absorbed by the students (i.e., teaching effectiveness) is uncertain.
>
> There have been a large number of studies on the effect of the "classroom atmosphere" or the form of teaching, dealing with such matters as the authoritarian or democratic, dominative or integrative approach of the teacher and the relative emphasis on subject or student. But apparently there are no clear conclusions. Here is a recent summary of the summaries:

Even though there is a vast body of research on the relation of teacher characteristics to effectiveness in teaching, the reviews of this research (Domas and Tiedeman, 1950; Barr, Eustice, and Noe, 1955) show no consistent relation between any characteristics, including intelligence, and such teaching effectiveness (Brim, 1958, p. 32).[1]

Since many other authors have written in a similarly gloomy vein, why is this paper being attempted? Why not reply negatively to the request for a summary of what research has to say about the desirable behavior of teachers, on the grounds that there simply is nothing constructive to be said?

The answer is twofold:

1. The desperate need to improve education in depressed urban areas inclines us to look upon our research knowledge more charitably, since even rather shaky findings may have some value in our present extremity.

2. The recent upsurge in the amount and quality of research on teaching may have rendered obsolescent the dismal conclusions of previous reviews of the literature.

At any rate, let us now look at what can be said about the desirable behaviors of teachers. In doing so, we shall omit any attempt at adequate documentation, we shall generally state conclusions without adequate defense or qualification, and we shall of necessity be anything but exhaustive. What follows is offered as a more or less personal and hurried effort to perform a service for a working group—and not as a careful, scholarly, and definitive sifting of the evidence.

Desirable Behaviors

Granted the provisos already stated, we find it possible to offer the following teacher behaviors (or characteristics of behavior) as "desirable" on the basis of correlational or experimental evidence of their relationship with desirable outcomes or aspects of teaching: warmth, cognitive organization, orderliness, indirectness, and ability to solve instructional problems.

Warmth

By warmth we mean the tendency of the teacher to be approving, to provide emotional support, to express a sympathetic attitude, and to accept the feelings of pupils. When observed by trained, reliable observers using Flanders' *Categories for Interaction Analysis* (11) to study their verbal behavior, "warm" teachers often make statements that are classified under these categories: "Accepts feeling . . . in a non-threatening manner" or "Praises or encourages . . . jokes (in ways) that release tension, not at expense of another individual." "Warm" teachers would also be likely to have high scores on the *Minnesota Teacher Attitude Inventory* (8). Indeed, such teachers seem to have an inveterate incapacity to think poorly of other persons, especially children. On the *California F Scale* (17), which is intended to measure authoritarianism, such teachers score at the nonauthoritarian end. On Ryans' *Teacher Characteristics Schedule* (22), such teachers believe that

[1] Reproduced by permission of Harcourt, Brace & World, Inc. from *Human Behavior: An Inventory of Scientific Findings* by B. Berelson and G. Steiner, copyright 1964.

"very few (less than 1 percent) high school students intentionally try to tax the patience of the teacher" and that "very few people (not more than about 10 percent) are influenced in their attitudes toward others by feelings of jealousy." On an inventory filled out by pupils, such teachers are often described as what Cogan (7) calls "Inclusive," or causing pupils to feel that their goals, sensibilities, abilities, and interests are taken into account.

In at least half a dozen studies, this kind of "warmth" has correlated positively with pupils', principals', and observers' favorable ratings of teachers (8, 17, 22). It sometimes goes along with the teacher's pupils getting higher scores on achievement tests, but not always. Flanders (11) found that pupils of "warm" teachers scored higher in mathematics and social studies, but Medley and Mitzel (18) failed to find such a correlation in reading tests. "Warmth" tends to correlate positively with the amount of required and also voluntary schoolwork done by pupils (7) and, in general science classes, with interest in science (21).

For pupils with high "cognitive values," who consider the teacher's ability to explain things clearly to be of primary importance, teacher warmth may be less relevant, even in the elementary school (9). At the secondary school and college levels, it is also less relevant (12), especially when students are quite secure emotionally. Nonetheless, it seems safe to say that the teacher-pupil relationship in our society is such that warm teachers are more effective, by and large, in eliciting favorable attitudes from pupils. Social-psychological theory (15:174–217) suggests that our tendencies toward consistency and homogeneity in our ideas, i.e., toward cognitive balance, push us toward liking someone whom we perceive as liking us. Pupils realize that the warm teacher likes them, and they tend to like him in return. And when they like him, they tend to identify with him, to adopt his values more readily, and even to learn subject matter from him more effectively. Whatever it may lack in surprise value, the finding that teacher warmth is desirable must be considered to be fairly well established.

Cognitive Organization

Insofar as a teacher aims to have his pupils acquire understanding, or meaningful learning, rather than mere rote knowledge, he should possess and exhibit the kind of intellectual grasp of his subject matter that I am here terming "cognitive organization." Such a teacher understands the processes and concepts of, say, multiplication, such as the reason for moving each sub-product one digit to the left when the multiplier has more than one digit (20). He has an understanding of the logical properties of a good definition, explanation, or conditional inference (19). He carries with him a set of "organizers" for his subject matter that provides him, and so his pupils, with "relevant ideational scaffolding" that discriminates new material from the previously learned and integrates it "at a level of abstraction, generality, and inclusiveness which is much higher than that of the learning material itself" (1:214).[2]

Although disagreements still exist as to the reasons for the findings and

[2] Reproduced by permission of the author, David P. Ausubel, and the publisher, Grune & Stratton, Inc. from *The Psychology of Meaningful Verbal Learning* by David P. Ausubel, copyright 1963, p. 214.

as to the nature of "meaningfulness" and "organization," the broad propositions concerning the value of these factors in learning are strongly established. Katona (16), Brownell and Moser (5), and Ausubel (1), among many others, have documented the great importance for learning, retention, and transfer of clear, logical, and integrated organizations of ideas.

Most of the research on this kind of variable has not, however, been concerned with teacher behavior. Rather, it has dealt with learning materials—the content, passages, texts, reading matter, etc.—given to pupils. It is possible, however, to make inferences about desirable teacher behavior from such research. For example, toward the end of his report on social-interaction variables in teaching, Flanders felt compelled to comment, "There is no substitute for knowledge of what is being taught" (11:117). According to Ausubel, "The art and science of presenting ideas and information meaningfully and effectively—so that clear, stable, and unambiguous meanings emerge and are retained over a long period of time as an organized body of knowledge—is really the principal function of pedagogy" (1:19).[3] Gagné (13) has formulated a theory of knowledge acquisition involving the analysis of tasks into hierarchies of subtasks and learning sets. But I am unable to cite research on the cognitive organization of teachers in the use of oral language—as distinguished from written language—that bears on this point. Wright and Proctor (25) developed a procedure for the systematic observation of verbal interaction in comparing mathematics lessons but did not correlate their measures with pupil learning. Bellack and Davitz (2) studied the language of the classroom in terms of "pedagogical moves," such as "structuring," and in terms of substantive categories, such as "instructional-logical" meaning, but again there was no investigation of achievement as a function of these aspects of the discourse. We are forced to rely on studies of subject matter rather than teachers for our conviction that the teacher's behavior should reflect a clear and valid cognitive organization of what he is trying to teach.

Orderliness

By "orderliness" we mean the teacher's tendency to be systematic and methodical in his self-management. Cogan (7) called this a part of the "disjunctive-conjunctive" category of teacher behavior. In part it consists of teacher effectiveness in classroom management. It was also Ryans' (22) Pattern Y_0—one of the three major "patterns" of elementary and secondary school teacher behavior, which he derived in large part from factor analyses of observers' ratings of teacher behavior. Pattern Y_0 is the dimension of "responsible, systematic, businesslike *vs.* evading, unplanned, slipshod teacher behavior" (22:108). Coffman's (6), French's (12), and Gibb's (14) factor analyses of college students' ratings of their instructors have yielded similar factors.

Cogan found no support for the hypothesis that mean pupils' ratings of their teachers' "conjunctivity" (i.e., orderliness) correlate with the mean amount of work reported by the pupils. But he did find positive within-classroom correlations between the ratings of a teacher's conjunctivity by individual pupils and the

3 *Ibid.*, p. 19.

amount of work reported by the pupils. Ryans (22:260–265) found that teachers' scores on an inventory designed to measure correlates of Pattern Y_0 were significantly different for teachers nominated by their principals as superior in "systematic, responsible behavior" than for teachers rated as inferior in such behavior. Some of his other findings suggested that "the principals' conceptualization of the poor elementary teacher is heavily influenced by unplanned, slipshod, irresponsible classroom behavior" (22:265). The same was true of secondary school principals' concepts of poor mathematics, science, English, and social studies teachers.

Indirectness

A tendency toward indirect methods of teaching consists in giving pupils opportunities to engage in overt behaviors, such as talking and problem solving, relevant to the learning objectives rather than merely listening to their teacher and to discover ideas and solutions to problems rather than merely receiving them from the teacher. In Flanders' (11) categories, already mentioned, such teachers often say things classifiable as "Accepts or uses ideas of student" or "Ask questions." In their classrooms will be found relatively many instances of "Student talk—response" and "Student talk—initiation." In Ryans' terms such a teacher would be high on Pattern Z_0, which reflects "stimulating, imaginative, and original *vs.* dull and routine" teacher behavior and is "associated with the teacher's ability to encourage pupil participation and initiative" (22:97). The idea of teaching concepts and generalizations by permitting pupils to discover underlying principles for themselves and of giving them less direct guidance is also related to the present concept of indirectness. In brief, indirectness consists in a teacher's realizing that it is not always desirable merely to tell a pupil what you want him to know and understand but that it is sometimes better to let the pupil become active, seek for himself, participate in the interplay of ideas, and make some "provisional tries." Indirectness in teaching represents a willingness to forbear furnishing the pupil with everything he needs to know. It does not, however, mean abandoning the pupil to his own devices.

Flanders (11) found that indirectness in teachers went along with greater achievement on the part of their pupils in units on geography and geometry. Correlated highly with Ryans' Pattern Z_0 were observers' ratings of pupil behaviors on such dimensions as "apathetic-alert" and "dependent-initiating" (22:106). Ausubel concluded from his review of the experiments on learning by discovery that "Providing guidance to the learner in the form of verbal explanation of the underlying principles almost invariably facilitates learning and retention and sometimes transfer as well. *Self*-discovery methods and the furnishing of completely explicit rules, on the other hand, are relatively less effective" (1:171).[4] The phrase, "the furnishing of completely explicit rules," characterizes the opposite of indirectness, and it is such teaching, unfortunately far too prevalent, that we consider undesirable. As Flanders put it, "Our

[4] Reproduced by permission of David P. Ausubel and of Grune & Stratton, Inc., from *The Psychology of Meaningful Verbal Learning* by David P. Ausubel, copyright 1963.

theory suggests an indirect approach; most teachers use a direct approach" (11:114).

Ability To Solve Instructional Problems

By "ability to solve instructional problems" we mean the teacher's ability to solve problems unique to his work in a particular subdivision of the profession. The teacher should have more of such ability than persons peripheral to that subdivision (24). For example, teachers of intermediate-grade arithmetic should be better at solving problems in teaching such arithmetic than, in order of increasing peripherality, teachers of primary-grade arithmetic, secondary school teachers of non-mathematical subjects, or college-educated persons who do not teach at all.

What kinds of problems should a teacher of intermediate grade arithmetic be especially able to solve? Turner's test (23) contained a task in which the teacher was given a set of arithmetic exercises. The teacher's task was to judge how closely related the set was to each of ten statements of skill or understanding, such as "To increase skill in using division to answer practical questions involving money" and "To develop skill in discriminating which arithmetic process is most efficient in solving a problem." In another task the teacher is given a set of solutions by Jimmy B. to ten long-division examples and is asked to decide "whether Jimmy B., whose work is shown below, has made any errors significant enough to hold an interview with him concerning those errors. If you decide he has, your next problem is to decide which errors seem most significant, and should thus be the focus of the interview with Jimmy." After the teacher decides, he must judge whether each of ten kinds of errors (e.g., errors in subtraction facts) should: (a) be the focus of the interview; (b) possibly be included in the interview, but not focally; or (c) not be included.

Turner reported that intermediate grade teachers of arithmetic scored significantly higher on his test than did forty-one non-teachers of elementary school arithmetic (nurses, businessmen, housewives, and secondary teachers). Similarly, the "problems showed some power to differentiate among teachers of varying training and experience ... (and) teachers who were rated by supervisors significantly above average in skill in teaching arithmetic had significantly higher mean problem-solving scores than did teachers rated distinctly below average. Pupils taught by high-scoring, problem-solving teachers achieved significantly more than pupils taught by low-scoring teachers" (10:245–246).

Although the work of the Indiana University group is continuing in an effort to refine and extend this approach, results thus far seem adequate to support the altogether plausible proposition that good teachers possess ability to solve technical problems in instruction. Apart from the social-emotional aspects of teaching behavior, the more strictly cognitive-intellectual ones, and the managerial phases of their work, good teachers need a unique body of problem-solving skills.

References

1. Ausubel, D. P. *The Psychology of Meaningful Verbal Learning: An Introduction to School Learning.* New York: Grune & Stratton, 1963.

2. Bellack, A. A., and Davitz, J. R., in collaboration with Kliebard, H. M., and Hyman, R. T. *The Language of the Classroom: Meanings Communicated in High School Teaching.* New York: Institute of Psychological Research, Teachers College, Columbia University, 1963. U.S. Cooperative Research Project No. 1497.

3. Berelson, B., and Steiner, G. A. *Human Behavior: An Inventory of Scientific Findings.* New York: Harcourt, Brace & World, 1964.

4. Brim, O. G., Jr. *Sociology and the Field of Education.* New York: Russell Sage Foundation, 1958.

5. Brownell, W. A., and Moser, H. E. *Meaningful Versus Mechanical Learning: A Study in Grade III Subtraction.* Duke University Research Studies in Education, 1949, No. 8.

6. Coffman, W. E. "Determining Students' Concepts of Effective Teaching from Their Ratings of Instructors," *Journal of Educational Psychology,* 1954, 45:277–286.

7. Cogan, M. L. "The Behavior of Teachers and the Productive Behavior of Their Pupils: I. 'Perception' Analysis; II. 'Trait' Analysis," *Journal of Experimental Education,* 1958, 27:89–105, 107–124.

8. Cook, W. W., Leeds, C. H., and Callis, R. *The Minnesota Teacher Attitude Inventory.* New York: Psychological Corporation, 1951.

9. Della Piana, G. M., and Gage, N. L. "Pupils' Values and the Validity of the Minnesota Teacher Attitude Inventory," *Journal of Educational Psychology,* 1955, 46:167–178.

10. Fattu, N. A. "Exploration of Interactions among Instruction, Content, and Aptitude Variables," *Journal of Teacher Education,* 1963, 14:244–251.

11. Flanders, N. A. *Teacher Influence, Pupil Attitudes and Achievement: Studies in Interaction Analysis.* Minneapolis: University of Minnesota, College of Education, November 30, 1960. U.S. Office of Education Cooperative Research Project No. 397.

12. French, G. M. *College Students' Concepts of Effective Teaching Determined by an Analysis of Teacher Ratings.* Seattle: University of Washington, 1957. Mimeographed.

13. Gagné, E. M. "The Acquisition of Knowledge," *Psychological Review,* 1962, 69:355–364.

14. Gibb, C. A. "Classroom Behavior of the College Teacher," *Educational and Psychological Measurement,* 1955, 15: 254–263.

15. Heider, F. *The Psychology of Interpersonal Relations.* New York: Wiley, 1958.

16. Katona, G. *Organizing and Memorizing.* New York: Columbia University Press, 1940.

17. Mcgee, H. M. "Measurement of Authoritarianism and Its Relation to Teachers' Classroom Behavior," *Genetic Psychology Monograph,* 1955, 52:89–146.

18. Medley, D. M., and Mitzel, H. E. "Some Behavioral Correlates of Teacher Effectiveness," *Journal of Educational Psychology,* 1959, 50:239–246.

19. Meux, M., and Smith, B. O. *Logical Dimensions of Teaching Behavior.* Urbana: Bureau of Educational Research, University of Illinois, 1961. Mimeographed.

20. Orleans, J. S. *The Understanding of Arithmetic Processes and Concepts Possessed by Teachers of Arithmetic.* New York: Board of Education of the City of New York, Division of Teacher Education, Office of Research and Evaluation, Publication No. 12, 1952.

21. Reed, H. B., Jr. "Teacher Variables of Warmth, Demand, and Utiliza-

tion of Intrinsic Motivation Related to Pupils' Science Interests: A Study Illustrating Several Potentials of Variance-Covariance," *Journal of Experimental Education*, 1961, 29:205–229.

22. Ryans, D. G. *Characteristics of Teachers*. Washington, D.C.: American Council on Education, 1960.

23. Turner, R. L. *Intermediate Grade Mathematics Teaching Tasks, Form F.* Bloomington: Institute of Educational Research, Indiana University, 1961. Mimeographed.

24. Turner, R. L., and Fattu, N. A. *Skill in Teaching, Assessed on the Criterion of Problem Solving.* Bloomington: Bulletin of the School of Education, Indiana University, 37, Publication No. 3, 1961.

25. Wright, E., Muriel, J., and Proctor, Virginia H. *Systematic Observation of Verbal Interaction as a Method of Comparing Mathematics Lessons.* St. Louis: Washington University, 1961. U.S. Office of Education Cooperative Research Project No. 816.

3. PERSONAL THOUGHTS ON TEACHING AND LEARNING

CARL ROGERS

This is the shortest chapter in the book but if my experience with it is any criterion, it is also the most explosive. It has an (to me) amusing history.

I had agreed, months in advance, to meet with a conference organized by Harvard University on "Classroom Approaches to Influencing Human Behavior." I was requested to put on a demonstration of "student-centered teaching"—teaching based upon therapeutic principles as I had been endeavoring to apply them in education. I felt that to use two hours with a sophisticated group to try to help them formulate their own purposes, and to respond to their feelings as they did so, would be highly artificial and unsatisfactory. I did not know what I would do or present.

Carl Rogers, "Personal Thoughts on Teaching and Learning," ON BECOMING A PERSON *(Boston: Houghton Mifflin Company, 1961), pp. 273–75. Reprinted by permission.*

At this juncture I took off for Mexico on one of our winter-quarter trips, did some painting, writing, and photography, and immersed myself in the writings of Søren Kierkegaard. I am sure that his honest willingness to call a spade a spade influenced me more than I realized.

As the time came near to return I had to face up to my obligation. I recalled that I had sometimes been able to initiate very meaningful class discussions by expressing some highly personal opinion of my own, and then endeavoring to understand and accept the often very divergent reactions and feelings of the students. This seemed a sensible way of handling my Harvard assignment.

So I sat down to write, as honestly as I could, what my experiences had been with *teaching*, as this term is defined in the dictionaries, and likewise my experience with *learning*. I was far away from psychologists, educators, cautious colleagues. I simply put down what I felt, with assurance that if I had not got it correctly, the discussion would help to set me on the right track.

I may have been näive, but I did not consider the material inflammatory. After all the conference members were knowledgeable, self-critical teachers, whose main common bond was an interest in the discussion method in the classroom.

I met with the conference, I presented my views as written out below, taking only a very few moments, and threw the meeting open for discussion. I was hoping for a response, but I did not expect the tumult which followed. Feelings ran high. It seemed I was threatening their jobs, I was obviously saying things I didn't mean, etc., etc. And occasionally a quiet voice of appreciation arose from a teacher who had felt these things but never dared to say them.

I daresay that not one member of the group remembered that this meeting was billed as a demonstration of student-centered teaching. But I hope that in looking back each realized that he had lived an experience of student-centered teaching. I refused to defend myself by replying to the questions and attacks which came from every quarter. I endeavored to accept and empathize with the indignation, the frustration, the criticisms which they felt. I pointed out that I had merely expressed some very personal views of my own. I had not asked nor expected others to agree. After much storm, members of the group began expressing, more and more frankly, their own significant feelings about teaching—often feelings divergent from mine, often feelings divergent from each other. It was a very thought-provoking session. I question whether any participant in that session has ever forgotten it.

The most meaningful comment came from one of the conference members the next morning as I was preparing to leave the city. All he said was, "You kept more people awake last night!"

I took no steps to have this small fragment published. My views on psychotherapy had already made me a "controversial figure" among psychologists and psychiatrists. I had no desire to add educators to the list. The statement was widely duplicated however by members of the conference and several years later two journals requested permission to publish it.

After this lengthy historical buildup, you may find the statement itself a letdown. Personally I have never felt it to be incendiary. It still expresses some of my deepest views in the field of education.

I wish to present some very brief remarks, in the hope that if they bring forth any reaction from you, I may get some new light on my own ideas.

I find it a very troubling thing to *think*, particularly when I think about my own experiences and try to extract from those experiences the meaning that seems genuinely inherent in them. At first such thinking is very satisfying, because it seems to discover sense and pattern in a whole host of discrete events. But then it very often becomes dismaying, because I realize how ridiculous these thoughts, which have much value to me, would seem to most people. My impression is that if I try to find the meaning of my own experience it leads me, nearly always, in directions regarded as absurd.

So in the next three or four minutes, I will try to digest some of the meanings which have come to me from my classroom experience and the experience I have had in individual and group therapy. They are in no way intended as conclusions for someone else, or a guide to what others should do or be. They are the very tentative meanings, as of April 1952, which my experience has had for me, and some of the bothersome questions which their absurdity raises. I will put each idea or meaning in a separate lettered paragraph, not because they are in any particular logical order, but because each meaning is separately important to me.

a. I may as well start with this one in view of the purposes of this conference. *My experience has been that I cannot teach another person how to teach.* To attempt it is for me, in the long run, futile.

b. *It seems to me that anything that can be taught to another is relatively inconsequential, and has little or no significant influence on behavior.* That sounds so ridiculous I can't help but question it at the same time that I present it.

c. *I realize increasingly that I am only interested in learnings which significantly influence behavior.* Quite possibly this is simply a personal idiosyncrasy.

d. *I have come to feel that the only learning which significantly influences behavior is self-discovered, self-appropriated learning.*

e. *Such self-discovered learning, truth that has been personally appropriated and assimilated in experience, cannot be directly communicated to another.* As soon as an individual tries to communicate such experience directly, often with a quite natural enthusiasm, it becomes teaching, and its results are inconsequential. It was some relief recently to discover that Søren Kierkegaard, the Danish philosopher, had found this too, in his own experience, and stated it very clearly a century ago. It made it seem less absurd.

f. As a consequence of the above, *I realize that I have lost interest in being a teacher.*

g. When I try to teach, as I do sometimes, I am appalled by the results, which seem a little more than inconsequential, because sometimes the teaching appears to succeed. When this happens I find that the results are damaging. It seems to cause the individual to distrust his own experience, and to stifle significant learning. *Hence I have come to feel that the outcomes of teaching are either unimportant or hurtful.*

h. When I look back at the results of my past teaching, the real results seem the same—either damage was done, or nothing significant occurred. This is frankly troubling.

i. As a consequence, *I realize that I am only interested in being a learner, preferably learning things that matter, that have some significant influence on my own behavior.*

j. *I find it very rewarding to learn,* in groups, in relationships with one person as in therapy, or by myself.

k. *I find that one of the best, but most difficult ways for me to learn is to drop my own defensiveness, at least temporarily, and to try to understand the way in which his experience seems and feels to the other person.*

l. *I find that another way of learning for me is to state my own uncertainties, to try to clarify my puzzlements, and thus get closer to the meaning that my experience actually seems to have.*

m. This whole train of experiencing, and the meanings that I have thus far discovered in it, seem to have launched me on a process which is both fascinating and at times a little frightening. *It seems to mean letting my experience carry me on, in a direction which appears to be forward, toward goals that I can but dimly define, as I try to understand at least the current meaning of that experience.* The sensation is that of floating with a complex stream of experience, with the fascinating possibility of trying to comprehend its ever changing complexity.

I am almost afraid I may seem to have gotten away from any discussion of learning, as well as teaching. Let me again introduce a practical note by saying that by themselves these interpretations of my own experience may sound queer and aberrant, but not particularly shocking. It is when I realize the *implications* that I shudder a bit at the distance I have come from the commonsense world that everyone knows is right. I can best illustrate that by saying that if the experiences of others had been the same as mine, and if they had discovered similar meanings in it, many consequences would be implied.

a. Such experience would imply that we would do away with teaching. People would get together if they wished to learn.

b. We would do away with examinations. They measure only the inconsequential type of learning.

c. The implication would be that we would do away with grades and credits for the same reason.

d. We would do away with degrees as a measure of competence partly for the same reason. Another reason is that a degree marks an end or a conclusion of something, and a learner is only interested in the continuing process of learning.

e. It would imply doing away with the exposition of conclusions, for we would realize that no one learns significantly from conclusions.

I think I had better stop there. I do not want to become too fantastic. I want to know primarily whether anything in my inward thinking as I have tried to describe it, speaks to anything in your experience of the classroom as you have lived it, and if so, what the meanings are that exist for you in *your* experience.

4. THE MODEL OF GOOD TEACHING

MARIE M. HUGHES & ASSOCIATES

What is good teaching? The teacher-learner situation in its complexity, its flow, and its multiple relationships requires creativity on the part of the teacher. If teaching may be described as decision-making in interaction, then the product of the teacher's decision is the response he makes to the child or group with whom he is interacting. When the response is not routine or stereotyped, it is creative. The occasion is never quite the same and won't be again. The effort made to understand and to respond within the meaning of a specific and unique child must be a creative act to be successful. The measure, then, of good teaching is the quality of the response the teacher makes to the child or group with whom he is interacting. It is the child who is reaching out, seeking, raising the questions, trying out his ideas.

How does the teacher respond so that he can be used as a resource by the child? To become a man of autonomy and initiative, to become a man with confidence in himself, the child needs to have opportunities to try himself out by initiating ideas and actions which are successful most of the time. This he can do only if the teacher makes the appropriate response. The responses of the teacher may include:

Giving the child support by telling him things are going along well, by assuring him that his is a good idea

Giving him a direct answer to a question that he asks, or helping him locate the answer if it is not known by the teacher

Giving him a chance to elaborate his idea by asking him more about it in a nonthreatening and nonevaluative manner

Giving him an evaluation, either posi-

Marie M. Hughes and Associates, "The Model of Good Teaching," DEVELOPMENT OF THE MEANS FOR THE ASSESSMENT OF THE QUALITY OF TEACHING IN ELEMENTARY SCHOOLS. *U.S. Office of Education Cooperative Research Project No. 353 (Salt Lake City: The University of Utah, 1959), pp. 215–22. Reprinted by permission.*

tive or negative, that points up specifically what is correct or incorrect; or by

Giving him a chance to relate to his own experience

If the child is to become a man who is "open to his experience," a man who can encompass much of reality, then as a child he must relate positively to more people, things, and situations. The teacher's response to him must be such that he wants to reenter the situation. When failure is more or less continuous, one reduces his level of aspiration and oftentimes withdraws from the situation. Therefore, the teacher's response must include:

Requiring from the child only that which he is capable of doing

Opening new possibilities to him without coercion

Withholding all sarcasm and ridicule

Interpreting to him the data in the situation of which he is aware

If the child is to become a man who has positive feelings toward himself and cherishes uniqueness in others, then the teacher's response to him must respect his own individuality. Such responses may include:

Giving the child some choice in what he is doing; for example, what he writes about, what he reads, the picture he paints

Expressing a belief in the child as a person

Listening to him

Accepting most of his ideas

Helping him gain competence in the things he cherishes

If the child is to grow into a man who possesses highly developed communicative skills, he must have opportunity to talk and to listen to others. The teacher's responses must include:

Seeking for his opinion and experience

Giving him an opportunity to use a variety of media of communication

Giving him a model of standard language usage

Providing him with a variety of books and other reading materials

Seeking to further his purposes in reading

Giving him opportunity to compare his reading with his new experience, to draw inferences and generalizations from his reading

Seeking the child's own idiomatic response in writing and other media of expression

If the child is to grow into a man who acts with an attitude of social responsibility the teacher's responses must include:

Setting of limits with him and for him

Clarifying standards with public criteria

Structuring the situation with clarity

Reprimanding with public criteria

Giving the child responsibility for others

Evaluating with discrimination

Good teaching, then, requires appropriate responsiveness to the data the child and group are placing in the situation. It is in this way that the exploring and searching activities of the child or group can be rewarded properly. When their own seeking activities are rewarded, they become involved and commit themselves further to the activity. We believe: "The child's capacity to create new and challenging problems for himself is his most potent source of continuous growth and development."[1] It is his own desire for growth that makes possible the constructively creative man.

Good teaching requires a reduction in the controlling functions exercised continuously by the teacher. We have shown how these controls extend to the exact wording of answers, to the minutiae of a problem for attention. We have shown that the child's explorations in the way of looking ahead, of relating to his own experiences are usually crushed as the teacher restructures the child back into the narrow path laid out for him. The stereotyped and repetitive question and answer blocks children's use of higher mental processes. They recall and repeat; they do not synthesize or generalize.

The extensive and pervasive control under which children live in the classroom keeps them dependent and prevents them from full participation in the subject matter (content) of the school.

Good teaching requires that the classroom be well managed so that the business of learning may receive full attention. This means that the teacher perform the functions of controlling with clarity and with consistency. It does mean that in the position of teacher with its superior-subordinate relationship, the power component be ameliorated through relating the direction or the command to situational factors or to the larger society.

It is quite probable that most teaching would be improved by the reduction of the present large number of controlling acts to one-third or one-half of what they now are.

Good teaching requires that the human environment be accepting of each individual, that in some way it tell him that he is important. This suggests that teachers not "pit" one group of children against another, but find ways to integrate the wide range of differences that are always present. It suggests a personal rapport between teacher and child. This personal rapport is built upon many little things. For example, the granting of a request other than routine says to the child, "I care for you. You count with me." Psychologists have noted that gratification in one area tends to instigate a feeling of well-being that extends into other areas of an individual's life.[2]

Individual rapport is built through empathy and support from one who is a significant person in one's life. It is developed with interpretation of reality that enriches or makes the situation more for one.

Good teaching keeps the interpersonal relationships supportive within the classroom. There are common problems, concerns, and agreements because people have had a chance to talk and to listen to one another. There has been time to explore the opinions and wants of the group. Out of this, a shared-problem-solving attitude develops. To maintain a supportive climate the negative acts of sarcasm and threat must be abolished. A reduction in the number of admonishments and reprimands will make those used more effective, es-

[1] Manual Barkan, *Foundations of Art Education* (New York: The Ronald Press Company, 1955).

[2] Louis Barclay Murphy, *Personality in Young Children* (New York: Basic Books, Inc., Publishers, 1957), Vol. II, Chap. IV; and Bruno Bettleheim, *Love Is Not Enough* (New York: Free Press of Glencoe, Inc., 1950).

pecially when they are linked to clearly stated situational factors.

The concept of functions performed in the classroom by the teacher in interaction makes it possible to relate action to the objectives toward which one is working.

The effects on children of the pattern of teaching functions to which they are subjected day after day and year after year are accumulative. Whether or not the "life space" permitted them in the classroom is sufficient to allow them to explore their own ideas, to solve problems of many kinds, to have some choice as to their own activities makes a real difference in their own involvement in the subject matter (content) of the school, in their attitude toward learning, and in their development of autonomy. Whether or not they are respected as individuals makes a difference in their development of confidence and positive self-concept.

What teachers do in the classroom makes a difference.

Good teaching requires that the teacher be a well educated, mature person who has the insight and energy for this demanding job. Every decision made in the classroom should be a considered one. This undoubtedly means a smaller number of students in each classroom. Growth is wavering and uneven as well as forward; it goes by leaps as well as crawls. The specifics for a growing child are not entirely predictable. To provide for the differences that are the hopes of each generation requires more than a textbook and a dictionary. It requires the responsive human environment that fosters exploration and initiative.

5. THE N.E.A. CODE OF ETHICS

Preamble

Believing that true democracy can best be achieved by a process of free public education made available to all the children of all the people; that the teachers in the United States have a large and inescapable responsibility in fashioning the ideals of children and youth; that such responsibility requires the services of men and women of high ideals, broad education, and profound human understanding; and, in order that the aims of democratic education may be realized more fully, that the welfare of the teaching profession may be promoted; and, that teachers may observe proper standards of conduct in their professional relations, the National Education Association of the United States proposes this code of ethics for its members. The term "teacher" as used in this code shall include all persons directly engaged in educational work, whether in a teaching, an administrative, or a supervisory capacity.

"Ethics for Teachers: The N.E.A. Code," Personal Growth Leaflet No. 135 (Washington, D.C.: Senior Citizens of America, n.d.). Reprinted by permission.

Article I—Relations to Pupils and the Home

Section 1

It is the duty of the teacher to be just, courteous, and professional in all his relations with pupils. He should consider their individual differences, needs, interests, temperaments, aptitudes, and environments.

Section 2

He should refrain from tutoring pupils of his classes for pay, and from referring such pupils to any member of his immediate family for tutoring.

Section 3

The professional relations of a teacher with his pupils demand the same scrupulous care that is required in the confidential relations of one teacher with another. A teacher, therefore, should not disclose any information obtained confidentially from his pupils, unless it is for the best interest of the child and the public.

Section 4

A teacher should seek to establish friendly and intelligent cooperation between home and school, ever keeping in mind the dignity of his profession and the welfare of the pupils. He should do or say nothing that would undermine the confidence and respect of his pupils for their parents. He should inform the pupils and parents regarding the importance, purposes, accomplishments, and needs of the schools.

Article II— Relations to Civic Affairs

Section 1

It is the obligation of every teacher to inculcate in his pupils an appreciation of the principles of democracy. He should direct full and free discussion of appropriate controversial issues with the expectation that comparisons, contrasts, and interpretations will lead to an understanding, appreciation, acceptance, and practice of the principles of democracy. A teacher should refrain from using his classroom privileges and prestige to promote partisan politics, sectarian religious views, or selfish propaganda of any kind.

Section 2

A teacher should recognize and perform all the duties of citizenship. He should subordinate his personal desires to the best interests of public good. He should be loyal to the school system, the state, and the nation, but should exercise his right to give constructive criticisms.

Section 3

A teacher's life should show that education makes people better citizens and better neighbors. His personal conduct should not needlessly offend the accepted pattern of behavior of the community in which he serves.

Article III— Relations to the Profession

Section 1

Each member of the teaching profession should dignify his calling on all occasions and should uphold the importance of his services to society. On the other hand he should not indulge in personal exploitation.

Section 2

A teacher should encourage able and sincere individuals to enter the teaching profession and discourage those who plan to use this profession merely as a stepping-stone to some other vocation.

Section 3

It is the duty of the teacher to maintain his own efficiency by study, by travel, and by other means which keep him abreast of the trends in education and the world in which he lives.

Section 4

Every teacher should have membership in his local, state, and national professional organizations, and should participate actively and unselfishly in them. Professional growth and personality development are the natural product of such professional activity. Teachers should avoid the promotion of organization rivalry and divisive competition which weaken the cause of education.

Section 5

While not limiting their services by reason of small salary, teachers should insist upon a salary scale commensurate with the social demands laid upon them by society. They should not knowingly underbid a rival or agree to accept a salary lower than that provided by a recognized schedule. They should not apply for positions for the sole purpose of forcing an increase in salary in their present positions; correspondingly, school officials should not refuse to give deserved salary increases to efficient employees until offers from other school authorities have forced them so to do.

Section 6

A teacher should not apply for a specific position currently held by another teacher. Unless the rules of a school system otherwise prescribe, he should file his application with the chief executive officer.

Section 7

Since qualification should be the sole determining factor in appointment and promotion, the use of pressure on school officials to secure a position or to obtain other favors is unethical.

Section 8

Testimonials regarding teachers should be truthful and confidential, and should be treated as confidential information by school authorities receiving them.

Section 9

A contract, once signed, should be faithfully adhered to until it is dissolved by mutual consent. Ample notification should be given both by school officials and teachers in case a change in position is to be made.

Section 10

Democratic procedures should be practiced by members of the teaching profession. Cooperation should be predicated upon the recognition of the worth and the dignity of individual personality. All teachers should observe the professional courtesy of transacting official business with the properly designated authority.

Section 11

School officials should encourage and nurture the professional growth of all teachers by promotion or by other appropriate methods of recognition. School officials who fail to recommend a worthy teacher for a better position outside their school system because they do not desire to lose his services are acting unethically.

Section 12

A teacher should avoid unfavorable criticism of other teachers except that formally presented to a school official for the welfare of the school. It is unethical to fail to report to the duly constituted authority any matters which are detrimental to the welfare of the school.

Section 13

Except when called upon for counsel or other assistance, a teacher should not interfere in any matter between another teacher and a pupil.

Section 14

A teacher should not act as an agent, or accept a commission, royalty, or other compensation, for endorsing books or other school materials in the selection or purchase of which he can exert influence, or concerning which he can exercise the right of decision; nor should he accept a commission or other compensation for helping another teacher to secure a position.

Article IV— Standing Committee on Professional Ethics

There is hereby established a Standing Committee on Professional Ethics consisting of five members appointed by the president.

It shall be the duty of the Committee to study and to take appropriate action on such cases of violation of this Code as may be referred to it. The Committee shall be responsible also for publicizing the Code, promoting its use in institutions for the preparation of teachers, and recommending needed modifications.

If, when a case is reported, it is found to come from a state which has an Ethics Committee, such case shall immediately be referred to said state committee for investigation and action. In the case of a violation reported from a state which has neither a code nor an ethics committee, or from a state which has a code but no ethics committee, the NEA Ethics Committee shall take such action as seems wise and reasonable and will impress members with the importance of respect for proper professional conduct. Such action shall be reported to the chief school officers of the community and the state from which the violation is reported.

The Committee is further vested with authority to expel a member from the National Education Association for flagrant violation of this code.

ACTIVITIES

1. If you were to observe a teacher practicing his profession, what are some aspects of the classroom, the climate, the planning, the interaction between teacher and students, etc. to which you would pay particular attention?

2. What bases did you use to identify the areas named in answer to Question 1? Did research evidence give much direction? Did learnings from previous Education courses suggest crucial areas to be observed?

3. Nathaniel Cantor[1] has suggested that the following statements are assumptions that serve as the basis for orthodox teaching:

The Assumptions of Orthodox Teaching

a. It is assumed that the teacher's responsibility is to set out what is to be learned and that the student's job is to learn it.

b. It is assumed that knowledge taken on authority is educative in itself.

c. It is assumed that education can be obtained through disconnected subjects.

d. It is assumed that subject matter is the same to the learner as to the teacher.

e. It is assumed that education prepares the student for later life rather than that it is a living experience.

f. It is assumed that the teacher is responsible for the pupil's acquiring of knowledge.

g. It is assumed that pupils must be coerced into working on some tasks.

h. It is assumed that knowledge is more important than learning.

i. It is assumed that education is primarily an intellectual process.

[1] Nathaniel Cantor, *The Teaching Learning-Process* (New York: The Dryden Press, 1953), pp. 59–72.

Would teachers who taught in the way of Carl Rogers accept these assumptions? Would they add or eliminate some? How would you answer these questions in terms of the teaching described by Gage; Hughes; L. Raths?

4. Collect from readings, conversations, or questionnaires opinions about teachers and teaching. Classify the specific comments found in these evaluations according to the five categories advanced by Gage. How many comments fall outside of the categories Gage proposed? What new categories need to be constructed to handle the comments remaining?

5. In the introduction to this chapter, Green's distinction between acts and responses was briefly discussed. Attempt to identify several teacher acts that might be subsumed by each of Gage's five categories.

6. Play the role of a teacher and instruct some fellow students. Listen to a tape recording of your lesson. What behaviors would you classify as "acts" using the Green schema presented in the introduction to this chapter? What behaviors would you classify as "responses"?

7. Common to most professions is a code of ethics; for the teaching profession such a code is advanced by the NEA. To what extent do each of the sections of the code reflect the current trends toward teacher militancy found in the profession?

INTERACTION IN THE CLASSROOM

CHAPTER TWO

Educational researchers have been working on the problem of describing classroom behaviors in a systematic fashion for over three decades. They have identified two ways of observing a classroom. One method is referred to as a "sign system"—a system in which isolated events are scheduled in advance to be the object of the observation. Some examples of this method might be the number of times the teacher asks questions, the number of times the teacher praises students, or the number of times the teacher shifts the topic under discussion. A sign system is effective if the categories describe, in the present tense, (1) single events and (2) positive occurrences. Thus, "teacher praises the contribution of a student" is a better category than "teacher failed to praise students' contributions."

A second approach is the "category system." This method places various classroom behaviors in one of several categories instead of only counting a few behaviors specified in advance. As an illustration, all questions a teacher asks could be classified by distinct categories—*e.g.* convergent and divergent. Other examples of category systems will be discussed in this chapter.

Regardless of whether a sign system or a category system is employed, two problems of observation need to be surmounted. First, neither approach describes the totality of the classroom activity. Some behavior is always overlooked and who is to say that the unrecorded aspects of the teaching act are not more important than those which are recorded? Second, efforts to describe teaching are often interpreted as evaluations of the teaching act and of the teacher. While descriptions may be used as a basis of evaluation, judgments can be made only after additional value assumptions are identified and applied to the data.

This chapter presents several procedures for observing teaching and suggests various behaviors that are significant to observe. Hopefully, you will find in the readings several techniques which will facilitate your observation of classrooms. As you read about them, you might ask yourself how a teacher could employ them to monitor his own teaching practices.

6. WHAT IS TEACHING? ONE VIEWPOINT

MARIE M. HUGHES

Psychologists, other researchers, and curriculum workers are in agreement that a most important variable in the classroom is that of the teacher.

The teacher behavior in the classroom that is most pervasive and continuous is, of course, the verbal action. The verbal and the nonverbal behavior of teachers is, according to Mary Aschner, "the language of responsible actions designed to influence the behavior of those under instruction" (1).

Indispensable data then for a description and analysis of teaching are verbatim records of what the teacher said and did and the response made by a child or group, including children's initiatory actions directed toward the teacher.

Marie M. Hughes, "What Is Teaching? One Viewpoint," Educational Leadership, *XIX, No. 4 (January 1962), 251–59.*

Data of this Study

The data of this study (2) were secured from 41 elementary teachers —7 men and 34 women. These teachers had classrooms in 19 buildings in 8 school districts.

The representativeness of the group may be judged from the fact that they received their training degrees in 22 different states. Their age range was 25 to 50 years; their teaching experience, 5 years to 30 years; with a bimodal distribution at the ninth and fifteenth years. They were career teachers and judged good by supervisory and consultant staff members.

Three 30-minute records were secured from each of the teachers by two observers working at one time in the classroom with the teacher's cooperation and knowledge of the exact time the observers would arrive to take the record. In general, the records were taken several days apart.

A brief episode from one 30-minute record may provide a more adequate picture of the data with which we worked:

Record #2620, Page 2:

T.: Carl, do you remember the day you came to school and said you could play a tune on the piano? It was a tune we all knew and so we sang it with you. You found out you could play the same tune on the tone bells. I wonder if you'd play the same tune for us today.

T.: My! We liked to sing with you. Can we start our music time by your playing again and our singing with you? Why don't you play it on the tone bells?

Carl: I'd like to play it on the piano.

T.: Well, all right, you may play it on the piano if you'd rather. Do you want to play it all through once or shall we start right off together?

Carl: I'll play it through. (Played on piano "Mary Had a Little Lamb" with one hand.)

T.: That was very nice!

Carl: I think you could sing with me.

T.: All right, we'd be glad to. (Carl played and children sang.) Thank you, Carl.

Carl: You could even do all of it.

T.: You mean we could sing all of the verses?

Carl: I can even do "followed her to school one day . . . etc."

T.: I'm sure you can, Carl. Thank you very much.

What does the teacher do? It is obvious what there is a wide repertoire of behavior open to the teacher.

The teacher *tells* people what to do.

The teacher *sets* goals, the specifics of attention. "Today, we shall do the 25 problems on page 90."

The teacher *gives* directions. "Take your books out and open them to page 90." "Do not write your name."

The teacher *reprimands.* "Take your seat, Johnny."

The teacher *accuses.* "You didn't work very hard."

The teacher *admonishes.* This is, of course, before anything happens. "Don't forget to close the door." "Make sure you look up your words."

The teacher *supports* and *encourages.* "That's nice." "Good." "Fine." "OK." "I knew you could do it."

The teacher *grants* or *denies* requests.

The teacher *clarifies* and *elaborates* on the problem or content under discussion.

The teacher *asks* questions.

The teacher *gives* cues.

There are many ways to categorize or organize the verbal behavior and nonverbal behavior of a teacher. It is the point of view of this investigator that the superior-subordinate rela-

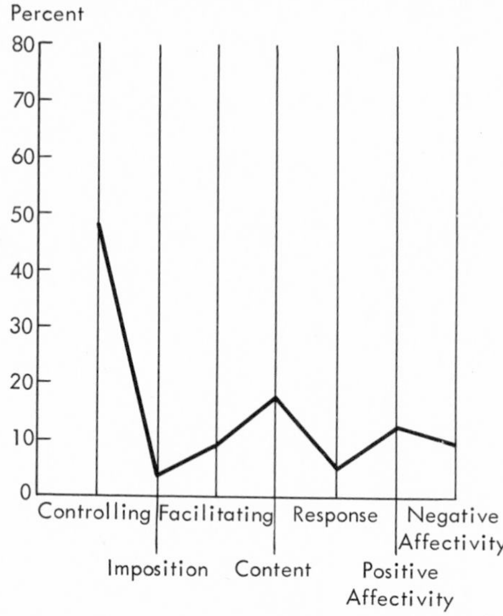

Figure 1.
Mean Distribution of Teaching Acts for 90 Minutes Observation for 35 Teachers.

tionship in the teacher-learner situation, with its culturally bestowed power position over the child, makes it impossible for the teacher to act in the classroom without performing a *function* for some child, group, or the entire class as recipients. It is the teacher who holds the power to give aid or withhold aid; to judge and to punish; to gratify or to deny; to accept or to ignore the response of a child.

Actually, children who are not participants in a given episode of interaction with the teacher do respond to his behavior (3, 4).

The presumptuousness of looking at teacher behavior from the standpoint of functions performed for the child is recognized. The 30-minute consecutive record often made it possible to follow actions and reactions through an episode, and many times several episodes. In addition, for a four year period there has been consistent effort through interviews and paper and pencil tests to discover children's views of typical classroom situations. To date, responses have been secured from some 1400 fifth and sixth graders in three states (5, 6). Interviews have been held with younger children, and with junior high youths.

As expected, children react in an individual manner; however, there is a great range of intensity of reaction. In general, there is a high degree of emotionality, with children responding to elements in the situations that were not intended or foreseen by adults. Another tentative finding was that for any given teacher behavior, from 7 to 20 per cent of those to whom it was directed appeared to make no response. They were not involved or they failed to identify with the situation when given the opportunity in interviews or paper and pencil test. The mode for this non-

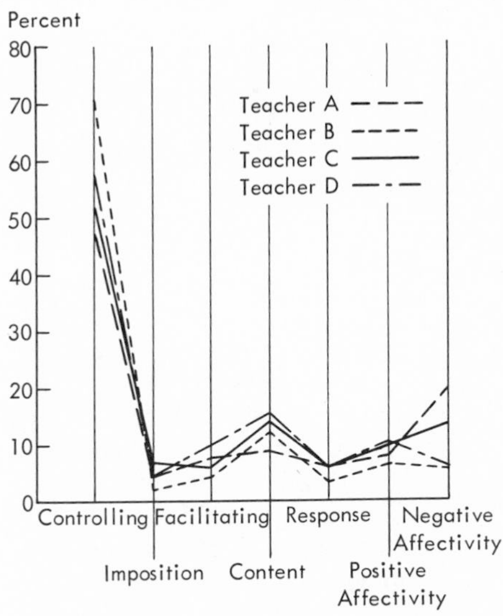

Figure 2.
Distribution Patterns of Teaching Acts for Four Teachers High in Controlling.

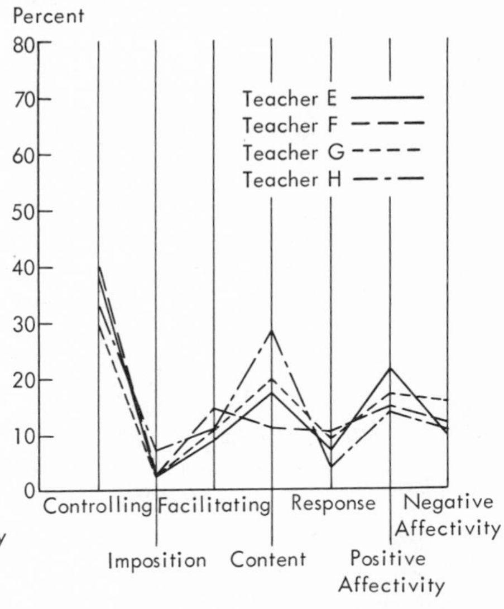

Figure 3.
Distribution Patterns of Teaching Acts for Four Teachers Low in Controlling.

involvement was 14 per cent. Most of the teachers are, of course, aware of the phenomenon of one or more children seeming not to be "with it."

Description of Teaching

Figure 1 presents the mean distribution of teaching acts performed by the teachers during three 30-minute periods of teaching. It is immediately clear that the largest number of teaching acts falls within the category of controlling functions. Figures 2 and 3 present the mean distributions of teaching acts for teachers who are among the highest and those who are among the lowest in the exercise of control in the classroom. Since the present report is devoted largely to an exposition of Controlling Functions, and the Development of Content, a brief definition of the other categories may be useful.

Teacher Imposition

These are acts where the teacher projects himself into the situation. For example: In a few classrooms without routine procedures for supplies, the teacher might say over and over again, "Keep your seat, I'll bring it to you." Another is the expression of evaluation e.g., on reading a story in a foreign locale, "Their names are certainly queer." Moralizing is another act that falls in this category. As may be noted in the figures, very few teaching acts fall in this category.

Facilitating

These acts may be thought of as management functions that are relatively neutral. All statements that designate time, change of schedule, and so forth. Those information seeking acts that are nonevaluative; that is, the child is free to have or not have it, e.g.: "Who brought lunch money?" Rhetorical questions of "Wasn't that fun?" "Did you enjoy it?" "We're finished, aren't we?" Such questions, if they evoke a response, secure a chorus of "yes" or "no" as expected. More often than not the teacher does not wait for an answer.

These management functions differentiate least among teachers and are the most stable with a teacher's series of records.

Personal Response

This includes meeting the individual requests of children, listening to their personal interests and experiences unrelated to the content under consideration.

These are all positive responses and most often are interactions between a teacher and a single child.

Positive and Negative Functions

These need little comment since they are the praise and reproof categories. It is realized that the use of positive and negative reinforcement controls behavior; however, by their very nature these teaching acts are, as a group, more affectivity-laden. Therefore, it was deemed desirable to trace them out separately.

Although space does not permit an elaboration of these last three categories, it is hypothesized that they have much to do with the personal liking or not liking of the teacher. There is something in a personal response that conveys the idea, "You count—you are important enough for me to listen to you, and to do something just for you."

Approval and acceptance were expressed most often in a stereotyped manner: "Fine," "Yes," "O.K." "Good," "All right." Such expressions without a definite referent served the purpose of allaying tension. It was one way of saying, "All is well."

It is hypothesized that the acceptance of reprimands of any degree of intensity depends to a large extent on the teacher's use of *public criteria.* If he makes clear the elements in the situation that call for certain required behavior, children may protest, but they can accept the reprimand as just. Consistency of teacher behavior is another element in fairness.

In general, more acts of positive affectivity were recorded for teachers than of negative affectivity; however, Fig. 2, depicting teachers high in control, shows two teachers who were more negative than positive in their teaching. The gross differences in distribution of teaching acts shown in Figs. 2 and 3 suggest that the classroom is quite different for the children in attendance.

Controlling Functions

Our study showed that the teaching acts most frequently performed were those of control. By control, reference is not limited to discipline. Since these teachers were considered good teachers, their classes were well organized and generally attentive. By control is meant goal setting, directing the children to the precise thing to which they give attention. Not only is the content named for childen, but they are held to a specific answer and processes of working. Such control is firm and pervasive. In many classrooms the control might be considered implacable. Sixty-eight per cent of the teachers had one or more of their records with 50 per cent or more of their teaching acts categorized as controlling.

The teacher most often wanted only *one* answer and refused all others. For example, a third grade was reporting on books read, then classifying them according to theme. One little girl made a few remarks about her book and then said, "It's a fantasy." The teacher immediately replied, "You mean imaginative, don't you?" No reward for the use of a divergent word or a suggestion of any relationship or differentiation between the two.

The control of content is exercised by the teacher in the structure of the *what* to give attention to. In a third grade arithmetic class each child had a foot rule. The teacher structured the group by saying. "Today, we are going to study the middle line. What is it called?" Several children answered. "One-third," "a fourth," "a half." One boy was busy measuring some paper on his desk and said, "This is 6¼ inches." (Correct) The teacher replied, "Just the middle line today. We just talk about the half."

As long as the question or statement that structures the class or the individual requires but *one* answer, the teacher is in absolute control. Nothing more may properly occur until the next question is asked. Such structure of content appears to evoke memory but little more in mental activity.

When structure is open, more than one answer is possible. Indeed, there may not be an absolutely right answer. For example, "What might happen if the new highway went across the state by one route instead of another?" Closed structure of content resulted in question and answer between teacher and class—it was strictly recitation. Open structure, with more than one answer possible, resulted in participation of several pupils before re-entry of the teacher in the situation. In other words, more ideas were generated and more pupils became involved in the work.

Control as Regulation of Who

Another phase of controlling behavior is that of regulating who will do what, answer questions, give the report, take lunch money to the office, etc. Such regulation can serve indirectly as punishment or as reward.

"Your work is finished, so you take the books to Mrs. Jones." At least a criterion of choice, "your work is done," is made public. In one episode the children were sharing their stories with one another and the teacher regulated after each story with, "Whom shall I choose, whom shall I ask to go next?" A child would then be named. As teacher choices followed one another, the excitement mounted over the who was to be next and not over the content of the stories.

Other teachers set up some *neutral* manner of regulating. "Write your names on the board when you are ready and we shall take them in order." Another teacher had children put a slip on a spindle. Their stories were then read in order of completion. Some teachers made charts of committees who worked at the various housekeeping and management chores a week at a time.

We found in one sixth grade that the students considered the teacher unfair. He was perplexed, so we tried to find out why this perception. It turned out that Lou and Hazel always got to answer the telephone. They sat next to the office and could answer without moving about unduly. This fact had not been shared with the children; consequently, all they saw was unfairness.

The use of *Public Criteria* for the controlling actions of the teacher is suggestive. It ameliorates the power of the teacher. It gives the authority an impersonal embodiment.

Control Over Many Activities

The controls exercised are expressed in all kinds of activities. It was difficult to get hold of the criteria used by teachers in their expression of control.

A child was making cut-out paper pears to be placed in a cornucopia poster filled with fruits and vegetables. The teacher said, "Why don't you make them bigger?"

Child: I made them like they are on my grandfather's farm.

T.: Get the picture from my desk and make them big like that.

The teacher judged in cases of altercation or conflict of interest. Incidentally, the conflict of interest was frequently between teacher and child or group. To illustrate, a teacher said:

T.: Who do you wish to have help you with your reading?

Child: Madeline.

T.: How about Susan?

Child: Jane.

T.: Let's see. Mary would be a good one. Yes, go sit with Mary.

A junior high school teacher working with the English class putting out a paper said:

T.: Here are some interesting things

about the Navy that we could put in the paper. Who wants to write it?

Agnes: I will. I read it and thought the the boys might like it.

T.: No, you already have three things in. I'll write it myself.

We hypothesize that consistent use of *Public Criteria* might aid in reducing the conflicts with authority. *Public Criteria* are situationally placed:

T.: There is time for *one* story before noon.

T.: We had trouble with a certain kind of problem yesterday; therefore, we will work on similar problems today.

T.: The children using the saws are on the barn committee and must have them until they finish; therefore, you have to wait.

Public Criteria can also express the conventions and accepted ways of doing. "You have too many erasures on your paper to read it easily," instead of "*I* won't take a paper that looks like that."

Place of Controlling Functions

This investigator believes that it is the business of the teacher to manage (control, if you prefer) the classroom so that learning for all the children present may proceed. Controlling functions will undoubtedly constitute between 30 and 40 per cent of a teacher's behavior; however, the power component may be ameliorated through the use of:

Open-structure that permits some choice or requires more than one answer

Increased Regulation (*who* is to respond) that is neutral or done with public criteria that express the reason for the choice

Directions that are clear with limits set to reduce repetition of directions and lessen the number of reprimands

Rules that are group developed, situationally oriented, and enforceable. They should make sense to children

Development of Content

There is a relationship between the development of content and the nature of the control exercised by structure. When the structure permits no exploration on the part of children it serves to delimit and restrict.

A primary class was reading about a baby elephant. They discussed its age and other things pertaining to the picture of the baby elephant. Finally Ben spoke up and said:

Ben: Look, here is an elephant with a tusk.

T.: Yes, that elephant is on the other page. Read this page and find out what Baby Elephant did when she got to the monkey cage.

It might have been profitable to raise the question why one elephant had tusks and the other did not. It can be hypothesized that the mental processes evoked by the different situations are likewise different.

In another class the teacher and class were looking at a large map of the two hemispheres, when one child asked where the local town was. The teacher replied, "It is about here, but can't be seen on this map. I'll get you one and you can find it and other towns you know."

The teaching acts that develop

content elaborate and add to the content or problem under consideration. Response is made to the data placed in the situation by the children. It is believed that children involved in content have something to say. They are encouraged in this by the teacher who respects their efforts. The teacher *stimulates* by offering several suggestions of ideas or of activities that might be done. The choice of doing, however, remains with the child. (It is, of course, proper to give a direction or an assignment, which then would be an act of control.)

Evaluation that keeps content as a referent is in this category. To illustrate, "You have used several kinds of sentence structure in your composition. Very good." The phrase, "That's good," spoken after a child has read the composition does not tell him whether he was good to have written it at all, or good to have read it, or just good to have gotten through the episode. In terms of compositions, he has received nothing definite that helps him move ahead with his writing. He has received teacher approval. With most of the evaluation made in the form of generalized approval or disapproval, such expressions foster dependence on teacher instead of judgment and interest in the content.

If children and youth are to become interested in subject matter for its own sake, do they not need to link their own experience and make their own personal inquiry in relationship to it? If children are not listened to, how can one know what concepts are developed or what interpretations are made?

An upper grade discussion had been going on concerning early California Indians.

T.: Incidentally, did the California Indians have a pretty easy life?

Arthur: No.

T.: Yes they did, Arthur. Don't you remember? Who can tell me about it?

What logic was Arthur using in his reply? Was it strictly subjective, "I wouldn't have liked it," or had he assessed the situation with some judgment?

When do children use a variety of mental processes such as making comparisons, explaining with some logic, noting relationships, generalizing from a series of data? What kind of questions and teacher responses evoke what mental activity (7)?

Perhaps teachers need to develop what might be called *creative use of interruptions*.

Not long ago a mother reported the disgust of her kindergarten son whose teacher allegedly told him that he couldn't talk about dinosaurs until third grade. The child had been to the Dinosaur Monument and Museum with his family. While there, the father had bought each boy a book which had been read at home.

One can conjecture all kinds of reasons why the teacher did not wish to get off on dinosaurs. However, the question remains, "In what situations do teachers act in ways that children can see them as people who *aid* in their personal quest for knowing? Since this child's dinosaurs were tied to Vernal, Utah, it might have been very stimulating to listen to his story and also mention the La Brea Tar Pits within the city of Los Angeles, as another locale where bones had been found.

It is, of course, possible that the child wanted attention only. Even so, the school can meet such personal needs of children through the use of their explorations and inquiries in the development of content. It is suggested that children's questions and remarks be integrated with the lesson plan of the teacher.

The present study of teaching found that the most prevalent series of teaching acts were in question-answer test or recitation situations. Far too many such situations were spent in working for the specific answer wanted by the teacher.

Of the total group of 41, only 3 teachers had all of their records with 20 or more of their teaching acts in this category of development of content. Seventy-four per cent of all records had 20 per cent or less of teaching acts falling in this category of exploration, amplification, utilization of children's questions and remarks, evaluation and stimulation. This category has been described as working with the content or problem and called *development of content.*

Some relationships of one category to another may be of interest. Development of Content and Negative Affectivity correlate −.42 significant at the .001 level in social studies. This relationship is not unexpected, since teachers who use many acts of Negative Affectivity are not responsive to children's ideas and explorations even in subject matter.

Personal Response is correlated −.35 with Controlling and a −.38 with Negative Affectivity. Again, this is not unexpected and it holds for all records regardless of kind of work the classes were doing.

The point of view expressed in this report is that teaching may be described in terms of functions the teacher behavior, verbal and nonverbal, performs for the child, group, or class to whom it is directed. It was found possible to categorize such teaching acts in seven categories: Controlling, Imposition, Facilitating, Development of Content, Personal Response, Positive Affectivity, and Negative Affectivity.

Control of the class was exercised in varied activities, but particularly in terms of *what* to give attention to and *who* was to do what; also, the *how* of doing was prescribed and enforced.

Management of the classroom for learning is the teacher's job; therefore, control functions are necessary. It was suggested, however, that the power component the teacher holds may be reduced with changes in verbal behavior.

In dealing with subject matter, little attention was given to children's exploratory remarks or their questions. The questions teachers used for structure were usually closed; that is, asked for one *right* answer. It was suggested that one right answer evoked the use of recall as a mental process instead of stimulating a larger range of mental activity.

It was suggested that *responsiveness* on the part of the teacher to children's remarks, questions, personal experience (data they place in the situation) would lead them to greater involvement in content (subject matter) and stimulate use of higher mental processes.

Teachers demonstrated different patterns in teaching. Different patterns do affect the learning of children (8, 9).

References

1. Aschner, Mary Jane, "The Language of Teaching," in *Language and Concepts in Education*, ed. by B. O. Smith and R. Ennis. Skokie, Ill.: Rand McNally & Co., 1961.

2. Hughes, Marie M. and Associates, *The Assessment of the Quality of Teaching: A Research Report.* U. S. Office of Education Cooperative Research Project No. 353. Salt Lake City: The University of Utah, 1959.

3. Kounin, J. and P. Gump, "The Ripple Effect in Discipline," *The Elementary School Journal* (Fall 1958), pp. 158–62.

4. Kounin, J., *et al.*, "Explorations in Classroom Management," *Journal of Teacher Education* (June 1961), pp. 235–46.

5. Carin, Arthur, "Children's Perceptions of Selected Classroom Situations." Doctoral Dissertation, University of Utah, June 1959.

6. De Vaney, Elena, "Perceptions Among Teachers and Students of Varying Cultural Backgrounds." Doctoral Dissertation, University of Utah, October 1960.

7. Aschner, Mary Jane, "Asking Questions to Trigger Thinking," *N.E.A. Journal* (September 1961), pp. 44–46.

8. Flanders, Ned, *Teacher Influence: An Interaction Analysis.* U. S. Office of Education Cooperative Research Project No. 397. Minneapolis: University of Minnesota, 1960.

9. Sears, Pauline, "What Happens to Pupils Within the Classroom of Elementary Schools." Paper read at American Educational Research Association meeting, Los Angeles, June 30, 1960.

7. TEACHER INFLUENCE, PUPIL ATTITUDES, AND ACHIEVEMENT

NED. A. FLANDERS

Communication and Teacher Influence

Step inside a classroom and what do you hear? The chances are better than 60 per cent you will hear someone talking if you are in an elementary or secondary school classroom.

If someone is talking, the chances are that it will be the teacher more than 70 per cent of the time. Yes, the teacher talks more than all the students combined. He manages class activities by giving directions. He expresses his ideas by lecturing. He stimulates student participation by asking questions. He clarifies student ideas by applying them to the solution of a problem. He praises and encourages students from time to time. On rare occasions he may clarify or diagnose the feelings and attitudes expressed by students or inferred from their behavior. He may also criticize the behavior of a student or class. All are types of teacher statements that can be heard in a classroom.

Most of the functions associated with teaching are implemented by verbal communication. Of course, nonverbal communication does exist and is not unimportant. The nod of the head to encourage student participation, the finger to the lips to warn against talking, the smile, and the frown, these all communicate to students. But nonverbal communication occurs less frequently than verbal communication and the two are usually highly correlated. The frown is most often associated with statements that express disapproval, the smile with statements of approval.

The first step toward systematic classroom management is made when a teacher understands how to control his verbal communication so that he can use his influence as a social force.

Ned A. Flanders, TEACHER INFLUENCE, PUPIL ATTITUDES, AND ACHIEVEMENT, *Cooperative Research Monograph No. 12, Office of Education, U.S. Department of Health, Education and Welfare. (Washington, D.C.: Government Printing Office, 1965), 1–23, 111–21.*

Unfortunately, this kind of knowledge and the corresponding skill don't always go together. As one teacher put it, "I know what I'm doing and I am usually aware of most mistakes that I make, but I don't know what to do about it."

The research reported in this monograph concerns the verbal statements of teachers as they occur in the spontaneous interaction of the classroom. We will explain what has been called a system of classroom interaction analysis, our method of recording and analyzing teacher statements. A theory of teacher influence or, more modestly, some hypotheses of teacher influence will be developed and tested. The data were obtained from research carried out in the Minneapolis and St. Paul public schools before March 1957 and after March 1958. Additional data came from research in Wellington, New Zealand, carried out under a Fulbright Research Scholarship during 1957.

Our basic purpose is greater understanding of the teacher's role, the control he provides while teaching, and the patterns of influence he uses in classroom management.

There are at least two theoretical models that are currently being used to understand interaction analysis data collected in a classroom. One model makes use of the logical steps of problem-solving and draws heavily from what we know about inductive and deductive reasoning, scientific method, procedures for defining terms, level of abstraction, and principles from the field of semantics. This approach is being used in the research of B. Othaniel Smith (14) at the University of Illinois.

The second model, the one we use, is based less on the intellectual skills mentioned above and more on a set of social skills used by teachers to control and manage class activities. This model is based on a psychology of superior-subordinate relationships, adapted to fit classroom conditions. An earlier development can be found in the 59th Yearbook, National Society for the Study of Educational Research (9).

The differences between these two models can be illustrated by the teacher's orientation to classroom behavior. Suppose a teacher becomes aware of intellectual confusion in the remarks of a student because the student uses the same word as if it had two quite different meanings. The teacher's knowledge and skill in defining words and his understanding of level of abstraction will help in diagnosing the intellectual aspects of the problem in terms of the first model. Just how he chooses to provide this information—by lecturing, by asking a series of questions so that the student can "discover" the difficulty, or by directing the student in some semantic exercise—is the kind of choice on which the second model is based. Here the teacher is concerned with his own behavior and how he can best use his authority to enhance student learning.

Neither model is "right" or "wrong," and an understanding of both models is likely to improve teaching. Each model is a frame of reference for organizing ideas about behavior; such an organization guides research. Research within either frame of reference is difficult and tedious; to work in both simultaneously would require more resources than were available at Minnesota when the research reported in this monograph was planned and conducted.

To summarize, this monograph is concerned with analyzing the spontaneous verbal communication of the teacher. A system of interaction analysis is used for this purpose. The procedure involves the classification of statements every 3 seconds and the tabulation of data in special matrices for later analysis. Measures of academic achievement and student attitudes are correlated with the verbal patterns observed in the classroom. Most of the conclusions refer to the role of the teacher in classroom management.

Early Research on Classroom Climate

Most research programs have antecedents in the work of other researchers. The research reported in this monograph is no exception. We are indebted to a number of individuals whose work has contributed to our thinking.

The term "classroom climate" refers to generalized attitudes toward the teacher and the class that the pupils share in common despite individual differences. The development of these attitudes is an outgrowth of classroom social interaction. As a result of participating in classroom activities, pupils soon develop common attitudes about how they like their class, the kind of person the teacher is, and how he will act in certain typical situations. These common attitudes color all aspects of classroom behavior, creating a social atmosphere, or climate, that appears to be fairly stable, once established. Thus, the word "climate"[1] is merely a shorthand reference to those qualities that consistently predominate in most teacher-pupil contacts and in contacts among the pupils in the presence or absence of the teacher.

The earliest systematic studies of spontaneous pupil and teacher behavior that relate directly to classroom climate are those of H. H. Anderson and his colleagues, Helen and Joseph Brewer and Mary Frances Reed (2, 3, 4, and 5 in the bibliography at the end of this paper); these studies are based on the observation of "dominative" and "integrative" contacts. It is essential to understand the qualitative differences between an integrative and a dominative social contact, because most of the research on classroom climate makes similar behavioral distinctions.

> A preliminary study showed that it was possible to devise reliable measures of behavior of young children. Behavior was recorded as "contacts" divided into two groups of categories. If a child snatched a toy, struck a playmate, or commanded him, or if he attempted to force him in some way, such contacts were included under the term "domination." By such behavior he ignored the rights of the companion; he tended to reduce the free interplay of differences and to lead toward resistance or conformity in responding or adapting to another.
>
> Other contacts were recorded which tended to increase the interplay of differences. Offering a companion a choice or soliciting an expression of his desires were gestures of flexibility and adapta-

[1] Climate is assessed either by analyzing teacher-pupil interaction and inferring underlying attitudes from the interaction, or by the use of a pupil-attitude inventory and predicting the quality of classroom interaction from the results. Its precise meaning, as commonly used, is seldom clear—just as its synonyms, "morale," "rapport," and "emotional tone," are also ambiguous. To have any meaning at all, the word is always qualified by an adjective, and it is in the choice of adjectives that researchers become reformers and too often lose their objectivity.

tion. These tended in the direction of discovering common purposes among differences. Such contacts were grouped under the term "socially integrative behavior." (5, p. 12)

The findings of Anderson are based on the study of preschool, primary school, and elementary school classrooms involving five different teachers and extending over several years. The imaginative research of Anderson and his colleagues has produced a series of internally consistent and significant findings: First, the dominative and integrative contacts of the teacher set a pattern of behavior that spreads throughout the classroom; the behavior of the teacher, more than of any other individual, sets the climate of the class. The rule is that a climate of domination incites further domination, and one of integration stimulates further integration. It is the teacher's tendency that spreads among pupils and is continued even when the teacher is no longer in the room. Furthermore, the pattern a teacher develops in one year is likely to persist in his classroom the following year with different pupils. Second, when a teacher has a higher proportion of integrative contacts, pupils show more spontaneity and initiative, more voluntary social contributions, and more acts of problem-solving. Third, when a teacher has a higher proportion of dominative contacts, the pupils are more easily distracted from schoolwork, and show greater compliance to, as well as rejection of, teacher domination.

A year or so after Anderson started his work, Lippitt and White (12), working with Kurt Lewin, carried out laboratory experiments to analyze the effects of adult leaders' influence on boys' groups. The laboratory approach used had certain advantages in studying the effects of the adult leader's behavior. First, the contrasting patterns of leader behavior were purified and made more consistent as a result of training and role-playing. Second, differences in the underlying personality and appearance of the adult leaders were minimized through role rotation. Third, the effect of the pattern of leader behavior was intensified, compared with the effect in an ordinary classroom, since there were only 5 boys to a group. Roughly speaking, the pattern Lippitt and White named "authoritarian leadership" consisted of dominative contacts; "democratic leadership" consisted of an integrative pattern; and "laissez-faire" consisted of irregular and infrequent integrative contacts with an element of indifference to the total group that is seldom found in a classroom and was not present in the Anderson *et al.* studies.

Most of the conclusions of the Lippitt and White study and others confirm or extend the general conclusions of Anderson *et al.*, with some semantic modification but very little change, if any, in behavioral meaning. From the point of view of classroom teaching, one interesting extension was the conceptualization of "dependence on the leader" by Lippitt and White. This is a state of affairs in which group members are unable to proceed without directions from the leader. Anderson *et al.* used the category "conforming to teacher domination" and thus noted similar events, but in the more concentrated social climates of the laboratory experiments, it was clearly seen that extensive compliance occurs when there is a generalized condition of dependence.

These two mutually supportive and independent studies aroused considerable interest in the notion of social climate. Additional research revealed minor variations of the central theme already established. Withall (15) showed that a simple classification of the teacher's verbal statements into 7 categories produced an index of teacher behavior almost identical to the integrative-dominative (I/D) ratio of Anderson *et al.* Flanders (8) created laboratory situations in which contrasting patterns of teacher behavior were exposed to one pupil at a time. A sustained dominative pattern was consistently disliked by pupils: it reduced their ability to recall the material studied, and it produced disruptive anxiety, as indicated by galvanic skin response and changes in the heartbeat rates. The reverse trends were noted as pupil reactions to integrative contacts. Perkins (13), using Withall's technique, studied groups of teachers organized to discuss the topic of child growth and development. He found that greater learning about child growth and development occurred when group discussion was free to focus on that topic; groups with an integrative type of leader were able to do this more frequently than were groups led by a dominative type of leader.

In a large cross-sectional study that did not use observations of spontaneous teacher behavior, Cogan (6) administered to 987 eighth-grade students in 33 classrooms a single paper-and-pencil instrument that contained three scales: (*a*) a scale assessing student perceptions of the teacher; (*b*) a scale on which students reported how often they did required schoolwork; and (*c*) a scale on which students reported how often they did extra, nonrequired schoolwork. Cogan's first scale assessed traits which he developed in terms of Murray's list of major personality needs. There were two patterns in this scale. The items of one pattern were grouped as "dominative," "aggressive," and "rejectant." The second pattern was "integrative," "affiliative," and "nurturant"; these correspond to Anderson's dominative and integrative patterns. Cogan found that students reported doing more assigned and extra schoolwork when they perceived the teacher's behavior as falling into the integrative pattern rather than the dominative pattern.

All together, these research projects support the definition given earlier of classroom climate. The two teacher behavior patterns that create the contrasting classroom climates are shown below:

The Integrative Pattern

a. Accepts, clarifies, and supports the ideas and feelings of pupils.

b. Praises and encourages.

c. Asks questions to stimulate pupil participation in decision-making.

d. Asks questions to orient pupils to schoolwork.

The Dominative Pattern

a. Expresses or lectures about own ideas or knowledge.

b. Gives directions or orders.

c. Criticizes or deprecates pupil behavior with intent to change it.

4. Justifies own position or authority.

Concepts for Understanding Classroom Interaction

One contribution of research on classroom climate has been the identification of different kinds of verbal statements that the teacher uses. This information has been used in the development of our system of interaction analysis.

A less consistent contribution of this early research concerns the words used to designate patterns of teacher behavior. In fact, there is quite a choice: Anderson (2)—"dominative" and "integrative"; Lippitt and White—"authoritarian," "democratic," and "laissez-faire" (12); Withall (15), Flanders (8), Perkins (13)—"teacher-centered" and "student-centered"; and Cogan (6)—"preclusive" and "inclusive." All these come from a short stroll in the conceptual garden of psychology; an overnight hike could extend the list indefinitely. Faced with such a choice, we might first pause to discuss the concepts used in this type of research.

Concepts used to describe teacher influence refer to a series of acts occurring during some time period. When a particular series occurs again and again, it becomes familiar to an observer and he can identify it. We call such a series of "pattern" of influence.

It is interesting to distinguish between an influence pattern and the concept of "role," as it is commonly used in the literature of social psychology. The difference is in the degree of behavioral specificity that is implied. For example, it may be said that a teacher plays in the classroom a "democratic" or "authoritarian" role. These concepts not only connote value judgments, but they are so abstract that they fail to denote very much about the behavior of the teacher. If someone tries to create either role, his choice of influence patterns depends primarily on his personal and often unique understanding of the concept. Such a choice involves too many alternatives; specificity is lacking.

The only path through these difficulties is to increase understanding by insisting that the concepts used have explicit behavioral meaning. In the rest of this section, certain concepts that refer to the teacher's behavior, the student's reactions, and the nature of the learning goals will be presented. In each instance, a description of behavior in a social setting will be given first. Next, concepts will be used to abstract the behavior events, and in the process, a theoretical definition of the concept will become clear. Finally, the procedures used in this study to measure or quantify the concept will be briefly stated.

The reader may wish to evaluate the development of these concepts by applying the following criteria. First, what are the concepts that are given theoretical meaning by analysis of the behavior that commonly occurs in a classroom? Second, are the procedures used for quantifying behavior that is associated with a concept (a) practical: that is, can they be used in a classroom; (b) representative: that is, do they adequately sample all behavior that could logically be associated with the concept; and (c) reliable: that is, can the error factor be determined and is it low, compared with the differences studied? Third, can the concepts be organized into hypotheses or principles (cause and effect statements) to predict behavior or the consequences of behavior?

Concepts for Describing Teacher Influence

Teacher influence exists as a series of acts along a time line. It is most often expressed as verbal communication. In this study we assume that verbal communication constitutes an adequate sample of the teacher's total influence pattern. A single act of a teacher occupies a segment of time. Before this act a particular state of affairs exists; after the act is completed, a different state of affairs exists. Some acts are more potent than others and have greater consequences. Furthermore, a long series of similar acts may have more extensive effects than just an isolated few.

A researcher is free to choose concepts that will be used to describe the state of affairs before and after an act, and concepts that will be used to describe the act itself.

Suppose a teacher says, "Please close the door," to a student. The chances are that the student will close the door. Before this act of influence, the student was engaged in some activity, such as thinking or reading. But since he was expected to comply with the teacher's command, he interrupted his train of thought to get up and close the door.

Actually, this sequence of behavior is as complex as we wish to make it. We could theorize about the social expectations that exist when a teacher makes what adults call a reasonable demand of a student. Much could be said, if we had the facts, about how past contacts with other authority figures have helped to form this particular student's reactions to a command. It might be that the student resented this intrusion and chose to push the door so that it slammed, rather than gently closing it. A lesser degree of resentment could be expressed by an audible sigh followed by slow movements.

Because of all the concepts that could be used to describe behavior, there is a choice here along a continuum. The genotypic concepts that describe inner motives or feelings are at one end, and the phenotypic concepts that describe more superficial aspects of behavior are at the other end. The choice should fit the purpose. A psychiatrist would prefer certain concepts for his purposes that would probably be too genotypic for the majority of interpretations that a teacher needs to make.

Our choice in this instance leads to the following explanation. The teacher exerted *direct influence*, which restricted the *freedom of action* of the student, making him momentarily more *dependent* on the teacher. From this illustration we hope the reader will understand that an act of direct influence restricts freedom of action, usually by focusing on a problem and, in this case, it made the student more dependent on teacher influence for a short period of time.

By the way, you the reader may have felt uneasy when you thought of a teacher's restricting the freedom of action of a student. These are terms that often elicit value judgments. However, it seems sensible to assert that a student's freedom of action is restricted when he is told to shut the door. Nevertheless, it is difficult to make an objective description of such events.

Now, suppose the same door is closed, but with a completely different script. The teacher asks, "Does anyone feel a draft in here?" Johnny says, "Yes, it's cold. I think it's coming from this open door." The teacher says, "Well, since it seems cold, please close the door." So Johnny gets up and closes the door.

The second example includes the same command and ultimately leads to the same compliance, yet most of us would agree that the state of affairs would be different at the termination of the episode. Consider, too, differences after a series of such episodes extending over hours, days, weeks, or the school year.

Again we face a choice in conceptualizing the behavior. Our choice is as follows: The command, "Close the door," was modified first by a question, "Does anyone feel a draft in here?"; second, by a student response, "Yes, it's cold. I think it's coming from this open door," the latter phrase being a student-initiated idea; and third, by the teacher's acknowledging the student's idea, "Well, since it seems cold. . . ." Taken all together, the teacher's acts of influence are more indirect than direct. While the student's freedom of action was restricted, his perception of this restriction was probably modified in the second example because he was solving a problem that he had helped to identify, rather than merely complying with the command of an authority figure. In fact, the teacher's behavior encouraged the student's initiative and, in this sense, his freedom of action was expanded. Later on, after more examples are given, we hope it will become clear that an act of indirect influence expands freedom of action and usually makes a student less dependent on the teacher. He often has greater orientation to a problem, because he helped to identify it.

Most teachers who hear these ideas expressed immediately conclude that indirect influence is superior to direct influence. We believe that the basis of this value judgment lies less in the ideas just expressed than in the social pressures that affect teachers' self-concepts. Most teachers apparently want to believe that they are "indirect teachers," even before they hear how these concepts are defined or are told about any research findings. If being an indirect teacher means consistently using indirect influence, we can state categorically that no such teacher exists, because no teacher employs a pure pattern of influence. All teachers establish some kind of balance based on a combination of direct and indirect influence.

At this point, further objection often arises. It seems obvious that any "intelligent teacher" would prefer to have his students "problem-oriented," as illustrated in the second episode, rather than "authority-oriented," as illustrated in the first episode. (The quotation marks are used here to emphasize how quickly abstract value judgments enter the discussion.) Our experience would suggest that, in the long run, most teachers want the students in their classes to react to the demands of problem-solving rather than to their own authority. Yet does it necessarily follow that indirect influence is superior to direct influence? Is the student in the first illustration any less "problem-oriented" than the student in the second?

Our system of interaction analysis provides an explicit procedure for quantifying direct and indirect influence that is closely related to the teacher behaviors identified by research on classroom climate. Direct influence consists of those verbal statements of the teacher that restrict freedom of action, by focusing attention on a problem, interjecting teacher authority, or both. These statements include lecturing, giving directions, criticizing, and justifying his own use of authority. Indirect influence consists of those verbal statements of the teacher that expand a student's freedom of action by encouraging his verbal participation and initiative. These include asking questions, accepting and clarifying the ideas or feelings of students, and praising or encouraging students' responses.

Concepts for Describing Student Dependence

One way to start describing student reactions to teacher influence is to postulate that dependence is always present in some degree in any teacher-pupil relationship. The maturity and power advantages of a teacher, reinforced by social expectations, are such that the student anticipates teacher direction and supervision. The student is more often ready to comply with teacher influence than not, and when he does not comply, his anxiety increases because the teacher can control an effective system of rewards and punishments.

One way to describe the process of instruction is to say that the teacher strives to change the response pattern of a student from mere compliance to independent action, determined by the student's own analysis of the problems confronting him. A student who recognizes no learning problem is much more dependent on the teacher in deciding what is or is not acceptable behavior, and will solicit direction. On the other hand, a student hard at work on a problem responds to the requirements for its solution; these requirements form a set of criteria with which to evaluate his own behavior as well as that of the teacher.

The first complication of this oversimplification is that students differ in their ability to give up dependence on the teacher by shifting orientation to the problem-solving requirements. Some students can hardly separate the problem-solving requirements from teacher approval, and continually seek teacher support at nearly all stages of their activities. We call such students *dependent-prone*. Even the most skillful teachers find it difficult to stimulate self-directed problem-solving among highly dependent-prone students. Dependence-proneness is a personality trait that is established early in childhood, and the extent to which it can be modified by school experiences is unknown.

We must distinguish here between *compliance* and *dependence*. When a teacher directs, demands, or forces, compliance is not voluntary. But when a student imagines or expects that the teacher wants a job done in a particular fashion and voluntarily does what he imagines the teacher wants, his reaction is an act of dependence.

By way of illustration, let us apply the concepts of dependence-proneness, compliance, and dependent behavior to the episode of the boy closing the door. Most students, whether they are dependent-prone or not, will comply when told or asked to do something by the teacher. Most students, for example, will get up and close the door. This is an act of compliance. Suppose, however, that we could turn this episode into a little experiment in which closing the door gradually becomes more and more of an imposition. Suppose that we could move the door farther and farther away, put flights of stairs in the way as physical barriers, and, in general, make the task increasingly cumbersome and difficult. Even when the task became most difficult, a highly dependent-prone student would probably get up and close the door, but a student with low dependency-proneness might be stimulated to think of an alternative, such as, "Let's close the window. That will stop the circulation of cold air." The dependent-prone student has a lower threshold or resistance to compliance than the independent-prone.

Illustrating acts of dependence within the context of this episode becomes a bit absurd, since the episode involves only a simple act of common courtesy. But suppose that the student, with no sign from the teacher, simply volunteers to close the door, and that we can prove he wasn't doing it for his own comfort. Such an action is not compliance, but an act of dependence. A more typical dependent act in the classroom consists of soliciting approval and permission. For example, a student does an arithmetic problem and then asks the teacher; "Is this the way you wanted it done?"

Over a long period of time, continuous compliance will increase the incidence of dependent behavior. Students begin to anticipate teacher demands and respond dependently. Being ordered to act in a certain way and being subjected to standards of behavior imposed by an authority figure will, in the long run, set these expectations. The more dependent-prone respond with compliance and acts of dependence. The more independent-prone will comply when forced, and, depending on other factors, may engage in subtle and not so subtle acts of aggressive counter-dependence, or rebelliousness.

Compliance, then, consists of doing what one is told to do by an authority figure. This type of behavior is best quantified by the analysis of spontaneous behavior, for example, by analyzing a tape recording or developing a system of observation.

Dependent behavior consists of voluntarily bowing to expected teacher influence or to imagined restraints associated with the teacher's authority. The problems of measurement are difficult, since acts of dependence must be separated from acts of compliance on the basis of difference in intent.

We might note here that conformity to group standards, real or imagined, often has a self-initiated and thus voluntary aspect to it. In this sense, acts of conformity and acts of dependence both differ from compliance because of the absence of a teacher directive and the presence of the pupil's intent to please. The imagined directive or group force-field that creates conformity and dependence can be just as potent and seem just as real for the pupil as those creating compliance.

Dependence-proneness is a personality trait representing the tendency of a student to engage in dependent acts. Dependence-proneness is a concept necessary to explain why some children respond dependently, and others do not, when exposed to identical social stimuli. Dependent behavior may be caused by a number of psychological forces, one of which is dependence-proneness.

In past laboratory experiments dependent behavior has been successfully measured by observing teacher-pupil contacts and noting, in particular, requests for help and solicitations of approval. Filson (7) used a paper-and-pencil questionnaire on which students indicated their need for approval and help, or their lack of it, during a teacher-directed learning task. We have been particularly unsuccessful in developing procedures for measuring dependent behavior in the classroom under field conditions.

In this study, dependence-proneness is measured by an attitude inventory consisting of 45 items. The reliability and validity of this scale have been cited by Flanders, Amidon, and Anderson (10) for seventh-grade and eighth-grade boys and girls.

Concepts for Describing Learning Goals

Learning goals are usually described in terms of curriculum organization and content. In all classroom activities the learning of certain skills, understandings, or facts is central to a plan for which the teacher has ultimate responsibility.

However, certain dimensions of learning goals, particularly the goal perceptions of the students and the teacher, can be conceptualized and measured without specifying the curriculum content involved. For example, the following dimensions of students' goal perceptions seem independent of content. First, there is a dimension of motivation; how attractive and interesting are these goals? Second, there is a dimension of realism; are the resources of time, ability, and energy adequate to reach a goal? Third, there is a dimension of clarity; how well do students understand the steps necessary to reach a goal and how clearly is the end product visualized?

The last-named dimension, goal clarity, received special emphasis in this paper because variation of this variable is crucial to our hypotheses about teacher influence. In the analysis of results, we will distinguish between situations in which goals are presumed to be clear and those in which goals are presumed to be less clear.

The first two dimensions, motivation and realism, are ignored in our studies, even though they are important, because the consequences of their variation are more self-evident. Lewin (11) and many others have discussed goals with high positive valence which create strong motivation and result in greater progress in learning. The consequences of sufficient or insufficient time, ability, and energy are self-evident. The assumption that motivation and realism are approximately equal among the groups being compared later [in our research] seems to us quite reasonable. Certainly the students all had an equal opportunity for work, they often had more than enough energy, and individual differences were distributed within each class in a manner that did not seriously affect our results.

We assume that the dimension of goal clarity can be described by conceiving of a continuum that extends from *clear goals* at one end to *ambiguous goals* at the opposite end. We define having *clear goals* as a condition in which a student knows what steps are necessary to reach the goal and has a clear picture of the end product. Having *ambiguous goals* is defined as a condition in which a student is not sure of the steps necessary to reach the goal and has an uncertain picture of the end product. The perceptions of the students, not the teacher, are essential to any measure of the clarity or ambiguity of goals.

As goals become clear, a student at work on a problem can use his understanding of the problem-solving requirements to guide his own behavior or to evaluate teacher influence. In either case, he is less dependent on teacher influence. It seems reasonable to suppose that a student will benefit most from problem-solving experiences when he works at the lowest level of dependence on the teacher that both he and the teacher can tolerate and that permits necessary coordination and maintenance of classroom learning activities. A certain amount of dependence is desirable and will always be present in the classroom, but the teacher can and should control the general level of dependence by appropriate use of teacher influence.

The level of dependence at some moment in the classroom is a function of the student's dependence-proneness, the restraints set by the teacher's pattern of influence, and the student's perception of the learning goal. In a specific situation, we assume the dependence-proneness of the student is "given," that is, fixed by the personality trait. The restraints set by the teacher are a function of his use of direct and indirect influence and the perception of this influence held by the student from past experience. When goals are ambiguous, the student is more likely to respond to teacher influence in a dependent fashion. When goals are clear, he can evaluate teacher influence by analyzing the intent of the teacher in terms of the problem-solving requirements.

It takes time to establish a learning goal, to identify the steps of problem-solving, and to begin work activities. During this period of time, clear goals gradually emerge from ambiguous goals. Because the student expects to comply with the teacher's authority, an expectation founded on past experience with authority figures, he responds initially in a dependent manner or at least with compliance. The natural tendency of a teacher, when faced with a situation in which goals are ambiguous, is to establish clarity by using a pattern of influence that is primarily direct. Direct influence, under these circumstances, leads to higher levels of dependence that can interfere with self-directed problem-solving. In effect, the student must take into consideration both the demands of the teacher and the demands of the problem. A dependent-prone student remains oriented to the demands of the teacher, even when goals become clear. Dependence, once established under these conditions, is difficult to reduce.

The case of closing the door can again serve as an illustration. When the teacher said, "Please close the door," the student's orientation to action was in terms of compliance. In one sense, problem-solving was not possible for him unless he chose to make an issue out of complying. Repeated over and over again, such compliance increases dependence. In the second example of closing the door, the action taken was a solution to the problem of eliminating a cold draft. The teacher's indirect approach permitted the student to participate in the identification of the problem; when such an approach is used, students are more likely to suggest an alternative solution, such as closing a window. Dependence-proneness is thus held constant rather than being intensified. The point here is that the teacher's choice of direct or indirect influence while goals are still ambiguous is crucial to the control of dependence.

When the activity under consideration is an important part of the curriculum and not a routine closing of a door, the consequences of alternative teacher influence patterns are much more significant. Our observation of teachers in many classrooms gives us the conviction that teachers are more likely to exert direct influence while goals are ambiguous or when progress is halted and diagnosis needed. Add to this the tendency of students to comply and to become dependent, and a good deal of the dependent behavior that occurs in the classroom is explained.

Amidon (1) has successfully measured the goal perceptions of students during laboratory experiments involving eighth-grade students learning geometry. He manipulated the initial conditions by presenting information on tape recordings: one to create goal ambiguity and the other, goal clarity. At different points during the learning activities, a paper-and-pencil scale was used to assess the students' perceptions of next steps and end products.

In the field studies to be reported in this paper, conditions of greater goal ambiguity are presumed to exist during the initial two days of the 2-week units of study and during those periods in which the teacher introduces new material. During the middle and terminal phases of the 2-week unit of study, excluding the introduction of new material, greater goal clarity is presumed to exist.

Concepts for Describing Teacher Flexibility and Homogeneous Classroom Activities

Anyone who has observed many hours in a classroom soon notices that classroom interaction occurs in a sequence of activity periods. First, there may be a routine 3 to 5 minutes for settling down to work. Next, perhaps, homework is corrected and handed in. Next, a student or group may give a report. This may be followed by a 15-minute discussion, and so on. We have found it advantageous to tabulate interaction analysis data separately for these periods.

The main reason for separating data from different activities is that we can then discover whether a teacher shifts his balance of direct and indirect influence in various activity periods. Is a teacher more indirect when new material is being introduced? Is he more indirect when helping diagnose difficulties? Is he more direct when supervising seatwork? What about evaluating homework or test results?

Identifying activity periods is almost a second system of categorization that is superimposed on the system for classifying verbal statements. In junior-high academic classrooms, we use 5 activity categories: introducing new material; evaluating homework, tests, or learning products; other class discussion; supervising seatwork or group activities; and routine clean-up, passing of materials, or settling down to work. In general, a change from one activity to another is indicated by the statements made, a change of class formation, or a change in the communication pattern.

Tabulating data separately for homogeneous activities permits us to define teacher flexibility and measure it. Teacher flexibility is a measure of the change a teacher makes in his verbal influence from one activity period to another. We measure this by noting the ratio of indirect influence (I) to direct influence (D) in one activity period and comparing it with the corresponding ratio in other activity periods.

Hypotheses of Teacher Influence for This Study

In the preceding section, a series of concepts necessary to understand teacher influence was described and defined. Included among these concepts were direct and indirect teacher influence, freedom of action of the student, dependent and independent behavior, the personality trait of dependence-proneness, clear and ambiguous goals, and teacher flexibility. These concepts are tools for thinking about teacher behavior.

In the long run, the purpose of testing hypotheses about teacher influence is to establish principles of teacher behavior that can guide a teacher who wishes to control his own behavior as part of his plan for classroom management. Each principle, if it is to be useful, must be a cause-and-effect statement. Accordingly, this report will express principles in statements that adhere to the following general pattern: if such and such is true, then action "X" will produce result "Y."

This study is concerned with the following hypotheses, which will be stated in terms of the concepts described in the preceding section:

HYPOTHESIS ONE: Indirect teacher influence increases learning when a student's perception of the goal is confused and ambiguous.

HYPOTHESIS TWO: Direct teacher influence increases learning when a student's perception of the goal is clear and acceptable.

HYPOTHESIS THREE: Direct teacher influence decreases learning when a student's perception of the goal is ambiguous.

In these three hypotheses, the concept *learning* refers to the development of skills and understandings that can be measured by pre- and post-tests of achievement. In this project, tests were administered before and after a 2-week unit of study, so that an operational definition of learning consists of final achievement, adjusted for initial ability.

By way of brief review, the dynamic explanation of these hypotheses rests on the following reasoning: First, indirect influence increases learning when goals are ambiguous because less disabling dependence develops. During the initial stages of learning, goals are ambiguous. Indirect influence increases student freedom of action, allowing the student the opportunity to question goals and the procedures for reaching them. The net effect of this participation in clarifying goals is less compliance to authority per se and more attention to problem-solving requirements, or at least a more balanced orientation for those students who have high dependence-proneness.

Second, direct influence increases learning when goals are clear because the criteria for accepting or rejecting teacher influence as well as various alternative actions can be recognized in terms of the problem-solving requirements. The student is presumably oriented toward the problem; direct teacher influence is likely to be oriented toward the problem and be helpful; and the net effect is more efficient action toward problem solution. Dependence on the teacher remains steady or is decreased as a result of successful progress toward the goal.

Third, direct influence decreases learning when goals are ambiguous because it increases dependence sharply. The primary response of the student is compliance with teacher authority when goals are unclear. This, in turn, develops dependence. Unless the student understands the goal that the teacher has in mind, he has no other acceptable alternative, given our present cultural expectations. The high dependence that quickly develops means that the student is oriented more toward pleasing the teacher than toward meeting the problem-solving requirements.

These hypotheses are generalized predictions across a range of individual differences. The interaction between a teacher and a particular student in a specific situation is modified by unique personality characteristics and situational factors.

Classroom Interaction Analysis

The spontaneous behavior of a teacher is so complex and variable that an accurate description of it is most difficult to obtain. Even trained observers struggle with the same biases that distort the testimony of witnesses at the scene of an accident. Too often an observer's preconceptions of what he thinks should happen allow him to perceive certain behaviors but prevent him from perceiving others. Interaction analysis is an observation procedure designed to minimize these difficulties, to permit a systematic record of spontaneous acts, and to scrutinize the process of instruction by taking into account each small bit of interaction.

Classroom interaction analysis is particularly concerned with the influence pattern of the teacher. This might be considered a bias, but it is a bias of purpose and interest. Our purpose is to record a series of acts in terms of predetermined concepts. The concepts in this case refer to the teacher's control of the students' freedom of action. Our interest is to distinguish those acts of the teacher that increase students' freedom of action from those acts that decrease students' freedom of action, and to keep a record of both. The system of categories is used by the observer to separate those acts which result in compliance from those acts which invite more creative and voluntary participation; at the same time, it prevents him from being diverted by the subject matter which is irrelevant to this study.

Interaction analysis is concerned primarily with verbal behavior because it can be observed with higher reliability than most nonverbal behavior. The assumption is made that the verbal behavior of the teacher is an adequate sample of his total behavior; that is, his verbal statements are consistent with his nonverbal gestures, in fact, his total behavior. This assumption seems reasonable in terms of our experience.

The Procedure

The observer sits in the classroom in the best position to hear and see the participants. At the end of each 3-second period, he decides which of a prescribed set of numbered categories best represents the communication events just completed. He writes this category number down while simultaneously assessing communication in the next period. He continues at a rate of about 20 to 25 observations per minute, keeping his tempo as steady as possible. His notes are merely a sequence of numbers written in a column, top to bottom, so that the original sequence of events is preserved. Occasionally, marginal notes are used to explain the class formation or any unusual circumstances. When there is a major change in class formation, the communication pattern, or the subject under discussion, the observer draws a double line and indicates the time. As soon as he has completed the total observation, he retires to a nearby room and writes up a general description of each separate activity period. This includes the nature of the activities, the class formation, and the position of the teacher. The observer also notes any additional facts that seem pertinent to an adequate interpretation and recall of the total observation period.

The Categories

There are 10 categories in the system. Seven are assigned to teacher talk and two to student talk. The 10th category covers pauses, short periods of silence, and talk that is confusing or noisy. The category system is outlined in Table 1.

Of the seven categories assigned to teacher talk, categories 1 through 4 represent indirect influence, and categories 5, 6, and 7, direct influence.

Indirect influence encourages participation by the student and increases his freedom of action. To ask a question (category 4) is an invitation to participate and express ideas, opinions, or facts. It is true that a question can be so phrased as to leave very little freedom of action, but at least the student can refuse to answer, a reaction which reflects more freedom than does passive listening. The more general a teacher's question, the greater the opportunity for the student to assert his own ideas.

When the teacher accepts, clarifies, or uses constructively the ideas and opinions of students (category 3), they are encouraged to participate further. Often teachers act as if they do not hear what a student says; to acknowledge and make use of an idea is a powerful form of recognition. To praise or encourage student participation directly (category 2) is to solicit even more participation by giving a reward. The ability to use the feeling tone of a student constructively, to react to feeling and clarify it (category 1), is a rare skill. Teachers with this ability can often mobilize positive feelings in motivation and successfully control negative feelings that might otherwise get out of hand.

All the actions falling into categories 1 through 4 tend to increase and reward student participation, and to give students the opportunity to become more influential. The net effect is greater freedom of action for the students.

Direct influence increases the active control of the teacher and often stimulates compliance. The lecture (category 5) focuses the attention of the students on ideas chosen by the teacher. To give directions or commands (category 6) is to direct the activities of the class with the intent of obtaining compliance. Category 7 refers to criticizing student behavior or justifying the teacher's use of authority. These actions concentrate authority in the hands of the teacher. Direct influence tends to increase teacher participation and to establish restraints on student behavior. The ensuing restriction of freedom may occur in the form of compliance to the teacher or of adjustment to the requirements of problem-solving activities. The net effect is less freedom of action for the students.

The division of student talk into categories 8 and 9 provides an automatic check on freedom of student action within the system of categories. Ordinarily, but not always, a pattern of direct teacher influence is associated with less student talk, which generally consists of responses to the teacher (category 8). A pattern of

TABLE 1

Categories for Interaction Analysis, 1959

Teacher Talk	Indirect Influence	1.* ACCEPTS FEELING: accepts and clarifies the tone of feeling of the students in an unthreatening manner. Feelings may be positive or negative. Predicting or recalling feelings are included.
		2.* PRAISES OR ENCOURAGES: praises or encourage student action or behavior. Jokes that release tension, but not at the expense of another individual, nodding head or saying "um hm?" or "go on" are included.
		3.* ACCEPTS OR USES IDEAS OF STUDENT: clarifying, building, or developing ideas suggested by a student. As teacher brings more of his own ideas into play, shift to category 5.
		4.* ASKS QUESTIONS: asking a question about content or procedure with the intent that a student answer.
	Direct Influence	5.* LECTURING: giving facts or opinions about content or procedure; expressing his own ideas, asking rhetorical questions.
		6.* GIVING DIRECTIONS: directions, commands, or orders which students are expected to comply with.
		7.* CRITICIZING OR JUSTIFYING AUTHORITY: statements intended to change student behavior from unacceptable to acceptable pattern; bawling someone out; stating why the teacher is doing what he is doing; extreme self-reference.
Student Talk		8.* STUDENT TALK—RESPONSE: talk by students in response to teacher. Teacher initiates the contact or solicits student statement.
		9.* STUDENT TALK—INITIATION: talk initiated by student. If "calling on" student is only to indicate who may talk next, observer must decide whether student wanted to talk.
Silence		10.* SILENCE OR CONFUSION: pauses, short periods of silence, and periods of confusion in which communication cannot be understood by the observer.

* There is NO scale implied by these numbers. Each number is classificatory, designating a particular kind of communication event. To write these numbers down during observation is merely to identify and enumerate communication events, not to judge them.

indirect influence is ordinarily associated with more student talk, which is often initiated by the students (category 9). The use of only two categories to record all kinds of student talk neglects a great deal of information, but the major purpose of these categories is the analysis of teacher influence. The greatest information will accrue from observation if category 9 is used sparingly and only on those occasions when the communication is truly student-initiated.

For example, the act of a student in answering a specific question asked by a teacher obviously falls into category 8. Even the act of giving an oral report may be placed in this category when the student is restricted to a specific outline and probably responding to the teacher's directions.

Category 9 should be used by the observer only to indicate the student's spontaneous expression of his own ideas. General questions are often a clue that a student may be initiating his own ideas. When a teacher calls on a student who voluntarily raised his hand to speak and asks, "Have you anything to add, Robert?" the chances are that the use of category 9 is correct.

The purpose of category 10 is to record short pauses, silences, and periods of confusion as they occur during classroom interaction. It is not intended to record periods of silence or confusion lasting for more than 2 minutes. The continuous use of this category to designate long periods of silence serves no useful purpose.

The system of categories is designed for situations in which the teachers and the students are actively discussing schoolwork. It is an inappropriate tool when the verbal communication is discontinuous, separated by fairly long periods of silence, or when one person is engaged in prolonged lecturing or in reading aloud to the class. In situations in which two-way communication does not exist and is not likely to exist, the observer should stop and make a note of the exact time at which spontaneous interaction lapsed and the reasons for the interruption. The observer must remain alert to the resumption of spontaneous interaction.

Marking Activity Periods

Teacher influence is a pattern that is constantly changing over time. The most effective teachers, in fact, have a large repertoire of behaviors, and systematic observation shows that they can present many different influence patterns.

The identification of activity periods is one way that flexibility can be studied. In effect, a second system of categories is superimposed on the 10 interaction categories; this second system is likely to be different in each research study. For example, it may be sufficient in a study of high school mathematics classes to indicate periods of (*a*) settling down to work, (*b*) introducing new material, (*c*) teacher-directed discussion or work on material that is not new, (*d*) supervision and direction of individual seatwork, and (*e*) periods of evaluation, in which homework and test results are discussed.

In an elementary classroom, it would be reasonable to keep interaction data collected during show-and-tell separate from reading instruction, and these in turn from arithmetic, music, games, penmanship, etc.

If interaction analysis is to be used to discover whether a teacher's pattern of influence in planning work with students is different, for example, from his influence pattern while supervising work already planned, then even finer discriminations would be necessary to identify the boundaries of the required time periods.

One way to develop sensitivity to these different activity periods is to train the observer to draw a double line whenever there is a change in the class formation, the communication pattern, the subject matter to be learned, or in the presumed purpose of instruction. After the classroom visit is completed, the observer can use his double lines and marginal notes to recreate a brief chronology of the classroom activities. Interaction data gathered by this procedure can be grouped in a variety of ways for special comparisons.

No matter whether one is discussing a set of categories for interaction analysis or a set of categories for classifying activity periods, there are two requirements that must be satisfied in order to make generalizations about total class interaction. First, the system should be designed to include all possible events, that is, the categories should be totally inclusive. Second, a single event must be recorded in one, and only one, category so that the categories will be mutually exclusive.

Any system of observation that fails to meet the first requirement is selective, and under it the data are not representative of all the events that occurred. Failure to meet the second requirement produces an inconsistent enumeration of events; the comparison of category frequencies then becomes meaningless or at least biased in some unknown way.

Conclusions of the Project

Metatheory

Theorizing about theory is not a common pastime, especially in the field of education, but some questions should be raised about the theoretical hypotheses around which this project is organized. What kind of theorizing will be of most help in creating a theory of instruction? Can the present hypotheses contribute to a theory of instruction? These two questions will occupy our attention for a page or two before we go on to discuss the conclusions and implications of the project.

To theorize about the behavior of a classroom teacher, one must draw from the fields of learning theory, motivation, personality, group dynamics, sociometry, and practically everything else, and direction signs are not well-posted.

Educators are not yet ready to start the ambitious task of developing a theory of instruction that takes into account all behavior that occurs in a classroom. In one bold step of oversimplification, we postulated that a theory of instruction must at least concern itself with the teacher's acts of influence and the reactions of the students, using the goals of learning as a reference for interpretation. There must be concepts that describe teacher influence, concepts that describe student reactions, and concepts that describe learning goals. In the analysis of behavior, the order is reversed. Given particular learning goals, students' perceptions of these goals are developed through classroom interaction. The work that follows also involves interaction. The analysis of student and teacher interaction is carried out in terms of the learning goals. We found that classroom behavior makes the most sense when viewed within this frame of reference.

In order to contribute to a theory of instruction, a hypothesis must propose dynamic cause-and-effect relationships among learning goals, teacher behavior, and student behavior. If the hypothesis is verified empirically, it can become a principle of instruction that a teacher can then use to predict the consequences of his own behavior under certain conditions. To illustrate, one of our hypotheses is that direct influence when goals are ambiguous produces high dependence on the teacher and less learning. Direct influence is a concept describing teacher behavior; it is operationally defined as the enumeration of a series of verbal statements occurring in sequence and theoretically defined as those acts which restrict alternative actions of the student. Goals are conceptualized along a continuum from ambiguous to clear, and are operationally defined in terms of the student's perceptions. Acts of dependence and learning are aspects of the student's behavior. Each can be assessed and given operational meaning by either paper-and-pencil tests or observation.

The ultimate value of this kind of engineering research will be tested by pragmatic criteria. As this chapter is being written, arrangements have been completed for an inservice training program in a nearby school district. The project will attempt to answer the question, if teachers learn our theories about the consequences of indirect and direct influence, will this help them control their behavior and become more effective teachers? The results of the present project will become part of the content of this inservice training.

Some Assumptions Inherent in Our Approach

Certain assumptions are necessary in our analysis of teacher influence. First, acts of influence are expressed primarily through verbal statements. Nonverbal acts of influence do occur, but are not recorded by interaction analysis. The reasonableness of this assumption rests on the assertion that the quality of the nonverbal acts is similar to the verbal acts; to assess verbal influence therefore is to adequately sample all influence.

Second, how much teachers talk and what they say determine to a large extent the reactions of the students. This is another way of saying that the teacher is an influential authority figure. Given the teacher's position of authority, his greater maturity, and the common expectations of students, we find this assumption reasonable.

Third, an assumption necessary to the application of these research results in any program designed to increase teacher effectiveness is that teachers can control their verbal participation in the classroom. We believe that the average teacher can control his behavior and use it as a psychological force in classroom management. He can be indirect if he chooses, or direct, according to his assessment of the situation. What we hope to provide are principles which he can use in making the choice.

These assumptions focus our attention on the verbal participation of teachers and students. We are in the business of evaluating classroom communication in terms of the teacher's control. Our procedures tend to emphasize control processes and to ignore subject matter, or content. The latter is important, but so is the former, and we prefer to work on one thing at a time at our present stage of development.

Major Conclusions of the 1955–57 Studies

The purpose of the early studies was to develop research tools and to use these tools to study relationships between teacher statements and average classroom scores on a pupil attitude inventory. These early studies were conducted in eighth-grade combined English/social studies in Minnesota and Standard Four elementary classrooms in New Zealand. A sample of Minnesota elementary classrooms provided additional interaction analysis data.

These early studies establish clear and significant relationships among teacher statements, pupil attitudes toward the teacher, and the classroom learning activities. Furthermore, the same relationships were shown to exist in more formal and less formal classroom situations in two countries some 8,000 miles apart.

It was shown that when a class scored higher on scales of teacher attractiveness, motivation for schoolwork, fair rewards and punishments, independence, and lack of disabling anxiety, its teacher showed more acceptance of, interest in, and constructive use of the student ideas expressed in classroom discussion. In New Zealand, the teachers of higher-scoring classes also gave fewer directions and made fewer criticisms. The incidence of corporal punishment was also much lower in high-scoring New Zealand classrooms. In the lower-scoring classrooms, the opposite trends occurred. The findings of these early studies were consistent with the research carried out almost 20 years before the present studies by H. H. Anderson and his colleagues.

If one accepts the assumptions and theoretical formulations presented in the first part of this monograph, one sees that these studies demonstrate a cause-and-effect relationship between teacher influence, as expressed by the verbal statements of teachers, and pupil attitudes, as measured by our paper-and-pencil instruments. At the different age levels that exist at primary, elementary, junior high, and senior high grade levels, across different combinations of pupil personality and individual differences, with different types of teaching styles, and even in two countries which differ in the formality of teacher-pupil relationships, students react similarly to the same differences in teacher influence.

These early studies did not include any measure of subject matter achievement. Such measures were purposely delayed until the larger field study could be conducted with the necessary experimental controls.

The Major Conclusions Regarding Achievement

In this project we have isolated situations in which students learned more, and have compared these with situations in which students learned less. Our method of isolation was not to administer a test of achievement first and then study the differences in teacher behavior. Instead, we made theoretical predictions of the following sort.

First, we assessed acts of teacher influence as they occurred spontaneously in the classroom. By using the technique of interaction analysis, we were able to isolate teachers who had an above-average pattern of indirect influence. We found that they were far more flexible than those teachers who exerted below-average indirect influence. That is, they could be just as direct as the latter teachers in certain situations, but they could be far more indirect in other situations. The net effect was a higher average of indirect influence.

Second, we predicted certain patterns would occur among the more flexible teachers: (1) they would be most indirect while goals were being clarified and new content material was being introduced; (2) they would be most direct after goals had been clarified, while work was in progress.

Finally, we predicted that the students of those teachers who were less flexible would learn less, as measured by our achievement tests. It was on this basis that we isolated classes of higher achievement and classes of lower achievement.

When we initially contacted teachers to solicit their participation in the project, we expected certain types of students to learn more while working with direct teachers and other types of students to learn more while working with indirect teachers. We were wrong. All types of students learned more while working with the more flexible teachers. We also thought that classes in the field of mathematics might learn more while working with a direct teacher and that classes in the field of social studies would learn more while working with an indirect teacher. Again we were wrong. It is true that teachers of mathematics use time and methods differently than do teachers of social studies, but students of the more flexible teachers scored higher on the achievement tests in both content areas.

We are not yet prepared to discard the notion that particular types of students work more effectively toward learning goals with particular types of teachers even though our field studies failed to support it. In a series of experiments with geometry classes, we found significant differences indicating that dependent-prone students learned more than independent-prone students while working with a more indirect teacher. Perhaps subsequent experiments will reveal what types of students learn the most while working with direct teachers. Furthermore, there are a number of improvements that can be made in our methods of classifying students into types, and these should be tried out before discarding expectations which at first glance seemed quite reasonable.

Some Implications of the Research

Implications for Classroom Teachers

To those of us on the staff, the most interesting implication of the project concerns the timing of direct and indirect influence. We find this most interesting because our theoretical predictions are contrary to accepted teaching practice. Nearly all teachers agree that immediate action should be taken in any situation in which the learning goals are ambiguous and students do not know what to do. "Students who are unable to go on with their work are wasting time," the reasoning goes, "Something should be done!" So far we are all in agreement.

Should the initial contacts made by a teacher in such a situation be direct or indirect? Our theory suggests an indirect approach; most teachers use a direct approach. Teachers can find many justifications for their direct approach. Often they think that to tell the students what to do is only to remind them of something they already know. Sometimes teachers are quite sure that the students are lazy or are pretending confusion. A direct approach seems more efficient at the moment, and a teacher is a busy person. These and many other reasons are often mentioned by teachers as a justification for the following pattern: (*a*) the teacher decides students are confused; (*b*) the teacher makes his best guess on the cause of this confusion; and (*c*) the teacher, acting on his own diagnosis, proceeds to give information, direction, and, in some cases, criticism in order to reestablish patterns of work.

The two most common situations in which a teacher faces this choice are those in which new material is being introduced, such as a new topic, a new procedure, or a new method of problem-solving, and those in which a group already at work runs into difficulty—when Johnny won't cooperate, information cannot be found, the answer doesn't check with an independent proof, materials are missing, and so forth.

It is obvious to any person with teaching experience that no valid generalizations can be made on how the teacher should handle these and similar situations. That is, it is obvious that there are some situations in which a teacher should be primarily direct and others in which he should be primarily indirect. However, we make a statistical generalization which will hold for 100 such situations. In this study, the teachers of students who learned less employed a pattern of direct influence more often in such a situation. Our theory predicts higher achievement and less dependence when goals are clarified by an indirect approach.

An indirect approach stimulates verbal participation by students and discloses to the teacher students' perceptions of the situation. Such an approach not only provides the teacher with more information about students' understanding of a particular problem, but also often encourages students to develop more responsibility for diagnosing their difficulties and for suggesting a plan of action.

A direct approach increases student compliance to teacher opinion and direction. It conditions students to seek the teacher's help and to check with the teacher more often to be sure they are on the right track.

A second implication for classroom teachers is that the major differences in the use of influence between the teachers whose students learned the most and those whose students learned the least are illustrated by the use of actions classified under categories 1, 2, and 3. The direct teachers lack those social skills of communication that are involved in accepting, clarifying, and making use of the ideas and feelings of students. The indirect teachers have these skills, even though they are not in use most of the time. Although these skills are used sparingly, they are employed when needed.

Associated with this increased social skill is less need for directions and criticism. The most direct teachers give twice as many directions as the most indirect, and express eight times as much criticism. These figures are consistent with what has been said about dependence. Lack of clarifying and using student ideas places the teacher in a position of giving more directions; in short, he must work harder to keep his students working successfully. When dependence is higher, progress by students depends much more on continuous teacher supervision.

There are interesting comparisons to be made between what we have found in this project and some of the more common criticisms of the public schools that have attained national prominence during the last several years. Some critics of the public schools have advocated that teachers "get tough," tell students what to do, and demand high standards. Our data show that higher standards can be achieved not by telling students what to do in some sort of misguided "get tough" policy, but by asking questions and then using student ideas, perceptions, and reactions to build toward greater student self-direction, responsibility, and understanding. If "getting tough" means helping students face the consequences of their own ideas and opinions, as contrasted against living with the consequences of the teacher's ideas and opinions, then indirect teachers are much tougher.

The third implication for classroom teachers that we would like to mention is that variability in teacher influence, or flexibility, is associated with teachers whose students learned the most. One consequence of this finding is that our better teachers were less alike and our poorer teachers were more alike. It suggests that creative teaching is an expression of a particular teacher's personality, working with a particular group of students, in a particular subject.

We should emphasize again that our six most indirect social studies teachers fell clearly into two types. Three lectured much more and placed greater emphasis on content material, but all six shared the common characteristic of a higher I/D ratio. The more content-oriented teachers worked with student ideas less, but when they did, their pattern was essentially indirect. The other three teachers worked in a very different style that included 31.6 per cent student talk, the highest average in the entire study. The average student achievement of this latter group was a nonsignificant one-half point higher, indicating that achievement was high for two rather different styles of teaching. It also indicates that a variation from 20 per cent student talk in the content-oriented style to 31.6 per cent student talk in the other three classrooms is not associated with a significant difference in achievement.

The differences between the direct and indirect teachers may be interpreted in terms of the different roles the teacher is able to play in the classroom. The direct teachers could not shift their style of interaction as much as the indirect teachers. Because the direct teachers had fewer ways of working with students, they could provide only a limited number of roles. On the other hand, the indirect teachers were able to adopt many different roles, and they shifted from one to another in a manner consistent with the theories that have already been stated.

Implications for Preservice and Inservice Education

There is no substitute for knowledge of what is being taught. Two of the mathematics teachers were not adequately trained. One of these two classes showed an average mean gain in achievement that was last in rank order and *one-sixteenth* of the mean gain of the highest-ranking class. The other class was ninth in rank order. The teacher of this latter class used more social skill in guiding classroom communication. His attitude was, "I'm no math teacher, but we'll have to make the best of it and learn this material together." While his class exceeded the achievement of one or two other classes whose teachers had more extensive training in mathematics, the achievement could not match that of those classes whose teachers were both socially skillful and well-qualified.

The two cases just described illustrate a general implication of this project for the training of teachers. Teachers who are qualified in a content area should be exposed to some type of human relations training that will help them attain the following objectives: first, the ability to use the social skills of accepting, clarifying, and using the ideas of students in planning work and diagnosing difficulties; second, knowledge of those acts of influence that restrict student reactions and those that expand student reactions; and third, understanding of a theory of instruction that he can use to control his own behavior as he guides classroom communication.

It is reasonable to suppose that these objectives cannot be reached without supervised practice. The person supervising this practice should be able to provide the practice-teacher with information about his own behavior. One way to do this is to use the technique of interaction analysis. The procedure is likely to involve threat for the practice-teacher and will require skillful, indirect approach on the part of the supervisor.

One possible procedure would permit practice-teachers to try out different patterns of influence. Suppose that on one occasion the practice-teacher tried introducing material with a highly direct pattern and that on another occasion he tried with an indirect pattern. A qualified observer could collect interation analysis data, tabulate the two matrices, and discuss the resulting communication patterns with the practice-teacher. This could be done if all practice-teachers were trained to become reliable observers so that they could alternate between the roles of observer and teacher in teams of two.

Implications for Merit Pay

In the present decade, the issue of merit pay for gifted teachers will probably receive more and more attention. Already many school districts are experimenting with different systems. Since this study deals with teacher effectiveness, inferences about the merit pay issue are inescapable.

Two warnings should be issued to anyone who reads this project report and then makes inferences about merit pay. The first warning is that it is easier to identify poor teaching than good teaching. This study found that teachers were quite similar whose students learned the least and had the poorest attitudes toward the teacher and class activities. The teachers who presented the opposite picture were more flexible. By refining the research techniques of this project, reliable distinctions between high- and low-scoring classrooms could be made concerning the amount of students' talk, teachers' use of their time, and the distinction between the 8 and 9 categories of student talk (i.e., student response versus student initiation). The possibility of making such distinctions looks promising, but much more preliminary work will be necessary.

The second warning is that the correlations between various measures derived from interaction analysis, student attitude inventories, and tests of achievement are still so low that evaluation of an individual teacher is subject to considerable error, even though the general trends of the research are statistically significant. So much for the warnings.

The major aim of all systems of merit pay is to reward competence in such a way that all teachers who can improve their teaching skills will do so. A secondary objective, which is to give higher pay for more difficult jobs, must await a more dramatic modification of school organization leading to specialized teaching functions.

Our staff, after making such a close analysis of teacher-pupil contacts, has developed a number of basic beliefs about some of the issues of merit pay. First, programs for the improvement of instruction should be designed and controlled by teachers as part of their professional responsibility. Teacher control, rather than administrative control, is necessary because changing one's methods of teaching is very personal, often involves emotional adjustments, cannot be coerced by administrative fiat, and therefore must be a voluntary, self-directed process.

Second, no system of teacher evaluation will be accepted by teachers until it has been tested and found satisfactory by the teachers whose professional welfare will be affected. Teachers must have confidence in the valuative methods, criteria, and control before they will cooperate.

Third, a system of inservice training that teachers think is successful in helping improve their own ability to teach can become, with care, a stepping-stone to a satisfactory system of rewarding the exceptionally competent. In our opinion, this means that merit pay would normally follow a 4- to 6-year active, voluntary inservice training program that, in the opinion of the majority of teachers, has been successful. As teachers experience success in improving their teaching and develop confidence in the criteria used to identify improvement, they will be closer to accepting a system that provides monetary reward for those who make the best progress.

It is our opinion that whenever systems of merit pay are forced from "the top down," the program will fail to meet its major objectives. Administrators and school boards following this path will meet with failure. In the same breath, it can be predicted that teachers who resist schedule policies that have served well in the past will be confronted with increasing criticism from the public and from school board members. Sooner or later the minimum teachers' salary will stop improving in relation to the general economy, and it will then be in the best interests of the profession to raise the ceiling of teacher income for those who are most qualified and most effective.

It follows from the foregoing assertions that the development of objective criteria and procedures to evaluate teacher effectiveness is a professional responsibility. The most rugged test of any procedure is an objective research program that not only provides evidence of the highest quality attainable, but also employs procedures that nearly all teachers can understand and use in a self-improvement program.

The Implications of Interaction Analysis

The system of interaction analysis used in this study is content-free. It is concerned primarily with the social skills of classroom management, as expressed through verbal communication. It is costly and cumbersome, and it requires some form of automation in collecting, tabulating, and analyzing the raw data. It is not yet a finished research tool.

Nevertheless, our staff has experienced minor triumphs that we will never forget. We have, for instance, played the following game with considerable success: A single observer collects interaction analysis data, tabulates a matrix, and presents the matrix at a staff meeting. The only information supplied to the staff is the presumed objective of the lesson, the grade level of the class, and the sex of the teacher. The observer who collected the data remains silent as the rest of the staff reconstruct the social interaction. Conclusions about the tempo or speed of interaction, the relative domination of the teacher, whether he asks long or short questions, how much he lectures, and many other aspects of interaction are listed. After the group has finished crawling out on the end of a limb, the observer corrects any misconceptions that may have developed. The number of correct speculations is usually very high, well over 80 per cent. Occasionally, a single misconception colors other guesses until a picture develops that is quite incorrect, but these latter outcomes are remarkably infrequent.

Much of the inferential power of this system of interaction analysis comes from tabulating the data as sequence pairs in a 10 × 10 matrix. This is a time-consuming process. It can be and should be done mechanically by electronic computers. Once the high cost of tedious tabulation is under control, the problem of training reliable observers and maintaining their reliability will still remain.

We have reason to be optimistic about the value of interaction analysis. Its potential as a research tool, however, for a wide application to problems in education remains to be explored.

References

1. Amidon, E. and N. A. Flanders, "The Effects of Direct and Indirect Teacher Influence on Dependent-Prone Students Learning Geometry," *Journal of Educational Psychology*, LII, No. 6 (December 1961), 286–91.

2. Anderson, H. H., "The Measurement of Domination and of Socially Integrative Behavior in Teacher's Contact with Children," *Child Development*, X, No. 2 (June 1939), 73–89.

3. —— and H. M. Brewer, "Studies of Teachers' Classroom Personalities, I: Dominative and Socially Integrative Behavior of Kindergarten Teachers," *Applied Psychology of Monographs*, No. 6, 1945.

4. —— and J. E. Brewer, "Studies of Teachers' Classroom Personalities, II: Effects of Teacher's Dominative and Integrative Contacts on Children's Classroom Behavior," *Applied Psychology Monographs*, No. 8, 1946.

5. —— and M. F. Reed, "Studies of Teachers' Classroom Personalities, III: Follow-Up Studies of the Effects of Dominative and Integrative Contacts on Children's Behavior," *Applied Psychology Monographs of the American Psychological Association*, Stanford, Calif.: Stanford University Press, No. 11, December 1946.

6. Cogan, M. L., "Theory and Design of a Study of Teacher-Pupil Interaction," *The Harvard Educational Review*, XXVI, No. 4 (Fall 1956), 315–42.

7. Filson, T. N., "Factors Influencing the Level of Dependence in the Classroom." Unpublished Ph. D. Thesis, University of Minnesota, 1957.

8. Flanders, N. A., "Personal-Social Anxiety as a Factor in Experimental Learning Situations," *Journal of Educational Research*, XLV (October 1951), 100–110.

9. ——, "Diagnosing and Utilizing Social Structures in Classroom Learning," 59th Yearbook of the National Society for the Study of Educational Research, *Part II, The Dynamics of Instructional Groups*. Chicago: University of Chicago Press, 1960. Chap. IX, pp. 187–217.

10. —— and J. P. Anderson and E. J. Amidon, "Measuring Dependence Proneness in the Classroom," *Educational and Psychological Measurement*, XXI, No. 3 (Autumn 1961), 575–87.

11. Lewin, K., *A Dynamic Theory of Personality*. New York: McGraw-Hill Book Company, 1935. Chap. IV, pp. 114–70.

12. Lippitt, R. and R. K. White, "The

'Social Climate' of Children's Groups," in R. G. Barker, J. S. Kounin, and H. F. Wright, eds., *Child Behavior and Development.* New York: McGraw-Hill Book Company, 1943, pp. 458–508.

13. Perkins, H. V., "Climate Influences Group Learning," *Journal of Educational Research,* XLV (October 1951), 115–19.

14. Smith, B. O., "A Concept of Teaching," *Teachers College Record,* LXI, No. 5 (February 1960), 229–41.

15. Withall, J., "The Development of a Technique for the Measurement of Social-Emotional Climate in Classroom," *Journal of Experimental Education,* XVII (March 1949), 347–61.

8. NONVERBAL COMMUNICATION

CHARLES M. GALLOWAY

When second-grade teacher Ruth Harris was getting dressed for school one dull Monday, she hesitated between a black suit and a bright print dress. Choosing the print, she thought, "It will brighten the day for me and the children." Things did seem to go well all day. . . .

As Paul Trask entered the school building, he saw the principal at the end of the hall. Expecting a smile and a wave, he was surprised to get a curt nod and the sight of a disappearing back. Paul wondered what could be wrong. . . .

Annette Webster looked at her fourth-year arithmetic group as they bent over the problem she had presented to them. She noticed Chris scowling at his paper and biting his lip and moved to help him. . . .

What happened with these teachers? Each one either sent or received a message without saying or hearing a word. What happened was nonverbal communication.

Nonverbal communication is behavior that conveys meaning without words. It can be symbolic or non-

Charles M. Galloway, "Nonverbal Communication," THE INSTRUCTOR, *LXXVII, No. 8 (1968), 37–42. Reprinted by permission. From Instructor, © Instructor Publications, Inc., and the author.*

symbolic, spontaneous or managed. It can be expressive, transmitting emotion; or it can be informative, transmitting facts. It can be as specific as a gesture or as general as the atmosphere of a room. It can be either dynamic or static.

Nonverbal communication takes a certain amount of time and occurs at a certain tempo. It can be quick or slow. It can be negative or positive—something that doesn't happen as well as something that does. Or it can be a combination of any of these—and there's even a nonverbal component in verbalisms.

All human beings are compelled to send and receive messages. They try constantly to discover information which lessens confusion or increases understanding. When messages are carried by words, the participators are consciously aware of hearing or seeing the words. But nonverbal communication is given much less conscious thought. The operations of giving information through nonverbal action and reading the meaning of another person's nonverbal behavior usually occur without deliberate reflection.

The clothing you wear, your posture, or how you walk transmits a message to others. You may be saying, "I am a teacher; I am meeting your expectations (and mine) of how a teacher should look." Depending on your emotional needs, you may also be trying to say, "I am an alert, modern teacher," or even, "I may be a teacher, but at heart I'm a swinger!"

So we can say that nonverbal clues are evident in any situation where people are with other people. In fact, the most subtle and covert kinds of information can be discovered in this way. Here are three examples:

Nonverbal phenomena establish the status of interaction. At a party you are talking to someone, but his eyes are following someone else around the room. His posture and manner indicate his desire to be off. What conclusion do you come to?

Nonverbal behavior indicates what the other person thinks of us. You are discussing a controversial topic with a small group. Everyone is reacting politely, but you are aware of those who approve of your ideas and those who disagree. How do you know?

Nonverbal clues are used to check the reliability of what is said. You had mailed a coupon indicating interest in an expensive set of books. The man who shows up at your door is poorly groomed and shifty-eyed. Although his credentials seem in order, you hesitate even to let him in.

The significance of nonverbal behavior in the classroom is an idea about teaching that is growing in importance. Until now, it has seldom been recognized or understood, at least in a formal, specific way. Now persons interested in improving the teaching act are studying the implications of nonverbal communication —implications that are important for you to understand.

Assignments

1. Think of at least one classroom situation in which of each the three conditions described above occurred.

2. Review the last two days of school. Can you recall an incident in which a child's behavior belied his remarks?

3. When a nonverbal cue disagrees with or contradicts a verbal remark, we tend to accept the nonverbal message as representative of the real meaning. Discuss why this occurs.

Nonverbal Phenomena

Nonverbal behavior consists of such events as facial expression, posture, gestures, movement, even the arrangement of space or objects around the behaver. It involves use of the body, use of space, and even the use of time.

Although we are often unaware of the process, we are very conscious of the eloquence of nonverbal cues. We all agree that "actions speak louder than words," and realize that *how* we say something can be as important as *what* we say. We also know the feeling of being "in tune" with someone—immediately understanding him and having him understand us.

Most of us believe that the most personal and valid kinds of information are discovered by what we call intuition. What really happens is that we subconsciously respond to nonverbal clues transmitted by other persons.

During the school day, many graphic portrayals of nonverbal phenomena occur. Here are some common ones, and as you read them, think about your class. Undoubtedly you will recall many examples like them, and will be able to add others.

Substitute Expression

A child strugs his shoulder in an "I don't know" manner after being accosted in the hallway for running. Probably this means he feels guilty at being caught, yet he hesitates to engage the teacher in a verbal debate. This is especially true if his verbal defense is likely to be employed against him later in the conversation. One of the places events like this occur repeatedly is in inner-city schools, where children are already conditioned to express their frustrations and defiance in a nonverbal way.

Qualifying Expression

Ann says, "I don't sing well," but what does she mean? Stated one way, it suggests that she *does* sing well; or it may mean that she *would like* to sing well; or, that she truly *does not* sing well. The intent of verbal remarks is usually qualified through intonation and inflection. Facial expressions and gestures also qualify verbal language.

Nonverbal Symbolic

John observed the teacher watching him. Now he is painting with large dramatic strokes, one eye on the teacher, hoping she will look his way again. When we know we are being observed, our behavior is designed to have intent or purpose for the observer. It symbolizes our thoughts or intentions. Eyes alone may beckon or reject. Many gestures and facial expressions symbolize our deepest feelings.

Nonverbal Nonsymbolic

You are watching a child who is observing another child, totally unaware that you are watching him. His behavior is considered nonsymbolic since it is free of overt intent. When you observe the unobserved observer, it is a profound process—for his reactions are genuinely his own with no desire to create an impression. Observing a person who is unaware of our presence is both informative and fun.

Attentive or Inattentive

Your students are pretending to listen while their minds wander in fields of fantasy, and when they respond it is in a bored fashion. Nonverbally they are being inattentive. As an experienced teacher, you are able to detect such reactions and use them to change the pace and direction of what is being taught. Observing when students are involved and interested and when they are not is a skill that teachers learn. But teachers vary widely in their ability or willingness to use these pupil reactions as directions for their own behavior.

There are other nonverbal occurrences, but these are good ones to start with. Undoubtedly you can add other specific types from your own experiences.

Assignments

1. Identify children in your class who typically react nonverbally to either reprimand or approval. Do you know what they are really trying to communicate?
2. Experiment with positive body and facial qualifying expressions, especially when you feel a need to support a request or judgment you are making.
3. Think of a nonsymbolic situation in which your observation was later confirmed; another one which later proved wrong.

Classroom Cues

Nonverbal behavior is not limited to personal practices. Many classroom phenomena serve as nonverbal communicators. Their impact on the course and direction of an activity can strongly affect the contextual meaning that is derived from it.

Methods of distributing materials can affect the activity that follows; the way a group is formed influences its practices; even the degree of neatness required suggests behavior to the pupil.

Nonverbal cues either reinforce or minimize verbal messages. They become the focus of attention and *carry conviction that lingers long after the verbal event has passed.* Why this is so is difficult to answer, but the strong influence of nonverbal cues is unmistakable.

Classroom phenomena often play a more significant role in students' learning than the formal teaching which takes place. In any classroom, the extent and duration of teacher-pupil contacts are great. It is vital to have mutual understanding in the exchange of the messages that are nonverbal in character and import.

Consider phenomena that are typical of any classroom:

Use of Space

Classrooms are divided into territories. Both teacher and students occupy space. Some arrangements of territorial rights are traditional, with the teacher's desk at the front of the room and students seated in rows. Other arrangements are more imaginative. Some uses of space are static.

Space arrangement shows the teacher's priorities—what she thinks important; what she thinks about her children; how she envisions her own position. A change in a spatial arrangement influences the potential meaning of a learning context.

Teacher Travel

Where and when a teacher chooses to travel in a classroom is significant. In the past, teachers usually moved around their own desks as if they were isles of security. They rarely ventured into territories of student residence, unless they wished to check up on or monitor seatwork. Today that picture has changed. Some teachers have done away with desks; others have put them in less focal places.

To move toward or away from students signifies relationships. Teachers may avoid some students or frequent the work areas of others. All of those movements have meaning that students recognize.

Use of Time

How teachers use their time indicates the value and importance they place on types of work, on subject areas, and on acceptable activities. Spending little or no time on a topic indicates a lack of interest in or knowledge about it so that even little children are aware of teachers' preferences.

Teachers often fail to recognize the implications of their use of time. One teacher spends two hours marking papers. A teacher in the next room spends the same amount of time in helping children mark their own papers. Certainly these teachers have different concepts of evaluation, and it is revealed by their uses of time.

Control Maneuvers

Teachers engage in various nonverbal tactics to control the behavior of students. These silent expressions serve as events reminding students of teacher expectations. Some typical examples of nonverbal maneuvers: the teacher indicates inability to hear due to classroom noise; places finger to lips; stands with hands on hips and stares in silence; scans room to see who is not working; records in grade book while student is making a report. Negative maneuvers tend to "put children in their place." Similarly, positive maneuvers can give encouragement, help a child overcome fear, put a nervous child at ease, or resolve a tense situation.

As the teacher works to establish better classroom phenomena, he must be careful to avoid *incongruity*. This is an event where there is a contradiction between what is said and what is done, and it may occur many times in a day. The thing to remember about an incongruity is that it is nonverbal behavior that makes the impression that is most lasting and most difficult to overcome.

Incongruous behaviors occur frequently during times of praise or encouragement. Teachers use words such as "good" or "nice job" but the praise can appear false or unbelievable. When we are not honest with children, it is the nonverbal clues that trip us up.

Nonverbal phenomena should not be thought of primarily in negative terms. Many classrooms are well arranged. The teacher's approach to an activity provides excellent motivation. Or, through meeting a child's eyes or with a small gesture, a teacher builds confidence. Such nonverbal events can be highly conducive to good classroom climate.

Nonverbal qualities that contribute to effective classroom interaction are suggested:

Attention

The event of listening to pupils when they talk. This is essential. When a teacher fails to listen, a pupil is likely to believe that what he says is unimportant.

Reception

Behavioral evidence that a teacher is listening, by maintaining eye contact while a pupil is talking. The event of attending to pupils when they talk assures pupils and encourages them to believe that their verbal communication is valued by the teacher.

Reinforcement

A look or gesture to reinforce approval of an act by a student. Not only the timid but also the seemingly forward child may need reinforcement if he is to go ahead on his own.

Facilitation

A movement toward a student for the purpose of helping or assisting. Teachers quite often detect needs or unexpressed feelings by students, and initiate a move toward the student to alleviate his concern. Teachers engage in such events because, either consciously or subconsciously, they have become sensitive to the nonverbal cues given by their students.

We all recognize that expressive cues are fleeting and transitory. Nonetheless, they transmit emotion and feeling, and are detected as indications of meaning far more quickly than speech. *It is the appearance of such cues that especially suggests to others the attitudes we hold at a given time.* Therefore, they are particularly important in establishing the classroom environment and in working out good rapport with each child.

Assignments

1. Draw some alternate layouts for your classroom. List changes in nonverbal phenomena that each layout would imply.

2. Make a two-day study of how often you contact each child in any of many ways. Keep a list of children's names and devise a simple code to indicate times of approving or disapproving, individual or group sharing, listening, or other interaction.

Feedback

Improving classroom nonverbal behavior is not easy, especially in discovering incongruity. Yet we probably all agree that such improvement should be a conscious goal for any teacher.

One enlightening and sometimes disconcerting way to check your present behavior is by watching yourself on film or video-tape. Another way is to listen to the comments and suggestions of an observer whose judgment you trust. *A teacher's major source of feedback, however, is the responses of students.*

To become more knowledgeable about the nonverbal reactions of your youngsters to your behavior is a difficult quest. Even when you begin to recognize the reactions, it is naïve to believe that change is imminently possible. Most of us have been observing and behaving in patterned ways for a long time. Ridding oneself of past habits and attitudes is a difficult undertaking and must be a continuing process.

The best way to start is to develop an attitude of *openness.* Openness to one's experience and the realization that a rich and available source of data exists in the classroom is crucial. Openness is necessary if an improvement of perceptual skills and style of behaving is to be effected.

Assuming that a teacher has an open attitude toward self and others, the steps for becoming better informed involve *awareness, understanding*, and *acceptance*. To be aware is to observe more fully and to be open to the nonverbal reactions of others and oneself. To understand implies the need to analyze the meaning of your observations and to suspend judgment until you are reasonably certain of their real meaning. To accept is to acknowledge that your behavior means what it does to students, even though the meaning is not what you intended to imply.

This last step is especially difficult because most of us do not like to admit even to ourselves that others perceive us differently. But once you can accept what your behavior represents to others, the door is open to behaving differently. (Does it seem odd to be talking about the *behavior* of teachers? That is a word usually reserved for children, yet the teacher's conduct in the classroom is of vital importance to every child.)

In being open to nonverbal cues, it is useful to recognize behavior as a cultural, social, and psychological phenomenon. The behavior of a teacher or of students arises from experiences that have been learned over a period of time. Here are some points to consider as you view students' reactions:

SIMILAR EXPERIENCES CAN MEAN DIFFERENT THINGS. A pat on the back to one child may imply friendliness and support, whereas to another exactly the same behavior may be interpreted as an aggressive and threatening gesture. Similarly, an aggressive act by a child may be in defiance of controls, or in response to something in your classroom climate that has encouraged him to go ahead on his own.

REACTION TO PHYSICAL CONTACT VARIES. To some children who are accustomed to adults' maintaining a physical distance from them, too close a proximity by the teacher might well stifle and embarrass. Conversely, other children prefer the close contact and warmth of teacher-pupil contacts. One broad cultural understanding among us that you may not have realized is that we do not stand too close to one another while talking in public. When the appropriate distance is broken, talking ceases.

NONVERBAL EXPRESSIONS AMONG RACIAL, ETHNIC, AND SOCIAL CLASSES CAN DIFFER MARKEDLY. Similarly, the behaviors of suburban, rural, and inner-city children vary. The teacher must be sensitive to behavior differences and seek to learn what they imply rather than coming to premature conclusions.

MEETING EXPECTATIONS APPEARS TO BE A DEVELOPMENT ABILITY. If meeting expectations is a learned process, it explains why the behavior of young children appears so unaffected and natural. Much of their behavior is spontaneous and unrehearsed. With older children, activities of pretending to listen in class, appearing busy during seatwork assignments, and putting on a front of seeming to be interested, may all be games that they have learned to play.

There are perhaps many such games that children learn to play in school, and the longer they go to school the better their skills develop. This is a necessary step in preparing for adult roles; but on the other hand, children who do need help may be able to conceal their need.

RESPONSIVENESS MAY BE MISLEADING. Parents who want their children to succeed often stress the importance of "pleasing the teacher." In actuality, the student less overt in his responsiveness may be more receptive to what is going on. Nonverbal clues are the best way to judge responsiveness.

DEPRIVED CHILDREN MAY BE INCAPABLE OF MEETING THE BEHAVIORAL EXPECTATIONS OF THE TEACHER. They may neither understand the rules of the school game nor be able to control their behavior satisfactorily. Indeed, many teachers do not facilitate their fumbling efforts, but, rather, try to catch them in the act. Such students need practice in what it means to be a student.

Awareness of the behavior of yourself and your students and what it means does not come all at once. Interpretations change as realization increases. But the processes of awareness and realization are concomitant. You perceive to greater depths, you are more attuned to those around you, and you begin to employ nonverbal clues for positive purposes. Having opened the door, you realize you have the ability to change and improve.

Assignments

1. A company selling video-tape recorders may be willing to give a demonstration of its product in your school. Volunteer to be photographed. It may take courage! Or make a class movie, letting children take footage with a movie camera. (Don't try to be in the film. Chances are you will be automatically included.) Study it to see how your nonverbal behavior could improve.

2. Make a study of the feedback at times when you are an observer—for example, of children's reactions to the librarian, music teacher, or other classroom visitors.

3. Discuss feedback in a teachers' meeting. Let teachers anonymously mark profile sheets showing impressions they have of other teachers, including yourself. (The results may amaze you.)

Experimenting

Since nonverbal communication is so basic and certainly old as mankind, why the recent interest in its role in education? Are teachers now expected to search for hidden meanings behind everything that happens in their classrooms? Must they become overly sensitive to ordinary behavior? Not at all.

Teachers need not set out to discover meanings that lurk in the subterranean caverns of the mind. Indeed, they shouldn't. Instead, the purpose is to become more aware of nonverbal cues because they operate as a silent language to influence teacher-student understandings and interactions. And it is through these understandings and interactions in the classroom that the business of teaching and learning goes forward.

Your final assignment in your nonverbal course is an invitation to experiment in every phase of classroom nonverbal communication. The possibilities are limitless:

1. If you customarily work with small groups of children, experiment with the spread of the chairs. When the

chairs are touching each other, do children react differently from when they are a foot apart? What about two feet? Does it make a difference whether you sit on a higher chair or one the same height?

2. Nonverbal acts are often preferable to words, and many studies show that the teacher's voice is heard far too often. Without telling the children of your intentions, experiment with giving nonverbal instead of verbal directions. Use devices such as a tap of a bell to tell children you want their attention, or the flick of lights to show that a period is about to end.

3. Make a definite attempt to react more effectively to signals. A kindergarten teacher found that she could avoid calamity by observing more closely a boy with bathroom problems. The child chewing his pencil may be hoping you will come to his desk. Or, the one wanting to sharpen his pencil may be lacking an idea to write about.

4. Try to match your degree of nonverbal behavior to the child's and examine the results. For instance, sometimes teachers tend to be overarticulate with a nonarticulate child, subconsciously compensating for his lack. In contrast, a child who sits quietly beside the teacher may be getting warmth and comfort from the teacher's sitting quietly beside him. Matching the nonverbal behavior of a child is a kind of approval.

5. Experiment with light and heat—both important factors in classroom climate. Some teachers flick the switch as soon as they open the door, yet in most classrooms, any artificial light is not necessary on a normal day. Light affects mood, and so does heat. Deliberate changes in temperature can also be an effective device for changing classroom atmosphere.

6. Use nonverbal displays. The old adage that a picture is worth a thousand words applies in establishing classroom climate, especially if you employ humor and relaxation. One teacher experimented with two signs. The first said, "Pick up paper and put it in the wastebasket." The second was a silhouette of a child neatly dropping paper in the wastebasket. The second proved to be by far the better reminder.

7. Provide opportunities for children to express emotions by nonverbal means. Pantomimes are not only highly expressive for the actors but also give teachers insight into their feelings and emotions. Various forms of rhythm and creative dance are good nonverbal expressions, and so of course are all types of art work.

8. Talk about nonverbal patterns with your children, but do it astutely. Give them the opportunity to express themselves about nonverbal behavior on the part of adults that gives them pleasure or causes them frustrations.

9. Increase your practice of looking students in the eye. Experiment with glance exchanges for individual-to-individual contact.

10. Increase the frequency of your relevant gestures. They are an excellent way of underlining points you are trying to make.

11. Check your relevancy by checking your degree of effectiveness in transmitting ideas. This is not easy to do but it is especially important. Do you often feel misunderstood? Does a particular point you tried to make fail to get across? Your nonverbal behavior may have an incongruity that cancels out the effectiveness of your words.

12. Experiment with new movement patterns. Things you have been doing, do differently for a while. You may be making yourself too available or not available enough. Be sure, however,

that your accessibility is not just a sneaky way to maintain close supervision.

13. Let children experiment with furniture arrangement that involves group interaction. One teacher tried putting desks in groups of four with the children facing each other. Two days later the desks were reversed so that this time the children faced away from each other.

14. Individualize your attention. You can't listen to all of the children all of the time, so experiment with listening very intently to a child for a brief period. As long as he is talking, look directly at him.

These suggested experiments aren't new. You've known about them all before. What's new is the emphasis on their nonverbal aspects. Considering them from this new point of view can help you understand their impact. Your goal is to use nonverbal communication more effectively in your quest for better ways of teaching.

9. FEEDBACK IN CLASSROOMS: A STUDY OF CORRECTIVE TEACHER RESPONSES

MORTON D. WAIMON

The efforts described in this paper grew out of an attempt to help prospective teachers study and understand interaction in classrooms, and to help them become more aware of pupil behavior in classrooms, and more sensitive to its meaning for teachers. It was felt that this could best be done by studying the teaching-learning process in actual classrooms. A method was developed, therefore, for describing, analyzing and interpreting observed classroom behavior.[1]

Basic to this observation of the

Morton D. Waimon, "Feedback in Classrooms: A Study of Corrective Teacher Responses," JOURNAL OF EXPERIMENTAL EDUCATION, *XXX, No. 4 (June 1962), 355–59. Reprinted by permission.*

[1] Morton D. Waimon, "Observing the Classroom Action System," *Journal of Teacher Education*, XII (December 1961), 466–70.

teaching-learning process is the conceptualization of the classroom as an action system; that is, a phenomenon whose separate elements exist in dynamic relationship to one another and to the environment in which they are found. The model developed for this work depicts three elements in the classroom action system: the teacher, the learners, and the behavior or classroom setting. It was used to demonstrate that a teacher's behavior influences the behavior setting and the behavior of learners; that a learner's behavior has an effect on the behavior setting and on how the teacher will act; and that the behavior setting itself limits the behavior of both teacher and learners. In other words, the three elements are mutually dependent each upon the others.

Although the education students involved in this investigation of the classroom studied the total action system, this paper is chiefly concerned with the way in which teachers are influenced by pupil behavior.

The learner obviously affects teacher behavior when he solicits help or asks a question. Less obviously, but perhaps of greater importance, all the learner's behavior provides the teacher with information about himself relative to that learning situation. He provides the teacher with clues about his present readiness to learn. This information, which is in the nature of a feedback to the teacher, is what prompts a teacher to change or modify something in the situation so that learning can occur.

When a teacher perceives that learning is not taking place, he makes corrective responses by changing something in the learning environment or by attempting to change some aspect of the learner's readiness. If we think of learning as occurring when learner's readiness and environment are brought into harmony, then we may view a teacher's corrective responses as maximizing the balance in the teaching-learning system.

This, then, is the conceptual framework which led us to ask the following questions:

1. What proportion of teacher behavior is corrective; that is, is made in response to pupil behavior which indicates that learning is not taking place?
2. What proportion of teachers' corrective responses is directed toward changing the environment?
3. What proportion of teachers' corrective responses is directed toward changing some aspect of the learner's readiness?
4. Which aspect of the environment is most frequently manipulated?
5. Which aspect of the learner's readiness is most frequently manipulated?

Procedures

After an initial orientation and training period, teams of four members each were established to make classroom observations, and observation guides were distributed to each team. One member was to concentrate and record data on the teacher, two were to concentrate on the learners, the fourth on the behavior setting. Time sheets blocked off in five-minute intervals were used for recording, and an entire observation period lasted thirty minutes. Immediately following the observation period, team members coalesced their data.

Teams were responsible for recording everything which took place during an observation period. Working as teams and having each member concentrate on one element of the action system helped in making the recorded accounts more complete and more accurate. The member responsible for the behavior setting had to identify the kind of lesson, unit or activity engaged in; the apparent goals and subgoals of the activity; the selection and organization of content; and the procedures followed, including the materials and equipment available for use. The member responsible for the teacher was to record everything the teacher said to an individual learner or to the class; all the teacher's nonverbal behavior relative to an individual learner or to the class; all the teacher's apparent feelings relative to an individual learner or to the class. The other two members divided the class between them to make observation easier, and were to record everything any learner said to the teacher or to the class; all significant nonverbal behavior of learners (that is, all behavior which was noticeable to the teacher and to the observers), and all apparent feelings expressed by any learner. At the end of the observation period, team members combined their records into a running account of everything that happened during the observation period. Observations were made in nineteen classes of the Laboratory School of Illinois State Normal University.

Treatment of the Descriptive Data

The descriptive records gathered by teams were divided into smaller units of behavior which were called behavior episodes. Behavior episodes may best be explained as samples of behavior, within the larger stream of behavior, which have a discernible beginning and end. For example, during an arithmetic lesson a pupil discovers he has no pencil; he tries to borrow one from his neighbor without success; he informs the teacher of his difficulty; is told to take one from the teacher's desk; he does so and returns to his seat to continue work. All the action aimed at securing a pencil is a behavior episode.

Classifying the Data

Team members then analyzed and classified their data several ways. First the records were read over to find pupil behavior, both verbal and nonverbal, which indicated that the pupil was not ready to learn in that situation. Each such response was starred. Expressions of boredom, disinterest or confusion, inattention, irrelevant behavior, questions regarding procedures or content were regarded as indications that a learner was not ready to learn; that is, not ready to make the correct response called for. Next the records were checked for teacher behavior which was made in response to starred pupil behavior. An "X" was placed beside each such teacher response.

Behavior episodes were then classified into three categories: Type A episodes are those episodes in which there was no evidence that any learner lacked readiness to learn in that situation. Learning proceeded smoothly without any apparent blocking. Type B episodes are those episodes in which a learner indicated a lack of readiness to learn, but in which the teacher did *not* respond to that specific pupil behavior. Type C episodes are those episodes in which a learner indicated a lack of readiness to learn and in which the teacher *responded* to the specific pupil behavior.

Type C episodes were further

evaluated to determine how often teachers responded to pupils' lack of readiness by attempting to change something in the environment, and how often the teacher's response tended to be directed toward the pupil himself.

When a teacher response was directed toward the environment, it was further classified into responses that change the goal, responses that change the content, or responses that change the procedures.

When a teacher response was directed toward the learner, it was further classified into responses that act on the pupil's equipment (that is, affect his physique, sense organs, or mental abilities), responses that act on pupil's needs and goals (that is, his need for affection, approval, independence, self-respect, or his immediate personal goals), or responses that act on the pupil's learned ideas and skills (that is, his previous learnings).

The following are examples of each type episode:

Type A—(All pupils ready. No corrective teacher responses made.)

T: "What is the first number? Lynn?"

Lynn: "Three."

T: "Three what?"

Lynn: "Three tens."

T: "What does the 2 mean?"

Lynn: "Two ones."

T: "And what is the whole number? Three?"

Lynn: "Tens."

T: "And two . . . ?"

Lynn: "Ones."

T: "Make?"

Lynn: "Thirty-two."

T: "Good for you, Lynn."

Type B—(Lack of readiness shown, but no corrective responses made by teacher.)

T: (Reviewing spelling words.) "*Every*. Look at your own paper. If you look at someone else's paper that tells me you don't know how to spell it. *Begin, yesterday*, . . ."

Ricky: (Repeats all words without being asked.)

Scott, Jim, Brad: (Talked to each other.)*

Kerry: (Dropped his pencil; picked it up.)

Paul: (Opened his book before he was supposed to.)

Toni: "I got scared last night."*

Sandy: "My mommy made some popcorn balls for Halloween."*

T: "The last word is *invite*. All right, there are your words. Open your book to page 80 and check your words, and I will come around to see if you are a good checker-upper."

Type C—(Lack of readiness shown, and teacher makes corrective responses.)

T: (Writes 14 on the board.) "What is the name of this number? Anybody? Anyone can answer because the group is small."

Steve: "Twenty-four."*

T: "No, Steve, let's begin at one and count until we reach the number." X L(l.i.s.)

Steve: "1 . . . 2 . . . 3 . . . 4 . . . 5 . . . 6 . . . 7 . . . 8 . . . 9 . . . 10 . . . 11 . . . 12 . . . 13 . . . 14"

T: "Fine, now we know how to proceed."

Polly: (Not paying attention)*

T: "Polly, look at this number right

here. You're too busy watching over there. How many tens?" X L(n.g.)

Polly: "One."

T: "How many ones?"

Polly: "One."

T: "Now, ten and one are 11 in all."

T: (Reading to class from *Who's Who in Supermarket*. The Produce Department is mentioned.) "Do you all know what a Produce Department is? It's the name given to the department where fresh fruits and vegetables are sold.
"Name something that is sold in the Produce Department. Steve?"

Steve: "Lettuce."

T: "Good. Janie?"

Janie: "Grapefruit."

T: "Yes. Willy?"

Willy: "Greeners."

T: "Greeners? What do you mean, Willy?"

Willy: "Greeners."

T: "Could you draw a picture of your vegetable? I'm afraid we don't quite understand your word." X E(p)

Willy: (Draws on board. His vegetable turns out to be a green onion.) "At our house, we call them greeners."

Findings

We found that out of a total of 865 behavior episodes, 402 were Type A episodes. That is, 46.5 per cent of the episodes observed were instances in which there was *no* evidence of lack of readiness on the part of learners. Learners indicated a lack of readiness in 463 episodes or 53.5 per cent of the total. In 96 episodes, or 11.1 per cent of the total, teachers made no response to the evidence of lack of readiness to learn in that situation (see Table 1).

The average number of episodes recorded in nineteen classes was 46 episodes. The average percentage of Type C episodes was 41 per cent with a standard deviation of 15 per cent.

Type C episodes totaled 367. Of these, 82 episodes or 22.3 per cent were episodes in which the teacher responded to pupils' lack of readiness by attempting to change something in the environment (E). In 285 episodes, or 77.7 per cent, the teacher responded to pupils' lack of readiness by attempting to change something about the learner himself. The average percentage of learner-directed teacher responses was 76 per cent with a standard deviation of 13.4 per cent.

Of a total of 82 teacher responses which attempted to change something in the environment (E), 53 responses, or 65 per cent, were a change of procedures; 25 responses, or 30 per cent, were a change of content; and only 4 responses, or 5 per cent, were a change of goals (see Table 2).

Of a total of 285 teacher responses which attempted to change some aspect of the learner's readiness (L), 140 responses, or 49 per cent, sought to change the learner's needs and goals; 138 responses, or 48 per cent, to change the pupil's learned ideas and skills; and only 7 responses, or 3 per cent, were related to pupil's equipment (see Table 3).

The ratio of one subcategory of teacher response to the others varied widely among the observed nineteen classes, and no significant central tendency was found to exist.

TABLE 1

Classification of Behavior Episode

Type of Behavior Episode	Number	Per cent
Type A	402	46.5
Type B	96)	11.1)
	463	53.5
Type C	367)	42.4)
Total	865	100.

TABLE 2

Classification of Environment-Directed Teacher Responses (E)

Aspect of Environment	Number	Per cent
Goals (g)	4	5.
Content (c)	25	30.
Procedures (p)	53	65.
Total	82	100.

TABLE 3

Classification of Leaner-Directed Teacher Responces (L)

Aspect of Learner's Readiness	Number	Per cent
Pupil's equipment (e)	7	3.
Pupil's needs and goals	140	49.
Pupil's learned ideas and skills (l.i.s.)	138	48.
Total	285	100.

Conclusions

A conceptualization of the classroom as an action system wherein pupil behavior is viewed as feedback information used by teachers to make corrective responses is a promising one for the study of the teaching-learning process.

The stream of interaction between teacher and learners can be divided into episodes and these episodes can be classified into three types: (1) Episodes in which there is no evidence of lack of readiness on the part of the pupils; (2) Episodes in which pupils indicate a lack of readiness, but in which teachers do not respond; (3) Episodes in which pupils indicate lack of readiness and in which teachers directly respond to that specific behavior.

In approximately 40 per cent of the instances observed, teachers' behavior was a direct response to learner behavior. This teacher behavior can be classified into (1) behavior which attempts to change the environment to suit the readiness of the learner (E), or (2) behavior which attempts to make the learner more ready for the environment. There is a tendency for teachers to try to change the learner's readiness when learning does not occur.

Teacher responses which manipulate the environment can be classified into the subcategories we used; that is, responses which (1) changed the goal, (2) changed the content, (3) changed the procedures.

Teacher responses which manipulate the learner can be classified into two of the subcategories which we used; that is, responses which act on (1) pupils' needs and goals, and (2) pupils' learned ideas and skills. The third category, pupils' equipment, is of questionable value since so few responses went into this category.

The ratio of one subcategory of teacher response to the others varied widely among the nineteen classes, as we have said. This wide variation suggests that type of teacher response may be related to some aspect not studied at this time, such as, subject matter being taught, grade level being taught, or years of teaching experience.

As a final conclusion, it is felt that direct study of the teaching-learning process in actual classrooms by prospective teachers is a valid and advantageous method of teacher training. And, it is feasible through the use of system analysis and the development of models to help in the conceptualization.

ACTIVITIES

1. Consider the following teaching episode. Do you think it demonstrates good teaching? What are some ways you might describe the teaching, withholding judgment for awhile? Use the Flanders framework and compare your ratings with those of your classmates. Devise your own scheme for cataloging interaction patterns. (Perhaps Chapter 6 of the *Handbook for Research on Teaching*, N. L. Gage, ed., will suggest alternatives for your analysis.)

Class: 30 ninth-grade social-studies students.
Topic: Civil War

Teacher: Do you think the Southern States were morally right in leaving the Union? Bob—

Bob: No. They joined the Union—and they should have known they were going to have to stay in the Union in thick and thin. It's just like a marriage.

Teacher: You feel the relationship of South Carolina to the United States was similar to that of husband and wife?

Bob: I didn't say that—I meant the Constitution was like a wedding promise—it is binding.

Teacher: Does it say in the Constitution that joining the Union is binding?

Bob: It must. At least it's implied.

Teacher: (taking to whole class) Shhh! Bob has brought up an interesting point—and very few of you are listening to it. Some of you don't even seem to care. You'll care next Friday when we have a quiz on this. Bob, would you repeat your position for the benefit of those who weren't listening.

Bob: I think the South was wrong in quitting the Union.

Sue: Why do you think so?

Teacher: He just told us why—if you had been listening. Any other person like to state his position?
Andy: I disagree with Bob.
Teacher: Tell us about your point of view.
Andy: I think South Carolina did the right thing—if you don't stand up for what you believe in—other people may push you around.
Sally: What time does this period end?
Teacher: Will you people please keep your mind on the topic at hand. Andy—is it always "right" to take a stand?
Andy: Yes—that's what I was taught.
Teacher: Do you *always* take a stand on whatever you believe?
Andy: I sure do.
Teacher: Oh. I appreciate how you feel, Andy. Many others feel as you do. We have heard two views about the Civil War. Any others? (pause) Perhaps we should review some of the facts during the rest of the period. Who was the Republican candidate for President in 1860?
Carolyn: Abraham Lincoln.
Teacher: OK! Who was the Democratic candidate?
Tom: U. S. Grant?
Teacher: No—but was Grant ever a candidate for President?
Richard: Yes—twice and he won.
Teacher: Good for you Richard. Do you know who the Democratic candidate for President in 1860 was?
Richard: Stephan Douglas.
Teacher: Good.
. . . *and on*

2. Collect, by tape recorder or other means, or make up similar classroom episodes. Avoid trying to label the episodes good or bad—but try to devise ways of describing the actual teaching.

3. Can you think of some ways a teacher could monitor his behavior in class other than those reported here?

4. If, after obtaining a description of a classroom activity, you wished to evaluate the quality of the teaching or the learning, what criteria would you employ?

5. Some of the observation scales may be too complex for convenient application. Can you suggest alternative scales which will emphasize those aspects of classroom interaction which seem most important to you?

6. Lead a discussion either by teaching fellow students or by teaching in your own classroom. Attempt to keep the discussion flowing by using mainly non-verbal communications techniques.

DECISIONS IN PLANNING

CHAPTER THREE

Many times teachers feel that a majority of the planning decisions usually considered a part of the teaching act are determined by forces in the community, in the school administration, or by the authors of textbooks. However, in spite of all these influences, teachers do have a great deal of freedom in making decisions about what will be taught and what students are to do in the classroom. In fact, a teacher communicates his values and beliefs about education in the way he plans and in the plans themselves.

For example, a teacher may plan his teaching by counting the pages in the text, dividing that number by the minimum number of classroom sessions, and using the quotient as the size of the each days' reading assignment. Every Thursday could be a movie day, with one quiz a week and one major test every marking period. Such an approach demonstrates this teacher's attitude toward learning and toward education itself.

The way in which a teacher resolves the problem of justifying the choices he makes in planning is another manifestation of his beliefs. Some teachers advocate that activities can only be justified in terms of the objectives to which they lead. Others argue that activities which meet certain well defined criteria can have intrinsic value. Of course, both positions can be used as guidelines in making curriculum decisions.

This chapter presents readings that reflect various positions teachers may consider in making planning decisions.

10. THE AIMS OF EDUCATION

ALFRED NORTH WHITEHEAD

Culture is activity of thought, and receptiveness to beauty and humane feeling. Scraps of information have nothing to do with it. A merely well-informed man is the most useless bore on God's earth. What we should aim at producing is men who possess both culture and expert knowledge in some special direction. Their expert knowledge will give them the ground to start from, and their culture will lead them as deep as philosophy and as high as art. We have to remember that the valuable intellectual development is self-development, and that it mostly takes place between the ages of sixteen and thirty. As to training, the most important part is given by mothers before the age of twelve. A saying due to Archbishop Temple illustrates my meaning. Surprise was expressed at the success in after-life of a man, who as a boy at Rugby had been somewhat undistinguished. He answered, "It is not what they are at eighteen, it is what they become afterwards that matters."

In training a child to activity of thought, above all things we must beware of what I will call "inert ideas"—that is to say, ideas that are merely received into the mind without being utilised, or tested, or thrown into fresh combinations.

In the history of education, the most striking phenomenon is that schools of learning, which at one epoch are alive with a ferment of genius, in a succeeding generation exhibit merely pedantry and routine. The reason is, that they are overladen with inert ideas. Education with inert ideas is not only useless: it is, above all things, harmful—*Corruptio optimi, pessima.* Except at rare intervals of intellectual ferment, education in the past has been radically infected with inert ideas. That is the reason why uneducated clever women,

Alfred North Whitehead, THE AIMS OF EDUCATION *(New York: The Macmillan Company, 1929), pp. 1–3, 8–15.*

who have seen much of the world, are in middle life so much the most cultured part of the community. They have been saved from this horrible burden of inert ideas. Every intellectual revolution which has ever stirred humanity into greatness has been a passionate protest against inert ideas. Then, alas, with pathetic ignorance of human psychology, it has proceeded by some educational scheme to bind humanity afresh with inert ideas of its own fashioning.

Let us now ask how in our system of education we are to guard against this mental dryrot. We enunciate two educational commandments, "Do not teach too many subjects," and again, "What you teach, teach thoroughly."

The result of teaching small parts of a large number of subjects is the passive reception of disconnected ideas, not illumined with any spark of vitality. Let the main ideas which are introduced into a child's education be few and important, and let them be thrown into every combination possible. The child should make them his own, and should understand their application here and now in the circumstances of his actual life. From the very beginning of his education, the child should experience the joy of discovery. The discovery which he has to make is that general ideas give an understanding of that stream of events which pours through his life, which is his life. By understanding I mean more than a mere logical analysis, though that is included. I mean "understanding" in the sense in which it is used in the French proverb. "To understand all, is to forgive all." Pedants sneer at an education which is useful. But if education is not useful, what is it? Is it a talent, to be hidden away in a napkin? Of course, education should be useful, whatever your aim in life. It was useful to Saint Augustine and it was useful to Napoleon. It is useful, because understanding is useful.

* * *

I appeal to you, as practical teachers. With good discipline, it is always possible to pump into the minds of a class a certain quantity of inert knowledge. You take a textbook and make them learn it. So far, so good. The child then knows how to solve a quadratic equation. But what is the point of teaching a child to solve a quadratic equation? There is a traditional answer to this question. It runs thus: The mind is an instrument, you first sharpen it, and then use it; the acquisition of the power of solving a quadratic equation is part of the process of sharpening the mind. Now there is just enough truth in his answer to have made it live through the ages. But for all its half-truth, it embodies a radical error which bids fair to stifle the genius of the modern world. I do not know who was first responsible for this analogy of the mind to a dead instrument. For aught I know, it may have been one of the seven wise men of Greece, or a committee of the whole lot of them. Whoever was the originator, there can be no doubt of the authority which it has acquired by the continuous approval bestowed upon it by eminent persons. But whatever its weight of authority, whatever the high approval which it can quote, I have no hesitation in denouncing it as one of the most fatal, erroneous, and dangerous conceptions ever introduced into the theory of education. The mind is never passive; it is perpetual activity, delicate, receptive, responsive to stimulus. You cannot postpone its life until you have sharpened it. Whatever interest attaches to your subject-matter must be evoked here and now; whatever powers you are strengthening in the pupil, must be exercised here and now; whatever possibilities of mental life your teaching should impart, must be exhibited here and now. That is the golden rule of education, and a very difficult rule to follow.

The difficulty is just this: the apprehension of general ideas, intellectual habits of mind, and pleasurable interest in mental achievement can be evoked by no form of words, however accurately adjusted. All practical teachers know that education is a patient process of the mastery of details, minute by minute, hour by hour, day by day. There is no royal road to learning through an airy path of brilliant generalizations. There is a proverb about the difficulty of seeing the wood because of the trees. That difficulty is exactly the point which I am enforcing. The problem of education is to make the pupil see the wood by means of the trees.

The solution which I am urging is to eradicate the fatal disconnection of subjects which kills the vitality of our modern curriculum. There is only one subject-matter for education, and that is Life in all its manifestations. Instead of this single unity, we offer children—Algebra, from which nothing follows; Geometry, from which nothing follows; Science, from which nothing follows; History, from which nothing follows; a Couple of Languages, never mastered; and lastly, most dreary of all, Literature, represented by plays of Shakespeare, with philological notes and short analyses of plot and character to be in substance committed to memory. Can such a list be said to represent Life, as it is known in the midst of the living of it? The best that can be said of it is, that it is a rapid table of contents which a deity might run over in his mind while he was thinking of creating a world, and had not yet determined how to put it together.

Let us now return to quadratic equations. We still have on hand the unanswered question. Why should children be taught their solution? Unless quadratic equations fit into a connected curriculum, of course there is no reason to teach anything about them. Furthermore, extensive as should be the place of mathematics in a complete culture, I am a little doubtful whether for many types of boys algebraic solutions of quadratic equations do not lie on the specialist side of mathematics. I may here remind you that as yet I have not said anything of the psychology or the content of the specialism, which is so necessary a part of an ideal education. But all that is an evasion of our real question, and I merely state it in order to avoid being misunderstood in my answer.

Quadratic equations are part of algebra, and algebra is the intellectual instrument which has been created for rendering clear the quantitative aspects of the world. There is no getting out of it. Through and through the world is infected with quantity. To talk sense, is to talk in quantities. It is no use saying that the nation is large—How large? It is no use saying that radium is scarce,—How scarce? You cannot evade quantity. You may fly to poetry and to music, and quantity and number will face you in your rhythms and your octaves. Elegant intellects which despise the theory of quantity, are but half developed. They are more to be pitied than blamed. The scraps of gibberish, which in their school-days were taught to them in the name of algebra, deserve some contempt.

This question of the degeneration of algebra into gibberish, both in word and in fact, affords a pathetic instance of the uselessness of reforming educational schedules without a clear conception of the attributes which you wish to evoke in the living minds of the children. A few years ago there was an outcry that school algebra was in need of reform, but there was a general agreement that graphs would put everything right. So all sorts of things were extruded, and graphs were introduced. So far as I can see, with no sort of idea behind them, but just graphs. Now every examination paper has one or two questions on graphs. Personally, I am an enthusiastic adherent of graphs. But I wonder whether as yet we have gained very much. You cannot put life into any schedule of general education unless you succeed in exhibiting its relation to some essential characteristic of all intelligent or emotional perception. It is a hard saying, but it is true; and I do not see how to make it any easier. In making these little formal alterations you are beaten by the very nature of things. You are pitted against too skilful an adversary, who will see to it that the pea is always under the other thimble.

Reformation must begin at the other end. First, you must make up your mind as to those quantitative aspects of the world which are simple enough to be introduced into general education; then a schedule of algebra should be framed which will about find its exemplification in these applications. We need not fear for our pet graphs, they will be there in plenty when we once begin to treat algebra as a serious means of studying the world. Some of the simplest applications will be found in the quantities which occur in the simplest study of society. The curves of history are more vivid and more informing than the dry catalogues of names and dates which comprise the greater part of that arid school study. What purpose is effected by a catalogue of undistinguished kings and queens? Tom, Dick, or Harry, they are all dead. General resurrections are failures, and are better postponed. The quantitative flux of the forces of modern society is capable of very simple exhibition. Meanwhile, the idea of the variable, of the function, of rate of change, of equations and their solution, of elimination are being studied as an abstract science for their own sake. Not, of course, in the pompous phrases with which I am alluding to them here, but with that iteration of simple special cases proper to teaching.

If this course be followed, the route from Chaucer to the Black Death, from the Black Death to modern Labour troubles, will connect the tales of the medieval pilgrims with the abstract science of algebra, both yielding diverse aspects of that single theme, Life. I know what most of you are thinking at this point. It is that the exact course which I have sketched out is not the particular one which you would have chosen, or even see how to work. I quite agree. I am not claiming that I could do it myself. But your objection is the precise reason why a common external examination system is fatal to education. The process of exhibiting the applications of knowledge must, for its success, essentially depend on the character of the pupils and the genius of the teacher. Of course I have left out the easiest applications with which most of us are more at home. I mean the quantitative sides of sciences, such as mechanics and physics.

Again, in the same connection we plot the statistics of social phenomena against the time. We then eliminate the time between suitable pairs. We can speculate how far we have exhibited a real causal connection, or how far a mere temporal coincidence. We notice that we might have plotted against the time one set of statistics for one country and another set for another country, and thus, with suitable choice of subjects, have obtained graphs which certainly exhibited mere coincidence. Also other graphs exhibit obvious causal connections. We wonder how to discriminate. And so are drawn on as far as we will.

But in considering this description, I must beg you to remember what I have been insisting on above. In the first place, one train of thought will not suit all groups of children. For example, I should expect that artisan children will want something more concrete and, in a sense, swifter than I have set down here. Perhaps I am wrong, but that is what I should guess. In the second place, I am not contemplating one beautiful lecture stimulating, once and for all, an admiring class. That is not the way in which education proceeds. No; all the time the pupils are hard at work solving examples, drawing graphs, and making experiments, until they have a thorough hold on the whole subject. I am describing the interspersed explanations, the directions which should be given to their thoughts. The pupils have got to be made to feel that they are studying something, and are not merely executing intellectual minuets.

11. THINKING IN EDUCATION

JOHN DEWEY

1. The Essentials of Method

No one doubts, theoretically, the importance of fostering in school good habits of thinking. But apart from the fact that the acknowledgement is not so great in practice as in theory, there is not adequate theoretical recognition that all which the school can or need do for pupils, so far as their *minds* are concerned (that is, leaving out certain specialized muscular abilities), is to develop their ability to think. The parceling out of instruction among various ends such as acquisition of skill (in reading, spelling, writing, drawing, reciting); acquiring information (in history and geography), *and* training of thinking is a measure of the ineffective way in which we accomplish all three. Thinking which is not connected with increase of efficiency in action, and with learning more about ourselves and the world in which we live, has something the matter with it just as thought. . . . And skill obtained apart from thinking is not connected with any sense of the purposes for which it is to be used. It consequently leaves a man at the mercy of his routine habits and of the authoritative control of others, who know what they are about and who are not especially scrupulous as to their means of achievement. And information severed from thoughtful action is dead, a mind-crushing load. Since it simulates knowledge and thereby develops the poison of conceit, it is a most powerful obstacle to further growth in the grace of intelligence. The sole direct path to enduring improvement in the methods of instruction and learning consists of centering upon the conditions which exact, promote, and test thinking. Thinking *is* the method of intelligent learning, of learning that employs and rewards mind. We speak, legitimately enough, about the method of thinking, but

John Dewey, DEMOCRACY AND EDUCATION *(New York: The Macmillan Company, 1916).*

the important thing to bear in mind about method is that thinking is method, the method of intelligent experience in the course which it takes.

I.

The initial stage of that developing experience which is called thinking is *experience*. This remark may sound like a silly truism. It ought to be one; but unfortunately it is not. On the contrary, thinking is often regarded both in philosophic theory and in educational practice as something cut off from experience, and capable of being cultivated in isolation. In fact, the inherent limitations of experience are often urged as the sufficient ground for attention to thinking. Experience is then thought to be confined to the senses and appetites; to a mere material world, while thinking proceeds from a higher faculty (of reason), and is occupied with spiritual or at least literary things. So, oftentimes, a sharp distinction is made between pure mathematics, as a peculiarly fit subject matter of thought (since it has nothing to do with physical existences) and applied mathematics, which has utilitarian but not mental value.

Speaking generally, the fundamental fallacy in methods of instruction lies in supposing that experience on the part of pupils may be assumed. What is here insisted upon is the necessity of an actual empirical situation as the initiating phase of thought. Experience is here taken as previously defined: trying to do something and having the thing perceptibly do something to one in return. The fallacy consists in supposing that we can begin with ready-made subject matter of arithmetic, or geography, or whatever, irrespective of some direct personal experience of a situation. Even the kindergarten and Montessori techniques are so anxious to get at intellectual distinctions, without "waste of time," that they tend to ignore—or reduce—the immediate crude handling of the familiar material of experience, and to introduce pupils at once to material which expresses the intellectual distinctions which adults have made. But the first stage of contact with any new material, at whatever age of maturity, must inevitably be of the trial and error sort. An individual must actually try, in play or work, to do something with material in carrying out his own impulsive activity, and then note the interaction of his energy and that of the material employed. This is what happens when a child at first begins to build with blocks, and it is equally what happens when a scientific man in his laboratory begins to experiment with unfamiliar objects.

Hence the first approach to any subject in school, if thought is to be aroused and not words acquired, should be as unscholastic as possible. To realize what an experience, or empirical situation, means, we have to call to mind the sort of situation that presents itself outside of school; the sort of occupations that interest and engage activity in ordinary life. And careful inspection of methods which are permanently successful in formal education, whether in arithmetic or learning to read, or studying geography, or learning physics or a foreign language, will reveal that they depend for their efficiency upon the fact that they go back to the type of situation which causes reflection out of school in ordinary life. They give the pupils something to do, not something to learn; and the doing is of such a nature as to demand thinking, or the intentional noting of connections; learning naturally results.

That the situation should be of such a nature as to arouse thinking means of course that it should suggest something to do which is not either routine or capricious—something, in other words, presenting what is new (and hence uncertain or problematic) and yet sufficiently connected with existing habits to call out an effective response. An effective response means one which accomplishes a perceptible result, in distinction from a purely haphazard activity, where the consequences cannot be mentally connected with what is done. The most significant question which can be asked, accordingly, about any situation or experience proposed to induce learning is what quality of problem it involves.

At first thought, it might seem as if usual school methods measured well up to the standard here set. The giving of problems, the putting of questions, the assigning of tasks, the magnifying of difficulties is a large part of school work. But it is indispensable to discriminate between genuine and simulated or mock problems. The following questions may aid in making such discrimination. (*a*) Is there anything but a problem? Does the question naturally suggest itself within some situation or personal experience? Or is it an aloof thing, a problem only for the purposes of conveying instruction in some school topic? Is it the sort of trying that would arouse observation and engage experimentation outside of school? (*b*) Is it the pupil's own problem, or is it the teacher's or textbook's problem, made a problem for the pupil only because he cannot get the required mark or be promoted or win the teacher's approval, unless he deals with it? Obviously, these two questions overlap. They are two ways of getting at the same point: Is the experience a personal thing of such a nature as inherently to stimulate and direct observation of the connections involved, and to lead to inference and its testing? Or is it imposed from without, and is the pupil's problem simply to meet the external requirement?

Such questions may give us pause in deciding upon the extent to which current practices are adapted to develop reflective habits. The physical equipment and arrangements of the average schoolroom are hostile to the existence of real situations of experience. What is there similar to the conditions of everyday life which will generate difficulties? Almost everything testifies to the great premium put upon listening, reading, and the reproduction of what is told and read. It is hardly possible to overstate the contrast between such conditions and the situations of active contact with things and persons in the home, on the playground, in the fulfilling of ordinary responsibilities of life. Much of it is not even comparable with the questions which may arise in the mind of a boy or girl in conversing with others or in reading books outside of the school. No one has ever explained why children are so full of questions outside of the school (so that they pester grown-up persons if they get any encouragement), and the conspicuous absence of display of curiosity about the subject matter of school lessons. Reflection on this striking contrast will throw light upon the question of how far customary school conditions supply a context of experience in which problems naturally suggest themselves. No amount of improvement in the personal technique of the instructor will wholly remedy this state of things. There must be more actual material, more *stuff*, more appliances, and more opportunities for doing things, before the gap can be overcome. And where children are engaged in doing things and in discussing what arises in the course of their doing, it is found, even with comparatively indifferent modes of instruction, that childrens' inquiries are spontaneous and numerous, and the proposals of solution advanced, varied, and ingenious.

As a consequence of the absence of the materials and occupations which generate real problems, the pupil's problems are not his; or, rather, they are his *only* as a pupil, not as a human being. Hence the lamentable waste in carrying over such expertness as is achieved in dealing with them to the affairs of life beyond the schoolroom. A pupil has a problem, but it is the problem of meeting the peculiar requirements set by the teacher. His problem becomes that of finding out what the teacher wants, what will satisfy the teacher in recitation and examination and outward deportment. Relationship to subject matter is no longer direct. The occasions and material of thought are not found in the arithmetic or the history or geography itself, but in skillfully adapting that material to the teacher's requirements. The pupil studies, but unconsciously to himself the objects of his study are the conventions and standards of the school system and school authority, not the nominal "studies." The thinking thus evoked is artificially one-sided at the best. At its worst, the problem of the pupil is not how to meet the requirements of school life, but how to *seem* to meet them—or, how to come near enough to meeting them to slide along without an undue amount of friction. The type of judgment formed by these devices is not a desirable addition to character. If these statements give too highly colored a picture of usual school methods, the exaggeration may at least serve to illustrate the point: the need of active pursuits, involving the use of material to accomplish purposes, if there are to be situations which normally generate problems occasioning thoughtful inquiry.

II.

There must be *data* at command to supply the considerations required in dealing with the specific difficulty which has presented itself. Teachers following a "developing" method sometimes tell children to think things out for themselves as if they could spin them out of their own heads. The material of thinking is not thoughts, but actions, facts, events, and the relations of things. In other words, to think effectively one must have had, or now have, experiences which will furnish him resources for coping with the difficulty at hand. A difficulty is an indispensable stimulus to thinking, but not all difficulties call out thinking. Sometimes they overwhelm and submerge and discourage. The perplexing situation must be sufficiently like situations which have already been dealt with so that pupils will have some control of the meanings of handling it. A large part of the art of instruction lies in making the difficulty of new problems large enough to challenge thought, and small enough so that, in addition to the confusion naturally attending the novel elements, there shall be luminous familiar spots from which helpful suggestions may spring.

In one sense, it is a matter of indifference by what psychological means the subject matter for reflection is provided. Memory, observation, reading, communication are all avenues for supplying data. The relative proportion to be obtained from each is a matter of the specific features of the particular problem in hand. It is foolish to insist upon observation of objects presented to the senses if the student is so familiar with the objects that he could just as well recall the facts independently. It is possible to induce undue and crippling dependence upon sense-presentations. No one can carry around with him a museum of all the things whose properties will assist the conduct of thought. A well-trained mind is one that has a maximum of resources behind it, so to speak, and that is accustomed to go over its past experiences to see what they yield. On the other hand, a quality or relation of even a familiar object may previously have been passed over, and be just the fact that is helpful in dealing with the question. In this case direct observation is called for. The same principle applies to the use to be made of observation on one hand and of reading and "telling" on the other. Direct observation is naturally more vivid and vital. But it has its limitations; and in any case it is a necessary part of education that one should acquire the ability to supplement the narrowness of his immediately personal experiences by utilizing the experiences of others. Excessive reliance upon others for data (whether got from reading or listening) is to be depreciated. Most objectionable of all is the probability that others, the book or the teacher, will supply solutions ready-made, instead of giving material that the student has to adapt and apply to the question in hand for himself.

There is no inconsistency in saying that in schools there is usually both too much and too little information supplied by others. The accumulation and acquisition of information for purposes of reproduction in recitation and examination are made too much of. "Knowledge," in the sense of information, means the working capital, the indispensable resources, of further inquiry; of finding out, or learning, more things. Frequently it is treated as an end itself, and then the goal becomes to heap it up and display it when called for. This static, cold-storage ideal of knowledge is inimical to educative development. It not only lets occasions for thinking go unused, but it swamps thinking. No one could construct a house on ground cluttered with miscellaneous junk. Pupils who have stored their "minds" with all kinds of material which they have never put to intellectual uses are sure to be hampered when they try to think. They have no practice in selecting what is appropriate, and no criterion to go by; everything is on the same dead static level. On the other hand, it is quite open to question whether, if information actually functioned in experience through use in application to the student's own purposes, there would not be need of more varied resources in books, pictures, and talks than are usually at command.

III.

The correlate in thinking of facts, data, knowledge already acquired is suggestions, inference, conjectured meanings, suppositions, tentative explanation—*ideas*, in short. Careful observation and recollection determine what is given, what is already there, and hence assured. They cannot furnish what is lacking. They define, clarify, and locate the question; they cannot supply its answer. Projection, invention, ingenuity, devising come in for that purpose. The data *arouse* suggestions, and only by reference to the specific data can we pass upon the appropriateness of the suggestions. But the suggestions run beyond what is, as yet, actually *given* in experience. They forecast possible results, things *to* do, not facts (things already done). Inference is always an invasion of the unknown, a leap from the known.

In this sense, a thought (what a thing suggests but is not as it is presented) is creative—an incursion into the novel. It involves some inventiveness. What is suggested must, indeed, be familiar in *some* context; the novelty, the inventive devising, clings to the new light in which it is seen, the different use to which it is put. When Newton thought of his theory of gravitation, the creative aspect of his thought was not found in its materials. They were familiar; many of them commonplaces—sun, moon, planets, weight, distance, mass, square numbers. These were not original ideas; they were established facts. His originality lay in the *use* to which these familiar acquaintances were put by introduction into an unfamiliar context. The same is true of every striking scientific discovery, every great invention, every admirable artistic production. Only silly folk identify creative originality with the extraordinary and fanciful; others recognize that its measure lies in putting everyday things to uses which had not occurred to others. The operation is novel, not the material out of which it is constructed.

The educational conclusion which follows is that *all* thinking is original in a projection of considerations which have not been previously apprehended. The child of three who discovers what can be done with blocks, or of six who finds out what he can make by putting five cents and five cents together, is really a discoverer, even though everybody else in the world knows it. There is a genuine increment of experience; not another item mechanically added on, but enrichment by a new quality. The charm which the spontaneity of little children has for sympathetic observers is due to perception of this intellectual originality. The joy which children themselves experience is the joy of intellectual constructiveness—of creativeness, if the word may be used without misunderstanding.

The educational moral I am chiefly concerned to draw is not, however, that teachers would find their own work less of a grind and strain if school conditions favored learning in the sense of discovery and not in that of storing away what others pour into them; nor that it would be possible to give even children and youth the delights of personal intellectual productiveness—true and important as are these things. It is that no thought, no idea, can possibly be conveyed as an idea from one person to another. When it is told, it is, to the one to whom it is told, another given fact, not an idea. The communication may stimulate the other person to realize the question for himself and to think out a like idea, or it may smother his intellectual interest and suppress his dawning effort at thought. But what he *directly* gets cannot be an idea. Only by wrestling with the conditions of the problem at first hand, seeking and finding his own way out, does he think. When the parent or teacher has provided the conditions which stimulate thinking and has taken a sympathetic attitude toward the activities of the learner by entering into a common or conjoint experience, all has been done which a second party can do to instigate learning. The rest lies with the one directly concerned. If he cannot devise his own solution (not of course in isolation, but in correspondence with the teacher and other pupils) and find his own way out he will not learn, not even if he can recite some correct answer with one hundred per cent accuracy. We can and do supply ready-made "ideas" by the thousand; we do not usually take much pains to see that the one learning engages in significant situations where his own activities generate, support, and clinch ideas—that is, perceived meanings or connections. This does not mean that the teacher is to stand off and look on; the alternative to furnishing ready-made subject matter and listening to the accuracy with which it is reproduced is not quiescence, but participation, sharing, in an activity. In such shared activity, the teacher is a learner, and the learner is, without knowing it, a teacher—and upon the whole, the less consciousness there is, on either side, of either giving or receiving instruction, the better.

IV.

Ideas, as we have seen, whether they be humble guesses or dignified theories, are anticipations of possible solutions. They are anticipations of some continuity or connection of an activity and a consequence which has not as yet shown itself. They are therefore tested by the operation of acting upon them. They are to guide and organize further observations, recollections, and experiments. They are intermediate in learning, not final. All educational reformers, as we have had occasion to remark, are given to attacking the passivity of traditional education. They have opposed pouring in from without, and absorbing like a sponge; they have attacked drilling in material as into hard and resisting rock. But it is not easy to secure conditions which will make the getting of an idea identical with having an experience which widens and makes more precise our contact with the environment. Activity, even self-activity, is too easily thought of as something merely mental, cooped up within the head, or finding expression only through the vocal organs.

While the need of application of ideas gained in study is acknowledged by all the more successful methods of instruction, the exercises in application are sometimes treated as devices for *fixing* what has already been learned and for getting greater practical skill in its manipulation. These results are genuine and not to be despised. But practice in applying what has been gained in study ought primarily to have an intellectual quality. As we have already seen, thoughts just as thoughts are incomplete. At best they are tentative; they are suggestions, indications. They are standpoints and methods for dealing with situations of experience. Till they are applied in these situations they lack full point and reality. Only application tests them, and only testing confers full meaning and a sense of their reality. Short of use made of them, they tend to segregate into a peculiar world of their own. It may be seriously questioned whether the philosophies . . . which isolate mind and set it over against the world did not have their origin in the fact that the reflective or theoretical class of men elaborated a large stock of ideas which social conditions did not allow them to act upon and test. Consequently men were thrown back into their own thoughts as ends in themselves.

However this may be, there can be no doubt that a peculiar artificiality attaches to much of what is learned in schools. It can hardly be said that many students consciously think of the subject matter as unreal; but it assuredly does not possess for them the kind of reality which the subject matter of their vital experiences possesses. They learn not to expect that sort of reality of it; they become habituated to treating it as having reality for the purposes of recitations, lessons, and examinations. That it should remain inert for the experiences of daily life is more or less a matter of course. The bad effects are twofold. Ordinary experience does not receive the enrichment which it should; it is not fertilized by school learning. And the attitudes which spring from getting used to and accepting half-understood and ill-digested material weaken vigor and efficiency of thought.

If we have dwelt especially on the negative side, it is for the sake of suggesting positive measures adapted to the effectual development of thought. Where schools are equipped with laboratories, shops, and gardens, where dramatizations, plays, and games are freely used, opportunities exist for reproducing situations of life, and for acquiring and applying information and ideas in the carrying forward of progressive experiences. Ideas are not segregated, they do not form an isolated island. They animate and enrich the ordinary course of life. Information is vitalized by its function; by the place it occupies in direction of action.

The phrase "opportunities exist" is used purposely. They may not be taken advantage of; it is possible to employ manual and constructive activities in a physical way, as means of getting just bodily skill; or they may be used almost exclusively for "utilitarian," i.e., pecuniary, ends. But the disposition on the part of upholders of "cultural" education to assume that such activities are merely physical or professional in quality is itself a product of the philosophies which isolate mind from direction of the course of experience and hence from action upon and with things. When the "mental" is regarded as a self-contained separate realm, a counterpart fate befalls bodily activity and movements. They are regarded as at the best mere external annexes to mind. They may be necessary for the satisfaction of bodily needs and the attainment of external decency and comfort, but they do not occupy a necessary place in mind nor enact an indispensable role in the completion of thought. Hence they have no place in a liberal education—i.e., one which is concerned with the interests of intelligence. If they come in at all, it is as a concession to the material needs of the masses. That they should be allowed to invade the education of the elite is unspeakable. This conclusion follows irresistibly from the isolated conception of mind, but by the same logic it disappears when we perceive what mind really is—namely, the purposive and directive factor in the development of experience.

While it is desirable that all educational institutions should be equipped so as to give students an opportunity for acquiring and testing ideas and information in active pursuits typifying important social situations, it will, doubtless, be a long time before all of them are thus furnished. But this state of affairs does not afford instructors an excuse for folding their hands and persisting in methods which segregate school knowledge. Every recitation in every subject gives an opportunity for establishing cross connections between the subject matter of the lesson and the wider and more direct experiences of everyday life. Classroom instruction falls into three kinds. The least desirable treats each lesson as an independent whole. It does not put upon the student the responsibility of finding points of contact between it and other lessons in the same subject, or other subjects of study. Wiser teachers see to it that the student is systematically led to utilize his earlier lessons to help understand the present one, and also to use the present to throw additional light upon what has already been acquired. Results are better, but school subject matter is still isolated. Save by accident, out-of-school experience is left in its crude and comparatively irreflective state. It is not subject to the refining and expanding influences of the more accurate and comprehensive material of direct instruction. The latter is not motivated and impregnated with a sense of reality by being intermingled with the realities of everyday life. The best type of teaching bears in mind the desirability of affecting this interconnection. It puts the student in the habitual attitude of finding points of contact and mutual bearings.

Summary

Processes of instruction are unified in the degree in which they center in the production of good habits of thinking. While we may speak, without error, of the method of thought, the important thing is that thinking is the method of an educative experience. The essentials of method are therefore identical with the essentials of reflection. They are first that the pupil have a genuine situation of experience—that there be a continuous activity in which he is interested for its own sake; secondly, that a genuine problem develop within this situation as a stimulus to thought; third, that he possess the information and make the observations needed to deal with it; fourth, that suggested solutions occur to him which he shall be responsible for developing in an orderly way; fifth, that he have opportunity and occasion to test his ideas by application, to make their meaning clear and to discover for himself their validity.

12. THE PROCESS OF EDUCATION

JEROME S. BRUNER

* * *

To recapitulate, the main theme of this chapter has been that the curriculum of a subject should be determined by the most fundamental understanding that can be achieved of the underlying principles that give structure to that subject. Teaching specific topics or skills without making clear their context in the broader fundamental structure of a field of knowledge is uneconomical in several deep senses. In the first place, such teaching makes it exceedingly difficult for the student to generalize from what he has learned to what he will encounter later. In the second place, learning that has fallen short of a grasp of general principles has little reward in terms of intellectual excitement. The best way to create interest in a subject is to render it worth knowing, which means to make the knowledge gained usable in one's thinking beyond the situation in which the learning has occurred. Third, knowledge one has acquired without sufficient structure to tie it together is knowledge that is likely to be forgotten. An unconnected set of facts has a pitiably short half-life in memory. Organizing facts in terms of principles and ideas from which they may be inferred is the only known way of reducing the quick rate of loss of human memory.

Designing curricula in a way that reflects the basic structure of a field of knowledge requires the most fundamental understanding of that field. It is a task that cannot be carried out without the active participation of the ablest scholars and scientists. The experience of the past several years has shown that such scholars and scientists, working in conjunction with experienced teachers and students of child development, can prepare curricula of the sort we have been considering. Much more effort in the actual preparation of curri-

Jerome S. Bruner, THE PROCESS OF EDUCATION *(Cambridge, Mass.: Harvard University Press, 1961), pp. 31–32. Reprinted by permission.*

culum materials, in teacher training, and in supporting research will be necessary if improvements in our educational practices are to be of an order that will meet the challenges of the scientific and social revolution through which we are now living.

There are many problems of how to teach general principles in a way that will be both effective and interesting, and several of the key issues have been passed in review. What is abundantly clear is that much work remains to be done by way of examining currently effective practices, fashioning curricula that may be tried out on an experimental basis, and carrying out the kinds of research that can give support and guidance to the general effort at improving teaching.

* * *

13. CURRICULUM DECISIONS AND PROVISION FOR INDIVIDUAL DIFFERENCES

VIRGIL E. HERRICK

A teacher makes a number of educational decisions when dealing with the problem of individual differences in his classroom. These decisions are in different classes.

One class of decisions has to do with the selection of objectives, the topic being studied, the organizing center being used, the instructional plan considered appropriate, and the nature of the evaluation desired.

A second class of decisions has to do with how individual children are recognized and respected, how teacher and pupil roles are determined, and how the interpersonal dynamics of the classroom are directed to more adequate personal, social, and educational ends.

A third class of decisions has to do with the way children and teachers are grouped, the way time and space are used, and the way instructional materials and resources are obtained and related.

Every teacher has to deal with all

Virgil E. Herrick, "Curriculum Decisions and Provision for Individual Differences," THE ELEMENTARY SCHOOL JOURNAL, *LXII, No. 6 (1962), 313–20.*

three of these classes of decisions in the teaching that he does. Most, if not all, of the provisions for dealing with individual differences in the classroom fall in these categories.

It is the thesis of this article that all these classes of decision-making are important and related. No one class can be omitted from adequate educational planning for individual differences. Further, decisions in Class 1, which deal with goals and instructional strategies to accomplish them, and decisions in Class 2, which deal with individuals and with human dignity and respect, have first priority and should precede and control rather than follow decisions in Class 3, where administrative arrangements for children, teachers, time space, and materials are dominant considerations.

Too often we start with an administrative commitment to a teaching machine, to a teaching team and a group of ninety children (or for that matter, to a group of twenty-five children); and then we consider what directives these decisions have for instruction rather than vice versa.

This thesis can be documented by examining briefly two decisions in Class 1 that confront every teacher every day that he teaches. These two decisions have to do with determining the nature and the level of the teacher's instructional objectives and the nature and the characteristics of the organizing centers he selects for teaching and learning.

Several other decisions in curriculum could have been used for this discussion. The nature and the priorities of the screens for selecting learning activities and the nature and roles of the teacher and the learner in the evaluation process in instruction would have served equally well. The conclusions growing out of the two areas selected will illustrate the point being made.

One of our most ancient and most persistent notions about the teaching-learning act is that it ought to be purposeful—goal-centered—and directed by significant educational objectives. Few disagree with this general proposition.

If this conception of the teaching-learning act is sound, a careful study of these objectives, their nature, and their use in making educational decisions should furnish many suggestions for providing for individual differences.

Nerbovig's (2) study of how teachers use objectives, Lund's (1) preliminary analysis of teacher-learning episodes, and our own studies of classroom behavior suggest several conclusions about how many teachers see and use objectives in their instructional practices.

1. Many teachers do not understand the difference between topics, areas, and objects as definitions of scope or of organizing centers for learning activities and important understandings and intellectual processes as definitions of instructional objectives. (*Addition* is a topic. *Chicago* is an area. The *earthworm* is an object.)

Teachers state their objective as "to teach Chicago" rather than seeing understandings like "Man works with other men to meet their common needs" as the objective and Chicago as a representative city that can be used to achieve some appreciation of this generalization.

Thus the phrases "to educate children," "to teach Chicago," or "to develop an understanding of the simple sentence" are not objectives. The first is a generality that states the total task of the school. The second is a possible organizing center to be used to develop certain understandings or objectives. The third avoids the issue: the objective is the understanding or idea of the simple sentence itself.

A teacher's statement of instructional objectives is more useful in making curriculum decisions if this statement does not include principles of learning, important organizing centers, a list of instructional materials, propositions about the good life, and the kitchen sink.

If a teacher can distinguish between important understandings and intellectual processes as objectives and the other necessary components of curriculum, he is freer to think imaginatively about many different topics, areas, objects, and centers of interest that can be used to include the individual differences of children and yet deal with the important understandings and thought processes of the educational program.

In providing for individual differences in the classroom, teachers must realize that in any comprehensive teaching act, several important curriculum decisions have to be made. Determining instructional objectives is only one of these decisions. Equally important is the realization that objectives can perform certain curriculum functions and that they cannot perform others. Failure to make these distinctions creates obstacles to providing adequately for the individual differences of children.

2. Many teachers fail to distinguish between objectives seen as facts and specific skills, and objectives seen as major concepts of the subject area and as key intellectual and social processes.

How a teacher sees and defines his instructional objectives plays an important part in determining how he will provide for the individual differences of children.

Stenographic records of classroom episodes were used to examine how teachers perform their many instructional tasks. The records used were taken from schools in "Prairie City," a typical midwestern community studied by the Committee on Human Development of the University of Chicago, and from schools in communities in Texas, Michigan, Illinois, and Wisconsin. Our analysis of these records shows three important findings.

First, many teachers see their content objectives at the level of the specific fact and thus deal with such objectives as "Robins have red breasts," "5 fours are 20," "the letter *h* is formed with a straight line and a half loop," and "Chicago is on Lake Michigan."

When a teachers sees his instructional objectives in this way, adaptations for individual differences are forced in certain directions. The teacher may vary the speed with which children move through these particulars. The teacher may make adaptations in instructional materials, workbooks, drill exercises, flash cards —so that the child can work on those things which he does not know. The teacher may devise grouping procedures that will bring together children who are at about the same place in this hierarchy of things to know and to verbalize.

Some teachers see their objectives, however, at the level of such concepts as "a number may express either the idea of how many or the idea of relationship" or "the area of any rectangular surface is dependent upon the length of its base and height" or "man influences and is influenced by his environment."

When a teacher sees his instructional objectives on this more general level, his classroom provisions for individual differences tend to use a wider variety of related activities and experiences to help children deal with these understandings on many levels of conceptualization and in respect to many different sets of particulars. The teacher tends to see no single learning experience as having a one-to-one relationship to the mastery of these concepts. The way is opened for many possible adaptations in the learning experiences of children. If the teacher does not see how he can achieve his objectives through many possible instructional means, the only alternatives open to him for variation in his teaching are children, time, and materials.

With this latter perception of objectives, teachers are more likely to see these broader objectives as having meaning for both the kindergarten child and the high-school senior. No time is spent in curriculum committees trying to define the level of understanding to be reached by first-, fourth-, or sixth-grade children. This important fact is always being defined by the children themselves. Thus, the child himself becomes an important agent in determining many of the necessary provisions for his own learning. Actually he is the only one who has much of the necessary information.

Second, many teachers who see their instructional objectives at the level of the fact tend to organize their instruction around these specifics directly and use instructional procedures that stress recognition, verbalism, and memory.

Thus, this kind of teacher sees no problem in teaching "3 fours are 12" as "3 fours are 12" or "air has weight" as the verbalism "air has weight." His objective, therefore, becomes the unit of instruction to be taught directly.

Our analysis indicates that when a teacher sees his instructional objectives as learning specifics, this perception limits the possible ways in which he can provide for pupils' individual differences.

Third, many teachers who see their instructional objectives at the level of the fact tend to ignore the importance of the whole array of skills—language skills, thinking skills, social skills, and skills in the use of instructional materials that are regarded as important instructional objectives in every curriculum program.

Again, our data seem to indicate that when a teacher sees process objectives as a necessary part of any classroom activity, he tends to organize his classroom instruction around organizing centers that properly include these skills. His organizing centers thus tend to be more comprehensive and provide more opportunity for various levels of skill use, for many different vehicles for skill development, and for many more appropriate areas of skill application—all important conditions that would make possible desirable instructional provisions for individual differences.

In our examination of learning episodes, the importance of the role of the organizing center in the instructional process soon became apparent. The more we thought about objectives and their nature and directives for instruction, the more we realized that if instructional objectives are important understandings and learning processes, then you did not teach them directly, but you had to select some vehicle or vehicles to provide the means for their accomplishment.

These vehicles—the questions the teacher asked, the example or problem posed, the objects to be examined, and the zoo to be visited and observed—all formed organizing centers to which the children and teacher related their activities and to which they applied their thinking, generalizing, and personal action.

An organizing center for instructional purposes is any object, idea, person, question, or instructional material used to relate and focus the thinking and the action of an individual or a group. Organizing centers can be defined better by their organizing functions than by their nature.

A picture is not an organizing center for instruction because it is a picture. Rather, it is an organizing center because the eyes and thoughts of a class of children focus on it and their learning behavior is related to it in some kind of active fashion.

If a picture is not the object of attention and educational action by some individual or group, it is not an organizing center. An object becomes an organizing center only when it becomes the focus for such action by these individuals. The nature of a center does not of itself make it a center; its nature merely permits and enhances such focusing and organizing behavior.

Nerbovig in her study found that teachers talked about teaching addition, the farm, electricity, and the seven basic foods as their objectives rather than identifying the understanding and the processes commonly assumed to be objectives (2 p. 122).

To us this finding indicated that many teachers start their educational planning with their organizing centers rather than with their objectives. Actually, this is a much more realistic and useful curriculum decision in their eyes than the decision that "a simple sentence is a single complete unit of thought."

These analyses forced the author to hypothesize that perhaps the most critical single decision a teacher makes about his teaching is the one dealing with the identification and the selection of a desirable set of organizing centers for giving meaning and scope to the learning activities of a group of children.

If an organizing center is to make it possible to meet the individual needs of the children who participate in its development, it should have the following characteristics:

1. *More than one dimension of accessibility.*

If an organizing center can be attacked in more than one way by the learner, its power to provide for individual differences is increased.

If a teacher poses a question as a center for thought and action and presents the question orally, he limits its accessibility. If he asks the question orally and also writes it on the chalkboard, he increases the accessibility of the question for learning. None of the child's energy has to go into remembering the question so that if the question has any significance for him, he is freer to concentrate his full attention on studying and resolving it.

Even though the teacher speaks and writes the question on the board, if the necessary information to deal with the question is provided only by the teacher, he limits its accessibility to children. If however, the necessary information to deal adequately with the question can be acquired by children through observation, manipulation, reading, and other sources of knowing, the accessibility of the organizing center to children for learning is correspondingly increased.

If the question is such that responses to it are limited to one word, *yes* or *no*, the capacity of the question to deal with individual differences is more limited than if this were not true.

If the map on the board is large enough for all to see and is placed properly, its accessibility to more than one child is increased. If the map is too small or is poorly placed, its accessibility for learning is decreased. Or, if work is to be done on the map, the map is more accessible to children if each child can have a copy than when this is not true.

An organizing center is more accessible to more than one child if it properly involves the participation of two or more individuals. Sending a note to the principal does not require the five children we sometimes send with it. One child can run this errand. We sometimes justify this action by claiming that the other four are getting better acquainted with their school environment. Organizing centers that consist of spelling words, vocabulary words in reading, combinations in arithmetic seldom involve more than one child and thus permit only certain limited adjustments to individual differences.

All that has been said may sound simple-minded, but it has become obvious to me that irrespective of how we manipulate the variables of ability and accomplishment, the number of individuals involved, the pacing of the learning process, and the materials and physical space, unless the organizing center for the learning is accessible to the children, no real provision for individual differences can be made.

2. *More than one level of accomplishment.*

If an organizing center is to have the capacity to provide for individual differences, it must have low catch-hold points and high ceilings. An earthworm can provide a challenge to a kindergarten child and to a college senior; to a child with limited experience and limited capacity to learn, as well as to a child with rich experience and gifted capacities. This principle applies to organizing centers like the common and persistent problems of living in social studies, creative writing in language arts, and learning more about our weather in science.

Many teachers, however, use organizing centers that have narrow limits for knowing and learning, such centers as spelling the word *cat*, locating the capital of Illinois, naming the parts of speech, or working examples in arithmetic. Each of these centers limits the child to one level of accomplishment. Each provides little opportunity for individual differences. The teacher's alternatives are to try these specific centers until he finds one the child can do or to spend enough time on one until the child finally grasps the proper response.

3. *More than one dimension of mobility.*

One of the most important problems in curriculum planning is to know how to insure proper continuity in a child's learning. Every teacher wants one lesson in reading to contribute to the next one. Every teacher wants to help every child transfer his knowledge of his own community to his attempts to understand the lives of people more remote in space and time.

If a teacher can select organizing centers that have the capacity to move in time, in space, in cultures, and in logic, these centers have greater capacity to provide for individual differences than when this is not true.

In social studies, for example, such centers as great people, great documents, cities, states, or countries are commonly used as organizing centers, but they have limited mobility. It is hard to move Madison, Wisconsin, anywhere else. But social functions, common geographic characteristics, or the common and persistent problems of living, all have the capacity to move in time, in space, in cultures, and in logic. They have greater capacity, therefore, for providing room and opportunity for encompassing meaningfully differences in children's background, ability, and development than centers that lack this capacity.

If we checked proposed organizing centers in social studies programs against this criterion, we would go a long way toward providing a more effective instructional base for dealing with individual differences in this field. Unless instruction is organized around centers that provide room for individuals to vary and to zoom in understanding as far as they can go, few effective instructional provisions can be made for individual differences.

4. *More than one degree of organizing capacity.*

Some teachers favor a main organizing center that has several important subcenters that have to be studied if the children are to get a proper understanding of the whole. The *home* is one good example. As children study the home, such subcenters as the responsibilities of children and parents in the home; how such problems as food, clothing, earning money, and recreation are handled; how the different rooms of the house are used; and how the house is placed in a community of houses—all provide a means for individual and/or small group study and exploration. Yet all these enterprises are seen as important and relevant parts of the main area of concern. It was felt that this kind of organizing center provided many more opportunities for providing for individual differences than an organizing center like *pets.* Yet a center like *pets* provides greater organizing scope than naming locations, describing objects, and drawing up lists—centers commonly used by many teachers.

This examination of how decisions in two common areas of curriculum planning can contribute to more adequate provisions for individual differences suggests the following conclusions:

1. The decisions the teacher makes about the important components of curriculum direct and limit the nature of the provisions that can be made for dealing with individual differences.

2. Teachers who see their instructional objectives at the level of factual specifics tend to provide for individual differences through variations in time, in amount to be learned, in numbers of children, and in instructional materials. The things to be learned tend to remain constant at the specific level for all children.

3. Teachers who see their instructional objectives at the level of important generalizations and key intellectual and social processes are more willing to explore a wider variety of means for accomplishing those objectives and are more willing to accept a wider range of levels of understanding and accomplishment.

4. The capacity of a learning center to provide for individual differences depends on the extent to which such centers meet the following criteria: they need to have more than one dimension of accessibility, more than one level of accomplishment, more than one aspect of mobility, and more than a single degree of organizing capacity.

When these conditions are met, the teacher has an organizing base for instructional activities that will include more than one child, provide room for many levels of contribution, permit children to move in many important directions, and help them explore an adequate number of important relationships. To me, the provision of this kind of instructional base lies close to the heart of our problem of providing adequately for the individual differences of children.

References

1. Herrick, Virgil E., and Grace Lund, "The Curricular Analysis of Teaching-Learning Episodes." Madison: University of Wisconsin, 1960, p. 25.

2. Nerbovig, Marcella H., "Teacher's Perception of the Functions of Objectives." Unpublished Ph.D. Dissertation, Department of Education, University of Wisconsin, 1956, p. 228.

14. PERFORMANCE OBJECTIVES

THORWALD ESBENSEN

Performance Objectives

Probably the best way to begin an individualized instruction program is by writing instructional objectives expressed in terms of observable student behavior. This is often a difficult thing for teachers to learn to do. The main reason for this would seem to be that in education the word "objective" has generally meant *purpose*; and when educators speak of purpose, they almost invariably use words such as "understanding," "comprehension," and "appreciation." These words point to noble aims; no question about that. But, *when left wholly in this form*, they do not refer to anything that is *directly observable* and, therefore, do not permit us to evaluate how well we are doing whatever it is we are trying to do.

The trick is to supplement each

Thorwald Esbensen, "Performance Objectives" in WORKING WITH INDIVIDUALIZED INSTRUCTION: THE DULUTH EXPERIENCE *(Palo Alto, California: Fearon Publishers, 1968), pp. 1–14. Reprinted by permission.*

announcement of purpose with a statement of criterion performance. That is to say, each declaration of an instructional aim should be accompanied by a clear description of what the learner must be able to do in order to demonstrate his accomplishment of the objective.

The emphasis here is on the word "do," and the doing must be observable—a warm feeling in the pit of the stomach is not sufficient. For example, which of the following two statements is expressed in terms of observable student performance?

A. The student will have a good understanding of the letters of the alphabet, A through Z.

B. The student will be able to pronounce the names of the letters of the alphabet, A through Z.

Statement B tells what it is that the student will be able to *do*. He will be able to *pronounce* the names of the letters of the alphabet, A through Z. Statement A tells us that the student will have a good *understanding* of the letters of the alphabet. But this is not very clear. We cannot tell what it is that the student is supposed to be able to *do* as a result of this understanding.

Let's try another pair of statements. Which of these statements is expressed in terms of observable student performance?

A. The student will have an adequate comprehension of the mechanics of punctuation.

B. Given a sentence containing an error in punctuation, the student will correct the mistake.

Statement B tells what it is that the student will *do*; he will *correct* the error in punctuation. Statement A, which says that the student will have an adequate *comprehension* of the mechanics of punctuation, is rather cloudy. We cannot tell what it is that the student is supposed to be able to *do* as a result of his comprehension.

Mental Activity

At this point, an objection may be raised. Isn't the person who is *comprehending* something *doing* something? Isn't intellectual performance an acceptable kind of student performance? Certainly. The difficulty is that mental activity, *as such*, is not directly observable. We cannot literally open up a person's head and see the thinking that is going on inside. If it is to be of *use* to us, a statement of performance must *specify* some sort of behavior that *can be observed*.

This does not mean that we are not concerned about intellectual performance. It does mean that since mental activity, as such, is not directly observable, some sort of behavior that *is* observable will have to stand for, or represent, the intellectual performance we have in mind. For example, suppose we are interested in having students "know something about the writing style of Ernest Hemingway." Whatever may be intellectually involved in the attainment of this goal, it should be apparent that our aim, *as stated*, leaves much to be desired. What is the student who knows able to do that the student who does not know is not able to do? This is the important question, for we cannot measure the accomplishment of our instructional purpose until we have specified the relevant behavior. Although there is no single answer to the question we have posed (our objective of "knowing something" is too vague for that), here is a possible statement of desired performance:

> Given ten pairs of short prose passages —each pair having one selection by Ernest Hemingway and one by a different author—the student is able, with at least 90 per cent accuracy, to choose the ten selections written by Hemingway.

Conditions of Performance

A well-written statement of desired performance should not only say what it is that a student who has mastered the objective will be able to *do*, it should also say under what *conditions* the student will be able to do this.

Here is one of our earlier statements concerning the alphabet:

> The student will be able to pronounce the names of the letters of the alphabet, A through Z.

We have said that this statement is expressed in terms of student performance. Does this statement also set forth the conditions under which the performance is to take place? No, it does not. For one thing, we cannot tell from our statement whether the student is to pronounce the names of the letters at sight or from memory. If the letters are to be shown, we do not know whether the student is to work with capital letters, small letters, or both. Nor do we know whether the student is to work with these letters in regular sequence or in random order. Each set of conditions is substantially different from the rest, and will make its own special demands upon the student who attempts to accomplish the objective.

Let's examine two more statements. Which of these statements sets forth the *conditions* under which a certain kind of performance is to take place?

> A. Given the Dolch list of the 95 most common nouns, the student will be able to pronounce correctly all the words on this list.
>
> B. The student will be able to pronounce correctly at least 90 per cent of all words found in most beginning reading books.

Statement A, which tells us that the Dolch list of the 95 most common nouns will be used, sets the conditions for the demonstration of student mastery. We are told that these particular words, and no others, are the ones at issue for this objective. Statement B, offering us only the dubious clue of "words found in most beginning reading books," does not tell us enough. Our conditions need to be defined more precisely than this.

Level of Performance

We come now to the matter of performance *level.* A well-written statement of performance will establish, when appropriate, an acceptable minimum standard of achievement. Look at this statement:

> Given 20 sentences containing both common and proper nouns, the student will be able to identify, with very few mistakes, both kinds of nouns.

Does this statement establish a minimum standard of achievement? No, it does not. To say that the student is to perform "with very few mistakes" does not tell us enough. How many are "very few"? Here is the Hemingway example we looked at earlier:

> Given ten pairs of short prose passages —each pair having one selection by Ernest Hemingway and one by a different author—the student is able, with at least 90 per cent accuracy, to choose the ten selections written by Hemingway.

Does this establish a minimum standard of achievement? Yes, it does. The student is expected to be able, "with at least 90 per cent accuracy, to choose the ten selections written by Hemingway." This constitutes a minimum standard of achievement.

Let's try one more example:

> The student should be able to pronounce from memory, and in sequence, the names of the letters of the alphabet, A through Z.

Does this establish a minimum standard of achievement? Yes, it does. The statement implies that we are looking for 100 per cent mastery. However, we could, if we wanted to be explicit, restate the desired performance in this way:

> The student should be able to pronounce from memory, in sequence, and with 100 per cent accuracy, the names of the letters of the alphabet, A through Z.

In a related manner, some learning tasks justifiably present the student with an all-or-nothing situation. For example, if the learner is supposed to be able to tie his shoe laces, it would not make sense to talk about his being able to do this with 90 per cent accuracy. Here the proposition is absolute: He either can tie his shoelaces or he cannot. There is nothing useful in between.

Instructional Materials for Objectives

An instructional objective should not ordinarily be limited to specific *means* (particular materials or methods), but should be stated in terms that permit the use of various procedures. Look at this statement of performance:

> Given the California Test Bureau's E-F level programmed booklet on capitalization, the student is able to work through the exercises in this booklet with at least 90 per cent accuracy.

Is this statement limited to the use of a particular instructional item or procedures? Yes, it is. The desired performance is expressed exclusively in terms of work with a specific booklet. Although the particular kind of skill development that is promoted by this booklet is presumably also fostered by other instructional materials and methods, no such options are available under the terms of the statement of performance as it is now written.

Look at this statement of desired performance:

> Given 20 sentences containing a variety of mistakes in capitalization, the student is able, with at least 90 per cent accuracy, to identify and rewrite correctly each word that has a mistake in capitalization.

Is this objective limited to the use of a particular instructional item or procedure? No, it is not. The desired performance, as now stated, permits the use of a number of instructional items that show promise in being able to help students attain the objective. These items might include not only the California Test Bureau's E-F level material, but also the somewhat simpler C-D level presentation, a programmed booklet by D. C. Health, Unit 11 of English 2200, Unit 9 of English 2600, Lessons 87 and 88 of English 3200, several filmstrips on capital letters, and so on.

Measuring Accomplishment

A well-written instructional objective will suggest how its accomplishment can be measured. This follows from our view that a well-written objective specifies under what *conditions* and, when appropriate, to what *extent* a certain kind of student *performance* can be expected to take place.

Look at this objective:

The student should know the alphabet.

Does this objective suggest how its accomplishment can be measured? No, it does not. The reason for this is that knowing the alphabet can mean different things to different people. Therefore, depending upon what is meant, the measuring of this knowing will take different forms.

Suppose we elaborate upon our objective so that it reads:

Shown the letters of the alphabet in random order (in both upper- and lower-case forms), the student is able to say the name of each letter with 100 per cent accuracy.

Does the objective now suggest how its accomplishment can be measured? Yes, it does. It tells us that the student will be shown the letters of the alphabet, that he will be shown these letters in both upper- and lower-case forms and in random order, and that he will be called upon to say with 100 per cent accuracy the name of each letter shown. The objective, in other words, makes plain how its accomplishment can be measured. If teachers at all levels of schooling would be this explicit in writing instructional objectives, they might reasonably hope to eliminate almost immediately one cause of learning failure among students: the traditional fuzziness of classroom assignments.

Format for Developing Objectives

Our in-service work in connection with individual instructional projects in the Duluth Public Schools has gradually led to the creation of a six-point format for developing instructional objectives, which follows.

Instructional Objective
1. Content classification.
2. Purpose.
3. Criterion performance.
4. Sample test situation.
5. Taxonomy category.
6. Resources.

We have already touched briefly on the matters of purpose, criterion performance, and sample test situation. Perhaps the best way of reviewing these elements, as well as explaining the remaining points listed above, is to construct an example that will illustrate in detail what we mean.

We shall choose an objective from the magic realm of creativity. There is a reason for doing this. Many people have the feeling that objectives expressed in terms of observable student behavior can be put together for some of the basic skills areas (map reading, spelling, etc.), but that nothing much can be done in this way when it comes to the humanities. If, therefore, our example can help to disprove this notion, we shall have served in double measure the cause of performance objectives.

The objective we have in mind has to do with the writing of haiku, Japanese poetry that contains three rhymeless lines of five, seven, and five syllables, respectively, for a total of seventeen syllables. Far from being an anemic academic exercise, the discipline of haiku somehow releases creative energies that are often imprisoned within the unlimited boundaries of student prose.

Let us turn to the task of setting forth our haiku objective under the headings of (1) content classification, (2) purpose, (3) criterion performance, (4) sample test situation, (5) taxonomy category, and (6) resources.

Content classification simply means the placement of an objective somewhere in a course or subject matter outline. In the present instance, we might treat this heading as follows:

Content Classification

I. Imaginative use of language.
  A. Poetry.
    1. Haiku.

The purpose of our objective:

Purpose

To engage students in a formal poetic exercise that will encourage brevity, relevance, and the use of words in fresh, new ways.

We have discussed criterion performance at length:

Criterion Performance

Given any item of experience (music, literature, films, an observed event, a recollection), the student will be able to make a personal response in the form of a haiku (seventeen syllables, 5-7-5, in three lines) of his own creation.

Next is the sample test situation. As our criterion performance makes plain, we have plenty of latitude here. One interesting possibility is to present the student with a literal English translation of some Japanese haiku and ask him to write his own haiku based upon whatever this translation suggests to him.

Sample Test Situation

Here is the literal English translation of a Japanese haiku: Cagedbird/butterflies envy/eye-expression. Look at the words carefully. Then write a haiku of your own, capturing whatever meaning the literal translation suggests to you.

If you are wondering just what a student might do with this problem, here is what one ninth grade girl came up with:

> The caged yellow bird
> envies the spring butterflies'
> remorseless freedom.

In keeping with our six-part format, we come now to the task of identifying the taxonomy category that most nearly fits our instructional objective. In developing this feature, we have been strongly influenced by Bloom.* The Bloom taxonomy uses six categories: knowledge, comprehension, application, analysis, synthesis, and evaluation. Although we have found Bloom's suggested heirarchy stimulating to explore and most

* Benjamin S. Bloom (ed.), *Taxonomy of Educational Objectives. Handbook I: Cognitive Domain.* New York: David McKay, Inc., 1956. [see selection 16, Eds.]

helpful in making us keenly aware of a broad range of intellectual activities, we have gradually come around to working with a simpler taxonomy of our own construction.

Our classification scheme employs four categories: knowledge, comprehension, application, and invention. As is true of the Bloom taxonomy, our categories for classifying intellectual tasks are not as clear and distinct as one might wish. This is partly because cognitive accomplishments often include activities that are, in turn, appropriate to different categories. Perhaps the best way to resolve this difficulty is to focus upon the main thrust of an instructional objective and to classify it accordingly.

It should also be remembered that an intellectual task is frequently defined by the nature of the test items or situation used to measure its achievement. For example, if items identical to those the student has practiced on are used in the test situation, the subsequent feat of learning is probably one of simple recall or recognition.

Let us consider each of our four categories. The emphasis in our knowledge category is on simple recall and recognition—in other words, on memory. The student remembers specific items, such as names, statements, objects, procedures, etc. For example, the student who learns to arrange the letters of the alphabet in order from A to Z has acquired knowledge. That is to say, the order of the letters is arbitrary and, therefore, must be memorized. Similarly, the student who is able to list a minimum of ten characteristics for each of the nine planets has acquired knowledge. The learning task involved is presumably largely one of memorization.

Perception, rather than memory, is the hallmark of our comprehension category. Here, the student identifies and continues patterns. He does not do this by remembering them, but by observing them. He matches or completes equivalencies and nonequivalencies, and he perceives other relationships in material presented to him. If, for example, when given two objects, the student is able to indicate a length comparison (longer than, shorter than, same length as), he has demonstrated comprehension. Or, given a list of ten latitudes numbered in degrees, if the student is able to categorize them correctly under the headings "Region of High Temperatures," "Region of Middle Temperatures," and "Region of Low Temperatures," he has demonstrated comprehension.

For our application category, the student selects and then uses one or more principles to produce or alter something. For example, if a student decides upon and then uses a certain formula to solve a problem, he has shown that he can apply what he has learned. He works upon material according to definite rules that he perceives as being appropriate. Nevertheless, he does not go beyond these rules and principles. Initially, and as a learning task, application is a deliberate and highly conscious act, although in time it may become merely a routine operation scarcely above the threshold of awareness.

A student qualifies for our invention category when he produces, uses, or alters something in a form or manner that in some way goes beyond any existing structures or principles of which he is aware. For example, after having studied the physical structure of insects, if the student is able to construct a taxonomy of his own that consists of categories into which all of the insects studied can be sorted according to their structures, he has invented something.

Examining our haiku objective in the light of these considerations, it would seem that creative writing falls naturally into the category of invention. So let's put it there.

Taxonomy Category Invention.

Resources are the final part of our format. What is needed here is a listing of various instructional means (tapes, films, records, filmstrips, printed matter, activities) that may be used to help students achieve the criterion performance. Resource items should not simply be assigned en masse; in each instance they should be used selectively, depending on the situation for any given student. In the case of our haiku objective:

Resources
An Introduction to Haiku (an anthology of poems and poets from Basho to Shiki, with translations and commentary by Harold G. Henderson).
Borrowed Water (a book of American haiku by the Los Altos Writers Roundtable).
American Haiku Magazine (a magazine devoted exclusively to the development of English-language haiku).
Good Night, Socrates (film).
The Red Balloon (film).
The Golden Fish (film).
The Smile (film).
Nahanni (film).
Eugene Atget (film).
Etc.

The three items of printed matter listed above provide a certain amount of background information about the nature of haiku, and some examples of this form of poetry. The film listings, which could be expanded almost indefinitely, can be used to trigger the responses of students; and when what they have to say is shaped by the discipline of haiku, the results are often gratifying and sometimes moving.

Let's take the film, *Good Night, Socrates,* as an example. In bland, diluted prose, here is how one student reacted to what she saw:

> This movie was something different from anything I have ever seen. I didn't realize there are people living like that in the United States. It wasn't the condition of the buildings or anything. They weren't the best but at least they were home. It was that they lived in their own world. That boy was growing up in a totally Greek atmosphere. The people were satisfied with it too. In fact they liked it. It was very hard to be thrown out of their home and town for something like better looks. They will never live the same way again. Maybe it would have been better if they stayed that way. At least there wasn't much discrimination.

Later, in haiku, here is what this girl wrote about *Good Night, Socrates*:

> The fragile bubbles
> tremble and break before me.
> I see my world fall.

Same student, same film. The difference is due to the form of expression.

However, the pleasure of promoting haiku as a worthy exercise in the mother tongue is not to our main purpose. The point is this: We have talked at some length about the need for expressing instructional objectives in terms of observable student behavior. It would be difficult to overemphasize the importance of doing this; for, once this has been accomplished, other problems can be solved more easily. We have already indicated how this is so when it comes to the construction of test items or the selection of appropriate instructional materials and procedures. Beyond this, the usefulness of performance objectives carries over into the matter of classroom management, which, in its largest sense, is the operational problem of individualized instruction.

15. SYSTEMATIC PLANNING AND CLASSIFYING OBJECTIVES

JOHN R. PANCELLA

In order for lesson and unit objectives to be meaningful to the teacher the objectives should support and be supported by the method and technique of the teaching act. This is not always obvious from looking at lesson plans. Objectives may contain comments such as "teaching for understanding of world problems," "providing experiences for better citizenship," or "to help the students understand the physical world." Comments such as these may be difficult to rationalize in terms of the content being taught if only facts and knowledge are emphasized. Usually the finale is a test which measures achievement of the facts, and does not reveal whether or not the goals and objectives were attained. How can teachers identify objectives and relate them to content? How can the objectives be planned so that they can be taught successfully? How can teachers determine their success or failure in reaching their goals? The latter might be indicated by testing what was taught. Such a notion will be explored in Chapter Four. There are techniques, however, which might help the teacher prepare for the total sequence of planning-teaching-testing.

One means of systematically plan-

CRITICAL ABILITY / CONTENT AREA	Identify Central Issues	Recognize Underlying Assumptions	Evaluate Evidence or Authority	Recognize Limitation of Data	Establish Relationships	Draw Warranted Conclusions
CULTURE CONCEPT (10 per cent)						
ECONOMIC AFFAIRS (40 per cent) Systems Business Organizations Labor Problems Agriculture Consumer						
POLITICAL AFFAIRS (40 per cent) Systems Government and Business Civil Liberties International Relations						
SOCIAL AFFAIRS (10 per cent) Family Education						

Figure 1.

Grid Form for the Construction of the Test of Critical Thinking in Social Science. The aim of the Social Science Committee was that the number of items for each ability would be approximately equal. P. L. Dressel and L. B. Mayhew, *General Education: Explorations in Evaluation* (Washington, D. C.: American Council on Education, 1954), p. 48, Fig. 1.

ning a unit of work is to use a grid form for the outlay of content versus abilities. Such a matrix is illustrated above.

By indicating the number of lessons or activities in the appropriate boxes a teacher can see at a glance whether or not all the abilities desired as objectives are being implemented. The matrix also will visually portray the degree to which emphasis is being placed on certain areas. The decisions to teach for the selected abilities and the items to be stressed are made by the teacher.

If it becomes important later that the test questions closely parallel the pattern on the grid form, a plot of test items can be compared with the unit plan. For example, suppose most of the information is presented for students to memorize and evaluate, i.e., columns headed "Identify Central Issues" and "Evaluate Evidence of Authority." Would it be useful to construct an examination which contains mostly questions on the other columns? Would it be useful to have most of the questions on the content area of "Culture Concept"? It would seem unlikely that such a plan would reflect to the teacher how effective the teaching was for reaching goals and objectives such as "To have the students learn critical abilities for analyzing situations."

Thus, two reasons for classifying objectives might emerge:

1. For monitoring the teaching of

skills, abilities, and thinking tasks which students are to gain with the content.

2. To use the planning at a later time for testing and determining whether or not successful teaching for goals has occurred.

A major difficulty in identifying the objectives is communicating the differences between types of thinking tasks. One system of classifying objectives according to a cognitive hierarchy is the "Taxonomy of Educational Objectives" (see condensed version in this chapter). The Taxonomy was developed on the presupposition that there is a structure to the cognitive process which is analyzable. Thus each thinking level builds on the previous ones. Six levels are defined: Knowledge (1.00), Comprehension (2.00), Application (3.00), Analysis (4.00), Synthesis (5.00), and Evaluation (6.00). This system is unlike the Dewey decimal classification for categorizing library materials, which is based on arbitrary divisions. The Taxonomy is a ladder of thought. Analysis (4.00) includes the first three levels; knowledge (1.00) is the base for all the levels.

These levels could be substituted for the column headings for critical abilities in the grid form. The plan could then be developed emphasizing selected content for those levels chosen by the teacher as goals. It may be that only the first three levels are applicable to a subject topic. The decision to use various levels should be left to the teacher. This necessarily depends upon whatever rationale the teacher selects.

The following are examples of objectives from a literature unit, classified by the six major levels of the Taxonomy.

1.00 To name and identify the contemporary poets and their writing styles.

2.00 To interpret the writings of contemporary poets.

3.00 To use the rules of writing verse to describe selected poems.

4.00 To study poems and determine how they were constructed from their component parts.

5.00 To write creatively in a style unique to each student.

6.00 To evaluate writings for internal consistency of writing style and word usage.

There are other systems of classifying objectives such as the "Levels of Performance" by Bradfield and Moredock (see "Levels of Performance in Teaching," by Fred W. Fox, in this chapter). A system could be simplified to (1) Knowledge and Understanding, (2) Application, and (3) Inquiry or Invention. How would these systems be used to classify the objectives given above?

As will be discussed in Chapter Four, test items can be similarly classified according to the levels in order to plan tests for monitoring what was taught. The grid form and systems of classifying objectives, although flexible enough to be adapted by the individual teacher for each analyzable situation, do not constitute the only methods for planning. Instead, they are techniques for helping the teacher answer his own question, "What are some ways I can evaluate my planning.

16. TAXONOMY OF EDUCATIONAL OBJECTIVES

BENJAMIN S. BLOOM, EDITOR

Cognitive Domain

Knowledge

1.00 Knowledge. Knowledge, as defined here, involves the recall of specifics and universals, the recall of methods and processes, or the recall of a pattern, structure, or setting. For measurement purposes, the recall situation involves little more than bringing to mind the appropriate material. Although some alteration of the material may be required, this is a relatively minor part of the task. The knowledge objectives emphasize most the psychological processes of remembering. The process of relating is also involved in that a knowledge test situation requires the organization and reorganization of a problem such that it will furnish the appropriate signals and cues for the information and knowledge the individual possesses. To use an analogy, if one thinks of the mind as a file, the problem in a knowledge test situation is that of finding in the problem or task the appropriate signals, cues, and clues which will most effectively bring out whatever knowledge is filed or stored.

1.10 Knowledge of Specifics. The recall of specific and isolable bits of information. The emphasis is on symbols with concrete referents. This material, which is at a very low level of abstraction, may be thought of as the elements from which more complex and abstract forms of knowledge are built.

1.11 Knowledge of Terminology. Knowledge of the referents for specific symbols (verbal and nonverbal). This may include knowledge of the most generally accepted symbol referent, knowledge of the variety of symbols which may be used for a

Benjamin S. Bloom, ed., "Condensed Version of the Taxonomy of Educational Objectives," in Taxonomy of Educational Objectives: *Handbook I, Cognitive Domain (New York: David McKay Co., Inc., 1956), pp. 201–7. Reprinted by permission.*

single referent, or knowledge of the referent most appropriate to a given use of a symbol.

*To define technical terms by giving their attributes, properties, or relations.

*Familiarity with a large number of words in their common range of meanings.

1.12 KNOWLEDGE OF SPECIFIC FACTS. Knowledge of dates, events, persons, places, etc. This may include very precise and specific information such as the specific date or exact magnitude of a phenomenon. It may also include approximate or relative information such as an approximate time period or the general order of magnitude of a phenomenon.

*The recall of major facts about particular cultures.

*The possession of a minimum knowledge about the organisms studied in the laboratory.

1.20 KNOWLEDGE OF WAYS AND MEANS OF DEALING WITH SPECIFICS. Knowledge of the ways of organizing, studying, judging, and criticizing. This includes the methods of inquiry, the chronological sequences, and the standards of judgment within a field as well as the patterns of organization through which the areas of the fields themselves are determined and internally organized. This knowledge is at an intermediate level of abstraction between specific knowledge on the one hand and knowledge of universals on the other. It does not so much demand the activity of the student in using the materials as it does a more passive awareness of their nature.

1.21 KNOWLEDGE OF CONVENTIONS. Knowledge of characteristic ways of treating and presenting ideas and phenomena. For purposes of communication and consistency, workers in a field employ usages, styles, practices, and forms which best suit their purposes and/or which appear to suit best the phenomena with which they deal. It should be recognized that although these forms and conventions are likely to be set up on arbitrary, accidental, or authoritative bases, they are retained because of the general agreement or concurrence of individuals concerned with the subject, phenomena, or problem.

*Familiarity with the forms and conventions of the major types of works, e.g., verse, plays, scientific papers, etc.

*To make pupils conscious of correct form and usage in speech and writing.

1.22 KNOWLEDGE OF TRENDS AND SEQUENCES. Knowledge of the processes, directions, and movements of phenomena with respect to time.

*Understanding of the continuity and development of American culture as exemplified in American life.

*Knowledge of the basic trends underlying the development of public assistance programs.

1.23 KNOWLEDGE OF CLASSIFICATIONS AND CATEGORIES. Knowledge of the classes, sets, divisions, and arrangements which are regarded as fundamental for a given subject field, purpose, argument, or problem.

*To recognize the area encompassed by various kinds of problems or materials.

*Becoming familiar with a range of types of literature.

1.24 KNOWLEDGE OF CRITERIA. Knowledge of the criteria by which facts, principles, opinions, and conduct are tested or judged.

*Familiarity with criteria for judgment appropriate to the type of work and the purpose for which it is read.

*Knowledge of criteria for the evaluation of recreational activities.

* Illustrative educational objectives selected from the literature.

1.25 KNOWLEDGE OF METHODOLOGY. Knowledge of the methods of inquiry, techniques, and procedures employed in a particular subject field as well as those employed in investigating particular problems and phenomena. The emphasis here is on the individual's knowledge of the method rather than his ability to use the method.

*Knowledge of scientific methods for evaluating health concepts.

*The student shall know the methods of attack relevant to the kinds of problems of concern to the social sciences.

1.30 KNOWLEDGE OF THE UNIVERSALS AND ABSTRACTIONS IN A FIELD. Knowledge of the major schemes and patterns by which phenomena and ideas are organized. These are the large structures, theories, and generalizations which dominate a subject field or which are quite generally used in studying phenomena or solving problems. These are at the highest levels of abstraction and complexity.

1.31 KNOWLEDGE OF PRINCIPLES AND GENERALIZATIONS. Knowledge of particular abstractions which summarize observations of phenomena. These are the abstractions which are of value in explaining, describing, predicting, or in determining the most appropriate and relevant action or direction to be taken.

*Knowledge of the important principles by which our experience with biological phenomena is summarized.

*The recall of major generalizations about particular cultures.

1.32 KNOWLEDGE OF THEORIES AND STRUCTURES. Knowledge of the body of principles and generalizations together with their interrelations which present a clear, rounded, and systematic view of a complex phenomenon, problem, or field. These are the most abstract formulations, and they can be used to show the interrelation and organization of a great range of specifics.

*The recall of major theories about particular cultures.

*Knowledge of a relatively complete formulation of the theory of evolution.

Intellectual Abilities and Skills

Abilities and skills refer to organized modes of operation and generalized techniques for dealing with materials and problems. The materials and problems may be of such a nature that little or no specialized and technical information is required. Such information as is required can be assumed to be part of the individual's general fund of knowledge. Other problems may require specialized and technical information at a rather high level such that specific knowledge and skill in dealing with the problem and the materials are required. The abilities and skills objectives emphasize the mental processes of organizing and reorganizing material to achieve a particular purpose. The materials may be given or remembered.

2.00 COMPREHENSION. This represents the lowest level of understanding. It refers to a type of understanding or apprehension such that the individual knows what is being communicated and can make use of the material or idea being communicated without necessarily relating it to other material or seeing its fullest implications.

2.10 TRANSLATION. Comprehension as evidenced by the care and accuracy with which the communication is paraphrased or rendered from one language or form of communication to another. Translation is judged on the basis of faithfulness and accuracy, that is, on the extent to which the material in the original communication is preserved although the form of the communication has been altered.

*The ability to understand nonliteral statements (metaphor, symbolism, irony, exaggeration).

*Skill in translating mathematical verbal material into symbolic statements and vice versa.

2.20 INTERPRETATION. The explanation or summarization of a communication. Whereas translation involves an objective part-for-part rendering of a communication, interpretation involves a reordering, rearrangement, or a new view of the material.

*The ability to grasp the thought of the work as a whole at any desired level of generality.

*The ability to interpret various types of social data.

2.30 EXTRAPOLATION. The extension of trends or tendencies beyond the given data to determine implications, consequences, corollaries, effects, etc., which are in accordance with the conditions described in the original communication.

*The ability to deal with the conclusions of a work in terms of the immediate inference made from the explicit statements.

*Skill in predicting continuation of trends.

3.00 APPLICATION. The use of abstractions in particular and concrete situations. The abstractions may be in the form of general ideas, rules of procedures, or generalized methods. The abstractions may also be technical principles, ideas, and theories which must be remembered and applied.

*Application to the phenomena discussed in one paper of the scientific terms or concepts used in other papers.

*The ability to predict the probable effect of a change in a factor on a biological situation previously at equilibrium.

4.00 ANALYSIS. The breakdown of a communication into its constituent elements or parts such that the relative hierarchy of ideas is made clear and/or the relations between the ideas expressed are made explicit. Such analyses are intended to clarify the communication, to indicate how the communication is organized, and the way in which it manages to convey its effects, as well as its basis and arrangement.

4.10 ANALYSIS OF ELEMENTS. Identification of the elements included in a communication.

*The ability to recognize unstated assumptions.

*Skill in distinguishing facts from hypotheses.

4.20 ANALYSES OF RELATIONSHIPS. The connections and interactions between elements and parts of a communication.

*Ability to check the consistency of hypotheses with given information and assumptions.

*Skill comprehending the interrelationships among the ideas in a passage.

4.30 ANALYSIS OF ORGANIZATIONAL PRINCIPLES. The organization, systematic arrangement, and structure which hold the communication together. This includes the "explicit" as well as "implicit" structure. It includes the bases, necessary arrangement, and the mechanics which make the communication a unit.

*The ability to recognize form and pattern in literary or artistic works as a means of understanding their meaning.

*Ability to recognize the general techniques used in persuasive materials, such as advertising, propaganda, etc.

5.00 Synthesis. The putting together of elements and parts so as to form a whole. This involves the process of working with pieces, parts, elements, etc., and arranging and combining them in such a way as to constitute a pattern or structure not clearly there before.

5.10 Production of a Unique Communication. The development of a communication in which the writer or speaker attempts to convey ideas, feelings, and/or experiences to others.

*Skill in writing, using an excellent organization of ideas and statements.

*Ability to tell a personal experience effectively.

5.20 Production of a Plan, or Proposed Set of Operations. The development of a plan of work or the proposal of a plan of operations. The plan should satisfy requirements of the task which may be given to the student or which he may develop for himself.

*Ability to propose ways of testing hypotheses.

*Ability to plan a unit of instruction for a particular teaching situation.

5.30 Derivation of a Set of Abstract Relations. The development of a set of abstract relations either to classify or explain particular data or phenomena, or the deduction of propositions and relations from a set of basic propositions or symbolic representations.

*Ability to formulate appropriate hypotheses based upon an analysis of factors involved, and to modify such hypotheses in the light of new factors and considerations.

*Ability to make mathematical discoveries and generalizations.

6.00 Evaluation. Judgments about the value of material and methods for given purposes. Quantitative and qualitative judgments about the extent to which material and methods satisfy criteria. Use of a standard of appraisal. The criteria may be those determined by the student or those which are given to him.

6.10 Judgments in Terms of Internal Evidence. Evaluation of the accuracy of a communication from such evidence as logical accuracy, consistency, and other internal criteria.

*Judging by internal standards, the ability to assess general probability of accuracy in reporting facts from the care given to exactness of statement, documentation, proof, etc.

*The ability to indicate logical fallacies in arguments.

6.20 Judgments in Terms of External Criteria. Evaluation of material with reference to selected or remembered criteria.

*The comparison of major theories, generalizations, and facts about particular cultures.

*Judging by external standards, the ability to compare a work with the highest known standards in its field—especially with other works of recognized excellence.

17. LEVELS OF PERFORMANCE IN TEACHING

FRED W. FOX

New developments in science programs are being received generally with enthusiasm. Teachers feel that good science is being taught, and in addition there is the satisfaction to students and teachers alike that the courses are intellectually stimulating. One is taught to think as well as to learn about the world of nature. Even apart from "the new programs" any teacher gains satisfaction from moving his teaching from the end of the spectrum which demands rote learning, imitation, or repetition of facts presented, to the other end which promotes critical thought and analysis, discovery, or creativity.

At which end of the spectrum do we as teachers perform or expect our students to perform? Are we satisfied to teach as we were taught, or do we use our teaching abilities uniquely and imaginatively according to our personal and community resources and the special needs of our students? Do students sit at their desks day in and day out simply giving back to us what is in their texts, or are they investigating with materials and equipment, testing, gathering data, making judgments, predicting, and discovering? What is the level of performance in our classes?

One of the most imaginative and striking analyses by which we may quickly judge our teaching has been devised by James M. Bradfield and H. Stewart Moredock.[1] It is titled "Levels of Performance" for this discussion. Look at Table 1, p. 130, and ask yourself: At which level do I expect my students to perform?

It has been the writer's experience that both practicing teachers and teachers in training have been caught up by Bradfield and Moredock's imaginative ordering of potential classroom experiences. Science teachers

Fred W. Fox, "Levels of Performance in Teaching," THE SCIENCE TEACHER, *XXXII, No. 4 (April 1965), 31–32. Reprinted by permission.*

[1] James M. Bradfield and H. Stewart Moredock, *Measurement and Evaluation in Education* (New York: The Macmillan Company, 1957), p. 204.

who have studied the analysis have suggested a variety of implications for their teaching. Some of these follow:

"Levels of Performance" Uses for the Analysis

1. Evaluation

The original authors entitled the outline as "Performances Indicating Different Levels of Understanding of a Given Subject." Thus the "levels" were to be considered as standards or criteria against which to judge the work of our students. It is probably safe to say that our tests and examinations usually measure our students' abilities at Levels I and II. Bradfield and Moredock, of course, suggest that we evaluate student performance on more data than are accumulated through tests, quizzes, and examinations.[2] Our students work in the laboratory, enter discussions, prepare reports, read, and engage in a variety of activities beyond mere recitation (usually a Level I performance) and test-taking. In using the "Levels of Performance" analysis in evaluation, key questions become: What sources of evidence of student performance are there for rendering teacher judgments, and how do I make a record of such evidence of student behavior?

2. Goals for Science Teaching

It is quite apparent that we cannot evaluate student effort at the upper levels of performance if we never arrange for our students to operate there. Converting these levels of performance to teaching goals is a distortion of the original authors' intent. Science teaching objectives should be in a context of the field of science knowledge, the means of deriving it, its social implications, and its application to the solution of our daily problems. But many of us could improve our teaching simply by stating and living up to such a statement as: "I am going to teach science in such a manner that students have to explain, justify, predict, estimate, interpret, and make critical judgments."

3. Method of Teaching

The tremendous implication of raising the level of performance in our classroom is that we must change our method of teaching. Obviously it would be unfair to evaluate student behavior at the upper levels if students had not been permitted to develop skills at those levels. Evaluation apart, the significance of the "levels" is that laboratory work must become more vital, challenging, stimulating. Demonstrations can no longer be routine. Students will have to be given opportunity to solve problems for which there are no simple solutions. They will have to read, discuss, investigate, try out, argue, take trips, look at, listen to, improvise, succeed, fail. Only by changed methods in most of our classes will students have opportunity to compare, discriminate, reformulate, interpret, predict, discover, create—that is, to perform at a "higher level."

4. Finding Satisfaction in Teaching

No teacher likes to be accused of teaching as he was taught, nor does he like to believe that he teaches in

[2] For an additional discussion of sources of evidence for judging student work, see John S. Richardson, *Science Teaching in Secondary Schools* (Englewood Cliffs, N.J.: Prentice-Hall, Inc., 1957), Chap. VII.

TABLE 1

*Levels of Performance**

Level	Performance
I	Imitating, duplicating, repeating. This is the level of initial contact. Student can repeat or duplicate what has just been said, done, or read. Indicates that student is at least conscious or aware of contact with a particular concept or process.
II	Level I, plus recognizing, identifying, remembering, recalling, classifying. To perform on this level, the student must be able to recognize or identify the concept or process when encountered later, or to remember or recall the essential features of the concept or process.
III	Levels I and II, plus comparing, relating, discriminating, reformulating, illustrating. Here the student can compare and relate this concept or process with other concepts or processes and make discriminations. He can formulate in his own words a definition, and he can illustrate or give examples.
IV	Levels I, II, and III, plus explaining, justifying, predicting, estimating, interpreting, making critical judgements, drawing inferences. On the basis of his understanding of a concept or process, he can make explanations, give reasons, make predictions, interpret, estimate, or make critical judgments. This performance represents a high level of understanding.
V	Levels I, II, III, and IV, plus creating, discovering, reorganizing, formulating new hypotheses, new questions and problems. This is the level of original and productive thinking. The student's understanding has developed to such a point that he can make discoveries that are new to him and can restructure and reorganize his knowledge on the basis of his new discoveries and new insights.

* James M. Bradfield and H. Stewart Moredock, *Measurement and Evaluation in Education* (New York: The Macmillan Company, 1957), p. 204. Copyright © 1957 by The Macmillan Company. Reprinted by permission.

a dull and perfunctory manner. The teacher who is gaining personal satisfaction from his teaching, who talks enthusiastically to his colleagues about his work, or who has a reputation among his students as a top teacher in the school, is exactly the same teacher who is himself teaching at a high level of performance. He compares the variety of teaching techniques he knows are available for his use and with discrimination selects those most suitable for his students and his experience and resources. He critically judges the content of the many science courses he may choose for his students. At his best, the teacher resourcefully departs from the traditional and the routine and creates new and imaginative approaches to both content and method in teaching. He critically questions the commonplace teaching doctrines of his time (and even the not-so-commonplace) and searches for unique ways to solve teaching problems. And in this spirit of his own creativity he finds at the same time poise and confidence that his profession is worthy of his energy and devotion and that education under his direction is serving its proper ends.

What is your "level of performance"?

18. WORTHWHILE ACTIVITIES

*JAMES RATHS**

My view is simply this: A large part of every child's school day should include his participation in activities that allow him to make choices; that provide opportunities for sharing; that involve him in the consideration of profound ideas; and that include the application of rules, standards, and disciplines that can be made meaningful to him. Activities that meet these criteria are, in my view, worthwhile regardless of the instructional objectives to which they are directed. To give emphasis to my view, let me place it in the context of current issues of curriculum planning. A given instructional activity can no longer be justified solely on the grounds that it leads to specific well defined instructional objectives, as those who espouse the behavioral objective approach would contend. I do not mean to imply that teachers need not plan, that planning need not be disciplined, nor that school programs need not be evaluated. On the contrary, what is important is that teachers strive to involve children in worthwhile activities throughout most of every school day—a most rigorous and demanding task.

* The author acknowledges the thoughtful criticisms he received from Mrs. Ilene Albert of earlier drafts of this manuscript. He also recognizes the influence of the writings of Professor Richard S. Peters cited in the references. Of course, no one but the author is responsible for the way in which the ideas are expressed here.

Observations

My view is based on several observations I have made of the present situation in the field of curriculum planning and in numerous visits to classrooms over the past few years. First, everyone agrees that curriculum planning involves a serious consideration of values. One of the strong points of those who argue for specificity in stating objectives is that it is difficult, if not impossible, to make distinct value judgments about an objective if the meaning of the objective is not clear. (9, 14). Thus, while all of us would presumably applaud an objective dealing with the development of a student's appreciation for poetry, it is only as that objective is made operational that we can intelligently discuss the values that are relevant to its selection as an objective. Our decisions about this particular objective may change as one teacher translates it into memorization objectives, while another treats it as though it referred to knowledge of the biographies of well-known poets. Clearly value statements may be assigned more definitely to either of these objectives than to an objective stated as broadly as "teaching for appreciation." However, what I see happening is that the value of operationalism is dominating the curriculum scene. Once a teacher has written an objective, it is evaluated as good if it is behavioral and poor if it is not. The value question, so important to curriculum planning has apparently become telescoped into one asking: "Is the objective stated behaviorally or not?" Thus, while writing objectives in behavioral language was intended to increase our sensitivity to the value question in curriculum planning, it has, in fact, dulled our concern for issues of values.

My second observation is that many behaviorists feel that almost any procedure that is effective in accomplishing an instructional objective is appropriate for classroom use. Of course, these advocates rule out electric shock and other extreme methods, but they do not rule out conditioning, the use of authority, or training procedures. In my view, some concern must be shown for the activities teachers assign in the classroom. Some may be more worthwhile than others. As R. S. Peters, an eminent British philosopher has remarked: "The Puritan and the Catholic both thought they were promoting God's kingdom, but they thought it had to be promoted in a different manner. And the different manner made it quite a different kingdom." (8) This is to say that any discussion of goals can be made meaningful only by a discussion of procedures elected to achieve those goals.

My third observation from which the view of this paper is derived deals with what is currently going on in our schools. Whitehead's eloquent critique, delivered almost 53 years ago, still suffices: "When one considers in its length and breadth the importance of this question of the education of a nation's young, the broken lives, the defeated hopes, the national failures, which result from the frivolous inertia with which it is treated, it is difficult to restrain within oneself a savage rage." (15) I find that my rage is not triggered by the fact that my own children may not score as high as they might on the College Boards, nor that their high school GPA might be below their predicted average. My anger is elicited by the lack of enthusiasm my children, and many other children, have for the day-to-day school activities in which they are asked to engage. School is seen by most students as an endless parade of assignments organized by sincere teachers who perceive their task as one of getting children prepared for the next grade, for senior high school, for college or even for graduate school. Children are being prepared for schooling—and not for life. Such a system of education asks children to work toward educational objectives arbitrarily deemed valuable by scientists, mathematicians, and the like and, for the most part, still undiscussed and unevaluated by educators. Also, the methods that many teachers use to help children reach these objectives involve largely the use of reward and punishment techniques and drill and grill procedures. As John Dewey once remarked of another similar educational plan, "It takes everything educational into account save its essence." (3)

Criteria for Worthwhile Activities

If my observations are valid, it would seem important to consider some criteria for differentiating between worthwhile activities and those that are not worthwhile. I am not suggesting that the criteria set down below are the only ones that can be used. Teachers, parents, and students should be asked to share in the development of alternative sets of criteria to the one I am presenting here.

1. The topics, areas, and objects under study in a classroom must be seen by both teachers and students as illustrative of important understandings, intellectual processes and/or problems. (4) If this criteria were met, a teacher and his student would not be studying Brazil for Brazil's sake alone, but perhaps to illustrate some ideas related to unstable governments. No class would deal with the Pilgrims simply to learn about the Pilgrims. Instead, the Pilgrims would be studied to illustrate, for instance, ideas of religious freedom. A class in science would not study the amoeba for the sake of learning about pseudopoda, but would be using the study of amoeba to illuminate ideas about evolution. In short, I am arguing that educational activities be intellectual—that they be planned to illustrate ideas of obvious importance. I would not hold that there exists a finite list of ideas of which all children should become aware. The location of a school in time and space might make some ideas more relevant than others. For instance, problems of pollution might be of special concern to children living in the East while issues associated with conservation may be more relevant in the Far West. My view is that ideas such as these are profound and need to be studied and discussed in our schools.

2. Second, a worthwhile activity is one which provides children with opportunities for making choices. The quality of possible choices may range from the mundane to the profound. On this continuum, I would, of course, opt for choices toward the profound end—but for the moment I would be satisfied with any opportunity children have for making choices. Let me suggest several kinds of choices that might be offered to students:

a. Scheduling:
   Can a student choose when to work on his assignment? When it is due? Whether or not it must be done at all?
b. Resources:
   Can a student choose the specific content he will study to illustrate the idea under consideration? If the idea and the content are determined, may

he elect from various sources for studying the content?

c. Modes of Presentation:
Can a student select the manner in which the results of his inquiry are shared with the teacher or with his fellow students—art work, drama, graphs, poetry, *etc*?

d. Conclusions:
Are students free to determine their own conclusions? Can they decide which piece of literature is enjoyable? Which trend is most pronounced?

This criterion rests on the assumption that it is through making choices that students manifest their individuality. Life itself is nothing if it is not a succession of choice-making opportunities. I would argue that, with few exceptions, a school activity that does not give children a chance to make choices is not one to be prized regardless of the "end" it guarantees.

3. A third criterion for worthwhileness is that activities should involve the application and mastery of meaningful rules, standards, and/or disciplines. Panel discussions should be disciplined by procedures which allow for interaction among panel members and the audience; an experiment must be disciplined by a semblance of control; the writing of poetry needs to be disciplined by some sense of meter and rhyme; reporting of data needs to be disciplined by considerations of measurement; the citing of authorities needs to be disciplined by standards of accuracy; dramas and speeches must be disciplined by rehearsals; essays must be disciplined by logic and standards of style and syntax. In all of these examples, and many more that can be given, the standards and rules may be derived from students as well as from authorities. Students might be encouraged to discuss their reasonableness and pertinence. Perhaps students might be able to make choices as to which of several sets of standards they wish to discipline their own work. In any case, some element of discipline should be a part of an activity in order to say that it is worthwhile.

My argument rests on two assumptions. The first is that discipline actually increases the enjoyment of an activity. A duffer on the golf course who never is able to discipline his swing or coordination and who shoots in the high 100's will probably give up the game in disgust. The activity becomes a chore. In a similar sense, participation in chemistry experiments by students who are unable to keep equipment clean, or who are unable to describe accurately what they observe, will soon cause the students to dislike the activity. The very mundane act of eating is enhanced by certain rules and standards of etiquette. Presumably, none of us would enjoy eating if food were dumped in a trough—even though the objective of ingesting so many calories a day were met. (8).

The second assumption is very closely related to the first. Bloom (2) reports that evidence from his study of "mastery" supports the assertion that "when a student has mastered a subject and when he receives both objective and subjective evidence of the mastery, there are profound changes in his view of himself and of the outer world. . . . He begins to "like" the subject and desire more of it. . . . Conversely to do poorly in a subject closes an area of further study." My argument here is not that mastery be reflected in recall of subject matter so much as in proficiency in experimenting, inquiring, explicating, demonstrating, communicating, *etc.*

4. My final criterion for presentation in this paper deals with giving students an opportunity to share the results of their work. As students investigate problems or ideas, their unique solutions should be shared with the group. The notion of freedom for inquiry carries with it an obligation to share ideas. Ideas must be tested in an open marketplace where colleagues have a chance to challenge the ideas and to act on them. My feelings on this point are so strong that I would argue that students should not have the choice of not sharing their ideas. They may choose when to share them or with whom or in what manner, but the notion that findings may be hidden from public view is alien to the notion of scholarship as I understand it. Admittedly, the annals of intellectual history include accounts of some scholars who have chosen not to publish their findings—most notably perhaps the famous mathematician Gauss, who enjoyed pulling his unannounced discoveries from his files when other scholars made public their discoveries. My feeling is that this approach to scholarship should be discouraged—and that all students must learn the importance and joy found in the sharing of ideas.

Problems

I would be remiss if I did not include in my discussion a few of the problems that accompany the acceptance of the views presented in this article. The first problem that must be raised about any advocate of "worthwhileness" is: "Worthwhile for whom?" My response to that would probably be similar to the response of an advocate of the behaviorist approach to writing objectives—"worthwhile to the student and to society." I would agree that students in elementary school, perhaps even many students above that level, would not be interested in studying ideas, sharing, or in being disciplined. Of course, that will be the case no matter what curriculum design is chosen. Some students frankly are not even interested in making choices—they don't want to do what they want to do. As in all teaching, teachers must make an effort to "get students interested" in the assignments they deem worthwhile. The ways of doing this right now lie in the province of "the art of teaching" and more systematic study needs to be exerted in this area to make it a more exact procedure.

A second problem is perhaps more serious to anyone thinking of applying this view to curriculum planning and evaluation. It is rather difficult to define the word "activity". Is an activity a unit lasting several weeks? Is an activity any five minute segment of the school day? Could an activity be both? Ecological researchers have been working on this problem, and indeed a decision about "units" is usually one of the first steps an ecologist takes as he is working to analyze his data. In my preliminary work with teachers trying to encourage their examination of the view of curriculum presented here, I found them able to respond fruitfully to the request "Name one activity you assigned to children today." Evidently most teachers have their classroom organized around activities of various lengths—and seem to think in those terms. A perusal of the responses I received from several groups of teachers led me to the following two-part definition of activity: 1. An activity is characterized by a teacher inviting children to focus their attention on some task, material, or idea. 2. Students responses to the teacher's invitation must last for at least fifteen minutes. The first criterion rules out times of aimlessness that children find themselves in between assignments or during periods of the teacher's absence from the room. The second criterion seems to stabilize teacher's responses to my request—away from the short range ("I asked Johnny to sit down") and the long range ("We are working toward self-realization"). If a school's curriculum is to be studied using the criteria stated in this paper, and using the self-reports of teachers, a system of sampling teacher's assignments needs to be devised. It would seem quite easy to devise a time-sampling procedure for collecting teacher's reports of the activities they assign and to devise a procedure for testing the validity of the reports received.

A third problem is associated with the application of the criteria. How many of the criteria must an activity meet to be considered worthwhile? My answer to that is as follows: if the choosing, the disciplining, or the sharing deal with subject matter that is not related to important understandings, intellectual processes or problems, then I would consider the activity as not worthwhile. I wouldn't care how many choices a student had to make or how much opportunity he had to share, if these activities were not related to important ideas. Therefore, for an activity to be worthwhile, according to my framework, it would have to meet the first criterion and any other of the remaining three. My answer sounds definite and positive. Of course, the criteria and the methods of applying them are merely working hypotheses at this time—subject to revision based on experience, insight, and shifts in values. I hope that the dogmatism of this approach does not impede others from considering other criteria or other ways of applying those presented here.

Summary

In summary, the argument has been presented that an activity needs to be justified beyond the instrumental value it possesses for attaining certain specified objectives. The article presented a set of criteria for evaluating activities and issued an invitation for others to present a set of their own. Most of all, it asked that some concern be directed toward the activities assigned to our youngsters in school.

References and Related Readings

1. Barker, Roger C. *The Stream of Behavior.* New York: Appleton-Century-Crofts, 1963. (Chapter 1).

2. Bloom, Benjamin S. "Learning for Mastery," *Evaluation Comment.* Los Angeles: University of California at Los Angeles, Center for the Study of Evaluation of Instructional Problems, Vol. I, No. 2, May, 1968.

3. Dewey, John. *Democracy and Education.* New York: Macmillan, 1916.

4. Herrick, Virgil E. "Curriculum Decisions and Provision for Individual Differences." *Elementary School Journal,* March, 1962, pp. 313–20.

5. Leonard, George B. *Education and*

Ecstasy. New York: Delacorte Press, 1968.

6. Nossiter, Bernard D. "Defense Firms Leery of Civilian Work" *Washington, Post*, December 9, 1968, p. 1.

7. Peters, Richard S. *Authority, Responsibility and Education*. London: George Allen and Unwin Ltd., 1959. (Chapter 7).

8. Peters, Richard S. *Ethics and Education*. Chicago: Scott, Foresman and Co., 1967.

9. Popham, James. *The Teacher-Empiricist*. Los Angeles: Aegeus Press, 1965.

10. Raths, Louis E. *Teaching for Learning*. Columbus: Charles Merrill, 1969.

11. Raths, James. "Specificity as a Threat to Curriculum Reform." *FASCD Mailbag*. Florida: Association For Supervision and Curriculum Development, December, 1968.

12. Skinner, B. F. *The Technology of Teaching*. New York: Appleton-Century-Crofts, 1968.

13. Vincent, William S. "Indicators of Quality," *Research Bulletin*. Institute of Administrative Research, Teachers College, Columbia University, May, 1967.

14. Walbesser, Henry. *Constructing Behavioral Objectives*. College Park, Md.: Bureau of Educational Research and Field Services, University of Maryland, 1968.

15. Whitehead, Alfred N. *The Aims of Education*. New York: Macmillan, 1929.

ACTIVITIES

1. What educational values might you attribute to teachers who planned in the ways described in the brief paragraphs below?

a. Teacher A religiously follows the school system's curriculum guide, complete with suggested activities, films, and timed units. The questions he asks in class and the examinations he uses are all taken from the teachers' guide which accompanies the text.

b. Teacher B rejects the idea of planning in a formal way. He attends class, listens to the conversations of youngsters, and on that basis encourages students to inquire, to study, and to communicate about their own concerns. For instance, if a butterfly were to fly in the window and catch the attention of several students, Mr. B would encourage students to study butterflies.

c. Teacher C makes use of a very formal and systematic lesson plan. Each day students respond to oral questions dealing with a reading assignment completed at home the night before and take a short quiz on the material at the close of the period. The cycle is then re-initiated by a new reading assignment for homework.

d. Teacher D chooses to justify his activities on the basis of the marks his students receive on a standardized examination that is given to all the students in the community. He has identified the skills needed to score high on the test, and he has patterned his planning to maximize students' scores on those tests.

2. For the paragraphs in question one above, contrast the values identified here with those presented by the authors of the articles found in this chapter.

3. Assume that a parent has asked you to explain your planning procedures. Write a paragraph similar to those found in question 1 which describes your planning procedures. Write an additional paragraph identifying the values you hold that are reflected in your planning procedures.

4. Identify some objectives given by a school system or objectives listed at the beginning of a course of study. Classify these according to Bloom's *Taxonomy* or to the levels of performance cited in Fox's article.

5. Using the grid-form technique, develop a unit in your teaching field.

6. Classify the "Critical Abilities" of the Dressel and Mayhew grid form according to Bloom's *Taxonomy*.

7. Review the lesson plans at the end of this chapter in the light of Herrick's discussion.

a. What decisions has the teacher made in each lesson plan according to each of the three classes mentioned in Herrick's article on organizing centers?

b. Has the teacher differentiated between topics and important understandings?

c. Has the teacher differentiated between concepts and skills?

d. What has the teacher used as an organizing center?

8. Classify the goals of the lesson plans at the end of this chapter according to the *Taxonomy*.

a. Discuss differences in the classification that are found in your group.

b. Most of the goals in traditional teaching can be classified under Knowledge (1.00). Why do you suppose this is true? How could you find out if your answer to this question is valid?

9. What are some generalizations worth teaching? What content would best illustrate these generalizations?

Sample Lesson Plan 1

Tenth-Grade Biology—Introduction to Classification Systems

OBJECTIVE

Students are to discover the structure of a classification system.

MATERIALS

Student data book.
Each table has a small pan which contains approximately fifty mixed buttons.

PROCEDURES

Each pair of students is to group the buttons in any way they wish according to specific characteristics. (Some may begin with color, or size, or number of holes, etc.)

Toward the last 15 minutes of the class period several students will present their classification scheme. (Ask for their rationale for selecting their grouping.)

Look for the following ideas to emerge from student discussions.

1. Before a classification system can be developed, materials must be present to be classified.
2. A system will proceed from general to specific, or from simple to complex.
3. The basic elements of the different systems developed by different students will probably include *shape, size, color,* and *form and/or structure.* (These four categories are common to other systems of other items, such as school buildings, automobiles, plants, and animals, etc.)

ASSIGNMENT

Read Chapter 6—"Classifying Living Things."

Answer the following question: In what way is the system for classifying living things related to your system for classifying buttons?

Sample Lesson Plan 2

Twelfth-Grade American Literature

ASSIGNMENT FOR TODAY

Learn spelling words, p. 73.

METHODS

1. Give spelling quiz
2. Show filmstrip on ship "Constitution"
3. Play record of poem "Old Ironsides"
4. Role-play how the crew of the "Constitution" would have reacted to the poem.
5. Questions to ask in class:
   a. What words are unclear?
   b. Where did the author live?
   c. Why did the author write the poem?
   d. Would a poetry editor print this poem if it were written today?
   e. Did you like the poem?

ASSIGNMENT FOR TOMORROW

Look up the words you do not know in the poem "Old Ironsides" and learn the correct meanings.

Memorize the first stanza of "Old Ironsides."

Read "Casey at the Bat."

Sample Lesson Plan 3

Eleventh-Grade U.S. History

STUDENT ASSIGNMENT FOR TODAY

Bring in two news stories and one editorial dealing with the same subject or event.

CLASSROOM ACTIVITIES

1. Show aerial and ground photographs of New York City. Then show artists' sketches of the same areas. Discuss similarities and differences.
2. Select a panel of students to read their articles and editorials. Have the students consider whether the news stories presented the same picture. Was the difference of purpose evident in the editorial as compared to the news story?
3. Give out three groups of in-class assignments:

Group 1: Write a news story on the basis of the information given on a handout sheet (to be given to students).
Group 2: Write a favorable editorial dealing with some aspect of the news story outlined on the handout sheet.
Group 3: Write an unfavorable editorial dealing with some aspect of the news story outlined on the handout sheet.

4. Have various students in Group 1 read their news stories and call on students in Groups 2 and 3 to state whether they would accept them for publication in their paper.
5. Reconsider some of the news stories and editorials read by the panel.

ASSIGNMENT FOR TOMORROW

Read the selection in the book: "Propaganda and the American Revolution."

TESTING AND GRADING

CHAPTER FOUR

Evaluating student work is one of the most pressing realities of teaching. Teachers and students alike recognize that most tests are given for the purpose of grading. At times, the grade a student receives may affect his life deeply. Grades may determine job opportunities, chances for admission to college, or perhaps even more important, concepts of self adequacy. Because of this, and because of the great emphasis currently placed on tests as a source of grades, it is incumbent upon each teacher to monitor his testing practices carefully. This section suggests some ways teachers may examine the tests they use in evaluating students' progress. While this chapter is not a course in tests and measurements, the ideas presented here are aimed at providing some means by which teachers can review their testing and grading procedures and consider alternatives.

While test scores are often used to appraise quality of teaching, it is also possible to describe the values of a teacher by examining the test itself. This approach is based on the premise that there exists an almost universal agreement between students and teachers that a test should reflect the teaching emphases that preceded it. If the class focused on facts of the colonial period, a test would be considered unfair if it asked for something else. Because teachers almost always test for what they have taught, tests themselves may describe the objectives of the course. Thus, here is another way a teacher is able to reflect on the value decisions he is making in his teaching.

19. PLANNING TESTS

JOHN R. PANCELLA

Once a teacher has his teaching objectives well in mind, his next efforts are usually directed to the question, "How may I evaluate the teaching and learning in my class to determine if the objectives have been obtained?" Most teachers answer this question to their own satisfaction by using tests. This section deals with ways a teacher may evaluate his tests to see if they are at all adequate for the purposes for which they are used.

Face Validity

A most important question asks, "Is the test measuring what I want it to measure?" To determine this is exceedingly difficult in most measuring situations involving the assessment of personality traits, motivation, curiosity, etc. In achievement testing, however, the answer is not quite so difficult. It is a fairly easy matter to establish "face" validity of an achievement test. Face validity, in a few words, is merely proof that the test "covers" the material. Perhaps we will be able to illustrate a way of establishing face validity by considering a specific example. Let us assume that of ten lessons in a science unit, four had lesson objectives concerned with the teaching of applications (level 3.00) and that the lessons were planned to accomplish these objectives through laboratory techniques. It would hardly seem consistent for a teacher, wishing to design a test to measure the attainment of these objectives, to make all questions on his test recall questions (level 1.00). The same logic would suggest that a test composed of synthesis questions (level 5.00) would be equally inappropriate. A teacher may establish the content validity of a test by categorizing the questions according to a taxonomic scheme such as Bloom's—and thereby demonstrate that indeed his test is measuring at a cognitive level that is congruent with his purposes.

Along another dimension—that of content. Again, consider a teacher devising a test for a unit dealing with

TABLE 1

	Knowledge (per cent)	Comprehension (per cent)	Evaluation (per cent)
Causes of the War	5	10	10
Military Campaigns	5		10
Life on the Home Front			10
International Diplomacy	5	5	5
National Politics	5		5
Reconstruction	5	10	10
Total	25	25	50

a Shakespearean play. Class objectives may have dealt with many aspects of the play—the author, the historical setting, the imagery, the plot, the characters, etc. Clearly a test would not have face validity if it concentrated most of its questions in any one of these important areas. Just as a test should reflect the cognitive level goals that a teacher sets, so it must reflect the content covered in class. A test that meets these objectives is said to have face validity.

Teachers examine the face validity of the tests they write, by making use of a grid described below. On one dimension, the teacher may enter various process dimensions. (Our example has made use of those of the Taxonomy.) Along a second dimension, content topics and areas of study are listed. Before writing an examination, the teacher may indicate how many questions he wants in every cell of the grid. This decision gives direction for the writing of items. For example, suppose a history unit on the Civil War is the focus of a teacher's concern for writing a test. He may identify the cognitive levels that reflect his teaching purposes and the content areas that he feels received the most emphasis in his teaching. His grid might look as shown in Table 1.

Of course there is nothing magical about the percentages assigned to each cell. Each teacher must decide which content objectives and cognitive objectives most suitably reflect the emphases given in the teaching of the unit. A perusal of lesson plans may be of some help in making the determination. Now, if the teacher is planning a 100 item test, the grid suggests that 5 items concern recall of information concerning the causes of the war; 5 items dealing with the facts and figures, etc., of the military campaigns, and so on.

A grid such as this one guards against an imbalance in the writing of a test—that would be the case if all the items were dealing with the military campaigns or if all the questions were recall questions. A test such as that may be appropriate in terms of its face validity for a course dealing centrally with the remembering of facts and figures of the military campaign, but not for the course reflected in the assignment of percentages in the grid.

The idea of "test banks" is seemingly becoming popular. A test bank is an accumulation of test items, usually categorized by subject topic and classified as to thinking task. Occasionally, performance data on each question are included. Teachers may draw question samples from the bank to construct their tests. The

FRONT

Testing and Grading
Mid-term exam

1.00

Choose the answer which to you represents the best alternative among those listed.

14. In using the Standard Deviation (SD) method for assigning grades it is assumed that the distribution of scores is normal. This assumption is most realistic in which of the following situations?

a. students are homogeneously grouped
b. students elect to take the course
c. students are heterogeneously grouped
d. a and b above

BACK

Nov. 1964

	a	b	c*	d
Upper 6	0	0	6	0
Lower 6	3	0	3	0

Fair discriminator. Fair difficulty. Choices b and d not powerful distractors. This information was in an assigned reading, not discussed in class.

Nov. 1965

	a	b	c	d
Upper 8	1	0	7	0
Lower 8	0	0	7	1

Overtaught idea this term in class. Not a good discriminator. Only fact recall item. Reject question in further exams for thinking.

Taxonomy is often used for constructing and classifying test questions in the test item bank.

The classroom teacher can easily initiate and build a test bank in a simple, retrievable form. Test questions from an extra exam paper can be pasted to one side of a 5 × 7 inch card. For convenience the acceptable answer(s) should be marked. The card can now be labeled at the top edge according to lesson topic, book chapter, unit plan, etc. It can also be identified as to thinking level according to the Taxonomy. The item analysis can be placed on the reverse side of the card, with appropriate teacher comments or evaluations. These cards can now be stored and categorized as desired. The next time a test question is needed it can be selected from the bank of items. If the item was not valid or useful (e.g. it did not discriminate) it may be revised or rejected. Easy and difficult items can be quickly located. Questions which require different thinking processes can be selected to build exactly the type of test the teacher wishes. Of course, the test item file improves with use and with additional tests which contribute to the total different cards on file. Groups of teachers would build a test bank quickly. See p. 146 for an example of a test bank card.

Testing is ordinarily considered a chore in teaching. Perhaps the suggestions outlined here might foster renewed interest in classroom testing and help teachers monitor their own teaching decisions through a review of the questions they ask on tests.

References

1. *Making the Classroom Test: A Guide for Teachers,* 2nd ed., Evaluation and Advisory Service Series No. 4, Princeton, N.J.: Educational Testing Service, 1961.

2. Diederich, Paul B., *Short-cut Statistics for Teacher-made Tests,* 2nd ed., Evaluation and Advisory Service Series No. 5, Princeton, N.J.: Educational Testing Service, 1960.

3. Wood, Dorothy Adkins, *Test Construction: Development and Interpretation of Achievement Tests.* Columbus, Ohio: Charles E. Merrill Books, Inc., 1961.

20. INTERPRETATION OF TEST RESULTS

KENNETH F. MCLAUGHLIN

Error Analysis Made Inside the Classroom

Paul B. Diederich suggests that an error analysis of a test can be done during classroom time by having each pupil *watch* a paper other than his own.[1] If the teacher is only interested in an overall "error analysis," i.e., in how many pupils chose any one of the *wrong* responses to a test question, then the teacher only needs to call out, "Item 1, 'b' is the correct answer. Each of you holding a paper in which item 1 was *missed*, raise your hand." Then he, or a class monitor, can quickly count the raised hands, record the number beside the test question, and proceed to the other questions. Thus, in a few minutes, the items missed by the greatest number have been identified. After the papers are returned to the students, the teacher can quickly go over those questions which were missed most often and explain why they are incorrect.

Kenneth F. McLaughlin, INTERPRETATION OF TEST RESULTS, *Bulletin 1964, No. 7, U. S. Department of Health, Education, and Welfare (Washington, D.C.: Government Printing Office, 1964), pp. 34–46.*

[1] Paul B. Diederich, *Short-Cut Statistics for Teacher-Made Tests*, Evaluation and Advisory Service Series, No. 5 (Princeton, N.J.: Educational Testing Service, 1960), p. 3.

Item Analysis Methods

There are several methods for analyzing objective test results which make it possible to determine one or more of the following points:

1. *Difficulty* of an item—The per cent of the students of the class answering the question correctly.

2. *Discriminating power* of the correct answer—The capacity of an item to distinguish between good and poor students; the per cent of the highest scoring students answering the question correctly as compared with the per cent of the lowest ranking students answering the question correctly.

3. *Effectiveness* of each response for each test item—The *number* of students selecting each response (each response should be chosen at least once).

4. *Identification* of each student making a correct or incorrect choice for each item—Permits an individually designed corrective procedure for each student.

In a few school systems it is now possible to carry out an item analysis entirely by means of an attachment to a test scoring machine or by the use of automatic data processing equipment. In other schools where such services are not available it may be necessary to use other methods. In fact, much student interest may be aroused by carrying out such procedures during the classroom period when the scored papers are returned. It has been found that pupils at all grade levels, from the primary grades through graduate school, cooperate willingly. The students are interested in learning how many of their peers missed each item, why they made an incorrect choice, and the best answer for each question. If such an analysis has been completed for the teacher's own objective test, he immediately has information which can assist him to improve his test items for future use. He can then build up a test file of items of a known quality and difficulty which will discriminate between his good and poor students.

"High-Low" Analysis

For some tests the teacher will find it helpful to use the classroom procedure which Diederich calls a "high-low" type of item analysis.[2] This method will reveal both the difficulty and the discriminating power of each item.

To determine the discriminating power of an item, it is necessary to split the class into two sections—those with high scores and those with low scores. The separation point is the middle or median score for the class. To find the median score the following steps are necessary. Determine the range of scores of the class, that is, the highest and lowest scores, and record them at the top and bottom of the blackboard. Write all possible scores occurring in this interval in a column, beginning with the highest score at the top of the board and continuing to the lowest. Divide the number of class members by two to determine how many papers must be tallied in order to find the middle one. Beginning with the highest score, ask how many students made each score and record the results. As soon as the cumulative total number of papers equals half the class, the middle score can be determined without completing the distribution of scores.

If there are several students' papers at this middle score, collect these papers first. Then collect all papers in two groups—those above the middle score and those below. Distribute all papers above the median score on one side of the room, and those below the median score on the other side. Then assign the several papers with the median score to the high and low sides at random so that the total number of papers on each side is the same. If there should be an odd number of papers in the class so that they cannot be evenly divided, the discarding of the one paper remaining will leave one student to act as a recording monitor at the board.

It is possible to get a certain amount of teamwork in this operation

2 *Ibid.*, pp. 3–10.

if a captain is appointed for each of the two groups. The teacher, or the class member with no paper, can write the question numbers in a column on the board and make four column headings:

H L H + L H − L

These headings stand for:

H—the number of the "high" group who mark the item correctly
L—the number of the "low" group who mark the item correctly
H + L—"difficulty index," the total number who marked the item correctly
H − L—"discrimination index," how many more of the "high" group than of the "low" group marked the item correctly

When the teacher asks, "How many have item No. 1 correct?" each student with the correct answer on the paper he is watching raises his hand. The captain of the high group calls his number—the "H" score. The captain of the low group calls his number—the "L" score. These two numbers are written on the board and then the recorder computes and calls out the two scores for "H + L" and "H − L."

These four numbers are always obtained in the same order. Each student writes these four numbers on the answer sheet below each question as it is computed by the board monitor. Each member of the class checks on the sum and difference. With a little practice, Diederich[3] says, this item analysis can be carried out for a one-period test in about 10 to 20 minutes depending on the number of items. This is much faster than the operation could be completed by the teacher. At the same time, an excellent learning situation develops since each student becomes involved in the test results for the class as a whole and wishes to know why he has missed some of the items.

If an item is acceptable for inclusion in later tests, "high-low" differences should be equal to at least 10 per cent of the size of the class.[4] For example, with a class of 36 the differences should be equal to at least 4. However, because of the large value of the "standard error," an item, the "true" difference of which would turn out to be 6, might in some cases give a value of less than 4. In other words, if the difference is small, one should examine the item closely. If it seems to be a well-constructed item, it should be retained. Diederich suggests that "not more than a fifth of the items in the final test should fall below the suggested standard and the *average* high-low difference should be above 10 per cent of the class, preferably 15 per cent or more."[5]

The H + L number, which indicates the total number of students choosing the correct answer, indicates the *difficully* of the item for the class. The larger the number, the easier the item. In most cases, an item which 90 per cent of the class marks correctly is too easy. On the other hand, if less than 30 per cent of the class marks it correctly, it is probably too difficult.[6]

Occasionally, especially with a teacher-made objective test, a greater

[3] *Ibid.*, p. 7.

[4] *Ibid.*, p. 8.
[5] *Ibid.*, p. 9.
[6] *Ibid.*, p. 8.

number in the low group will obtain the correct answer than in the high group. Then the H − L becomes negative, as in question 4 in Table 1, which is called "negative discrimination." When this occurs, the item needs further investigation. Careful examination of such an item may reveal that a few changes will improve it so that it need not be discarded. To determine what changes are necessary, the teacher might ask each member of the class why he chose one of the incorrect responses, and determine whether or not the key response was poorly written. For example, the correct response of the answer key might not attract the better students if some of the supposed incorrect choices, or distractors, were actually correct. A rewritten item may be placed in the teacher's item file and tried again in a later examination.

In Table 1 the results of the analysis of several test questions are given for a class with 36 students. Item 1 is an easy item (H + L = 36), since all members of the high and low group marked it correctly. It has the highest possible difficulty index—36—which indicates an easy item. (The lower the H + L score, the more difficult the item.) Since all students in each half marked the correct answer, it certainly will have no influence in discriminating between the high and low groups. Unless one desires to begin the test with an easy item, this item would not be used in another test.

Item 7 is harder than item 1, with a difficulty index of 18. Since H = 9 and L = 9, H − L is 0. Therefore, this item will not discriminate between the two groups and would not be used in its present form.

Item 2 is of average difficulty and is the most discriminating item illustrated, with H − L = 12.

Item 3 and 8 just barely meet the criteria for the level of discrimination (H − L) with the suggested value of 4 (i.e., 10 per cent of 36 is 3.6, which is rounded to 4). Item 8 is more difficult than item 3, as shown by the indices of 8 and 22, respectively. In fact, a test should not include many items as difficult as item 8. The teacher might examine this item to determine whether it is measuring a fundamental concept which must be taught again, or if it is referring to an insignificant detail which should not have been included.

Items 4 and 6 are examples of "negative discrimination." More students in the *lower* group selected the right answer than in the upper group. Although the difficulty indices sug-

TABLE 1

Examples of High-Low Item Analysis [N=36]

Question	H	L	H+L	H−L
1	18	18	36	0
2	16	4	20	12
3	13	9	22	4
4	7	13	20	−6
5	9	7	16	2
6	5	7	12	−2
7	9	9	18	0
8	6	2	8	4

gest that the items are not easy, these items should be rejected until they are examined and rewritten.

Item 5 is more difficult than questions 1 through 4; however, since the discrimination index is only 2, it would not be used in future tests without some revision.

"Alternate Response" Analysis

The alternate responses, or choices, prepared for multiple-choice items often include those responses which students have been known to make most often in short-answer or free-response questions. For example, in mathematics or science the most frequent incorrect answer choices are those which would result if common errors were made in arriving at a solution. (In order to prevent a student from spending too much time on a problem, the last choice is often "none of the above.") The teacher may be more interested in the *kinds* of student errors than he is in knowing merely that a certain number of students missed a question. In this situation, the analysis would be carried out in this manner by the teacher: "Question No. 1—How many students selected choice 1?" (pause and record), "How many students selected choice 2?" (pause and record), and so on, for each of the choices for each question. Since in most cases the majority of the class will choose the correct response, the response count takes only a few minutes.

Item Analysis by Test Scoring Machine

If a school system or a school has the IBM 805 Test Scoring Machine, it may have available the attachment called the Graphic Item Counter. This attachment provides one of the quickest and most accurate ways for making an item analysis. After separating the scored test papers into upper and lower groups on the basis of the total test scores, the machine operator can obtain the number of students in each group marking each response to each question. This information can be obtained for 18 5-choice questions at one time, since there are 90 counters available. If 4-choice, 3-choice, or 2-choice questions are asked, one run of the answer sheets through the machine will handle 22, 30, or 45 questions, respectively. If one wishes to learn only how many students answered each question correctly, as many as 90 questions may be analyzed at one time.

The procedures suggested before are for use with a single class or a department in one school. In developing and standardizing a new test, more cases would be needed than those of a single classroom and the procedures should be followed which are described briefly in *Understanding Testing*[7] or given in detail in *Educational Measurement*.[8] In making an item analysis for a single classroom, it seems appropriate to divide the class into halves—upper half and lower half. If an item analysis is based upon a test administration to 400 or more students, then the upper and lower 27 per cent of the total group will give the best results.

7 Kenneth F. McLaughlin, "How Is a Test Built?" in *Understanding Testing* (Washington, D.C.: U.S. Government Printing Office, 1962), pp. 4–7. U.S. Office of Education, OE–25003.

8 Frederick B. Davis, "Item Selection Techniques," in *Educational Measurement* (Washington, D.C.: American Council on Education, 1951), pp. 266–328.

An Item Analysis Sheet can be mimeographed with the headings and form given in Fig. 1. By using legal size paper, it is possible to analyze 10 questions in each column.

The figures for the "No." columns under "Upper Group" and "Lower Group" are obtained directly from the Graphic Item Count Record. The "No." under "Total Group" is the sum of the quantities under "No." in the Upper Group and Lower Group. The per cents are obtained by dividing the recorded numbers by the number in the upper or lower groups and in the total group. An example will make these calculations clear.

Suppose that there are 40 students in a class and the division into halves places 20 students in the Upper Group and 20 students in the Lower Group. In item 1, choice 1 was marked by 15 students in the Upper Group and 5 students in the Lower Group. In the Total Group, 20 (15 plus 5) marked choice 1. Choice 2 was marked by 1 student in the Upper Group and 1 student in the Lower Group which gives a sum of 2 for the Total Group. This procedure continues for each choice for each item in the test.

For rapid computation one can easily construct a table of per cents corresponding to the number of students in half of the total group, going from 1 (which is 5 per cent) to 20 (which is 100 per cent). Then one fills in the % columns in the item analysis sheet for the Upper Group and Lower Group. (If this is done with a colored pencil, later analysis will be easier. In Fig. 1 the % columns have been shaded.) In item 1 this becomes for choice 1, 75 and 25; for choice 2, 5 and 5; for choice 3, 15 and 35; etc. The sum of the per cents in either of these columns should not exceed 100 by more than 3 per cent, which is the maximum which might occur in some classes because of rounding errors. The total may be less than 100 if one or more students omit a question.

Another table of per cents should be constructed corresponding to the number of students for the total group, in this case going from 1 (which is 2.5 per cent, rounded to 3 per cent) to 40 (which is 100 per cent). Then one fills in the % column under Total Group. (One can save these tables and develop new ones as they are needed when class size changes—because of absences at test time or changes of class size in a new school year.)

It has been shown in the literature that the test best able to put a class of students in rank order is one which has item difficulties spread over most of the range, but which has an average item difficulty of 50 per cent, with the greatest number clustering about 50 per cent.

As the next step, examine each test item in figure 1 and code it as suggested: A circle (O) around the correct answer choice; no further mark if the item appears satisfactory; a single check (√) if the item discrimination is less than desired; a double check (√ √) if there is negative discrimination; and an "X" if a "large number" select the same incorrect choice.

In item 1 the correct answer is choice 1; 75 per cent of the Upper Group and 25 per cent of the Lower Group marked it correctly. Since there is a difference of 50 per cent (75 minus 25), which is much greater than the suggested minimum difference of 15 per cent, this item discriminates satisfactorily and would be

ITEM ANALYSIS SHEET

Item No.	Choice	Upper Group		Lower Group		TOTAL GROUP		Item No.	Choice	Upper Group		Lower Group		TOTAL GROUP	
		No.	%	No.	%	No.	%			No.	%	No.	%	No.	%
	①	15	75	5	25	20	50		1	3	15	1	5	4	10
	2	1	5	1	5	2	5		2	1	5	2	10	3	8
1	3	3	15	7	35	10	25	11	3	6	30	4	20	10	25
	4	1	5	5	25	6	15		4	2	10	1	5	3	8
	5			2	10	2	5	✓✓	⑤	8	40	12	60	20	50
	1								1						
	②	20	100	18	90	38	95		2			1	5	1	3
2	3			1	5	1	3	12 ✓	③	8	40	6	30	14	35
	4							X	4	10	50	12	60	22	55
	5			1	5	1	3		5	1	5			1	3

○ Correct Item Choice

✓ Item Discrimination Less Than Desired

✓✓ "Negative" Discrimination

X A "Large Number" Choose the Same Incorrect Choice

Example: Choice 1 is the correct answer for item No. 1. 75% of the upper group and 25% of the lower group choose choice 1. These values lie in the 20–80 range, requiring a difference of 15% or more to be acceptable (75–25 = 50). Therefore, the item discriminates satisfactorily. The total group % for the correct answer, choice 1, is 50. Hence the difficulty index is 50%.

Requirements for
Satisfactory Item Discrimination
(for correct choice)

Range of Values (Upper Group and Lower Group)	Difference (Upper Group minus Lower Group)
90–100	5 or more
80–90	10 or more
20–80	15 or more
10–20	10 or more
0–10	5 or more

Figure 1.
Sample Item Analysis Sheet

a good one to include in future tests—if its other responses are satisfactory. Each of the other choices was operating since each was chosen at least once by some member of the class.

Item 2, with choice 2 as the correct one is an easy item—95 per cent of the total group of students marked it correctly. The *larger* the per cent the *easier* the item. The item does discriminate satisfactorily at this level, since there is a difference of 10 per cent (100 minus 90). Choices 1 and 4 should be reexamined, since no one chose them. Some test constructors believe that a few easy items of this difficulty level at the beginning of a test helps to put the examinees at ease. Almost every student's score is raised one point by such an item and his relative rank may not be changed at all when one considers the complete test.

Item 11, the number of the item at the top of the second column in the Item Analysis Sheet, shows that each choice was selected by some of the students. The double check (√ √) indicates that there is a "negative discrimination" with this item, which means that more students in the Lower Group chose the keyed answer than in the Upper Group. As a result, one obtains a discrimination index of minus 20 per cent (40 minus 60). This item does not assist in ranking the students in the proper order, but rather makes the rankings less dependable. The difficulty index, as shown in the Total Group % column is 50 per cent, the same as item 1—but this item 11 should *not* be used. One should examine items of this type to be sure that one has not made an error in developing the answer key. Because of rounding the Total Group % for all choices is 101.

Item 12 is an example of a question which does not discriminate at the desired level of 15 per cent but only 10 per cent (40 minus 30). However, if reconsideration of the item shows that it is a good item and important to the course, retain it. Choice 1 should be changed—it was so poor that no one selected it. Choices 2 and 5 are chosen by only one student each and are much weaker than choice 4. Choice 4 must be considered, since it has been marked with an "X." Why did so many students in both the Upper and Lower Groups select it? Is it the statement of a commonly accepted fallacy? Is it so ambiguous that in one sense it may really be correct? Does this question cover a basic part of the course which needs reteaching? Has this question been keyed properly? If choice 4 should be determined to be correct rather than choice 3, then one would have "negative discrimination" as in question 11. Since one student in each group omitted the question the Total Group % is 96.

Comments should be made concerning test items omitted by the student. As one becomes experienced in examining an Item Analysis Sheet, he quickly becomes aware of the few items which many students failed to answer because of the low numbers in the Total Group % column. If the test is timed, these items would come, in most cases, near the end of the test. If they occur randomly throughout the test, the teacher should examine the lesson plans to be certain that they have been previously covered—and then reteach them if necessary.

When the item analysis has been completed, a summary table of marks may be made of the number of single or double checks or X's. As one becomes more skillful in constructing one's own tests and using again items which have been tried out and found successful he will discover the number of marks diminishing. However, it will be a rare occasion when, for any given class, there will be no marks. This would also be true of standardized tests which can be analyzed in a similar manner in order to discover the weak points and errors in thinking of the students.

If each item used on a test is typed or pasted on a separate card, cataloged as to topic, and the aforementioned kinds of information concerning discrimination and difficulty recorded, it is possible to build a pool of *good* items which can be used in later classes. By recording when the item is used, the repetition of the same items in succeeding terms or years can be avoided. If the foregoing analysis shows that an item is poor, it should not be used unless it is rewritten.

21. EVALUATION IN SOCIAL SCIENCES

HARRY D. BERG

The Use of Tests in Instruction

Tests are intended to evaluate the outcomes of instruction. The kinds of questions discussed in this chapter, then, will be most valid if the learnings and skills needed to deal with them are subjects of instruction. When emphasis on note taking in the classroom is followed by the thought type of examinations, the results will be destructive of student morale and disquieting to the teacher. Thought-provoking classroom discussions followed by memory tests will cause students to refrain from discussion in favor of listening for the instructor's remarks and explanations. Neither is good educational practice. Instruction and evaluation should reinforce each other.

This chapter does not intend to go into methods of instruction. However, it should not be presumptuous to point out a few ways in which test items and exercises, themselves, may be used for nontesting purposes. Such procedure is particularly valid if the testing materials come close to defining the behavior we are interested in developing.

A common practice is to discuss a

Harry D. Berg, "Evaluation in Social Sciences," in Evaluation in Higher Education, *ed. Paul L. Dressel and Associates (Boston: Houghton Mifflin Company, 1961), pp. 109–11. Reprinted by permission.*

test in class as soon after giving it as possible. (It would be most desirable, of course, if students could learn of their errors at the time of making them. But without special devices this is not feasible.) Motivation is usually high, and if the test has been made up of thought items a good deal of learning can be expected to take place. A thought item, incidentally, might be defined as one which is worth discussing in class after testing.

Test items can also be used profitably for nongrading purposes at the time a topic is being discussed. The value of this procedure can be increased if the students are given study questions geared to the item exercises. In such cases the latter might be used as a study self-check.

A more formalized method of diagnosing student difficulties for instructional purposes involves the use of a 5″ × 8″ index card on which the student is to record the reasons for selecting a particular answer to an objective test item. In effect, the item becomes the subject of an essay—a device occasionally appropriate for use in essay tests. The student's response may then be evaluated as indicated below. The technique is also useful in revising items for future use.

Name____________ Date________
Question No.________ Choice 1 2 3 4 5
(Circle one)
Reasons for choice (Use back of card if necessary.)

The completed cards may be scored in terms of four categories:

1. R-R. These cards have the correct answers and the students' justifications are sound (right answer—right reasoning).

2. R-W. These cards have the correct answers, but the described reasoning is weak or wholly irrelevant and could not have led to the choice of the correct answer (right answer—wrong reasoning).

3. W-R. These cards have incorrect answers, but seemingly the reasoning is sound. In other words, looking at the reasoning alone would lead one to believe that the student had reasoned well and should have chosen the correct answer (wrong answer—right reasoning).

4. W-W. These cards have incorrect answers and the reasoning is wholly inappropriate (wrong answer—wrong reasoning).

These results are useful for class discussion as well as for instructional planning.

Summary

Instruction and testing are sometimes viewed as dichotomous, with instruction being devoted to providing answers and the student's mastery being later determined by questions directly pointing to the answers already provided. Instruction should be aimed at development of student abilities to relate knowledge to problem situations, and testing should both encourage this development and determine whether and to what extent it has taken place. The number and scope of social science problems in the world today to which such ability is both relevant and necessary are sufficient reason to orient instruction to the objectives and approaches to them suggested in this chapter.

22. GRADING ALTERNATIVES

JOHN R. PANCELLA

One of the paradoxes of the teaching profession is that almost every teacher can intuit which students are really good, which are really poor, and which are mediocre. Therefore a problem arises in grading tests, because the mores of the teacher-student relationship almost forbid a teacher to make grade assignments on an intuitive basis. Classroom ethics demand that teachers consider more than their intuition in handing out rewards and punishments. The guidelines for this procedure are based on more than mere whimsy or circumstance. There is a great deal of evidence in support of the idea that as teachers make public their criteria for distributing rewards and punishments, anxiety levels are lower and children seem to learn more effectively. The question, then, is not so much whether one method of distributing grades is better than another, but rather, whether students understand the methods that the teacher is planning to use. This section will include a brief résumé of several alternatives a teacher may consider for assigning grades to students.

1. One way to grade is to mark according to fixed percentages selected in advance. For instance, 90 per cent and above is A, 80–89 per cent is B, and so on. The scores of other pupils are not considered as a basis for comparison. Each student competes against a fixed standard. This method is used quite often by teachers in schools and colleges; however, it has several serious drawbacks. First, the difference between an 89 and a 90 may be small compared to the standard error (precision) of the test, and yet vastly different grades will be assigned unfairly and invalidly to pupils receiving those scores. Secondly, there is nothing magical about 90 per cent alone. The question "90 per cent of what" directs us to examine the test itself. How difficult were the items and how strictly was the key applied to the students' answers? Almost any teacher in any situation can write a test that everyone will pass or that everyone

will fail. This means that the rigid standards of 90 per cent, etc. are not so rigid but merely reflect a flexibility in writing tests rather than in assigning grades.

2. A second means of grading which is just as arbitrary as that discussed above, but which gives the illusion of being quite sophisticated is the "normal" curve technique. This procedure assumes that the class reflects ability grouping similar to the distribution of intelligence in the general population. More specifically, the assumption asserts that there are few students in the class in the A and F categories; more students in each of the B and D categories; and most of the students fall in the C range. A teacher calculates the standard deviation[1] of the distribution of test scores and assigns grades on a basis similar to this:

A—Mean plus 1 1/2 standard deviation units

B—Mean plus 1/2 standard deviation units

C—Mean plus and minus 1/2 standard deviation units

D—Mean minus 1/2 standard deviation units

F—Mean minus 1 1/2 standard deviation units

This procedure almost always assumes someone is going to get A and someone is going to fail. The basis for assigning grades is one of comparing one student's achievement with the class record. This method would suggest that two students with identical achievement levels assigned to two different classes might end up with completely different grades. This would occur if one student were in a "bright" section while the other student were in a "slow" section. The latter student's score would look good in comparison to his student colleagues, whereas the first student's grade might suffer when compared to his fellow students.

3. Another method for assigning grades incorporates aspects of both of those previously mentioned. It consists of placing the raw scores of a test along a continuum. Teachers using this procedure make two decisions. First, where are there significant enough gaps between scores to draw lines distinguishing students who deserve one level of grade and those deserving another level? Second, once the lines have been drawn, which letter grade will be assigned each group recognized by the gap-scanning (see Table 1)? It is possible for a teacher to decide that while he

[1] See Paul B. Diederich, *Short-Cut Statistics for Teacher-Made Tests* (Princeton, N.J.: Educational Testing Service, 1960), pp. 19–20, for suggestions for calculating the standard deviation of a distribution.

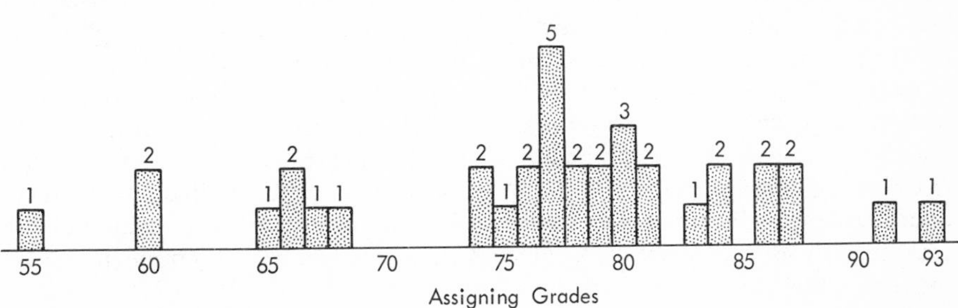

TABLE 1

recognizes three groups, they achieved so well he will label the groups A+, A and A−. On another test, he may feel that the performance was particularly weak, and he might assign only C, D, and F grades to the groups.

Nothing in this paragraph is meant to imply that this procedure is strictly objective. It is our contention that all methods are subjective—with the subjective element taking effect in various dimensions of the testing-grading process. Some subjectivity enters into the writing of the test in the first alternative mentioned, specifically, at the level of judging the quality of work the various groups represent. Teachers using this method must plan their tests in such a way that the middle person in the group gets approximately 50 per cent of the test correct. Only if this condition is met will the gaps between groups be wide enough to allow teachers to draw meaningful distinctions between groups. We are assuming that the purposes of tests of this sort are essentially for the assigning of grades.

4. An alternative to assigning letter or numerical grades is to indicate only whether or not a student has completed the course requirements. For example, a student will receive a certificate of accomplishment in a typing course when the student can type eighty words a minute, with a minimum of three errors. The student either masters the task, or does not. There is no provision for 78 per cent of a certificate.

Such an approach to grading is not readily accepted by administrators, teachers, or parents when it is applied to the academic, or "solid" courses such as mathematics, English, and science. To a parent who has planned and saved for years for his child's college experiences, the grade "pass" does not satisfy the parent's eagerness to have his child produce A's and B's, in order to compete for the best colleges. The task of convincing students that letter grades can be eliminated is also not without difficulty. Students who have been indoctrinated in elementary school that their major goal should be to work hard and get high marks will not be easily comforted by their first "pass" in U.S. History.

Despite the seeming inertia of public education to break away from the present grading system, many schools are tentatively trying courses without marks. Arrangements with colleges and universities can be made to admit students based on college board scores and personal recommendations, rather than on class rank and grade point average. In short, if the commitment to change is earnest enough, the way to effect a change can be identified and made operational.

The decision to grade for mastery is not a difficult one to make, providing it is permitted by school authorities. The difficulty comes in planning a system which is valid. The teacher will need to decide the tasks and learnings that a student must manifest, as a result of the instruction, in order for the teacher to say the student has satisfactorily completed the course. One way to accomplish this is to describe the tasks in behavioral terms, or as behavioral objectives. Thus stated, the behavior should be easily identified and duly recorded as the student exhibits competency in that objective. For example, suppose the teacher of Grade 6 mathematics has identified a series of four activities related to solving fraction problems by multiplication. The teacher has decided that in order for a student to be able to solve fraction problems, the student must be able to identify what fractions are; to name the different types of fractions; to be able to arrange fractions and construct a problem; and to be able to apply the rules of multiplication in their solution. The behavioral objective for the last might be stated as: "The child will *apply a rule* of multiplying numerators and denominators to obtain a correct product for 90 per cent of the problems when given sets of simple and mixed fractions." Similarly stated objectives would be given, in unambiguous terms, for the other activities to indicate who is to exhibit the behavior, what the person is to do, and how, or under what conditions the behavior is to be done. Collections of such tasks could be identified as a course. Once all the tasks are successfully completed, the student has mastered the course regardless of the time it takes. An uncomfortable implication of this system is that, if the student fails to learn, it may be because the teacher failed to teach, or at least failed to properly organize the instructional units necessary to help a student master the tasks.

Grading for mastery simplifies the teacher's chore of reporting progress, or giving a final mark. The end product could be a simple "acceptable" versus "not acceptable," or pass-fail, or "A" (meaning completed), versus "Incomplete" (meaning not completed). The last system of *A* or incomplete, is used by at least one University of Maryland professor in his graduate course, much to the chagrin of the campus registrar. If a student does not complete the established number of tasks by the end of the semester, the student receives a grade of "Incomplete," and takes the course again, without charge, and again, if necessary, until the tasks are completed, in which event his grade is changed to "A."

With the use of behavioral objectives, as stated above for mathematics, a simple checklist of behaviors for each student, using a two-category differential of "acceptable" versus "not acceptable" would suffice. The checklist might look something like Table 2.

TABLE 2

Name: Tommy Timely

Math 6

Task 2.3 Fractions		ACCEPTABLE	NOT ACCEPTABLE
	A) identify fractions	1 (1/7/70)	
	B) name types	1 (1/8/70)	
	C) construct problems	4 (1/20/70)	1,2,3
	D) apply rule and obtain products, 90%		1,2

The summary above indicates that Task 23 consists of four distinct parts. Tommy completed parts A and B on the first attempt. He had a little trouble with part C, but then he mastered it on the fourth attempt. Perhaps the teacher helped Tommy understand a concept, or interpret some piece of the instruction, or directed Tommy to a remedial activity in order to help him master the objective. Tommy is still to master part D.

A parent might find the above report of Tommy's progress, much more sensible and more easily interpreted than a report card mark of "C" or "78%."

In sum, no method is foolproof or perfectly objective. We hope that someday teachers will be able to lay aside the impossible task of labeling students' work with *A*'s or *B*'s while they continue to describe the quality of a student's work in grosser and perhaps more valid ways, e.g., pass or fail. Until that time, teachers need to know the assumptions underlying the grading system they are using and to be aware of the importance of making their system public to their students.

23. TEACHING BY CONTRACT AND INDEPENDENT STUDY METHODS: PROGRAMMING YOUR COURSE

WILLIAM D. ROMEY

Learning behavioral skills lends itself well to various forms of programmed instruction, although many existing programmed textbooks involve a highly structured group of questions stressing learning of vocabulary and factual information. These will not be treated here, for they are mainly an aid to memorization. Memorization of factual information should be a minor goal of any science course.

Well-planned programs with proper behavioral objectives enable a teacher to ascertain that no student leaves a particular unit of study until he has demonstrated a minimum level of competence. Teaching by program or contract can be done in many ways, ranging from an approximation of traditional group teaching to a completely independent study program. For variety, a course may be divided into modules, some of which involve programmed, independent study and others of which involve more conventional group teaching. As you begin to experiment with programmed study, choose small units of study and gradually work toward more complete programming.

One convenient way of programming a unit of study is to have your students sign learning *contracts.* In one kind of contract, students are given a list of tasks and informed that their grades for the particular unit of study depend directly on the number of tasks that they perform satisfactorily. The tasks may include laboratory exercises, problems, reading assignments, written papers, and quizzes. Rate each task on a pass-or-fail basis. If the students do not perform the task satisfactorily, they must do it over or revise their materials in some way before resubmitting them if they wish to get credit for that par-

William D. Romey, "Teaching by Contract and Independent Study Methods: Programming Your Course" in INQUIRY TECHNIQUES FOR TEACHING SCIENCE *(Englewood Cliffs, N.J.: Prentice-Hall, Inc., 1968), pp. 77–86. Reprinted by permission of Prentice-Hall, Inc., Englewood Cliffs, New Jersey.*

ticular section of the unit. Certain essential parts of the unit should be required in order for the students to pass. Other activities are made optional, and the number of these activities satisfactorily completed determines the level of the passing grade: A, B, C, or D. The students are not allowed to submit optional tasks until they have satisfactorily completed the required work.

Why is the word "contract" applied to these programs? At the beginning of the unit each student is given a complete list of the requirements, both required and optional, and is asked to sign a statement such as the following:

> I understand that in order to receive a minimum passing grade (D) for this unit of study, I must complete all of the tasks marked "required" on the above list. In order to receive a grade of C, B, or A, I must in addition complete the optional tasks specified above as required for those grades.
>
> Signed __________

Some teachers carry the contract a step further and require each student to contract for a specific grade by completing a sentence such as:

> The grade I wish to contract for is ____
>
> Signed __________

This statement can be used in one of two ways:

1. As a nonbinding contract. Here the contract merely informs you generally about the level of effort various students intend to put forth, and it helps you to know something about how each student rates himself.

2. As a binding contract in which the student receives an extra grade penalty if he fails to meet the grade requirements he signed for and in which he must do special extra work if he decides to try for a higher grade than the one for which he initially contracted.

Making your students contract for a specific grade has the advantage of forcing them to evaluate their own abilities and to learn how to estimate their capabilities in realistic terms, but if penalties are established for not meeting the terms of the contract, tension in the classroom is raised. If a student has underestimated his ability and has no way of renegotiating for a higher grade, he may lose interest in the subject and create problems. Therefore, it might be profitable for the student to allow him to renegotiate his contract halfway through the period of time allowed for completion of the unit. Once he has signed this final contract, he must either meet its terms or be penalized. This enables the student who thought he could do B work but has realized that he cannot reach this goal to complete the rest of the unit at the C level. It also permits a student who suddenly discovers that he loves the subject and is able to do well in it to receive without penalty of extra work the higher grade his performance merits.

An example of a binding contract used by Kilburn is on pp. 165–169.

Using a contract unit of the type reproduced in this example makes it possible to be sure that every passing student in the class has attained a certain minimum level of achievement in a given time period. It is also possible to keep the members of the class working on approximately the same topic for the same period of time. Thus, although different students may be working on different activities during laboratory periods and reading different materials in class and at home, it is still possible to schedule regular group discussions and arrange for students doing special projects to report their results to the rest of the class.

One important pitfall to avoid if possible is to put your students so much on a plane of independent study that they do not have a chance to interact with each other in group activities. Science is not a one-man affair, and students must learn to cooperate and exchange information as well as to work independently.

Another approach to programmed teaching is a system used by L. H. Parsons of Central Technical High School, Syracuse, New York. No actual contract is signed in this approach. Each student is provided at the beginning of each unit of study with a sheet of specific directions, and problems relating to the unit of study. Each student must complete all of the specified activities and problems and submit an appropriate written report on the unit. Upon satisfactory completion of the program and completion of a unit test taken by each student individually when he is ready for it, the student proceeds to the next study unit. No attempt is made to keep the whole class working together. The better students can proceed to the end of the course at a rapid pace and have time for certain optional work at the end of the school year. The slower students may lag behind a specified number of chapters. Grade in the course is based on the total amount of work completed satisfactorily.

A CONTRACT UNIT ON ROCKS AND MINERALS*

NAME ______________________________

The grade you will receive depends on the work you do!! Contract to work for a letter grade as listed below.

F—Required work incomplete
D—Complete only required work
C—Required work + 2 from I.
2 from II.
2 from III.

B—Required work + 4 from I.
4 from II.
6 from III.
A—Required work + 6 from I.
6 from II.
10 from III.

Place a check mark opposite the work you select. Keep an account on one copy of the contract and return the other with your work plan and contracted grade. Contract terms:

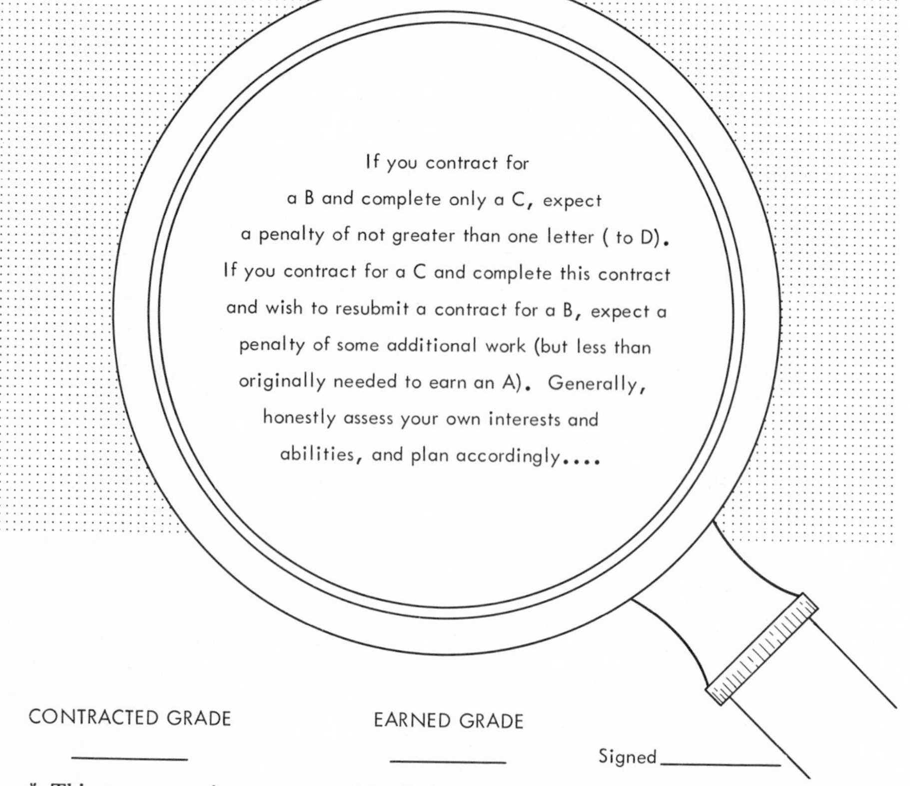

CONTRACTED GRADE ________ EARNED GRADE ________ Signed ____________

* This contract unit was prepared by Robert E. Kilburn, formerly of the Fayetteville-Manlius New York School district and presently a supervisor of science education in the Newton, Mass. school system. I wish to thank Mr. Kilburn for permission to reproduce this material.

Selections	Contracted	Completed	Selections	Contracted	Comp.	Selections	Contracted	Comp.
I Reading and Writing			II Rock and Mineral Identification Skills			III Activities		
Required			Required			Required		
A			A			A		
B			B			B		
C			C			C		
D			D			D		
E						E		
F						F		
						G		
						H		
						Any 12 { I		
						J		
						K		
						L		
						M		
						N		
						O		
						P		
						Q		
Optional			Optional			Optional		
A			A			A		
B			B			B		
C			C			C		
D			D			D		
E			E			E		
F			F			F		
G			G			G		
H			H			H		
I			I			I		
J			J			J		
K			K			K		
L			L			L		
M			M			M		
N			N			N		
			O			O		
			P			P		
			Q			Q		
						R		
						S		
						T		
						U		
						V		
						W		

CONTRACT UNIT ROCKS AND MINERALS

The following lists contain the course content for the next few weeks. The grade for this time will be determined by the amount of this work you successfully complete in the next four weeks.

I. Reading and writing

Required

A. Read N&S, 8–18; submit list briefly defining each italicized word: Due ________

B. Read T&K, 209–234, submit answers to review questions. Due ___

C. Read N&S, 20–40 major ideas, not ital. words, examined orally, due before D.

D. Read T&K, 242–268; submit answers to review questions. Due ___

E. Read N&S, p. 43–55; submit key-styled outline of all rocks mentioned in text. Due ______

F. Read one of the selections from the optional list. Due at end of the unit.

KEY

N&S: Namowitz and Stone, *Earth Science Text*

T&K: Thurber and Kilburn, *Exploring Earth Science*, Allyn and Bacon Inc., 1965

R&R: Read and report orally

OE: Oral Exam

Optional

A. "Interaction Between Light and Minerals," *Nat. Hist.*, 53–57, Oct. '65, R&R.

B. "Sediment. Origins of Rock Layering," *Nat. Hist.*, 50–55, Dec. '65, R&R.

C. "Time's Traces in Sediments," *Nat. Hist.*, 53–61, Feb. '63, R&R.

D. "Diamonds in Meteorites," *Sci. Am.*, p. 26, Oct. '65, R&R.

E. "Rocks and Minerals," in *The Crust of The Earth*, pp. 128–146, R&R.

F. "The Formation of Mineral Deposits," same as E, 146–154, R&R.

G. "Rockhounds Uncover Earth's Natural Beauty," *Nat. Geog.*, p. 631, Nov. '51, R&R.

H. Read one issue of "Rocks and Minerals" for one-hour report on its worth.

I. "Notes on the Clintonville Dikes, Onondaga County, NY," NYS Museum Pub. #286, p. 119. OE including locating local deposits on top sheet.

J. Skim "Gypsum Resources and Gypsum Industries of New York," reading all local references. OE including locating local deposits on top sheet.

K. Skim either NYS Museum Pub. #434, 343, or 14 or ________. Brief written summary.

Reading and writing (cont'd.)

Optional

L. Read and understand organization of U.S. Geol. Survey Bulletin 1072 F. Written summary.

M. "Minerals and Mineral Ores" in *The Earth* (Fenton). Written summary.

N. "The Great Treasure Hunt" in *The Earth* (Life). Written summary.

II. Rock and mineral identification skills

Required

A. Learn names of minerals in collection. Tested by identifying same mineral types. Passing score —90%

B. Learn names of Hardness Scale of Mohs and devise a method to remember it.

C. Learn names of rocks in collection. Test as in above.

D. Pass test in identifying microchips of minerals.

Optional

A. Prepare a display of unweathered surfaces of fifteen local rocks. Identify all you've studied.

B. Same as in A (above), with minerals.

C. Learn six additional important minerals. OE.

D. Learn five important additional ores. OE.

E. Learn five different varieties of quartz. OE.

F. Collect minerals from two sites listed in "Field Trip Guide to Onondaga County" (or other sites you know).

G. Make a display of cardboard models of different crystal shapes.

H. Perform chemical tests to identify several minerals (tests such as bead tests, charcoal block tests, flame tests).

I. T&K p. 235 #3

J. 236, #4

K. 237, #12

L. 238, #7

M. 269, #3

N. 271, #5

O. 271, #6

P. 271, #9

III. Activities (T and K)

Required (A + 12 others)

A. 211, include color, luster, hardness, streak, cleavage-fracture, and specific gravity of galena, hematite, gypsum.

B. 218–219[1]

C. 221

D. 222

E. 223

F. 225 (2 analyses)

G. 227[1], 227[2] (any one chemical)

H. 235, #2 (do heating at home)

I. 236, #5 (at home or school)

J. 243[1]

K. 244[2]

L. 246

M. 255

N. 258[2]

O. 270, #1

P. 271, #3 (locally important) or (NY State important)

Q. 237, #11

Optional

A. Compare the specific gravity of two rocks by three different methods.

B. Attend Syracuse Gem and Mineral Soc. meeting. Write report.

C. Attend Syracuse University Dept. of Geology outside lecture.

D. Determine weight and volume of eight different pieces of a mineral. Graph and explain.

E. Calculate % of weight lost when gypsum is heated. Calculate % of water in $CaSO_4 \cdot 2H_2O$. Propose and defend possible explanations for the difference in these two values.

F. Analyze six or more different rock samples from a cliff for % calcite.

G. 217[23]

H. 220[3]

I. 235, #3

J. 236, #4 prepare a collection

K. 237, #9

L. 237, #13 or 14

M. 238, #6

N. 239, #13

O. 247

P. 249 sketch observations

Q. 250

R. 266–7 (counts as two)

S. 269, #1

T. 269, #3

U. 269, #6 (5 different igneous or metamorphic rocks)

V. 270, #10

W. 271, #6

In an elementary college geology course that the author teaches at Syracuse University, he is presently experimenting with a contract of the nonbinding type. This contract is a full-semester contract involving about thirty required tasks, each graded on a pass-or-fail basis. Required tasks include regular weekly laboratory reports, regular outside problem sets, field trip reports, short essays, and short, single-skill quizzes (mineral identification, rock identification, map study, and so forth). Each of these tasks must be satisfactorily completed in order for a student to receive a minimum passing grade. When quizzes are retaken, the second quiz is not a repeat of the first quiz, but a new one. This discourages rote learning of answers to the first quiz and puts emphasis on the ability to apply skills to new situations.

In addition to the required tasks, an additional thirty optional tasks are designated, including optional readings, film viewings, attendance at approved lectures, participation in independent or extra field trips, and approved independent research projects (either original or library research). Satisfactory performance of optional tasks is evaluated in short oral interviews between individual students and course instructors. Students may propose their own optional readings and other tasks in keeping with their own interests. Some students try to spread their optional work over several topics. Others select one or two main areas of interest and do studies in depth. In order to qualify for a course grade of C students must in addition to completing all of the required tasks submit five optional tasks. A grade of B requires fifteen optional tasks, and an A requires twenty optional tasks. Further check on quality of performance is maintained by a mid-term and a final examination. No credit is attached to the mid-term examination, but in addition to completing the appropriate number of required and optional tasks a student must obtain an A or B on the final examination in order to receive an A or B in the course.

Advantages to this type of contract are:

1. The class as a whole can be kept working on the same general required topics, although the slower students may also be finishing work formerly judged unsatisfactory.
2. The better students are able to get appropriate credit for doing outside work in areas of special interest to them.
3. No student passes the course without achieving a certain minimum competence in certain critical skills.
4. Passing the course becomes a matter of hard work and application rather than of skill in taking examinations. Examination pressure is lower (except, of course, for the A and B students).

Elaborate independent study systems involving study in carrels equipped with audiovisual materials, laboratory equipment, programmed study material, and tape-recorded instructions are being introduced in some schools. Other institutions have begun experimenting with computer-monitored analysis and response techniques. Such systems will allow teachers to handle heterogeneously grouped classes in optimum fashion. But even when elaborate machinery and facilities are available, teachers must still provide opportunities for student—group interaction and student—teacher interaction. Good independent study programs also can be designed and put into operation without elaborate equipment. Contract systems provide a means of being sure that behavioral goals set up for your classes are achieved, even in heterogeneously grouped classes. Note, however, that you will usually have to set up the details of your own programs. You must be certain that you have developed adequate behavioral goals before you begin setting up a contract.

24. MARKS ON TERM PAPERS IN THE LIBERAL ARTS

ARNOLD M. ROTHSTEIN

It has been said that "... the ideal training for the ideal citizen [is a] good sound liberal education."[1] To provide ideal training requires, in the first place, liberal teachers. Unfortunately, according to one view, the education of teachers "is corrupted by a curriculum, a program of pedagogy which is a methodology of teaching."[2]

The implication here is that exposure to a liberal arts curriculum will have a broadening and liberating effect. This investigation attempted to explore how this effect is achieved.

A professor's assignments often reflect his conception of course purpose(s). Accordingly, markings by professors on term papers which *they* had assigned were examined, with a view to ascertaining the relationship between the assignments and the purposes of the liberal arts course.

Thirty-six undergraduate term papers from the humanities, natural

Arnold M. Rothstein, "Marks on Term Papers in the Liberal Arts," JOURNAL OF TEACHER EDUCATION, *XVI, No. 2 (June 1965), 249–50. Reprinted by permission of the publisher.*

[1] Center for the Study of Democratic Institutions, "The University—An Interview with A. Whitney Griswold, President of Yale University" (New York: Fund for the Republic, 1961), p. 21.

[2] *Ibid.*, p. 14.

sciences, and social sciences were read and carefully analyzed.[3] The students received eight A's, twenty-two B's, five C's, and one P (passing). If one considers B a good grade, at least 80 per cent of the papers were rated as good, while *no* paper was rated as poor. The professors' markings and comments were catalogued and tabulated. Fifty-three per cent of a total of 329 markings related to mechanics of writing: spelling, punctuation, grammar, and usage; 23 per cent consisted of value statements such as "Good," "Weak," "Tighten your organization," "Improve your style," "Be less superficial," "Reveal yourself more"; 13 per cent endorsed or questioned the assertions of the students; 5 per cent dealt with matters of form and style. Commentary tended to be profuse when the professor disagreed with the student or appeared to be justifying his assignment of a particular grade. Both markings and commentary appeared to be used merely as a record of achievement symbolized by the letter grade.

In assaying what further work could have been done on the papers, they were subjected to detailed analysis.[4] Altogether, 1,558 additional markings might have been made which would have called attention to thinking processes.

The papers were coded according to the following scheme.[5]

1. Attributive statements were identified—those which ascribed or imputed motivation or feeling to another.
2. Extreme statements were marked—superlatives, all, none, always, never.
3. Generalities were scored—people, we, they, Negroes, groups, nations.
4. Qualifying statements were checked—maybe, perhaps, might, probably.
5. If-then hypotheses were identified, e.g., "If I didn't see them, they weren't there."
6. *Or* statements were identified—"There are only two possibilities," the polarization of issues into two values.
7. Analogies were underscored—just as, like, the same as, you might as well say.

It is significant that the range of ratios of possible markings to actual markings was from 2:1 to 100:1, with a mean potential of nearly 5:1. Under the coding analysis for expressions relating to thinking processes, *no* paper had less than a total of seven markings. In contrast, in the tabulation of the markings of the professors (excluding the letter grade), twenty-one of the thirty-six papers contained less than a total of seven markings, and five of the twenty-one contained no markings at all.

The writer has employed the system of coding papers indicated herein with much success in several undergraduate courses. Parts of the system

3 The papers were written by thirty-six students and marked by thirty-six different professors. Twenty-five students were from a private liberal arts college in a metropolitan area and eleven were from a public liberal arts institution in the same area. Seventeen sophomores, eleven juniors, five freshmen, and three seniors produced seventeen papers for courses in the humanities, thirteen for courses in the social sciences, and six for courses in the natural sciences.

4 Each paper was read three times: once for general comprehension and twice for distinctive analysis, the cataloguing of the professors' markings, and the coding scheme used by the investigator.

5 Acknowledgment of indebtedness is made to Louis E. Raths, distinguished professor of education, Newark State College, who developed the scheme.

are gradually introduced until, over the period of a semester, students are able to react to the entire system. The writer has found it provides students with an opportunity to analyze what they say, to uncover their assumptions, and to draw inferences therefrom. They get a chance to reflect on and react to what they have written. From student reactions in general, an impression has been received that little attention has been given in previous training to the forms of thinking. To be sure, teachers claim that they teach students to think,[6] but one can only wonder *how*. For example, it would be instructive to know how the hortatory injunctions, "Improve your style" and "Reveal yourself more," actually help the student to think.

Should the mechanics of writing, form and style, the writer's assertions —what the professors looked for in the papers—not have been looked for? Without doubt, these matters deserve attention. The question is rather what else might have been looked for. More than 50 per cent of the investigator's markings identified extreme statements, found in all but one of the papers studied, and attributive statements, found in all but two. Here was potential for instruction.[7]

The implications of language for revealing the mental processes of students dare not be overlooked, and a means is here proposed whereby an assignment is not terminated, either for professor or student, merely because a grade has been recorded. Exhortations, such as "Improve your thinking," are relegated to the scrap heap; instead markings are used which lay the exercise open to further analysis and reflection to provide practice in using important mental processes.

Objections and criticisms may be anticipated. Admittedly, the investigation is limited in scope and method, but it can serve as a springboard for future exploration. Some may object that the thirty-six professors did not mark papers very well, that this may be *just* an indication of poor teaching. Another criticism might point to purpose: The investigator analyzed the papers in one way and the professors in another. It might also be argued that concern with mental processes as such provides the structure for an entire course, probably logic or composition. But should not *all* course have logic? At least one professor of logic believes it is precisely because schools do not emphasize thinking that we need courses in logic.[8] Moreover, compartmentalization is not a little to blame for the student's seeing spelling and punctuation as belonging within the confines of the appropriate course—"Spelling counts only in the spelling course." The perversity of student nature being what it is, could one hope for transfer of grandiose proportions if logic courses were made mandatory? Is it not likely that student reaction would be—"Thinking counts only in the thinking course?"

The criticism of the liberal arts

[6] Thinking involves several mental processes.

[7] Perhaps we all need training in differentiating between what is observational and what is inferential; confusion of the ascriptive and the descriptive is often the hallmark of the undisciplined. Upon momentary reflection, the symbiotic nature of certain ways of speaking (thinking) and prejudice becomes evident.

[8] Cynthia Schuster, "Can We Teach the High School Student to Think?" *Educational Research Bulletin* No. 37 (April 1958).

champion contains an implied objection to the investigation. Referring to the need for gifted teachers, he states: ". . . the solution to the problem of an adequate number of properly trained teachers in the universities lies first in the change of the curriculum for the training of high school teachers."[9] The question is, How is the curriculum to be changed?

The common conception of curriculum views it as organization of content: the means by which the content is disseminated is considered subsidiary. And so, traditionally, curricular revision has been seen as an augmenting, deleting, or shifting of the content. A curriculum is made liberal by widening the number and scope of course offerings; rarely is change in method conceived of as a means of liberalizing.

As one examines the way in which the term papers were marked by the professors, one can see that their teaching practices reflect more of a parochializing effect than an encouragement of thoughtfulness. On the other hand, the analysis undertaken by the investigator, requiring a shift not in content but in method, has a liberalizing effect, with autonomy as a distinct goal.

The investigation tends to reaffirm what has long been known. It is not the specific course nor the specific content within a course that is crucial. What is all-important is the quality of the work pursued.[10] Teaching practices determine to a significant degree whether effects shall be parochial or liberal. There may be faith that a liberal arts course broadens, releases, and emancipates, but some evidence should be forthcoming that the liberalizing *effect* is distinct from method, that it depends upon *arts* which are liberal and not upon a teacher who is liberal.

9 Center for the Study of Democratic Institutions, *op. cit.*, p. 15.

10 Lamar Johnson, "Criteria for Defining New Type Courses," *School and Society*, XLII (September 14, 1935); Lawrence A. Lowell, "College Studies and Professional Training," *Educational Review*, XLII (October 1911). President Lowell pointed out that it made little difference what specific courses were taken in preparation for advanced study, since transfer of the knowledge was questionable, but that it did matter whether attention was paid to mental processes, the skills of which could be transferred widely.

ACTIVITIES

1. Categorize each of the following according to Bloom's *Taxonomy*. (Suggested answers follow.) Also, try out the category systems suggested by the Fox article included in this section.

a. List five reasons why the assembly-line method of manufacture is so widely used by American industry.

b. The "initiative," "referendum," and "recall" were incorporated into state constitutions primarily during the:
(a) New Deal
(b) Progressive era
(c) Civil War
(d) Jacksonian era

c. Briefly outline relations between America and Mexico over Texas to 1836.

d. What are the implications in the case of the Charles River Bridge vs. Warren Bridge (1837)?

e. You turned four pieces of work 8″ between centers, and all pieces showed a taper on the end nearest the tailstock. In order to correct this inaccuracy (eliminate the taper) you should adjust the taper attachment:
(a) away from you
(b) toward you
(c) to your left
(d) to your right

f. What were the proslavery arguments? Were they realistic?
(a) historical justification
(b) scriptural justification
(c) benefits whites and Negroes alike
(d) economic advantages of the institution
(e) necessary to the Southern way of life

g. Evaluate the qualities of agar as a culture medium for growing bacteria.

h. What disadvantages could you see in using live animals as "cultivating media" for growing bacteria?

i. Would these dsiadvantages outweigh the advantages? Why?

j. Why can bacteria be used in industry?

k. In 1795 the Conspiracy of Equals led by one Grachus Babeuf failed badly and would earn little more than a mention in a history of the Revolution except that, in retrospect, Babeuf appears as the first modern exponent of what system? Can you see this system in operation today?

l. In your opinion what were the six most important political and social features brought about by the French Revolution?

m. The fight for American independence has been called a revolution, an international war, and a civil war. Which one of these three interpretations do you agree with, and why? I will accept any answer if you can give valid reasons for your choice.

n. Do you feel that the treatment received by the Loyalist from the Colonist was fair or unfair? State your reasons. I will accept any answer if it is well thought out and substantiated.

o. What suggestion would you make to help spur the feudal economy most?

p. Which of the following can be concluded from Jefferson's "principles of government?"

(a) Honest friendship with all nations rules out the necessity of entangling alliances.
(b) State governments should have the supreme power in dealing with foreign countries.
(c) All men are equal in the eyes of the law of the land.
(d) None of the above.

q. Match the following:

Peaceable Coercion	Embargo Act
Continental System	Charles Pinckney
Election of 1800	Louisiana Purchase
Election of 1804	Thomas Pinckney
Treaty of San Ildefonso	Napoleon

r. If ex-President DeGaulle had suddenly begun to practice impressment of American seamen, what would America's course of action have been? Briefly explain, giving reasons for your conclusion.

s. In your own words, explain how you would construct a "soundproof" room. Evaluate the problem carefully and give the types of materials used and the reasons for their use.

t. What alternative courses of action would you seriously consider and which one would you choose concerning the Negro problem. This includes such issues as Negro troops, slaves in rebel states, slaves in loyal states, etc.

u. You are asked to formulate a bill in which the voting age is reduced to 18. Explain how you would go about getting advocates for your bill in both a state and a national situation.

v. Describe briefly women's rights and how they have increased since 1789. Do you think women should have equal rights with men? Explain.

w. You are in the South Atlantic and you are in a warm current. Are you near South America or Africa?

x. You read in a book that penguins have been found on some islands parallel to Central America. What conclusion could you draw concerning ocean currents?

y. Write two or three sentences to tell what you have found most interesting about your study of ocean currents.

Suggested Answers for Activity 1

a. 1.00
b. 1.00
c. 1.00
d. 2.00
e. 3.00 or 4.00
f. 1.00 and 6.00
g. 6.00
h. 4.00
i. 6.00
j. 2.00
k 1.00 and 5.00
l. 2.00
m. 2.00
n. 6.00
o. 4.00
p. 2.00
q. 1.00
r. 4.00
s. 3.00
t. 5.00
u. 5.00
v. 2.00 and 5.00
w. 3.00 or 4.00
x. 3.00 or 4.00
y. ? May be 6.00 or in Affective Domain

Note: These "solutions" are not professed to be irrevocably correct. In some cases the level of the question will depend on what is assumed to be the intended thinking task, and not what has actually occurred in answering the questions. Readers may justify other levels than those shown here.

2. A class of 32 students was given an objective mastery test of ten multiple choice questions with five alternatives each. The following is the analysis of correct answers for each test item. What conclusions do the data suggest for each item?

(Test Item)

	1	2	3	4	5	6	7	8	9	10
Correct Answer in Upper 16	16	16	10	2	12	0	13	4	10	8
Correct Answer in Lower 16	16	12	5	12	10	0	3	6	4	4

Suggested Answers for Activity 2

Students may recognize that test items, 1, 2, and 5 are too easy for discriminating between high and low ability students. Numbers 3, 7, 9, and 10 look acceptable. Numbers 4, 6, and 8 are questionable. Number 4 may have been miskeyed; number 6 may be too difficult; and number 8 may be ambiguous or miskeyed. Based on a 10 per cent minimum high-low difference between students in the top half and those in the bottom half, then, 2, 3, 7, 9, and 10 are acceptable for degree of discrimination. Number 5 is questionable and 4, 6, and 8 are suspect.

3. The following are analyses of three of the test items indicated above. Correct key answer is marked with asterisk (*). What conclusions do the data suggest for each item?

Item 8

	1*	2	3	4	5
Upper 16	4	1	1	8	2
Lower 16	6	0	3	3	4

Item 9

	1	2	3	4	5*
Upper 16	0	3	2	1	10
Lower 16	1	7	4	0	4

Item 10

	1	2*	3	4	5
Upper 16	0	8	1	6	1
Lower 16	3	4	2	2	5

Suggested Answers for Activity 3

In activity 5, analysis of item 8 indicates a suspected miskeying of choice 1, when choice 4 may have been the correct answer. This is indicated since so many good students selected choice 4. The other choices for this question are fair distractors.

Item 9 analysis shows the question is acceptable for discrimination and difficulty. Choices 1 and 4 were not powerful distractors. Choices 2 and 3 were adequate distractors.

Item 10 analysis looks satisfactory except that choice 4 seems too powerful a distractor. Perhaps the question and answers are ambiguous. The other choices were fair distractors.

4. The following scores represent the number correct out of 100 items on midsemester tests in various courses. What decisions would you make concerning the assignment of letter grades?

Course A	Course B	Course C	Course D
98	93	75	55
97	89	75	54
97	88	75	53
96	88	75	53
95	88	75	50
95	87	74	50
94	81	74	50
93	81	74	50
92	81	74	50
88	80	74	49
84	80	74	49
81	80	73	49
77	79	73	48
75	79	73	47
74	79	73	47
68	79	70	46
68	75	70	46
68	75	70	46
67	75	70	46
67	75	69	46
65	74	65	45
64	73	65	45
59	73	65	45
59	73	64	45
58	73	63	45
57	68	62	
57	67	62	
50	67	49	
40	66		
	64		
	64		

5. Check the face validity of several classroom tests. How well do the tests conform to the goals of the course?

6. Collect papers handed back by professors in various courses. Do the professors' comments on these papers support or refute Rothstein's thesis articulated in his article in this chapter?

7. Write several test questions for each of the categories in Bloom's Taxonomy.

8. Collect tests administered by teachers and professors. Classify the questions according to the Taxonomy.

9. Examine several standardized tests in your subject area. For what purposes were the tests designed? Do the items seem to contribute to the purposes?

10. The scope of this text is necessarily limited in the measurement area. Find several sources deal with measurement and testing and compare their definitions of validity, reliability, objectivity, and practicality. Apply these definitions to the tests examined above.

11. Devise another scheme for classifying test items other than the ones mentioned in this chapter. Try it on the sheet of practice questions.

12. Do you find it easier to select the level and write the test question or to assign levels to questions already written? Explain your choice.

13. Look at the end-of-chapter questions in textbooks popular for the course you will teach. What levels are they? What might the results reflect about the text content?

14. Could a system of classification such as Bloom's be useful in evaluating textbooks? How could this aid in planning?

15. Can you cite examples of teaching in which the test questions may not reflect the goals of the course?

16. Consider the following dialogue between two teachers.

Smith: "In my English classes an 'A' is 90 per cent and above. I teach a tough course."

Jones: "My standards are a little higher. I have college prep kids and it takes 95 per cent or above to get an 'A.' "

What are your comments on these assertions? Do you agree or disagree that Jones is a "tougher" grader than Smith? Does Jones have higher standards than Smith? What suggestions could you offer to help these teachers clarify their statements?

17. Working in pairs, write an essay question and administer it to a group of students. (The question might deal with the content of the course in which you are currently registered and it might be administered to a small group of students in your own class.) With your partner develop criteria for grading the essays. Apply the criteria to the essays independently. Compare your grades with those assigned by your partner. Suggest ways the criteria or the question might be improved.

18. For a unit or lesson that you might teach, develop a contract that you would present to students following the ideas presented by Romey.

19. Assume that you are using the "grading for mastery" technique described by Pancella. For a unit or lesson that you might teach, identify those objectives upon which you would set "mastery" criteria. Defend your choices.

TEACHING METHOD

CHAPTER FIVE

A teacher once began a lesson by asking, "What should we talk about today?" as he leaned on a huge lump of coal he had placed on his desk. Needless to say, the students' questions were directed toward the lump of coal and coincidently to the teacher's lesson plan on carbon. This is an example of a gimmick that teachers discover for themselves, steal from colleagues, or share in professional meetings. "Schemes" such as these help motivate students, assist teachers in making their teaching more individual, and clearly are a part of every successful teacher's repertoire. However, it is impossible to particularize successful stratagems for young teachers to use. They are either so specific to a definite topic or so reflective of the individual's personality that they defy cataloging.

As an alternative to describing gimmicks such as the one identified above, this section presents ideas on a more general level concerning teaching methods that teachers may consider. The final selection structures several of these ideas and others found in the educational literature, in paradigms that encourage one to compare and contrast the various elements of each approach.

No value judgements are made here about which method of teaching is good or bad. The selection of a particular model must depend on factors which vary from time to time and from place to place: characteristics of curricula, objectives, children, facilities, etc. We have assumed that the teacher who is capable of using more than one teaching strategy is in a better position to work successfully with children than is the teacher limited by commitment or ability to only one approach.

25. METHOD AND TECHNIQUE IN TEACHING

EARL S. JOHNSON

Between the "immanent future" and the "immanent past" stands the "insistent present." "The present contains all there is. It is holy ground; for it is the past, and it is the future."[1] The question to be faced is, what to do *now*? Teachers have to understand what it means to teach. To this co-experience, for it is always teaching-learning, there are four faces: what to teach? why teach it? whom do we teach? and how? The quick answers to these questions are: reliable and useful knowledge, a philosophy of life, all God's children, and method and technique.

But quick answers are not good enough. Teachers have suffered too long from quick answers. They need to know with the utmost clarity, insight, and precision what the teaching-learning act is and what happens in and because of it.

It is necessary to start with a definition. The teaching-learning act in the social studies is a *transaction* between reliable and useful knowledge and immature human beings who are in the process of becoming better and wiser selves; this transaction is mediated by the process of *psychologizing* through which the subject matter of the social sciences and the humanities is restated into experience. Whatever else it be, this is certainly not a quick answer. But it is the one about which teachers of the social studies must be clear, insightful, and precise. It may be

Earl S. Johnson, "A View of the Future of the Social Studies," in New Viewpoints in the Social Sciences, *ed. Roy A. Price (Washington, D.C.: National Council for the Social Studies, 28th Yearbook, 1958), pp. 225–32. Reprinted by permission of the author and the publisher.*

[1] These are Whitehead's words to which may be added: "The communion of saints is a great and inspiring assemblage, but it has only one possible hall of meeting, and that is the present." *The Aims of Education and Other Essays* (New York: New American Library of World Literature, Inc.), pp. 14–15.

found in John Dewey's *The Child and the Curriculum.*[2]

Here, Dewey's "the child" and "the curriculum" will be replaced by "the need for knowledge" and "reliable and useful knowledge." Between these two polar terms the shuttle of the process of psychologizing weaves an education. It is this dialectic which will be dealt with. The polar terms and their subterms may be juxtaposed as follows.[3]

The Need for Knowledge

1. "an immature, underdeveloped" human being
2. "a somewhat narrow world of personal contacts"—"a world of persons with their personal interests"
3. "affection and sympathy"
4. the "little span of personal memory and tradition"
5. a "familiar physical environment"
6. "things held together by the unity of the personal and social interests which carry life along"
7. "the child's own world . . . the unity and completeness of his own life"
8. "the vital ties of affection, the connecting bonds of activity"

Reliable and Useful Knowledge

1. "certain aims, meanings, values incarnate in the matured experience of the adult"
2. "a realm of facts and laws"—"material stretching back indefinitely in time, and extending outwardly indefinitely in space"
3. "truth, in the sense of conformity to external fact"
4. "the long centuries of the history of all peoples"
5. "the wide world—yes, even to the bounds of the solar system"
6. "facts torn away from their original place in experience and arranged with reference to some general principle"
7. "various studies [which] divide and fractionize the world for him"
8. "logically ordered facts . . . to be interpreted in relation to [a] principle"

What a distance apart these poles and their subterms are. The task of teaching is, as has been suggested, to effect a transaction between them. This is the process of psychologizing, the process of restating subject matter into human experience. But it is a joint and mutual process, a two-way street on which teacher and taught meet. This is the "feed" and "feedback" process as it relates to pedagogy rather than to technology. But this is a genuine "feed" and "feedback," not rote teaching or rote learning, not teacher citing and student re-citing but a joint adventure in ideas and ideals. How, from such a conception, anyone could derive the cliché, "teach the child and not the subject matter," escapes the wildest and most irresponsible imagination.[4]

But this process goes on between unequals. They are a "superior" teacher and an "inferior" student. What these words mean is implicit in the subterms given. The teacher's obligation is to reduce these inequalities or disparities or, in so far as possible, abolish them. This obliga-

2 This essay, along with *The School and Society*, may now be had in the Phoenix Books paperback series of the University of Chicago Press.

3 The subterms are taken, verbatim, from John Dewey, *The Child and the Curriculum* (Chicago: University of Chicago Press, 1902), pp. 5–6.

4 This cliché states the view of "either-or." The facts demand the view of "both-and." For this see Dewey, *op. cit.*, pp. 9–11.

tion falls upon the teacher as the person in the transaction who is "able to see the end in the beginning." Dewey observes that "to see the outcome is to know in what direction the [student's] present experience is moving, provided it move normally and soundly." Here is where present and future are joined, for "the faraway point, which is of no significance to us simply as far away, becomes of huge importance the moment we take it as defining a present direction of movement. Taken in this way it is no remote and distant result to be achieved, but a guiding method in dealing with the present.[5]

The four faces of teaching-learning again claim attention. The order in which they were stated is meant as no fixed order—from most to least important. Any attempt to arrive at a fixed and hierarchical order would be preliminary to impotence; hence, they are treated in the order which is *convenient* rather than "right," that is, according to some "first principles" which the writer does not know.

First, what to teach? However much it is conditioned by why, for whom, and how, and each of these in turn conditioned by every other, there is something called reliable and useful knowledge. This the teacher ought to know. If this can, in the first instance, be acquired in terms of its teachability as well as in terms of its reliability and usefulness, well and good. But there is much doubt that it can be, at least *ab initio*. It should be voted against whenever it appears to be serving the principle that the education of teachers of the social studies should be merely task-oriented. Such a principle is too *ad hoc*, too practical, and too restricted. This is not to say that teachers need less education in the practice of their art. It is, rather, to emphasize the prior need for profound substantive knowledge and skill in analysis, so that the teacher has a firm place to stand in the social sciences and the humanities. If these fields are taught by masters of their art, so much the better. But there is need for insistence upon the prerequisite that substantive knowledge and analytical skill be attained in a program whose focus and purpose are with the theory and practice of loving and thinking about the Great Oughts of democratic humanism, not in the "training" of teachers. If it contributes to their *education*, it will contribute to their preparation *for* teaching. This philosophy is based on the motto, *Primum vir esto*—First, let him be a man. This demands a general education, about which more will be forthcoming.

So much and all too briefly about what is taught. Next, why teach it? The answer, which will have to be too quick to suit the demands of the question, is this: because it is necessary for the student's growth in goodness and wisdom in a society which is dedicated to the philosophy of democratic humanism. But what and why are interdependent as means and ends. H. G. Wells tells of the conditions and means which will help understand better the why of teaching.

> I want simply this world better taught. . . . I will not suppose that there is any greater knowledge of things than men actually possess today, but instead of its being confusedly stored in many minds and books and many languages, it has

[5] *Ibid.*, p. 13.

> all been sorted and set out plainly so that it can be easily used. . . . When I ask you to suppose a world instructed and educated in the place of this old traditional world of unguided passion . . . a world taught by men instead of a world neglected by hirelings, I do not ask you to imagine any miraculous change in human nature. I ask you only to suppose that each mind has the utmost enlightenment of which it is capable instead of its being darkened and overcast. Everyone is to have the best chance of being his best self. Everyone is to be living in the light of the acutest self-examination and the clearest mutual self-criticism.[6]

Next, for whom? Again, the answer must, perforce, be too quick. The boys and girls from both sides of the tracks; those whose fathers support the family by the use of their hands and those who support it by the use of their heads; the sons and daughters of those who borrow and those who lend; those who come from life circumstances with little or no margins of moral or material security and those who, for whatever reason, have an abundance of both; those with only a blurred picture of their careers and those whose picture is clear; those who view the school as something only to be endured until they can "get a job" and those who genuinely enjoy and respect it; those who have a distaste for, or at best an attitude of sufferance toward the teacher and those who respect the person and the role of the teacher; those who are "dull" and those who are "bright"; and those who are "hand-minded" and those who are "head-minded." All and each are to get the education which their talents and capabilities warrant which is not the *same* education, except that it be one which permits both appreciation and understanding of the values of a human life as each can love and know them.

And now, to the *how* of it. In this face, to a degree not found in any other single one, all the faces are reflected. It traces to and depends on the *what* from which it gets the substance that is to be psychologized—restated into experience. Thus it traces to and depends on the *for whom*, the many kinds of human beings whose experience the substance is to affect. It also traces to and depends on the spirit and philosophy of democratic humanism, that which must pervade the climate in which teaching-learning goes on and from which it gets it dedication and its goals.

It is desirable now to trace the *how* of teaching-learning along the axis of *what* and *for whom*. In order to do this, it is necessary to explore the meaning of the terms, *method* and *technique*. One does not need to accept them as terms; only to follow the argument through which this author undertakes to show that each has a unique meaning, and how they become integrated in the process of psychologizing. In effect, the terms are *accidents*, but the processes which they symbolize are *essences*.

By the term *method* is meant that phase of the education of the teacher, as *intellectual*, by which substantive knowledge, analytical skill, and insight are acquired. That it combines both science and art is not only admitted but affirmed. Proof of this is given by Professor Robert Redfield in his paper, "The Art of Social Science," in which he recognizes "the

6 H. G. Wells, *The Undying Fire* (New York: The Macmillan Company, 1919), pp. 182, 184.

relationship of social science to humanistic endeavors and include[s] in the preparation of social scientists, as such, a humanistic education.[7]

The term *technique* here refers to that phase of the education of the teacher, as *teacher*, by which the science and art of instruction is acquired and continually improved in practice. It is the teacher's tool as "psychologizer." Note the term, "psychologizer" not *psychologist*. That the former requires knowledge of psychology is admitted, but that it also requires knowledge in the other social sciences and in the humanities is mandated. William James wrote that, "To know psychology . . . is absolutely no guarantee that we shall be good teachers."[8] "Psychology," he says, "is a science, and teaching is an art; and sciences never generate arts directly out of themselves. An intermediary inventive mind must make the application, by using its originality.[9] The application of what? The application of substantive knowledge, analytical skill and insight into human experience as the social sciences and the humanities deal with it. All the subterms under the poles of *Useful and Reliable Knowledge* and *The Need for Knowledge* are now brought into interaction. The transaction between them is now in process. In this process "for whom" becomes "with whom"—teacher and taught engaged in the mutual and reciprocal experience of teaching-learning.

What is processed in this process? A character? Yes, but in the very long run, for learning to be the architect of a character is the task of life, not only the assignment of school. Is the moral-intellectual independence of the student from the teacher also processed? It is, for it is one of the great ends of schooling and, in the measure in which it is achieved, the inequality between teacher and student is reduced and, we hope, ultimately abolished.

What else? In the words of John Dewey:

> Events turn into objects, things with a meaning. They may be referred to when they do not exist, and thus be operative among things distant in space and time, through vicarious presence in a new medium.[10]

This is the process by which percepts are put into families and become concepts—the acid test of education wherever and under whatever auspices it goes on. This is the process in which the transfer of learning goes on, through which useful and reliable knowledge is transmuted into ideas, attitudes, ideals, and patterns of action. This is the process by which issues are settled, anxieties relieved, desires subjected to critical and disciplined examination, and curiosities satisfied. This is the process by which the Word becomes flesh, all in the context of the rhythm of "romance, precision, and generalization."

Thus it is that "teaching has to

[7] Robert Redfield, "The Art of Social Science," *The American Journal of Sociology*, LIV, No. 3 (November 1948), 181–90.

[8] William James, *Talks to Teachers on Psychology: And to Students on Some of Life's Ideals* (New York: Holt, Rinehart & Winston, Inc., 1914), p. 9.

[9] *Ibid.*, p. 7. He continues: "The science of logic never made a man reason rightly, and the science of ethics (if there be such a thing) never made a man behave rightly. . . . A science only lays down lines within which the rules of art fall, laws which the follower of the art must not transgress. . . ." *Ibid.*, p. 8.

[10] Dewey, *Experience and Nature, op. cit.*, p. 166.

depend on learning for its technique."[11] This is the learning of the *learned* as well as of the *learner*, of both the teacher and the taught. Thus, method and technique are joined until one can hardly tell which is which.[12]

But if they become almost indistinguishable why bother to separate them and treat them as if they were things apart? Because we ought to know what is joined if we would fashion and control the joining. Furthermore, technique (wrongly conceived) is, far too often, held to be enough. This is implied in the cliché "teach 'em what they know" which presumes that the teacher does not need to know other than or more than what "they" know. If this is all the teacher needs to know it isn't much, if anything, beyond commonsense knowledge. If so, Heaven help the students! There is, however, just enough truth in this cliché to make it dangerous. If it means that the teacher ought to *begin* with what "they" know it makes sense. But if it there, it makes nonsense. What "they means that the teacher ought to *stop* know" they often don't know as to its factuality but more importantly as to its meaning.

Technique must not be used as a lame and inadequate substitute for method, as these terms have been defined previously. Nor can it, now defined in its lowest terms, be permitted to be only devices and tricks of procedure with which the "trained" but still uneducated teacher tries to eke out inadequate knowledge.[13]

Criticism of those who hold that technique is enough, good or bad in quality, should be complemented by criticism, equally forthright, of those who hold that method is enough. There is nothing "just as good as" either technique *or* method. Teachers must have both.

11 See Whitehead, *op. cit.*, Chap. III.

12 Whitehead's observations on this process are: "You cannot put into life any schedule of general education unless you succeed in exhibiting its relation to some essential characteristic of all intellectual or emotional perception.... The process of exhibiting the application of knowledge must, for its success, essentially depend on the character of the pupils and the genius of the teacher." *Ibid.*, pp. 20, 21.

13 See Fred Clarke, *Foundations of History-Teaching* (London: Oxford University Press, 1929), p. 25. To commit this error is tantamount to one's redoubling his efforts when he has forgotten his aims or never had the knowledge which would give them to him. To commit the error of "only *method*" is equivalent to believing that students are intellectually superior to their teachers.

26. THE ACT OF DISCOVERY

JEROME S. BRUNER

Maimonides, in his *Guide for the Perplexed*,[1] speaks of four forms of perfection that men might seek. The first and lowest form is perfection in the acquisition of worldly goods. The great philosopher dismisses such perfection on the ground that the possessions one acquires bear no meaningful relation to the possessor: "A great king may one morning find that there is no difference between him and the lowest person." A second perfection is of the body, its conformation and skills. Its failing is that it does not reflect on what is uniquely human about man: "he could [in any case] not be as strong as a mule." Moral perfection is the third, "the highest degree of excellency in man's character." Of this perfection Maimonides says: "Imagine a person being alone, and having no connection whatever with any other person; all his good moral principles are at rest, they are not required and give man no perfection whatever. These principles are only necessary and useful when man comes in contact with others." "The fourth kind of perfection is the true perfection of man; the possession of the highest intellectual faculties. . . ." In justification of his assertion, this extraordinary Spanish-Judaic philosopher urges: "Examine the first three kinds of perfection; you will find that if you possess them, they are not your property, but the property of others. . . . But the last kind of perfection is exclusively yours; no one else owns any part of it."

It is a conjecture much like that of Maimonides that leads me to examine the act of discovery in man's intellectual life. For if man's intellectual excellence is the most his own among his perfections, it is also the case that the most uniquely personal

Jerome S. Bruner, "The Act of Discovery," Harvard Educational Review, *XXXI, No. 1 (Winter 1961), 21–32. Reprinted by permission of the author and the publisher.*

[1] Maimonides, *Guide for the Perplexed* (New York: Dover Publications, Inc., 1956).

of all that he knows is that which he has discovered for himself. What difference does it make, then, that we encourage discovery in the learning of the young? Does it, as Maimonides would say, create a special and unique relation between knowledge possessed and the possessor? And what may such a unique relation do for a man —or for a child, if you will, for our concern is with the education of the young?

The immediate occasion for my concern with discovery—and I do not restrict discovery to the act of finding out something that before was unknown to mankind, but rather include all forms of obtaining knowledge for oneself by the use of one's own mind—the immediate occasion is the work of the various new curriculum projects that have grown up in America during the last six or seven years. For whether one speaks to mathematicians or physicists or historians, one encounters repeatedly an expression of faith in the powerful effects that come from permitting the student to put things together for himself, to be his own discoverer.

First, let it be clear what the act of discovery entails. It is rarely, on the frontier of knowledge or elsewhere, that new facts are "discovered" in the sense of being encountered as Newton suggested in the form of islands of truth in an uncharted sea of ignorance. Or if they appear to be discovered in this way, it is almost always thanks to some happy hypotheses about where to navigate. Discovery, like surprise, favors the well prepared mind. In playing bridge, one is surprised by a hand with no honors in it at all and also by hands that are all in one suit. Yet all hands in bridge are equiprobable: one must know to be surprised. So too in discovery. The history of science is studded with examples of men "finding out" something and not knowing it. I shall operate on the assumption that discovery, whether by a schoolboy going it on his own or by a scientist cultivating the growing edge of his field, is in its essence a matter of rearranging or transforming evidence in such a way that one is enabled to go beyond the evidence so reassembled to additional new insights. It may well be that an additional fact or shred of evidence makes this larger transformation of evidence possible. But it is often not even dependent on new information.

It goes without saying that, left to himself, the child will go about discovering things for himself within limits. It also goes without saying that there are certain forms of child rearing, certain home atmospheres that lead some children to be their own discoverers more than other children. These are both topics of great interest, but I shall not be discussing them. Rather, I should like to confine myself to the consideration of discovery and "finding-out-for-oneself" within an educational setting—specifically the school. Our aim as teachers is to give our student as firm a grasp of a subject as we can, and to make him as autonomous and self-propelled a thinker as we can—one who will go along on his own after formal schooling has ended. I shall return in the end to the question of the kind of classroom and the style of teaching that encourage an attitude of wanting to discover. For purposes of orienting the discussion, however, I would like to make an overly simplified distinction between teaching that takes place in the *expository mode* and teaching that utilizes the *hypothetical mode*. In the former, the decisions concerning the mode and pace and style of exposition are principally determined by the teacher as expositor; the student is the listener. If I can put the matter in terms of structural linguistics, the speaker has a quite different set of decisions to make than the listener: the former has a wide choice of alternatives for structuring, he is anticipating paragraph content while the listener is still intent on the words, he is manipulating the content of the material by various transformations, while the listener is quite unaware of these internal manipulations. In the hypothetical mode, the teacher and the student are in a more cooperative position with respect to what in linguistics would be called "speaker's decisions." The student is not a bench-bound listener, but is taking a part in the formulation and at times may play the principal role in it. He will be aware of alternatives and may even have an "as if" attitude toward these, and as he receives information he may evaluate it as it comes. One cannot describe the process in either mode with great precision as to detail, but I think the foregoing may serve to illustrate what is meant.

Consider now what benefit might be derived from the experience of learning through discoveries that one makes for oneself. I should like to discuss these under four headings: (1) The increase in intellectual potency, (2) the shift from extrinsic to intrinsic rewards, (3) learning the heuristics of discovering, and (4) the aid of memory processing.

1. *Intellectual Potency*

If you will permit me, I would like to consider the difference between subjects in a highly constrained psychological experiment involving a two-choice apparatus. In order to win chips, they must depress a key either on the right or the left side of the machine. A pattern of payoff is designed such that, say, they will be paid off on the right side 70 per cent of the time, on the left 30 per cent, although this detail is not important. What is important is that the payoff sequence is arranged at random, and there is no pattern. I should like to contrast the behavior of subjects who think that there is some pattern to be found in the sequence—who think that regularities are discoverable—in contrast to subjects who think that things are happening quite by *chance.* The former group adopts what is called an "event-matching" strategy in which the number of responses given to each side is roughly equal to the proportion of times it pays off: in the present case R70:L30. The group that believes there is no pattern very soon reverts to a much more primitive strategy wherein *all* responses are allocated to the side that has the greater payoff. A little arithmetic will show you that the lazy all-and-none strategy pays off more if indeed the environment is random: namely, they win 70 per cent of the time. The event-matching subjects win about 70 per cent on the 70 per cent payoff side (or 49 per cent of the time there) and 30 per cent of the time on the side that pays off 30 per cent of the time (another 9 per cent for a total take-home wage of 58 per cent in return for their labors of decision). But the world is not always or not even frequently random, and if one analyzes carefully what the event-matchers are doing, it turns out that they are trying out hypotheses one after the other, all of them containing a term such that they distribute bets on the two sides with a frequency to match the actual occurrence of events. If it should turn out that there is a pattern to be discovered, their payoff would become 100 per cent. The other group would go on at the middling rate of 70 per cent.

What has this to do with the subject at hand? For the person to search out and find regularities and relationships in his environment, he must be armed with an expectancy that there will be something to find and, once aroused by expectancy, he must devise ways of searching and finding. One of the chief enemies of such expectancy is the assumption that there is nothing one can find in the environment by way of regularity or relationship. In the experiment just cited, subjects often fall into a habitual attitude that there is either nothing to be found or that they can find a pattern by looking. There is an important sequel in behavior to the two attitudes, and to this I should like to turn now.

We have been conducting a series of experimental studies on a group of some seventy school children over the last four years. The studies have led us to distinguish an interesting dimension of cognitive activity that can be described as ranging from *episodic empiricism* at one end to *cumulative constructionism* at the other. The two attitudes in the choice experiments just cited are illustrative of the extremes of the dimension. I might mention some other illustrations. One of the experiments employs the game of Twenty Questions. A child—in this case he is between 10 and 12—is told that a car has gone off the road and hit a tree. He is to ask questions that can be answered by "yes" or "no" to discover the cause of the accident. After completing the problem, the same task is given him again, though he is told that the accident had a different cause this time. In all, the procedure is repeated four times. Children enjoy playing the game. They also differ quite markedly in the approach or strategy they bring to the task. There are various elements in the strategies employed. In the first place, one may distinguish clearly between two types of questions asked: the one is designed for locating constraints in the problem, constraints that will eventually give shape to a hypothesis; the other is the hypothesis as question. It is the difference between, "Was there anything wrong with the driver?" and "Was the driver rushing to the doctor's officer for an appointment and the car got out of control?" There are children who precede hypotheses with efforts to locate constraint and there are those who, to use our local slang, are "potshotters," who string out hypotheses noncumulatively one after the other. A second element of strategy is its connectivity of information gathering: the extent to which questions asked utilize or ignore or violate information previously obtained. The questions asked by children tend to be organized in cycles, each cycle of questions usually being given over to the pursuit of some particular notion. Both within cycles and between cycles one can discern a marked difference on the connectivity of the child's performance. Needless to say, children who employ constraint location as a technique preliminary to the formulation of hypotheses tend to be far more connected in their harvesting of information. Persistence is another feature of strategy, a characteristic compounded of what appear to be two components: a sheer doggedness component, and a persistence that stems from the sequential organization that a child brings to the task. Doggedness is probably just animal spirits or the need for achievement—what has come to be called *n-ach*. Organized persistence is a maneuver for protecting our fragile cognitive apparatus from overload. The child who has flooded himself with disorganized information from unconnected hypotheses will become discouraged and confused sooner than the child who has shown a certain cunning in his strategy of getting information—a cunning whose principal component is the recognition that the value of information is not simply in getting it but in being able to carry it. The persistence of the organized child stems from his knowledge of how to organize questions in cycles, how to summarize things to himself, and the like.

Episodic empiricism is illustrated by information gathering that is unbound by prior constraints, that lacks connectivity, and that is deficient in organizational persistence. The opposite extreme is illustrated by an approach that is characterized by constraint sensitivity, by connective maneuvers, and by organized persistence. Brute persistence seems to be one of those gifts from the gods that make people more exaggeratedly what they are.[2]

Before returning to the issue of discovery and its role in the development of thinking, let me say a word more about the ways in which information may get transformed when the problem solver has actively processed it. There is first of all a pragmatic question: What does it take to get information processed into a form best designed to fit some future use? Take an experiment by Zajonc[3] as a case in point. He gives groups of subjects information of a controlled kind, some groups being told that their task is to transmit the information to others, others that it is merely to be kept in mind. In general, he finds more differentiation and organization of the information received with the intention of being transmitted than there is for information received passively. An active set leads to a transformation related to a task to be performed. The risk, to be sure, is in possible over-specialization of information processing that may lead to such a high degree of specific organization that information is lost for general use.

I would urge now in the spirit of a hypothesis that emphasis upon discovery in learning has precisely the effect upon the learner of leading him to be a constructionist, to organize what he is encountering in a manner not only designed to discover regularity and relatedness, but also to avoid the kind of information drift that fails to keep account of the uses to which information might have to be put. It is, if you will, a necessary condition for learning the variety of techniques of problem solving, of transforming information for better use, indeed for learning how to go about the very task of learning. Practice in discovering for oneself teaches one to acquire information in a way that makes that information more readily viable in problem solving. So goes the hypothesis. It is

[2] I should also remark in passing that the two extremes also characterize concept attainment strategies as reported in *A Study of Thinking* by J. S. Bruner *et al.* (New York: John Wiley & Sons, Inc., 1956). Successive scanning illustrates well what is meant here by episodic empiricism: conservative focusing is an example of cumulative constructionism.

[3] R. B. Zajonc (Personal communication, 1957).

still in need of testing. But it is an hypothesis of such important human implications that we cannot afford not to test it—and testing will have to be in the schools.

2. *Intrinsic and Extrinsic Motives*

Much of the problem in leading a child to effective cognitive activity is to free him from the immediate control of environmental rewards and punishments. That is to say, learning that starts in response to the rewards of parental or teacher approval or the avoidance of failure can too readily develop a pattern in which the child is seeking cues as to how to conform to what is expected of him. We know from studies of children who tend to be early over-achievers in school that they are likely to be seekers after the "right way to do it" and that their capacity for transforming their learning into viable thought structures tends to be lower than children merely achieving at levels predicted by intelligence tests. Our tests on such children show them to be lower in analytic ability than those who are not conspicuous in over-achievement.[4] As we shall see later, they develop rote abilities and depend upon being able to "give back" what is expected rather than to make it into something that relates to the rest of their cognitive life. As Maimonides would say, their learning is not their own.

The hypothesis that I would propose here is that to the degree that one is able to approach learning as a task of discovering something rather than "learning about" it, to that degree will there be a tendency for the child to carry out his learning activities with the autonomy of self-reward or, more properly, by reward that is discovery itself.

To those of you familiar with the battles of the last half-century in the field of motivation, the above hypothesis will be recognized as controversial. For the classic view of motivation in learning has been, until very recently, couched in terms of a theory of drives and reinforcement: that learning occurred by virtue of the fact that a response produced by a stimulus was followed by the reduction in a primary drive state. The doctrine is greatly extended by the idea of secondary reinforcement: any state associated even remotely with the reduction of a primary drive could also have the effect of producing learning. There has recently appeared a most searching and important criticism of this position written by Professor Robert White,[5] reviewing the evidence of recently published animal studies, of work in the field of psychoanalysis, and of research on the development of cognitive processes in children. Professor White comes to the conclusion, quite rightly I think, that the drive-reduction model of learning runs counter to too many important phenomena of learning and development to be either regarded as general in its applicability or even correct in its general approach. Let me summarize some of his principal conclusions and explore their applicability to the hypothesis stated above.

I now propose that we gather the

[4] J. S. Bruner and A. J. Caron, "Cognition, Anxiety, and Achievement in the Preadolescent," *Journal of Educational Psychology*, unpublished.

[5] R. W. White, "Motivation Reconsidered: The Concept of Competence," *Psychological Review*, LXVI (1959), 297–333.

> various kinds of behavior just mentioned, all of which have to do with effective interaction with the environment, under the general heading of competence. According to Webster, competence means fitness or ability, and the suggested synonyms include capability, capacity, efficiency, proficiency, and skill. It is therefore a suitable word to describe such things as grasping and exploring, crawling and walking, attention and perception, language and thinking, manipulating and changing the surroundings, all of which promote an effective—a competent—interaction with the environment. It is true of course, that maturation plays a part in all these developments, but this part is heavily overshadowed by learning in all the more complex accomplishments like speech or skilled manipulation. I shall argue that it is necessary to make competence a motivational concept; there is *competence motivation* as well as competence in its more familiar sense of achieved capacity. The behavior that leads to the building up of effective grasping, handling, and letting go of objects, to take one example, is not random behavior that is produced by an overflow of energy. It is directed, selective, and persistent, and it continues not because it serves primary drives, which indeed it cannot serve until it is almost perfected, but because it satisfies an intrinsic need to deal with the environment.[6]

I am suggesting that there are forms of activity that serve to enlist and develop the competence motive, that serve to make it the driving force behind behavior. I should like to add to White's general premise that the *exercise* of competence motives has the effect of strengthening the degree to which they gain control over behavior and thereby reduce the effects of extrinsic rewards or drive gratification.

The brilliant Russian psychologist Vigotsky[7] characterizes the growth of thought processes as starting with a dialogue of speech and gesture between child and parent; autonomous thinking begins at the stage when the child is first able to internalize these conversations and "run them off" himself. This is a typical sequence in the development of competence. So too in instruction. The narrative of teaching is of the order of the conversation. The next move in the development of competence is the internalization of the narrative and its "rules of generation" so that the child is now capable of running off the narrative on his own. The hypothetical mode in teaching by encouraging the child to participate in "speaker's decisions" speeds this process along. Once internalization has occurred the child is in a vastly improved position from several obvious points of view—notably that he is able to go beyond the information he has been given to generate additional ideas that can either be checked immediately from experience or can, at least, be used as a basis for formulating reasonable hypotheses. But over and beyond that, the child is now in a position to experience success and failure not as reward and punishment, but as information. For when the task is his own rather than a matter of matching environmental demands, he becomes his own paymaster in a certain measure. Seeking to gain control over his environment, he can now treat

6 *Ibid.*, pp. 317–18.

7 L. S. Vigotsky, *Thinking and Speech* (Moscow, 1934).

success as indicating that he is on the right track, failure as indicating he is on the wrong one.

In the end, this development has the effect of freeing learning from immediate stimulus control. When learning in the short run leads only to pellets of this or that rather than to mastery in the long run, then behavior can be readily "shaped" by extrinsic rewards. When behavior becomes more long-range and competence-oriented, it comes under the control of more complex cognitive structures, plans and the like, and operates more from the inside out. It is interesting that even Pavlov, whose early account of the learning process was based entirely on a notion of stimulus control of behavior through the conditioning mechanism in which, through contiguity, a new conditioned stimulus was substituted for an old unconditioned stimulus by the mechanism of stimulus substitution, that even Pavlov recognized his account as insufficient to deal with higher forms of learning. To supplement the account, he introduced the idea of the "second signaling system," with central importance placed on symbolic systems such as language in mediating and giving shape to mental life. Or as Luria[8] has put it, "the first signal system [is] concerned with directly perceived stimuli, the second with systems of verbal elaboration." Luria, commenting on the importance of the transition from first to second signal system, says: "It would be mistaken to suppose that verbal intercourse with adults merely changes the contents of the child's conscious activity without changing its form. . . . The word has a basic function not only because it indicates a corresponding object in the external world, but also because it abstracts, isolates the necessary signal, generalizes perceived signals and relates them to certain categories; it is this systematization of direct experience that makes the role of the words in the formation of mental processes so exceptionally important."[9, 10]

It is interesting that the final rejection of the universality of the doctrine of reinforcement in direct conditioning came from some of Pavlov's own students. Ivanov-Smolensky[11] and Krasnogorsky[12] published papers showing the manner in which symbolized linguistic messages could take over the place of the unconditioned stimulus and of the unconditioned response (gratification of hunger) in children. In all instances, they speak of these as *replacements* of lower, first system mental or neural processes by higher order or second-system controls. A strange irony, then, that Russian psychology that gave us the notion of the conditioned response and the assumption that higher order activities are built up out of colligations or structurings of such primitive units, rejected this notion while much of American learning psychology has stayed until quite recently within the early Pavlovian fold (see, for exam-

8 A. L. Luria, "The Directive Function of Speech in Development and Dissolution," *Word*, XV (1959), 341–464.

9 *Ibid.*, p. 12.

10 For an elaboration of the view expressed by Luria, the reader is referred to the forthcoming translation of L. S. Vigotsky's 1934 book being published by John Wiley & Sons, Inc., and the Technology Press.

11 A. G. Ivanov-Smolensky, "Concerning the Study of the Joint Activity of the First and Second Signal Systems," *Journal of Higher Nervous Activity*, I (1951), 1.

12 N. D. Krasnogorsky, *Studies of Higher Nervous Activity in Animals and in Man*, Vol. I (Moscow, 1954).

ple, a recent article by Spence[13] in the *Harvard Educational Review* or Skinner's treatment of language[14] and the attacks that have been made upon it by linguists such as Chomsky[15] who have become concerned with the relation of language and cognitive activity). What is the more interesting is that Russian pedagogical theory has become deeply influenced by this new trend and is now placing much stress upon the importance of building up a more active symbolical approach to problem-solving among children.

To sum up the matter of the control of learning, then, I am proposing that the degree to which competence or mastery motives come to control behavior, to that degree the role of reinforcement or "extrinsic pleasure" wanes in shaping behavior. The child comes to manipulate his environment more actively and achieves his gratification from coping with problems. Symbolic modes of representing and transforming the environment arise and the importance of stimulus-response-reward sequences declines. To use the metaphor that David Riesman developed in a quite different context, mental life moves from a state of outer-directedness in which the fortuity of stimuli and reinforcement are crucial to a state of inner-directedness in which the growth and maintenance of mastery become central and dominant.

13 K. W. Spence, "The Relation of Learning Theory to the Technique of Education," *Harvard Educational Review*, XXIX (1959), 84–95.

14 B. F. Skinner, *Verbal Behavior* (New York: Appleton-Century-Crofts, 1957).

15 N. Chomsky, *Syntactic Structure* (The Hague: Mouton & Co., 1957).

3. Learning the Heuristics of Discovery

Lincoln Steffens,[16] reflecting in his *Autobiography* on his undergraduate education at Berkeley, comments that his schooling was overly specialized on learning about the known and that too little attention was given to the task of finding out about what was not known. But how does one train a student in the techniques of discovery? Again I would like to offer some hypotheses. There are many ways of coming to the arts of inquiry. One of them is by careful study of its formalization in logic, statistics, mathematics, and the like. If a person is going to pursue inquiry as a way of life, particularly in the sciences, certainly such study is essential. Yet, whoever has taught kindergarten and the early primary grades or has had graduate students working with him on their theses—I choose the two extremes for they are both periods of intense inquiry—knows that an understanding of the formal aspect of inquiry is not sufficient. There appear to be, rather, a series of activities and attitudes, some directly related to a particular subject and some of them fairly generalized, that go with inquiry and research. These have to do with the *process* of trying to find out something and while they provide no guarantee that the *product* will be any *great* discovery, their absence is likely to lead to awkwardness or aridity or confusion. How difficult it is to describe these matters—the heuristics of inquiry. There is one set of attitudes or ways of doing that has

16 L. Steffens, *Autobiography of Lincoln Steffens* (New York: Harcourt, Brace & World, Inc., 1931).

to do with sensing the relevance of variables—how to avoid getting stuck with edge effects and getting instead to the big sources of variance. Partly this gift comes from intuitive familiarity with a range of phenomena, sheer "knowing the stuff." But it also comes out of a sense of what things among an ensemble of things "smell right" in the sense of being of the right order of magnitude or scope or severity.

The English philosopher Weldon describes problem solving in an interesting and picturesque way. He distinguishes between difficulties, puzzles, and problems. We solve a problem or make a discovery when we impose a puzzle form on to a difficulty that converts it into a problem that can be solved in such a way that it gets us where we want to be. That is to say, we recast the difficulty into a form that we know how to work with, then work it. Much of what we speak of as discovery consists of knowing how to impose what kind of form on various kind of difficulties. A small part but a crucial part of discovery of the highest order is to invent and develop models or "puzzle forms" that can be imposed on difficulties with good effect. It is in this area that the truly powerful mind shines. But it is interesting to what degree perfectly ordinary people can, given the benefit of instruction, construct quite interesting and what, a century ago, would have been considered greatly original models.

Now to the hypothesis. It is my hunch that it is only through the exercise of problem solving and the effort of discovery that one learns the working heuristic of discovery, and the more one has practice, the more likely is one to generalize what one has learned into a style of problem solving or inquiry that serves for any kind of task one may encounter —or almost any kind of task. I think the matter is self-evident, but what is unclear is what kinds of training and teaching produce the best effects. How do we teach a child to, say, cut his losses but at the same time be persistent in trying out an idea; to risk forming an early hunch without at the same time formulating one *so* early and with so little evidence as to be stuck with it waiting for appropriate evidence to materialize; to pose good testable guesses that are neither too brittle nor too sinuously incorrigible; etc., etc. Practice in inquiry, in trying to figure out things for oneself, is indeed what is needed, but in what form? Of only one thing I am convinced. I have never seen anybody improve in the art and technique of inquiry by any means other than engaging in inquiry.

4. Conservation of Memory

I should like to take what some psychologists might consider a rather drastic view of the memory process. It is a view that in large measure derives from the work of my colleague, Professor George Miller.[17] Its first premise is that the principal problem of human memory is not storage, but retrieval. In spite of the biological unlikeliness of it, we seem to be able to store a huge quantity of information—perhaps not a full tape recording, though at times it seems we even do that, but a great sufficiency of impressions. We may

17 G. A. Miller, "The Magical Number Seven, Plus or Minus Two," *Psychological Review*, LXII (1956), 81–97.

infer this from the fact that recognition (i.e., recall with the aid of maximum prompts) is so extraordinarily good in human beings—particularly in comparison with spontaneous recall where, so to speak, we must get out stored information without external aids or prompts. The key to retrieval is organization or, in even simpler terms, knowing where to find information and how to get there.

Let me illustrate the point with a simple experiment. We present pairs of words to twelve-year-old children. One group is simply told to remember the pairs, that they will be asked to repeat them later. Another is told to remember them by producing a word or idea that will tie the pair together in a way that will make sense to them. A third group is given the mediators used by the second group when presented with the pairs to aid them in tying the pairs into working units. The word pairs include such juxtapositions as "chair-forest," "sidewalk-square," and the like. One can distinguish three styles of mediators and children can be scaled in terms of their relative preference for each: *generic mediation* in which a pair is tied together by a superordinate idea: "chair and forest are both made of wood"; *thematic mediation* in which the two terms are embedded in a theme or little story: "the lost child sat on a chair in the middle of the forest"; and *part-whole mediation* where "chairs are made from trees in the forest" is typical. Now, the chief result, as you would all predict, is that children who provide their own mediators do best—indeed, one time through a set of thirty pairs, they recover up to 95 per cent of the second words when presented with the first ones of the pairs, whereas the uninstructed children reach a maximum of less than 50 per cent recovered. Interestingly enough, children do best in recovering materials tied together by the form of mediator they most often use.

One can cite a myriad of findings to indicate that any organization of information that reduces the aggregate complexity of material by embedding it into a cognitive structure a person has constructed will make that material more accessible for retrieval. In short, we may say that the process of memory, looked at from the retrieval side, is also a process of problem solving: how can material be "placed" in memory so that it can be got on demand?

We can take as a point of departure the example of the children who developed their own technique for relating the members of each word pair. You will recall that they did better than the children who were given by exposition the mediators they had developed. Let me suggest that, in general, material that is organized in terms of a person's own interests and cognitive structures is material that has the best chance of being accessible in memory. That is to say, it is more likely to be placed along routes that are connected to one's own ways of intellectual travel.

In sum, the very attitudes and activities that characterize "figuring out" or "discovering" things for oneself also seems to have the effect of making material more readily accessible in memory.

27. AUSUBEL'S SUBSUMER THEORY OF LEARNING: A BASIS FOR THE TEACHING OF MEANINGFUL VERBAL MATERIAL

JAMES RATHS

While there are clearly many educational philosophies and theories of learning from which a teacher may choose to use a guide for selecting and planning educational experiences, it is clear that a profusion of reality factors found in today's schools strictly limit the choices a teacher may make operational in a classroom. Whether dedicated to the humanist view, the progressive philosophy, or the phenomenological position, a teacher is faced with classes of 30 to 40 students and with community pressures to teach content that is fairly well set and standardized. These obstacles, and many similar reality factors associated with schools and teaching, serve to inhibit the introduction of many modern notions into the classroom.

Many educationists deplore the existing state of affairs. These people have made a major effort through preservice programs to affect changes in the teaching practices found in public schools. It is the author's point of view that many of the ideas advocated in preservice courses in education are inconsistent with the realities found in the schools. To implement change in the current basic organizational patterns of the schools by training preservice teachers in the ideas of progressive education for instance is clearly ineffective in its impact on the schools and on the teachers.

The original ideas presented in this paper stem from the work of two leaders in the field of learning, D. P. Ausubel and Walter B. Waetjen. Professor Ausubel has written a very stimulating book summarizing his theory for the teaching and learning of meaningful material. Most of this paper is drawn from this source. Professor Waetjen has contributed a paradigm postulating the relationship of the cognitive structure to new stimuli and the role that epistemic behavior plays in incorporating new material into the cognitive structure. A slightly modified version of Professor Waetjen's paradigm is included in this paper.

While the author gives credit to both these men for their contributions, it is clear that neither of them can be held responsible for the manner in which their original ideas are expressed in this paper.

This paper will attempt to elucidate a theory of learning that seems more relevant to teachers faced with the following givens—a rather well defined curriculum that must be "covered" and hopefully taught to a large group of youngsters. At best, the implications of this theory for teaching are vague and obscure, but the fact that this is a theory of learning that seems quite relevant to the existing situation that our students face in classrooms makes it a worthwhile one to examine and pursue.

The purpose of this paper is to clarify and expand some of the statements found in Ausubel's theory of learning (1). C. D. Hardie once suggested that the structure of theory in the natural sciences consists of statements or postulates about unobservable entities that direct researchers in their observation of observable phenomena (5). Ausubel's theory presupposes such a nonobservable entity—the cognitive structure. A cognitive structure is the totality of an individual's existing knowledge organized in terms of highly generalized concepts under which are subsumed concepts of a less generalized nature as well as specific facts. The major organizational principle of the cognitive structure, in other words, is that of progressive differentiation of a body of knowledge from regions of greater generality to lesser generality—each linked to the next higher step in the hierarchy through a process of subsumption. It is important to point out that Ausubel does not mean that the levels are deductively related—one being derivable from another. The relationship is rather analogous to a filing system or an outline in that one concept is included within another more general one.

As a learner internalizes new material he places a value on it along a continuum going from highly general and inclusive to not very general and specific. Another dimension of material found in the cognitive structure is that of abstractness. This continuum, ranging from the concrete to the abstract, is different than the continuum going from the general to the specific.

If this theory adequately describes the way a student internalizes new material, then teachers must organize their teaching in such a way that they are confident their students possess in their cognitive structures highly general concepts under which they may subsume new material. Ausubel refers to these general elements as "advanced organizers."

For example, Ausubel used as an advanced organizer for a lesson dealing with the metallurgical properties of carbon steel, a passage placing emphasis on the major similarities and differences between metals and alloys. He found this material effective in anchoring the content of the lesson (2). As another example more relevant to the secondary school, teachers of geometry may teach the basic elements of proof—axioms, definitions, and theorems in mathematical and nonmathematical contexts before geometric proofs are introduced. This prior learning may serve to anchor the geometric concepts presented later in the year.

Advance organizers, Ausubel suggests, may be expository or comparative in nature. An expository organizer provides a hierarchical series of organizers in descending order of inclusiveness—each organizer preceding its corresponding unit of detailed material in the lesson. The comparative organizer suggests ways the previously learned concepts are basically similar or different from the new material. Historically relevant material or summaries or overviews which are presented at the same level of inclusiveness as the material to be learned are not considered to be advance organizers.

If a person has no cognitive structure relevant to the new material that is being presented to him, he will use strategies to master the material that can be found in the psychologies of rote learning. However, such knowledge of rote learning, it is held, does not give teachers insights into the dynamics of learning potentially meaningful material. Ausubel's theory is an attempt to fill that gap.

The following diagram endeavors to explain ways in which new material is incorporated into cognitive structure. Example A suggests that the material is not really new and that it is so readily subsumed into existing cognitive structure that a student may incorporate it almost immediately without much effort on his part. Example B portrays the internalization of material that is incorporated by a student only after some active process designed to fit the material into the existing cognitive structure. This active process may be one of asking questions or testing ideas or merely thinking about how this new idea relates to the familiar material. The new learnings in this case do not fit the structure immediately, and a student plays an active role in trying to organize it into his structure.

Example C shows new material that does not fit the cognitive structure at first and even after an active

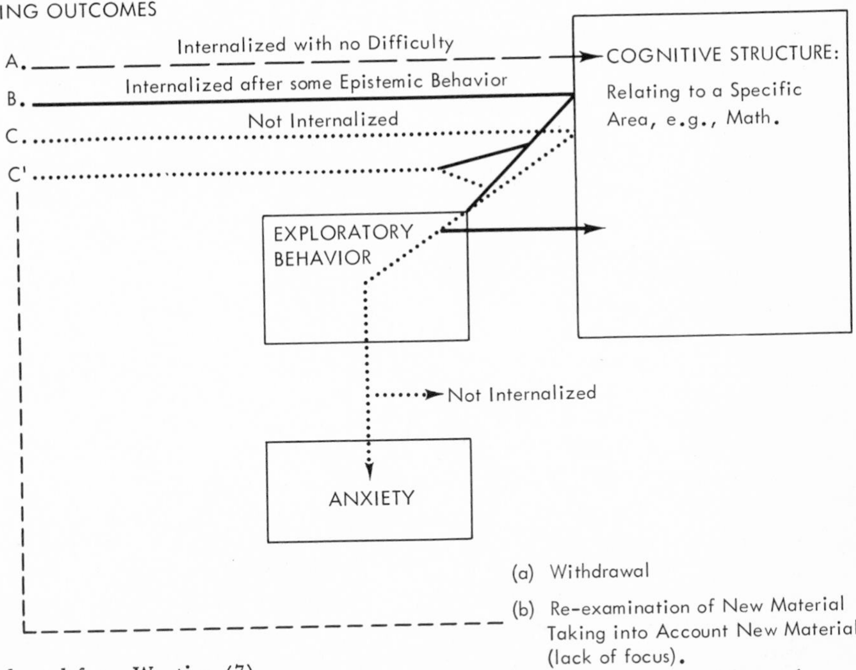

* Adapted from Waetjen (7).

Figure 1.
The Incorporation of Material into Cognitive Structure

process on the student's part to make it fit. The material is not internalized. Two outcomes may result in this case. First, generally anxiety is aroused. Feelings of anxiety may cause a student to withdraw from the learning situation. Sometimes we say he becomes blocked. Secondly, as shown in the line marked C′, a student may review the new material with a wider focus than at first, taking into account more and more details in an effort to incorporate the new material into his structure (7). The lowering of discrimination that is reflected in this behavior may serve to alter the material through additions of perceptions and biases in a way that facilitates its incorporation into his cognitive structure. In these cases, C and C′, the student is manifesting symptoms of learning disabilities. According to Ausubel's theory, they can be remedied by a teacher's strategy in organizing his presentation of content.

Implications

The theory of learning stated above seems to have implications for many areas of a teacher's concern. These implications are briefly spelled out as follows:

Readiness

It follows from this theory that readiness for learning is a function of previous learning experiences as well as maturity. Do youngsters have in their cognitive structure elements of a degree of inclusiveness that will enable them to subsume or incorporate the new material? Do youngsters have in their cognitive structure elements of a degree of abstractness that will enable them to handle the new material that is to be presented? If either of these questions is answered in the negative, it may be said that the youngsters are not ready for the learning experience. Both requisites, that of maturity (a factor in determining the ability of a student to handle abstract concepts, [6]), and previous learnings (a factor in establishing advanced organizers), must be met before a youngster is "ready" to learn.

Attention Span

Attention span may be considered to be the amount of time a person spends fitting novel material into his cognitive structure. His attention span may appear short if he has no difficulty incorporating the new material into his cognitive structure. An example of this is the bright student in a review class. He shows signs of inattention. Another example is the case in which an individual has little or no existing cognitive structure under which to subsume the new material. An illustration of this would be a student naïve to mathematics sitting in on an advanced mathematics seminar. He, too, would show signs of inattentiveness. If after much effort a student is still unable to incorporate new material into his cognitive structure, he may develop anxieties leading to signs of withdrawal.

Psychology of Self

The extent to which a person can tolerate the anxieties of being unable to fit the new material into the existing cognitive structure may be related to current notions of the psychology of self that have become prevalent in the literature. Psychologists have for some time been puzzled by the discrepancies in learning abilities of people with equal intelligence. Nonintellectual factors have been surveyed to explain the observed differences. The psychology of self suggests that individuals have a unique attitude or stance that reflects attitudes toward thinking, learning and problem solving. Cartwright (3) has called this stance an "address of life." There may be a relationship between the ability to tolerate new material that does not fit into the cognitive structure and this quality.

Curiosity

Curiosity can be defined as a drive to fit new material into the current cognitive structure of the individual. The extent to which a student puzzles, manipulates, studies, and reflects on new material in order to fit it into his cognitive structure may be an indicator of his curiosity. If this indicator is valid, then it would follow that curiosity is not an all-pervasive trait. A person must be curious about *something*. He is curious about those things for which he has a tentative cognitive structure that includes highly general elements under which new phenomena can be incorporated.

Research Suggested by Ausubel's Theory of Learning

A major problem in the examination of Ausubel's theory is to find hypotheses that stem from the theory that are testable. The problem is intensified in this case because of the obscure nature of the concept "organizer." Does an organizer function equally effectively for everyone? If Ausubel is saying that everyone has his own personal organizer, then his theory certainly would give little direction for teachers in the classroom. If, on the other hand, he is saying that a teacher can find organizers for students naïve to the new material to be taught, and that these organizers will facilitate learning, then teachers may find his ideas very productive and useful in a classroom. A first step may be one of trying to identify students who seem to learn using a style that reflects use of cognitive organization. The following procedure may produce two samples of youngsters with different learning styles. First, match secondary school youngsters on self-concept and general anxiety variables. Next, select those pairs of youngsters matched on these variables who show markedly different test anxiety scores. It may be reasonable to assume that the two populations of youngsters—one with high test anxiety and the other with low test anxiety—but with equivalent self-concept and general anxiety scores will use different learning styles in mastering new material. Interviews or schedules may be used with each of the pairs of students to find indicators of the use of advance organizers in a particular learning exercise. Such populations may also be generated by identifying those students with nearly equal test scores on a given achievement test but whose retention scores are vastly different. We may assume that the ways in which these students mastered the new material were quite different and the group that was able to retain the information made use of advance organizers. Perhaps these organizers could be discovered through an interviewing process.

References

1. Ausubel, D. P., *The Psychology of Meaningful Verbal Learning*. New York: Grune & Stratton, Inc., 1963.

2. Ausubel, D. P., "The Use of Advance Organizers in the Learning and Retention of Meaningful Verbal Material," *Journal of Educational Psychology* (October 1960).

3. Cartwright, Roger, "Promoting Student Thinking," *Journal of Educational Sociology* (September 1963).

4. Dewey, John, *Democracy and Education.* New York: The Macmillan Company, 1916.

5. Hardie, C. D., "Reply to George L. Newsome, Jr.," *Studies in Philosophy and Education* (September 1963).

6. Inhelder, Barbel, and J. Piaget, *The Growth of Logical Thinking from Childhood to Adolescence.* New York: Basic Books, Inc., Publishers, 1958.

7. Waetjen, Walter B., "Curiosity and Exploration: Roles in Intellectual Development and Learning." Paper presented to A.S.C.D. Research Institute, Washington, D.C., April 1963.

28. TEACHING SOCIAL STUDIES THROUGH DISCOVERY

BYRON G. MASSIALAS / JACK ZEVIN

The study reported here is grounded in some of the hypotheses advanced by Jerome Bruner in his recent work. According to him, the highest state of human autonomy and perfection is achieved when the child begins to discover for himself regularities or irregularities in his physical and sociopolitical environments. While no earthshaking scientific discoveries should be expected, the person who is engaged in this process is given the opportunity to make leaps into the unknown and uncontrolled world, and he learns the value of formulating plausible hypotheses about human interactions. It is maintained that when facts and details are put into

Byron G. Massialas and Jack Zevin, "Teaching Social Studies Through Discovery," SOCIAL EDUCATION, *XXVIII, No. 7 (November 1964), 384–87, 400. Reprinted by permission of Dr. Massialas and the publisher.*

a structured pattern, they are retained longer and can be retrieved easier when needed.[1]

The study was conducted in a Chicago public high school over a period of one academic year, and it attempted to explore further the dimensions and the implications of teaching a course in world history through discovery or, what Bruner calls, the process of "figuring out." While the general nature of the study was exploratory, some questions provided the focus of the investigation. Some of these questions were: (1) To what extent are high school sophomores with slightly above average ability capable of participating in discovery and in inquiry? (2) How can historical materials be presented in such a way that while some cues will be offered, the story will not be given away, and the student will be prompted to study independently and to acquire the heuristics of learning? (3) To what extent do the style and method of discovery operate as a potent motivational device in learning? Before dealing with these questions and presenting relevant classroom discussion, let us briefly identify some instructional procedures and classroom mechanics which will help the reader reconstruct the teaching experience.

The class was composed of 35 students, most of them about 15 years old, enrolled in a required modern world history course. The course began with the Reformation, and it generally followed the sequence of historical topics; selected social events were chosen to be investigated in some depth. All the aesthetic products of culture including art, music, literature, and architecture were drawn upon for classroom material; however, the study emphasized the use of historical documents in developing the student's ability to discover and explain his political and social environment. Secondary sources—e.g., textbooks, excerpts from monographs, magazine articles—were used only insofar as they related to the problem under attack, and they were introduced after the initial encounter with the "discovery episode." On the average, a new discovery episode was introduced every two weeks, and in the main, it consisted of a historical document, the origin, referent, and author of which were carefully deleted. The students were challenged to gather all the missing information. Although a discovery episode presupposed some general knowledge, it was not necessary for the student to have had special training or familiarity with the problem under consideration. In a situation such as this, the instructor performs a nondirective role in that he explicitly refuses to answer any of the students' questions. His task in the classroom is twofold: (1) to instigate and challenge the students, and (2) to moderate the discussion.

In order to illustrate the flow of classroom discussion during a discovery session, parts of the student dialogue are here reproduced. In this particular case, the students were

[1] Jerome S. Bruner, "The Act of Discovery," *Harvard Educational Review*, XXXI (Winter 1961), 21–32. (See Reading 26 this vol.) For more details on the philosophical and psychological assumptions underlying the method, see B. G. Massialas, "Teaching History as Inquiry," in Shirley H. Engle, editor, *New Perspectives in World History*. Thirty-Fourth Yearbook (Washington, D.C.: The National Council for the Social Studies, 1964).

given ten brief poems[2] and were asked to read them carefully. The participants were encouraged to discover a plausible choice for the cultural origin of the following poems.

1.

My Thoughts turn to the Ancient Capital
Long life and peace during your reign
O, Emperor.

2.

The beginning of all art
A song when planting a rice field
in the country's inmost part.

3.

Is there, I wonder
A man without a pen in hand—
The moon tonight!

4.

On the temple bell
Resting, sleeping,
a firefly.

5.

A Great Lord—And Who
makes *Him* get off his horse?
—cherry blossoms do!

6.

Snow yet remaining
The mountain slopes are hazy—
It is evening.

[2] These poems were taken from Harold G. Henderson, *Introduction to Japanese Haiku* (New York: Doubleday & Company, Inc. [Anchor Books], 1962). The selection of material was based primarily on two criteria: (a) availability of data pertaining to a central or common theme, e.g., the feudal system in Japan; and (b) careful avoidance of clues which would "give away" the puzzle.

7.

A crossroad sermon! True,
It's rigamarole—but then
It's tranquil too!

8.

So brilliant a moonshine
When I am born again—
A hilltop pine!

9.

To the Great Lord's hall
Five or six horsemen hurry hard—
A storm wind of fall.

10.

As he snoozes, the mountain stream he uses
To wash his rice,
No simple peasant, this!

The discussion that ensued was tape-recorded and transcribed. Selected parts of the transcription are given below.

First Day

Teacher: Please read this. (*five minutes of silence*) Well now, everyone finished? What do you think of this reading? What are these?

Tim: This must be a collection of poems.

Teacher: Why?

Tim: Because each of these little pieces is in verse. Some rhyme.

George: But they're so vague. What are we supposed to do with them?

Teacher: Whatever you like. Are they really vague?

Gwen: I don't think so. Some of the poems are very interesting, maybe difficult to interpret, but interesting.

Sylvia: Yes, I think we can find clues if we try.

George: Clues for what? All this is still vague.

Bill S.: Yes, what are we supposed to find out? What do these mean? Where are they from? Who wrote them? When were they written?

Teacher: All of you should be able to supply your own answers to these questions. Who would like to make the first attempt? (*a moment of silence*)

Carolyn: Well, they're all poems, so they must have been written by a poet.

Bill S.: That's some help! How do you know they're not written by one and the same poet? They all look the same to me, same three lines, same style, all short and vague.

Carolyn: But they're on different subjects and they give different feelings. Each one gives me a different feeling.

Bill S.: Does that mean they can't be by one poet expressing himself on different subjects?

Sylvia: I have a different idea. Maybe these poems are all by different poets, but may seem to be the same because of the style. What I mean is that maybe these are the usual kind of poem for this country.

Gwen: Or, it could just be the style of a particular poet.

John: I think this is getting us nowhere. Let's forget about the poet and try to find out where it's from.

Bob: But these poems are too vague.

Diane: We're back to that again.

Teacher: Well, does everyone agree with this, or can someone offer advice or evidence to help us out? Where are these from?

Sharon: They are from Europe because an Emperor is mentioned, and lords are also mentioned a couple of times. This means there must have been an autocracy in this country. Many countries of Europe had monarchs and lords.

Bernard: At one time almost every European country had this kind of government. Maybe these poems are from Russia. Russia had an Emperor and nobles running it for a long, long time.

Diane: I think that this is from France or Germany, or Austria during the Middle Ages, because the lords seem to be very powerful; they are able to command cavalry men and to own large halls. Maybe the emperor referred to is Charlemagne.

Gwen: I think you're getting on the wrong track. This is no European set of poems, certainly not American!

Teacher: Why?

Gwen: Well, you're missing a lot of important parts of the poems that seem not to be European at all. What about the mention of a temple? Since when are Medieval churches called temples? And what about the reference to rice in one of the poems? Rice wasn't one of the European's main dishes, at least as far as I know.

Eddie: Rice is from the Orient, from China. The Chinese eat lots of rice. The poems must be translated from Chinese.

Steve: They could also be from Japan or India. I've read somewhere that these two countries produce and eat rice as their main dish.

Mary: I read recently that Southeast Asia produces a lot of rice. Vietnam exports rice, and eats some of it.

Helen: I have a suggestion, but not of another country. I think we should try to get the meaning and message of each poem and then find out where they're from. Let's start with poem 1 and work our way down.

It is apparent that the first day is spent on orientation and organization of the material at hand. During the introductory phases of the discovery episode, the students are encouraged to come to grips with the responsibility of exercising independent judgment in pursuing a course of action. The teacher and the material, which includes only limited clues, create a sense of puzzlement. The students begin to suggest modes of attack and try to capitalize on the available springboards. For example, John proposes that the focal point of investigation should change from a quest to identify the poet to an inquiry into the national origin of the poems. This suggestion is taken up by several members of the class—e.g., Gwen, who in her first reaction to the poem, offers a hypothesis which harmonizes several problematic bits of data and refutes previous conjectures. At this point other students attempt to validate and to narrow down the proposition that the poems are of non-Western source. Helen, following up this line of investigation, concludes the deliberations of the first day by suggesting that each poem be thoroughly scrutinized and analyzed before returning to the main source of perplexity.

Second Day

Here the students are considering Helen's suggestion, and they are studying each poem in depth. Only discussion relating to three of these poems (8, 9, and 10) is reproduced here.

Helen: This poem (Number 8) is written by a Buddhist or a Hindu because it contains a belief in rebirth. As far as I know, only these two religions teach this belief.

George: I think it's called reincarnation. That means that you are born over and over again into new bodies or forms, although your soul remains the same.

Helen: Well, I think this poet is a Buddhist or Hindu because he believes this idea. He wants to be born again as a pine tree on a hilltop so he can enjoy beautiful moonlit nights. Does anyone disagree?

Mary: I don't. Now we have a better idea of where these poems are from. They have to be from the Orient, and they have to be from a country with Buddhists or Hindus living in it. They can't be from anywhere else.

Gwen: Yes, and according to the ninth poem, these would have to be from a country in which great lords are important people. The ninth poem repeats the fourth poem, and the great lord is said to own a hall. This must be like a castle.

Steve: The lord seems to have soldiers or cavalry working for him. Then the poem changes subject and tells of a storm wind of the fall.

Gwen: Maybe the poet is trying to tell us in a roundabout way that a war or fight is brewing. That's why the cavalry is reporting to the great lord. I don't think his poem is peaceful like the others at all. It's a poem that tells us of troubles in the country. People were fighting each other and each great lord probably had soldiers working for him.

Sharon: That's called a feudalistic system. These poems have to be from a feudalistic country. We have to find out which Oriental countries were feudalistic—or still are.

George: That might be a help. Find out which Oriental countries had feuding societies and feudal lords.

Sharon: I agree about the wars, but I don't think your suggestion will help because all those feudal societies used to have little wars.

Steve: Like England during the War of the Roses and France during the tenth and eleventh centuries?

Tim: I think you are right. You have also missed something important. If there are great lords in this country, there are most likely other lords, lesser ones in the setup as well. This sounds very close to feudalism. Usually, however, feudalism is a system of many powerful nobles and a weak king.

Sharon: Well, that fits pretty well. We definitely know that the lords of this country are powerful, armed, and have castles of some kind, while the emperor is spoken of as being in his ancient capital. It seems to me that he's out of the picture.

Bill: But we really can't tell for sure.

Sharon: Well, at least we know that the nobility is powerful, and if that's true, then the emperor must have that much less power or say-so on everything.

Teacher: Good point. Now what about a volunteer for the last poems?

Bernard: The last one is about a lazy peasant. I guess it's a kind of joke because the peasant is taking a nap while the water washes his rice, which I guess is in some sort of sack hanging in the water. Say! That's pretty clever.

Diane: Some people, including the poet, must have thought peasants were simpleminded, and the poet is showing us that this isn't so, because here's a peasant who can get his work done and sleep at the same time.

Bernard: By the way, I think this poem and the second one about rice prove that rice is very important in the life of the people of this country, and it also shows that these two poems are by different people.

Mary: Why do you say that? We decided before that we couldn't be sure of that.

Bernard: Well, in the second poem those who plant the rice are praised and in the last poem peasants are made fun of.

Karen: That could still be that same poet in a different place or mood.

In the above discussion the students are subjecting the poems to a detailed examination. All shades of meaning and locational clues are explored. In part, they seem to be working in sequential steps or plateaus; once they have determined that the poems are of Buddhist or of Hindu origin then they strike out to reach a new plateau which would incorporate more data and eliminate fruitless speculations. In their attempt to explain the existence of "great lords" they begin to draw certain logical inferences, e.g., if powerful lords are in control the monarch must be correspondingly weak. It should also be noted that in the process of "figuring out" the puzzle, the participants draw from personal accumulated knowledge which, on several occasions, provides the missing parts and clarifies certain ambiguities and vagueness in the material. For example, they are trying to interpret the poems in terms of a theory of feudalism. The discussion pertaining to the last poem is a clear illustration of an attempt to reconcile contradictory information and place it in the framework of a more inclusive and warranted hypothesis.

Third Day

Teacher: Now that you've analyzed all of the poems, where do you think they're from?

George: We've ruled out the West, and this has to be from countries under the influence of Buddhism or Hinduism, the only religions preaching reincarnation.

Eddie: That limits our choices to India, China, or Japan.

Eileen: Or Southeast Asia. The question is which one?

Steve: It seems as though each of these places fills the bill. All are countries that are literate, religious, feudalistic at one time or another, and dependent on rice for a main part of their diet.

Eddie: Well, wait a minute. Now that I think of it, China may not be a good choice. It doesn't fit in with what we've been saying about these poems. China had a very powerful emperor who ruled through a civil service. As far as I know there was no nobility in China except for the emperor's household.

Bill V.: But wasn't there an earlier period in Chinese history in which feudalism was the form of government?

Mary: Well, at least we can eliminate most of Chinese history.

Tim: I think it's India. Great Lord could be a translation for Maharaja, but I'm not sure if India has had emperors. Did it?

Teacher: You can find out, can't you?

Bill S.: Oh, please tell us where it's from. I can't wait any longer.

Teacher: But why should I when you can find out for yourself? Doesn't someone have any helpful suggestions?

Diane: I think it's from India, too. The mention of rice, temples, peasants, and the religious tone to several of the poems make me think of India.

Gwen: But what you've said could apply to almost all of Asia, India, and the East.

Tim: I think we can rule out China altogether because I remember reading that Buddhism and the idea of rebirth were introduced into China after

China already had a system of absolute emperors who ruled through a civil service, and I think there were no powerful nobles.

Bob: If all of that is correct, then China is ruled out, but that still leaves us with Japan, India, and Southeast Asia.

Mary: These poems must be from a mountainous country because of the mention of mountains in several of them.

Gwen: Northern India is very mountainous, so are parts of Southeast Asia, and all of Japan is that way.

Randy: Maybe it's Japan. Up until very recently Japan was a feudal country with lords, barons, and soldiers called Samurai, including a very shy, weak emperor. It is also a Buddhist country filled with ancient temples and preachers of religion. Japan sounds like a very good choice.

Bill S.: It could still be Northern India or Southeast Asia some time long ago.

Bernard: I believe there were emperors in India rather recently, called Moguls, or something like that.

Karen: What about the style of these poems? They seem pretty unusual. Maybe we can check into this by looking at sample poems from all over Asia until we hit on the same type. Maybe that will help us find a definite answer.

(Bell rings.)

During the third day of class deliberations, the students begin to limit the range of alternative choices or hypotheses; based on the previous analysis, they assert that the country in question will have to be Oriental, and that it will have to be under the cultural influence of Buddhism and/or Hinduism. Once this has been determined, a search for specific countries within the given cultural region takes place. Here they attempt to match alternative countries with the criteria that they have established. They further delimit the field of choice by rejecting those Oriental nations which deviate from the image they have constructed based on their interpretation of the poems. Throughout this process, they draw inferences which aid them in the defensible elimination of unwarranted hypotheses, e.g., the rejection of China as a possible choice by Tim and Bob, which takes the form of what Hunt and Metcalf call an "if-then generalization."[3] The primary goal of the group is the discovery of an answer that harmonizes all the evidence and integrates the ten poems. However, they soon realize that whatever data are at their command, they are not sufficient to support conclusively any of the proposed solutions. The realization of this difficulty motivates them to seek additional sources, especially those which include more detailed and authoritative information.

Fourth Day

Bill W., Steve, Tim, and Karen: We have final proof. We found it.

Karen: We checked these poems against Indian, Chinese, Japanese, and any other Oriental types of poems we could find, and we found out that this

3 Maurice P. Hunt and Lawrence E. Metcalf, *Teaching High School Social Studies* (New York: Harper & Row, Publishers, 1955).

> type of poem is Japanese only, and is called a *haiku*.

During the last phase of the discussion, the students offer concluding suggestions which are based on newly obtained evidence. For the most part, the additional proof was the result of the collation of the poems under investigation with all other relevant material which was accessible in the library. This line of inquiry was in part instigated by Karen's suggestion at the conclusion of the third day, which directed attention to the form and style in addition to the content of the poems.

Summary

The following four points provide the major results of this research:

1. Without exception the students were able to participate directly in the process of discovery and inquiry. This process entailed a number of related tasks—identifying and defining the problems at hand, devising alternative plans of attack, formulating working hypotheses from the given data and their previous learning experiences, testing the hypotheses by drawing logical inferences and by gathering relevant information, and arriving at a theory or "grand generalization" which draws together all bits of data and supporting hypotheses. It is interesting to note that the process of discovery moves from a stage of hunch and intuition to a stage of in-depth analysis and, finally, to the point where knowledge-claims are based on concrete, documentary evidence. While this is the general direction followed in the discovery episode, speculative or "intuitive" thinking may be found, to a great or lesser degree, in all of the phases; when there is a gap in knowledge the student reaches out into unchartered and largely unknown realms of interpretation and thinking. From this observation the complementary nature of intuitive and analytic thinking may be seen.

2. Historical materials are used as raw data or as archeological remains from which students may reconstruct a society at a given place and period. The historical document furnishes the springboards for inquiry into human thought and action and the evolution of social institutions. In the process of reconstructing the event, historical hypotheses are often checked against contemporary phenomena; the students employ both historical and social science concepts, research techniques, and methods of analysis.

3. The way material is presented, coupled with the nondirective behavior of the teacher, leads to the creation of a new psychological climate. The students now become increasingly independent and they begin to question the authority of secondary material. They generally adopt an attitude of intelligent doubt, and they tend to propose new ideas and explanations that must be carefully defended. The class is given the opportunity to exchange ideas and analyze different views and interpretations.

4. The method of discovery has a highly motivating effect on students. Almost without exception, the students, directly or indirectly, demonstrate a great deal of personal involvement with the material under discussion. During the duration of the study there was wide classroom participation and intensive utilization of library resources. The motivating effect of the discovery episode is due, in large part, to the game-like situa-

tion which reinforces the element of perplexity and incentive to explore. The teacher indirectly encourages student exploration by stubbornly refusing to provide ready-made answers.

The reader should keep in mind the exploratory nature of this study and the fact that the writers are offering observations based on rather limited samples. This research should, hopefully, provide a point of departure for further experimentation in this area. It would be advisable to undertake further study in which a variety of materials is given to students who represent all levels of education and who have a wide range of intelligence.

29. THE ILLINOIS STUDIES IN INQUIRY TRAINING

J. RICHARD SUCHMAN

We have been trying to develop inquiry skills in elementary school children. This began back in 1957 when we were disturbed by the findings of some studies. One of these found that 97 per cent of the questions asked in the classroom were asked by the teacher. Another found that as children moved from the first grade to the sixth grade, they become less empirical and based more hypotheses and tests of hypotheses on conclusions of authorities and less on their own empirical operations.

Over a period of years we have identified what seem to be necessary conditions for inquiry to occur in classroom settings, and we have tried to build a program that creates these conditions. The conditions are essentially these:

1. We find that the children need some kind of *focus* for their attention, some kind of problem or stimulus, and preferably, although not necessarily, one that is discrepant to the schemata or conceptual systems of the child. In other words, one that cannot be readily assimilated.

J. Richard Suchman, "The Illinois Studies in Inquiry Training," JOURNAL OF RESEARCH IN SCIENCE TEACHING, II, No. 3 (September 1964), 230–32. Reprinted by permission.

2. They need the condition of *freedom.* We have broken freedom down into two parts, one of which is a kind of external freedom, that is, physical freedom to reach out for desired data and information and to acquire it at any rate in any sequence the child wishes. This is antiprograming in a sense. Internal freedom is something that follows as a consequence. We found that when you give children external freedom, they are inhibited for a time and do not avail themselves of it because they have been conditioned to follow the teacher's lead and to conform. But eventually, as they explore and find that external freedom does exist, they begin to build up what we call autonomy in their operations. They make decisions and try to satisfy their own cognitive needs by gathering the kinds of information they want. They also exercise freedom in trying out ideas.

Two kinds of scanning are used: scanning the field for data, and scanning the store of ideas for conceptual models. These comprise two parts of the inquiry cycle. A child absorbs a percept and he tries to find a model he can use to assimilate it. Then, providing assimilation is incomplete, he performs some action to generate new data. At the same time that he acquires new data, he scans for new models on which to test the data. He endeavors to match the data coming in with the models being tried out. At some point the match between the data and a model is made.

3. The third condition is what O.K. Moore calls the "responsive environment." The child needs to have an environment where, when he reaches out for data, he procures something. He does not return with empty hands.

These, then, are three conditions for inquiry: the focus, the freedom to operate, and the responsive environment. If we provide these conditions we find that children inquire at elementary school age, and that inquiry will progress at a rate that far exceeds what would happen if one did not have these conditions. I am not going to say that they are necessary, but they are clearly conducive.

I would like to comment briefly on the motivation operating in this situation. One of the outcomes of creating these conditions is that you obtain a shift in motivation. When you have a teacher programing the learning experiences of the children (deciding what happens next), and when you have children following the teacher's lead, much of the motivation falls into what we call the social-ego category. The children look for rewards from the teacher and from the situation, extrinsic to the learning activity itself. When you go into the inquiry mode, you start with a problem and the children are free to attack it and build their constructs as they see fit. The motivation becomes more cognitive and takes two forms. One is the motivation of closure—to close the gap and to make the match between what is perceived and what is known. But we found that beyond this, after the children had found a reasonable degree of closure, they continued to inquire, to pull in data, and to process them. They were motivated, it seemed, by the act of inquiry itself. We were particularly curious about this.

The motivation seems to have different flavors. One is a pleasant sense of confidence a child gets in processing data even if no great problems bother him. The child picks away at an old alarm clock, takes it apart, and puts it back together, not because he is trying to build a grand theory of alarm clocks but because it is fun and because processing the kinds of data he is getting from these manipulations is very satisfying to him. He continues to do it without any real problems to prod him. There is also a sense of power and excitement in being able to do this. To borrow a phrase that J. McV. Hunt at Illinois uses, "we see in children a motivation inherent in information processing and action" and it seems to be a growing kind of motivational force that after a while tends to supplant the motivation of closure. In the beginning it seems highly important to give children problems that are discrepant in order to provide strong early interest. But after a while it becomes less necessary and children start structuring problems for themselves without having to be given one to start.

The procedure used for making children aware of the inquiry process is something we once termed Inquiry Training. (We have been sorry about the word "training" ever since.) We have produced a series of film starting with physics (we now have economics and biology, also) which are designed as discrepant events. They pose episodes which the children cannot assimilate without accommodating, or at least analyzing the event itself until assimilation is possible. The film is then the focus and offers the initial motivation. Next, we provided the freedom by allowing the children to ask yes-and-no questions to gather their data. These are questions phrased to be answered by "yes" or "no," but the teacher may qualify the answers where necessary. The questions are not attempts to elicit explanations or theory from the teacher but are strictly for data gathering, e.g., "Was the blade made of steel?"

One of our films is about a bimetal blade. When it is heated it bends downward, and when it is inserted into a tank of water, it straightens out. The demonstrator turns it over and puts it back on the flame. This time it bends upward, and when placed in water it once more straightens out. To the children who do not know anything about a bimetal blade, this is a discrepant event.

They continue from there, using "yes" or "no" questions. They cannot ask "was it because." If they start such questioning we tell them that it is their job to find explanations. "See if you can construct a theory. If you have one, you ought to be able to test it experimentally." Their experiments, too, are conducted through "yes" and "no" questions. "If we put the blade into a refrigerator would the same thing happen?" Such a question is the equivalent of an empirical test of a hypothesized relationship. The responsive environment is created by the teacher who answers the questions. As the children ask questions they build little theories which they test themselves.

We are now doing a study of the transfer of the effects of Inquiry Training with physics films, to see what influence this has on the ability to inquire into economics and biology problems. This is being done as a controlled study, in which we are comparing children who had experiences with physics to those who had not and checking the effects. So far, although the data are not all in, one thing is very clear: inquiry skills do transfer, not method per se, but a kind of attitude, a sense of self-confidence that the child has in his own ability to handle data and to build and test theories. The trained child is more willing to try out ideas after he has had this kind of experience. As far as transfer of method or approach is concerned, we do not know how much carries over. Such strategies are very hard to identify and to measure, so I am not so sure if we are going to see evidence of the transfer of methods.

We conducted a pilot study last summer with approximately 14 children to investigate the effects of cognitive style on inquiry. We had about 49 variables dealing with cognitive style, such as schematesizing, leveling, sharpening, field dependency, etc., in addition to data from the Primary Mental Abilities test. An intercorrelation matrix, including inquiry and other cognitive variables, yielded three correlation clusters suggesting three factors relevant to success in inquiry. One is the cognitive control dimension: the ability to handle and manipulate data. A second correlation cluster suggested the existence of an impulsivity factor, the capacity to leap beyond data to generate abstractions. Impulsivity leads to moving away from the data rather than "zeroing in" on it. In the inquiry process the child must shift back and forth from high cognitive control to impulsivity. If you never leave the data you will never construct theory. This ability is related to a third factor which we have identified as autonomy. If the child is high on cognitive control, impulsivity, and autonomy, we find him to be a more effective inquirer than a child who is low on any one of the three.

30. STRATEGY FOR LEARNING

HILDA TABA

From the educational tumult of the past decade, certain trends and patterns are now emerging that promise much more interesting teaching for all of us and more enthusiastic learning by our students. For example, research in education is shifting from laboratory to actual classroom situations. New concepts of learning processes offer clues to better understanding of how people learn. We can even begin to think of "strategies" of learning. Teaching, too, is developing strategies—to fit the newer concepts of learning. There is much here that is of special interest for teachers of science in the elementary grades.

An important effect of the shift to classroom-based research is the new perception of the idea of the unlimited potentiality of human learning—including the learning of those whose abilities we currently do not rate too high. The notion of a fixed IQ is being questioned, and the idea of a "functioning IQ" is developing. While no one pretends to know what the upper limit of human potentiality is, there seems to be a fairly widespread agreement that it is much higher than we have known how to realize. Gardner Murphy's book *Freeing Intelligence Through Teaching* (Harper and Brothers, New York, 1961) offers excellent reading on this subject.

From observations of what happens in classrooms in which both the curriculum and teaching concentrate on developing the use of thinking-cognitive powers, I believe that in twelve years of schooling we could achieve a level of maturity about four years beyond what we now attain. This would be especially true if our techniques of studying learning were refined to include some factors that we do not study now because they seem statistically insignificant. Some of

Hilda Taba, "Strategy for Learning," SCIENCE AND CHILDREN, *III, No. 1 (1965), 21–24. Reprinted by permission.*

these could well be the "trigger" factors that set off processes which could reorganize the entire approach of an individual to learning. By studying the effects of these factors, we may be able to determine more precisely the effect of certain strategies of teaching. For example, how does a certain strategy affect the learning of individuals who have certain abilities, certain types of social-cultural background, or certain motivational patterns? Such knowledge would be invaluable at all grade levels. We need to be alert to findings in this area and to contribute to such research whenever possible.

Recent studies are also revolutionizing the concept of readiness to learn by shifting attention from what readiness individuals *have* to how to *build* readiness—certainly an area of special interest to teachers in the elementary grades. In the first flush of enthusiasm about readiness studies, the findings that children can learn more and earlier have been translated into programs of acceleration. Eventually, it is hoped, these ideas will be translated into creating more potent learning in depth, rather than merely a more rapid covering of the same ground.

Perhaps the most interesting and productive consequence of the new studies of the teaching-learning processes has been the restoration of a balance between content and process as ingredients of learning. In the past, too much time has been spent on conflict between these two areas. Recent emphasis on analyzing the structure of content clarifies the function of the different levels of content in curriculum, in teaching, and in learning. We are analyzing more clearly the processes of learning.

Today, we can identify more precisely the four targets of learning: knowledge, thinking, attitudes, and skills. We need to recognize that only the objective of knowledge can be implemented through organizing curriculum content. The other three depend upon process or the kind of learning experiences that are made available to children. For example, an objective such as thinking has remained in the realm of "pray and hope," because almost anything from daydreaming to inventing the concept of relativity could be, and has been, classified as thinking. This lack of analysis of what constitutes thinking has naturally resulted in uneconomical and ineffective teaching and learning of "thinking." It was too easy to assume that thinking is an automatic by-product of mastering "a subject matter" or of a "natural ability for it." True enough, a small percentage of children did learn some things on their own. Now that all kinds of children remain in school longer, we have an obligation to help all children learn to think.

Because of an inadequate behavioral analysis of thinking as an objective and ingredient of learning, we have relied on accumulating descriptive knowledge in order to enable learners to "think with it" later. Our curriculum in many areas, and especially so in the social studies, has been extremely descriptive. It has called for the same level of thinking, no matter what shifts have been made in content at successive grade levels. These shifts in content have not always been accompanied by systematically escalating the opportunities (or demands) to apply more complex and abstract modes of thinking.

We need to develop categories of the processes of thinking which can be learned and taught. The study of

Concept Formation

Overt Activity	Covert Mental Operation	Eliciting Question
1. Enumeration and listing	Differentiation	What did you see? Hear? Note?
2. Grouping	Identifying common properties, abstracting	What belongs together? On what criterion?
3. Labeling, categorizing	Determining the hierarchical order of items; super- and sub-ordination	How would you call these groups? What belongs under what?
	Interpretation of Data	
1. Identifying points	Differentiation	What did you note? See? Find?
2. Explaining items of identified information	Relating points to each other Determining cause-and-effect relationships	Why did so-and-so happen?
3. Making inferences	Going beyond what is given Finding implications, extrapolating	What does this mean? What picture does it create in your mind? What would you conclude?
	Application of Principles	
1. Predicting consequences Explaining unfamiliar phenomena Hypothesizing	Analyzing the nature of the problem or situation Retrieving relevant knowledge	What would happen if . . . ?
2. Explaining, supporting the predictions and hypotheses	Determining the causal links leading to prediction or hypothesis	Why do you think this would happen?
3. Verifying the prediction or hypothesis	Using logical principles or factual knowledge to determine necessary and sufficient conditions	What would it take for so-and-so to be true or probably true?

thinking in elementary school children attempts to do this.[1] It deals with three cognitive tasks: (1) concept formation, or the organizing of specific information into conceptual systems; (2) interpretation of data, or the inductive process of developing generalizations and inferences from specific data; and (3) the application of principles and facts, or the deductive process of using knowledge to explain unfamiliar phenomena, to predict, and to hypothesize. These are learnable and teachable targets, because each represents a cluster of skills that can be identified and taught. They are surely especially pertinent to the teaching of science in the elementary grades. In fact, the science teacher should feel particular responsibility for developing these skills. Let us look briefly at each of these targets.

Concept formation involves essentially a way of putting unorganized

[1] Hilda Taba, S. Levine, and F. F. Elzey, *Thinking in Elementary School Children*, Cooperative Research Project No. 1574. U.S. Office of Education, Washington, D.C., 1964.

information into some kind of mental filing system by grouping together an array of dissimilar objects or events on the basis of some common property that they possess, such as grouping together climate, weather, altitude, and topography, because all represent some elements of climate.

Interpretation of data is essentially a process of evolving generalizations from an analysis of concrete data. This is an inductive way of processing data and making inferences from the data. It involves the ability to go beyond that which is directly given and to arrive at a larger meaning, such as putting together the data on species of animals in a particular area and the data on water and vegetation in the same areas and inferring that generally certain species of animals are found in certain types of environments.

Application of principles and facts to new situations involves a deductive sequence. It starts when either a problem or a set of conditions is presented and hypothesizing regarding the possible solutions or consequences is required, such as asking students who have studied nomadic life in a desert to hypothesize what changes would occur in the way of life in the desert if water became available. It also involves a support or verification of these hypotheses and predictions by the application of relevant factual knowledge or generalizations, such as that the presence of water makes possible the growing of crops and, therefore, also a form of settled life and growth of cities.

Each of these cognitive tasks involves several levels of overt activity and of covert mental operations. Therefore, there must also be corresponding teaching strategies which elicit these processes. The three levels of the three dimensions of the teaching-learning process are shown in the chart on the previous page.

Some Principles for Strategies of Learning

Several theoretical principles underlie the identification of these skills and especially the formulation of teaching strategies for helping students master them.

1. Learning is a transactional process

An individual organizes whatever he receives by way of information, from whatever source, according to his current conceptual system. This system may be faulty, partial, productive, or unproductive. For example, in his inquiry training, Suchman shows a filmed "episode" in which what appears to be a plain metal blade is put over a flame. The blade bends downward. The students tend to interpret this phenomenon in terms of the concept that metal softens with heat and therefore bends downward. They are, therefore, baffled when the same blade bends upward when it is turned over and inserted into the flame again.[2]

Or, the third graders who see in a film a girl in a jungle village putting the coins she received from the sale of carved figures into a pot and then burying it in the floor of the hut may interpret this act as "keeping the money safe from baby sitters," because this is part of their concept reasons for keeping money safe, inappropriate as it is to the jungle situation. In a sense, then, an individual

[2] J. R. Suchman. *The Elementary School Training in Scientific Inquiry*, Illinois Studies in Inquiry Training. Title VII, Project No. 216, U.S. Office of Education, Washington, D.C., 1962.

"remakes," or reorganizes, reality according to his conceptual scheme. The information does something to the individual, and the individual does something to the information.

To aid students acquire increasingly more productive conceptual systems for organizing information, we need to devise learning-teaching strategies designed to help them learn to organize knowledge and not just present them with organized knowledge. One important aspect of these strategies is to stress the asking of questions instead of the giving of answers. The types of questions the teacher asks determine what students can or will be allowed to do.

2. The learning of cognitive skills is a developmental process

Each cognitive task involves a series of hierarchical skills that represent sequential steps in mastering the task. Each preceding step is a prerequisite to mastering the next one, and each successive step should capitalize on what preceded. The development of cognitive skills is not instantaneous learning. Each subsequent step requires the use of more complex and more sophisticated operations than did the preceding step. The success with each subsequent step depends on the mastery of the cognitive operations involved in the preceding one.

The concepts themselves are hierarchical in the sense of representing different degrees of complexity, abstractness, and generality. This introduces still another development sequence: that of combining concepts of a lower order into those of a higher order.

In an ideal overall sequence, one would rotate tasks which require assimilating new information into an already established conceptual organization with tasks that require a reorganization and stretching of that scheme.

3. Maturation of learning requires escalation both of content and of cognitive processes

The planning of learning experiences to promote thinking of this type requires planning on two tracks. One is the sequence and escalation of the basic concepts, ideas, and the required information. The other is the sequence and the escalation of the processes by which information is organized and used. These need to progress together; the neglect of either may prevent or hinder the development of autonomous thinking. Sequences must be planned for both content and mental operations. If not, the pacing of learning is likely to be faulty in the sense that either more or less is required than is possible for the student. The result in the first case is the loss of the autonomy of student thinking, because the student must revert to passive absorption. In the second case the students are bored because the performance required represents repetition of concepts and skills which are already mastered.

Strategies of Teaching

What strategies of teaching should the teacher apply for this type of learning? First, the teacher needs to construct for himself two sets of cognitive maps by which to guide the process of learning: (1) the map of the content topics, of the dimensions of the topics, and of the basic ideas and concepts that the study of these topics is to produce, and (2) of the nature of intellectual skills involved and of the ways in which these skills are mastered.

Second, teachers need to change their role from the customary answer-giving to question-asking. Cognitive operations are stimulated only as the students are required to *search* for answers and to invent and discover the processes by which to deal with the tasks proposed by the questions.

Third, such a concept of learning introduces a different approach to handling content topics. The direct emphasis is not on "covering" a quantity of specific content but on sampling judiciously the specific instances which are valid examples of certain basic ideas and concepts. These instances must then be explored in sufficient detail to make it possible for students to "discover" the basic idea, generalization, or a concept. A teaching strategy which leads to mastery of powerful inductive generalizations and the necessary application of the corresponding skills is teaching for transfer, because transfer can occur only through the mediation of generalizations.

If these cognitive processes are learned in an interactive process, such as classroom discussion, students have a new source of learning new modes of thinking. In an interactive classroom, students are aided in extending their models for thought processes by "taking off from each others' shoulders," so to speak.

Finally, teachers need to understand and to accept the fact that it takes both time and practice to acquire new skills in thinking. This is especially true when preceding instruction has cultivated habits which are inconsistent with the processes required in thinking.

However, the results in our study of thinking suggest that, given adequate teaching strategy and a curriculum design which facilitates the stepwise development of concepts and ideas, even a student who is considered a "slow learner" will learn to master the higher levels of cognitive skills. All students make great strides both in the mastery of essential knowledge and in the mature use of reasoning power which is considerably beyond the level usually attained. At first the pacing will be slow for all because of the additional task of learning cognitive skills. Later the progress in both content mastery and thinking is cumulatively accelerated.

31. THE LEARNING REQUIREMENTS FOR ENQUIRY

ROBERT M. GAGNÉ

One of the most interesting and important ideas which has ben given emphasis in recent discussions of science education is the idea of enquiry. It has been stated to be perhaps the most critical kind of activity that the scientist engages in, and for that reason to represent one of the most essential objectives of science instruction. Accordingly, there appears to be a very widespread agreement that enquiry is a worthwhile objective—something that our various educational efforts should deliberately try to achieve. And there is a widespread consensus that an instructional program for the student of science most clearly achieves this rightful goal when it enables such a student to adopt the procedures of scientific enquiry in response to any new unsolved problem he encounters.

Along with this emphasis on the importance of the method of enquiry there has been an accompanying realization that many traditional courses in science, at all levels of education, exhibit serious deficiencies insofar as they fail to get across to students the elements of this method. Many such courses seem to be neglecting the student in the most important sense that they do not encourage him to acquire the attitudes of enquiry, the method of enquiry, the understanding of enquiry. They may provide him with a great many facts, with knowledge of important principles, even with the capability of using previously discovered principles in situations novel to him. But they omit this essential part of his education as a scientist, or even as an informed citizen, by not establishing within him the disposition which makes him able to employ enquiry in the manner so well-known to scientists.

Perhaps no writer has described this deficiency in science education so

Robert M. Gagné, "The Learning Requirements for Enquiry," JOURNAL OF RESEARCH IN SCIENCE TEACHING, *I, No. 2 (1963), 144–53. Reprinted by permission.*

cogently and so thoroughly as has Schwab. It is worthwhile to quote here a short passage from his Inglis Lecture.[1]

> It is the almost total absence of this portrayal of science which marks the greatest disparity between science as it is and science as seen through most textbooks of science. We are shown conclusions of enquiry as if they were certain or nearly certain facts. Further, we rarely see these conclusions as other than isolated, independent "facts." Their coherence and organization—the defining marks of *scientific* knowledge—are underemphasized or omitted. And we catch hardly a glimpse of the other constituents of scientific enquiry: organizing principles, data, and the interpretation of data.

The problem, then, seems pretty well-defined and agreed upon. It is, "How can one go about introducing, or perhaps restoring, to the process of instruction the necessary conditions which will make it more probable that the student learns about science as enquiry?" Obviously this is not as simple a matter as is "adding material" on neutrinos in atomic structure, or even as is "revising material" such as that on the reactivity of inert chemical elements. It is more complicated than either of these, because it is more difficult to identify and specify what it is that the student must learn. Yet this is the task that must be faced, complicated or not, if the desired change is to be brought about.

Let us assume, then, that there is general agreement about the problem and about the objective to be sought in its solution. Now, what, if anything, can the methods and results of research on the learning process contribute to this problem? This is the interest of the student of learning theory. Obviously, dealing with science as enquiry must be something that is learned. What do we know about learning that is relevant in establishing such a capability in the student?

Analysis of the Problem

As is the case with other users of scientific methods, the investigator of human learning customarily begins by defining or specifying what the problem is in terms which have served this function in the past. These terms serve to separate the general aspects of the problem situation from the specific and therefore incidental ones, and thus enable him to think about it in a rigorous fashion.

When this basic method is applied to the problem, the first distinction which becomes apparent is this: First, there is something we may call a *terminal capability*, something that the student is able to do after he has learned. That is to say, if we have been successful in establishing the correct conditions for learning, we will be able to infer that the student is or is not capable of employing the methods of scientific enquiry. To make this inference possible, of course, we must observe some kind of behavior, which may also be specified, and we might refer to these observed events as *terminal behaviors.*

Second, the other major category of events with which we must deal in this problem is a set of conditions which are used to bring about a *change* in the student's capability. These we may call the *instructional conditions.* Potentially these conditions include everything that is done to or by the student from some initial point in time (when he does not possess the desired capability) to some other point in time (when he does). But more specifically, they are all the aspects of the instructional situation which can be shown to affect this change, including the events that take place in classrooms, laboratories, libraries, at his desk, or elsewhere.

Perhaps this distinction seems obvious to you—the terminal capability, on the one hand, and the instructional conditions which accomplish the change between initial and terminal capability, on the other. But this distinction has not always been carefully maintained in thinking about this problem, even by people who think profoundly about it. It is nonetheless an essential distinction, and one which will be referred to again later.

The Terminal Capability

In order to understand and specify the problem further, we need to ask again, what is the nature of this desired capability of using the approach of enquiry towards the solution of problems? Having read the authors who have written on this subject, one concludes that they have spent many more words describing what it is *not* than in describing what it *is*. What it is not, all agree, is an activity which deals with scientific concepts as things rather than abstractions, or with scientific hypotheses and theories as fixed facts rather than as convenient models subject to empirical test. I judge them to mean, that what it *is* is a set of activities characterized by a problem-solving approach, in which each newly encountered phenomenon becomes a challenge for thinking. Such thinking begins with a careful set of systematic observations, proceeds to design the measurements required, clearly distinguishes between what is observed and what is inferred, invents interpretations which are under ideal circumstances brilliant leaps, but always testable, and draws reasonable conclusions. In other words, it is the kind of activity that might be called the essence of scientific research (neglecting for the moment such clearly relevant components as obtaining research funds and writing good scientific reports, among others).

Can such inferred capabilities as these be observed as behavior? It does not seem unreasonable that this is possible, provided we accept the fact that the sample of behavior we may be able to observe is somewhat limited and therefore somewhat unreliable. This appears to be the kind of behavior the university science faculty tries to observe in its graduate students. It uses various methods of doing this, such as requiring the execution of an initial problem before the dissertation, or requiring the completion of a series of partial problems, or by asking the student to "think through" how he would approach an already reported investigation, or in some other manner. In many instances, more and better observation of this sort could actually be done, if some greater thought were given to it.

Observation of such behavior is also done with increasing frequency at the undergraduate college level. Here we find programs of independent study, honors programs, and other devices which require students to take an independent approach of enquiry towards a scientific problem. Again, the frequency and representativeness of this kind of observation of "enquiry behavior" can be improved. A number of authors suggest, for example, that the laboratory be made the setting for the practice of this approach, by designing and using the kinds of laboratory problems which are invitations to careful thought, rather than "standard exercises."

Can this kind of activity of scientific enquiry be extended downward to the secondary school and even into the primary grades? Of course it can, in some sense, since we know that even elementary students are quite capable of some pretty good thinking. But whether it should or not may involve some other considerations which we have not yet touched upon.

Conditions of Instruction

We are now ready to look more closely at the other part of the problem—how do we effect a change such that a student who doesn't initially employ the approach of enquiry toward problems will employ this approach? What are the conditions of instruction which are likely to effect this change?

Practice in Enquiry

One of the conditions emphasized by several writers on this question is that of *practicing strategies* in proceeding from the known to the unknown. Bruner,[2] for example, calls this "learning the heuristics of discovery," and states that although the form that such learning should take is not known in detail, it seems reasonable that improvement in the technique of enquiry should depend upon practice in enquiry. Schwab[1] points out the ways that such practice can be conducted in the laboratory and in the classroom. The import of these writings for the design of instructional conditions is clear: the student should be provided with opportunities to carry out inductive thinking; to make hypotheses and to test them, in a great variety of situations, in the laboratory, in the classroom, and by his own individual efforts.

It is impossible not to agree with this prescription in a specific sense. The student who has been given practice merely in the recall of ideas, or in their application in particular situations, will not necessarily acquire these important techniques of enquiry. In physics, for example, the setting of problems like this one is a common practice in many textbooks: "A box slides down a 30° inclined plane with an acceleration of 10 ft./sec.^{2}. What is the coefficient of friction between the box and the plane?" Now the student obviously is getting practice from performing such problems, but the question is, what kind of practice? Obviously not the same kind he would get if this kind of problem were stated: "A box slides down an inclined plane. Can this event be shown to be compatible with Newton's second law of motion?" In this second case, what is being required of the student is that he relate some observed events to a general principle (or "law"), and that he himself *think out* what these relationships are. First he must identify the forces at work, specify the mass and acceleration, and then induce how these specific variables may be related to the general equation $F = ma$. And in carrying out this enquiry, he is obtaining valuable practice which will doubtless be transferable to other problems, not necessarily within the field of physics alone. A similar technique, or thinking strategy, may be useful in quite a different situation—in thinking about the reactions of chemical solutions, or about the metabolism of a cell, or even about the relation of national income to productivity.

If there are any limitations to the value of *practice in enquiry*, they are probably to be found in this fact: such practice is *not the whole story.* Establishing conditions for practice in enquiry does not by any means exhaust the requirements for the instructional conditions needed for the achievement of the desired terminal capability. And there are real dangers in thinking that such practice does constitute the entire set of requirements for this purpose.

Some scholars have perceived this danger. In a recent interview recorded in the newspapers, the noted physicist Dr. C. N. Yang[3] states his concern about the increasingly common practice of starting students on basic research early in their college careers. Students who are educated in this way, he says, will not be able to stand away from their work and see it in perspective; they will think of research as a study of a single problem rather than as a broad attack on the entire frontier of the unknown. In dealing with new problems, such students will lack the deep understanding on which to draw for help.

Dr. Yang's concern is essentially the same as that just mentioned. There is nothing wrong with practicing enquiry, and surely enquiry is the kind of capability we want students of science to attain in some terminal sense. But practicing enquiry too soon, and without a suitable background of knowledge, can have a narrowing and cramping effect on the individual's development of independent thinking. And if this is true at the level of the college sophomore, surely this danger must be all the more severe if we consider the instructional situation in the high school and the elementary school.

Is this a valid objection? If practice in enquiry can be given too soon, or too exclusively, what other parts are there to the instructional situation? What else is there to learn, if one does not practice the strategies of thinking?

Two Other Components of Instruction

There are two other major capabilities which are of importance as objectives of instruction. It is possible to think that they are at least as important as practice in enquiry, and it is possible to argue that they are even more *essential*, in the sense that they represent *prior requirements*, if the practice of enquiry is to be carried out successfully. These two other capabilities may be characterized as follows:

(*1*) the capability of *generalizing* the principles of knowledge to the variety of situations to which they are applicable (and have been shown to be applicable by earlier scholars) ; and

(*2*) the capability of *discriminating* the probable and improbable applicability of hypotheses to new problem situations.

In general terms, the reasons why these kinds of capability need to be fostered by the instructional situation are easy to understand. If an individual is to try to solve new problems, he must have a knowledge of a great variety of principles which can be potentially applicable to these problems. The best guarantee that these principles are available will be to insure that he has acquired generalizable knowledge, in other words, that he has *broad knowledge*. And when he does make the inductive leap that characterizes enquiry, he should be able to know that he is doing something that has a probability of being right, rather than of just being silly. He must discriminate the good ideas from the bad, in accordance with their probable consequences. One might call this *critical or incisive knowledge*. But both of these are needed *before* practice in enquiry can have the positive effects that are expected of it.

Generalizable Knowledge

Consider again the student who is asked to use the sliding of a weight down an inclined plane as an instance compatible with Newton's second law. It is obvious, isn't it, that the student must have a rather sizeable amount of broad knowledge before he can be successful at this problem? Among other things, he must know (*1*) what Newton's second law is, in terms which make sense to him; (*2*) what acceleration is, and its relation to velocity, time, and distance; (*3*) what mass is, and how it is related to weight; (*4*) how the angles of an inclined plane can lead to a conceptualization of the magnitude and direction of the forces at work. Others could undoubtedly be mentioned. It is senseless to think that these principles of knowledge are trivial, or that the student can easily have "picked them up" incidentally to some other learning, including perhaps previous practice in enquiry. It is surely wrong to believe that the student can *think* without *knowing* these principles. This would be like asking him to play chess without ever having learned what the rules are. And it is probably quite contrary to the interests of learning to ask the student to undertake "enquiry practice" without knowing these principles. As evidence for the latter statement I refer to some work of my own and my colleagues on learning in mathematics, which has shown clearly that learning to solve new problems is critically dependent upon the acquisition of previous knowledge.[4]

Broad, generalizable knowledge is a prerequisite for the successful practice of enquiry, whether as a part of the total instructional process or as a terminal capability. How does the student acquire this broad knowledge? Well, that is a question of great interest to a student of human learning. And some things are known about it, some things not yet. Here are some observations about this broad, generalizable knowledge that are relevant.

1. Such knowledge cannot all be attained by a student by the use of the method of enquiry itself. Were we to follow this suggestion, we should have to put the student back in the original situation that Newton found himself in, and ask the student to invent a solution, as Newton did. It would be difficult to achieve this situation, in the first place, and presumably not all students would achieve what Newton did, even then. But the major difficulty with this suggestion is that it would be a most terrible waste of time. Are we going to have students rediscover the laws of motion, the periodic table, the structure of the atom, the circulation of the blood, and all the other achievements of science simply in order to ensure that instructional conditions are "pure," in the sense that they demand enquiry? Surely no one seriously proposes that this method should be followed.

2. The possession of broad and

generalizable knowledge is an admirable capability, and not to be equated with "knowing facts." There is quite a difference between knowing a *fact*, such as "Newton invented the laws of motion," and a *principle*, such as might be exhibited if we asked a student to describe a situation which could be used to test Newton's second law of motion. One might call the ability to repeat verbally the statement, "If an unbalanced force acts upon a body, the body will accelerate in proportion to the magnitude, etc.," knowing a fact. But to know such a fact is not the same as knowing this law of motion as a principle, as the previous example has indicated. Knowledge of principles is generalizable; one expects a student who knows Newton's second law as a principle to be able to describe a wide variety of specific situations in which the validity of the law can be tested. Such knowledge is of tremendous value, not just in and of itself, but because it constitutes an essential basis for acquiring other knowledge. To an equal degree, it is an essential basis for the practice of the strategies of enquiry.

3. As to how knowledge is acquired, one should not assume that this has to be done, or is best accomplished, by "routine drill." Repetition does indeed appear to be one desirable condition for instruction, but only one. At least equally important, if not more so, is the condition which fosters the use of *discovery* on the part of the student. In its simplest form, this means simply that it seems to be better for learning if one can get the student to respond to a situation in his own way, and in a way which is also correct, rather than having him "copy" or "echo" something that the teacher says or that the book says.[2, 5] In other words, discovery appears to be a very fundamental principle of good instruction. It applies to *all* conceptual learning, the learning of principles and generalizations, and may even apply to the learning of a simpler sort such as the memorizing of names or facts. But discovery, as a very fundamental condition of most learning, should not be equated with enquiry, which is the exercise of all the various activities making up what we have identified as the terminal capability. The construction of a response by a learner, something that happens nearly every step of the way in the process of learning, is what usually has been called discovery. In contrast to this, enquiry is the terminal thinking process we want the student to be able to engage in, *after* he has taken all the necessary previous steps in learning.

In summary then, it appears that broad, generalizable knowledge is best conceived as knowledge of principles. As such, it may be attained in the context of instructional conditions which include "discovery" on the part of the learner. Knowledge of principles is not what is usually referred to in a deprecating manner as "knowledge of mere facts," nor is such knowledge best acquired under conditions of sheer repetition. But knowledge of principles is prerequisite to the successful practice of the techniques of enquiry.

Incisive Knowledge

The other kind of capability we have identified as prerequisite to successful enquiry is the possession of critical or incisive knowledge. In terms that the psychologist uses, this is the capability of *discriminating* between a good idea and a bad one, or between a probably successful course of action and a probably unsuccessful one.

Just for variety of illustration, let us take a new example. Suppose we set the student this problem in enquiry: "How does the picture of an object get 'into the head' in the sense of being experienced as a picture and retained from one occasion to another?" Suppose that the student has a certain amount of generalizable knowledge about the eye, and its function as a camera, so that he is able readily to recall the principles which get the picture onto the retina. But now, how does it get "into the head?" If he has no more knowledge than this, he may think of a variety of mechanisms, each of which may be brilliantly inventive, but some of which may be silly. Perhaps it is carried by a scanning mechanism similar to television. Perhaps the frequencies of various light waves are transmitted directly over nerves. Perhaps the pattern of neurones stimulated corresponds to the pattern of physical energy. Perhaps the stimulation is carried in some mechanical way. Perhaps there are differences in the strength of electrical transmission. Perhaps the pattern of brightness is transmitted as a pattern of frequencies, different from those of the light waves themselves. And so on. Any fairly bright student can probably think of quite a large number of possibilities.

Is there an instructional value to encouraging students to make such guesses? Probably so, but *only when* the means are simultaneously provided for the student to estimate that an idea is probably good or probably bad. The wildness of the guesses, or perhaps even the frequency of wild guesses, is a most doubtful criterion. (People whose guesses are extremely wild are called schizophrenics.) It seems to me that if the student is encouraged to form hypotheses, even to follow hunches, as a part of practice in enquiry, that these hunches and guesses should be *disciplined* ones. This does not mean at all that hypotheses need to be restricted in scope or simple in content. On the contrary, they can be as elaborate as his abilities and his generalizable knowledge will permit. But he should be able to estimate their consequences. Any hypothesis is subject to the discipline of ultimate verification.

What kind of knowledge is it that makes possible the discrimination of good ideas from bad? Well, it is not very different in kind, although it is different in content, from the other kind of knowledge we have described. Generally speaking, it is knowledge of principles, sprinkled here and there, perhaps, with a few facts. In the case of our example of the picture in the head, the student needs to know at least the following principles: (*1*) the relation between intensity of stimulation and frequency of neural response; (*2*) the frequency and strength of neural responses; (*3*) the rapidity of the nervous impulse; (*4*) the relation between distribution of nerve endings and distribution of frequency of nervous impulses; and a number of others. Each of these principles and facts provides him with a means of checking the compatibility of the hypotheses he generates in terms of their probability or improbability.

Here again, then, in this capability for *self-criticism of ideas*, we come upon another essential need for knowledge, prior to the exercise of enquiry. From a base of knowledge of principles, enquiry takes off. Where it comes to rest is also dependent upon the possession of knowledge. Enquiry which cannot be checked against estimates that hypotheses are probably good or probably bad will be undisciplined enquiry, possibly as satisfying as the daydreams of Walter Mitty, but of no greater social importance. Likewise, the practice of enquiry which lacks the discipline of self-criticism may be expected to be of no positive value to the development of the individual, and could even be harmful. Which teacher of science has not encountered the student who is constantly willing to display a bubbling fountain of ideas, almost all of them worthless? Is this what we want to encourage?

The Instructional Basis of Enquiry

This analysis of the instructional conditions required to establish the capabilities for enquiry emphasizes that the major essential is the possession of a body of organized knowledge. On the whole, the more highly organized this knowledge is, the better; it will be better retained that way.

What are the implications of this line of reasoning for the science curriculum and for science instruction? It may be of greatest meaningfulness if the answer to this question is attempted by considering what science instruction might be like, not at some particular level of development, such as high school or college, but throughout the entire range of the educational sequence from kindergarten onwards. However, this might be better done "from the top down," because the interrelationships of problem-solving, knowledge, and fundamental skills are most clearly revealed by such an analysis. Accordingly, let us consider what seem to be approximately definable "levels" of science instruction. Of course these are not hard and fast distinctions, nor are they exclusive categories. Learning takes place during the entire course of an individual's lifetime, and it is only the relative priorities which can be indicated by such an analysis.

The Independent Investigator

At the highest level of development we have the student who is beginning to take all of the responsibilities of an independent scientist. He has broad knowledge, not only within his specialized field, but of others as well. Furthermore, he understands and has practiced the methods of enquiry sufficiently so that he knows what he is doing, and understands his own limitations. He is able to begin a new line of investigation in a disciplined, responsible manner, with deliberate attention to what has gone before, but with a mind unhampered by tradition. Currently, we think of this capability as being possessed by the second- or third-year graduate student. If our educational system were reasonably effective, this level could perhaps be achieved by people of the age of present college juniors.

The Scientific Enquirer

At the next lower level, we find the student who has acquired enough broad subject-matter knowledge to be able to learn to speculate, to form and test hypotheses about scientific problems which are not trivial, and which he himself can subject to the discipline of self-criticism. In other words, the emphasis at this level of instruction might profitably be upon the method of enquiry. This should be practiced in the discussion class, in the laboratory, as well as in individual study. Again, making the assumption of a reasonably efficient educational system, the study should probably be able to begin this phase of instruction at the age of present 11th graders.

But in order to do this successfully, we have argued, he must have acquired a great deal of broad and incisive knowledge. The latter kinds of knowledge are not confined to the facts and principles of content, it should be noted. They also include knowledge about methods—of observing, classifying, describing, inferring, and conceptual invention.

The Student of Knowledge

This level of instruction emphasizes the learning of broad and critical knowledge, particularly of what previous generations of scientists have found out about the world, as well as the more fundamental principles which have led to the formulation of modern scientific conceptions. At this stage, the student needs to begin to acquire large masses of previously formulated principles of knowledge. At the same time, he needs to learn to engage deliberately and systematically in the fundamental activities used by the scientist, in as wide a variety of contexts as possible. Such activities include controlled observation, classification, measurement, inference, the formulation of models. Accordingly, there is definite need for the "laboratory" at this level. But the activities resemble those of the "laboratory exercise" more than they do the "independent enquiry." If he is encouraged to do the latter, he will fail because he doesn't *know* enough to behave like a scientist. Accordingly, his activity will either be extremely narrow in scope or will tend to be ridiculous, neither of which outcomes will have salutary effects upon his learning.

Does this suggestion of an emphasis on acquiring broad knowledge carry the implication of "stifling curiosity?" Not at all. There are plenty of rewards for curiosity, in discovering new things about the world, in exploring previously unknown paths of knowledge, in trying one's hand at new kinds of classification, in finding out how indirect measurements can be made and verified, in seeing how one can best communicate scientific information, and in many other areas. Curiosity is not the special possession of the fully trained scientist. Neither is the method of discovery in learning, as has been pointed out previously.

This level of instruction could probably have its inception around the age level currently attending the 6th or 7th grade.

The Competent Performer

Acquiring broad knowledge in the way that it should be acquired, and particularly knowledge of the methods of the scientist, is in turn based upon a stage of instruction which extends downward to the kindergarten (and informally, farther than that). For what is needed first of all in science instruction are certain kinds of performance capabilities. The word *skills* should carry no negative aura, but it seems to for some people, so let us avoid it and refer to *competencies*. At this level, the question is not so much "Does the student *know* something," but "Can he *do* something." We are used to thinking of these competencies as "reading, writing, and arithmetic," but what an inadequate description that is! When one considers the competencies needed for learning about science, it is quite probable, first of all, that this set of three leaves some important ones out. Beyond this, they do not adequately convey what kinds of specific capabilities are really intended.

No one seems to have adequately faced up to the necessity for identifying and describing these fundamental competencies which underly all of learning about science. A good list would include not only number computation, but also spatial and manipulative skills, and the capabilities of observing, classifying, measuring, describing, inferring, and model conceptualizing. In general, there should be good agreement that these competencies are important to science instruction. Shouldn't the high school student know how to *describe* an unfamiliar object seen for the first time? More than this, though, the suggestion made here is that the later acquisition of broad and incisive knowledge about science will be inadequate and unsuccessful unless the student has already acquired the capability of observing and describing what he sees. How can he acquire such knowledge unless he is able to distinguish clearly, and in terms of his own behavior, the description of an observed object or event from the description of a conceptual model?

As stated earlier, instruction in these fundamental capabilities so essential to the understanding of science carries no implication of the "routinizing of instruction" or the "deadening of curiosity." A child simply has to learn to read before he can understand printed texts. Similarly, an individual needs to know how to observe, to classify, to describe, to conceptualize, before he can understand science or the activities of scientists. All of these competencies can be acquired through his own efforts, motivated by his own curiosity, and by means of his own discoveries.

At the same time, it seems to be totally erroneous to look upon these early attainments as having anything but a specious resemblance to the activities of disciplined enquiry, or to contend that they can be acquired by "practice in enquiry." One doesn't learn to be a scientist, or to appreciate science, by pretending to be a scientist. What is the difference, in principle, between trying to "practice enquiry" in the second grade, and trying to practice "being a physician" at the same age level? Why should anyone be led, perhaps by wishful thinking, to give serious consideration to the former, while at the same time chuckling patronizingly at the latter? Engaging in enquiry of a successful, productive, and useful variety can be undertaken when the individual has acquired a store of broad and critical knowledge, and this in turn can be acquired when he has learned some prerequisite but very important fundamental capabilities. At the earliest stage of instruction, one needs to be most concerned with these latter competencies, which will remain with the student all his life.

Having described a sequence of acquired competencies from top to bottom which is based upon the best generalizations from studies of the learning process, one must be careful not to imply that there is no overlap among the kinds of capabilities to be acquired at each of these four "levels" of instruction. At the earliest stage, for example, the child is certainly acquiring some knowledge of principles, and even a litle bit of the strategy of clear thinking, even though the major part of what he most needs to learn are the competencies (or skills) mentioned. And similar comments could be made about other stages. None of them is "pure." Even at the highest of these levels, as we know, the student may often have to "catch up" on some broad knowledge he somehow missed at a much earlier level. If he has missed some of the important competencies at the earliest level, the chances are very good that he has some time previously decided to major in some field other than science.

In summary then, let us consider what would happen in science instruction, this time beginning at the bottom, if it were seriously designed to establish the terminal capability of enquiry. This is not an attempt to describe what *does* happen, because we are far from that condition, but what *should* happen. At the earliest level of instruction, the individual needs to learn how to observe, how to figure, how to measure, how to orient things in space, how to describe, how to classify objects and events, how to infer, and how to make conceptual models. These capabilities he will use all of his life. If he becomes a student of science, they will make possible the acquiring of broad knowledge of principles, the incisive knowledge which makes possible the self-criticism of new ideas, and the disciplined exercise of the method of enquiry. If he chooses some other field as a career, they will provide a fundamental understanding of science which is quite independent of any particular scientific knowledge he may read about. At the next level, he needs to make a thoroughgoing start at acquiring broad knowledge and critical knowledge of the principles of science, throughout the various disciplines, and including knowledge of both content and method. This knowledge is essential if he is later going to practice making reasonable hypotheses and testing them; in other words, if he is later to practice enquiry. The practice of enquiry itself might begin at the next stage, along with a continuation of the learning of substantive knowledge, perhaps with a somewhat greater degree of specialization. This enquiry practice will, on the one hand, be soundly derived from suitably broad knowledge; and on the other, it will be carried out so as to make possible discriminations between "good" and "bad" ideas. But it will nevertheless be genuine enquiry, in which the student is encouraged to solve problems by means of unrestrained inductive thinking, and in which he is rewarded for his ingenuity. Having done all this, the student is then ready for the final stage, learning to assume the full responsibilities of the scientific investigator. At this stage, he must learn to depend upon himself, and to trust himself, to look upon problems objectively; to have new ideas; and to be able to judge them critically. In all of these activities he will be enormously aided by his previous practice in enquiry, as well as by his knowledge of scientific principles and methods, and by the fundamental capabilities he acquired early in his educational career.

It must be quite clear that "practice in enquiry" for the student of science has great value. But to be successful it must be based upon a great variety of prerequisite knowledges and competencies which themselves are learned, sometimes by "discovery," but inconceivably by what is called "enquiry."

References

1. Schwab, J. J., "The Teaching of Science as Enquiry," *The Teaching of Science*, Harvard University Press, Cambridge, 1962.

2. Bruner, J. S., "The Act of Discovery," *Harvard Educational Review*, **31,** 21–32 (1961).

3. Yang, C. N., quoted in article in *Pittsburgh Post-Gazette*, Friday, December 28, 1962.

4. Gagné, R. M., J. R. Mayor, H. L. Garstens, and N. E. Paradise, "Factors in Acquiring Knowledge of a Mathematical Task," *Psychol. Monographs*, **76,** No. 7 (Whole No. 526) (1962).

5. Gagné, R. M., "The Acquisition of Knowledge," *Psychol. Rev.*, **69,** 355–365 (1962).

32. MODELS FOR TEACHING

BRUCE R. JOYCE

Describing Teaching Strategies

Since the function of a teaching strategy is to provide a model or a paradigm around which an educational environment can be built, it has to establish a blueprint on which a curriculum, or a media package, can be built, or on which the teacher can model his behavior so as to achieve desired effects. It is important, then, that a teaching strategy be constructed so that it can be *acted on.* Curriculum workers, teachers and media specialists have to be able to do the things it asks, or it will not work for them.

In this paper,* we will look at

Bruce R. Joyce, "Models for Teaching," from THE TEACHER-INNNOVATOR: A PROGRAM TO PREPARE TEACHERS, *U.S. Office of Education FS5.258:58021 (Washington, D.C.: Government Printing Office, 1968), pp. 197–238.*

N.B. The models identified in the Joyce paper do not exhaust all of the models teachers may consider. As other models are identified, teachers may find it useful to emulate the systematic approach Joyce has used to describe the model's elements. Moreover, it may be necessary to consult the original document for additional readings related to the theoretical bases of the models discussed in this excerpt from the Joyce paper.

several aspects of teaching strategies that provide us categories that can be acted on. In the first case, we will describe teaching strategies in terms of their *syntax*, or structure, by which we mean the phases of activity and the purpose of each phase, and the relationships between phases of activity. Second, we will describe the *social system, or social structure*, which is to be created. We will describe that in terms of the sharing of initiatory activity by teacher and learner, and the amount of control over the activities that emerges from the process of interaction. Third, we will describe the *principles which govern the reactions or responses by teachers or materials to the activity of the learner*. For example, in some strategies, the teacher attempts to respond to a learner's activity by being extremely supportive of what the learner does and attempting to reflect it back to the learner so that the student himself can be assisted in deciding what to do next. In other strategies, the teacher corrects the learner and reshapes his behavior along a pre-determined line, or a set of prescriptions that have been prepared in advance. The principles, in short, tell the teacher or the materials-maker how to program his behavior as a learning activity or unit develops. A fourth aspect of a teaching strategy is the *optimal support systems* which are needed to facilitate the teacher's and learner's behavior. Strategies vary widely in the support they need, and some support systems are highly specific. For example, one can construct an inductive teaching strategy in history which requires learners to reconstruct historical events by making inferences from original source documents. That strategy must be supported with sets of original documents in some kind of storage system where learners have access to them, otherwise obviously the major activity cannot take place. Similarly, strategies which employ individualization of learner activity require appropriate materials by which many learners of differing capacities and achievement levels, perhaps even learning styles, can engage in activity which is suited to their particular needs and make-up. Yet other strategies need to be supported by teachers who have a high degree of subject-matter or pedagogical competence. For instance, some strategies for teaching foreign languages specify the need for teachers of virtually "native" fluency. Others do not, but depend on teachers who have the skill to administer highly complex sets of self-instructional materials or "language laboratories." *It is worth noting that a great many attractive teaching strategies never come to fruition because support systems are not developed to back them up.*

* * *

Taba's Inductive Strategies

A Model Derived from Analysis of a Mental Process

The late Hilda Taba was probably more responsible than any one else for the popularization of the term "teaching strategy," and in her work with the Contra Costa school district she provided a first rate example of the development of a teaching strategy from a model of an intellectual process. The strategy formed the backbone of a social studies curriculum. (1)

Taba analyzed thinking from a

psychological and logical point of view, and came to the following conclusion. "While the processes of thought are psychological and hence subject to psychological analysis, the product and the content of thought must be assessed by logical criteria and evaluated by the rules of logic." (1:36) She identified several postulates about thinking, beginning with the notion that thinking can be taught; second, that thinking is an "active transaction between the individual and the data in the program."

"This means that in the classroom setting the materials of instruction become available to the individual mainly through his performing certain cognitive operations upon them: organizing facts into conceptual systems, relating points in data to each other and generalizing upon these relationships, making inferences and using known facts in generalization to hypothesize, predict, and explain unfamiliar phenomena. From this it follows that the conceptual schema and the mental operations which an individual acquires cannot be taught in the sense of being 'given by a teacher' or of being acquired by absorbing someone else's thought products. The teacher can only assist the processes of internalization and conceptualization by stimulating the students to perform their requisite processes while offering progressively less and less direct support from the external stimulator." (1:34) Taba's third idea was that the processes of thought evolve by a sequence which is "lawful." She postulated that, in order to master certain thinking skills, you had to master certain others earlier and that the sequence could not be reversed. Therefore, "this concept of lawful sequences requires teaching strategies that observe these sequences." (1:35) In other words, Taba concluded that specific teaching strategies needed to be designed for specific thinking skills and that, furthermore, these strategies need to be applied sequentially because thinking skills arise sequentially.

She then developed a set of cognitive tasks, or thinking tasks, and then developed sets of teaching moves, called teaching strategies, which would induce those tasks. To illustrate this, let us look at one of these—the task of concept formation. This cognitive task involves grouping items according to some basis of similarity and the development of categories and labels for the groups. In order to cause students to engage in each one of these activities within the tasks, Taba identified teaching moves in the form of questions which she called "eliciting questions" which would be likely to cause the student to engage in the appropriate type of activity. For example the question, "What did you see?" might induce the student to enumerate a list. The question, "What belongs together?" is likely to cause people to group those things which have been enumerated or listed. The question, "What would you call these groups?" would be likely to induce people to develop labels or categories.

Thus, the *syntax*, or structure, of the concept-formation strategy is designed around the process of concept formation which serves as the model for the strategy. The first phase is "enumeration," the second is "grouping," and the third is "developing categories." The teacher guides the development by the use of the appropriate eliciting questions. The *social system* is cooperative, with much pupil activity, but the teacher is the

Summary Chart #1

Taba's Inductive Strategies

Syntax	Phase One (Collect Data)	Phase Two (Identify Similarities and Differences)	Phase Three (Make and Label Groups)
Reaction by Teacher	Supportive, must shape distinctive activity in each phase, however. (For example, if a group is working together, data collection must be completed before analysis begins.)		
Social System	—Cooperative, but teacher initiates and controls movement. Intellectual tasks, however, are performed by children. *Moderate Structure*		
Support Systems	—Sources of raw, ungrouped data.		

initiator of phases and controls information flow. The teacher's *principles for reacting and responding* are to be sure to match his moves or eliciting questions to the specific cognitive tasks, and to be sure that the cognitive tasks occur in order. That is, the teacher should not direct a grouping question to a person who has not yet enumerated or listed, and if the teacher is operating with a group, he must be sure that the enumeration and listing is completed and understood by all before proceeding to the grouping questions. The prominent moves by the teachers are questions, and they are eliciting questions modelled after the cognitive functions. The support systems which are necessary are sources of raw data which can be organized. For example, statistics about economic factors in various nations of the world could provide the raw data for concept formation lessons which induce children to build categories of economic comparison and contrast among the nations.

Taba developed strategies to function in curricular systems and also to guide teachers as they developed and carried out units and lessons. In all probability, the same strategies could be adapted to structure media-based instructional systems. For example, television-mediated lessons could follow the concept-formation paradigm which Taba described. However, because teacher and learner would not be in direct contact, the strategy would have to be modified by employing in certain roles teachers who work directly with the learners.

There are many other interesting examples of teaching strategies which are designed from a model of an intellectual process, dating from Dewey's early work. Torrance's in identifying teaching strategies for use with the gifted has proceeded from an analysis of creative processes or divergent thinking. Hullfish and Smith have developed extensively strategies developed from conceptions of "reflective" thinking, and Massialas and Cox have done the same with respect to inductive thinking. (2)

Concept Attainment

A Model of Teaching Drawn from a Description of the Cognitive Process

In recent years, many psychologists have begun to turn their attention to the study of the ways in which humans acquire and process information about their environment. In this section we will concentrate on the work reported by Bruner, Goodnow and Austin in 1956. (3)

Bruner, Goodnow and Austin studied the process by which humans form concepts of categories which enable them to describe similarities and relationships among things in the environment. They begin (3:1) with the assertion that the environment is so tremendously diverse and man is able to discriminate so many different objects that "were we to utilize fully our capacity for registering the differences in things and respond to each event encountered as unique, we would soon be overwhelmed by the complexity of our environment." In order to cope with the environment, therefore, we engage in the process of categorizing, which means that we "render discriminately different things equivalent, . . . group the objects and events and people around us into classes, and . . . respond to them in terms of their class membership rather than their uniqueness." (3:1) In other words, we invent categories. We use these categories to manipulate our confusing world. This process of categorizing or forming concepts benefits us in five ways. First, it "reduces the complexity of the environment." Second, it gives us the means by which we identify objects in the world. Third, it reduces the necessity of constant learning. For example, once we have learned what an automobile is, we do not have to discover, at each encounter with an automobile, that it is an automobile. We simply need to find out whether or not it has certain identifying properties. In the fourth case, it gives us direction for activity. If we know that we've liked eggs before and that they are nutritious, it helps us select eggs rather than some other substances that we we might eat for breakfast. In the last case, it helps us to organize and relate classes of events, for example, the subject disciplines, or cognitive maps, or sets of interacting categories that we use for rendering the world comprehensible, ordering it, and making decisions about investigations and their meaning. (3:12, 13)

Bruner, Goodnow, and Austin devote their major work to the description of a process which is called concept attainment, which is the process by which we discriminate the attributes of things, people, events and place them into categories. In the discussion, they identify (p. 41 ff) three types of concepts. One is conjunctive, which means that the category is defined by the joint presence of several attributes, or characteristics. For example, red-haired boys is an example of a conjunctive category. When we find a boy who is also red-haired, we have an example of the concept. We also describe disjunctive categories and relational concepts (those in which there is a certain relationship between defining attributes). A relational category, for example, is that there are more accidents when people drive at higher speeds on narrow roads. Holding narrowness of road constant, drivers at higher speeds will have more accidents.

Concept attainment, according to Bruner, Goodnow, and Austin, occurs by making decisions about what attributes belong in what categories. The process of attaining a concept which has been invented by someone else is the process of determining the criteria by which they have placed certain attributes into certain categories. For example, let us suppose that a college senior is trying to describe (to someone who is trying to get him a blind date) the kind of girl that he would like to be matched up with. In order to do this, he is trying to *communicate* his concept and his friend is trying to *attain* the concept. Our senior communicates by identifying to his friend several girls both know who fit his concept of a desirable date and several who do not. In the middle of his description, his friend interrupts him and finally says, "Ah, I see." "Aha!" he says. "You like girls who are shorter than you are and prefer blondes," his friend said. "You also like girls who laugh a lot, and you tend to avoid girls who are very good students and are very intelligent."

"You've got it, but how did you know?"

"All the time you were talking, I kept thinking about why you had put each girl on the preferred and not-preferred lists. Gradually, I began to get the idea that those were the reasons why you did it. For example, most of the preferred girls were short and only one was a good student."

The above process by the matchmaker was one of concept attainment. His friend has the concept of the girls he liked to date, and they could be defined by several attributes. As soon as his friend began to see by what concepts the girls were being discriminated into the two classes, he had attained the concept and was able to act.

Now, let us look at some examples of teaching concepts to children, and then proceed to describe the model.

Teaching the Concept of a Concept

Quite frequently students have difficulty developing concepts. A promising approach is to teach them, as closely as possible, what a concept is. An interesting approach is to provide the students with samples of information, some of which contain examples of a concept and some of which do not. The students know only which samples example the concept and which do not. Gradually, they are presented with more samples until everyone has developed an opinion about the concept. Then, by analyzing the process each student went through, one may be able to help them understand the nature of a concept and strategies for forming them. Let us try an example of this procedure. Each of the following passages is labelled "yes" or "no" depending on whether it represents a concept that I have in mind. As you read the passages, think of the concepts that the "yes" passages might represent: the principle by which they were designated "yes" and the others were designated "no".

* * *

A group of children are playing on the playground. One of the students makes an error that lets the other side win a point. The other children crowd around him, shouting at him. Some take his side. Gradually, the hubbub subsides, and they all return to the game.	YES

* * *

The above passage *does* provide an example of the concept. What concept? Is it playground, or games, or punishment, or children? What are the other possibilities? Let us turn to another passage in which the concept is *not* contained.

* * *

Four children are sitting on the floor of a room. There is a rug, and they are shooting marbles. At one point there is a dispute over a shot. However, the problem is soon settled, and the game resumes. NO

* * *

This passage contained a game, so we have to eliminate that concept. There was an argument, so we have to eliminate *that* possibility. What are some of the other concepts that are and are not exemplified in this passage and the previous one? Let us look now to another example in which our concept *is* represented.

* * *

It is bedtime. A harried mother is putting the children to bed. It is discovered that one of the children has not scrubbed his teeth. The mother berates the child, sending her back to the bathroom and her toothbrush. When she returns, the mother smiles, the children crawl into bed, and the lights are put out. YES

* * *

What is our concept? Is it punishment? Is it, possibly, simply children? Let us look at one more passage in which the concept is present?

* * *

It is a track meet. One boy crosses the finish line in the one mile race far ahead of his competition. Yet, the next two runners cross the line, straining all the way as they vie for second place. As they slow down after the race, their parents and friends crowd around them, praising them for their effort. YES

* * *

Now, we must rule out punishment. However, if we develop a larger concept, such as "things people do to influence one another's behavior" or "sanctions," or some concept that includes, "approval and disapproval," then we have one that could describe the principle on which the selections were made.

This "game" could continue through several more passages. However, we have included enough to illustrate its principle. It focuses attention on the basis on which we have made a categorization. Because that basis is not revealed clearly at first, we have to keep several possibilities in mind. Gradually we receive more information that enables us to eliminate some possibilities and think of some new ones. Hence, we are involved in a search for the concept on which the division was made, a search that helps throw light on the nature of concepts that provide a basis for categorizing events. It helps us identify the mental process that we must go through if we are to make categories.

Before turning to the usefulness of this "concept of a concept," let us look at a more difficult example of the exercise. The following list of nations is marked "yes" or "no" beside each nation. The task is to determine the principle on which the yeses and noes were assigned.

Ghana	yes
France	no
Kenya	yes
Germany	no
Chad	yes
Denmark	no
Egypt	no

At this point, if "African" was

thought to be the basis for the division, it has to be discarded. What possibilities remain?

Peru	yes
Japan	no
England	no
Ecuador	yes

Have you arrived at a concept? Are the nations being divided on a basis of the extent of their economic development? Is it their voting patterns in the United Nations? What possibilities remain?

Russia	no
Polynesia	yes
Indonesia	yes
Canada	no

And on and on we might go, developing and discarding principles. Students who begin to get the idea can begin to make their own categories and examples and try them out on each other.

However, the real payoff of this concept game occurs when we begin to apply it to materials which are not arranged so as to help us be conscious of the categories that are being employed, but when, for example, we turn to the analysis of passages in which authors have grouped material without a complete explanation of the basis for the grouping. For example, consider the following passage.

"Despite the ceremonial talk about the common destinies of the peoples of the Western Hemisphere, and the shared blessings of representative government and democratic ideals, and so forth, there never had been any real rapport between Anglo-Americans and Latin Americans. Anglo-American culture was derived from the British Isles and the European countries of the North Atlantic, and it was Protestant, commercial, middle-class, prosaic and static.

Latin American culture was derived from Spain, Portugal, and Rome, and it was Catholic, non-commercial, caste-ridden, humanistic, colorful, and passionate.[1]

Let us see what principles Carleton has used for identifying Anglo-American (United States and Canadian) culture:

Protestant	yes
Catholic	no
Commercial	yes
Single Class	yes
Prosaic	yes
Passionate	no
Colorful	no

But, we say immediately, there are many Catholics in Anglo-America, there are many classes and castes! His stereotype doesn't hold up very well, although there may be some truth in it. Whereas his prose is interesting and persuasive, a careful analysis of the concept he is using bids us take caution and equally, helps us see more precisely just what he is saying.

The following passage from a fifth grade social studies text will bear the same kind of analysis:

"Cuba is the world's largest producer and exporter of sugar. The United States has been one of the largest consumers of Cuba's sugar. Would Haiti and the Dominican Republic import Cuban sugar? Why or why not? Tobacco is Cuba's second most important crop.

"We have had many links with Cuba. The United States helped Cubans win their independence from Spain. We enjoy Cuban music and

[1] William G. Carleton. *The Revolution in American Foreign Policy* (New York: Random House, Inc., 1965), p. 100.

we like the rhumba and other Cuban dances. Cuban baseball players play on our big league teams. Thousands of people from the United States have spent their vacations in Cuba. Many of our nation's businessmen have invested money in Cuban enterprises.

"Cuba has been a free nation less than a hundred years. Its people have not had a long time to learn to govern themselves. Several times dictators have gained control of the government. Each time, the people of Cuba have overthrown the dictators and attempted to establish a government 'of the people'."[2]

It seems that this passage has as its intent to create (or avoid creating) an attitude toward the Cuban people. Let us examine the concept that the authors had toward the friendliness of the relations between the United States and Cuba.

United States is a customer of Cuba with respect to sugar
(Implies at least working relations.)

United States helped Cuba win their independence
(Implies that relations were very close.)

"We" enjoy Cuban music and dances
(Implies that we are favorably disposed toward their leisure culture.)

Cuban baseball players play professional baseball in the United States
(Implies that they have imported and are successful at one of the games that originated in the United States.)

United States citizens have spent many vacations in Cuba
(Implies friendship again, since one hardly vacations where he is not wanted.)

United States businessmen have invested much money in Cuban enterprises
(Again implies stable relations.)

Cuban politics are a struggle between democracy and tyranny
(Again implies kinship with United States aspirations.)

Now, we may note that many of the statements in these paragraphs were put in the past tense—the unwary reader might not notice this—and nowhere is there an outright statement about Cuban-United States relations. The concept, however, that the reader is allowed to reach, if he is not careful, is that extremely cordial relations exist between Cuba and the United States. Yet, as we all know, that is not quite the picture of reality —one needs a good bit more information before his concept will fit the case as it is.

It is worthwhile for a teacher to include early in the year some lessons intended to establish an understanding between himself and his students of what a concept is and then to apply this as they analyze resources, whether books, films, or visitors.

Students also can develop their own categories, as we have illustrated—and concept-building activity should probably be one of the major activities in any social studies unit.

Describing the Concept Attainment Teaching Model

Syntax or Structure

The first phase of the model involves presenting data to the learner. The data may be events or people or any other discriminable unit. The units of information are delineated to the learner as belonging or not be-

2 Paul R. Hanna, Clyde F. Kohn, and Robert A. Lively. *In the Americas* (Chicago: Scott, Foresman & Company, 1962), p. 310.

longing as examples of the concept. The learner is encouraged to speculate about the concept or principle or discriminatory concept which is being used as the basis of selection of units of data. In the next phase, students may be encouraged to compare their hypotheses concerning the concepts and their reasons for their choices. In succeeding phases, further units of data may be presented as before, and the above procedure may be repeated until there is consensus about the concepts. In succeeding phases, learners begin to analyze their strategy for attaining concepts. For example, some learners initially try very broad constructs and then gradually narrow the field or become more specific in their statement of the concept. Others move rather quickly to specific concepts and combinations of them. Concept attainment strategies are particularly interesting when relational concepts are being considered. Suppose that units of data are presented which compares countries by agricultural productivity in relation to technological level (use of fertilizer, and so on), climate, general level of development of the country, and so on, and the students are attempting to attain concepts of relationship among the several factors. In such a complex case the strategies students will use will be varied and interesting. (See *A Study of Thinking* for examples of different strategies.)

Social System or Structure

In the initial phase the teacher presents data and designates it as belonging or not belonging as an exemplar of the concept. (This designation is in sharp contrast to the typical move of the teacher when he tells people what a concept is.) In the latter stages, when students are beginning to analyze and compare their strategies for attaining the concept, the teacher shifts to an analytic role, but again draws the students into analysis, being exceedingly careful not to provide them with the criteria by which they can judge their strategies. If it is desired to improve students' efficiency in attaining concepts, successive concept attainment lessons are necessary with subsequent analyses of the effectiveness of various strategies. The teacher is the controller, then, but the atmosphere is cooperative and the procedures of the lesson stay closely in tune with the learners.

Principles of Teacher Reaction and Response

During the flow of the lesson, the teacher wants to be supportive of the students' hypotheses about concepts, but to emphasize that they are hypothetical in nature and to create a dialogue in which the major content is a balancing of one person's hypotheses against another. In the latter phases of the model, the teacher wishes to turn the attention of the students toward analysis of their concepts and strategies, again being very supportive. He should encourage analysis of the merits of various strategies rather than attempt to seek the one best strategy for all people in all situations.

Optimal Support Systems

Concept attainment lessons are extremely difficult unless data sources are available and have been classified according to concept. It should be stressed that the student's job in a concept attainment strategy is not to invent new concepts, but to attain the ones that have been previously attained by the teacher or teaching agent. Hence, the data sources need to be *known* beforehand.

Utility of the Model

The concept attainment model is widely useful. In many senses, much of language learning can be viewed as concept attainment in as much as the society has already devised categories of things and labels for those categories, and the language learner attains those concepts and learns those labels. The same is true in the learning of the vocabulary of a foreign language. It is even true in terms of the grammar or the syntactic structure of every language in that the linguistic structure consists of relational concepts of various kinds that need to be attained. To learn the structure of the disciplines is to attain the concepts of that discipline. In mathematics, for example, the basic properties of integers, the commutative, the associative and distributive properties, are existing concepts which become attained by the mathematics student. Whenever students seem not to be understanding something, the concept attainment strategy can be brought into a play in an effort to establish the fundamental ideas which are at the root of the difficulty. Because of its great flexibility, the concept attainment model can be adapted to entire curriculums in the various disciplines and it can be the basis for extensive man-machine systems. It can function as a model for television teaching, both when the teacher is seen and when the medium is used to carry an instructional sequence without a visible teacher.

An Advance Organizer Strategy

A Model Derived from a Theory of Verbal Learning

The psychologist David Ausubel tends to accept the view expressed in Bruner's *Process of Education* (4) that each of the academic disciplines

Summary Chart #2

Concept Attainment Strategy

Syntax	Phase One Present Data—Indicate Positive and Negative Exemplars.	Phase Two Students Present and Analyze Concepts.	Phase Three (May repeat one and two presenting more exemplars and revising concepts.)
Reaction by Teacher	Supportive. In Phase Two must turn discussion to concept-attainment strategies. Care must be taken to be sure students are clear about *their* task in Phase One.		
Social System	*Moderate Structure*. Teacher controls action, but may develop into a free dialogue in Phase Two.		
Support Systems	Data are needed in the form of discrete units that can be labeled as exemplars. Or—as students became sophisticated, *they* can share in making of data units (as when analyzing a document).		

has a structure of concepts which can be identified and taught to the learner and which provide an intellectual map which can be used to analyze particular domains and solve problems in those domains. For example, Bruner would assume that political science contains sets of concepts that can be used to analyze political events and that these can be taught to learners in such a way that when they try to analyze political behavior and to solve political problems this structure will be available to them. For a complete view of this position, the reader should familiarize himself with Bruner's *Process of Education* and *The New Curricula* (5) in which various authors apply the Brunerian hypotheses to the specific subject disciplines. It is worth noting that nearly all of the curriculum projects of the late '50s and 1960s which are described as the new math, the new science, the new social studies, the new English, and so on, have made the same assumption and attempted to organize their materials accordingly.

Ausubel accepts this view, but attempts to extend it in terms of two principles which he says should govern the programming of content in the subject fields. The first is the idea of *progressive differentiation.* "The most general and inclusive ideas of the discipline are presented first, and are then progressively differentiated in terms of detail and specificity." (6:79) "The assumption we are making here, in other words, is that an individual's organization of the content of a particular subject matter discipline in his own mind, consists of a hierarchical structure in which the most inclusive concepts occupy a position at the apex of the structure and subsume progressively less inclusive and more highly differentiated subconcepts and factual data." (6:79)

Ausubel feels that "optimal learning and retention occur when teachers *deliberately* order the organization and sequential arrangement of subject matter along similar lines." (6:79) By similar lines he means the type of hierarchical organization of concepts that has been described earlier.

The second principle Ausubel operates on is that of "integrative reconciliation" which means that new ideas are reconciled and integrated with previously learned content. In other words, the sequence of a curriculum is organized so that successive learning builds on what has gone before. (See Tyler, *Basic Principles of Curriculum and Instruction*, University of Chicago Press, 1951 for a thorough exposition of principles of sequence and the way they function in curriculum and instruction.)

The Essence of the Model

The salient feature of Ausubel's "Organizer Technique of Didactic Exposition," as he puts it, is to program sequences of content for learners so that each segment of learning material is preceded by a conceptual "organizer" which we can think of as an advance organizer. The organizer has a higher level of "abstraction, generality and inclusiveness of" the material and is selected on the basis of its "suitability for explaining, integrating, and interrelating the material." (6:81) An organizer is not to be confused with an overview or summary which is ordinarily at the same level of abstraction, as the material which is to be learned. An organizer is an idea, a general idea, which is fairly abstract relative to the material and which precedes the material. It functions cognitively to organize the material as it is presented; that is, it provides a kind of conceptual framework into which the learner will integrate the material. Ausubel recommends that in terms of unfamiliar material to the learner that a general "expository" organizer should be used to provide a wholistic conceptual structure to which the learner can relate the new material. The organizer provides "ideational anchorage in terms that are already familiar to the learner." (6:83)

When relatively familiar material is being presented to the learner, Ausubel recommends a "comparative" organizer which will help the learner integrate new concepts with "basically similar concepts in cognitive structure, as well as to increase discriminability between new and existing ideas which are essentially different but confusable." (6:83)

Let us look at an example of this. Suppose that the material that is to be presented to learners is a matrix of multiplication facts. This matrix might be presented by the commutative property with respect to multiplication (that is that $A \times B = B \times A$). Then the exposition of the material in the multiplication matrix can be at least partly organized by the learner in terms of commutation; that is, he will be prepared for ideas like $3 \times 2 = 2 \times 3$, and his memory task will be considerably reduced. The organizer, the commutative property, is more abstract than the multiplication facts themselves, but they are explainable in terms of it. In fact, they could be presented in commutative pairs. Later on, when the learner is being introduced to long division, a comparative organizer might be introduced that would stress the similarity and yet differentness of the division facts from the multiplication facts. For example, whereas in a multiplication fact, the multiplier and multicand can be reversed without changing the product, that is 3×4 can be changed to 4×3, the divisor and dividend cannot be reversed in division without affecting the quotient, that is 6 divided by 2 is not the same as 2 divided by 6. This comparative organizer can help the learner see the relationship between multiplication and division and therefore anchor the new learnings about division in the old ones about multiplication, but at the same time can help him discriminate the new learnings so that he does not carry over the concept of commutativity to a place where it does not belong.

Let us look at the advance organizer model in terms of our four dimensions of a teaching model or strategy.

Syntax or Structure

The first phase of the activity is the presentation of the organizer which must be at a more general level than the material that is to follow. The second phase is the presentation of the material itself. In a sequence of learning activities, the first organizer and its materials should be hierarchically more abstract than the succeeding ones which get more and more specific and elaborate the original one. For example, in English, if the content were to deal with metaphors, the first organizer would deal with the general idea of metaphor and the content would illustrate that general idea. The next lessons would go into more and more specific kinds of metaphors and the ways they are used, so that the first unit of work with its organizer would intellectually anchor the material that was to come in the successive unit activities.

The Social System of the Model

Many people at first find startling Ausubel's proposition that an abstract idea should precede material rather than being discovered by learners who have analyzed the material. Ausubel is not an advocate of discovery learning, to put it mildly, and the really striking feature of the model is the presentation of that abstract idea ahead of the content which is to be learned. The social system, then, is controlled entirely by the teacher.

Principles of Reaction or Response by the Training Agent

In the flow of the lesson, the training agent can function to point out the conceptual anchorages for the material and to help learners see the relationship between the material that is being presented and the organizer. The teacher or the instructional material is the controller in the situation. The content has been selected for the learner, and the teacher should function to hem the discussion in around the material at hand.

Optimal Support Systems

Well organized material is critical. The advance organizer depends on an integral relationship between the conceptual organizer and the rest of the content. It may be that it works best as a paradigm around which to build instructional materials so that the time can be taken to insure complete relevance of content and organizer. *However*, the model was designed for use by the face-to-face teacher and can be, if the time is given to prepare lectures or other types of material carefully.

Applicability of the Model

The advance organizer model is another extremely versatile model in the sense that it can be applied to any material that can be organized intellectually. It can be used in nearly every subject area, although it was

Summary Chart #3

Advance Organizer Model

Syntax	Phase One Presentation of Organizer.	Phase Two Presentation of Verbal Material to be Learned.
Reaction by Teacher	Teacher is seen as presenter. No consistent principles characterize the model.	
Social System	*High Structure*. Teacher defines roles and controls norms. Learner roles carefully defined.	
Optimal Support Systems	Development of organizer and system for presenting it is crucial. Material, however, must be organized so it *pertains* to the organizer.	

designed for use with verbal material rather than with skills and the mastery of problem solving paradigms. However, Ausubel assumes that it will be useful in the transfer of materials to new problem settings, and he presents some evidence to that effect.

As a model it provides very good discipline for lectures for reasons which were outlined above, especially because the content of the lecture would have to be very carefully related to the organizer, and the lecturer would not be permitted to ramble or digress without cause. Also it can serve very well in the analysis of expository materials in textbooks and other instructional materials where abstractions and information alternate in various patterns. It is worthwhile to examine lessons and units in several of the disciplines, and look for the ways in which organizers are handled either consciously or unconsciously, for, it should be obvious by now, a teacher who is not careful can unwittingly present a poor organizer that will actually confuse the learner.

The Inquiry Training Program

A Model Derived from an Analysis of Scientific Inquiry

The inquiry training model was developed by J. Richard Suchman when he was at the University of Illinois. The primary reference is J. Richard Suchman, *The Elementary School Training Program in Scientific Inquiry*, the University of Illinois, 1962, a Report to the United States Office of Education on Title VII Project No. 216. Suchman, as do Bruner and Hunt, operates from information processing theories of cognitive behavior. His model comes partly from a model of scientific inquiry. As such, however, it is generalized, in that it is not specific to physics, or anthropology, or any other single discipline, but comes from a general analysis of the methods employed by creative research personnel. The objectives of the inquiry training model are, in Suchman's words: "to develop the cognitive skills of searching and data processing, and the concepts of logic and causality that would enable the individual child to inquire autonomously and productively; to give the children a new approach to learning by which they could build concepts through the analysis of concrete episodes and the discovery of relationships between variables; and to capitalize on two intrinsic sources of motivation, the rewarding experience of discovery and the excitement that is inherent in autonomous searching and data processing. We wanted inquiry training to consist of activities that were for the most part autonomously controlled and intrinsically rewarding." (p. 28) The critical element of the strategy was to put the students into a situation where they would have to try to find out the answer to a puzzling situation. "The children were confronted by an episode to explain, or in other words, a series of discrepant events to be assimilated. We used short physics demonstrations as the problem episodes. They were recorded on motion picture film and accompanied by a title which simply asked why a particular outcome of the demonstration had resulted." (7:29) Suchman uses the example of a bimetallic strip which is bent when it is held over a Bunsen burner flame. "The strip is made of a lamination of unlike strips of metal (usually steel and brass) that have been welded together to form a single blade. With a handle at one end it has the appearance of a narrow knife or spatula. When this apparatus is heated, the metal in it expands, but the rate of expansion is not the same in the two metals. Consequently, half of the thickness of this laminated strip becomes slightly longer than the other half and since the two halves are attached to each other the internal stresses force the blade to assume a curve of which the outer circumference is occupied by the metal which has expanded the most.

"The child who encounters this problem must contend with the following variables: the temperature of the blade, the shape of the blade, the structure and composition of the blade, the length of the blade. These are all highly relevant to the problem at hand and the inquirer must sample them at various times during the demonstration to determine changes. In addition there are innumerable other variables which, although irrelevant to the bending, must be considered by the child before he can determine this fact. The position in which the blade is held during the heating, the composition of the handle, the source of heat, the upward pressure of the gas flame are just a few of the variables which concern the typical inquirer, but which do not affect the bending appreciably. If the child immediately tries to hypothesize complex relationships among all the variables that seem relevant to him, he could go on testing indefinitely without any noticeable progress, but by isolating variables and testing them singly he can eliminate the irrelevant ones and discover the relationships that exist between each relevant independent variable (such as the temperature of the blade) and the dependent variable (which in this case is the bending of the blade)." (7:15–16)

It is the kind of episode, that is the bending of the strip when it is held over the flame, that is used to confront the learner and to begin the inquiry cycle. Suchman and his collaborators deliberately selected episodes that would have sufficiently surprising outcomes that it would be difficult for a child to remain indifferent after the encounter. How does the child proceed? He proceeds by asking questions of the teacher, and the teacher attempts to respond to the child's questions by facilitating his discovery. However, he structures the situation. "First, the questions must be so structured as to be answerable by 'yes' or 'no.' This eliminates all open-ended questions and forces the children to focus and structure their probes. In a sense each question becomes a limited hypothesis. For example, the child *may not* ask: 'How did the heat affect the metal?' but he *may* ask, 'Did the heating change the metal into a liquid?' In the first instance the child does not state specifically what information he wants, he is asking the teacher to conceptualize relationships for him, to teach him something." (7:30) The child is permitted to continue to ask questions, and whenever he phrases one which cannot be answered in a "yes" or a "no," the teacher or training agent reminds him of the "rules of the game" and waits until he finds a way of stating the question in the proper form. The teacher also, as the child attempts to inquire in the above fashion, tries to lead the children to a strategy whereby they confine their early questions to an analysis of the situation they have observed, trying to find out what things have been made of, what actually happened, and that kind of thing. Next they turn their questions to relationships among variables. Then, even later, the teacher works with the children to help them analyze their inquiry and to try to formulate principles about "the logical structure of causality and strategies of inquiry. Each time, the children check their performance against these rules, against this background of very concrete experiences, revived and made immediate through the recordings, the children can begin to conceptualize the structure of inquiry and see the the shape of the strategies they are being urged to use and the consequences of using them or not. With each session, the children see more clearly the success they achieve by following the pattern which reinforces the use of these systematic and productive operations." In addition, the teacher attempts to help the students learn a set of concepts, or a structure, as Suchman calls it, for the analysis of causality. (See 7:35–37 for a description of the structure which can be taught to the children.)

Analysis of the Model

Syntax or Structure

The model usually has three phases. In the first phase comes the confrontation with the problem. In the second phase is the period of children's questioning with the teacher responding only to questions that can be answered with "yes" and "no" answers. The third phase is the analysis of the children's strategy with emphasis on pointing out the consequences of their strategies and helping them become more causal in their questioning and to follow the general schema of establishing facts first, determining what is relevant second, and building concepts of relationship or explanation third.

Social System of the Model

Critical moves are those by the teacher which move the inquiry sessions from phase to phase. Probably most important is the insistence of the parameters of the game in the second phase, and shifting the level of discussion to an analysis of inquiry strategy in the third phase. Hence, the structure is very high and the social system is controlled entirely by the teacher.

Principles of Responding or Reacting to the Children

The most important principle is to refuse, but in a supportive way, to give information during the second phase unless the questions are properly phrased, and during the third phase, when the children are analyzing their inquiry, to be extremely supportive and yet draw them toward an analysis of the consequences of their particular patterns of endeavor.

Optimal Support Systems

Two things are needed. One is prepared sets of materials that cause the vivid and ambiguous confrontations, and second a training agent who understands strategies of inquiry and can help the students to analyze their patterns and work toward greater effectiveness.

The Applicability of the Model

The model was designed and is most useful for attempts to teach

Summary Chart #4

Inquiry Training Model

Syntax	Phase One Confrontation with Ambiguous Situation.	Phase Two Inquiry by asking questions.	Phase Three Analysis of Inquiry Strategies.
Principles of Teacher Reaction		Establishes "Rules." Gives information only in response to properly phrased questions.	Deals with inquiry strategies—turns discussion toward analysis of alternatives.
Social System	*Highly structured,* especially in early phases. Moderate in last phase. As Students gain experience, can become mutual.		
Support Systems	Problem-Confronters are needed. (See Suchman for specifics.)		

children scientific methods of inquiry. Particularly, it helps them to analyze their own inquiry and compare the effectiveness of various strategies. The particular content can be drawn from any of the scientific disciplines, or a part of it from any domain when one is concerned with the improvement of thinking ability.

References

1. Hilda Taba, *Teaching Strategies and Cognitive Functioning in Elementary School Children* (San Francisco, Calif.: San Francisco State College, 1966), Cooperative Research Project No. 2404.

2. Byron Massialas and Benjamin C. Cox, *Inquiry in Social Studies* (New York: McGraw-Hill Book Company, 1966).

3. Jerome S. Bruner, Jacqueline J. Goodnow, and George A. Austin, *A Study of Thinking* (New York: Science Editions, Inc., 1967). (Originally published in 1956.)

4. Jerome S. Bruner, *The Process of Education* (Cambridge, Mass.: Harvard University Press, 1961).

5. Robert W. Heath, ed., *The New Curricula* (New York: Harper & Row, Publishers, 1963).

6. David P. Ausubel, *The Psychology of Meaningful Verbal Learning* (New York: Grune and Stratton, Inc., 1963).

7. J. Richard Suchman, *The Elementary School Training Program in Scientific Inquiry* (Urbana, Ill.: The University of Illinois, 1962), Reporting United States Office of Education Title VII Project No. 216.

ACTIVITIES

1. By what means are you able to evaluate the method you are using in your teaching?

2. In both the inquiry and discovery processes the students collect and evaluate data. What is the main difference by which data are collected in the two methods? Are there other differences as well as similarities?

3. Design teaching situations for your subject area which utilize organizing centers for (*a*) the process of discovery, (*b*) the process of inquiry.

4. What is the relationship between an organizing center (Herrick) and an advanced organizer (Ausubel)?

5. Suppose you are observing the following: A sixth-grade teacher has provided students with sealed cigar boxes which contain objects unidentified to the students. The students are busily shaking, tilting, and revolving the boxes in an endeavor to determine as much as possible about the contents. Is this method or technique? What thinking is going on? Speculate as to the lesson objective. Explain your answers in terms of what you have read.

6. You are observing a tenth-grade math class. The teacher previously has related to you that students have been having some difficulty understanding fractions. In this class the teacher has posted two full-page newspaper advertisements of different automobiles. The students were asked, "What do you see here that is similar? What do you see here that is different?" What do you think the teacher is trying to accomplish? Is this method or technique? Why? Could it be an advanced organizer?

7. Select an instructional objective you might use in your own teaching. Develop four different lesson plans for getting at that objective using the four models identified in Joyce's paper.

8. Observe a teacher either in person or on video tape. Attempt to iden-

tify the model of teaching he is using. If the model is apparently not one of those described by Joyce, construct a paradigm similar to those found in this section which does identify the basic elements of the observed teaching style.

9. Examine courses of study or the products of new curriculum studies in your subject matter area. To what extent is the model of teaching fixed by the approaches suggested in the materials?

10. Do the lessons portrayed in the Massialas and Zevin article exemplify any of the models described by Joyce? Discuss.

TEACHING FOR VALUING AND THINKING

CHAPTER SIX

For many years, poor teaching was described in terms of the apparent effects it had on the psyches of students. Accounts of cruelty, sadism, insensitivity, and the like usually are characteristics of stories concerning inferior teachers. As of late, more and more investigators of teaching are beginning to realize that poor teachers have been inflicting "intellectual" injury upon students too.

The teaching profession has dedicated itself to the task of helping students develop a sense of values and a habit of critical thinking. In fact, these attributes are considered of such importance that the Educational Policies Commission of the National Education Association has made each of them the subject of its recent yearbooks. Although such statements are intended to stimulate, teachers occasionally may have a feeling of frustration because they do not always see how their teaching contributes to the achievement of the goals they have set for themselves.

Many educators believe that to promote thinking and valuing, teachers must allow students to do a great deal of verbalizing about their experiences: what they have seen, what they have heard, what they have read, and what they have imagined. You may have perceived from earlier articles included in this collection that a student's chance to verbalize is at a minimum in many classrooms. It has also been found that in the areas of thinking and valuing, teachers can optimize their effectiveness by withholding critical judgments. Both of these aspects of the teaching-learning encounter, the amount of student talk and the amount of teacher criticism, may be used in monitoring teaching. The readings in Chapter 6 suggest some alternatives open to teachers in the areas of valuing and thinking.

33. SOCIOLOGICAL KNOWLEDGE AND NEEDED CURRICULUM RESEARCH

LOUIS E. RATHS

The Social Context of Values and Thinking

Throughout the free world most people believe that social arrangements, laws, and institutions are made for man. Not the other way round. We believe that these social arrangements are means for the creating of individuals. Not the only means, perhaps, but a powerful resource for the creation of changed personalities. In his *Reconstruction in Philosophy*, written more than forty years ago, Dewey viewed social institutions in their educative effect; with reference to the types of individuals they foster. "The question is one of specific causations. Just what response does *this* social arrangement, political or economic, evoke, and what effect does it have upon the disposition of those who engage in it? Does it release capacity? If so, how widely?"[1]

I shall assume that the curriculum research that is "needed" will be related to the "types of individuals whom we wish to foster," and that shortcomings are in some ways related to the social arrangements and institutions and laws of our society. In my discussion I shall focus upon the school, but any reference to personality development assumes the wider social matrix.

The sociological research relating to social class structure, based for the most part, on Warner's scheme of identifying class status, has been directly related to the functioning of the school. The evidence is clear that in its distribution of rewards and punishments, the former go out of all proportion to the middle and upper middle class students; the penalties,

Louis E. Raths, "Sociological Knowledge and Needed Curriculum Research," in Research Frontiers in the Study of Children's Learning, *ed. James B. Macdonald (Milwaukee: School of Education, The University of Wisconsin-Milwaukee, 1961), pp. 20–48. Reprinted by permission.*

[1] John Dewey, *Reconstruction in Philosophy.*

go, out of all proportion, to the lower social classes. There is evidence that our tests of intelligence are biased in the kinds of problems presented, and in the words chosen to present those problems. The bias is in the direction of favoring the middle and the upper class children. Participation in extracurricular activities is shown to distinguish between lower and middle class children. Prizes, honors, and awards go in much higher proportion than their numbers suggest to the middle and upper class children. The high grades on reports to parents, and reports to colleges, go to the children of the middle and upper classes in much larger numbers than their proportion of the school population. The curriculum materials represented by the beginning primers and readers are shown to be a product of middle class living; hence probably of more interest to middle class children than to others.

Other items might be added to this list. Taken together, what bearing do they have upon Dewey's question about specific causation? Granting that the schools are functioning in this way, are they, then, releasing capacity? What are the effects upon children who participate in this social institution?

The evidence indicates that the school is selective in *releasing capacity.* In its functioning, the school shows a sensitivity to the welfare of the children of the middle class. An examination of "dropouts" shows that many more of the lower class children leave school before finishing. We know also that for every high school graduate who goes to college, there are two with equal intelligence scores and scholastic background who do not go, and primarily because of inadequate finances.

The elementary schools, the junior high schools, the senior high schools, a teacher's college, all show a relatively consistent pattern in this regard. Those who write materials for the schools, those who make the tests, the teachers, the administrators, and even the guidance personnel, display a similar consistency in their higher regard for children of the middle and upper social classes. Given such a consistent pattern of functioning, is it possible that children of the lower social classes are unaware of the discrimination? What effects must this be having upon their development of *democratic* attitudes? upon loyalty to the school? upon their social relationships with each other? What rather large generalization might they draw about the "social system" in which they live? upon the integrity and sincerity of the status figures in the school?

And must it not also leave them with some sense of unworthiness? Year after year, in class after class, in academic and nonacademic matters of the school, they are rated low. As the years pass, must they not come to believe that they must in some ways merit these low ratings? that they are indeed inferior and unworthy? Instead of releasing capacity, I would infer that this treatment of many children restricts and constrains the release of capacity. We need curriculum research which explores a great variety of teaching and testing materials that are appropriate for lower class children. We need to know when and how to use these materials to release capacity. We need to reexamine the extracurricular programs to find ways of making them representative of the entire student population. We need annual accountings of ways in which high and how grades, rewards and penalties, praise and blame, are distributed to the children in the schools.

In the past few years there has been much talk of the lack of values in our children. Jacobs[2] summarized a series of studies which were concerned with the measurement of certain changes in college, and he concluded that in general not much change takes place. Judith Schoelkopf[3] found that children who were rated as severely overinhibited in their behavior showed little evidence of change between the years of two and one-half and six and one-half. Another group, characterized as severely underinhibited, made very few changes during the same four-year period. Those of us who have been visiting and observing schools for a period of years have experienced reports in faculty meetings which indicate that for a great many children the characterizations, year after year, are pretty much the same.

In these specific cases, some of the characterizations suggest the absence of release of capacity. One cannot say, however, that this is the fault of the school alone. In the absence of valid and reliable research evidence, we cannot make a claim against any one or several of the social institutions and arrangements of our society. We do know that certain undesirable kinds of behavior persist in the children under our care and tutelage.

What are some of the social conditions in general, which seem to have a bearing upon this lack of desirable change? We do know that about 20 per cent of our children move to a new residence every year, and we have little knowledge of the impact of this moving upon the growth and development of the children who move. We do know that approximately one in seven mothers is working, and that many of them will not be at home when children return from school. How does this affect the development of values? In approximately one-seventh of our families the home is "broken": either the father or the mother (or both) are not a part of the child's home; separation, divorce, mental illness and confinement to an institution, and death take a heavy toll and threaten the integrity of family life.

In terms of *where* our families are settling, the situation is again one that raises questions. One-fourth of our families now live in our new suburbs—and most of these cannot be called communities in the old sense of that term. We cannot depend upon these new centers of living to develop in our children a sense of values which will give direction to their lives. Almost 60 per cent of our families live in metropolitan centers; the cities are trying to squeeze their budgets for more adequate education of youth, for better housing and recreation, but, in general, they are fighting a losing battle, and they are now turning more and more toward the idea of securing federal assistance. What does this resettling of our families mean for the growth and development of the children, and what does it mean for curriculum research?

It must mean a great deal to the friendship and acquaintance problems of children. As we meet this new social phenomenon, can we not take an increased interest in the human relationships of these children, both in and out of school? Can we avoid the temptation of overorganizing the

[2] Jacobs, "*Changing Values In College*" (New York: Harpers Magazine, 1957).

[3] Schoelkopf. Unpublished Ph. D. Dissertation, New York University.

lives of these children? Can we provide more opportunities for them to be associated with each other in ways which they, themselves, might organize? How does all this affect junior and senior high school students as contrasted with those of elementary school age? We need this information and I suggest that we need it now.

In this century children have been exposed to ways of life that were alien to small communities at the turn of the century. It seems to me that it is now much more difficult for children to internalize the mores of their community. The movies, silent and talkies, have brought a bewildering variety of ways of life to nearly all of our children. Which is right? What is best? The new highways and other means of transportation have reshuffled our population and the ensuing new and different interactions have brought to the attention of the people involved many new ways of behaving. The radio, and later—television, increased greatly the range of choices in human behavior for hearing and viewing by children.

The press in American life is no longer what it once was. At the turn of the century our small town press was parochial and provincial. Today it is the purveyor of happenings the globe over. Moreover, it has lost a great deal of its respect and prestige. It probably stimulates little thought, and there is little or no consideration by the press of matters of values. The hodgepodge which the press now represents contributes to the confusion in values.

The place of work in the development of personality has lost much of its significance. It used to be that the struggle for survival gave meaning to life. Our children are largely divorced from the realities of that struggle, if indeed it continues to exist. In the absence of any such continuing motivation for work, we are inclined not to ask about the meaning of life. Then too, much of the work that many educated people do today could be done with much less schooling. Moreover, there is abroad in the land the idea that schools have little to do with the development of character: those who go to school many more years may indeed develop little more virtue. Our children see, daily, apparently well-educated persons extolling the advantage of one cigarette filter over another, one skin cream over another. Payola, bribes, rigged contests, surely must have effects on the kinds of children developing in our culture.

Could the children too be saying: "It isn't what you know, it's who you know that counts"; "it's money that talks"; "everything's a racket"; "you can't win"; "it's all right if you don't get caught"; "what's the gimmick?"

At any rate, the failure of our social institutions to free the capacities of the young for change, and the kinds [of] social conditions which are prevalent at home and abroad in our time, point toward two important foci for education: *the development and clarification of values, and the development of thinking processes.* We assume that both processes will be carried forward in a context of significant world problems, national and local problems, and problems that have great personal significance for the students.[4]

[4] See, for example, C. Wright Mills, *The Sociological Imagination*, and Allen Wheelis, *The Quest For Identity*, for meaningful statements of the need for value clarification in terms of a societal perspective.

Values

The many and conflicting patterns of life to which our children are exposed, the lack of a strongly integrated community, the reduced impact of the family and the church, the deterioration of the relation between education and virtue, the worldwide upheavals, all point to the realm of values as a needed research in curriculum.

How can we go about it? Attempts to identify the "values" of people have proved almost fruitless. In general pencil-and-paper procedures have been followed, and the results represent pencil-and-paper opinions of students. We may get a starting direction by examining the concept of health, physical health. It is almost impossible to define the term so that it has practical meaning for an individual. Our needs for rest vary greatly; in terms of food, there can be no universal standard in terms of particulars of diet; in terms of energy output, again, great differences.

Suppose, however, we ask about deviations from health? about sickness? Here, we secure a much greater amount of agreement. In the area of values, by analogy, we would not seek to identify the values of children. Instead, we would ask: *When children have not developed values, how might it show up in their behavior?* And, if there is a widespread lack of value development in our culture, might not the symptoms vary, and wouldn't many children be afflicted?

This would suggest that we must be guided by a concept of value. Even though doctors tend more to agree on symptoms of illness, in the background there is at least the assumption that a treatment of the causes will be associated with a diminution of the symptoms. We need a guide on which to base our educative work with students. I have borrowed heavily from Dewey and my additions seem to me to be necessary.

1. A value implies prizing and cherishing. We may indeed have an attitude toward the lower social class, and may be acting upon that attitude, but if we do not prize it, if it is an attitude which we wish were different, then it cannot be called a value. Prizing and cherishing are, therefore, a requirement of a value. In addition:

2. A value implies choice after deliberation. It involves answering the question: Should I choose this? It frequently involves the anticipation of consequences and a reflection upon the desirability of the choice. It is weighing, and judging, before the choosing. If a person is responding impulsively, instinctively, reflexively, we should not associate the response with valuing. There is involved an intellectual emphasis upon sizing-up, upon judging alternatives in relation to ends sought. In addition:

3. A value—as such—implies recurrence of the valuing act. To choose something *once*, is hardly indicative that the something has the status of a value. We associate the concept of value with trend, with repetition, with a certain style of life. We infer that Jones or Smith values something because there is some emphasis on kinds of choices by Jones and Smith. Thus far we have said that a value must be: prized and cherished, reflected-upon, and repeated. There is more to the concept. In addition:

4. A value penetrates our living. If it is indeed a value of ours, we may allot some of our finances to support what is valued; we plan our time so that the value may be experienced in our living; we may develop new ac-

quaintance and friendship patterns which are consistent with our values. We do reading, writing, speaking, collecting, and many other things, in support of values. We don't necessarily do all of these in support of any one value, but where we value, our lives are influenced. Values penetrate our living. In addition, and, finally:

5. When asked about our values, we affirm them. Having reflected upon them, prized them, repeatedly chosen them, having lived them—quite naturally—we affirm them when asked or challenged. We know what we are for. We have not only the moral courage, but in our lives we have demonstrated the moral energy.

This is a large order. If it takes *all five* criteria to determine a value, how many values do you have? It's my guess that you don't have many, and you are far from being alone in this regard. As was said earlier, it has become very difficult to develop values, and you and I are no exceptions.

The definition may be all the more welcomed if some time is given to some assumed synonyms of the word. Attitude is often associated with value. A father may have certain attitudes toward interracial marriage. As he examines them, he may feel that this is an awful risk. When asked for advice by his son, he might say, "This is a tremendously serious thing and you should think about it deeply." The son might then say, "What do you really think?" And the father might respond: "Frankly, I'm against it." But, if the son were to add, "Father, are you glad that you are of this opinion?" it is possible that the father would say that he wished he were different. In other words, he possesses an attitude that he does *not* prize, and in this case, as in many others, an attitude is not the equivalent of a value.

Beliefs are sometimes thought of as values. The point is here made that they are indeed values, if, and only if, they meet the five criteria which have been proposed. And I suggest that all of us have many so-called "beliefs" which are not values at all. They are securely compartmentalized and have little traffic with our lives.

So it is with many of our activities. There are many people who are in bridge clubs and play quite regularly, but who almost hate the thought of going—when the time comes for the game. They *do* things that look like interests, but which surely are not valued.

Here, the activity is carried out, but the prizing does not take place, and the reflection leads to another and quite different course of action.

Attitudes may become values, *when* they meet all five criteria. Interests may become values when they meet the criteria. Purposes, and aspirations too, may become values as they encompass the criteria. Feelings, activities, and beliefs may also become values. These are seven common ways in which personality expresses itself. Some of these expressions may be of the valuing kind. When they are not, it is suggested that we confine ourselves to the terms attitudes, interests, purposes, aspirations, feelings, activities, or beliefs. These are good terms, but there is no need to confuse any or all of them with the concept of value.

Youngsters with Value Problems

If we use these criteria as a basis for exploring the lives of children, what will we find in the behavior of children who have "missed out" in the creation of values? Shall we find, as we did in the case of children with emotional needs, that certain patterns of behavior are common to them? The preliminary evidence suggests that we may be on the right road if we think of the following kinds of persistent behavior as in some way a concomitant of the absence of values:

1. Children Who Are Apathetic, Listless, Dull

They don't care much about activities going on around them. They look out the window; they fool with things in their pockets; they stare at books instead of reading them attentively. Nothing seems to be giving any direction to their lives. It is suggested that these children are in need of value development.

Before listing other behaviors symptomatic of a lack of value development, let me add that in every case I would apply two precautions: first, there should be a careful physical examination, to be sure that the symptoms of apathy are not related to physical defect or malfunctioning; and second, there should be clear evidence that a child is not severely disturbed emotionally. It might be inferred that these two exceptions may very well include all or nearly all of the cases of apathy and indifference. There is some evidence to the contrary.

2. Extremely Flighty Children

They seem to be interested in almost everything but, just for a moment or two; then they shift to something else. They seem to have no stable interests or concerns. They flit from one thing to another, and their teachers are apt to say: "I wish to high heaven that they would settle down for just a few minutes." Here, and in all other cases, we must make sure that there is no physical malfunctioning which might be causing the behavior, and no serious emotional difficulty.

3. Children Who Are Extreme Overconformers

Not having any values of their own, these children carry on their lives by trying to identify the values of their teachers, and then giving a kind of lipservice to these concepts. They will say or write what the teacher seems to want or to prize.

4. Nagging Dissenters

These children are not rebels for a cause. They seem to pick on the teacher as a authority figure. They nag, carp, dissent. The teacher knows what they are against, but almost never does she know anything that they are *for*. One gets the clear feeling that these children are not dissenting after clear deliberation; that they are not dissenting because of conflict of principles. In other words, their dissent is not value-oriented. They are in need of guidance toward the development of values.

5. Extreme Hesitancy, Doubt, Uncertainty

In the presence of a choice-situation, they cannot make up their minds. They want help. They don't know what they want, what they like, and they don't know what they want to try. In the absence of a value-base, it is indeed difficult to make choices, and in almost every classroom there are children of this kind. It is suggested that they need help in the development of values.

6. Persistent, Continuing Underachievement

Where we have fairly clear evidence of ability, and almost chronic underachievement, it is a good hunch to suspect that guidance in value-development is needed. Having no values to guide their hour-by-hour, and day-by-day activities, these people are apt to aim at "getting by" and even to miss this goal on occasion. In our suburban schools especially, this category often includes 15 per cent, or more, of the children in the secondary levels. With the effort to help these children to develop values, will the pattern of underachievement change? As in all other cases, here too, we must take pains to investigate physical and emotional health before we decide that it is quite surely a value-related behavior.

7. The Role-Players and Poseurs

In our classrooms we not infrequently find children who seem to take the role of "the class fool." They mimic other children and sometimes the teacher; they pretend to be the characters in a story that is being read; or in a movie that is being seen. Having no real self to play, they play many selves. In their continuing trial of new and different roles they may be trying to find a role that suits them. They seem to need help in the creation of values, the ultimate basis for a *self*.

8. Very, Very Inconsistent Children

These children sem to change their beliefs, their attitudes, their feelings from day to day, and sometimes, from hour to hour. They are for integration, and a short time later, for segregation. Now they are loud for peace; yesterday it was for all-out war. There is little repetition of their views, and little penetration into life, and so far as we can infer, little or no deliberation before making their choices known. I suggest that here are children who need help in the development of values.

These *eight* behavior patterns (and there must be others) illustrate what may very well be the natural consequences of a culture that has been and is now in confusion. The family, the school, the church, the government, the communications media, the industries, seem less and less to stand for anything. In the absence of a unified outlook, there is little or nothing that can be internalized by our children as they grow through the culture. There is less "growing up" than we would want. It is becoming more and more difficult for children to acquire values which give direction and zest to life.

I think we must assume that the school, like every other institution, has some responsibility in this matter. We are, therefore, back to John Dewey's idea that the function of social institutions and arrangements is to help create personality; that in association with young learners we should be helping them to arrive at a sense of discrimination, a basis for making choices that are relevant to the worth of their lives.

What should the schools do? A good first step would be to make the best possible approximation concerning the frequency of these types of behavior in every classroom. We could indeed count the children who are like the ones described. Are teachers competent to identify them? With some help and some preparatory and exploratory activities, I believe they are in the best position. You must remember, too, that we are looking for the extremes of behavior. We are not asking teachers to make ultrafine discriminations, and whenever they are in doubt, we should advise them to exclude the child in question.

After the audit is made, we shall have some idea of the extent of the problem. Our own preliminary estimates in the upper grades of the elementary school suggest that about 30 per cent of the children are so-called value-related behavioral types. This, I submit, makes it a very serious problem indeed. It is, of course, possible, that first approximations will vary considerably from community to community, and that in some areas the problems will be more or less acute.

Developing Values

Let us assume that the problem is worthy of attention in terms of numbers of children involved. What next? Succeeding steps have to do with curriculum materials and teaching methods. If the social background has been reflected reasonably, there are some cues to follow. If we want these children to have a deeper understanding of themselves, and a better comprehension of their own epoch, it will be necessary to introduce curriculum materials which are consistent with these ends. And, in addition, the curriculum materials must provide the opportunity for children to express attitudes, feelings, beliefs, interests, purposes, aspirations, and to discuss their activities, in and out of school. When any of these are expressed by a child, the teacher listens, and her subsequent questioning represents an effort to find out if values are involved. She tries to find out if the child prizes or cherishes his belief or attitude or interest; she asks about one or two alternatives; she asks how long this has been a matter of concern: how often it comes up; she asks if he is doing anything about it in his life or if he needs any help to get it into his life's functioning; and she tries to sum up his views, thus giving him the chance to affirm or deny or reject what is attributed to him. This is the way in which the definition of value is useful in the clarifying processes.

There are many other ways to help children to clarify, and teachers have been using them for years; not in a systematic, focused way, perhaps—but with some effectiveness. We can repeat back to children, in exactly their own words, what they have said, and ask: "Is this what you mean?" When children *hear* what they have said, they often restate it with modifications which seem more clearly to express what they want to say.

We can say back to the children *in our words*, what we interpret as their meaning, and ask if this represents their point of view. Sometimes we quite consciously distort what they have said, and ask if this is what they mean.

On other occasions we ask children for definitions of a term they have used. We ask them to give examples or illustrations of the point they are trying to make. Our assumption is that as children try to make things more clear to us, they must first make them more clear to themselves, and this is the process of clarifying. We cannot do this, of course, unless children have an opportunity to say or to write about matters of concern to them; and we cannot carry the process forward unless we *listen* to what they are saying.

This *listening* is no easy task, and it is my opinion that we don't do nearly enough of it. There is an old saw to the effect that the best education would consist of Mark Hopkins at one end of a log, and a student at the other. No one takes the time to indicate what Mark did at his end of the log, and what the student *did* at the other end. To be effective, I think Mark would have to ask very intelligent questions, and then he would have to listen very carefully, and then he would have to react in ways which would help the student to clarify his meanings.

Sometimes we help the student to clarify by asking him to tell more about what he has said. We say, sometimes, that we don't see where it leads, what the consequences will be. We sometimes ask what is good about the particular interest, or attitude, or purpose, or activity. On occasion we ask if he believes that every one should accept his idea and why. At other times we raise questions about possible assumptions which he is making. We might ask about the importance or significance of the idea. We could ask him to tell us how he happened to get involved with the idea, or project, or belief.

There may be times when we sense some inconsistency in what the student is saying, and we bring this to his attention and ask him to try and straighten it out. If the occasion seems to warrant it, we might ask him to present the idea to the class, or to put it in writing. If he has talked for some length, we suggest that he boil it down into a summary. Sometimes we ask if he needs help in getting something started to test the idea.

There are two ideas to keep in mind about this questioning and clarifying procedure: (1) we never carry on an extended interview with a student in a classroom situation; one, two, or three questions at the most, consuming perhaps two or three minutes at the most; and (2) we don't argue with the student about what he says in reply and we don't reject it. Instead we say something to the effect that now we see it more clearly; now we understand him better. Where he has avoided replying we suggest that perhaps we might talk about it another time.

Thinking and Values

At this point, I must digress momentarily from the value theme, and address myself to some thinking processes. The two are always interlocked, if our concept of value is accepted. Hence, we believe that all value-type curriculum materials should have, and will have a problematic character. They present a situation which involves thinking. We can best insure this if we are guided by some criteria for making assignments which emphasize thinking.

What follows is only suggestive. There are many other kinds to consider, but these, I believe, are adaptable to all classes in the school, at every age level, and relevant to all subject areas without exception.

1. Comparing

When students are put in the position where two or more things must be contrasted and compared; where they must seek out similarities and differences, we assume that thought processes are called for. Comparing one demonstration with another; one proof with another; one short story with another; one character with another; one translation with another; one diet with another; one form of life with another, one art form with another; one symphony with another; one poem with another . . . all of these . . . involve sensitivity, dscrimination, judgment, and the support of that judgment by the materials under consideration. Moreover, if the student is asked what similarities and differences are significant, he is entering the world of value judgments. In his writing, he is almost certain to make a number of such value-type judgments, and one or two or three of these can be utilized by the teacher for clarification, using the types of questions suggested in preceding paragraphs.

2. Summarizing

When students are asked to summarize an experience, when they are asked to summarize a story, a discussion, a chapter in a text, or a demonstration, they have to make discriminations. What will they retain? What will they leave out? What will receive greatest emphasis in the summary? least emphasis? A few will try to avoid summarizing; they will attempt to restate every detail, and these students must be asked to try again, and to do it in summary form. Here again, the teacher is almost sure to find a number of value judgments, and the processes of clarification can begin.

3. Observing

If students are required to make observations of the world around them; if they must visit stores, and shops, and labs, and farms, and exhibitions, the problem of writing up one's observations requires organization, discrimination, emphasis. As they write, almost always, value judgments are made, and these become the basis for the clarifying procedures.

4. Classifying

To be required to make one's own categories is a rather high-level assignment, but it is within the abilities of most of us. In spelling, children might be asked to classify a list of words; in arithmetic, a list of problems. In a short story assignment, we might ask students to make a list of all the adjectives used in associations with a character, and to ask for some classification of the words. We could again classify diets; we could ask for discussion of a large area and, as different topics are mentioned, write them on the blackboard. If a large list results, we might ask the students to try to arrange the topics under headings which seem relevant to them. Here, as in the other cases, almost always value judgments are made, and can become the basis for the suggested clarification procedures.

5. Criticizing

Where students are asked to criticize, there are deep challenges to thought. The materials must be carefully examined and points selected for criticism; the criticism in turn must be defensible, and arguments against the criticism must be anticipated. Moreover, almost always some value judgments are made, and the teacher will find if relatively easy to try to clarify some of these statements.

6. Problem Solving

Students are presented with a problem and are asked: what would you do in this situation and give your reasons for your action; or they may be asked to anticipate the consequences when different solutions are presented. As in the other cases, this requires reflecting, weighing, identifying facts and assumptions, and a judgment which represents a synthesis of all the factors entering into the situation. Where students indicate choices, preferences, what they are for or against, what they like or dislike, what they hope or fear, they are using value-type expressions and these can be clarified by the teacher.

7. Analyzing

On some occasions we give to children a set of categories and ask them to analyze materials with those categories in mind. Often, this is done in the analysis of propaganda. Sets of pictures might be analyzed in terms of color, mood, media, space relations, and other criteria. Criteria for social class identification might be put forth, and the students required to apply them to characters in short stories and novels and plays. There are literally dozens of applications of this function, and in nearly all cases thought is required, and judgments are made. These can be clarified by the teacher.

8. Imagining

This category is limited only by the imagination of the teacher. Sometimes the so-called desert-island type of question is asked; or students are asked to tell what they would do if they had unlimited power and unlimited resources in certain situations; or, what they would do if they had twenty-four hours to live. They are asked to recall their most wonderful, or their most dire experiences, or the scariest, or the newest and most startling or surprising incident in their lives. In all of these, and hundreds more like them, students are making value-type expressions and these can be clarified.

9. Planning

This might involve the planning of a paper by making a preliminary outline; it might encompass the planning of a research. It might involve planning for the weekend, or for shorter and longer vacation periods. It might involve the planning of some money-raising project for the class or the school. It might deal with one or several kinds of possible civic improvements: safety and traffic control; recreation facilities and management, and a host of other ideas. In all of them there is opportunity for students to think and to express value judgments, some of which the teacher can attempt to clarify.

10. Interpreting Data

Here the idea is to present to students some systematic, organized data which have been collected and published. Only the data are given to students, and they are asked what inferences or conclusions can be drawn. After they have written their inferences, they are furnished with those inferences drawn by the writer of the article, and they are asked to compare their own, with those of the author. This is an exercise which requires precision in thinking, and when the comparisons are made, students often make value-type judgments which can then be clarified. The data may take the form of tables, graphs, charts, prose passages, cartoons, and maps. This form of assignment is excellent for teaching students some of the principles of interpreting data.

11. Doing Research

In some circumstances this can take the form of polling or interviewing; it might involve the construction of a questionnaire designed to find out how students spend their out-of-school hours, or how they spend their money. It might involve studies of soil productivity; it might encompass original problems which require the use of laboratory equipment and supplies. Whatever the problem proposed for inquiry, here again, there is great opportunity for thought, and as in all researches, many value-type judgments have to be made, and these can be identified and efforts made to clarify them.

12. Reacting to Coding

We have had great success with a method of coding the written papers of students. We put the symbol X in the margin wherever a student has used such extreme expressions as: all, every, never, none, always, each, etc., and we ask him to rewrite such sentences on a separate page and to answer two questions about them: (1) In what ways are these sentences alike? And (2) does he wish to change any of them, and if so—which ones—and what change does he wish to make. We use the code symbol Q in the margin where the student has used qualifying expressions: it seems, I feel, perhaps, maybe, could, might, some, etc., and we ask him to answer the same two questions about sentences so coded. We suggest that there is no necessity for him to change anything. If, after reexamining what he has written, he wants to make no changes, he is assured that this is his privilege, and that it is perfectly all right.

We use other code symbols for a great variety of thinking expressions: a V for value-type expressions; an A for attributions to other people. We use I-T for if-then sentences; E-O for either-ors. A mimeographed sheet containing fifty or more of these kinds of expressions is used as a guide for the reading of student papers. So far, we have made it a practice to take note of only a few types in each piece of writing completed by a student. Over a period of a semester, however, we try to bring to his attention just about all of the kinds which are on the mimeographed guide sheet.

We have found this as useful at the graduate level as at the elementary school level. It suggests that in our teaching, all along the line, not much attention has been given to forms of thinking represented in the writings of students. We do not read carefully what they have written; or if we do read it carefully we do not annotate it critically, and ask for reconsideration of coded sentences.

Thus far we have talked about values and the lack of value development, and what tends to show up in the behaviors of students as a consequence. Our hypothesis is a simple one: If students with behaviors of the kind put forth are exposed to thinking situations; if their written papers and oral comments are used as a basis for clarification with the questions suggested in the previous pages (and if the student's responses are accepted), then the frequency and intensity of these behaviors will diminish.

To test this hypothesis these students will have to be identified. Once or twice a day, for a period of an entire semester, some of the clarifying procedures will be utilized with these students. At the end of that time, the hypothesis states, these students will have changed their own behavior patterns. In other words, the teacher is not *trying* to change their specific acts. The teacher helps them to clarify their attitudes, their feelings, their purposes and aspirations, their interests and beliefs. As this is done, the student sees himself more clearly. He is now free to choose; to change or not to change.

Experimentation with this theory has been very, very limited. The available, and admittedly limited, data are encouraging. Students have changed significantly. It has been voluntarily commented upon by parents, by other teachers not aware that a hypothesis was being tested, and by the principal and counseling office. Underachievers have shown a significant gain at the high school level. In the elementary school at Scarsdale, N. Y., a number of children in Grades 3, 4, and 5, seemed to change markedly, in their school behavior.

We have no information on the stability of these changes. Our designs were such that we cannot even say that we have clarified the values of the experimental students. We can say: that as students are worked with in the specified ways, the behavior of the students changed. To bring zest and purpose into the lives of students; to reduce apathy, flightiness, overconforming, nagging dissent, role-playing, great uncertainly, and even extreme inconsistency is perhaps enough, and much more than we have been able to accomplish heretofore.

It is possible, too, that our experimental teachers are extraordinary persons, teachers of the genius type. They say, however, that in former years they did not succeed with children of the kind worked with. Moreover, it is their belief that the great majority of teachers can learn to work with children in ways that emphasize the clarifying processes.

Youngsters with Thinking Problems

And now, for a concluding section, which returns to the emphasis on thinking. Is there any analogy with the valuing process, in terms of behavioral types? We now hypothesize that there is. It is believed that through some combination of circumstances in the growing-up process, a number of children have not been required to master even some of the elementary thinking processes. Not having become proficient in them, not habituated to their use, how do these chronic "nonthinkers" behave in terms of characteristic patterns? We see some clearly recognizable cases, almost stereotypes of the poor thinking kind.

1. The Very Impulsive Child

First, assuring ourselves that there is no physical cause, and that the child does not have severe emotional difficulties, we proceed on the assumption that he needs frequent opportunity to think. Teachers often say about him: he jumps the gun; he flies off at the first suggestion; if he would only take time to think for a minute. We suggest that teachers improvise some of the twelve thinking situations for this kind of child every day for a period of a semester. Developing a curriculum for him, which requires comparing, summarizing, observing, criticizing, analyzing, classifying, imagining, problem solving, interpreting data, doing research, and reacting to coding, are the first steps in the reconstruction of his impulsivity. These thinking operations require the taking of thought, the consideration of alternatives, the anticipation of difficulties —all of which slow down the impulsive person. As he is helped with these operations, the hypothesis states, the impulsiveness will decline in frequency.

2. The Overly Dependent Child

This child very, very often asks the teacher for help. Over and over again, he seems to be stuck. He seems to need help at every stage. The teacher often urges him to try to think things out for himself, and this does little good. He has been told this many times. We suggest that what he needs is a great emphasis upon the thinking-type situations which have been outlined at some length. As he works on his own observations, his own summaries, his own comparisons, he will be learning how to use his intelligence, and the hypothesis implies that as this process goes forward, day after day, he will become more independent, more self-directing.

3. The Rigid, "In-a-Rut" Child

When this child makes a mistake of some kind and is asked to start over again, he is quite apt to repeat his errors. He doesn't like to try something new; to try *another* way. There is a lack of flexibility about his approach to thinking, a narrowness which almost precludes thinking. He seems to be in a rut of his own making. The theory suggests that he too needs a variety of assignments encompassing many diverse thinking functions, and as he carries on the required operations, he will get out of his rut.

4. He Misses the Meaning

Sometimes, when a joke is told in the classroom, and the children laugh, this child is apt to ask: "What are they laughing at?" He very frequently does not catch the meaning of a situation. In a summarizing situation, he is apt to repeat every tiny detail because he doesn't see the larger meanings. The causes may in some instances be physical or emotional, but if these can be ruled out, it may be inferred that he has not been required, nor has he learned to carry on the functions of interpretation, analysis, and criticism. Day after day, he needs a curriculum which is related to the twelve thinking assignments. His papers need to be scrutinized carefully and coded in terms of the thinking patterns he is using. Under these circumstances, it is hypothesized that he will come to see the significant meanings in situations in which he is a participant.

5. The Loud, Dogmatic, and Overassertive Child

In adult life he is a commonly appearing type. As arguments run low, or as the argument appears to be lost, his voice rises in volume, and perhaps, in stridency. He seems to be cocky; overly confident of his views, his conclusions, or recommendations. He wants to win or to dominate and cares little or nothing about logic and thinking if they happen to be in the way of winning. He often gets his way through his arrogance and he seems to conclude that his reasoning was the better kind. He is difficult to work with when reliance is placed upon exhortation, or cajolery. He reverts, again and again, to his characteristic behavior. To help him to reconstruct his habits, it seems necessary to get him on a regimen of thinking situations, and then to code his thinking so that he can see it, and appraise it for himself. Under these circumstances, he will probably reduce the bombast in his behavior, and introduce greater sensitivity to the analysis of the problematic situation.

6. The Underconfident Child

Assuming again, that physical and emotional causes have been eliminated, this child is probably in need of rigorous training in thinking. At the moment, he has little confidence in his ability to think. He is apt to say, at the close of the meeting that he wanted to suggest something, but he didn't know how it would be received. Perhaps he might be laughed at, or ridiculed. He isn't sure that his thoughts are worth listening to. He isn't able to appraise his own analysis, or his own recommendations. Habitually, he is quiet and withdrawn in thinking situations. He too, it is presumed, needs assignments, day after day, of the kind previously described, and as he carries these out, he will develop the courage to say what he thinks, what he believes, what he is for and against.

7. He can't Concentrate on Means and Ends

At the time and the moment when it is most needed, he fails to concentrate on the matter at hand; a mistake is made which often imperils the whole enterprise or ruins the project at hand. Means are not connected with ends at every step of the way; a kind of thoughtlessness enters in; carelessness takes over. The connections between the immediate doing, and the long-range goal are not sensed. He himself often says that he tries hard but he always makes some mistake; that he is never satisfied with the quality of his final product; that something always goes wrong. As a matter of routine we are apt to tell him that he must pay closer attention, that he has to be more careful, that he should concentrate, and even as we are thus trying to persuade him into more adequate action, we realize, deep down, that it isn't going to do much good. This child needs a rigorous and longrange exposure to thinking situations of the kinds previously outlined. Teachers need to examine his thinking carefully; to code it for him; to reflect it to him. We must face him with his own thinking; we must let him see it and appraise it. Under these circumstances he might reconstruct his careless habits, and change his behavior.

8. The "Anti-Think" Child

We have children who don't want to think. They're against it. They want things spelled out for them, on principle. "Isn't it the teacher's job to tell us what to do?" Confronted with the need for making some plan, alone, or in consort with others, he says, "Why all the talking? Why don't we just go ahead and *do* something?" They are action-oriented and in effect, lesson learners—in school. They dislike the need for suspending judgment, for considering alternatives, for examining the relationships of means to ends. In the parlance of our times, he is an anti-egghead. We suggest that this child has not had repeated opportunities to learn how to use reason. He needs the discipline of a curriculum which day after day focuses upon the thinking-type situations which have been presented in previous pages. Under that discipline, it is hypothesized that he will find satisfaction in pausing for reflection;

he will find stimulation in a situation that is puzzling; he will want the challenges that are inevitably associated with thinking one's way toward more adequate solutions.

Summary

The curriculum should contain many more opportunities for the clarification of values, and the clarification of thinking. These opportunities should be related to the world conflicts, the culture conflicts, to regional, state, and local issues, and to problems of great personal concern to students. Questions of a kind faciliating clarification have been set forth. Ways of handling student responses have been outlined. The kinds of assignments which put an emphasis upon thinking have been described, and a number of ways of coding student papers have been presented.

It was suggested that certain types of behavior are associated with lack of value development:

1. Apathy, dullness
2. Flightiness
3. Overconforming
4. Nagging dissent
5. Extreme uncertainty
6. Underachievement
7. Role-playing
8. Great inconsistency

When these kinds of children have been identified, it was hypothesized that if teachers will work persistently on the processes of value clarification, changes will take place in the behavior of children. These symptoms will decline and zest and purpose and direction will characterize the lives of the children. On the basis of very meager experimental evidence, there is hope that four out of five such children will change significantly.

It has also been suggested that certain types of behavior are associated with absence of, or neglect of thinking. These were listed as:

1. Impulsiveness
2. Overdependence
3. Rigidity, rut
4. Missing meaning
5. Loud, assertive
6. Fearful, underconfident
7. Lack concentration
8. The "anti-think"

Here it was hypothesized that if teachers were to see to it that these children were exposed over and over again to thinking-types of assignments, and that if the responses of the students were coded, and if the students were then confronted with instances of their own patterns of thinking, significant change would begin to take place in these designated behavior patterns.

If we assume the responsibility for the development of personality through our social institutions, and if we recognize the behavioral symptoms as a resultant of current social conditions, then we are obligated to do our part in carrying forward two major emphases: the exploration of the significance and meaning of life to our students, and requiring of them the continuing utilization of higher mental processes. Nothing less is good enough. Nothing less will prepare us for an understanding of ourselves, in relation to the epoch in which we live. Nothing less will prepare us for our awesome responsibilities on the world stage.

Those with responsibility for curriculum development and research in the area of curriculum may profitably experiment with these ideas from the kindergarten through the graduate levels of instruction.*

* N.B. Two more recent works by the author of this article elaborate upon the ideas expressed in this chapter: Louis E. Raths, Merrill Harmin, and Sidney B. Simon, "*Values and Teaching*" Columbus, Ohio: Charles E. Merrill Books, Inc., 1966, Louis E. Raths, Selma Wasserman, Arthur Jonas, and Arnold Rothstein, *Teaching for Thinking*. Columbus, Ohio: Charles E. Merrill Books, Inc., 1967.

34. THE REFLECTIVE TEACHER

LAWRENCE E. METCALF

It is easy for a modern educator to conclude that there are no horizons in the social studies today, except those that have been lost since the Eight Year Study. There are no large and exciting projects in social studies education such as are believed to be taking place in science and mathematics. With the assistance of Sputnik and the Cold War, science and mathematics have stolen all the headlines. Yet there are unrecognized horizons for the social studies in certain quiet developments now occurring at the level of basic research into the nature of teaching and subject matter. These developments are producing certain refinements in the theory and practice of reflective teaching.

The classical theory of reflective thinking as a method for teaching concepts and generalizations has been put by John Dewey.[1] Recent research on the logic and linguistics of teach-

Lawrence E. Metcalf, "The Reflective Teacher," PHI DELTA KAPPAN, *XLIV, No. 1 (October 1962), 12–20. Reprinted by permission.*

[1] John Dewey, *How We Think* (Boston: D.C. Heath & Company, 1910, 1933).

ing point toward certain refinements in Dewey's basic theory, although some of the investigators perceive themselves as anti-Dewey, or at least as having gone beyond Dewey. The import of these studies for teaching the social studies is not entirely clear, but at least two broad lines of development are beginning to suggest themselves. First, it is already clear that the traditional course in methods of teaching will have to give more attention than it has to the logical foundations of method. The methods course will become less technical and more theoretical in its content, a development that could silence those superficial critics of education who have claimed that all we need do to save the public schools is to eliminate courses in methods of teaching in favor of additional courses in "solid liberal arts content." The second development that is beginning to emerge is a preference for conceptual over factual content in both the elementary and secondary schools. No one has yet dared to suggest a similar reform at the college level.

The movement toward an emphasis upon the logical as well as the psychological aspects of teaching method, recent though it is, has already resulted in the publication of a methods textbook by Hullfish and Smith which assumes that reflective thinking is the only educational method.[2] This book is largely concerned with the problem of warranted belief, and how teachers may help students determine whether there is any warrant for holding certain beliefs. The authors of this book classify beliefs into three kinds, the analytic, synthetic, and evaluative. The procedures for verification of a belief vary with each type. In fact, verification has three different meanings. It is significant, particularly for the social studies, that the authors believe that all three kinds of belief can be verified, and they discuss the logical problems involved in each kind of verification.

Their discussion of the difference between the form and the function of a belief is also significant for the social studies teacher who favors reflection as a method of teaching. How is it possible for a statement that is synthetic in form to function as if its form were analytic? This possibility becomes a reality for the person who holds a synthetic belief not only without any evidential ground but also without any notion of the kind of factual knowledge that would make it necessary for him to give up his belief. A defining attribute of any belief that functions as analytic is that its possessor will not modify or reject it in the light of his experience with it. In Hullfish and Smith's terms, it is held in such a way that it is treated as true "come what may in experience." To illustrate the matter further, the principle of identity or noncontradiction as we find it stated in logic is analytic in both form and function. But a statement that is obviously synthetic in form, such as, "Negroes are intellectually inferior to whites," is held analytically by any person who lacks a concept of evidence. Many high-school students lack this concept, and a social studies teacher who would have students reflect upon their prejudices may first find it necessary to teach the nature of evidence.

[2] H. Gordon Hullfish and Philip G. Smith, *Reflective Thinking: The Method of Education* (New York: Dodd, Mead & Co., 1961).

In his essay on the uses of subject matter, Henderson has suggested a taxonomy of belief that is more complete than Hullfish and Smith's.[3] He has defined eight kinds of statements, and has labeled them as follows:

1. Statements
   - 1.1 Analytic
     - 1.11 Singular
     - 1.12 General
   - 1.2 Contingent
     - 1.21 Singular
     - 1.22 General
2. Prescriptions
   - 2.1 Singular
   - 2.2 General
3. Value Statements
   - 3.1 Singular
   - 3.2 General

Since he refers to these as statements of knowledge, he evidently shares with Hullfish and Smith the idea that value judgments and definitions, as well as propositions, may be verified in some way. He does not discuss the problems of verification where values and definitions are concerned, matters which receive considerable attention from Hullfish and Smith. It should be noted that Henderson uses the term *contingent* for those statements that Hullfish and Smith have called synthetic. Whether they are called contingent or synthetic, they amount to what logical positivists mean by testable propositions. Henderson also differs from Hullfish and Smith in making a distinction between prescriptions and evaluations, and between statements that are singular or general in their subject.

The Value of Classifying Statements

The classification of statements, whether the statements represent knowledge, belief, or opinion, is useful in at least one regard to all teachers of social studies who seek reflection. It would be a mistake for a teacher to ask a student to present evidence in support of his analytic statement. An analytic statement usually takes the form of a definition, and for such a statement it would be more appropriate to ask for an example or an illustration. Bruner's work on concept attainment also suggests the appropriateness of asking for defining attributes, and to note whether the student can distinguish between the defining attributes of a concept anl its nondefining or noisy attributes.[4] If a teacher wants a student to reflect upon a contingent statement, he will ask the student what else must be true if the statement is true. Hullfish and Smith make the same point when they say that every synthetic statement implies a prediction. The simple statement that "It is raining" implies that other things will be true if, indeed, it is raining. Ennis has defined critical thinking as the correct assessing of statements, and has identified 12 different kinds of judgment to be made by those who think critically about the statements

[3] Kenneth Henderson. "Uses of 'Subject Matter,'" in B. O. Smith and R. H. Ennis (eds.), *Language and Concepts in Education* (Skokie, Ill.: Rand McNally & Co., 1961).

[4] J. S. Bruner, Jacqueline J. Goodnow, and G. A. Austin, *A Study of Thinking* (New York: John Wiley & Sons, Inc., 1956).

they encounter.[5] The point must be well taken that a teacher who seeks reflection in his students cannot succeed if he treats all statements as if they were of the same kind.

Henderson's concept of a contingent general statement is especially significant for those teachers of history who claim that a reflective study of the past increases student's understanding of the present. A contingent general statement, *if it is expressed in the present tense*, is the only kind of statement in history that arches through time, and breaks down the wall of separation between past and present. The statement that "Unless American soldiers fought like Indians, the red men usually defeated them," is contingent general in form, but its subject matter is in the past. But a statement that "Roman Catholic loyalty helps a presidential candidate of the Roman Catholic faith more than Protestant prejudice hurts him" (a statement that has received some confirmation from Louis Bean's study of the election returns of 1928 and 1960), in addition to having a contingent general form is cast in the present tense, and thus has a subject matter that is not limited to the past. Courses in history that fail to emphasize the study of such statements, what they mean and whether they are true, cannot back up the teacher's claim that an understanding of history clarifies present-day problems.

One can infer from the textbooks that are popular with teachers of social studies that the teachers of these courses prefer contingent singular to contingent general content. These are the "facts" that teachers believe students must learn in order to acquire enough background to think about current problems. Typical content in high-school American history courses is illustrated by statements such as the following, each of which is taken from one of the leading textbooks in the field:

> After the capture of Mexico City it was some months before a Mexican government could be found to sign a peace.
>
> The most famous of the railroad consolidators was Cornelius Vanderbilt (1794–1877), who built up the New York Central system.
>
> The Roosevelt Corollary was first put into effect in Santo Domingo.
>
> The advance of labor unions was aided by the National Labor Relations Act (also called the Wagner Act) passed by Congress in 1935.
>
> World War II did not inspire the enthusiasm and idealism of either the War Between the States or World War I.

The usefulness of this kind of content is reduced to a minimum when teachers require that it be learned apart from and prior to reflection. Hullfish and Smith put the issue clearly and succinctly:

> . . . Some critics say, for instance, that, since thinking cannot go on in a vacuum, students must first be given the facts they may later use in thinking. Now, of course, the alternatives are not gaining facts apart from thought or thinking apart from facts. The question is how facts are to be best gained. This introduces a third alternative, using facts within a reflective process.

[5] R. H. Ennis, "A Concept of Critical Thinking," *Harvard Educational Review*, XXXII, No. 1 (Winter, 1962).

The use of facts within a process of reflection gives the facts some kind of order. There are two kinds of order suggested by Henderson, Hullfish, and Smith in their taxonomies. One kind results in concepts, the other in generalizations. Much of the literature on teaching the social studies has not distinguished between these two kinds of order. In fact, it is not unusual to find in a textbook on teaching the social studies that the teaching of concepts and generalizations is treated as a single topic. Bruner has defined a concept as a category, which suggests that the teaching of concepts would require students to engage in acts of classfication. Students, for instance, would use their information about events as part of the basis for grouping them according to their common attributes. If imperialism is defined by attributes, *a*, *b*, and *c*, then any event which possesses these attributes would be classified as an instance of imperialism. The author of this article has suggested that the sorting of events is one of the processes with which a teacher is concerned when he teaches a concept.[6] The kind of order which results from classification is basic to all thinking and cognition, and it focuses instruction upon the study of analytic statements. Such statements are never true in the sense that they have evidence to back them up, but rather they are what Hullfish and Smith have described as formal truths. Such statements are *necessarily* true because of the way in which terms are defined, and because of the way in which we have *chosen* to structure experience. Bruner puts the point well when he says that concepts are not discovered; instead, they are created.

6 L. E. Metcalf, "Teaching Economic Concepts in the Social Studies," *The Illinois Councilor,* XXI, No. 1 (March 1960).

Backing up Contingent General Statements

A second kind of order is obtained when contingent singular content is organized and presented according to the generalizations (contingent general statements) toward which they point. The statement that government deficits foster inflation under the conditions of full employment or imperfect competition is an example of contingent general content. This kind of statement may be tested empirically and found to be probably true or false. Sometimes evidence is unavailable, and in this case we reserve judgment. The teaching of generalization includes two aspects. One aspect is concerned with what the statement says. This requires the learning of analytic statements (concepts). In the example above, students must define deficit financing, full employment, and imperfect competition. From the subject matter of economics students can learn the correct meanings of these terms. Bruner calls these correct meanings official definitions, to set them apart from the opinions students may have about the meaning of full employment, etc. But the teaching of generalizations, unlike the teaching of concepts, does not stop with definitions. The second and crucial aspect is empirical. It seeks to answer the question: Is it true that deficit-financing has certain consequences under certain conditions? At this stage of instruction the reflective teacher wants to know whether students have evidence to back up their contingent general statements.

The "What," but Never the "Why"

If teachers of social studies insist upon teaching the facts out of all relationship to concepts or generalizations, they cannot expect students to grow in their understanding of social phenomena regardless of whether the phenomena are in the past or the present. If this kind of instruction occurs in a history course devoted to the pleasures of chronological narrative, the teachers may be entertaining, interesting, metaphorical, and even poetic, but their students will not develop any capacity to generalize their learning. They may at best learn a great deal about *what* happened, although this can hardly happen if terms are never defined, but they can never learn *why* anything happened, because their content has no power to explain or predict events. The reason why this is so is suggested clearly by Swift's study of the teaching of explanations.[7, 8, 9]

High-school social studies are so much devoted to contingent singular content that they seldom try to explain why events have occurred except in a descriptive sense, and Swift has observed that many teachers and textbook writers cannot tell the difference between an explanation and a description. In order to tell the difference, and also in order to assess the correctness and adequacy of any explanation, one needs a model from which to work. Swift has borrowed his model from Hempel, and has studied the problem of teaching historical explanations as an aspect of instruction in critical thinking.

Hempel's model, which he borrowed from the physical sciences, and which he suggests as a research tool for professional historians, casts explanations into the form of a syllogism, the major premise of which is a contingent general statement. For reasons already offered, the author of this article believes that this contingent general statement should be expressed in the present tense. Other criteria are implicit in Hempel's model. The major premise should be testable and true (Hempel refers to explanations that rest upon an untestable premise as a pseudo-explanation). The minor premise, which describes the existence of the antecedent conditions for the occurrence of the event to be explained, should also be historically true. Finally, a description of the event to be explained should follow logically from the truth of the major and minor premises. Swift has summarized the meaning of this kind of explanation as "a deductive argument possessed of empirical content."

The explanations offered by high-school social studies textbooks are usually incomplete by Hempel's standards, and require "filling in." These incomplete explanations usually imply, but do not state openly, a general law. Such explanations may abound even in the writings of historians who deny that there are any laws in history. A typical example of an incomplete explanation is the statement, "The Pilgrims came to the New

[7] L. F. Swift, "Explanation as an Aspect of Critical Thinking in Secondary School Social Studies." Unpublished doctoral dissertation, University of Illinois, 1959.

[8] L. F. Swift, "Explanation," in B. O. Smith and R. H. Ennis, eds., *Language and Concepts in Education* (Skokie, Ill.: Rand McNally & Co., 1961).

[9] L. F. Swift, "The Teaching of Explanation in History," 1958. (Unpublished.)

World to escape religious persecution." This sentence standing as it is will make sense to most high-school students. They will believe it in the sense of not doubting it, and may even commit it to memory as an item of information. If this incomplete explanation is cast as a syllogism, doubt flows in from all directions.

Major Premise:	If a group of people is persecuted for its religious beliefs, it will migrate to a new territory where it will be free to practice its religion.
Minor Premise:	In 17th-Century England a group of people called the Puritans were persecuted for their religion.
Conclusion:	The Puritans migrated to the New World.

The teacher needs to raise only a few questions about this syllogism before the students sense its inadequacy. Many people who have been persecuted for their religious and other beliefs have not migrated. In fact, many of the Puritans did not, and hence we reserve the term *Pilgrim* for those who did.

The discovery of negative cases always calls for the rejection or modification of a proposition. It is not easy in the social studies to find propositions for which there are no negative cases. It is even difficult to frame propositions precisely enough to distinguish between negative and positive cases. We often settle for propositions that are grossly probable in their truth. Sometimes we are no more precise than to distinguish between the possible and the impossible, or the probable and the improbable, without specifying except in a very rough form the probability that a certain kind of event will occur under certain conditions. If the major premise in the above syllogism is modified so that it becomes a probabilistic rather than a certain truth, it might read as follows: If a group of people is persecuted for its religious beliefs, it *usually* migrates to a new territory.

The term *usually* gives us trouble, for it leaves unanswered the question, "How many negative cases would make it necessary for us to reject the probable truth of our premise?" Clearly, we would have to reject the premise if the number of negative cases exceeds the number of positive cases. But this observation raises the further question, "What constitutes a representative and adequate sample of cases?" What history, and how much history, would students have to study in order to test fairly the truth of a premise? Teachers of social studies are not yet well trained in logic or sampling and probability theory, and this is the kind of content that belongs in the methods course of the future.

The use of a qualifying term gives us another kind of trouble. It destroys the logical tightness of a syllogism. A description of the event to be explained cannot be deduced from premises that are merely probable in their truth. At best we can conclude that a certain kind of event is likely to occur under certain conditions. Unless we can identify conditions that account for negative cases we are forced to treat the major premise as a plausible hypothesis rather than a principle or general law. This may be the only kind of truth commonly available from the subject matter of the social studies. Nagel's analysis of explanation in the social sciences has explored thoroughly the limits of knowledge in history.[10] Given this state of affairs, the use of Hempel's model helps students to learn the extent to which their social studies content is a reliable guide for conduct, and better grounded than "common sense," if not as well established as physics or chemistry content.

There are many other considerations to be faced by a reflective teacher of the social studies, and basic research has begun to explore their dimensions. Unfortunately, limitations of space do not permit their treatment in this article. But it should be clear from what has been reported here that the new horizons for the social studies are in methods of teaching. The suggested reforms in method also call for revisions in social studies content, and the teacher of the future, in addition to knowing a lot of history, will also need to know more social science than has been required of him in the past. It goes without saying that he will have to be well trained in logic, linguistics, and the philosophy of science. As long as the social-studies curriculum devotes most of its instructional time to history he will need to be a student of theories of history, and what history is, and what kinds of history there are, and how history is different from such social sciences as sociology and economics.

10 Ernest Nagel, *The Structure of Science* (New York: Harcourt, Brace & World, Inc., 1962).

35. DEVELOPMENT AND LEARNING

JEAN PIAGET

My dear colleagues, I am very concerned about what to say to you, because I do not know if I shall accomplish the end that has been assigned to me. But I have been told that the important thing is not what you say, but the discussion which follows and the answers to questions you are asked. So this morning I shall simply give a general introduction of a few ideas which seem to me to be important for the subject of this conference.

First I would like to make clear the difference between two problems: the problem of *development* in general and the problem of *learning*. I think these problems are very different, although some people do not make this distinction.

The development of knowledge is a spontaneous process, tied to the whole process of embryogenesis. Embryogenesis concerns the development of the body, but it concerns as well the development of the nervous system and the development of mental functions. In the case of the development of knowledge in children, embryogenesis ends only in adulthood. It is a total developmental process which we must re-situate in its general biological and psychological context. In other words, development is a process which concerns the totality of the structures of knowledge.

Learning presents the opposite case. In general, learning is provoked by situations—provoked by a psychological experimenter; or by a teacher, with respect to some didactic point; or by an external situation. It is provoked, in general, as opposed to spontaneous. In addition, it is a limited process—limited to a single problem, or to a single structure.

So I think that development explains learning, and this opinion is contrary to the widely held opinion that development is a sum of discrete learning experiences. For some psychologists development is reduced to a series of specific learned items,

J. Piaget, "Development and Learning," Journal of Research in Science Teaching, *II, No. 3 (1964), 176–86. Reprinted by permission.*

and development is thus the sum, the cumulation of this series of specific items. I think this is an atomistic view which deforms the real state of things. In reality, development is the essential process and each element of learning occurs as a function of total development, rather than being an element which explains development. I shall begin, then, with a first part dealing with development, and I shall talk about learning in the second part.

To understand the development of knowledge, we must start with an idea which seems central to me—the idea of an *operation*. Knowledge is not a copy of reality. To know an object, to know an event, is not simply to look at it and make a mental copy or image of it. To know an object is to act on it. To know is to modify, to transform the object, and to understand the process of this transformation, and as a consequence to understand the way the object is constructed. An operation is thus the essence of knowledge; it is an interiorized action which modifies the object of knowledge. For instance an operation would consist of joining objects in a class to construct a classification. Or an operation would consist of ordering, or putting things in a series. Or an operation would consist of counting, or of measuring. In other words, it is a set of actions modifying the object, and enabling the knowers to get at the structures of the transformation.

An operation is an interiorized action. But, in addition, it is a reversible action; that is, it can take place in both directions, for instance, adding or subtracting, joining or separating. So it is a particular type of action which makes up logical structures.

Above all, an operation is never isolated. It is always linked to other operations, and as a result it is always a part of a total structure. For instance, a logical class does not exist in isolation; what exists is the total structure of classification. An asymmetrical relation does not exist in isolation. Seriation is the natural, basic operational structure. A number does not exist in isolation. What exists is the series of numbers which constitute a structure, an exceedingly rich structure whose various properties have been revealed by mathematicians.

These operational structures are what seem to me to constitute the basis of knowledge, the natural psychological reality, in terms of which we must understand the development of knowledge. And the central problem of development is to understand the formation, elaboration, organization, and functioning of these structures.

I should like to review the stages of development of these structures, not in any detail, but simply as a reminder. I shall distinguish four main stages. The first is a sensory-motor, pre-verbal stage, lasting approximately the first 18 months of life. During this stage is developed the practical knowledge which constitutes the substructure of later representational knowledge. An example is the construction of the schema of the permanent object. For an infant, during the first months, an object has no permanence. When it disappears from the perceptual field it no longer exists. No attempt is made to find it again. Later, the infant will try to find it, and he will find it by localizing it spatially. Consequently, along with the construction of the permanent object there comes the construction of practical or sensory-motor space. There is similarly the construction of temporal succession, and of elementary sensory-motor causality. In other words, there is a series of structures which are indispensable for the structures of later representational thought.

In a second stage, we have pre-operational representation—the beginnings of language, of the symbolic function, and therefore of thought, or representation. But at the level of representational thought, there must now be a reconstruction of all that was developed on the sensory-motor level. That is, the sensory-motor actions are not immediately translated into operations. In fact, during all this second period of pre-operational representations, there are as yet no operations as I defined this term a moment ago. Specifically, there is as yet no conservation which is the psychological criterion of the presence of reversible operations. For example, if we pour liquid from one glass to another of a different shape, the pre-operational child will think there is more in one than in the other. In the absence of operational reversibility, there is no conservation of quantity.

In a third stage the first operations appear, but I call these concrete operations because they operate on objects, and not yet on verbally expressed hypotheses. For example, there are the operations of classification, ordering, the construction of the idea of number, spatial and temporal operations, and all the fundamental operations of elementary logic of classes and relations, of elementary mathematics, of elementary geometry, and even of elementary physics.

Finally, in the fourth stage, these operations are surpassed as the child reaches the level of what I call formal or hypothetic-deductive operations; that is, he can now reason on hypotheses, and not only on objects. He constructs new operations, operations of propositional logic, and not simply the operations of classes, relations, and numbers. He attains new structures which are on the one hand combinatorial, corresponding to what mathematicians call lattices; on the other hand, more complicated group structures. At the level of concrete operations, the operations apply within an immediate neighborhood: for instance, classification by successive inclusions. At the level of the combinatorial, however, the groups are much more mobile.

These, then, are the four stages which we identify, whose formation we shall now attempt to explain.

What factors can be called upon to explain the development from one set of structures to another? It seems to me that there are four main factors: first of all, *maturation*, in the sense of Gesell, since this development is a continuation of the embryogenesis; second, the role of *experience* of the effects of the physical environment on the structures of intelligence; third, social *transmission* in the broad sense (linguistic transmission, education, etc.); and fourth, a factor which is too often neglected but one which seems to me fundamental and even the principal factor. I shall call this the factor of *equilibration* or if you prefer it, of self-regulation.

Let us start with the first factor, maturation. One might think that these stages are simply a reflection of an interior maturation of the nervous system, following the hypotheses of Gesell, for example. Well, maturation certainly does play an indispensable role and must not be ignored. It certainly takes part in every transformation that takes place during a child's development. However, this first factor is insufficient in itself. First of all, we know practically nothing about the maturation of the nervous system beyond the first months of the child's existence. We know a little bit about it during the first two years but we know very little following this time. But above all, maturation doesn't explain everything, because the average ages at which these stages appear (the average chronological ages) vary a great deal from one society to another. The ordering of these stages is constant and has been found in all the societies studied. It has been found in various countries where psychologists in universities have redone the experiments but it has also been found in African peoples for example, in the children of the Bushmen, and in Iran, both in the villages and in the cities. However, although the order of succession is constant, the chronological ages of these stages varies a great deal. For instance, the ages which we have found in Geneva are not necessarily the ages which you would find in the United States. In Iran, furthermore, in the city of Teheran, they found approximately the same ages as we found in Geneva, but there is a systematic delay of two years in the children in the country. Canadian psychologists who redid our experiments, Monique Laurendeau and Father Adrien Pinard, found once again about the same ages in Montreal. But when they redid the experiments in Martinique, they found a delay of four years in all the experiments and this in spite of the fact that the children in Martinique go to a school set up according to the French system and the French curriculum and attain at the end of this elementary school a certificate of higher primary education. There is then a delay of four years, that is, there are the same stages, but systematically delayed. So you see that these age variations show that maturation does not explain everything.

I shall go on now to the role played by experience. Experience of objects, of physical reality, is obviously a basic factor in the development of cognitive structures. But once again this factor does not explain everything. I can give two reasons for this. The first reason is that some of the concepts which appear at the beginning of the stage of concrete operations are such that I cannot see how they could be drawn from experience. As an example, let us take the conservation of the substance in the case of changing the shape of a ball of plasticene. We give this ball of plasticene to a child who changes its shape into a sausage form and we ask him if there is the same amount of matter, that is, the same amount of substance as there was before. We also ask him if it now has the same weight and thirdly if it now has the same volume. The volume is measured by the displacement of water when we put the ball or the sausage into a glass of water. The findings, which have been the same every time this experiment has been done, show us that first of all there is conservation of the amount of substance. At about eight years old a child will say, "There is the same amount of plasticene." Only later does the child assert that the weight is conserved and still later that the volume is conserved. So I would ask you where the idea of the conservation of substance can come from. What is a constant and invariant substance when it doesn't yet have a constant weight or a constant volume? Through perception you can get at the weight of the ball or the volume of the ball but perception cannot give you an idea of the amount of substance. No experiment, no experience can show the child that there is the same amount of substance. He can weigh the ball and that would lead to the conservation of weight. He can immerse it in water and that would lead to the conservation of volume. But the notion of substance is attained before either weight or volume. This conservation of substance is simply a logical necessity. The child now understands that when there is a transformation something must be conserved because by reversing the transformation you can come back to the point of departure and once again have the ball. He knows that something is conserved but he doesn't know what. It is not yet the weight, it is not yet the volume; it is simply a logical form—a logical necessity. There, it seems to me, is an example of a progress in knowledge, a logical necessity for something to be conserved even though no experience can have lead to this notion.

My second objection to the sufficiency of experience as an explanatory factor is that this notion of experience is a very equivocal one. There are, in fact, two kinds of experience which are psychologically very different and this difference is very important from the pedagogical point of view. It is because of the pedagogical importance that I emphasize this distinction. First of all, there is what I shall call physical experience, and, secondly, what I shall call logical-mathematical experience.

Physical experience consists of acting upon objects and drawing some knowledge about the objects by abstraction from the objects. For example, to discover that this pipe is heavier than this watch, the child will weigh them both and find the difference in the objects themselves. This is experience in the usual sense of the term—in the sense used by empiricists. But there is a second type of experience which I shall call logical mathematical experience where the knowledge is not drawn from the objects, but it is drawn by the actions effected upon the objects. This is not the same thing. When one acts upon objects, the objects are indeed there, but there is also the set of actions which modify the objects.

I shall give you an example of this type of experience. It is a nice example because we have verified it many times in small children under seven years of age, but it is also an example which one of my mathematician friends has related to me about his own childhood, and he dates his mathematical career from this experience. When he was four or five years old—I don't know exactly how old, but a small child—he was seated on the ground in his garden and he was counting pebbles. Now to count these pebbles he put them in a row and he counted them one, two, three, up to ten. Then he finished counting them and started to count them in the other direction. He began by the end and once again he found ten. He found this marvelous that there were ten in one direction and ten in the other direction. So he put them in a circle and counted them that way and found ten once again. Then he counted them in the other direction and found ten once more. So he put them in some other arrangement and kept counting them and kept finding ten. There was the discovery that he made.

Now what indeed did he discover? He did not discover a property of pebbles; he discovered a property of the action of ordering. The pebbles had no order. It was his action which introduced a linear order or a cyclical order, or any kind of an order. He discovered that the sum was independent of the order. The order was the action which he introduced among the pebbles. For the sum the same principle applied. The pebbles had no sum; they were simply in a pile. To make a sum, action was necessary—the operation of putting together and counting. He found that the sum was independent of the order, in other words, that the action of putting together is independent of the action of ordering. He discovered a property of actions and not a property of pebbles. You may say that it is in the nature of pebbles to let this be done to them and this is true. But it could have been drops of water, and drops of water would not have let this be done to them because two drops of water and two drops of water do not make four drops of water as you know very well. Drops of water then would not let this be done to them, we agree to that.

So it is not the physical property of pebbles which the experience uncovered. It is the properties of the actions carried out on the pebbles, and this is quite another form of experience. It is the point of departure of mathematical deduction. The subsequent deduction will consist of interiorizing these actions and then of combining them without needing any pebbles. The mathematician no longer needs his pebbles. He can combine his operations simply with symbols, and the point of departure of this mathematical deduction is logical-mathematical experience, and this is not at all experience in the sense of the empiricists. It is the beginning of the coordination of actions, but this coordination of actions before the stage of operations needs to be supported by concrete material. Later, this coordination of actions leads to the logical-mathematical structures. I believe that logic is not a derivative of language. The source of logic is much more profound. It is the total coordination of actions, actions of joining things together, or ordering things, etc. This is what logical-mathematical experience is. It is an experience of the actions of the subject, and not an experience of objects themselves. It is an experience which is necessary before there can be operations. Once the operations have been attained this experience is no longer needed and the coordinations of actions can take place by themselves in the form of deduction and construction for abstract structures.

The third factor is social transmission-linguistic transmission or educational transmission. This factor, once again, is fundamental. I do not deny the role of any one of these factors; they all play a part. But this factor is insufficient because the child can receive valuable information via language or via education directed by an adult only if he is in a state where he can understand this information. That is, to receive the information he must have a structure which enables him to assimilate this information. This is why you cannot teach higher mathematics to a five-year-old. He does not yet have structures which enable him to understand.

I shall take a much simpler example, an example of linguistic transmission. As my very first work in the realm of child psychology, I spent a long time studying the relation between a part and a whole in concrete experience and in language. For example, I used Burt's test employing the sentence, "Some of my flowers are buttercups." The child knows that all buttercups are yellow, so there are three possible conclusions: the whole bouquet is yellow, or part of the bouquet is yellow, or none of the flowers in the bouquet are yellow. I found that up until nine years of age (and this was in Paris, so the children certainly did understand the French language) they replied, "The whole bouquet is yellow or some of my flowers are yellow." Both of those mean the same thing. They did not understand the expression, "some *of* my flowers." They did not understand this *of* as a partitive genitive, as the inclusion of some flowers in my flowers. They understood some of my flowers to be my several flowers as if the several flowers and the flowers were confused as one and the same class. So there you have children who until nine years of age heard every day a linguistic structure which implied the inclusion of a subclass in a class and yet did not understand this structure. It is only when they themselves are in firm possession of this logical structure, when they have constructed it for themselves according to the developmental laws which we shall discuss, that they succeed in understanding correctly the linguistic expression.

I come now to the fourth factor which is added to the three preceding ones but which seems to me to be the fundamental one. This is what I call the factor of equilibration. Since there are already three factors, they must somehow be equilibrated among themselves. That is one reason for bringing in the factor of equilibration. There is a second reason, however, which seems to me to be fundamental. It is that in the act of knowing, the subject is active, and consequently, faced with an external disturbance, he will react in order to compensate and consequently he will tend towards equilibrium. Equilibrium, defined by active compensation, leads to reversibility. Operational reversibility is a model of an equilibrated system where a transformation in one direction is compensated by a transformation in the other direction. Equilibration, as I understand it, is thus an active process. It is a process of self-regulation. I think that this self-regulation is a fundamental factor in development. I use this term in the sense in which it is used in cybernetics, that is, in the sense of processes with feedback and with feedforward, of processes which regulate themselves by a progressive compensation of systems. This process of equilibration takes the form of a succession of levels of equilibrium, of levels which have a certain probability which I shall call a sequential probability, that is, the probabilities are not established *a priori*. There is a sequence of levels. It is not possible to reach the second level unless equilibrium has been reached at the first level, and the equilibrium of the third level only becomes possible when the equilibrium of the second level has been reached, and so forth. That is, each level is determined as the most probable given that the preceding level has been reached. It is not the most probable at the beginning, but it is the most probable once the preceding level has been reached.

As an example, let us take the development of the idea of conservation in the transformation of the ball of plasticene into the sausage shape. Here you can discern four levels. The most probable at the beginning is for the child to think of only one dimension. Suppose that there is a probability of 0.8, for instance, that the child will focus on the length, and that the width has a probability of 0.2. This would mean that of ten children, eight will focus on the length alone without paying any attention to the width, and two will focus on the width without paying any attention to the length. They will focus only on one dimension or the other. Since the two dimensions are independent at this stage, focusing on both at once would have a probability of only 0.16. That is less than either one of the two. In other words, the most probable in the beginning is to focus only on one dimension and in fact the child will say, "It's longer, so there's more in the sausage." Once he has reached this first level, if you continue to elongate the sausage, there comes a moment when he will say, "No, now it's too thin, so there's less." Now he is thinking about the width, but he forgets the length, so you have come to a second level which becomes the most probable after the first level, but which is not the most probable at the point of departure. Once he has focused on the width, he will come back sooner or later to focus on the length. Here you will have a third level where he will oscillate between width and length and where he will discover that the two are related. When you elongate you make it thinner, and when you make it shorter, you make it thicker. He discovers that the two are solidly related and in discovering this relationship, he will start to think in terms of transformation and not only in terms of the final configuration. Now he will say that when it gets longer it gets thinner, so it's the same thing. There is more of it in length but less of it in width. When you make it shorter it gets thicker; there's less in length and more in width, so there is compensation—compensation which defines equilibrium in the sense in which I defined it a moment ago. Consequently, you have operations and conservation. In other words, in the course of these developments you will always find a process of self-regulation which I call equilibration and which seems to me the fundamental factor in the acquisition of logical-mathematical knowledge.

I shall go on now to the second part of my lecture, that is, to deal with the topic of learning. Classically, learning is based on the stimulus-response schema. I think the stimulus-response schema, while I won't say it is false, is in any case entirely incapable of explaining cognitive learning. Why? Because when you think of a stimulus-response schema, you think usually that first of all there is a stimulus and then a response is set off by this stimulus. For my part, I am convinced that the response was there first, if I can express myself in this way. A stimulus is a stimulus only to the extent that it is significant, and it becomes significant only to the extent that there is a structure which permits its assimilation, a structure which can integrate this stimulus but which at the same time sets off the response. In other words, I would propose that the stimulus-response schema be written in the circular form—in the form of a schema or of a structure which is not simply one way. I would propose that above all, between the stimulus and the response, there is the organism, the organism and its structures. The stimulus is really a stimulus only when it is assimilated into a structure and it is this structure which sets off the response. Consequently, it is not an exaggeration to say that the response is there first, or if you wish at the beginning there is the structure. Of course we would want to understand how this structure comes to be. I tried to do this earlier by presenting a model of equilibration or self-regulation. Once there is a structure, the stimulus will set off a response, but only by the intermediary of this structure.

I should like to present some facts. We have facts in great number. I shall choose only one or two and I shall choose some facts which our colleague, Smedslund, has gathered. (Smedslund is currently at the Harvard Center for Cognitive Studies.) Smedslund arrived in Geneva a few years ago convinced (he had published this in one of his papers) that the development of the ideas of conservation could be indefinitely accelerated through learning of a stimulus-response type. I invited Smedslund to come to spend a year in Geneva to show us this, to show us that he could accelerate the development of operational conservation. I shall relate only one of his experiments.

During the year that he spent in Geneva he chose to work on the conservation of weight. The conservation of weight is, in fact, easy to study since there is a possible external reinforcement, that is, simply weighing the ball and the sausage on a balance. Then you can study the child's reactions to these external results. Smedslund studied the conservation of weight on the one hand, and on the other hand he studied the transitivity of weights, that is, the transitivity of equalities if $A = B$ and $B = C$, then $A = C$, or the transitivity of the inequalities if A is less than B, and B is less than C, then A is less than C.

As far as conservation is concerned, Smedslund succeeded very easily with five-and six-year-old children in getting them to generalize that weight is conserved when the ball is transformed into a different shape. The child sees the ball transformed into a sausage or into little pieces or into a pancake or into any other form, he weighs it, and he sees that it is always the same thing. He will affirm it will be the same thing, no matter what you do to it; it will come out to be the same weight. Thus Smedslund very easily achieved the conservation of weight by this sort of external reinforcement.

In contrast to this, however, the same method did not succeed in teaching transitivity. The children resisted the notion of transitivity. A child would predict correctly in certain cases but he would make his prediction as a possibility or a probability and not as a certainty. There was never this generalized certainty in the case of transitivity.

So there is the first example, which seems to me very instructive, because in this problem in the conservation of weight there are two aspects. There is the physical aspect and there is the logical-mathematical aspect. Note that Smedslund started his study by establishing that there was a correlation between conservation and transitivity. He began by making a statistical study on the relationships between the spontaneous responses to the questions about conservation and the spontaneous responses to the question about transitivity, and he found a very significant correlation. But in the learning experiment, he obtained a learning of conservation and not of transitivity. Consequently, he successfully obtained a learning of what I called earlier physical experience (which is not surprising since it is simply a question of noting facts about objects), but he did not successfully obtain a learning in the construction of the logical structure. This doesn't surprise me either, since the logical structure is not the result of physical experience. It cannot be obtained by external reinforcement. The logical structure is reached only through internal equilibration, by self-regulation, and the external reinforcement of seeing that the balance did not suffice to establish this logical structure of transitivity.

I could give many other comparable examples, but it seems useless to me to insist upon these negative examples. Now I should like to show that learning is possible in the case of these logical-mathematical structures, but on one condition—that is, that the structure which you want to teach to the subjects can be supported by simpler, more elementary, logical-mathematical structures. I shall give you an example. It is the example of the conservation of number in the case of one-to-one correspondence. If you give a child seven blue tokens and ask him to put down as many red tokens, there is a preoperational stage where he will put one red one opposite each blue one. But when you spread out the red ones, making them into a longer row, he will say to you, "Now, there are more red ones than there are blue ones."

Now how can we accelerate, if you want to accelerate, the acquisition of this conservation of number? Well, you can imagine an analogous structure but in a simpler, more elementary situation. For example, with Mlle. Inhelder, we have been studying recently the notion of one-to-one correspondence by giving the child two glasses of the same shape and a big pile of beads. The child puts a bead into one glass with one hand and at the same time a bead into the other glass with the other hand. Time after time he repeats this action, a bead into one glass with one hand and at the same time a bead into the other glass with the other hand and he sees that there is always the same amount on each side. Then you hide one of the glasses. You cover it up. He no longer sees this glass but he continues to put one bead into it while at the same time putting one bead into the other glass which he can see. Then you ask him whether the equality has been conserved, whether there is still the same amount in one glass as in the other. Now you will find that very small children, about four years old, don't want to make a prediction. They will say, "So far, it has been the same amount, but now I don't know. I can't see any more, so I don't know." They do not want to generalize. But the generalization is made from the age of about five and one-half years.

This is in contrast to the case of the red and blue tokens with one row spread out, where it isn't until seven or eight years of age that children will say there are the same number in the two rows. As one example of this generalization, I recall a little boy of five years and nine months who had been adding the beads to the glasses for a little while. Then we asked him whether, if he continued to do this all day and all night and all the next day, there would always be the same amount in the two glasses. The little boy gave this admirable reply. "Once you know, you know for always." In other words, this was recursive reasoning. So here the child does acquire the structure in this specific case. The number is a synthesis of class inclusion and ordering. This synthesis is being favored by the child's own actions. You have set up a situation where there is an iteration of one same action which continues and which is therefore ordered while at the same time being inclusive. You have, so to speak, a localized synthesis of inclusion and ordering which facilitates the construction of the idea of number in this specific case, and there you can find, in effect, an influence of this experience on the other experience. However, this influence is not immediate. We study the generalization from this recursive situation to the other situation where the tokens are laid on the table in rows, and it is not an immediate generalization but it is made possible through intermediaries. In other words, you can find some learning of this structure if you base the learning on simpler structures.

In this same area of the development of numerical structures, the psychologist Joachim Wohlwill, who spent a year at our Institute at Geneva, has also shown that this acquisition can be accelerated through introducing additive operations, which is what we introduced also in the experiment which I just described. Wohlwill introduced them in a different way but he too was able to obtain a certain learning effect. In other words, learning is possible if you base the more complex structure on simpler structures, that is, when there is a natural relationship and development of structures and not simply an external reinforcement.

Now I would like to take a few minutes to conclude what I was saying. My first conclusion is that learning of structures seems to obey the same laws as the natural development of these structures. In other words, learning is subordinated to development and not vice-versa as I said in the introduction. No doubt you will object that some investigators have succeeded in teaching operational structures. But, when I am faced with these facts, I always have three questions which I want to have answered before I am convinced.

The first question is: "Is this learning lasting? What remains two weeks or a month later?" If a structure develops spontaneously, once it has reached a state of equilibrium, it is lasting, it will continue throughout the child's entire life. When you achieve the learning by external reinforcement, is the result lasting or not and what are the conditions necessary for it to be lasting?

The second question is: "How much generalization is possible?" What makes learning interesting is the possibility of transfer of a generalization. When you have brought about some learning, you can always ask whether this is an isolated piece in the midst of the child's mental life, or if it is really a dynamic structure which can lead to generalizations.

Then there is the third question: "In the case of each learning experience what was the operational level of the subject before the experience and what more complex structures has this learning succeeded in achieving?" In other words, we must look at each specific learning experience from the point of view of the spontaneous operations which were present at the outset and the operational level which has been achieved after the learning experience.

My second conclusion is that the fundamental relation involved in all development and all learning is not the relation of association. In the stimulus-response schema, the relation between the response and the stimulus is understood to be one of association. In contrast to this, I think that the fundamental relation is one of assimilation. Assimilation is not the same as association. I shall define assimilation as the integration of any sort of reality into a structure, and it is this assimilation which seems to me to be fundamental in learning, and which seems to me to be the fundamental relation from the point of view of pedagogical or didactic applications. All of my remarks today represent the child and the learning subject as active. An operation is an activity. Learning is possible only when there is active assimilation. It is this activity on the part of the subject which seems to me to be underplayed in the stimulus—response schema. The presentation which I propose puts the emphasis on the idea of self-regulation, on assimilation. All the emphasis is placed on the activity of the subject himself, and I think that without this activity there is no possible didactic or pedagogy which significantly transforms the subject.

Finally, and this will be my last concluding remark, I would like to comment on an excellent publication by the psychologist Berlyne. Berlyne spent a year with us in Geneva during which he intended to translate our results on the development of operations into stimulus-response language, specifically into Hull's learning theory. Berlyne published in our series of studies of genetic epistomology a very good article on this comparison between the results obtained in Geneva and Hull's theory. In the same volume, I published a commentary on Berlyne's results. The essence of Berlyne's results is this: Our findings can very well be translated into Hullian language, but only on condition that two modifications are introduced. Berlyne himself found these modifications quite considerable, but they seemed to him to concern more the conceptualization than the Hullian theory itself. I am not so sure about that. The two modifications are these. First of all, Berlyne wants to distinguish two sorts of response in the S-R schema: (*a*) responses in the ordinary, classical sense, which I shall call "copy responses"; (*b*) responses which Berlyne calls "transformation responses." Transformation responses consist of transforming one response of the first type into another response of the first type. These transformation responses are what I call operations, and you can see right away that this is a rather serious modification of Hull's conceptualization because here you are introducing an element of transformation and thus of assimilation and no longer the simple association of stimulus-response theory.

The second modification which Berlyne introduces into the stimulus-response language is the introduction of what he calls internal reinforcements. What are these internal reinforcements? They are what I call equilibration or self-regulation. The internal reinforcements are what enable the subject to eliminate contradictions, incompatibilities, and conflicts. All development is composed of momentary conflicts and incompatibilities which must be overcome to reach a higher level of equilibrium. Berlyne calls this elimination of incompatibilities internal reinforcements.

So you see that it is indeed a

stimulus-response theory, if you will, but first you add operations and then you add equilibration. That's all we want!

Editor's note: A brief question and answer period followed Professor Piaget's presentation. The first question related to the fact that the eight-year-old child acquires conservation of weight and volume. The question asked if this didn't contradict the order of emergence of the pre-operational and operational stages. Piaget's response follows:

The conservation of weight and the conservation of volume are not due only to experience. There is also involved a logical framework which is characterized by reversibility and the system of compensations. I am only saying that in the case of weight and volume, weight corresponds to a perception. There is an empirical contact. The same is true of volume. But in the case of substance, I don't see how there can be any perception of substance independent of weight or volume. The strange thing is that this notion of substance comes before the two other notions. Note that in the history of thought we have the same thing. The first Greek physicists, the pre-socratic philosophers, discovered conservation of substance independently of any experience. I do not believe this is contradictory to the theory of operations. This conservation of substance is simply the affirmation that something must be conserved. The children do not know specifically what is conserved. They know that since the sausage can become a ball again there must be something which is conserved, and saying "substance" is simply a way of translating this logical necessity for conservation. But this logical necessity results directly from the discovery of operations. I do not think that this is contradictory with the theory of development.

Editor's note: The second question was whether or not the development of stages in children's thinking could be accelerated by practice, training, and exercise in perception and memory. Piaget's response follows:

I am not very sure that exercise of perception and memory would be sufficient. I think that we must distinguish within the cognitive function two very different aspects which I shall call the figurative aspect and the operative aspect. The figurative aspect deals with static configurations. In physical reality there are states, and in addition to these there are transformations which lead from one state to another. In cognitive functioning one has the figurative aspects —for example, perception, imitation, mental imagery, etc.

The operative aspect includes operations and the actions which lead from one state to another. In children of the higher stages and in adults, the figurative aspects are subordinated to the operative aspects. Any given state is understood to be the result of some transformation and the point of departure for another transformation. But the pre-operational child does not understand transformations. He does not have the operations necessary to understand them so he puts all the emphasis on the static quality of the states. It is because of this, for example, that in the conservation experiments he simply compares the initial state and the final state without being concerned with the transformation.

In exercising perception and memory, I feel that you will reinforce the figurative aspect without touching the operative aspect. Consequently, I'm not sure that this will accelerate the development of cognitive structures. What needs to be reinforced is the operative aspect—not the analysis of states, but the understanding of transformations.

36. EXPRESSIVE THOUGHT BY GIFTED CHILDREN IN THE CLASSROOM

JAMES J. GALLAGHER

For many years there has been an unfortunate gulf between those professions whose purposes are to create or teach expressive thought, and psychologists whose goals are to attempt to understand more about man's thinking processes and developing intelligence. The psychologist has been fascinated with how a person can internally process information in such a way as to generate a product different from the information received. This interest in productive thought and the more specific subject area of creative thinking, has waxed and waned over the past few decades but now seems to be enjoying an important revival.

James J. Gallagher, "Expressive Thought by Gifted Children in the Classroom," ELEMENTARY ENGLISH, XXXXII, NO. 5 *(1965), 559–68. The research reported herein was made possible by Cooperative Research Grant #965 from the U.S. Office of Education. Reprinted with the permission of the National Council of Teachers of English and James J. Gallagher.*

A review of the research in this area (Stein and Heinze, 1960) has presented a fine picture of the two main avenues of approach to studying this problem, investigating the creative thinker and investigating the creative process. While the study of the creative person has resulted in many interesting hypotheses, it is also fraught with difficulty. Many of the great creative geniuses that we would wish to study have long since passed from the scene and biographers often tell us more about themselves than about their subjects. It is also difficult to weigh the life of a Wilde against the standards of modern society, or to try and determine whether Wagner's financial irresponsibility was an essential or irrelevant part of the total creative person.

Recent work by MacKinnon (8) and by Barron (1) in their studies of creative *vs.* noncreative persons have suggested that there are certain personality characteristics that seem closely related to the creative person. Those judged most creative deviated more from the norm on measures of maladjustment but also possessed more ego strength than the less creative. They have an openness to experience and intellectual risk taking that permits them to take the atypical view.

The educator cannot be satisfied merely with dealing with the once-in-a-lifetime student who is destined to place his mark on history or to create enduring literature. His duty is a broader one which entails increasing the productive potential in all students.

Many investigators felt the key to improvement of thinking abilities was the study of the process by which the individual generates new thoughts. In order to determine what factors might influence student productivity or nonproductivity in thought expression, one particular focus of this research interest has been the classroom environment. To study such a wide range of expressiveness as occurs in this special environment, one needs a method of cataloguing the classroom content and a theory of thinking ability that can aid in interpretation of the scene.

In this study, the theoretical model of Guilford (5, 6) was used as a basis for analyzing the expressive behavior. Guilford's structure of intellect was developed through a decade of research studies using factor analytic methodology. The parameters of this theoretical structure consist in the operations of thinking, the content within which these operations are performed, and the products which result from the performance of these operations upon the content.

Other investigators with similar approaches but different theoretical models are Smith and Meux (11); Flanders (3); Taba, Levine and Elzey (12); Medley and Mitzel (7); and Bloom (2), to mention only a few.

The purposes of the present study were to describe the kinds of thinking operations taking place in this variety of classrooms and to determine factors or variables that seemed to have influence on the expressive abilities of gifted students.

Subjects

The subjects in the present study were 118 boys and 117 girls, in junior and senior high school, placed in ten classes for gifted students. Each student was chosen for membership in these class groups on the basis of IQ scores and proven academic attainment. The mean verbal IQ was 131 for boys and 130 for girls; the mean nonverbal IQ score was 131 for the boys and 128 for the girls. Since group IQ scores were used in this instance and these scores often are found to be lower on group than individual tests, it was assumed that the groups chosen here represented at least the top five percent of their age group on this dimension. Gifted children were chosen for particular study due to their propensity to express themselves in the classroom setting.

Classification System

The present category system was constructed primarily on the operations of intellect as Guilford has described them. Five primary categories have been developed. These are: cognitive memory (C-M), convergent thinking (CT), divergent thinking (DT), evaluative thinking (ET), and routine (R). The routine category consists of the familiar and conventional interpersonal maneuverings of speakers in the management activities of the classroom setting, and in a number of categories defining behaviors—verbal and otherwise—expressing affect and feeling tone. In order that the reader have some idea of the dimensions of each of these areas of cognitive behavior in the classroom, a brief description is given below:

Cognitive-memory operations represent the simple reproduction of facts, formulae, or other items of remembered content through use of such processes as recognition, rote memory, and selective recall. Examples of cognitive-memory performance can be seen in the following:

T: What were some of the main points covered in our discussion about mercantilism?

Mary: One of the things we learned was that there was an attempt to keep a favorable balance of trade.

T: What is a conjunction?

The above examples of teacher-student interchanges do not require the student to integrate or associate facts; the questions can be handled by direct reference to the memory bank. The sole duty of the student is to select the appropriate response from his store of remembered items. While factual information is clearly indispensable to the development of higher thought processes, it is also obvious that it would be a sterile and uninteresting class that dealt exclusively with this type of question, never moving into the challenge and excitement of more complex operations.

Convergent thinking represents the analysis and integration of given or remembered data. It leads to one expected end-result or answer because of the tightly structured framework through which the individual must respond. Examples of convergent thinking are as follows:

T: If I were going to town A 170 miles away and drove at 50 miles an hour, how long would it take me to get there?

Bob: Three hours and twenty-four minutes.

T: Can you sum up in one sentence what you think was the main idea in Paton's novel, *Cry the Beloved Country?*

Pete: That the problem of the blacks and the whites in Africa can only be solved by brotherly love; there is no other way.

Thus, convergent thinking may be involved in the solving of a problem, in the summarizing of a body of material, or in the establishment of a logical sequence of ideas or premises—as, for example, in reporting the way in which a machine works, or in describing the sequence of steps by which the passage of a bill through Congress is accomplished.

Divergent thinking represents intellectual operations wherein the individual is free to generate independently his own data within a data-poor situation, or to take a new direction or perspective on a given topic. Examples of divergent thinking are:

T: Suppose Spain had not been defeated when the Armada was destroyed in 1588, but that instead, Spain had conquered England. What would the world be like today if that had happened?

Sam: Well, we would all be speaking Spanish.

Peg: We might have fought a revolutionary war against Spain instead of England.

Tom: We might have a state religion in this country.

These examples represent teacher-stimulated divergent thinking, but it need not always be teacher-generated. In a regular discussion of the "spoils system," a student may come up with the following:

Well, sure, the spoils system might be a good thing when a political party is getting started, but what about when there's no party system—like in the United Nations?

Here the student reveals his ability to take off from an established fact or facts and see further implications or unique associations that have not been requested or perhaps even thought of by the teacher. Instances of this type of self-initiated student behavior would also fall under the general category of divergent thinking.

Evaluative thinking deals with matters of judgment, value, and choice, and is characterized by its judgmental quality. For example:

T: What do you think of Captain Ahab as a heroic figure in Moby Dick?

Bob: Well, he sure was brave, but I think he was kind of mean the way he drove the men just because he had this crazy notion of getting back at Moby Dick.

T: Is it likely that we will have a hard winter?

Mary: Well, I think that the pattern of high pressure area suggests that we will.

T: Who was the stronger President, Jackson or Adams?

Mike: Adams.

In the first of the above examples, the student is asked to construct a value dimension of his own in terms of what he considers "heroic," and then to make a judgment as to where on this value dimension he would place Captain Ahab. In the second response, the student is asked to make an estimate or to give a speculative opinion or assessment of probability. A third possibility involves entering a qualification or disagreement, wherein the respondent would offer a modification of a prior judgment of another student; or he may state a counter-judgment, in which he declares direct opposition to the statement of the previous speaker.

The final category, Routine, contains a large number of miscellaneous classroom activities. Included here are the attitudinal dimensions of praise and censure of others and of self. Also present are dimensions of *structuring,* a kind of prefatory remark, telling in advance what the speaker intends to say or do, or what he expects someone else to say or do. Other characteristic occurrences, such as humor, as well as the ordinary "routine" classroom management behaviors—even to requests to close the door or asking what time it is—are included in this primary category.

Procedure

Each of the ten classes were tape recorded for five consecutive hour sessions (two classes were taped in the fall and again in the spring to check on classroom consistency). In addition to the tape recordings, two observers were present in the classroom and took extensive notes on classroom activities such as demonstration, charts, blackboard material, *etc.* In addition, they noted the more obvious attitudinal relationships in the classroom such as censure, praise, frustration, humor, *etc.* Each transcribed classroom session was classified statement by statement by trained judges working with the scoring manual described above. The results of this analysis were then compared with test findings and teacher ratings on the dimensions of cognition (IQ tests of divergent thinking), attitude (a semantic differential scale and sentence completion test), and sociability (teacher ratings).

Figure 1.
Proportion of thought processes asked for by the teacher

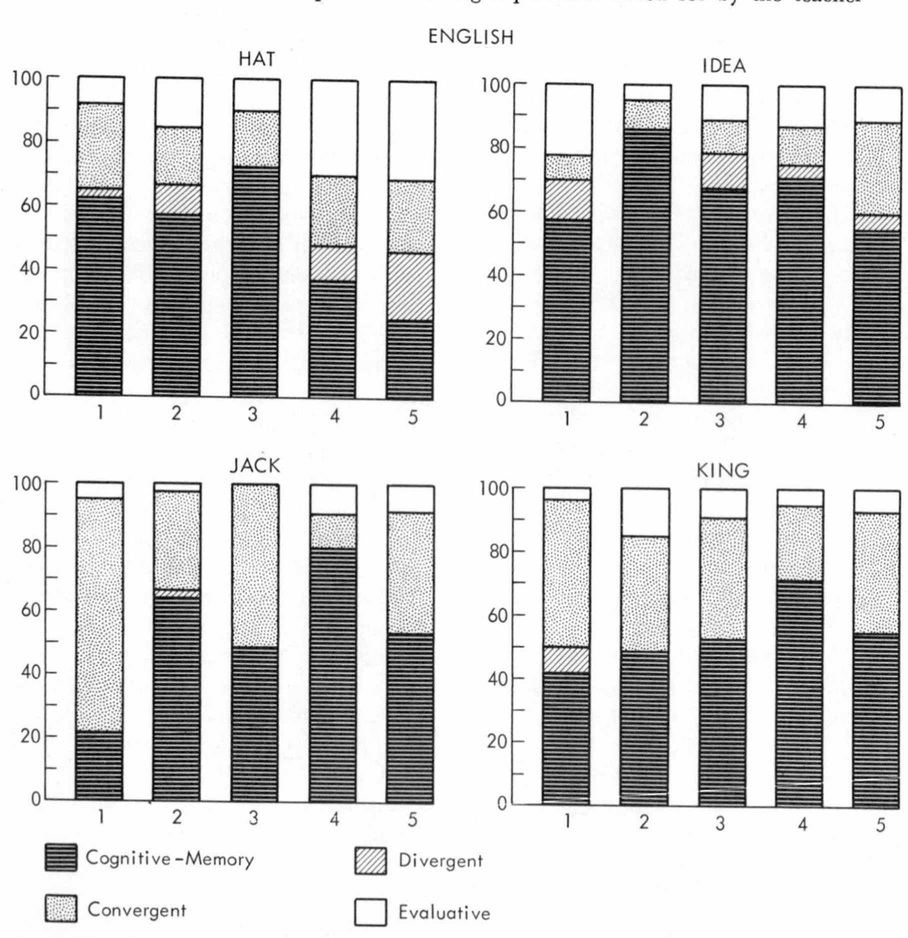

Results

Figures 1 and 2 indicate the proportions of each major thought operation produced by teacher and by the boys in class over five consecutive class sessions in two sections of social studies and two sections of English. Figure 2 represents only the boys' responses since the pattern of the responses were the same for the two sexes, although the total output was often different.

It will be noted that the majority of both teacher questions and student responses fell in the Cognitive-Memory area. There would seem to be an inescapable baseline of factual and memorized material that forms the basis of any classroom discussion. The more the class tends to a lecture type of operation, as opposed to discussion, the more the total responses lean in this direction.

The second most frequent category in terms of usage was Convergent Thinking. Much of the Convergent Thinking centered around explana-

Figure 2.
Proportion of thought processes given by students

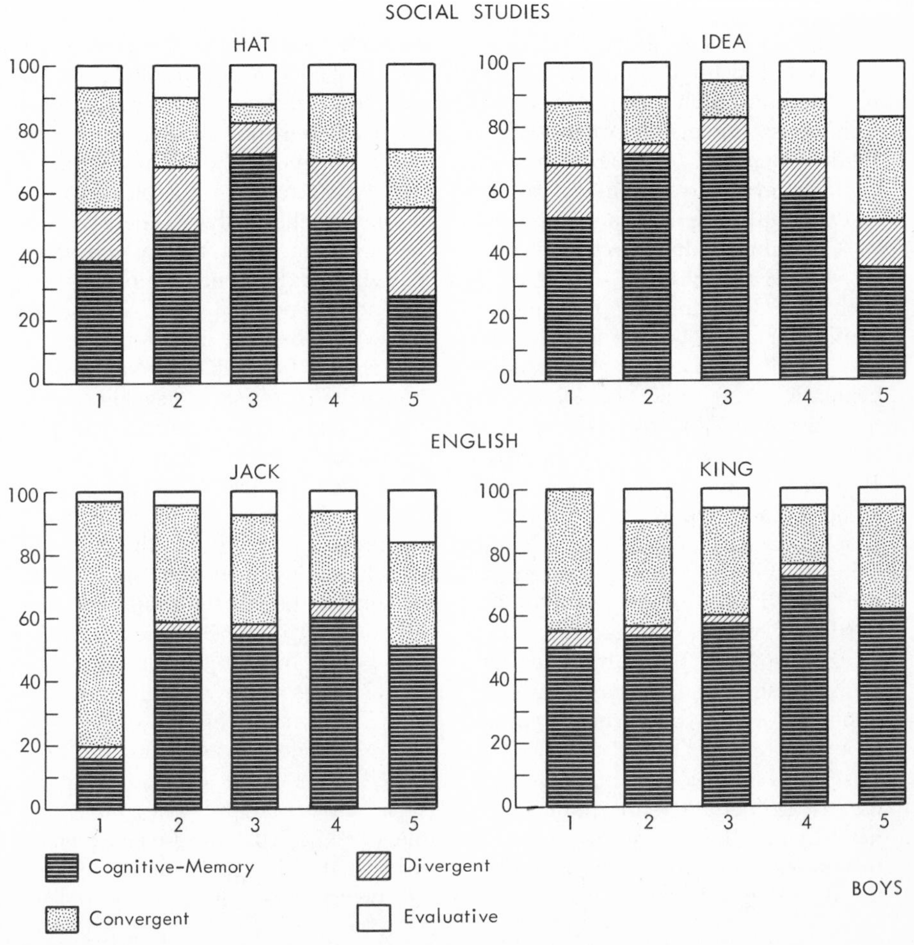

tions and conclusion drawing along one given line of thought and forms a recognizable part of most classroom discussions. It appears that class sessions can operate on these two thought operations alone, without much evaluative or divergent thinking. Indeed, in Jack 3 session the entire class hour was devoted to teacher questions only in these two categories. The evaluative and divergent categories appeared to be particularly dependent upon teacher stimulation. The percentage of responses in these two areas were low unless stimulated by deliberate teacher action.

A visual comparison of Figures 1 and 2 will indicate the close relationship between the patterns of teacher questions and the student responses. It is not difficult to understand why. A question such as, "When did Columbus discover America?" is hardly calculated to bring forth divergent or evaluative thinking by the student, although it is not impossible —"Columbus didn't discover America, Leif Erickson did." A question such as "Compare the performances of Olivier and Burton in Hamlet" can hardly fail to evoke student evaluative responses. In short, the teacher controls the expressive thought patterns of the class to a large extent. It will be noted that the English sections, Jack and King, were almost devoid of divergent thinking while being heavily loaded with convergent thinking. This was the result of this particular teacher's style rather than a direct result of the subject matter. Censure shouldn't be automatically applied for the absence of certain thought categories either. No standard exists to suggest that one teacher pattern is "better" than another. The definition of "better" in this case leads to very complex arguments related to the desirable outcome of teaching.

If divergent thinking *is* considered desirable, it can be inserted in any subject matter by changing the type of question asked. For example, the teacher in asking the students to outline a short passage or speech had one best way in mind. The students worked their way towards that best way through successive approximations (convergent thinking). If divergent thinking had been a goal of the teacher he could have posed the problem—How many ways could you reorganize this passage, keeping the same content, so as to meaningfully change the outline?

Other analyses suggest, as is obvious in the Hat series, that a teacher will modify his pattern from one class session to another in the same series and that one teacher's style is distinctively different from another teacher's. It is not possible to observe and catalogue one day's performance and expect to have a typical sample of one teacher's style. There also is the suggestion that the same teacher may show a different style of teaching depending upon the group he is working with (observe in Figure 1 the differences between Hat and Idea groups with the same teacher teaching the same content on the same day to two different sections).

In each of the classroom groups studied, boys were significantly more expressive in some of the thought dimensions used in this study than the girls, although the dimension and intensity of difference varied with the class group and subject matter. In no instance was there a significant difference in favor of the girls. The general conclusion then was that boys tended to be more expressive in the classroom situation. The male sex role of expected aggressiveness being learned at this age level was one of the possible explanations offered to account for this result. No sex differences were found on written expressiveness!

Although originally it had been expected that different students would show different expressive patterns (*i.e.*, one specializing in divergent thinking, another concentrating on evaluation), this was not found to be the case. Instead, the high intercorrelations of all of the categories in classroom expressiveness, mostly in the .80's, made it clear that there was one general factor of expressiveness that was operating and that if a student was expressive in divergent thinking the chances were very high that he scored high on the other categories also. There remained the interesting question as to what other variables might relate to this expressiveness factor.

An adjusted score for classroom expressiveness was obtained for each student by dividing his production for the five days by the total production for the whole class for those class sessions. For example, if Sam gave 10 divergent responses while his class gave 100 responses in this category, his adjusted score would be 010 for divergent thinking responses. If Mary gave 20 such responses while her class was giving a total of 200 responses in this category, her adjusted score would be 010, or the same as Sam's. In this way, it was possible to compare performance across class groups.

In order to compare the expressive *vs.* nonexpressive groups, the top third of the total sample recorded was chosen on the basis of their adjusted class scores and compared with the bottom third of the group on adjusted class scores on expressiveness. A part of this comparison can be found in Table I. The information for boys and girls was considered separately since interesting sex differences in patterns of performance were noted throughout the current study.

It might be expected that students scoring higher on verbal IQ would be

TABLE I

The Comparison of Expressive and Nonexpressive Gifted Students on Cognitive Factors and Teacher Ratings

		Expressive			Nonexpressive		
		N	Mean	σ	N	Mean	σ
Verbal IQ	B	27	133.00†	9.56	27	128.44	7.93
	G	27	128.22	10.46	29	127.24	9.36
Non-verbal IQ	B	27	129.33	7.62	27	129.89	8.45
	G	27	128.81	11.14	29	127.69	11.21
Uses Breadth	B	26	21.58	6.46	27	19.67	5.53
	G	27	19.96	8.03	29	17.48	5.67
Consequences	B	26	15.00	3.90	27	14.11	3.47
Breadth	G	27	13.78	2.65	29	13.48	2.89
Consequences	B	26	39.88	18.81	27	31.78	19.22
Solutions	G	27	41.04	20.05	29	47.52	17.82
Teacher Rating	B	26	8.65**	3.99	27	11.74	4.11
Cognition	G	27	10.56*	3.77	29	12.86	4.57
Teacher Rating	B	26	2.31	.79	27	2.41	.93
Sociability	G	27	2.00	.62	29	2.00	.76

† Significant at .10 level of confidence
* Significant at .05 level of confidence
** Significant at .01 level of confidence

the most expressive students in the classroom but this expectation held, in the present study, only for the boys. Table I shows that the mean I.Q. of the expressive boys was 133 as opposed to 128 for the nonexpressive boys and this difference exceeded only a probability level of <.10, but the differences between expressive and nonexpressive girls was almost nonexistent. No differences were found between the two groups, on nonverbal intelligence scores.

The Uses and Consequences tests were developed by Guilford and have been used as one of the key measures of divergent thinking in a number of other studies (4, 13). The students are asked questions such as, "How many different uses can you think of for a brick?" or "What would happen if everybody were born with three fingers and no thumb?" The answers are then considered in terms of the number of different categories the student can produce in his answers and in the style of answer given. In Table I it can be seen that none of the differences between these two groups for either sex reached a level of statistical significance. Thus, a test measure which was specifically designed for measuring written expressiveness does not seem to predict oral expressiveness in the classroom. On the Consequence Solutions score (on items like the "Three fingers" the student will answer, "Cars would have new types of steering wheels" instead of "You couldn't drive cars"), no statistically significant differences were obtained, but it can be noticed that the trends are in opposite directions for the two sexes. The most expressive boys give more solutions but the more expressive girls give less solutions to the Consequences questions.

The teachers were given the task of rating the students along two dimensions, cognitive abilities and sociability. In Table I, the teachers significantly distinguished in their ratings between the expressive and nonexpressive students of both sexes. Since a low score means favorable rating, this meant that the teachers significantly rated higher on cognitive abilities those students who were the most expressive. It can be argued that it is this very expressiveness in class that might be influencing and directing the teachers' judgments in this regard.

This favorable rating on cognitive area did not carry over into the social dimension. No statistically significant differences were found on ratings of social success between the two groups. In summary, in this general area, the expressive boys differed from the nonexpressive boys on a measure of verbal IQ and on teacher ratings of cognitive abilities. The only difference between the expressive and nonexpressive girls was found on teacher ratings of cognitive abilities. These differences were not as great as might be expected and led to the further supposition that other than strictly cognitive abilities were determining the amount of thought expressiveness in the classroom.

Each of the students in the present study was administered a semantic differential scale which previously had proven successful in distinguishing between gifted achievers and nonachievers (10). The semantic differential scale was developed from work by Osgood (9). Students are presented with a series of concepts in terms of a number of adjective pairs, such as cold-hot, good-bad, active-passive, *etc.* The concepts in the present study are listed in Table

TABLE II

The Comparison of Expressive and Nonexpressive Gifted Students on Semantic Differential Scale

Concept		Expressive N	Expressive Mean	Expressive σ	Nonexpressive N	Nonexpressive Mean	Nonexpressive σ
Mother	B	25	68.84	6.18	26	74.26**	5.41
	G	25	72.32	5.93	28	72.17	5.18
Father	B	25	66.36	9.40	26	70.50	7.93
	G	25	70.16	8.49	28	70.25	7.30
Student	B	25	63.88	9.71	26	65.34	7.51
	G	24	67.12	7.75	28	67.89	7.26
Work	B	25	63.60	6.54	26	67.73†	8.20
	G	25	66.56	7.87	28	64.92	8.66
Competition	B	25	66.28	9.32	26	67.61	13.77
	G	25	69.04*	6.57	28	64.53	8.85
Success	B	25	59.72	11.76	26	70.84**	8.07
	G	24	66.83	9.20	28	67.50	8.58
Love	B	25	66.76	9.81	26	70.65	9.02
	G	25	69.80	7.07	28	68.42	7.18
Faith	B	25	67.72	9.14	26	72.11	9.06
	G	25	76.66	8.29	28	73.17	7.60
Imagination	B	25	66.60	7.31	26	62.15	14.72
	G	25	68.96	9.63	28	65.85	7.39
School	B	25	65.72	10.40	26	71.69*	7.20
	G	25	70.24	7.10	28	68.46	7.52

† Significant at .10 level of confidence
* Significant at .05 level of confidence
** Significant at .01 level of confidence

II. Fourteen adjective pairs were used and the concept score for a student was the sum of his ratings on the fourteen pairs for that concept.

Table II reveals that differences were found between expressive and nonexpressive gifted boys on a number of the concepts. All of the differences were consistent in the same direction. On the concepts of Mother, Success, School, and Work the nonexpressive group were consistently higher than the expressive group in their ratings. The expressive group could not be said to be rating these concepts negatively, since a neutral score would be 49. It would be more accurate to say they are merely *less* positive in their ratings. One possible interpretation of these differences would be to suggest that the expressive boys possess more self-confidence and more assurance in themselves and do not have to give extreme positive ratings on these concepts.

Students who are less sure of themselves and less inclined to independent judgment, and thus less inclined to contribute to class discussions, might tend to overdo their positive ratings on such socially acceptable concepts (for gifted students) as those on which differences were obtained.

Consistent with other results in this study, the pattern noted for gifted boys is not repeated for gifted girls. Only one difference was found and that indicated a higher level of positive feeling for the concept of Competition for the expressive girls. On most of the other concepts the expressive girls were, on the average, more positive on these concepts than the nonexpressive girls. One suggested explanation would be that girls who are expressive accept the concept of Competition as a desirable factor and are willing to compete on equal terms for classroom recognition with the boys. If these results are confirmed by other studies it is clear that there are different patterns of motives and abilities lying behind the classroom expressiveness of boys and girls.

Summary

The expressive behavior of gifted children at the junior and senior high school level in ten different classrooms was studied through analyzing the tape recordings of five consecutive class sessions. A special classification system was developed as part of the project to allow the categorization of each teacher and student statement. It was found that certain types of thought operations were more common than others in all of the classrooms regardless of subject matter orientation.

Expressive behavior in the classroom in both kind and amount of thought output seemed dependent on the teacher's style of question asking, the sex of the student, the goals of the teacher in a given lesson, the composition of the class group, and the pattern of attitudinal and personality characteristics of the student. Consistent sex differences suggested that different patterns of attitudes and cognitive skills underlie expressive behavior in gifted boys and girls.

Bibliography

1. Barron, F., *Creativity and Psychological Health.* Princeton, New Jersey: Van Nostrand, 1963.

2. Bloom, B. S. (Ed.), *Taxonomy of Educational Objectives. Handbook I: Cognitive Domain.* New York: Longmans, Green, 1956.

3. Flanders, N. A., "Intent, Action and Feedback: A Preparation for Teaching," *Journal of Teacher Education,* 14 (1963), 251–260.

4. Getzels, J. W. and P. W. Jackson, *Creativity and Intelligence.* New York: John Wiley, 1962.

5. Guilford, J. P., "The Structure of Intellect," *Psychological Bulletin,* 53 (1956), 267–293.

6. Guilford, J. P., "Three Faces of Intellect," *American Psychologist,* 14 (1959), 469–479.

7. Medley, D. M. and H. E. Mitzel, "Measuring Classroom Behavior by Systematic Observation," in N. Gage (Ed.) *Handbook of Research on Teaching.* Chicago: Rand McNally, 1963.

8. MacKinnon, Donald W., "Fostering Creativity in Students of Engineering," *Journal of Engineering Education,* 52 (1961), 129–142.

9. Osgood, C. E., "Studies on the Generality of Affective Meaning Systems," *American Psychologist,* 17 (1962), 10–28.

10. Pierce, J. W. and P. Bowman, "Motivation Patterns of Superior High School Students," in *The Gifted Student.* Washington, D.C.: U. S. Office of Education, Cooperative Research Monograph, 1960, 33–66.

11. Smith, B. O. and M. O. Meux, *A Study of the Logic of Teaching.* U. S. Office of Education Cooperative Research Project #258. Urbana, Ill.: University of Illinois, Bureau of Educational Research, 1962.

12. Taba, Hilda, S. Levine, and F. Elzey, *Thinking in Elementary School*

Children. U. S. Office of Education Cooperative Research Project #1574. San Francisco, California: San Francisco State College, 1964.

13. Torrance, E. P., *Education and the Creative Potential.* Minneapolis, Minn.: University of Minnesota Press, 1963.

37. A STRATEGY FOR DEVELOPING VALUES

JAMES RATHS

This paper deals with a strategy for helping children to develop their own values. Recognition of the importance of children's values has been with us for years. "A great and continuing purpose of education has been the development of moral and spiritual values" (5). With this pronouncement, the Educational Policies Commission opened its 1957 report. As important as developing values seems to be to indignent citizens the area is even more important to us as educators, it seems to me, because of its implications for the learning process. Let me briefly spell out some of these implications.

First, Kubie (12) suggests that learning is swift, spontaneous and automatic. At times, learning is blocked—many times by what Kubie calls preconscious motives and drives. He recommends that teachers concern themselves with developing self-knowledge on their students' part to remove blocks to learning—to free children so that they may learn in a spontaneous fashion. Second, Ginsburg (7) suggests that good mental health, assumed to be a necessary condition for learning, is merely a process of living up to a set of values. Finally, several researchers, following the ideas of Louis Raths, have identified pupil behaviors associated with a lack of values (9, 11, 13,

James Raths, "A Strategy for Developing Values," Educational Leadership, *XXI, No. 8 (May 1964), 509–14.*

14). These classroom behaviors, including overconforming, indifference, flightiness and several others, it is argued, interfere with concentration, involvement, and openness in the learning process. Therefore, value development, it seems, should be one of the many central concerns of teachers.

While the area of value development has been a major concern of educators for many years, the public and many professional people, too, have had a feeling that our efforts in this area have not been too effective. The studies summarized by Jacob in his *Changing Values in College* tend to support this hunch (8). Teachers have been unable, it seems, to translate their genuine concerns about the value problem into effective patterns of action in their classrooms.

Essentially, there are four basic approaches to the development of values current in our schools. These methods include the teaching of values by the lecture method, by use of peer-group pressure, by finding or setting examples for children to respect and emulate, and by a reward and punishment rationale. These methods are neither mutually exclusive nor exhaustive of all the approaches we use in schools, but they seem to me to be among the most prevalent in our classrooms.

Methods in Use

Perhaps the most common approach is the use of lecture methods. Teachers seem ever ready to tell students what they should believe or how they ought to act. It is easy to burlesque this method in harsh tones. Actually, it may be employed by the kindest, most sincere teachers as well as by the overly self-righteous, would-be reformers found on some school faculties. While it is possible to cite cases in which a lecture or even a "bawling out" did bring about changes in students' values, basically this method is not too successful. Attesting to this is the common cry of many teachers—"You can't *tell* those kids anything." In general, this remark has been found to be accurate.

Teachers' judgments and convictions seem, from a student's point of view, to be out of the framework of things. (Analogously, it may be akin to the feelings teachers in the field have of the "should's and should not's" of professors from schools and colleges of education.) Jones (10) has suggested a basis for explaining the ineffectiveness of the lecture method. He states that a teacher must be emotionally accepted by his students before he can contribute much to their development of self. By their moralizing and preaching, teachers may set themselves apart emotionally from their students. To the extent that teachers are not accepted by their students, it can be presumed that they will have little effect upon students' values. Students may leave the lecture all full of enthusiasm about what the teacher said, but they may not internalize what they admire and all too often they do not.

A second approach to the value development problem has been in the main popularized by exponents of the core curriculum. During a special period of the school day, students address themselves to self-evaluations and group evaluations. They are encouraged to speak freely, frankly and openly to the entire class judging their own behavior, criticizing group performances, and perhaps pledging themselves to future improvements.

In general, such statements are accepted by the teacher with little or no comment while other pupils are free to make suggestions, recommendations, and comments.

The pressure of group approval or disapproval is a powerful force in bringing about changes in values. This method seems successful in some cases but it has some disturbing by-products. The most distressing of these is the tacit approval of the teacher of the notion that group consensus is correct or at least worthy of very serious consideration. This method, in effect, helps develop "other directed" persons. Another disadvantage inherent in this group technique is the passive role of the teacher. In a sense, the insight, experience, and skills of the teacher are muted. In their place, naïve students play the dominant role in value development, and they do it quite unconsciously.

A third approach for developing students' values is one of acquainting students with examples of exemplary behavior. Instances of model behavior may be drawn from history, literature, and legend or, more directly, from examples set by teachers.

Literature for all levels of schooling has been selected for the past several hundred years on the basis of the ethical and moral lessons with which it dealt. As in other methods discussed previously, some students are truly inspired by these vicarious experiences but we have little evidence that attributes found in a student's reading are readily transferred to daily life.

Teaching values by a living example is a related tactic. Here it is assumed that "values are caught, not taught." It is argued that as teachers demonstrate values, students will learn to prize these values. Surely people have been inspired by the goodness of a teacher with whom they have had the good fortune to be associated. However, teachers, especially in secondary schools, have little opportunity to demonstrate many key values. Problems that represent the real issues of life rarely present themselves in a 50-minute subject-matter period in such a way that students can observe their teacher's handling of them. It would truly be unfortunate if we had to rely on this approach as the only positive way teachers can help youngsters develop a set of values.

A fourth method deals with indoctrination and habit formation. Here it is assumed that when students are required to follow rules and regulations, when they are punished for infractions and praised for obedience, they will take on the values associated with the requirements. We are all familiar, however, with what students do when they are free *not* to obey the rules.

It is my contention that these four methods are rather ineffective. Perhaps their relative ineffectiveness arises partially because they are based on the assumption that the knowledge of ethical and moral choices necessarily leads to ethical and moral conduct. As pointed out many years ago by John Dewey (4), this assumption has little basis in fact.

Yet more important, these methods seem intent on utilizing external factors, such as lectures or peer-group pressures, to develop values. Friedenberg (6) analyzes the current problems in developing values as follows:

> ... it is the inner discipline that is lacking; the school fails to provide a basis for it. The undisciplined behavior which sometimes results is often a sign of the anguish which results from

having no core *of one's own.* [Emphasis added.]

The most promising approach would seem to be one that attempts to help each student build his own value system. This idea is supported by Allport (2) who asserts that no teaching is more important than that which contributes to a student's self. Clearly, this statement echoes the ideas of Kubie mentioned in the opening paragraphs. Are teachers able to help children in this way? B. O. Smith has said that teachers use little psychological knowledge beyond that found in common sense. What knowledge can we, as teachers, use in this area? Louis Raths has developed a teaching method designed to provide some direction for teachers who are interested in helping students develop their own value systems (15, 16, 17).

Use of Clarification Procedures

The teacher's role in this method is neither that of preacher nor that of passive listener. Instead the teacher strives to (*a*) establish a climate of psychological safety, (*b*) apply a clarification procedure. An elaboration of these procedures follows.

Establishment of Psychological Safety

Nonjudgmental Attitudes

It has been said that teachers have difficulty responding to an idea without saying, "That's good," "That's bad," or "What good is it?" To provide an atmosphere in which children will feel free to express themselves without threat of ridicule and derision, teachers must refrain from making harsh unnecessary judgments. Of course at times some judgments become necessary in situations in which the health and/or safety of students are threatened in any real sense.

Manifestations of Concern

While the teacher may be nonjudgmental, it is important for him to be concerned with the ideas expressed by his students. If the concern is apparently lacking, then often the number of student ideas shared with a teacher tends to diminish. Perhaps students are reluctant to share their ideas with someone who is not interested in them. One of the most effective ways to show concern for a student's ideas is to *listen* to them. Busy teachers sometimes overlook this basic and effective technique for communicating interest to their students. Another method for a teacher's communicating his concern for a student's ideas is to *remember* them. As a teacher is able to cite a student's idea in a later conversation, the student cannot help but feel genuinely flattered and impressed.

Opportunities for the Sharing of Ideas

Teachers must organize their courses in such a way that children have the opportunity to express their opinions, purposes, feelings, beliefs, hunches, goals, and interests about moral issues. These attitudinal-type statements may then be examined by the child who expressed them with the teacher acting somewhat as a catalytic agent in the process. Some methods used by teachers in various researches by classroom teachers include: (*a*) question-answer discussion periods involving moot questions for the class to consider; (*b*) special written assignments; (*c*) role-playing techniques; (*d*) behavior manifestations of individuals or groups that may indicate attitudes, e.g., cheating or being tardy.

The task of finding issues that children may react to is no small problem. While our lives are filled with many, many moral and ethical questions to consider, even within our formal disciplines, it is difficult to find these issues in our textbooks, or *Weekly Readers.* Alexander (1), a textbook consultant for the New York City schools, has found that "few or no serious problems" are present in our current textbooks.

Clarifying Strategies

Asking Questions

The teacher may attempt to clarify the ideas elicited from his students by asking probing questions. The key criterion for selecting these questions is that they must be questions for which only the student knows the answer. Of course, to be effective they must be asked in a nonjudgmental manner. If a student seems seriously challenged by one of the questions, the teacher should make efforts to "save face" by accepting his bewilderment. For example, the teacher may pass on by saying, "That's a hard question for anyone to answer, isn't it?" "Let's think about it for a while and maybe an answer will come to us later." A list of questions that a teacher may ask is included below. Of course, this list is not exhaustive, and teachers may add to it as they become more fluent in the use of this procedure.

1. Reflect back what the student has said and add, "Is that what you mean?"
2. Reflect back what the student has said with distortions and add, "Is that what you mean?"
3. "How long have you felt (acted) that way?"
4. "Are you glad you think (act) that way?"
5. "In what way is that a good idea?"
6. "What is the source of your idea?"
7. "Should everyone believe that?"
8. "Have you thought of some alternatives?"
9. "What are some things you have done that reflect this idea of yours?"
10. "Why do you think so?"
11. "Is this what you really think?"
12. "Did you do this on purpose?"
13. Ask for definitions of key words.
14. Ask for examples.
15. Ask if this position is consistent with a previous one he has taken.

It is important that teachers ask these questions of students who express ideas with which they agree as well as with those students who express ideas with which they disagree.

Coding Written Work

Researchers have found the coding of written work very effective in value clarifying. Whenever students seem to express an attitude, belief, goal, purpose, interest, or aspiration, teachers may mark a V+ or V− in the margin to reflect this idea to the student. This code works much like other more familiar codes we already use in our schools, e.g., WW for wrong word, or SP for misspelled word. There is one crucial difference. When a teacher marks WW in the margin, there usually *is* a wrong word. When a teacher marks V+ in the margin, it is understood that he is really asking, "Do you believe this?" or "Do you want to change it?"

Acceptance Without Judgment

It has been found that teachers feel awkward trying to draw the clarification exchange to a close. The verbal interaction between teacher and student is not to win an argument nor to gain a debating point. The purpose of the exchange is to clarify students' ideas. It is important that teachers find a way to accept the students' ideas without communicating agreement or praise of them. In a sense, the exchange does not have an ending. Neither the teacher nor the student arrives at a conclusion. Neither is there a need for summarizing. Questions left unanswered are thought about and dwelt on by the student (and perhaps the teacher) at night before going to sleep, or during moments of quiet during the day. Some ways that have been found successful in closing an exchange are as follows:

1. Silence with a nod.
2. "Uh-huh."
3. "I see."
4. "I understand you better now."
5. "I can see how you would feel that way."
6. "I understand."
7. "I can see that it was difficult for you to decide that way."

In summary, the clarification procedure developed by Louis Raths attempts to elicit from students statements of an attitudinal nature and to clarify these statements for the student. By developing an emotional acceptance of himself on the part of his students, and by asking students questions which will serve to clarify their own purposes, goals, attitudes, beliefs, etc., teachers can play an effective role in developing values in their classrooms.

This procedure can be time-consuming or it may also take just a few seconds. For example, consider the following hypothetical exchange:

Student: I hate math.
Teacher: You have never liked math?
Student: Well, I did like it at one time.
Teacher: What changed your mind?
Student: I don't know.
Teacher: Oh.

Without trying to lecture the student about what he "ought" to like, without preaching about the dangers inherent in not liking math, the teacher is attempting to help the student understand his own preferences and values.

In passing, it may be appropriate to add that several researches (9, 11, 13, 14) have successfully attempted to test these ideas in classrooms in New York State and Wisconsin. Other studies are needed, of course, to test further the efficacy of this procedure. The experiences of a number of researches in this field suggest also that learning to use the process of clarifying is not easy. It is clearly a difficult matter to enter into a significant interaction with a student. The problem is much less that of identifying with a student, but one of identifying with the student's concerns, of listening, and of taking seriously what he has said and reacting thoughtfully to it.

It must be clear that teachers who apply the clarification procedure must have a tremendous respect for their students. As teachers agree or disagree with students' expressed ideas they must be able to consider them as tenable ones to hold. If teachers believe it is their role to "convert" students to a "right way" of thinking, then it seems they must basically disrespect the view their students hold now. The distinction I am trying to make is one between accepting and respecting. It would seem possible for me to respect the views of a colleague, let us say, without accepting those views. This is the spirit that I believe must dominate a teacher's conversations with his students. Of course, this statement must be modified to the extent that a student's view may threaten the health or safety of himself or society. It is my contention that such cases are rare in classrooms. Yet there is still plenty of room for many safe differences of opinion and behavior between students and teachers.

Most of us have become accustomed to the association of teaching with changes in student behavior. Too frequently, quite without being aware of it, we look for "instant" changes. We hope for miracles on the "values front." We do not pay enough attention to the fact that it took many years for our students to learn their present almost valueless behavior, and that it may take a long sustained effort to help students to develop serious purposes and aspirations through the clarifying processes. For a free society, opportunities to clarify and to choose must be created again and again.

Norman Cousins (3) has written about his concern for the predatory quality of life in human form. He suggests that what makes our society so much like a jungle is the misfits who exert power over honest men.

> There are those . . . who insist on projecting their warped ideas to the people around them. They are the agents of chaos. . . . Maybe this is what makes a jungle a jungle.

Cousins continues to say that the way out of the jungle is not just emptying it of these misfits. "There must be some notion about what is to take the place of the jungle. That is why ideals and goals are the most practical things in the world. They conquer the jungle, make men mobile, and convert humans from fawning and frightened animals into thinkers and builders." As teachers learn to develop the ideals, goals, and values of students by applying the clarification procedures outlined in this paper, they may perhaps become truly "influential Americans."

References

1. Alexander, Albert, "The Gray Flannel Cover of the American History Text," *Social Education*, XXIV, No. 11 (January 1960).

2. Allport, Gordon, *Becoming: Basic Considerations for Psychology of Personality.* New Haven, Conn.: Yale University Press, 1955.

3. Cousins, Norman, "Hoffa, Hegel and Hoffer," *Saturday Review* (April 20, 1963).

4. Dewey, John, *Moral Principles in Education.* Boston: Houghton Mifflin Company, 1909.

5. Educational Policies Commission, *Moral and Spiritual Values in the Public Schools.* Washington, D.C.: National Education Association, 1957.

6. Friedenberg, Edgar Z., *The Vanishing Adolescent.* New York: Dell Publishing Co., Inc., 1962.

7. Ginsburg, Sol. W., "Values and the Psychiatrist," *American Journal of Orthopsychiatry*, XX (July 1950), 466.

8. Jacob, Philip E., *Changing Values in College*. New York: Harper & Row, Publishers, 1957.

9. Jonas, Arthur, "A Study of the Relationship of Certain Behaviors of Children to Emotional Needs, Values, and Thinking." Unpublished Ed.D. thesis, New York University, 1960.

10. Jones, Vernon, "Character Education," *Encyclopedia of Educational Research*, Chester Harris, ed. New York: The Macmillan Company, 1960.

11. Klevan, Albert, "An Investigation of a Methodology for Value Clarification: Its Relationship to Consistency of Thinking, Purposefulness, and Human Relations." Unpublished Ed.D. thesis, New York University, 1958.

12. Kubie, Lawrence, "Are We Educating for Maturity," *N.E.A. Journal* (January 1959).

13. Raths, James, "Underachievement and a Search for Values," *Journal of Education Sociology*, XXXIV, No. 2 (May 1961).

14. ——, "Clarifying Children's Values," *National Elementary Principal*, LXII, No. 2 (November 1962).

15. Raths, Louis E., "Values and Teachers," *Education Synopsis* (Spring, 1957).

16. ——, "Sociological Knowledge and Needed Curriculum Research," *Research Frontiers in the Study of Children's Learning*, J. B. Macdonald, ed. Milwaukee: School of Education, The University of Wisconsin-Milwaukee, 1960.

17. ——, "Clarifying Values," *Curriculum for Today's Boys and Girls*, R. S. Fleming, ed. Columbus, Ohio: Charles E. Merrill Books, Inc., 1963.

ACTIVITIES

1. What are some activities you may plan for your classes that would promote valuing and thinking?

2. Assume that a teacher's response to a student's statement of belief can be categorized as (1) accepting (without judgment); (2) judgmental, either plus or minus; (3) reflecting, or (4) argumentative—raising objections to the student's view. Observe a classroom and attempt to find if this category system is efficacious. Listen to a tape recording of your own teaching and attempt to categorize your responses.

3. Assume that the following comments are made by a student in your class. Assume also that the comment is relevant and germane to the class discussion. If you wished to clarify the student's idea, what would be your best response? Circle your judgment. (Assume all teacher statements are made in a nonemotional way.)

1. "I don't want to salute the flag."
   a. I'm sure some Americans feel that way.
   b. Do you think this is a patriotic attitude?
   c. Just this flag or any flag?
   d. I don't see how you can feel that way.
2. "Writing a letter to a congressman is a waste of time."
   a. Someday you'll learn to appreciate our form of government.
   b. Do you feel this way about all congressmen or special ones?
   c. Imagine a Russian writing to his government.
   d. What do some of you other children think about this?
3. "The government has no right to tell a private businessman what to do."
   a. What do you mean by the words "no right"?
   b. Is your father in business?
   c. Did the government ever tell your father what to do?

d. A great many people feel as you do.

4. "Negroes have made great contributions to our society."
   a. The history of America is a story of the contributions of persons of all races and religions.
   b. Give me some examples and tell why you think they are great.
   c. More and more people are beginning to realize this fact.
   d. Did you hear that on television?

5. "The Supreme Court has banned prayer in the public schools."
   a. I don't think that is exactly what the Supreme Court decision says.
   b. Was the Supreme Court decision unanimous?
   c. I can see that the decision makes you feel badly.
   d. What does this mean for your school?

6. "Let's demonstrate our view by picketing the White House."
   a. Should we bother the President with this now that he is so busy with other problems?
   b. Are there other ways to demonstrate your views?
   c. You certainly seem to think your views are important.
   d. Picketing really never accomplished anything, did it?

4. Some educators feel that it is most important to teach process-thinking, valuing, inquiring, etc. Sometimes this position is considered to be antithetical to that which emphasizes subject matter. In your view, are these positions inconsistent?

5. It has been said that no textbook or course of study contains "thinking." Thinking takes place when students "interact" with the content of a textbook. What assignments seem most productive to promote deep and intellectual interactions? Suggest some in the content areas in which you are most interested.

6. If it is desirable for a teacher to be acceptive of students' responses, what types of questions lead to students' responses that are most difficult to accept? What kinds of questions facilitate attaining the desired acceptable replies?

7. Write down some of your beliefs concerning teaching and education. Which of these beliefs are synthetic according to Metcalf's view; which of these are analytic? What evidence can be gathered or cited to support the synthetic beliefs you hold?

8. Gagné, in his article included on page 223, identifies the conditions needed for enquiry. Piaget, in this section, has reported his observations of the cognitive development of youngsters. Considering the ideas found in these articles, discuss the pros and cons of teaching by means of inquiry in primary grades.

MEETING THE EMOTIONAL NEEDS OF CHILDREN

CHAPTER SEVEN

A perennial issue on the educational scene is the degree to which a teacher should play "psychologist." On the one hand, it can be argued that elementary and secondary school teachers are not prepared to deal with the emotional problems of children, and any such problems that arise should be referred to the proper authorities. Although most teachers concede that they are not trained as psychologists, they do believe that they can act effectively and safely in giving students support and encouragement.

Activities designed to give support and encouragement to students have been subsumed under the broader heading of "meeting the emotional needs of students." Many curriculum plans over the past thirty years have been based on the premise that they were doing just that. But what are needs and how are they identified? Is there a distinction between a need for oxygen and a need for a feeling of belonging and group acceptance?

In addition, how important is it for a teacher to "know his students" in the area of meeting emotional needs? What information can increase the effectiveness of a sensitive teacher in meeting the emotional needs of his students? As a teacher becomes aware of feelings, revealed by students' behaviors, perhaps he can meet needs as effectivly as a teacher who "knows" all about the students' backgrounds. Perhaps there is little correlation between the knowledge that teachers have about students and what they do about this knowledge. Too often, "understanding of children" allows teachers merely to explain behavior in class rather than giving directions for the improvement of the learning climate. The readings in this chapter address themselves to these and other questions.

38. "NEED" AND THE NEEDS-CURRICULUM

B. PAUL KOMISAR

Individuals involved in all aspects of education reveal a considerable concern about needs. The administrator considers the needs of his faculty before submitting a budget. The school counselor decides the cases of academic tragedy and vocational aspiration with which he daily contends by recourse to his clients' needs. The curriculum supervisor exhorts teachers to meet the needs of their pupils, and it is announced to the public with dreary regularity that this is what teachers are doing. Programs at all levels of instruction from the nursery to the graduate school find their justification in the needs of the student or society or, more popularly, in both. Not to be outdone by the defenders of practice, the espouser of innovation employs similar warrant for *his* proposals. Nor is the critic (of theory or practice) a laggard in this regard; he is just as apt to castigate his victim for meeting needs as for failing to do so. And, of course, there is no dearth of candidates eager to list for us the pupils' needs. Indeed, no committee report or textbook seems to be considered complete without at least one such list, though their authors seem divided on whether it is brevity or profusion that indicates success in this endeavor.

It is not my intention to add to these agitations or lists of what students need. Instead I will examine what we *mean* when we say pupils need something. This will be a study of the ways the word "need" is used in education. In the final section of this essay I will go a step further and apply the results of the analysis to the claim that public education should meet the needs of students.

The senses of "need" we will examine fall roughly into two categories. The first includes what I will call the prescriptive uses. Here we find, for example, the cases where "he needs

B. Paul Komisar, "'Need' and the Needs-Curriculum," in LANGUAGE AND CONCEPTS IN EDUCATION, *eds. B. O. Smith and Richard Ennis (Skokie, Ill.: Rand McNally & Co., 1961), pp. 24–42. Reprinted by permission.*

discipline" is roughly equivalent to "he must have discipline" or "discipline is necessary for him." In the second category will fall the motivational uses of "need"; that is, its uses to refer in some way to motives. Here an assertion that pupils need affection is similar to saying that pupils want or seek out affection. This classification is crude but it will do for a beginning.

1. *Prescriptive Uses of "Need"*

A fruitful way of clarifying the use of an expression is by a study of the challenges which can be raised against statements made with the expression. I will be following this procedure in the subsequent examination. I will take up in turn some of the more important objections that might properly be raised against assertions of the form "he needs X." From these challenges and the accompanying answers, it will be possible to infer some of the criteria for the use of "need."

Objective

When we refer to something as a need (or say that a subject needs something), we might be asked what it is needed for. In the case of "this pupil needs to study," we might be asked what objective studying is to serve for the pupil. As a test of the assertion itself, this makes "he needs to study," different from "he is six feet tall." A request for the consequences of being six feet tall is simply a request for additional information; it is not an attempt to evaluate the statement "he is six feet tall." For the fact that being tall makes a boy a likely basketball prospect is not part of the criteria for saying "he is six feet tall." The opposite is true of "he needs to study." If we are told that no objective is to be served by studying, that studying is not needed *for* anything, then this does constitute grounds for a denial of the assertion itself ("if nothing is to come of it then he doesn't need to study").[1]

One of the criteria, then, for calling something a need is that it be related to some further state of affairs. I will refer to this state of affairs as the objective, although it may be a complex situation. The objective can be the achievement of a new state of affairs ("he needs drill to develop skills"). It may be the maintenance of an already existing state ("he needs to study in order to continue his fine record"). Or the objective may be the avoidance of some possible future state ("he needs recognition lest emotional frustration result").

Quite often we fulfill this criterion by making the objective part of the assertion itself ("he needs a course in history to graduate"). Even when we do not make the objective explicit, it is frequently implied by the context of our statement. But the absence of a challenge on this point only means that the condition has been fulfilled. Ultimately, if the objective is not made clear, or at least indicated, we can ask "what is that needed for?" We can press for an answer to our question, however elusive and difficult to articulate the objective may be. For by virtue of our language, that

1 "But what are 'requirements'? They are the things that must be done in order to secure certain ends; they do not exist except in relation to those ends. If different ends are sought, the 'requirements' become different." Bertrand Russell, "Reply to Criticism," in *The Philosophy of Bertrand Russell*, Paul A. Schilpp, ed. (Evanston, Ill.: The Library of Living Philosophers, Inc., 1946), p. 732.

which is not needed for anything is not needed.

Necessity

When we say that a pupil needs something, we are relating that thing to some objective. But *how* are they related—that which we call a need to the objective for which it is a need? Consider the claim "you need vitamin pills to improve your health." There are two ways of defeating it; that is, there are two ways of supporting the counterclaim that pills are not needed.

1. We might argue that vitamin pills have no effect on a person's physical or emotional state. If this argument could be made to stick, the prescription would stand refuted.

2. But even if we were to grant that the pills have a tendency to enhance health, we could defeat the claim by showing other feasible ways to achieve the same end. A demonstration of equally possible alternatives in some situation also refutes any claim that one alternative is *needed.*

Both of these cases involve a denial of necessity in some situation. The first claims that what is called a need will not assist in realizing the objective at all. The second claims that it is not the only way of helping to achieve the objective. It is clear now what the relation between need and objective must be. The object or activity or state of affairs we refer to as a need must be necessary to the objective, in the sense that its presence contributes to the achievement of the objective, while its absence renders the objective unattainable.

This second criterion is less stringent than it might appear. We are not called upon to guarantee the objective, except in very special cases in which we claim to be doing this ("*all* you need is practice").[2] Normally it is the necessary, not the sufficient conditions we prescribe (though a list of needs might satisfy both conditions). To announce that all candidates for graduation need twenty credits does not thereby guarantee graduation to all who fulfill the requirement. There may be additional requirements, other needs for the same objective. All we are committed to in our announcement is that with that many credits it remains possible to graduate, and that without them one cannot graduate.

But even this claim has an important reservation. When I say you need something, I mean that it is necessary in some more or less determinate situation. We are dealing with contextual necessity here. So what appear at first glance to be alternatives to needs, can often be eliminated by the practical exigencies of the specific situation. Take the case of a teacher who asserts that a pupil needs to join a special remedial class in order to accelerate his learning. It is no criticism of this assertion to say that the same result can be achieved with intensive personal tutoring. In most school situations this alternative is unrealistic, impossible to achieve. So in this situation it *is* the special class that is needed. There may be conceivable alternatives in some concrete situation, but if only one is feasible then that one is needed.

A word, finally, about two senses in which we might speak of something as necessary. There is the familiar notion of empirical necessity

2 All uses of "need" in questions which request requirements fall into this special class. In asking for needs, we always seem to be requesting the necessary *and* sufficient conditions. The significance of this fact, if it is a fact, eludes me.

which exists between events in the natural world. When an event regularly precedes another event which would otherwise fail to occur, we speak of the relation as an empirically necessary one. The same is true of analytic necessity or necessity by rule. Here also only one path can be followed to a certain result, but this is the "can" of custom or culture. Thus it is empirically possible for a man to steal money to support his family, but cultural rules (laws, in this case) proscribe this practice. We will be returning to this point in a later section for, as it turns out, rules play an important role in prescription.

Deficiency

There is a third way of challenging assertions of the form "he needs *X*." They can be countered with the claim that the condition has already been realized and hence not needed any longer. For example, the assertion "John needs to complete the final assignment" is wrong if the assignment is already complete.

From this we can infer a third criterion supervising the use of "need." Before we can properly say of someone that he needs something, the subject must be deficient in, or lack, whatever we prescribe. More accurately, the use of "need" presupposes a deficiency, without which it is a mistake to say a need exists.[3]

This third criterion seems to be trivial and obvious, but there is one consideration that makes it worth our attention. Educators occasionally define a need as "a condition of deprivation or lack." On this view, when we use "need" to prescribe for a student, we are merely reporting that the student is lacking in some respect. On this definition, the two assertions "John needs this book" and "John doesn't have this book" say the same thing. However, they do not. It is true that one *criterion* for saying successfully "John needs this book" is that John does not have the book, but the original assertion does not say this. For I could *agree* that John lacks the book yet *disagree* that he needs it. (One of the other conditions for making the prescription might be unfulfilled.)

This attempt to establish synonymity between statements of the form "*X* needs *Y*" and "*X* lacks *Y*" ignores the fact that whenever we are told that someone is bereft ("he is without a college education"), we can still properly ask if it is needed. This request is not meaningless, for there is an important difference between the two forms of expression. But the question "does John need attention?" *after being told he requires it, is* meaningless, heralding a failure in communication. For unless we are questioning the criteria ("does he *really* need it?"), the two assertions ("he needs . . ." and "he requires. . .") mean the same thing.

There are two temptations, I believe, which lead to this assimilation of "need" and "lack." First, there are some objectives so commonly accepted in a society that the mere realization that someone is deficient in them prompts us immediately to prescribe for alleviation of the condition. But this does not mean that *all* lacks are important. Nor does it mean that it is the deficiency alone which implies the need. It is only that the other conditions necessary for the use of "need" are obviously present and

3 This applies to the objective as well. If the objective is already attained, then clearly prescriptions made in its name are spurious.

taken for granted. Secondly, we sometimes employ "lack" in assertions that are very similar to prescriptions. For example, we say "he lacks adequate medical care" not only to report a deficiency but to point out such a condition is unjustified. This is still not the same as "he needs more medical care," but the two assertions are very close. The one recognizes an unacceptable situation; the other takes action to remove it. However, even this does not justify equating "lack" with "need," for it is the presence of such adjectives as "adequate" and "sufficient" which turns mere lacks into serious shortages.

Rules

There is, finally, a fourth condition which prevails when we use "need" in its prescriptive sense. Consider the case of a supervisor telling a teacher that members of her class need drill to improve their spelling. The teacher goes on to plan activities, demand student compliance, apply sanctions for failure, and generally evaluate students on their proficiency. The teacher is obviously not responding to the assertion "the class needs drill" as she would to a mere *report* that drill improves spelling.

In the above case the question of whether or not to increase the skill in spelling is simply not treated as a matter for debate. The decision has already been made. It is presupposed that the objective must be achieved. This introduces a new factor. Not only does the use of "need" presuppose an objective; it frequently presupposes an obligation or even a compulsion to achieve the objective as well.

Before discussing this point in greater detail, contrast the spelling situation with another which does not involve such a presupposition. An adviser tells a student, "You need more practice if you expect a career in music." There is no presupposition here concerning whether or not the student must go on in music. The adviser is simply giving information, reporting that some condition is necessarily dependent on another.

What is present in the spelling case and not present in the counseling situation is an underlying commitment to achieve the objective. As usual, the logical force of this point is revealed when we examine the challenge that might arise. Consider again the spelling example and suppose, simply for the sake of argument, that we did not care whether students spelled correctly. This would be sufficient grounds for denying that the class needs drill. Note that this kind of challenge is irrelevant in the counseling situation. Since the counselor does not assume an obligation to attain a goal, jeopardizing the goal does not invalidate the assertion.

In some cases then the correctness of a prescription hinges on whether the presupposition—that the objective must be achieved—is justified. When the presupposition is challenged, what sort of defense can be made for it? If a teacher is challenged on this point ("why must students learn to read?"), there is a sense in which the reply "because I say so" would not be wholly inappropriate. For what the teacher is saying, in effect, is that he is responsible for seeing to it that certain objectives are achieved. These general social expectations constitute the teacher's authority and justification for imposing further requirements, giving directives, prescribing needs.

This point is made clearer, I think,

when we look at a simpler case. A player in a card game may tell another that he needs to take one card. The person uttering the directive is presupposing that each player must have a certain number of cards. If someone were to challenge this assumption ("why must I have five cards?"), the objector would be referred to the rules of the game in which this was stipulated. In applying rules to persons clearly bound by them, we get directives. One needs to do X because X is itself dictated by the rules or because X is in some way necessary to what the rule does stipulate.

Though schools are more complicated than card games, they are in this respect similar. The host of social expectations and subordinate regulations comprising school policy function as do the rules in games to justify prescriptions.

Types of Prescriptions

Thus far I have been discussing prescription as if it were one job, a singular task which we do with language. Under the general rubric of prescription, however, different uses of "need" can be distinguished.

(1) "Need" occurs in assertions whose major function is to make rules or state them. An academic committee may decree, for example, that a certain average is needed for continued residence in a university. Here the committee is not reporting a requirement; they are literally making one. But "need" is also employed in the statement of a rule, in a report that such and such is a rule. I will call this the rule sense or rule use of "need."

(2) The application of general rules in specific situations to yield detailed requirements for particular subjects is what I called earlier the directive use of "need." There are variations in the way rules apply in different cases. I have been focusing attention on cases in which the objective is stipulated by rule or social expectation and "need" is used to prescribe the empirically necessary means. Other patterns are possible. In some cases rules may dictate both the objective and means. Finally, no objective may be involved, only a rule stipulated requirement.

In distinguishing the rule use of "need" from the directive use, I don't mean to be emphasizing the performatory character of rule making. The performatory element is important but there are directive cases also in which it is present. In some unusual circumstances "higher authority" must judge whether a rule applies to a subject, and even how it applies. But where the performatory element is common in the rule use, it is necessarily rare in the directive use. For we *make* rules of a general sort just to avoid the necessity for individual judgments in each specific case.

The differences I do want to emphasize between (1) and (2) are those that exist between a rule and the application of a rule. Typically, rules do not refer to particular subjects but to roles or positions. Also, but not invariably, rules differ from directives in that they stipulate only a *type* of required action or performance.

(3) In the counseling situation we encountered a third, the *informative* sense of "need." Here "need" is used to report, not impose, requirements. Thus we inform those not bound by rules what would be required of them if they were so bound ("if you join the club, you will need to attend

meetings"). Or we can specify what is necessary to some goal even though the goal is not being sought ("to get good grades, one needs to study").

The difference between (2) and (3) is the difference between the hypothetical and categorical mood. Cases of (3) tell us what *would* be needed *if* certain conditions existed. Cases of (2) state what we *do* need *because* these conditions *do* exist. However, the actual form of the prescription may be misleading. In some contexts "need" may be used informatively to make a seemingly categorical assertion. "Students need affection," for example, may be elliptical, a condensed version of the hypothetical "if students are to achieve emotional security, affection is necessary." We depend on the context of the utterance to determine whether the actual form of the assertion is misleading.

Despite the differences between these uses, they are all prescriptive in the ordinary sense of that term. A rule is said to prescribe or proscribe certain actions, and we are also said to prescribe when we apply the rules to specific individuals. Similarly a doctor is said to prescribe for a patient although the prescription is not binding on us. This reveals the ambiguity in the ordinary sense of prescription, but more importantly for present purposes, it helps explain why some challenges are not relevant to every case wherein "need" is used prescriptively.

In the preceding section it was shown that there are at least four possible challenges one can legitimately make to the prescription "these students need *X*." We can ask what objective *X* is to serve and question whether *X* is necessary to the attainment of the objective. Also an inquiry can be made as to whether the students really lack *X* or the objective. And finally we can ask for the rules or social expectations that make the achievement of *X* obligatory. Thus, in response to the claim "this class needs instruction in science," the following questions might be raised:

(a) What objective is served by science instruction? (Suppose that the objective is development of scientific attitudes.)

(b) Is science instruction necessary to achieve the attitudes? (Will it contribute to their development at all? Is it the *only* feasible way to develop them?)

(c) Have students already had the instruction? Do they already possess the attitudes?

(d) What rules or expectations make the attainment of these attitudes mandatory?

Now it can be seen that not all challenges are relevant or relevant in the same way to each prescriptive use. Let me list some of the exceptions.

(1) When "need" is functioning informatively, challenge (d), the request for justification, does not apply as it does in directive cases. In directive cases the rules justify the *demand* or *insistence* that something be achieved. In informative cases the rules justify my *claim* or *prediction* as to what will be demanded; the rules do not justify my imposition for there is no imposition.

(2) The deficiency challenge, challenge (c), is irrelevant to statements of rules. For example, the rule that all club members need to pay dues is properly asserted even when it has been obeyed. Actually the rule is the general formula which tells us what to say and do when dues have not been paid.

But if a rule does not presuppose an existent deficiency, it does assume the expectation of one. It would be pointless to establish rules for cases that are unlikely to arise (e.g., "all high school students need to know how to talk").

(3) On some occasions of the rule use it is inappropriate to invoke challenge (a) and request the objective of the need. For some needs are "ultimate." Some rules do not specify what must be done to achieve a given end; they simply assert what must be done. However, these cases are apt to be rare, for "need" tends to be a relative term. We reserve it for cases when "*X* is needed *for A*." To make simple demands or commands we tend to employ the more imperative expressions "must," "have to," and "is mandatory."

In addition to exceptions to the challenges, there are also additional challenges. The directive "you need to do *X*" is unjustified if you are not bound by the rules from which the prescription was generated. Similarly, any rules made by a group lacking legitimate authority are invalid.

These do not exhaust the exceptions or additional challenges but they round out the picture of prescriptive sense of "need."

2. *Motivational Uses of "Need"*

As far as his professional language is concerned, the educator stands at halfway house. Some of the concepts he uses have been borrowed from the social sciences. To this extent there tends to be disparity between the talk of the teacher and the layman. However, words common to everyone also find a place in educational discussions. No concept reveals this linguistic divergence better than the one we are presently scrutinizing. For there is nothing particularly technical about the use of "need" to prescribe. "He needs a job" is the kind of assertion anyone might properly make. But an educator who says that pupils need recognition may not mean pupils *require* it, in the prescriptive sense, but rather that pupils want or seek it out. This motivational sense of need we owe to the psychologist.

Here, as in the previous section, we we find not one but three uses:

(a) Sometimes "need" reports or refers to a motive, so that the assertion "John needs (or has a need for) *X*" is a report of what John desires.

(b) Also, it is often *claimed* that "need" is used to refer to "deficit states" or "conditions of lack."

In both (a) and (b) need is an event or occurrence. That is, need assertions on either use are reports of states of affairs transpiring at the time the assertion is made. Or suitably tensed, the assertion may report past or future *events.*

(c) "Need" can and does operate in a dispositional sense also, as when it is used to report that a subject is prone to want a certain thing from time to time. In this sense "John needs affection" does not mean that John now desires affection, only that he is inclined to desire it periodically. In the dispositional sense a need is a trait, a propensity, a predilection, not an event.

Despite the dual use of "need" as event and as trait, there has not been, to my knowledge, any attempt to alter the commonly accepted grammar of the term to give it a present continuous tense. Thus we do not say "he is needing" when reporting a contemporary episode, as we do with the terms "boxing," "running," "falling," etc. Consequently the same form—"he needs"—is utilized to report motives and dispositions.

We will be returning to this dispositional sense a little later, but I will give most attention to the first two senses of need—as motive and lack. These uses have been more widely recognized and discussed than the dispositional one.[4] Indeed one sometimes suspects that there is more talk about need as motive and need as deficit state than actual *use* of the expression in either way. At any rate, it will not be necessary to dwell on the much discussed aspects of these uses. In the discussion to follow I will concentrate on some of the special problems and puzzles which arise in connection with these uses. We will find that each use is plagued by conceptual difficulties that in one case at least render the very use itself questionable. Yet these difficulties are often ignored by educators who introduce the expression into all aspects of education.

Needs As Motives

Sporadically among educators generally and more commonly among educational psychologists in particular there has developed a practice of using the expression "need" to refer to a certain type of happening. This event has been characterized in a variety of ways—as a state of tension, a psychological condition of sensitivity to respond, a condition of disequilibrium, or less grandly, as an "inner urge" or desire or want, etc. Whatever we call it, "need" is being used to report the motive itself and not, as in the dispositional use, the tendency for the motive to recur.

Furthermore, in pedagogical language, "need" is usually a general motive expression; it is used to refer to any kind of motive or any goal-seeking behavior. The definition given by Gates and others illustrates this general applicability of "need":

> A need exists as a state of tension in a person which serves to direct his behavior toward certain goals.... "Need" ... is used as an inclusive term to embrace drives, impulses, goal sets, urges, motives, cravings, desires, wants, and wishes.[5]

The first point to note is that this usage is not encountered outside education (and the social sciences generally). In ordinary discourse, "need" is not a general motive expression but a specific one, referring only to a motive that is particularly persistent and compelling. Thus, one feels truly "driven" by a need, and if motives were scaled by reference to their intensity or strength, feelings of need would top the scale.

The restricted use is represented in education also. Cronbach, for example, speaks cryptically of needs as

[4] For a few of the discussions see Reginald D. Archambault, "The Concept of Need...," *Harvard Educational Review* (Winter, 1957), pp. 40f.; Donald C. Doane, *The Needs of Youth* (New York: Bureau of Publications, Teachers College, Columbia University, 1942), pp. 3f.; Ralph W. Tyler, *Basic Principles of Curriculum and Instruction* (Urbana, Ill.: University of Chicago Press, 1950), pp. 5f.; and Herbert F. Wright, "How the Psychology of Motivation Is Related to Curriculum Development," *Journal of Educational Psychology* (March 1948), pp. 149f.

[5] Arthur I. Gates, Arthur T. Jersild, T. R. McConnell, and Robert Challman, *Educational Psychology*, 3rd ed. (New York: The Macmillan Company, 1948), p. 617.

"persistent and recurrent wants," not simply as wants.[6] And the attempt made by some educators to separate needs from whims and "mere" desires indicates that the ordinary usage still retains followers in education.

The use of "need" as a motive expression has yet another feature which warrants particular attention. There is considerable variation in the type of word that can be employed to refer to the object of the motive. In the same or similar circumstances a relatively abstract term might be employed ("he has a need for recreation") or a more specific one ("he has a need to go fishing").

What makes this divergence particularly intriguing is that it concerns only the choice of word (or phrase) used to refer to the goal. It is not a disagreement over the criteria for the motivational use of "need" itself.

Let me explain this point a little more fully. The actual specific or concrete criteria for the use of motive expressions are numerous and differ (though not completely) from situation to situation. For example, the pleas of a boy to be taken fishing and the boy's preparations are all criteria for the assertion "he wants to go fishing." However, we can abstract from the *specific* criteria to form the *general* rule that a motive expression is used in a situation where some subject is actively pursuing a goal.

We recognize that a great variety of activities may constitute an active pursuit. In one case it may be asking a question and skimming through an encyclopedia ("he wants to know the area of Spain"). In another it may be spurts of running, or fretting over the lateness of the hour ("he wants to see the batting practice"). There is no reason to concern ourselves with this issue, for the disagreement we are discussing does not concern the presence or absence of the criteria. All would agree that a student must actively be pursuing (in some way) a goal before we say he has a need for that goal. In spite of this agreement, however, there might still be variations in the generality of the word employed to characterize the goal.

The more general terms like "status," "achievement," and "adventure" are also employed when "need" is used *dispositionally*. This is understandable, for in the dispositional use we are trying to summate, generalize from, many individual motivational episodes. A need in this sense is not a report of the actual goal being pursued. So the use of general terms in dispositional reports does not mean that the *goals* are necessarily general, only that the goals—whether they be specific or general—fall into a certain class.[7]

However, when exclusively general terms are used to refer to goals then we *are* committed to the proposition that motives themselves are general. And general motives are characterized by transitory goal-objects and wavering goal-directed behavior, among other things. The original choice of abstract terms implies the above as characteristics of human goal-seeking

6 Lee J. Cronbach, "The Learning Process and Text Specification," *Text Materials in Modern Education* (Urbana: University of Illinois Press, 1955), p. 66.

7 "Needs describe the relatively permanent tendencies in persons to be motivated in specific ways, and *we infer them from the commonalities among the goals that the person appears to be seeking* [italics not in the original]." Frederick J. McDonald, *Educational Psychology* (Belmont, Calif.: Wadsworth Publishing Company, 1959), p. 81.

behavior. Similarly one who employs only specific labels for goals is prejudging the empirical traits motivated behavior will be found to possess.

Furthermore, the fact that goals are given abstract labels has at least one other important consequence. We find that the same terms are applicable to many students and to the same student at various times in his career. Thus the step to the universality of motives (needs) is a smooth one. For example, a student who studies furiously for a test and requests guidance in eradicating errors is said to have a need to gain status. The same is said of the pupil whose antics gain the attention of his classmates. What is more natural than to conclude that both students are having the "same" need? The transition is more difficult when the more idiosyncratic expressions like "get an A in the spelling test" rather than "recognition" are used to label the goals. Thus many educators who claim to *discover* common motives in students may be deluding themselves. Their discovery may simply be a consequence of a previous *decision* to employ abstract language. The choice of words to report needs in the motive sense is a serious matter. For the choice itself may commit one to empirical claims concerning motivational phenomena.

Needs As Lacks

Considering the popularity of the notion of needs as a state of deficiency, it is surprising that there is so little agreement on descriptions of the use. However, many educators who agree on the notion diverge considerably in their more detailed accounts of it.

First, there seems to be no consensus on whether the need is the *object* that is lacking or the *condition* of absence.[8,9] But having noted this particular divergence, let me put it aside and adopt the language of "condition."

A more serious difficulty is revealed when we attempt to clarify the way in which motives are related to lacks in this conception. One view of the relationship has been described by James Olds as follows:

> The physiological phenomenon of need is this: without certain needed conditions the organism will perish. The animistic theory proceeds to make the following assumptions: (1) the organism wants the conditions that will permit survival. The conclusion is that when we say something is needed we mean not only (*i*) that without the condition the organism will perish, but also (*ii*) the organism will want and therefore pursue the condition.... My contention is that the term *need* refers only to the fact that the organism would perish without the needed conditions; and I believe the assumption that "need" is intrinsically related to "want" or "pursuit" is something akin to the presumption that an automobile low on fuel will always automatically head for the nearest gasoline station.[10]

[8] "Anything that is requisite to the maintenance of a state of affairs is a need." Asahel D. Woodruff, *The Psychology of Teaching*, 3rd ed. (New York: David McKay Co., Inc., 1951), p. 80.

[9] "A need is the lack of something that, if present, would further the welfare of the individual." Robert T. Beck, Walter W. Cook, and Nolan C. Kearney, *Curriculum in the Modern Elementary School*, 2nd ed. (Englewood Cliffs, N.J.: Prentice-Hall, Inc., 1960).

[10] James Olds, "A Physiological Study of Reward," in *Studies of Motivation*, edited by David C. McClelland (New York: Appleton-Century-Crofts, 1955), p. 135.

Putting aside for the moment Olds' proposal to restrict the expression, let us consider the view he criticizes. The claim (or assumption) that needs arouse motives has at least two interpretations. First, we might view it as an empirical assertion, as a prediction that a motivated state reliably follows a deficient one. Secondly, the claim could be taken as a defining characteristic of need. Thus "need" would be *defined* as a deficit state that reliably initiates a motive.

Educators seem to vacillate between these two interpretations. Thus, Stephens begins with the empirical position by making the factual assumption that needs and motives are related. But a little later he seems to be *defining* a need state as one which brings on action:

> Just as it is convenient to assume that some force or drive is giving direction and continuity to a series of individual acts, so it is convenient to assume that the drive is operating in the service of some *need.* A need is the thing which sets a drive in motion. . . . Need is a condition which calls for action toward a certain goal.[11]

On the other hand, Thayer and his associates, in their well-known study of secondary education, begin with the definitional conception:

> Hence a working concept of an educational need must always be both personal and social in reference; it must always incorporate both the present desires of the individual and what they should desirably become.[12]

However, in the second half of the study they slip back into the empirical view. The authors simply identify the important student deficiencies and seem to assume, as a matter of fact, that students will be motivated to overcome the lacks so identified.

But even if educators agreed on one view of the lack-motive relation, difficulties would not disappear. For "needs (lacks) arouse motives" as an empirical claim is manifestly false. The world is full of things we do not have and do not want. To retain at least the hope of truth, "need" will have to refer to a subclass of lacks. However, there has been little success in specifying this subclass. If "need" refers to a state of deprivation, a loss of things once possessed, the motivational claim fares no better. Chronic failure, disease, poverty, and submission are not typically in demand when absent from lives they once afflicted. There are other possibilities. We can take some norm or end-state and use "need" to refer to deviations from the norm or the absence of conditions necessary for achieving the end-state. Survival is the most common nominee for this role, but "the welfare of the individual"[13] and "comfortable adjustment in some stage in life"[14] have also been proposed. Survival, however, is too miserly a conception, since there are deficiencies which arouse us without the threat of death (e.g., affection). On the other hand, the other proposed norms are too vague to be used as criteria (what constitutes "comfortable" adjustment?).

The definitional interpretation

[11] J. M. Stephens, *Educational Psychology*, rev. ed. (New York: Holt, Rinehart & Winston, Inc., 1956), pp. 478f.

[12] V. T. Thayer, Caroline B. Zachry, and Ruth Kotinsky, *Reorganizing Secondary Education* (New York: Appleton-Century-Crofts, 1939), p. 38.

[13] Beck, *op. cit.*, p. 53.

[14] Woodruff, *op. cit.*, p. 81.

avoids most of these difficulties for on this view "need" is defined as a deficit state that initiates a motive. The price of this avoidance, however, is vagueness. For example, it is not clear whether this use of the expression requires present motivation or only past instances of motivation in similar circumstances. That is, when I say "*A* needs *X*" am I saying that *X* is now being sought or only that *X* is now lacking and has been sought in the past when absent? Discussion and use of "need" in education does not supply an answer. Yet if present motivation is required, then this use would differ very little from the motive use of "need."

Clarity is lacking on at least one other point. Here, as with motives, it is pertinent to ask about the degree of generality in the labels used to report the lacks. If I say someone needs *X*, precisely what is lacking? Do I say he lacks some particular friend, or just a friend, or affection? This question also goes unanswered in the literature. Yet if specific terms are allowable, it is possible that in some cases the teacher will encounter legitimate needs for things—like breaking windows—which go unrecognized in educational texts.

Finally, we can adopt Olds' suggestion and simply employ "need" to refer to deficiencies associated with certain norms or end-states. Any claim, definitional or empirical, that these deficiencies are related to motives could be dropped. What is immediately apparent is that such a practice would differ little from "need" in the prescriptive sense. We would then have two uses of "need," one to report deficiencies and another to prescribe for their alleviation. Surely this is linguistic luxury. We have discussed enough of the use of "need" as lack to suggest its confused state.

3. The Needs-Curriculum

The needs concept has been made to carry a heavy theoretical load in many areas of education. This is especially true in the area of curriculum theory, as witnessed by the popularity of the claim that the public school curriculum should meet the needs of the students. For ease of reference, let me refer to this view as the "needs-policy" and the resulting educational program as the "needs-curriculum." The needs-policy is considered to be a significant and certainly a controversial approach to public education. Thus it is not uncommon for someone to object to new proposals and practices by claiming that they will fail to meet some or all of the needs of some or all of the students. Also, some educational textbooks explicitly distinguish the needs-curriculum from other types of curricular organization.[15] And at least one major educational association has made need-meeting its clarion call.[16] By applying some of the results of the earlier analysis, I hope to show that this widespread belief in the significance of the needs-policy is unjustified. Depending upon the way "need" is interpreted, the needs-policy turns out to be sometimes trivial, sometimes

15 Kenneth H. Hansen, *Public Education in American Society*, 2nd ed. (Englewood Cliffs, N. J.: Prentice-Hall, Inc., 1963). Galen J. Saylor and William M. Alexander, *Curriculum Planning* (New York: Holt, Rinehart & Winston, Inc., 1955), Chap. 9.

16 National Association of Secondary-School Principals, *Planning for American Youth*, rev. ed. (Washington: The Association, 1951).

indeterminate, and sometimes unsupported, but always unimportant.

Prescriptive Meanings

When applying prescriptive meanings to the needs-policy, it is possible to treat the rule and directive uses together. We fulfill general requirements (rules) by applying them to specific cases (in directives), and the directives in turn presuppose rules. Therefore a curriculum derived from students' needs in either of these senses will inevitably invoke the other as well. When these uses are adopted, the needs-policy has two possible interpretations. The interpretation depends on whether *school* requirements or *social* requirements are employed for determining students' needs.

If the school requirements are viewed as the source of the curriculum, then the needs-policy is trivial. For, then, to say that the school should meet needs would be the same as asserting that the school should do what is necessary to fulfill its assigned tasks. No one could sensibly dispute this claim since it is a tautology. For the acceptance of something as one's objective already *implies* that one should do what is necessary to achieve it. And as expected, the denial of the needs-policy, so interpreted, involves a self-contradiction. With this interpretation, then, the needs-policy receives unanimous support, but only because it makes the trivial claim that schools should do what they should do.

If, on the other hand, needs are general social requirements, then the claim is significant (it says something), but what it says is either preposterous or incomplete. For affirming the needs-policy would now commit us to the view that the school should take responsibility for *all* the requirements imposed on children in our society. Such a school is barely conceivable.

Someone who supports this form of the needs-policy probably does not want us to take it literally. Rather he merely wants to emphasize that the school should assume a broader social responsibility. But if this is so, then the needs-policy is of secondary importance. For the real dispute arises not in answer to (1) "should the curriculum be based on needs of youth?" but in answer to (2) "which needs should the school be concerned with?" The needs-policy is an answer to (1) only; it is indeterminate with respect to (2), and a policy that does not offer an answer to (2) is incomplete.

There is one other prescriptive use of "need"—the hypothetical use. The adoption of this meaning, however, would also culminate in a policy that was either preposterous or indeterminate.

Motivational Meanings

The proposal fares no better when a motivational meaning is adopted. If we take needs to be very general motives or dispositions (need for recognition, affection, achievement, etc.), even then, as Bode has demonstrated, it is not enough to say that schools should meet needs. There are different ways of gaining affection, status, achievement, and the like,[17] that is, there is a great variety of "objects" that these general terms can cover. The needs-policy is again incomplete; it does not tell us which of these to teach. Yet debates arise over

17 Boyd H. Bode, *Progressive Education at the Crossroads* (New York: Newson & Company, 1938), Chap. 4.

the *mode* of satisfaction, not over satisfaction per se.

There is another point to note here. Looked at as a proposal about our most general goals or propensities (i.e., "basic needs"), the needs-policy once more resembles a mere truism. Any curriculum can be said to assist students in meeting their needs. Every curriculum is a needs-curriculum. Of course, the needs-policy is not a tautology; it would be possible to deny it without self-contradiction. But it would be decidedly odd to find a curriculum that is said to be unrelated to the students' basic needs. The reason is that the very conception of basic needs makes them so ubiquitous and all-embracing that no such sustained activity as schooling could be completely alien to them.

However, one can *choose* whether or not to talk the language of basic needs when discussing curricula. It is still possible to ignore the relation of schooling to students' needs without denying that there is some connection.

In contradistinction to the general approach, one can take a microscopic view and use "need" to refer to specific motives ("have a bicycle," "build a boat"). If "meet needs" is taken to mean "assist the student to reach his goal," then the needs-policy is more determinate and certainly not redundant. The difficulty with this interpretation is that it has no supporters.

To summarize the discussion thus far, I have tried to show that the general proposal that schools meet students' needs is trivial or indeterminate or unsupported, depending on what a need is taken to be. This might account for the popularity of the needs-policy. For by a nimble equivocation on the meaning of "need" a supporter of the needs-policy can feel as if he were making a daring proposal which could not possibly be wrong (no mean feat!).

These conclusions should not be overgeneralized. There are many specific contexts in education in which the claim "we should meet this need for *X*" is significant. This might be said, for example, to report the discovery of a condition necessary to the achievement of some accepted goal. Or on some particular occasion it might be uttered to warn a teacher against unnecessary activities. My strictures apply only to the attempt to use "need" in a general policy statement, but even here there may exist another way of saying it.

Thus far I have been treating the proposal "schools should meet needs" as a prescriptive generalization from which one can deduce that if *X* is a need then the schools should deal with it. This is certainly a reasonable approach to proposals of this sort. Thus, if someone proposed that schools develop intellectual discipline, our very first step would be to discover the meaning of "intellectual discipline." For this information is necessary if we are to deduce the kind of curriculum being proposed.

One sign of the usualness of this treatment is the widespread use of the *reduction ad absurdum* argument in educational debate. But to claim that some proposal is unjustified because one can deduce foolish consequences, is to assume that one can deduce consequences at all. To do so is to treat the proposal as a prescriptive generalization.

But suppose the needs-policy is not a prescriptive generalization. Then it would not necessarily have the weaknesses enumerated earlier. But what else could it be? It could be the *title* given to a set of curriculum practices. When the needs-policy is viewed as a title, it is not necessary that there be any logical relation between the policy itself and the parts of the proposed curriculum. The "relation" is similar to that which obtains between the title and content of a novel. Titles of novels are chosen because they are suggestive of the content (in *some* way) and appealing in their own right. So it is with the needs-policy (on this interpretation). Actually the needs-curriculum could conceivably ignore students' needs. The term "need" might be employed in the title because it suggests necessity, and necessity connotes importance, and the proposed studies are considered important. This example borders on the absurd, but it typifies the connection that exists between policy statement and curriculum in this view.

Other assertions in education seem to function similarly. "Education for life adjustment" and "teach the child, not the content" are ludicrous when cast in the role of generalizations. The first, because of the appalling vagueness and ambiguity of "adjustment." The second, because the notion of teaching someone without teaching him something is nonsense. We call such assertions slogans; they have the "logic" of titles and are chosen because of their appeal. I am suggesting that the needs-policy might belong to this group.

This interpretation becomes even more plausible when carried a step further. For it would explain why the ambiguous term "need" survives and even thrives in educational writing and discussion. Its vagueness and multiplicity of meaning, far from impairing its usefulness, enhances it. For its utterance in a slogan in a suitable setting may further or maintain some educational enterprises.

Consider the role of the administrator with its attendant conflicts and dilemmas. The person occupying such a position is frequently called upon to announce policy statements to a public replete with competing and incompatible educational expectations. The energy given in defense of a seemingly partisan policy would detract from other vital administrative functions. Such assertions as "our schools meet needs . . ." may help, in part at least, to avoid these impairments. For a task is performed and a "policy" announced which is least apt to require lengthy debilitating defense. Similarly, the administrator must maintain authority when dealing with teachers more competent in some subject than himself. What better directive can he give than "be sure to meet the needs of the student."

The appraisal of the needs-policy as a slogan calls for a new approach. For here the triviality, the vagueness, and the indeterminacy are boons, not failings. The terms employed in slogans must appeal, yet be flexible; they must arouse without suggesting anything definite. If "need" has become too closely identified with a definite and controversial program, as I believe it has, then whatever utility it once possessed as a slogan has vanished.

39. PRESSURES TO LEARN CAN BE BLOCKS TO LEARNING

JOHN I. GOODLAD

Certain pressures block children's learning. Sometimes these pressures stem from beyond the schools; they are part of the larger society. Sometimes these pressures arise inside the classroom; they are part of the teaching-learning environment. We shall concern ourselves here with the latter type.

Prepackaged Content and Inappropriate Rewards

Schools often proceed as though the thinking already had been done. Somebody, somewhere, thought up everything in advance. There's just no more thinking to be done. Or, worse still, nobody had anything to do with it in the first place. Ideas are the product of immaculate conception!

John I. Goodlad, "Pressures to Learn Can Be Blocks to Learning," CHILDHOOD EDUCATION, *XXXVI, No. 4 (December 1959), 162–65. Reprinted by permission of the Association for Childhood Education International, 3615 Wisconsin Avenue, N. W., Washington, D.C., and the author.*

The task of curriculum construction, following this concept of learning, becomes the prepackaging of content into neat, consumable bundles. These bundles are then stored away in a curricular deep-freeze and, ultimately, displayed before the eager eyes of hopeful pupils. But, alas, once removed from cold storage, the fast-thawing goods quickly spoil and swiftly smell. The pupils are less than enchanted.

Such a concept of learning leads naturally to fixed patterns of teaching. If the purpose of learning is to consume, then the purpose of teaching is to dispense. Successful consumption is easily recognized and approved.

In the process of dispensing and consuming, both teacher and learner often become confused over ends. For example . . . Miss Manton tells a story of her second-grade class. (Of course, there's no such thing as a "second-grade" class but we'll abide by the conventions.) Before completing it, she asks, "How do you think this story ends?" So far, so good. The children eagerly pose conclusions. To Tommy's response, Miss Manton answers, "No, I don't quite see how that could be." To Susan's, "No, I don't think so." To Mildred's, "No, that's not *what I'm thinking of*."

A shift has occurred, a subtle but significant shift. A process of inquiry, a process of putting ideas together to infer a logical conclusion, has shifted to a mere guessing game. Guess the right answer and the teacher's warm beam of approval floods down upon you. Learning becomes not a search for meaning, not an exciting pursuit whetted by surprise and the satisfaction of true accomplishment, but a search for responses that bring rewards. Press the right button and gain approval.

Some students learn the process well. They go through high school, college, and life burdened with this misguided conception of education. So many nods of approval add up to a B, so many B's add up to an A.B. and an A.B. opens certain doors. In graduate school they ask, "Mr. Professor, what do I need to do [to gain your approval] in your course?" In business they become good organization men.

This is education? I think not. This is pressure to conform, social pressure of the most insidious sort, worming its way like a bacterial infection into the heart of the learning-teaching process, distorting and contaminating it until true education withers and dies.

Some educators writhe in horror over the imminent danger of machines taking over part of the learning-teaching act. Perhaps, for some aspects of learning, machines are more promise than threat. At least they focus on learning for learning's sake. You press the button and you're right or you're wrong. No syrupy words of commendation, no halos, for guessing the teacher's mind. The machines, too, will become monsters to be feared when they dispense peanuts, candy and chewing gum for pressing the right button. Once more, the ends of education will be contaminated and distorted.

Perceptions of Coverage

A crippling perception of coverage often is part of the teaching-learning environment. We must be up to here by Hallowe'en, this much farther by Thanksgiving. Heaven help us if we aren't halfway there by Christmas. Halfway where? Don't ask silly questions. *There*, of course! On to Easter. By May, we're loping out in front, all by ourselves. And the children? Don't be ridiculous. We're almost *there*! A little prodding, a litle pushing, a little skipping—and it's June. We're *there* for another year.

Such a concept of coverage creates immeasurable pressures to learn. It, too, is based on a "sacred cow" view of the curriculum. Here are the important things to be learned, laid out in neat order, to be "covered" at a set pace one after the other in the process of getting an education.

There is, indeed, a fairly respectable theory of knowing to support this view of the curriculum. But imagine, for a moment, the problem of selection in today's world! How do teachers determine what is of most worth among all from which to select? The little that can be put into the curriculum in relation to all that is available is as a handful of straw in relation to thousands of silos filled with straw.

And yet, we often act as though

the most important content already had been selected for all time and appropriately arranged for consumption. We have, indeed, our sacred cow standing stubbornly in the path of reason. Do we dare to kill it?

External Standards

When one troubles to push beyond the criticisms, the panaceas, and the slogans mouthed in the name of educational betterment, one sees that many seeking to be heard conceive standards to be something external to the learning process. "Higher standards, more rigor, better quality," come the pleas. "If they can't learn," says one, "kick 'em out. That's what we did at West Point."

It is difficult (and unwise) for teachers to ignore the clamor, ever mindful as most are of the need to do better. But, sometimes, we ignore our own beliefs about learning. Short-route methods take on a special attractiveness. Drill replaces the search for meaning. Children repeat their incorrect responses along with correct ones. Teacher presentation replaces pupil exploration. Routes that *appear* to be most direct take precedence.

Learning is seldom the shortest distance between two points. Learning often is oblique and circuitious. The means that appear to be most roundabout often lead most directly to the ends sought.

The net result of the pressure of inappropriate standards is likely to be less, not more, learning.

True standards are found within, not outside of, the learning process. True standards relate means most appropriately to ends. True standards free rather than restrict the human mind in its search for order and truth. Standards perceived to be outside of learning itself are blocks to learning.

Some Ground to Stand on

Each of us readily identifies with some part of the foregoing. In recognizing ourselves we can in part right ourselves—but only in part. We're all caught up in a massive piece of machinery that answers not to our commands. Some basic changes are needed.

First, we need a concept of curriculum that better defines our freedoms. Freedom is a disciplined thing. It comes to the individual with increased understanding of his areas of choice as well as his areas of no choice. The sailor who sails strange waters is free to cruise and to explore if he possesses good charts. The sailor who lacks such charts must either pine away on the shore or then grope his way cautiously, ever fearful of lurking reefs.

A curriculum plan that better defines our freedoms separates the relatively variable from the relatively constant. A few facts—particularly in the linguistic and mathematical realms—are here for a while, unless the structure of knowing of which they are a part collapses. The learning of them does not call for undue imagination, as though there were wide degrees of choice. In fact, imagination may well be a block to the learning of such facts.

Some facts are transitory or, at best, quite incidental (even accidental) to the learning of larger concepts. Such facts should be subordinated to the larger ends of formulating and employing concepts.

The teacher is free to use whatever data seem appropriate to the clarification of larger concepts.

Most curriculum plans now in existence fail to recognize distinctions such as those suggested above. As a result, everything in a plan (even when labeled "for consideration only") becomes relatively constant—to be learned by all. Thus we get our sacred cow.

Second, we need a better understanding of the learner realities before us. We act as though there were only shades of difference among learners—as though, perhaps, the brightest child were twice as bright as the dullest. Actually, the differences in reasoning among slow and bright children almost defy mathematical comparison. One is thousands of times more proficient than the other in certain kinds of abstract reasoning.

In seeking appropriate teaching techniques, we do well to approach these differences as differences in kind (as between a cat and a human) rather than in degree. Thus, the pedagogical road to learning for the slow may not be more of what was good for the bright. Similarly, the best procedure for the bright may not be just a little less of methods that worked for the average. We need experimental studies designed to find the optimal learning conditions for many kinds and degrees of differences among learners. The studies needed will not be conducted until potential experimenters catch a vision of pupil variability radically different from the view presently in vogue.

Third, we need a concept of learning embracing unlimited expectancy for human creativity. We know little about the potential creativity inherent in the human organism. We know only that our school practices tend to recognize and reward certain abilities out of proportion to other abilities. In a very real sense, then, creativity comes to be defined sociologically rather than biologically and psychologically. What we value most shifts with the ebb and flow of societal tides. What we value in peacetime we value not in time of war.

There is little likelihood of social pressure ceasing to reward only certain kinds of creativity. Social pressure is part of a real world. But the schools can do much to keep open-ended the drive that is human creativity. Schools must avoid like the plague external rewards for certain kinds of learning that freeze the creative process in its infancy. They do well to encourage creativity as an end in itself—creativity in many things—rather than to promote and reward accomplishment in those limited aspects of human activity that happen to be currently popular.

There are appropriate as well as inappropriate pressures to learn. Somewhere along the educative and miseducative road that is life the learner must respond to compelling forces within him, forces seeking to repeat the satisfactory experience of coming to know for one's self. The best way to make sure that these forces never will hold sway is to substitute for them pressures from without—pressures to please, pressures to cover and pressures to conform.

40. INTELLECTUAL MASTERY AND MENTAL HEALTH

MILLIE ALMY

A pencilled slogan, "Kill mental health," has appeared on so many billboards of late that it no longer excites comment. Is the demise of "mental health" perhaps to date from the moment it became a cliché? So far as the schools are concerned, the answer seems all too clear.

Since the 1930's most American schools have had an avowed concern for children's social relations, their personal problems, and their personal adjustment. In many instances extensive psychological services have been developed for the early detection of emotional disturbance and mental illness. But the main responsibility for the promotion of mental health has lain with the teachers. Imbued with the notion that they must teach the "whole child" (as though there were some other kind), they have struggled to understand the complexities of a child growing up in his family and the intricacies of his life with his peers. Beyond this, many have attempted in various ways to help children to cope more or less directly with these problems.

Millie Almy, "Intellectual Mastery and Mental Health," Teachers College Record, *LXIII, No. 6 (March 1962), 468–78. Reprinted by permission.*

Limits on Teachers

But the teacher's influence, however good it may be, is spread over some 25 individuals (or in the case of many high school teachers, 125). How effective can he be? This question becomes particularly acute, in view of the fact that the mental health function of the teacher has so often been seen as something apart from his teaching functions. One of the first mental hygiene specialists to call attention to this was Ruth Kotinsky.

In an article with Jules Coleman (9), she put the issue very directly: What is the school's business? Have the schools the personnel, the facilities, the time to take on mental health responsibilities beyond those inherent in carrying through the functions traditionally accepted as their business? Are there not potentialities for influencing mental health in teaching the skills and understandings necessary to cope with the environment, the skills of communication, the ways of identifying and solving problems rationally, and the rudiments needed for a vocation?

The decade in which Ruth Kotinsky raised these questions was, by and large, a decade of retreat for the schools. Beset by criticism from within and without, many schools abandoned so-called frills and fads and placed renewed emphasis on the fundamentals, on skills and content and subject matter.

So far as mental health is concerned, the decade may perhaps be labeled one of beginning clarification. The appearance in 1958 of *Current Concepts in Mental Health* by Marie Jahoda (7) indicated initial progress toward the eventual establishment of some empirical indicators for mental health. One of the six components of the multiple criteria proposed by Jahoda seems especially relevant for the school. This is the component of environmental mastery.

Environmental mastery encompasses adequacy in love, work, play, and in interpersonal relationships, in adaptation and adjustment, and in problem solving. The child undoubtedly formulates his basic attitudes toward love, work, play, and other people in considerable part before he enters school, but the school confronts the child with new possibilities. It introduces him to persons whose ways of responding are different from those he has known at home. It provides him with knowledge of many sorts of work and play. It develops skills that enable him to investigate and to cope more effectively with the world of people and things. Although the knowledge and the skills the school offers can be acquired elsewhere, no other agency can be held so directly responsible for this aspect of mental health.

To say this does not deny that developments in other components of the personality may affect environmental mastery. Mastery obviously also involves attitudes toward self, the development of autonomy, and the perception of reality. Conversely, progress toward mastery has repercussions on each of the other facets of the mental health criterion.

Children's Reactions

We can only conjecture about how effectively the schools further environmental mastery at the present time. Everyone knows youngsters who have not only found satisfaction from their schooling, but have emerged from it with real convictions about their own abilities and their future. They anticipate mastery. One 15-year-old, shortly following the announcement of Sputnik, wrote this about his reactions:

> What a time to live! In five years we'll be on the moon!
>
> Every time I hear someone moaning about how he should have lived in the days of the Old West when men were men and about how the world today is a hopeless mess, I nearly throw up.
>
> And I want to be a part of it. So the Russians did it first. More power to them. They're going to need it to keep ahead of us now. 18,000 miles an hour. Ten years ago Bell had just finished going eight hundred and astonishing the world. Now, we're on our way. Vanguard will succeed, and Sputnik

> will have a couple of U.S.-type companions.
>
> And then in a few years, I come along. I and my generation are going to be the ones to see this thing off. We may not get to Mars, but the first men to leave the earth's atmosphere are going to be my contemporaries. Maybe me, if I can be so lucky. What a chance! How can a pioneer of three thousand miles of earth be compared to a pioneer of forty thousand miles of space? I'm on my way. Just watch my smoke!

But in contrast to the youngsters who regard the future with equanimity and see themselves taking active part in it, there are others who are resigned to passivity. They spend their days in waiting—waiting to be old enough for first grade, waiting to graduate from elementary school, waiting to graduate from high school, and then waiting for college, or waiting for marriage, or waiting for a job that involves waiting for quitting time. Then they wait for the coming of their children, who, unless war comes, will carry on the endless waiting, the endless rounds of meaningless activity. Or, as one commentator on the American scene has put it, "America will not perish from a bomb. It will perish from boredom."

The picture is exaggerated of course. But its prototype does exist. And to the extent that youngsters emerge from our schools without commitments, with little sense of personal challenge, beset by apathy, the schools appear to have failed in furthering environmental mastery. Furthermore, children who lack any real feelings of involvement, who evade using their intellectual powers, are probably to be found both in schools that are clearly traditional and in schools that still bear some of the trappings of progressivism.

The crucial test of any school's contribution to mental health lies not so much in the skills and knowledge it purports to teach as in its effectiveness in helping youngsters to incorporate these into their day-to-day living. It is a matter of using such skills and knowledge to strengthen and enhance each child's personal resources. But the question of whether the average school makes an appreciable difference in these respects is an open one. It is a question unlikely to be answered satisfactorily until certain basic issues have been resolved.

One such issue has to do with the matter of individuality in learning and thinking. To what extent can the school, predicated on the notion that children are to be taught in groups, provide adequately for each individual? Related to this is the problem of differences in the ways of learning and of thinking at different ages. When there is so much to be learned, how much leeway can the school have to adapt its instruction to these differences?

Still another issue relates to the fact that the glib use of words does not always reflect genuine understanding. Traditionally, the school has emphasized the verbal transmission of knowledge to the exclusion of other ways of knowing. How long can this continue if students are to develop the critical, creative thinking demanded for mastery in a complex modern world?

Teaching vs. Learning

An issue of somewhat different but nonetheless critical order has to do with the relationship between teaching and learning. Schools are prone to describe their curriculum in terms of what is taught. The more important question, of course, is "What has been learned?" But the nature of the learning very likely turns as much on *how* something is taught as it does on *what* is taught.

Around each of these issues are many questions that schools must face before they can hope to fulfill their mental health roles adequately.

First, the matter of *individuality in learning*. Although schools have long paid lip service to "individual differences," most school practice assumes common, average, or typical ways of learning. Yet, it is a specific emotional concern, a specific tendency to see a problem differently from the way others see it, a specific sensitivity to what one sees or hears or feels, that either inhibits or enhances learning. Clinical studies have shown that children's propensities for learning are related to their ways of coping with the emotional conflicts inherent in growing up. The accomplishment of a particular learning task may lead toward a constructive resolution of conflict for one child. The same task may be unproductive or even defeating for another child. Without training in recognizing the influence of these deeper motivations, can a teacher adequately diagnose the child's needs as a learner? To what extent can the curriculum provide leeway for the child to make the appropriate use of his unique ways of learning at the same time that he adapts to the ways of others? To further environmental mastery, where shall the balance between the nurturance of individuality and conformity to group trends be struck?

At a time when the furore of "keeping up with the Russians" puts a premium on the acceleration of learning, many persons press the schools to begin the "fundamentals" earlier, to start mathematics, science, and foreign languages sooner, and to push the "gifted" ahead. Although many children have already demonstrated their abilities to learn more than has typically been expected, many questions about pacing learning to development arise. For example, evidence from the administration of thousands of IQ tests, from other studies of conceptual development, from Piaget's research on children's thinking, as well as from psychoanalytic studies of young children, indicates that the young child's learning and his thinking is of an imaginative, manipulative, exploratory kind. Not until the middle school years does he begin to organize and systematize his knowledge in a truly logical fashion. Even then, he is still very much bound to the concrete in his thinking, and not until near adolescence do abilities to deal meaningfully with abstractions emerge.

Price of Hurry

What are the effects of the early introduction of generalizations and abstractions for which the child may have few experimental referents? Is it possible to further a kind of verbal environmental mastery at an early age, but at a price? The price, perhaps, of a lack of empathy toward one's fellows or what Jerome Bruner (4) has termed a lack of "passion" for ideas? Conversely, what happens to the child who is held in school to a concrete level when his mind is already taken up with the abstract? Is the concrete *always* enriching?

Many schools, from the kindergarten through the college, have reacted to current criticisms by putting more stress on "knowledge," which may be anything from the alphabet and the multiplication tables to the dates of the Punic Wars or the basic principles of atomic theory. Such knowledge often is acquired largely by memorization and repetitive drill and all too often is tested in similar fashion. No one doubts the importance of many of the facts youngsters are supposed to learn, but in relation to a mental health criterion of environmental mastery, the crucial question is their relevance to an individual coping with and understanding a changing world. A youngster needs to know facts; he also needs to know how and when to apply them. He needs, further, to know how to appraise and evaluate a given situation. Above all, he needs to know that there are many ways of knowing. The scientist does not always arrive at new ideas through processes of logical deduction. New insights often arise from undirected fantasy or from periods of conscious preoccupation with some other activity. A particular event can be "known" through direct sensory participation; it can be weighed, measured, analyzed into its components, put into a larger context, but often it may also be played with, painted, or danced.

Does the school contribute to environmental mastery when it leaves the student with the impression that there are so few ways of knowing? Or are *all* the ways of knowing not the business of the school?

With appalling frequency, many young teachers say today, "What I learned in my education courses does not help me in the classroom." Those of us who teach teachers often retort that they are merely looking for "recipes." But are they? Are they not saying that we have taught them about children, about learning, and about thinking without teaching them *how* to direct learning or *how* to change thinking?

In dealing with the nature of teaching as related to the nature of the learning and the thinking that ensues, we have come to what is likely the basic issue for mental health in the schools. Not until we know more specifically how teaching affects thinking can we know how extensively teachers can influence the development of environmental mastery.

When John Dewey formulated his ideas about learning and thinking, he surely intended to help youngsters toward a meaningful, intellectual mastery of the environment. But neither Dewey nor his followers spelled out in sufficient detail how a teacher may appraise the many kinds of thinking he encounters among his pupils, nor how he may help them to shift from ineffective to effective kinds. Too often the teacher, receiving his notions of Dewey's philosophy fourth or fifth hand, has been left with no better criterion for the value of a particular activity than "they learn by doing." Once a teacher loses sight of the intellectual goals to be realized in the pursuit of any activity, it often deteriorates into a free-for-all in which the immediate emotional concerns and needs of the youngsters dominate the situation. Many teachers are ill-equipped to deal directly with these and retreat from them to a more stereotyped and sterile but "safe" kind of teaching.

When the teacher's *primary* function is clearly seen to be that of teaching skills and understandings and ways of solving problems, it is clear that knowledge of children's ways of thinking and learning is an essential part of his professional repertoire. But, in addition, he needs skill in influencing that thinking and learning. Without such skills, it is doubtful that any teacher can effectively fulfill the mental health functions which are inherent in his role.

A few educators and psychologists are now beginning to examine the nature of the relationship between what the teacher does and what the children think. Such examination promises much for eventual understanding of the specific ways teachers can further environmental mastery. Current research programs at Bank Street College (3), for example, include an analysis of the teacher's involvement in the processes of the child's learning and thinking. Along with this goes study of the various ways the teacher offers emotional support to the child and helps him to build inner controls.

Many other centers are carrying on research related to thinking, and interest in the nature of teaching increases steadily. Examination of some of the research dealing with the nature of teaching on the one hand, and the nature of thinking on the other, suggests that both of these areas constitute important new resources for mental health in education.

Analyses of Teaching

Most of the research related to teaching is directed toward the questions of what it means to be a teacher and what it is that a teacher *does* in relation to his pupils that results in their learning and their thinking.

There is nothing new in the notion that effective teachers present material, ask questions, clarify understandings, and so on, in different ways from less effective teachers. What is new is the attempt to arrive at a framework for analyzing the teacher's behavior so that it becomes possible to pinpoint the places where his questions or his comments either enhance or forestall good thinking.

Interest in such analysis has arisen sponstaneously in several different centers. Bellack and Huebner (2), discussing the need for a theory of teaching, point out that in the 25 years prior to 1956 little if any research was directed specifically toward teaching. Apparently, in what would seem to be equally important activities in the school—the *giving* and the *taking* of instruction—much more systematic attention has been given to taking than to giving. B. O. Smith (14), an educational philosopher at the University of Illinois, is engaged in an attempt to describe and classify the actions, both verbal and expressive, that compose the teacher's repertoire. A colleague of Smith's, M. J. Aschner (1), describes the teacher as a strategist and tactician in the campaign for learning, noting that the teacher's repertoire includes not only what he does to instruct pupils, such as defining, explaining, showing, and admonishing, but also observing what his pupils do and say in response to these actions. "He does so in order to predict—to diagnose and adapt his teaching to the pupils' present state of comprehension and progress in learning, to appraise the quality of their reasoning and to assess their emotional reactions to the situation of the moment." This notion of prediction, Dr. Aschner cautions, is not the same as that implied in much current research in the psychological laboratory. Teachers do not see themselves as manipulators of student behavior by push-button techniques: "It is the teacher's task and purpose not to condition the responses or the learnings of his pupils, but to develop in them their own capacities to think and to act responsibly."

Marie Hughes (5) and her colleagues at the University of Utah have also attempted to analyze teachers' behavior in the classroom. They have studied teaching functions relating to the obviously intellectual content of the classroom experience, such as stimulating interest, clarifying content, and evaluating results, and also functions relating to the affective aspects of the learning situation. Many of the immediate outcomes of their study offer real cause for discouragement about the effectiveness of teachers in furthering active environmental mastery. Teachers judged "good" by their administrators exercised the controlling functions most frequently and most pervasively. They told the children both what they should do and how they should do it, what they should answer and how they should answer. The teachers gave the children very little opportunity to explore or expand ideas, or to make comparisons and inferences. The thinking processes they demanded were almost exclusively limited to identification and memory.

Dreary as these findings are, they also seem to hold some promise. These teachers were not "bad" teachers; they were not mean; they were simply ineffective. The reason for this probably lies in the fact that no one had ever helped them to see the variety of specific ways they could respond to children and, having so responded, the specific ways they could build on the ideas of the children. Given an opportunity to study an analysis of their own behavior and to discuss it with a nonthreatening consultant or counselor, could they not learn to modify their approach and to direct it toward opening new and richer avenues of inquiry?

Sauce for the Goose

Lawrence Kubie (10), in a devastating critique of education, has suggested that overemphasis on repetitive drill (and much that these teachers were doing *would* fall under the heading of repetitive drill) is symptomatic of anxiety, anger, and repression. But we may ask whether some (though by no means all) of the anxiety and the anger which teachers bring to the teaching situation may not arise in part out of the frustration involved in knowing that they are expected to do *something* about the learning of these children, while they remain basically uncertain as to *what* to do.

If we expect the acquisition of knowledge, skills, and understandings to enhance the ego development of youngsters, it is no less reasonable to anticipate that knowledge, skills, and understandings—provided always that their relevance to the teaching situation is clear—should also strengthen the teacher.

Some oblique evidence on this point comes from a current study by Jersild (8), relating to the effects of personal psychotherapy and psychoanalysis on teachers. Some of these teachers reported that as their therapy progressed, they were able to see more clearly and specifically how their own behavior in the classroom influenced the learning and the thinking of their pupils. At the same time, some of them noted an increasing ability to understand and hence to clarify the youngsters' confusions. Although, in these instances, the teachers' insights into their own functioning as teachers came only after therapy, their comments often suggested that they would not only have welcomed but could have benefited at an early point in their careers from a more penetrating analysis of what was involved in teaching.

Studies of teacher behavior by Levin (11) and others provide good evidence that teachers who have a high interest in children are most likely to remain in teaching. Such individuals, it would seem, would not be frightened but, rather, rewarded by an opportunity to examine their own techniques. They might welcome study of their own ways of relating to children with a view to seeing how these affect children's learning and thinking.

The notion that teachers and teachers-in-training would benefit from analysis of their teaching implies that such analysis would not be directed toward a single "right" way. Rather, consideration of the *variety* of ways one might respond in a given situation should lead to flexibility and help in the quick "on the spot" decisions which are part of the challenge and the fun of teaching.

Ultimately, of course, any analysis of the task of teaching leads back to the question of its effectiveness in relation to the achievement of the pupil. Some of the teacher's actions may further the pupil's learning and thinking. Others may serve only to block and confuse him. It is no accident that much of the current interest in the analysis of teaching comes from centers where there has also been continuing research related to thinking as revealed in the classroom.

Research on Thinking

The theoretical views on thinking held by two psychologists, Jean Piaget and Jerome Bruner, appear to have particular significance for the eventual resolution of some of the issues raised earlier.

Piaget's position, although well formulated, has been difficult for American investigators to interpret. But, many former skeptics are now impressed by his later work and by independent research validating a number of his ideas. These relate particularly to the question of developmental differences in thinking. Piaget uses the principles of formal logic as a basis for his analysis of thinking. He has arrived at a schematization of the emerging developmental stages of the abilities to deal either with increasingly complex problems or with simple problems in more efficient ways. Within the period covered by the years of schooling, there are three such stages. A preoperational or representational stage extends into the early childhood period. During this phase, much of the child's thinking is characterized by an inability to separate his own goals from the means for achieving them. In the later stage of concrete operations, extending from approximately 7 to 11 years, the child becomes increasingly able to organize the means for achievement of the goal independently of the goal itself. His operations are internalized and reversible, but he is still bound very closely to the immediately present object world. In the stage of formal operations, beginning around the age of 12, a stage which is preparatory to adult thinking, the ability to use hypothetical reasoning and controlled experimentation develops. The child is no longer bound to the concrete, but can deal directly with abstractions.

By and large, Piaget has seemed to his American colleagues to neglect the important role of motivation in thinking. Indeed, he has specified that the "structures" of intellect and affect must be regarded separately. Nevertheless, as various psychoanalytic writers have shown, and as he and his colleague, Inhelder (6), have brilliantly demonstrated in an analysis of adolescent thinking, the shift from one level of thinking to another is in many ways very closely bound up with the individual's life situation and with the changing nature of his needs, wishes, and desires.

Piaget is a genetic psychologist and biologist. He has never fully developed the implications of his position for the schooling of children. The main implication is, however, almost immediately apparent. If there are, as his theory indicates, built-in limitations in thinking at a particular level, then to confront the pupil with problems whose solutions are based on logical operations beyond his comprehension at that level must be to confront him with a meaningless task. If the solution his teacher expects is beyond him, it appears that for the moment at least, he and his teacher are really speaking in different languages. The student can, perhaps, if the teacher demands it, learn a solution by rote memory; but the words he mouths are little more than gibberish so far as real insight is concerned.

Jerome Bruner, unlike Piaget, does not deal with developmental differences in thinking, and his emphasis on motivation is somewhat different. Nevertheless, his viewpoint is in many ways compatible with Piaget's. His mode of attack on the nature of thinking seems likely to provide new insights into both the problem of individuality and that of the variety of ways of knowing.

Bruner views thinking as a complex process involving categorization, organization, transformation, and evaluation. Motivation is implied in and gives direction to each of these. This scheme for analyzing intellectual performance is currently being tested with children. Although children younger than ten years have not been involved in this study, the results are assumed to have general application, certainly to older children and probably to younger ones.

These youngsters under Bruner's observation have encountered a wide range of intellectual tasks, many of them clearly parallel to those usually involved in school learning. Examination of their performances in detail has indicated some of the dimensions on which this theory can be measured. One such dimension is *power*, which has to do with the youngster's perseverance and the range and order of approaches he uses in attempting to solve a problem. Another dimension involves individual *style* in thinking, a matter of the way the concepts the child brings to the problem are organized. A third, referred to as *conceptual distance*, reflects the child's ability to avoid becoming bound in the immediate and obvious and to keep his eventual goal in view. A dimension of *involvement* measures the degree of separation of the task from personal needs and demands. In this connection, it may be noted that some children appear to be almost exclusively task-oriented, whereas others are always much more directed toward pleasing the experimenter. Finally, there is a *rigidity-flexibility* dimension, related to the ability to recognize errors and change one's plans accordingly.

Bruner (4), has recently reported a study comparing learning effectiveness in normal children and in children with learning blocks—those with adequate or superior intelligence who were unable to learn in school.

Learning Blocks

The findings bear directly on the question of the school's responsibility for mental health. The children with learning blocks revealed cognitive organizations differing radically from those of the normal youngsters. Their thinking was dominated by what Bruner calls "preemptive metaphors," principles of organization biased toward overinclusion and overgeneralization. For example, a child whose early experiences have reinforced the idea that "things can hurt me" views his environment as a source of potentially disruptive events. A youngster of this sort is so busy reading possible destruction into the learning problems set for him and defending himself against it that he never copes with the reality problems.

Bruner believes that the thinking of persons who are "defenders" rather than "copers" has never moved beyond the action-and-affect-laden conceptualization characteristic of the young child. Such conceptualization, of course, also survives in the creativity of the artist and sometimes serves the disciplined thinking of the inventor and initiator. But it is not preemptive and distorting as it is in the child who thinks only defensively.

Bruner theorizes that the prevention of learning difficulties is dependent on three factors in the early history of the child. These include opportunities for play, opportunities for identification, and freedom from excessive drive and anxiety. Undoubtedly the family contributes most importantly to these, but the influence of the school is not negligible. A closer examination of these factors indicates some of the ways the school may function to further children's abilities to think adequately and to cope with their environment realistically rather than merely defensively.

Play, according to Bruner and others, reduces the pressures of impulse and incentive and makes intrinsic learning possible. Piaget also indicates that play is important, especially during the period when the child is developing basic notions about the nature of the world. Thus, a first step toward the conviction that intellectual activity has an inherent worth comes in doing things for fun, and an early childhood education program based on play takes on added significance.

So far as identification is concerned, the child first emulates the models he finds in his own family. But teachers, provided they are individuals for whom children can have warm and positive feelings, may also serve as models and, if they are competent, importantly influence children's ways of thinking.

The third factor mentioned by Bruner also relates to the behavior of the teacher. Excessive drive and anxiety inhibit effective thinking. Too much pressure on learning, too many external rewards and punishments, lead to blocking and functional stupidity on the part of the would-be learner.

Illustrative of the inevitable enmeshing of teaching and thinking is a recent six-year study by Sarason (12) and others. This inquiry revealed many children with good intellectual potential who were unable to function adequately in school. It appeared that very often the techniques used by their teachers mobilized rather than allayed these children's anxieties. Unfortunately, relatively few of the teachers were able to identify the anxiety-prone children in their classrooms. Nor were they able to avoid anxiety-arousing techniques in dealing with them.

Undoubtedly, many teachers are benignly unaware of the inhibiting effects certain comments and expressions have on many children. Others deliberately push and prod in the mistaken notion that they are thus providing needed motivation. They assume that learning is necessarily painful and overlook the fact that success in learning often provides a powerful incentive to further learning.

Learning by Machine

Evidence on this point comes from current research on teaching machines. This research also throws considerable light on many of the relationships between teaching and thinking. Teaching machines, as developed under the direction of B. F. Skinner (13), operate on the principle that a very complex concept can be broken down into a series of related ideas—learning these ideas step by step according to a "program" leads to eventual comprehension of the large idea. Unlike a textbook, which may skip an essential step for the student, each step in the program for the machine must be made explicit. The person who sets up a program must not only know the subject matter to be taught, but also the thinking processes through which it can be mastered. The record of the student's errors indicates the places where the programmer failed to anticipate confusion. The machines may thus contribute to improved knowledge of both teaching and thinking.

Many educators have taken a dim view of the development of the machines for a variety of reasons. The machines do involve the manipulation of student behavior by push-button techniques. Some of their appeal to the learner may depend on their novelty, and that appeal may diminish. They promote some kinds of thinking and learning, but are inappropriate for others. The effectiveness of any machine is entirely dependent on the nature of the program given it. This, in turn, depends on the person who develops the program, how well he understands the subject the machine is to teach, and the thinking processes involved in mastering it.

But the machines appear to have some very positive attributes. The student makes an active response. He does not parrot an answer, but must compose or select the appropriate idea. The machine is set up so that he makes progress through making the correct responses in a sequence intended to lead him to increasing competence and understanding. The machine eliminates the kinds of verbal and expressive behavior on the part of the teacher that may either enhance or confuse learning in the usual classroom situation. The child is "in contact" only with the person who made the program on which the machine operates. For some children, a machine may be considerably less threatening than a teacher! In general, however, the purposes of mental health and environmental mastery would seem best served only when the machine is used as an adjunct to the teacher. It could provide opportunities for individuals to proceed at their own rates, obviate much of the needless repetition which is now so prevalent, and free the teacher to function in a more truly creative and individualized way with youngsters.

In the long run, of course, the question of whether or not the school can promote mental health lies directly with the teacher. The teacher, more than most other persons can, I believe, further the youngster's efforts toward active, healthy mastery. He can help him with the specific skills and knowledge traditionally held to be the business of the school. He can also help him toward the critical, evaluative, creative kinds of thinking needed to cope with an environment that is ever changing.

But if the teacher is to accomplish these things, he too must have help. His mental health function needs to be clarified and reduced to comprehensible size. He needs more than a firm grasp of the skills and knowledge he is expected to teach his pupils. He needs to understand thinking processes. He needs to know very specifically what it means to teach and how what he does as a teacher influences the thinking and the learning of those he teaches.

References

1. Aschner, M. J., "The Language of Teaching," *Teachers College Record*, LXI (1960), 242–52.

2. Bellack, A. and D. Huebner, "Teaching," *Review of Educational Research*, XXX (1960), 246–50.

3. Biber, Barbara, "Integration of mental health principles in the school setting," in G. Caplan, ed., *Prevention of Mental Disorders in Children*. New York: Basic Books, Inc., 1961.

4. Bruner, J., "On coping and defending." Address to the American Psychological Association, September 1959.

5. Hughes, Marie *et al., Assessment of the Quality of Teaching in Elementary Schools*. Salt Lake City: University of Utah, 1959.

6. Inhelder, Barbel and J. Piaget, *The Growth of Logical Thinking from Childhood to Adolescence*. New York: Basic Books, Inc., 1958.

7. Jahoda, M., *Current Concepts of Positive Mental Health*. New York: Basic Books, Inc., 1958.

8. Jersild, A. T. and E. A. Lazar, *The Meaning of Psychotherapy in the Teacher's Life and Work*. New York: Bureau of Publications, Teachers College, Columbia University, 1962.

9. Kotinsky, Ruth and J. V. Coleman, "Mental Health as an Educational Goal," *Teachers College Record*, LVI (1955), 267–76.

10. Kubie, L., *Education and the Process of Maturation*. New York: Bank Street Publications, 1958.

11. Levin, H. *et al.*, "Studies of Teacher Behavior," *Journal of Experimental Education*, XXVI (1957), 81–92.

12. Sarason, S. B., *Anxiety in Elementary School Children*. New York: John Wiley & Sons, Inc., 1960.

13. Skinner, B. F. "Teaching Machines," *Science*, CXXVIII (1958), 969–77.

14. Smith, B. O., "A Concept of Teaching," *Teachers College Record*, LXI (1960), 229–41.

41. ARE WE EDUCATING FOR MATURITY?

LAWRENCE S. KUBIE

I am impatient with educators and psychiatrists, with scientists and artists—with all of us in fact—for our failure to implement criticism of education by an experimental search for new ways.

My central thesis here is that we do not need to be taught to *think*; indeed that thinking is something that cannot be taught. Memorizing (i.e., the recording and recalling of factual data) and also creative thinking (i.e., the assembling of such data in new combinations) are automatic, swift, and spontaneous processes, if these are allowed to proceed undisturbed by other influences.

Under ideal circumstances, memory and thinking are carried on neither consciously nor unconsciously but in the preconscious stream of automatic mentation, which proceeds at phenomenal speed. Of this swift stream, conscious processes provide us with tentative summaries and fragmentary samples; but conscious and, even more, unconscious processes combine to distort and delay and impede and sometimes wholly to block the processes of conscious summary and sampling by which the data from the preconscious stream can be put to work in human affairs.

For this, there is abundant clinical and experimental evidence, the crucial implications of which have been largely neglected by educators. What we need is to learn how to avoid interfering with this inherent preconscious capacity of the human mind.

This concept of a preconscious core of all human mentation is essential to my thesis. It implies that there is an incessant current of thought and feeling which is incredibly swift, which is neither conscious nor unconscious, which can learn, record, recall, and respond appropriately and also creatively, and all this without conscious awareness of any one of these steps.

We need also to be helped to im-

Lawrence S. Kubie, "Are We Educating for Maturity?" N.E.A. JOURNAL *(January 1959), pp. 58–63. Reprinted by permission.*

prove the tools of conscious sampling and communication: i.e., how to read and listen to words, how to speak and write them. Yet even this is only one component in the complex art of communication, since here again the imperative need is to learn how not to let unconscious conflicts, affects, and defenses distort the work of even the fully educated eye and ear and tongue and hand.

Eventually, education must accept the full implications of the fact that the free creative velocity of our thinking apparatus is continually being braked and driven off course by the play of unconscious forces. As long as educational procedures refuse to recognize this, they will continue to increase this interference from masked and unrecognized neurotogenic processes. This happens in school today from the first grade through the highest echelons of postgraduate study.

It has long been known that in early years children have extraordinarily inventive imaginations, and use delightful and original figures of speech and allegory. What happens to this poetic gift when it is exposed to formal education? Or to rephrase the question: What happens to the free play of preconscious (spontaneous, "intuitive") functions in the course of conventional education?

It has been the assumption of education that learning would make man wise, mature, and creative. It is my unhappy conviction that learning alone achieves none of these goals, but more frequently is a mask for immaturity, neurosis, and a lack of wisdom. Furthermore, much of the learning which has traditionally been looked upon as an essential attribute of the educated man has no necessary relevance either to creativity or to maturity. Instead many ingredients in the very process by which men become learned tend actively to prevent psychological growth. It is not learning or the learning process which matures men; it is maturity, however won, which makes it possible for men to learn and to be creative with their learning.

I must warn that I am not going to prescribe remedies for this state of affairs, or to describe preventive measures. We must diagnose before we can cure or prevent; and educators must first acknowledge that something is amiss, before they will even tolerate a search for remedies.

I will be content if I am able to convince even a few that there is something quite basically wrong with our approach to education, and then to define what is wrong in terms of the crippling influence on the creative process of much of what now occurs in school. Only at the end will I suggest a few directions in which it is reasonable to seek for corrective or preventive techniques.

This is as far as I will presume to go; but I hope that experienced educators, with their more intimate knowledge of the details of educational procedures, may be able to offer more definitive remedies. Indeed, some educators and certain special schools have begun to attack the problems that I will describe. But I must leave this to them. My function is to challenge, not to offer panaceas.

The premises from which I start are not happy ones. Nor are they pessimistic, since they carry the implication that if we face these problems, we can solve them and that if we solve them, we will open a new era in human culture. Let me then state my premises.

The great cultural institutions of human society, including art and literature, science, education in general, the humanities and religion, have three essential missions: namely, to enable human nature itself to change; to enable each generation to transmit to the next whatever wisdom it has gained about living; to free the enormous untapped creative potential which is latent in varying degrees in all men.

It is my belief that in all of these respects our great cultural efforts and institutions have failed, and will continue to fail until new techniques of education are developed.

Evidence for this is found in the fact that our knowledge of the external world and our ability to represent the world as it is or as we would like it to be has grown enormously, while our ability to meet wisely the challenge of how to be human beings has not developed. Everyone acknowledges this intellectually; yet few have accepted the full implications which this failure entails for education itself as an instrument of human growth.

The failure of education to make it possible for man to change is due to a specific component in human nature; to wit, that psychological rigidity which is the basic and universal expression of the neurotic process. Indeed, this neurotogenic rigidity is so universal that it is frequently accepted as normal (even among some psychiatrists), as though the mere fact that everybody is rigid in one or more aspects of his personality means that rigidity is normal.

Since all that I will say is predicated upon what I regard as this basic failure of human culture, I will list the indices of this failure:

1. There is the universality of the neurotic process itself, which is manifested with minor variations in every culture about which we know anything.

2. There is the resulting failure of the race as a whole, and of men as individuals, to evolve and change psychologically.

3. There is the failure of all traditional methods to impart to successive generations that wisdom about living which a few individuals in each generation slowly acquire. Specifically, the kinds of behavioral conventions which protect the association of men into livable societies are well known. We call these ethical principles. Yet we do not know how to perpetuate and inculcate such ethical principles, nor how to seat them firmly in the saddle of human affairs.

These are basic gaps in our knowledge of how to transmit the fruits of experience from one generation to the next. The consequence is that in forms which change only in detail, country after country and generation after generation repeat the errors of their predecessors.

These manifestations of the failure of culture signify that the universal masked neurotic component in "normal" human nature is the major obstacle to progress. No system of education which fails to accept this challenge can educate in any meaningful sense. Therefore, we must ask ourselves whether the educational process as we know it increases or decreases in the student the sway of hidden neurotic forces in his life. It is my contention that education as it is increases the power of the neurotic processes in our culture, and that this need not be true.

Every adult bears the imprint of the child. The unconscious projection of the years of childhood onto the screen of adult years anchors us to the past. Consequently, the educator who is interested in making education assist the individual to move toward maturity must study how such projections from the past influence education, and whether the educational process tends to perpetuate their influence.

First of all, we face the obvious fact that the schoolroom and school as a whole confront the child with substitute parents and siblings. This provides an opportunity to resolve the fateful and destructive conflicts of the nursery. Yet the opportunity is not utilized. Instead, the child in school merely relives and buries even deeper the hates and loves and fears and rivalries which had their origins in his home.

The schoolroom may partially balance or neutralize these conflict-laden feelings; but it fails utterly to render them less fixed and less rigid *by bringing them within the reach of conscious selection, direction, and control.* Self-control, as it is taught, is almost invariably concentrated on control of the secondary consequences of such conflicts, rather than focusing on the elimination of their inner sources.

One could choose at random a number of illustrations of the consequences of this. There is the child who in his struggle with authority becomes an obsessional dawdler. This will have begun in the nursery in dawdling about eating, washing, or dressing. Unless this neurotic deviation has been effectively resolved in the home before the youngster reaches school, it will warp his every activity in this new setting.

At the opposite pole from the obsessional dawdler is the compulsive rusher, the youngster who has to plunge headlong from one half-finished task to another, afraid to tarry long enough to complete anything lest he be overtaken by some nameless fate, some dreaded exposure. These two oppositely paced obligatory patterns may alternate in the same individual, and may arise out of almost identical unconscious conflicts.

The relevant and disconcerting point is that both of these opposing neurotic patterns (as well as others) tend to be reinforced and not lessened by the pressure of our formal educational processes. Yet instead of giving the child insight into and freedom from this reaction to authority, the school usually increases its paralyzing influence. Consequently, it persists to plague the lifework of potentially brilliant and creative adults.

Many such adults are seduced by the illusory freedom of a blind automatic rejection of all external authority. Yet because the road to external freedom is never found by submitting to irresponsible internal compulsion, these obligatory rebels pay for this in the stereotyped and repetitive quality of their pseudorebellious productions, whether these are in literature, art, music, politics, or science.

In considering how to deal with these difficult and ubiquitous problems, we do not need to conjure up a Utopian school in which no nursery battles would be reenacted. Whether the immediate and remote effects of such conflicts upon each child and adult are creative or destructive will depend not upon the mere fact that such struggles occur, but upon the *level on which they are waged*, i.e., whether this level is preponderantly conscious, preconscious, or unconscious.

Therefore the schools face the challenge to see what they can do to make sure that these battles will be fought out on conscious and preconscious levels. It would seem that an essential aspect of any truly educational experience would be to enable each child to face in himself those painful conflicts from which he shrinks, but which shape his character.

Neither traditional disciplinary education nor progressive education solves the technical problems which this goal involves. Disciplinary techniques alone, even when seemingly successful, give the child a sense that he must control *something*, but fail to make clear what there is inside that needs controlling or redirecting.

In its early years, progressive education encouraged the child to act out his problems, but failed to realize that acting out will not alone bring any increase in self-understanding or in self-mastery. Indeed, like blind discipline, blind acting out can distort and block insight—as it does in the case of the psychopath.

In addition to its failure to accept the challenge of buried neurotogenic processes, even at its current best, the educative process tends to reinforce the neurotic process through the misuse of the techniques of repetitive drill.

In the tangled interweaving of the processes of learning and the neurotic process, repetition plays a major role. By imperceptible gradations, the repetitive drills of the learning process shade over into the automatic involuntary repetitions of the neurosis. This intensification of the neurotic process through repetitive drill mars our educational system from primary grades through professional and graduate levels.

Limitless repetition without the guidance of insight is not merely self-defeating; it does deeper damage by hampering spontaneous, "intuitive," i.e., preconscious, functions.

Nevertheless, in the acquisition of skills, many teachers continue to place major emphasis on repetitive drill; and this in spite of the well-known and repeatedly demonstrated fact that the most efficient learning is essentially effortless and almost instantaneous.

For example, under hypnosis enormous amounts of material can be recorded effortlessly, almost as on a photographic plate. Here drill and repetition play no role, and their introduction would merely interfere with automatic recording and recall. In general, the degree to which learning depends upon repetitive drill is a measure of the degree to which guilt, anxiety, anger—whether conscious or unconscious—are blocking the assimilative component of education.

For a number of reasons, therefore, we are forced to conclude that there is a continuous conflict rather than a happy alliance between erudition and maturity. This conflict begins in the primary grades and continues unabated to and through postgraduate education.

Every educator knows scholars who lack the least quality of human maturity and wisdom, yet who are technical masters of their own fields, whether this field is the humanities, art, music, philosophy, religion, law, science, the history of ideas, or the languages by which men communicate ideas. The measure of our wisdom about living is determined neither by the breadth of the area of our knowledge nor by the sharpness of the focus of our specialization.

It might shed some light on the elusive relationship between formal education and maturation to consider what happens to medical students when they are brought into contact with the sufferings of patients. This is a moment which forces them to accept some measure of responsibility for human suffering other than their own. For each student, this is an experience which precipitates a powerful, if masked, internal struggle among conflicting impulses.

Shall he cling to the unrecognized prerogative of childhood to shut out the suffering of others or even secretly to exult in it? Or shall he yield to those simultaneous, powerful internal and external pressures of medical tradition to accept the challenge of human needs other than his own? Will it extricate him from the cocoon of his childhood to identify with other individuals through ministering to them?

This may give us a clue to other basic defects in our educational process. Perhaps above anything else, the adolescent needs not only to be exposed to human suffering, but also to be given the responsibility of ministering to it. Yet instead of this, the educational years cultivate in each student a maximal concentration on himself. Moreover, we know that the essence of maturity can come only through the insight which arises out of the interaction between living and blundering, and then of studying and dissecting our blunders. Neither living without self-study nor study without living is enough.

One obvious implication runs through everything I have said; namely, that if education is to become a matter not only of the mind but of the spirit, and if it is ever to facilitate the maturing process instead of limiting and distorting it, then it must deal with the universal, masked, neurotic ingredient in human nature. Clearly then, self-knowledge in depth is essential for any solution.

It is my conviction that education without this understanding can never mean wisdom or maturity; and that self-knowledge in depth is a process which, like education itself, is never complete. It is a process which goes on throughout life. Like the fight for external freedom, the fight for this inner freedom from the internal tyranny of unconscious processes demands eternal vigilance and continuous struggle.

This is because in every one of us, from the beginning of life until its end, active forces are at work which tend repeatedly to confuse and obscure our images of ourselves. Consequently, those who do not struggle continuously throughout life to attain and then to retain self-knowledge in depth cannot be creative. Without such knowledge, society has no adults, but only aging children, armed with words and paint and clay and atomic weapons, none of which they understand.

And since self-knowledge has been a neglected aspect of our educational system, and indeed of human culture in general, most scholars have been only erudite rather than wise. Wisdom when it has graced any one of us has come not by design but as a happy accident. This challenges us to have the courage to face this failure of education as we have always known it, with a determination to do something effective about it.

Even if we do not already possess the technique by which to implement fully our determination, we can at least formulate our goals.

The increasing duration of the

process of formal education tends to imprison the student for many decades in an adolescence of limited responsibility in which he lives on a dole from an adult world toward which—whether or not he manifests it openly—he harbors much unconscious hostility. Thus we obstruct the very processes of maturation for which we are striving.

I take it for granted that our educational processes must continue to last longer and longer. This means, however, that unless the student is exposed concurrently to maturing experiences, he will continue to end up as an erudite adolescent. The need to achieve the fullest degree of intellectual preparation without emotional stunting challenges us to find ways in which without limiting education we can facilitate those aspects of emotional maturity which emanate only from the direct experience of living and from carrying a sobering responsibility for others.

Yet the amount of data which every educated man must master is enormous already and is constantly increasing. Moreover, we know that if we hold him at the student level too long, the process of emotional maturation which is so essential an ingredient of education is in danger of being stunted. Obviously, then, some means must be found to remake the life of the student, so that in itself it will become a maturing experience. Alternatively, periods of study must be interspersed with periods devoted to other types of experiences, or techniques of psychotherapy must be adapted to the educational scene to supplement formal education in the service of greater emotional maturity.

When we meet the currently popular and all too easy assumption that the humanities will solve our problems, we should remind the optimist that the humanities have never served us that well in the past.

We cannot be wise, yet remain immature. Maturity requires the capacity to change, to become different, to react in varied and unanticipated ways. The emotional and intellectual maturity which the returning veteran brought to his studies after World War II, the subtle birth of maturity in the medical student as he first experiences the suffering of others and participates in its alleviation, what we have learned about the imprisoning of the human spirit by the neurotic process—all these indicate the directions toward which we must move as we seek solutions to these fundamental problems of how education for the first time in human history can enable the human spirit to grow and change. Progress will not come just from sitting back and hoping. It will come only as a reward for an uncompromising defense of the creative value of doubt, and from an unsparingly critical reexamination of every educational premise.

42. TEACHER TRAINING AND EMOTIONAL NEEDS

LOUIS E. RATHS

Within the past twenty-five years there has been a very great emphasis within professional education on the desirability of "meeting the emotional needs of children." It is probably true that throughout all recorded history there are writings which touch upon this point. It is also undoubtedly true that the pioneering work of Freud in the study of neurotic personalities contributed very greatly to an increased understanding of the role of emotional needs in the behavior of people, and it was also due to the work of Freud that educators came to see the great significance of experiences in early childhood on the later development of personality. Simultaneously, with the great depression of the early thirties, various leaders in education saw the necessity for some systematic, organized attack on the problem of how to identify these needs and how best to try to meet these needs.

The Progressive Education Association became the organizing center for this more and more, so far as this accelerated emphasis was concerned. Through the planning of people in the Association, with the aid of consultants from a number of fields, with the cooperation of many public and private school administrators, they submitted a plan which resulted in the organization of The Eight Year Study which included thirty secondary schools of the United States. A number of commissions and committees were organized to study and to report on significant developments that had bearing on the education of children. One of these commissions, under the untiring and intelligent leadership of Caroline Zachry, concentrated much of its attention on the needs of youth. At the same time, Dr. Alice Keliher headed up the Commission on Human Relations and she and her associates produced books, pamphlets, and motion picture

Louis E. Raths, "Teacher Training and Emotional Needs," JOURNAL OF EDUCATIONAL SOCIOLOGY, *XXIV, No. 7 (March 1951), 369–80. Reprinted by permission.*

excerpts which paid particular attention to some of the emotional problems of youth and growing up in our society. The work of these two outstanding leaders influenced considerably the educational thinking of that time. Other committees working within the framework of the Progressive Education Association produced a number of books and reports dealing with the role of various academic subjects in the education of youth, and nearly all of these writings stressed the great importance of certain needs of secondary-school students. At the same time, a number of educational leaders associated with The Eight Year Study were often invited to speak at meetings of educational associations, at faculty meetings, at particular schools, to parents' meetings, and over and over again there was a great stress on the role of emotional needs in the adjustment of adolescents. These leaders had been associated with psychologists, with psychoanalysts, with anthropologists, with sociologists, with physicians, with frontier thinkers in the field of teacher education, and with teachers, parents, and children. Out of these associations had come a firm conviction that emotions had been neglected in the educative processes; that attention had been given almost exclusively to intellectual factors in the learning process, and that a concern for the all-around growth and development of children required a reconstruction of our beliefs and practices as these related to the emotional needs that were pressing for recognition.

In many of these writings a great variety of such emotional needs were postulated and leaders were exhorted to pay more attention to meeting the needs of children. Among the needs most frequently mentioned were: (1) the need for belonging, (2) the need for achievement, and (3) the need for love and affection. Studies of delinquency seemed to show a correlation between the neglect of these needs and delinquent behavior. Studies of difficulty in the learning process seemed to indicate that emotional maladjustment was often associated with the blocking of normal progress in educational achievement. Studies of social acceptance and rejection seemed to indicate that students with frustrated emotional needs had greater difficulty in making friends and getting along with people. The theory was suggested that aggression directed toward minority groups might well have its origin in the frustrated needs of those who were aggressive. Because the depression was affecting family life so significantly, it was suggested that economic insecurity brought with it anxiety and tension, and that under these conditions adjustment was more difficult and learning more difficult too.

Over and over again it was suggested to teachers that one of their most important jobs was "to meet the needs of children." Just how this could be done was often left as an exercise for the individual teacher who had heard the speech or who had read the materials in which this directive was laid down. It was pretty clear that before one could meet the needs of children it was certainly necessary to be able to identify some of those needs. It was also pretty clear that some kind of systematic procedure had to be developed for teaching procedures and curriculum development, once the needs had been identified.

A significant contribution was made by H. A. Murray in his book,

Personality, a Psychological Approach. He listed 44 needs and described them in some detail. He also suggested ways of getting evidence bearing upon these needs, and his writings were widely discussed and many of his techniques were used in experimental researches. One of his methods included a projective procedure called the Thematic Aperception Test. He also called attention to a number of other projective types of procedures.

One important development of Keliher's work was represented by a series of motion picture film excerpts. These represented problems in human relationships, and the excerpting was done in such a manner that solutions were not presented. The audience, composed usually of secondary-school students, were then invited to discuss the excerpt that they had seen. In general, these discussions by adolescent youth tended to show that they projected their own problems and their own needs into the pictures thus shown. Skillful observers were able to note some of the more pressing needs of the discussants. Both the work of Murray and the work of Keliher seemed to depend upon very highly informed and very expertly trained leaders. The writer may be doing an injustice to these contributors, but it does seem clear that their work did not penetrate into the classrooms of the country to the extent that was expected.

It seemed evident that the rank and file of teachers were in need of some more direct attack on the problem of meeting needs. The rank and file of the teaching profession were hardly prepared to understand and to apply what had thus far been discovered. Moreover, no systematic proof was then available that these needs did exist or that they did have serious influence on learning and on the total growth and development of children. There was a wealth of illustrations, a wealth of anecdotes, but there was no conclusive evidence that attempts to meet needs would result in significantly changed behavior. There was a faith that this would happen, there was a faith that this could happen and that the effort should be made.

With respect to learning, the theory received support from a great many teachers who had met with failure as they repeatedly addressed themselves to the so-called "intellectual analyses" of difficulties in learning. The recommended techniques for the improvement of reading, for example, often resulted in little or no progress, and teachers who used these techniques came to see that emotional problems were involved in these learning difficulties. Here again there was no proof with respect to this point but there was a widespread sharing of experiences, and out of these experiences there came the feeling on the part of many leaders in education that more attention needed to be given to the emotional needs of children.

Twenty-five years have now passed since this trend began to assume importance in professional educational circles. It can truly be said that teachers all over the nation have become much more sensitive to the role of emotions in the learning process and in the social adjustment of children. It can also truly be said that even now we do not have any conclusive proof, experimental proof, of the existence of emotional needs and their direct relationships to learning, or to behavior. This relationship seems to be one "that everybody knows and that no one has demonstrated."

Moreover, there is no listing of needs which has received the blessings of leaders in psychology, anthropology, or education. Human personality is conceived to be infinitely varied. Needs are thought to be infinite in their number and widely varying in their expression. A concept so vague and so all-embracing with respect to personality leaves much to be desired with respect to the organization of teacher education, both preservice and in-service. The facts, however, seem to support such a generalization about the infinite variability of human needs and the expression of these needs in behavior.

Nonetheless, teachers were anxious and often expressed intense desire to have some organized systematic training in identifying needs and also some training in ways of helping to meet these needs. The practical problem which these teachers faced day by day was one which demanded attention. There was an urgent demand for some kind of training which would help teachers to gain some insight into the role of emotional needs, some systematic training in trying to identify some of the emotional needs of children who are having difficulty in school, and some systematic training in ways of trying to meet the needs of these youngsters. When one thinks of ways of helping teachers in these several directions, one thinks immediately about the necessity for a curriculum that has continuity and sequence to it; a curriculum that would focus directly upon some emotional needs, a curriculum which would illustrate the behavior of people who seem to have these needs, and a curriculum which would allow teachers to engage in activities that would test out different procedures in attempting to meet these needs.

Dollard and others had brought out a book entitled *Frustration and Aggression*. In their writings they postulated that aggressive behavior was an outcome of the frustration of emotional needs. They indicated also that submissive behavior was a possible outcome of the frustration of these needs. Flanders Dunbar conducted an investigation relating to psychosomatic illness and it was her conclusion that many of these illnesses had their origin in emotional disturbances. Amongst teachers it was widely held that the child who was an isolate, a fringer, a nonparticipant, was also a student whose emotional needs were not being met. With this basis it became possible to meet with groups of teachers and to ask them to identify children in their classrooms who were unusually and characteristically aggressive, who were unusually and characteristically submissive, who were unusually and characteristically withdrawn from the group, and who were unusually and characteristically "ill" when emotional pressures became intense. It was not a very difficult matter to identify children who represented extremes in these behaviors. They were the source of "trouble" in the classrooms, and they were more or less "problems" with the teachers. The most common, of course, were the so-called "aggressive" ones.

If the theory was sound, children exhibiting these behaviors to a marked extent were the children who were supposed to have intense emotional needs. The next step in the process was to try to study the behavior of these children and to identify, if possible, any emotional needs that seemed to be present. At this time, efforts were made, in working with groups of teachers, to have no finite list of needs which would direct observations. The long list suggested by Murray was singled out for attention. The writings of Prescott, of Zachry, of Kotinsky, and of Alberty and others became a basis for studying the behavior of children. In general, the attempts failed and the opinion was held that until some more simplified method of attack was developed, success was highly improbable so far as in-service teacher education was concerned. It seemed fairly clear that some listing of needs was necessary as a framework. It seemed clear also that materials had to be found which teachers could study and which would focus upon this simplified listing.

An attempt was then made to solicit from teachers their own opinions about needs which seemed to have direct relationships to problems in the classroom. In these discussions suggestions were made to the teachers which derived from Freud, Zachry, Keliher, Frank, Plant, Prescott, Rogers, and many others. Out of these discussions the writer generalized a list of eight emotional needs that seemed to find acceptance with teachers with whom he had worked, and that had some support in the literature that was then current. It was decided to concentrate upon the following needs:

1. The need for belonging
2. The need for achievement and recognition
3. The need for economic security
4. The need to be relatively free from fear
5. The need for love and affection
6. The need to be relatively free from intense feelings of guilt
7. The need for self-respect and sharing in the values that direct one's life
8. The need for guiding purposes in understanding of the world in which one lives

The decision to concentrate on these *eight* needs was a matter of convenience. The teachers with whom the writer was working seemed to agree that these offered a starting point and that if these could be defined fairly clearly, illustrated profusely, then attempts could be made to develop procedures which would be helpful in trying to meet those needs. The next problem became one of organizing some kind of curriculum for teachers out of which these understandings might come.

Professor Alberta Young of the University of Tennessee agreed to accept the major responsibility for undertaking this task. Over a period of two years she worked on the problem of developing a curriculum that could be used in the training of teachers with primary emphasis on an understanding of these eight selected needs. Her work resulted in a doctoral dissertation at Ohio State University. It was a pioneering work and of great importance in the subsequent chain of events.

After she had developed a resource unit in this area, Professor Anna Carol Fults, now with the University of Florida, used this curriculum as a basis for training teachers in an experiment which she conducted in Arkansas.[1] In her work with these junior high school teachers, the group identified the so-called "problems" in their classrooms. They then tried to identify some of the needs of these youngsters and they limited themselves to a study of the eight needs

[1] Anna Carol Fults, "Improving Learning Through an Emphasis on Human Relations in an In-service Teacher Education Program." Ph.D. Dissertation, Ohio State University, 1946.

listed above. Working together, they started to devise a list of "do's and don'ts" in working with children who had specific emotional needs. They tried to carry through a systematic educational treatment of these needs over a period of a semester. They took measures before and after, of academic achievement, of IQ, of social acceptance, and they kept anecdotal records of manifest behavior. The conclusions of the study pointed conclusively to the fact that the teachers' attempts to meet needs seemed to be accompanied by significant changes in the measurements that were made. This was not, of course, any proof of the existence of needs as such. It was a demonstration that if teachers worked with children in these ways, certain changes took place.

A number of similar studies were carried on at different age levels. One was done by Professor Katheryn Feyereisen now on the faculty at Wayne University in Detroit. Still a third was carried on by Professor Anna Porter Burrell now on the faculty of Buffalo State Teachers College. In these studies the same general procedures were followed and the curriculum materials developed by Professor Alberta Young were utilized in the in-service training of teachers. In general, again, the results showed positive changes in an overwhelming majority of the children selected for remedial work with respect to emotional needs.

In 1949 Professor Robert Fleming of the University of Tennessee attempted a study in which with the aid of nurses, physicians, teachers, and parents certain school children were identified as having chronic symptoms of psychosomatic illness. These children became the focus of further study in an attempt to identify whether or not any of the eight needs previously listed were being thwarted. The same curriculum materials were used for an in-service training program with teachers and in some instances with parents. . . . His conclusions support the general idea that if attempts are made to meet some of these emotional needs, the frequency of the symptoms and the intensity of the symptoms of illness tend to decline. Other gains were also reported.

Dr. Frank A. Mann, now of Temple University, set for himself the task of surveying a relatively large number of classrooms in order to determine the frequency with which needs made themselves manifest in the behavior of children and to determine how frequently teachers characterized children as overly aggressive, overly submissive, overly withdrawn or chronically ill in a psychosomatic sense. His results . . . tend to reinforce what has previously been expressed as opinion so far as the frequency of unmet needs are concerned and the frequency with which deviant behavior of a serious kind tends to assert itself.

In all of these studies, not one of the investigators has taken the position that these particular eight needs constitute the range of needs which are important in the lives of children. They have taken the position that among the many emotional needs of children these eight appear frequently, seem to be closely related to certain kinds of behavior, and tend to affect the learning process rather significantly. It follows from this that perhaps other needs should be given equal attention, should be clearly defined, should be illustrated in terms of children's behavior, and should be identifiable through close observation of behavior. In the same fashion, those "to be added" needs should be studied in terms of what teachers can do to help children more satisfactorily to meet these needs. The work of many of these graduate students and cooperating teachers, children and parents in the several studies have culminated in the publication of two booklets which have had extensive distribution in more than twenty-five states of the nation. The first of these, *An Application to Education of the Needs Theory,*[*] contains rather specific directions and procedures for trying to identify these eight emotional needs. The second booklet, *Do's and Don't of the Needs Theory,*[*] consists almost exclusively of hundreds of ideas for teachers who are anxious to make some attempt to meet the needs of children in their classrooms. The publications have proved to be of great help to classroom teachers who are seeking to bring about desirable change in the growth and development of their children. The booklets themselves, however, do not provide a design for "proving" the existence of a particular need or a pattern of needs. The various researches that have been carried on have not been designed to verify the existence of particular needs or groups of needs as such. Instead, all of these researches have had as their purpose an attempt to do something with children *who seem to have one or more of these needs.* The significance of each of these studies has consisted in demonstrating worthwhile changes which have occurred in the behavior of children. The studies have not proved that attempts to meet these needs caused the changes to occur; neither have these studies proved the existence of the needs. Over and over again, however, they have demonstrated that as teachers try to work with disturbed children in the ways that are suggested, in a very, very large proportion of the cases desirable changes have taken place. Perhaps we should not hope for more, and yet designs need to be worked out which extend this list of needs, and designs need to be worked out which will give us a better basis for estimating the causal character of needs in the learning process.

* * *

* N.B. The booklets referred to in this article are currently available under the following title: Louis E. Raths and Anna Porter Burrell, *Understanding the Problem Child,* West Orange, New Jersey: The Economics Press, 1963.

ACTIVITIES

1. Compare the articles by Kubie and Goodlad. On what issues do these authors agree? Where do they seem to disagree? What evidence from learning theory would support their premises? Which of their premises may be discredited by evidence from research in this area?

2. Read a section on "the needs of children" in an educational-methods text. How does the author define "need"? If his definition is not explicit—or perhaps not given at all—state your own, drawing on contextual clues. Compare the various meanings of the word as outlined in Komisar's discussion.

3. Consider, for example, that a new child has entered your class in the middle of the year and is having difficulty making friends. You assume that he has a need for belonging, as yet unmet. What are some things you might do as a teacher? What are some things you should try to avoid? Prepare lists of other needs similar to those mentioned by L. E. Raths in his paper.

4. Louis E. Raths has identified eight needs that are predominantly unmet in our students. Which of these needs do you consider the most unrealistic? Which do you think is the most important? Defend your choices.

5. The Supreme Court decision concerning the desegregation of public schools held that separate school facilities are inherently unequal. Do you imagine that the Court was referring to emotional needs in its decision?

6. Observe children's behavior in school or out of school. Attempt to identify either verbal or non-verbal behaviors that may indicate an emotional need. Attempt to label the need as one of the eight advanced by L. E. Raths.

7. Observe a teacher's behavior while he is actually teaching or on video

tape. Identify those behaviors that apparently are directed at meeting the needs of children. Describe in some detail the teacher behavior and the specific need that behavior is apparently meeting.

DISCIPLINE

CHAPTER EIGHT

For many new teachers, as well as for some who have been teaching for many years, one of the greatest concerns is whether or not the students will cooperate with them. They are fully aware—in fact, some have learned by experience—that the most imaginative ideas, the finest plans, the best intentions are of no value if a class is "out of control."

Just what is meant by classroom control? Obviously this term means something quite different to the art teacher, the science teacher, the math teacher, the physical education teacher, and the reading teacher. The definition which may generally apply is: students and teacher work toward a commonly held goal, and behave in a manner which is mutually acceptable. Now, while this means the students have to cooperate with each other and with the teacher, the important consideration for us here is the job of the teacher. And it should be apparent that there is no one prescription for success. Teachers' personalities vary a great deal, so that even identical approaches to the problem of class control do not always have the same results. The following articles offer several alternatives for consideration.

43. POWER IN SMALL GROUPS

LOUIS E. RATHS

All serious writers about power speak of its interpersonal nature and its reciprocal relationships: to have power one must be empowered. The power comes from others.

Much of the writing about power concerns itself with definitions and illustration of what is meant by one or more conceptions of power. What is communicated in these writings are the personal conviction and opinions of the writers. Many of these are intelligent guideposts for the researcher in the field, particularly the inference that *power* is not a simple unitary concept, and that its meanings and effects may differ from one situation to another.

It is probably true that all knowledge starts with opinion, but on many occasions it delays overlong at the starting position. Opinion may or may not be verifiable but the conscious increase of knowledge requires the reformulation of opinion into testable form.

With respect to the concept of power there have been two prevailing trends: the expressions of opinion and the tendency to simplify a very complex phenomenon: power is force; power is influence; power is the ability to get work done; power is what is behind the decision-making activity of the top-most level of a social hierarchy; power is authority.

Oversimplification is not necessarily to be condemned. There may be great advantage in focusing upon a single factor in a situation involving many variables. The restatement of opinion into the form of a hypothesis may or may not lead to further clarification, depending upon the designs of the researcher and also upon the relevance of the hypothesis to the *theory* under consideration.

We need an explicitly formulated theory from which hypotheses can be derived for experimental testing.

In the absence of experimental data or a systematized organization

Louis E. Raths, "Power in Small Groups," Journal of Educational Sociology, *XXVIII, No. 3 (November 1954), 97–103. Reprinted by permission.*

of fact we may take as a basis the informed opinion of authorities in the field, such as Bertrand Russell,[1] Lasswell and Kaplan,[2] de Jouvenel,[3] Homans,[4] and L. L. Whyte. The latter says, "The unity of society depends on the existence of a hierarchical order which gives each section its special status and function within the whole, and this order may be effective even when it is not recognized."[5]

Given the interpersonal nature of power, the *power-empowering* relationship, and the suggestion of the need for hierarchical order, we may formulate a theory as follows:

1. In a small group if everyone were equal in all respects to every other person, the potentials for the development of power would be at a minimum.
2. Effective social power arises out of the operation of inequalities present in small group situations.
3. These inequalities may be few or many in number and may relate to different status categories. They come into being through the consent of those in the group. In other words, differences in status in one or more categories are recognized by the group members.
4. To preserve itself, leadership utilizes these inequalities; in part it tends to preserve them.
5. The utilization and preservation of inequalities is more likely if the leader is *aware* of them.
6. Group effectiveness is likely to be superior in those situations where the operations of the group leader support the several status systems created by the members of the group.

This theory assumes that power is created when a status system is brought into being. The source of the power is the status system itself. The functioning of power is dependent upon the continuance of a stable status system.

Power, then, arises in situations where there is imbalance or inequality of status and where the inequality in status is recognized by the members of the group. A particular status leader is chosen on the assumption that he will preserve the inequalities in the status system. The leader will not "rock the boat" for if he does he threatens his own leadership position. A leader may seize the power which has been created by the status system but does not create it. It is recognized that in addition to the differences between the statuses within a system there may be significant status differences between the several different status systems.

It is argued that to be effectively utilized power must be channeled through the different status systems which exist in the groups. The group system is, of course, dynamic and with change in the focus of attention, developing status systems may assume more or less importance from time to time. As the situation changes certain individuals in the group may appear to have more status at one time than another.

[1] Bertrand Russell, *Power, A New Social Analysis* (London: George Allen & Unwin, 1938), p. 103.

[2] Harold D. Lasswell and Abraham Kaplan, *Power and Society* (New Haven, Conn.: Yale University Press, 1950), p. 67.

[3] Bertrand de Jouvenel, *On Power: Its Nature and the History of Its Growth* (New York: The Viking Press, Inc., 1949), p. 63.

[4] George C. Homans, *The Human Group* (New York: Harcourt, Brace & World, Inc., 1950), p. 59.

[5] L. L. Whyte, *The Next Development in Man* (New York: New American Library of World Literature, Inc., 1950), p. 102.

Another assumption is involved. Given a primary group whose associations are concerned with common problems, who meet under regularly prescribed conditions, and who get to know each other quite well on a "person to person" or "person to group" basis, *statuses become known.* Individuals "earn" a regard from their fellows in the group. Thus each person "comes to have status" and this status is a product of his interaction with others in that group. For any individual the status which he has achieved for himself may not be the one that he desires; moreover the status which he has earned may not be a sound reflection of his abilities. Status is used in the sense that it is that place or position in the hierarchy which members of the group bestow upon a participant.

In ordinary life we often see applications of this theory of power. A new man coming into an important post asks to be briefed on "Who's who around here?" The principal of a school has "to go through channels." Our bureaucracy, in one sense, represents an attempt to systematize, to mechanize, and perhaps to publicize the status levels within the several organizations in which bureaucracy is characteristic.

In many groups, however, this all takes place at almost an unconscious level. Individuals in a group, in some manner now unknown to us, come to identify the status level of individuals in the group with respect to many different categories. Also there is a sense in which one makes a kind of composite of all the status systems and tends to place people in dominant or deferential classifications. The theory suggests that this gradiation of status is the vehicle through which power is most effectively expressed in our culture. By implication there is the suggestion that an effective leader, one who gets work done and gets it done under circumstances where the group morale is high, is a person who distributes rewards directly in proportion to status and distributes penalties or neglect inversely in proportion to status. On the other hand there is the implication that the appointed or elected status leader who goes against the channels, who goes against the status systems, will get less work done and will do it less effectively, and will have problems of morale of a serious nature.

There is the further implication that as committees are chosen in such a way that all of the members seem to be of about equal status, or if they are ignorant of each other's status and if their continued efforts do not allow an opportunity for them to become aware of each other's status, the work of that group will be largely ineffective. The situation will be somewhat confusing to the members. They will be aware that things are not going along well and that they are not accomplishing much and often they will wonder why.

Are there some systems of status in group situations which are crucial for the development of the group's power potential? Lasswell has suggested eight status categories which he seems to believe are intimately associated with power. All eight seem to be interrelated but the correlations are not extremely high. Their actual impact upon classroom morale will be discussed in the other articles which follow.

1. *Well-being*: Refers to qualities of

physical strength and endurance, capacity for work and play, and to the general idea of well-being.

2. *Skills*: These refer to what we ordinarily think of as special abilities and special proficiencies.

3. *Enlightenment*: This refers to knowledge, insight, and information.

4. *Power*: The ability to influence the behavior of others and to participate in the making of decisions.

5. *Wealth*: Meaning the personal economic resources of the individual himself rather than family wealth.

6. *Rectitude*: Which includes uprightness, virtue, and conscience.

7. *Respect*: The term is related to social position and to favorable reputation.

8. *Affection*: Which includes not only social acceptance but friendship and regard.

If we may assume that in primary groups these different status categories are influential in relation to power, we are in a position to formulate research.

We need to get information from every one of the group members about his estimate of every other member in terms of these eight status categories. Having that information, we can combine these results and get the total status of each member in each category, or we can combine one or more categories into a larger composite.

We tend to associate effective group work with a desirable group climate. We may call this *morale* or social climate, or good group atmosphere. If the theory is sound it seems to follow that where there is good social climate, power is being effectively channeled through the status system. Another implication would be that where there is good social climate that status leader would be more *aware* of the differences in status among the group members with respect to these categories.

If the power is being effectively channeled it would imply that the status leader supports more frequently the individuals of higher status and supports less frequently those of lower status.

* * *

It should be possible to secure evidence of status in many different kinds of groups; it should be possible to secure data which indicate whether or not status leaders tend to support individuals with high status in the group and to give less support to individuals of lower status. It should be possible to identify groups which are *accomplishing* a great deal and other groups with the same tasks confronting them who are not *accomplishing* very much. An hypothesis related to the theory would suggest that where group accomplishment was high the theory is at work and where accomplishment is relatively low the theory is not being applied.

Space is too limited for an extensive discussion of related ideas but perhaps one or two words should be said about the relationships. The status systems as such are the results of the interaction of individuals in the group and hence were determined more or less by assent and consent. It seems to follow that these status systems cannot be imposed upon a group; they come from the group itself and are in that sense an expression of that group's experience.

In another sense the theory implies that as new status systems have opportunity to come into being, new sources of power are being created so far as group work is concerned. That teacher or leader who tries to limit the status systems to one or two which relate only to academicism is limiting opportunities for the development of group power. It is in this sense that a group or nation becomes powerful as it increases opportunities for a group to differentiate themselves, but to differentiate themselves in group situations where status may be earned—a *status* that is cherished and is also approved by other members of that group.

The theory opens up many opportunities for further research. It is possible that the committee system which is such a fundamental in our social operations might be considerably improved if we knew how to select a group whose self-accepted differentials might allow for a maximum of power with a maximum of social climate.

The theory might be very helpful in the organization of individual groups. The relationships of such groups to departments and departments to divisions and divisions to the central authority may all be examined if this theory is used as a tentative base for experimentation. It is indeed possible that problems of discipline in all of our social institutions including the school can be approached from this point of view and aid in the discovery of solutions.

Although it has been implied throughout, a final word might be said to the effect that hierarchy was not considered as something permanent, unyielding, or fixed. The concept here dealt with a multitude of hierarchies in a situation so flexible that change was an ever-present possibility. It may indeed be true that this is a great strength of our society as it is presently organized.

44. SOCIAL PERCEPTION AND TEACHER-PUPIL RELATIONSHIPS

N. L. GAGE / GEORGE SUGI

How two or more persons interact in a given situation depends on many variables, only a few of which have been isolated even conceptually. Properties of the persons and of their situations, all considered as interdependent aspects of a field of forces, obviously provide handles by which to grasp the interaction phenomena. This paper seeks to throw light on interactions between teachers and pupils as a function of one property of the teachers: the accuracy of their perception of pupils' attitudes.

We are concerned with the more affective dimensions of the interaction, rather than with cognitive ones. Our reasoning goes as follows: Behavior in any situation is a function of one's perception of the situation. The "appropriateness" of the behavior will hence depend, at least in part, on the correctness or accuracy of the perceptions. But mere perceptions do not govern behavior completely; the motivational system of the person will determine the ends to which his perceptions are used. Similarly, his "integration," or freedom from neuroticism, will determine how well he can control his behavior to accord with his motivations and perceptions. Thus, even if John perceives a stoplight accurately, he will not stop for it unless he wants to and is sufficiently unexcited to be able to react in time. If John perceives his date's boredom with a movie, he will not suggest that they leave unless he wants to please her and this motive is integrated in a given way with his own feelings about the movie.

So far, however, this formulation ignores the relationships between these determiners; motivation and perception, at least, are themselves linked together. As Bruner (1) recently summarized it:

> a. Personally relevant objects in the perceptual field, whether the relevance

N. L. Gage and George Suci, "Social Perception and Teacher-Pupil Relationships," Journal of Educational Psychology, *XLII (1951), 144–52. Reprinted by permission.*

> is a function of positive or negative value to the individual, undergo accentuation. . . .
>
> b. Perceptual selectivity . . . is shown to favor the recognition of valued objects and objects associated with the prevailing interests of the subject.

Applied to teachers' perceptions of pupils' attitudes and their interaction with pupils, this implies that the accuracy of teachers' perceptions will be a function of the way in which teachers value pupils and relationships with them. Miss Smith will tend to become aware of how her pupils feel about various issues to the degree that she is interested in those pupils and in getting along smoothly with them. Similarly, she will probably act upon her awareness of their attitudes in positive ways for the same reasons that motivated her to perceive them accurately. Thus certain patterns of motivation, perception, and behavior tend to go together. At the one extreme of a continuum, we may have teachers who do not value pupils positively, do not perceive their attitudes accurately, and behave in ways conducive to negative reactions. At the other extreme are teachers who "need" their pupils more, perceive them with greater sensitivity and understanding, and conduct themselves in ways that elicit positive affect from pupils.

But, it may be objected, need does not necessarily lead to accuracy of perception. The more an object is valued, the more indeed may perception of it be distorted. In our framework, this leads us to examine what it is we are asking teachers to perceive. This, as will be described below, was the attitudes of pupils as reported by themselves in answer to direct Yes-No questions. Whether the attitudes so reported are "true" or "real" ones, we cannot know. It is reasonable to suppose, however, that what pupils report about themselves in a nonclinical, classroom situation are probably opinions of an ego-supporting kind. The opinions of the pupils tended, in other words, to be those which would enhance their own view of themselves. When teachers are then asked to estimate these opinions, they are being asked to judge what are the ego-supporting responses of pupils. Teachers who value pupils positively then should come closer to the pupils' own picture of themselves. Such a "coming closer" is what we have here termed "accuracy of social perception."

In short, this should mean that teachers who perceive their pupils' attitudes more accurately should be regarded more favorably by their pupils. To test this inference, we need estimates of (*a*) the accuracy of teachers' perceptions of pupils' attitudes, (*b*) the favorableness of pupils' attitudes toward their teachers, and (*c*) the relationship between (*a*) and (*b*).

The Estimate of Accuracy of Social Perception

Ideally, we should deal with the teacher's perception of attitudes of individual pupils on matters that are deeply relevant to each pupil. This would mean, first, the identification of attitude-objects that are highly salient for each pupil and, second, asking the teacher to estimate that pupil's attitude toward those objects. The attitudes to be perceived would then differ from one pupil to the next. Such a procedure was manifestly too difficult for the present study. We compromised by selecting areas of attitude that we surmised to be significant to the pupils en masse, and we asked the teachers to estimate the group attitude on each topic. This procedure is admittedly gross; but whatever support for our hypothesis might emerge from such an approximation might then be considered an underestimate of its true validity.

Accordingly, we proceeded as follows: The 20 teachers of a high school were asked to estimate what per cent of the two hundred pupils in the school would respond affirmatively to a set of 67 opinion items. The items dealt with scholastic, recreational, and student government issues in their school.[1] An illustrative item of each kind follows:

Scholastic: Should students with high scholastic ratings be allowed to skip classes?
Recreation: Could the time spent in school activities be used better for studying or working?
Student government: Should Student Council members be appointed by teachers rather than elected by students?

The students responded anonymously, underlining "Yes" or "No" for each item. The pupils' "Yes" responses were tabulated and the percentage of Yes's found for each item. These percentages comprised the scoring key. Each teacher was scored by taking the difference between his estimate and the actual percentage for each item, summing, and, because a few teachers omitted some items, averaging overall items. The signs of the differences were disregarded. Such "mean error" scores were also obtained separately for each of the three subgroups of items.

These "mean error" scores are directly dependent on the absolute accuracy with which each percentage is predicted. But a teacher, although not able to predict accurately in terms of absolute percentages, may be able to rank the items in order of relative acquiescence of the pupils. Accordingly, we also computed for each teacher a Pearsonian r between actual and predicted percentages. This we called an "r" score. It correlated .77 with the "mean error" score, showing a possibly important difference between the two scoring methods.

Pupils' Interaction with Their Teachers

At a separate meeting, with the teacher absent, the pupils rated their 6 current teachers on 52 Yes-No items[2] typified by the following:

Is this teacher often "bossy"?
Does this teacher think he or she is always right and the student wrong?

Again the papers were unsigned and pupils were assured their responses would remain anonymous. A score for each teacher was obtained by scoring favorable and unfavorable pupil responses as 1 and 0, respectively, summing overall items and averaging overall pupils rating the given teacher. This measure we considered an approximation, adequate for this study, to the positive affect elicited in pupils by their interaction with a given teacher.

[1] These items were adapted from those used by Wood (4).

[2] These were a slight modification of those used by Leeds and Cook (3).

Furthermore, for an appraisal of each teacher's system of values in teacher-pupil relationships, we used the *Teacher Attitude Inventory* developed by Leeds and Cook.[3] The 239 items in this device had been empirically selected and weighted by Leeds and Cook for their ability to discriminate between teachers known to maintain very satisfactory and very unsatisfactory relations with pupils, in the judgment of the teachers' local school administrators.

Results

Our first task in analyzing the data was to estimate the generality over items, or the internal consistency, of our approach to accuracy of social perception. Table 1 shows the corrected odd-even coefficients for the "mean error" scores on all items and on each of the three subgroups. The coefficient for all items, .73, indicates that the accuracy of teachers in estimating percentages of acquiescence was fairly general over the items. Thus we have evidence that the task of judging opinion revealed individual differences among teachers that were substantially loaded with nonerror variance. For the subgroups of items, these estimates yielded much lower coefficients.

Secondly, what is the reliability of the pupils' ratings of their teachers? Table 2 shows the results obtained from an application of Horst's formula (2). This coefficient, .93, indicates that the mean ratings we obtained would correlate very highly with subsequent sets of similar ratings, when our estimate of the variability of such further mean ratings is based on an average of the standard errors of those obtained. In short, the variance among the mean ratings is even more a nonerror one; the ratings discriminated well among the teachers.

Having established these estimates of reliability, we turned to the relationships with which we were primarily concerned. Is social perception, defined operationally as mean error in estimating students' percentages of acquiescence to opinion items, related to acceptance of the teachers by pupils, defined as the mean rating of teachers by pupils? Table 3 shows the pertinent coefficients of correlation. The r's between mean rating and mean error for all items and for the three subgroups of items are $-.37$, $-.16$, $-.30$, and $-.18$, respectively. It is evident that all r's are in the direction inferred from our hypothesis: the greater the teacher's mean error in estimating student opinion, the lower his mean rating by students. None of these r's is statistically significant. Our interpretation of this fact may, however, be tempered somewhat by the consistency in direction and size of the three subtest coefficients. These subtests provide in a sense three semi-independent trials of our investigation. The consistency of their results may therefore be construed as favorable evidence in addition to that provided by the overall test's r.

When the teachers' estimates of student opinion were scored in terms of their correlation with, rather than their difference from, the actual percentages, we obtain the results also shown in Table 3. Here the relationships, using r and z_r as measures of accuracy of social perception, increase to .50 and .45, respectively. Both these coefficients meet the re-

[3] We are grateful to Professor W. W. Cook for permission to use this device.

TABLE 1

Corrected Odd-Even Reliability Estimates for the "Mean Error" Scores on Opinion Estimates. N=20

Type of Items	No. of Items	Odd Items Mean	Odd Items SD	Even Items Mean	Even Items SD	Corrected Odd-Even *r*
All Items 1–67	67	20.19	2.81	18.64	2.97	.73
Scholastic 1–23	23	22.50	5.03	19.74	4.05	.17
Recreation 24–45	22	15.47	3.13	18.16	4.28	.28
Student Government 46–67	22	20.50	5.07	17.26	4.95	.47

TABLE 2

Estimate by Horst's Method of the Reliability of Pupils' Ratings of Their Teachers

$$r = 1 - \frac{\sum \frac{\sigma_i^2}{n_i - 1}}{N \sigma_{M_i}^2} = 1 - \frac{47.45}{648.46}$$
$$= .93$$

where
N = number of teachers
n_i = number of pupils rating teacher i
M_i = mean of the ratings for teacher i
σ_i = standard deviation of ratings for teacher i
σ_{M_i} = standard deviation of means for the N teachers

TABLE 3

Means, Standard Deviations, and Intercorrelations of Various Measures*

	No. of Teachers	Mean	SD	(2)	(3)	(4)	(5)	(6)	(7)	(8)
1. Mean Rating by Pupils	20	33.20	5.49	−.37	−.16	−.30	−.18	.50	.45	−.20
2. Mean Error (All Items)	20	19.35	2.45					−.77		−.57
3. Mean Error (Scholastic Items)	20	21.65	3.54			.13	.18			
4. Mean Error (Recreational Items)	20	16.70	3.28				.48			
5. Mean Error (Student Government Items)	20	19.15	4.60							
6. r-score (All Items)	20	.67	.08							.46
7. z_r-score (All Items)	20	.82	.16							
8. Teacher Attitude Inventory	19	154.08	18.35							

* When N=20, an r of .44 is significant at the 5 per cent level.

quirement for statistical significance at the 5 per cent level.

Why do the *r* scores correlate more highly than the mean error scores with the pupils' ratings? We can only conjecture as follows: The *r* scores are not influenced, as are the mean error scores, by individual differences among teachers in "adaptation level," or "anchor point." The teachers differed very significantly beyond the 1 per cent level, in the means of their predicted percentages. The *r* scores eliminate the effect of these differences. They render the measure of accuracy in social perception dependent solely on relative rather than absolute judgments of degree of acquiescence.

Two further findings should be mentioned. First, as shown in Table 3, the scores on the Cook-Leeds inventory correlated .57 and .46 with our mean error and *r* scores, respectively. This indicates that the attitudes and understandings concerning pupils which are tapped by that test are significantly related to ability to estimate student's opinions. But what of the relation of the Cook-Leeds instrument to mean ratings by pupils? Contrary to the Cook-Leeds findings, our coefficient was negative, −.20, although not significantly different from zero. In this school, at any rate, this test did not yield results in corroboration of the significant positive relationships with pupils' ratings (about .45) previously reported by Cook and Leeds.

Discussion

All our conclusions must be tempered by an awareness of the smallness of our sample and its lack of replication in other schools. For example, our impression that a curvilinear relationship exists between pupil ratings and accuracy of perception cannot adequately be pursued. It should be reported, however, that six teachers with high mean ratings nevertheless made only mediocre "mean error" or "*r*" scores. None of the teachers with very low ratings made high accuracy in social perception scores. This could have occurred if some of the well-liked teachers did not attack the task of estimating pupils' opinions with sufficient motivation. Thus low ratings seem sufficient to indicate poor perception scores, but the converse is not true.

The instability of our results is further indicated when we omit one extreme case from calculations of the *r*'s between the two scoring methods and the mean ratings. With the one case retained, *r's* of −.37 and .50 were obtained with the "mean error" score and the "*r*" score, respectively. With the extreme case omitted, the *r*'s became −.24 and .18, respectively —a considerable reduction. Nevertheless some degree of correlation, in the expected direction, persisted.

Summary

To test the hypothesis that accuracy of social perception is positively related to effectiveness of interpersonal relations, we asked the 20 teachers of a high school to predict the percentage of the 200 students who would answer "Yes" to each of 67 items eliciting opinions on various aspects of the school. Teachers' predictions were scored in terms of (*a*) "mean error" from actual percentages and (*b*) correlation with actual percentages. The teachers were rated by their pupils on a 52-item inventory. Finally, the teachers filled out the Cook-Leeds *Teacher Attitude Inventory.*

Results support the hypothesis. The teachers' "mean error" scores had fair internal consistency (corrected odd-even r, .73) and correlated −.37 with mean rating by pupils. Their "r" scores correlated .50 with mean rating. The teachers' scores on the *Teacher Attitude Inventory* correlated .57 with the "mean error" scores but, unexpectedly, −.20 with mean ratings. (For $N = 20$, an r of .44 is significant at the 5 per cent level.)

Our results must, of course, be pursued through replications in other schools and other situations. Tentatively, however, we conclude that teachers' accuracy of social perception is positively related to their effectiveness in eliciting positive affect in pupils.

References

1. Bruner, J. S., "Social Psychology and Group Processes," in C. P. Stone and D. W. Taylor, eds., *Annual of Psychology,* I (1950), 119–50.

2. Horst, Paul, "A Generalized Expression for the Reliability of Measures," *Psychometrika,* XIV (1949), 21–31.

3. Leeds, C. H. and W. W. Cook, "The Construction and Differential Value of a Scale for Determining Teacher-Pupil Attitudes," *Journal of Experimental Education,* XVI (1947), 149–59.

4. Wood, Homer, "An Analysis of Social Sensitivity." Unpublished Ph. D. Thesis, Yale University, 1948.

45. A NEW LOOK AT CLASSROOM DISCIPLINE

DAVID P. AUSUBEL

A few years ago, in one of our better New England high schools, two members of the school's counseling staff happened to be walking in the building when their attention was drawn to sounds of a disturbance in an adjoining corridor. Investigating further, they found that two boys, surrounded by a knot of curious onlookers, were engaged in an all-out switchblade fight. One counselor quickly whispered to the other, "We'd better break this up in a hurry before there's bloodshed." The latter replied heatedly, "For heaven's sake leave them alone or you'll ruin everything! Do you want the kids to think we are *disciplinarians?*" Fortunately, however, the native common sense of the first counselor prevailed over the doctrinaire permissiveness of his colleague, and a near-tragedy was averted.

David P. Ausubel, "A New Look at Classroom Discipline," Phi Delta Kappan, *XLIII, No. 1 (October 1961), 25–30. Reprinted by permission.*

This true story is admittedly a bit extreme and unrepresentative of disciplinary attitudes in American public schools. Nevertheless, somewhat less extreme versions occur frequently enough to suggest that American teachers are more confused and disturbed about matters of discipline today than at any previous time in the history of our public school system.

It is true that superficial observation does not support this conclusion. On the surface, practically everything *appears* the same as it was ten years ago when, except in the so-called "Blackboard Jungles," these same teachers seemed supremely confident that the ideal of democratic discipline had been achieved in the American classroom. Substantially the same disciplinary philosophy is still preached in our teachers colleges; and teachers, by and large, still practice the same kind of discipline they practiced a decade ago.

To be sure, there is still an appreciable gap between the theory or discipline as taught in colleges of education and discipline as it is actually conceived and practiced in the schools. For example, in a recent survey conducted by the National Education Association, 72 per cent of the responding classroom teachers favored the judicious use of corporal punishment in the elementary school. But the gap is no greater now than it has ever been. In everyday disciplinary practice, American teachers have never gone along completely with the more extreme ideas of educational theorists. Elementary and high-school teachers, after all, have to be realistic in handling problems of discipline because they encounter them daily in doing their jobs. Unlike professors of education, who rarely if ever have to cope with disciplinary problems in the classroom, they can ill afford to be starry-eyed about these matters.

Why then should teachers be suddenly confused and disturbed about issues of discipline? Closer scrutiny reveals that everything is not *really* the same as it used to be. One important factor in the situation has undergone significant change: Although educational theory in the field of classroom discipline has remained virtually unchanged over the past two decades, the pendulum of public opinion in recent years has been swinging further and further away from the formerly fashionable cult of permissiveness. As a result, a growing estrangement has arisen between the general public, on the one hand, and educational and psychological theorists on the other—with the classroom teacher and the rank-and-file school administrator caught squarely in the middle. Teachers, of course, were also in the middle throughout the entire period of approximately 1935–1955, when American classroom discipline underwent a process of extensive democratization. But this middle position was decidedly more comfortable then than it is now, because all three groups—educational theorists, teachers, and the public at large—were moving toward the same culturally desirable goal of a less authoritarian classroom climate.

It is true that these three groups were moving toward this goal at quite different rates. Permissiveness, nondirective guidance, and the cults of extroversion, conformity, and social adjustment were much more extreme among child-centered educators, client-centered counselors, and psychoanalytically trained child-study experts than among American parents and teachers generally. By 1955, however, the entirely laudable objective of more democratic pupil-teacher relationships had been reached, and perhaps overreached. Public opinion began moving away from permissiveness, but educational and psychological theorists and professors of education, with few exceptions, stood their ground tenaciously. The same relatively extreme permissive doctrines of discipline are still dominant in teachers colleges, even though educational philosophy in the post-Sputnik era has generally become less permissive in most other areas, such as curriculum.

Now, it was one thing for teachers to swim in the middle of two streams moving in the same historically necessary direction, and to enjoy the approbation of both the general public and of their own professional leaders. It is quite another for them to be caught between two opposing streams, and to be faced with the problem of having to choose between the spirit of the times, on the one hand, and the historically obsolete ideological extremism of their former professors on the other.

Historical and Cultural Perspective

Before examining how particular concepts and practices of discipline have gone astray, it might be profitable first to view the problem in historical perspective within a broader cultural context. The revolution in classroom discipline that swept American schools between 1935 and 1955 was as necessary as it was inevitable. Teacher-pupil relationships had to be brought into closer alignment with the general spirit of adult egalitarianism in American society; and a more desirable balance had to be achieved between the actual dependence of children on adult direction and their realistic capacities for exercising self-direction and self-discipline. It was inevitable, of course, that we would go too far in redressing the balance—in overdoing the permissiveness and in cutting back adult control and guidance too drastically. Much more serious, however, were the deplorable consequences of deemphasizing certain other traditional American values in the enthusiasm of democratizing adult-child relationships.

Thus, in stressing the inherent right of children to receive the consideration to which they are entitled, we have neglected the equally valid claims of age and maturity. In debunking superficial and unilateral forms of etiquette, we have lost sight of the importance of genuine courtesy in human relationships. And in attacking despotic and abusive adult rule, we have failed to cultivate appropriate respect for just and rightful authority.

By respect for age I do not mean uncritical veneration or ancestor worship, but simply the consideration that is due all human beings at any stage in the life cycle. Yet our cultural attitude toward middle-aged and elderly persons tends to be patronizing and slightly contemptuous. Because they quite understandably lack the exuberance and venturesomeness of youth, they are often cavalierly dismissed as "has-beens" or as bumbling, ineffectual fuddy-duddies.

Courtesy is another of our most valuable cultural assets that was overlooked in the frenzy of extending democracy to home and school. It is fashionable in many quarters—not only among the younger set—to regard good manners and the more subtle amenities of interpersonal relationships as hollow formalities. But even the highly stylized bowing ceremony of the Japanese is far from being an empty gesture. It symbolizes deep and culturally ingrained respect for the dignity of the individual and genuine concern for his pride and feelings. Although bowing is obviously incongruous with our modern way of life, concern for the pride, feelings, and dignity of every human being is one of our most cherished American values. Hence, since courtesy is basically an institutionalized set of rules designed to safeguard and implement this legitimate cultural concern, those who sneer at courtesy, whether they realize it or not, sneer at nothing less than human dignity.

Finally, our culture has tended to put authority figures in an anomalous and untenable position, particularly in the school environment. We have assigned them the necessary and often distasteful task of authority figures the world over, that is, to enforce certain basic standards of conduct; but in too many instances we have failed to give them the respect, the authority, and the protection commensurate with this responsibility. When they conscientiously attempt to apply without fear or favor the community approved sanctions for violating these standards, we accuse them of being punitive, vindictive, and authoritarian. School administrators, of course, are not above criticism and reproach when they use poor judgment or exceed their authority; but society has an obligation to protect them from disrespect and abuse for simply doing their duty and exercising their just and necessary disciplinary prerogatives. In our present cultural climate, therefore, it is small wonder that many principals and superintendents of schools are more concerned with courting general popularity than with enforcing desirable norms of pupil behavior.

The Brighter Side of the Coin

In pointing out some of the failings of our recent approach to discipline, I do not mean to detract in any way from our genuine accomplishments. The latter are extremely impressive when compared with disciplinary practices in many other countries. I recently had an opportunity to study secondary schools in New Zealand, an English-speaking welfare state of British origin with a pioneering tradition not unlike our own. School discipline in New Zealand high schools connotes explicit subjection to authority and implicit habits of obedience that are enforced by a very heavy-handed set of controls and punishments. It implies a very identifiable atmosphere of classroom control which the teacher maintains with much deliberate effort—in much the same sense that he strives to have his pupils understand and assimilate the subject matter he teaches. For example, it is not uncommon for a New Zealand high-school teacher to begin the school year by exhibiting a cane to his class and announcing that he fully intends to use it on the first pupil who steps out of line.

By contrast, the American approach to discipline seems laudably incidental. Our teachers tend to feel that the cause of discipline is adequately served if pupils exercise sufficient self-control and observe a minimum set of rules with sufficient decorum to enable classroom work to proceed in an orderly, efficient manner. They do not, in other words, strive deliberately for discipline as an explicit goal in its own right. They assume instead that good discipline is *ordinarily* a natural by-product of interesting lessons and of a wholesome teacher-pupil relationship; that the vast majority of pupils respond positively to fair and kindly treatment; that respect for the teacher is a usual accompaniment of the latter's superior knowledge, experience, and status as a leader, and does not have to be reinforced by such artificial props and status symbols as differences in clothing, mode of address, and fear of the strap. Hence they treat adolescents as maturing young adults rather than as unruly children, and implicitly expect them to respond in kind—which they usually do. And it was a very gratifying experience to discover that despite the absence of strict authoritarian controls, American high-school students, on the whole, behave more decorously than their New Zealand counterparts—particularly when not under direct supervision.

Science or Opinion?

Discipline today is much less a science than a matter of opinion. It not only shifts in response to various social, economic, and ideological factors, but also manifests all of the cyclical properties of fads and fashions. Objective scientific evidence about the relative merits of different types of discipline is extremely sparse. Indeed it is highly questionable to what extent valid objective data are obtainable and even relevant in matters of discipline. Whether or not particular disciplinary practices are appropriate depends, in the first place, on the particular values, institutions, and kinds of personal relationships prevailing in a given culture; and, second, any definitve empirical test of appropriateness would have to be conducted over such an extended period of time that its conclusions would tend to be rendered obsolete by intervening changes in significant social conditions. For all practical purposes, therefore, the choice of disciplinary policy involves taking a rationally defensible and self-consistent position based on value preferences, on relevant considerations of child development, and on individual experience and judgment.

The fact that discipline cannot be placed on a largely scientific basis, however, does not mean that one position is as good as another or that no public policy whatsoever is warranted. Society is continually obliged to resolve issues of much greater moment with even less objective evidence on which to base a decision. Under the circumstances, all we can reasonably expect is greater humility and less dogmatism on the part of those engaged in formulating disciplinary policy. Thus, the most disturbing aspect of the entire problem is not the fact that there is precious little scientific evidence to support the disciplinary doctrines expounded in our colleges of education and educational journals and textbooks, but rather the ubiquitous tendency to represent purely personal opinions and biases as if they were the incontrovertibly established findings of scientific research.

The Definition and Functions of Discipline

By discipline I mean the imposition of *external* standards and controls on individual conduct. Permissiveness, on the other hand, refers to the absence of such standards and controls. To be permissive is to "let alone," to adopt a laissez-faire policy. Authoritarianism is an excessive, arbitrary, and autocratic type of control which is diametrically opposite to permissiveness. Between the extremes of laissez-faire permissiveness and authoritarianism are many varieties and degrees of control. One of these, to be described in greater detail below, is democratic discipline.

Discipline is a universal cultural phenomenon which generally serves four important functions in the training of the young. First, it is necessary for socialization—for learning the standards of conduct that are approved and tolerated in any culture. Second, it is necessary for normal personality maturation—for acquiring such adult personality traits as dependability, self-reliance, self-control, persistence, and ability to tolerate frustration. These aspects of maturation do not occur spontaneously, but only in response to sustained social demands and expectations. Third, it is necessary for the internalization of moral standards and obligations or, in other words, for the development of conscience. Standards obviously cannot be internalized unless they also exist in external form; and even after they are effectively internalized, universal cultural experience suggests that external sanctions are still required to insure the stability of the social order. Lastly, discipline is necessary for children's emotional security. Without the guidance provided by unambiguous external controls, the young tend to feel bewildered and apprehensive. Too great a burden is placed on their own limited capacity for self-control.

Democratic Discipline

The proponents of democratic classroom discipline believe in imposing the minimal degree of external control necessary for socialization, personality maturation, conscience development, and the emotional security of the child. Discipline and obedience are not regarded as ends in themselves but only as means to these latter ends. They are not striven for deliberately, but are expected to follow naturally in the wake of friendly and realistic teacher-pupil relationships. Explicit limits are not set routinely or as ways of showing "who is boss," but only as the need arises, i.e., when they are not implicitly understood or accepted by pupils.

Democratic discipline is as rational, nonarbitrary, and bilateral as possible. It provides explanations, permits discussion, and invites the participation of children in the setting of standards whenever they are qualified to do so. Above all, it implies respect for the dignity of the individual and avoids exaggerated emphasis on status differences and barriers between free communication. Hence it repudiates harsh, abusive, and vindictive forms of punishment, and the use of sarcasm, ridicule, and intimidation.

The aforementioned attributes to democratic classroom discipline are obviously appropriate in cultures such as ours where social relationships tend to be egalitarian. This type of discipline also becomes increasingly more feasible as children become older, more responsible, and more capable of understanding and formulating rules of conduct based on concepts of equity and reciprocal obligation. But contrary to what the extreme permissivists would have us believe, democratic school discipline does not imply freedom from all external constraints, standards, and direction, or freedom and discipline as an end in itself. And under no circumstances does it presuppose the eradication of all distinctions between pupil and teacher roles, or require that teachers abdicate responsibility for making the final decisions in the classroom.

Distortions of Democratic Discipline

Many educational theorists have misinterpreted and distorted the ideal of democratic discipline by equating it with an extreme form of permissiveness. These distortions have been dogmatically expressed in various psychologically unsound and unrealistic propositions that are considered sacrosanct in many teachers colleges. Fortunately, however, most classroom teachers have only accepted them for examination purposes—while still in training—and have discarded them in actual practice as thoroughly unworkable.

According to one widely held doctrine, only "positive" forms of discipline are constructive and democratic. It is asserted that children must only be guided by reward and approval; that reproof and punishment are authoritarian, repressive, and reactionary expressions of adult hostility which leave permanent emotional scars on children's personalities. What these theorists conveniently choose to ignore, however, is the fact that it is impossible for children to learn what is *not* approved and tolerated simply by generalizing in inverse from the approval they receive for behavior that *is* acceptable. Merely by rewarding honesty and good manners one cannot, for example, teach children that dishonesty and rudeness are socially unacceptable traits. Even adults are manifestly incapable of learning and respecting the limits of acceptable conduct unless the distinction between what is proscribed and what is approved is reinforced by punishment as well as by reward. Furthermore, there is good reason to believe that acknowledgement of wrongdoing and acceptance of punishment are part and parcel of learning moral accountability and developing a sound conscience. Few if any children are quite so fragile that they cannot take deserved reproof and punishment in stride.

A second widespread distortion of democratic discipline is reflected in the popular notion that there are no culpably misbehaving children in the classroom, but only culpably aggressive, unsympathetic, and punitive teachers. If children misbehave, according to this point of view, one can implicitly assume that they must have been provoked beyond endurance by repressive and authoritarian classroom discipline. Similarly, if they are disrespectful, then the teacher, by definition, must not have been deserving of respect. It is true, of course, that some pupil misconduct *is* instigated by harsh and abusive school discipline; but there are also innumerable reasons for out-of-bounds behavior that are completely independent of the teacher's attitudes and disciplinary practices. Pupils are also influenced by factors originating in the home, the neighborhood, the peer group, and the mass media. Some children are emotionally disturbed, others are brain-damaged, and still others are aggressive by temperament; and there are times when even the best-behaved children from the nicest homes develop an irresistible impulse—without any provocation whatsoever—to test the limits of a teacher's forebearance.

Both of the aforementioned distortions of classroom democracy are used to justify the commonly held belief among educators that pupils should not be reproved or punished for disorderly or discourteous conduct. I have, for example, observed classrooms where everybody talks at once; where pupils turn their backs on the teacher and engage in private conversation while the latter is endeavoring to instruct them; and where pupils verbally abuse teachers for exercising their rightful disciplinary prerogatives. Some educators contend that all of this is compatible with wholesome, democratic teacher-pupil relationships. Other educators deplore this type of pupil behavior but insist, nevertheless, that punishment is unwarranted under these circumstances. In the first place, they assert, reproof or punishment constitutes a "negative" and hence axiomatically undesirable approach to classroom management; and, secondly, the misbehavior would assuredly have never occurred to begin with, if the teacher's attitudes had been less autocratic or antagonistic. I have already answered the second group of educators, and to the first group I can only say that I am still sufficiently old-fashioned to believe that rudeness and unruliness are not normally desirable classroom behavior in any culture.

When such misconduct occurs, I believe pupils have to be unambiguously informed that it will not be tolerated and that any repetition of the same behavior will be punished. This action does not preclude in any way either an earnest attempt to discover why the misbehavior occurred or suitable preventive measures aimed at correcting the underlying causes. But, by the same token, the mere fact that a pupil has a valid psychological reason for misbehaving does not mean that he is thereby absolved from moral accountability or rendered no longer subject to punishment.

Still another related distortion of democratic discipline is reflected in the proposition that it is repressive and authoritarian to request pupils to apologize for discourteous behavior or offensive language. However, if we take seriously the idea that the dignity of the human being is important, we must be willing to protect it from affront; and apology is the most civilized and effective means mankind has yet evolved for accomplishing this goal. In a democratic society nobody is so important that he is above apologizing to those persons whom he wrongfully offends. Everybody's dignity is important—the teacher's as well as the pupil's. It is no less wrong for a pupil to abuse a teacher than for a teacher to abuse a pupil.

If apologies are to have any real significance in moral training, however, it is obvious that, even though they are explicitly requested, they must be made voluntarily, and they must be reflective of genuine appreciation of wrong-doing and of sincere regret and remorse. Purely formal and mechanical statements of apology made under coercion are less than worthless. Apologies are also without real ethical import unless their basis is reciprocal, i.e., unless it is fully understood that under comparable circumstances the teacher would be willing to apologize to his pupils.

A final distortion of democratic classroom discipline associated with the extreme child-centered approach to education is the notion that children are equipped in some mysterious fashion for knowing precisely what is best for them. "Scientific proof" of this proposition is adduced from the fact that nutrition is adequately maintained and existing deficiency conditions are spontaneously corrected when infants are permitted to select their own diet. If the child can successfully choose his diet, runs the argument, he must certainly know what is best for him in *all* areas, including curriculum and classroom management.

This doctrine, however, has even less face validity than the three other distorted concepts of school discipline. Because the human being is sensitive in early childhood to internal cues of physiological needs, we cannot conclude that he is similarly sensitive to complex intellectual and moral needs, or that he has sufficient experience, perspective, and judgment to make intelligent decisions in these latter areas. Even in the field of nutrition, self-selection is a reliable criterion of need only during early infancy. The current interests and opinions of immature pupils can hardly be considered reliable guideposts and adequate substitutes for seasoned judgment in designing a curriculum or in formulating rules of classroom behavior. Hence, while it is reasonable to consider the views of pupils in these matters, teachers and school administrators cannot abdicate their responsibility for making the final decisions.

What Needs to be Done

In seeking to correct these undesirable permissive distortions of classroom democracy, it would be foolhardy to return to the equally undesirable opposite extreme of authoritarianism that flourished in this country up to a quarter of a century ago, and still prevails in many Western nations. Democratic school discipline is still an appropriate and realistic goal for American education; hence there is no need to throw away the baby with the bath water. It is only necessary to discard the aforementioned permissivist doctrines masquerading under the banners of democracy and behavioral science, and to restore certain other traditional American values that have been neglected in the enthusiasm of extending democracy to home and school.

More specifically, we first have to clear up the semantic confusion. We should stop equating permissiveness with democratic discipline, and realistic adult control and guidance with authoritarianism. Permissiveness, by definition, is the absence of discipline, democratic or otherwise. We should cease instructing teachers that it is repressive and reactionary to reprove or punish pupils for misconduct, or to request them to apologize for offensive and discourteous behavior.

Second, we should stop misinterpreting what little reputable evidence we have about discipline, and refrain from misrepresenting our personal biases on the subject as the indisputable established findings of scientific research. The available evidence merely suggests that, in our type of cultural setting, authoritarian discipline has certain undesirable effects —*not* that the consequences of laissez-fair permissiveness are desirable. As a matter of fact, research studies show that the effects of extreme permissiveness are just as unwholesome as are those of authoritarianism. In the school situation a laissez-faire policy leads to confusion, insecurity, and competition for power among pupils. Assertive pupils tend to become aggressive and ruthless, whereas retiring pupils tend to withdraw further from classroom participation. The child who is handled too permissively at home tends to regard himself as a specially privileged person. He fails to learn the normative standards and expectations of society, to set realistic goals for himself, or to make reasonable demands on others. In his dealings with adults and other children he is domineering, aggressive, petulant, and capricious.

Third, we should stop making teachers feel guilty and personally responsible for all instances of misconduct and disrespect in the classroom. We do this whenever we take for granted, without any actual supporting evidence, that these behavior problems would never have arisen in the first place if the teachers involved were truly deserving of respect and had been administering genuinely wholesome and democratic discipline.

Finally, teachers colleges should terminate the prevailing conspiracy of silence they maintain about the existence of disciplinary problems in the public schools. Although discipline is the one aspect of teaching that the beginning teacher is most worried about, he receives little or no practical instruction in handling this problem. Colleges of education, as pointed out above, rationalize their inadequacies in this regard by pretending that disciplinary problems are relatively rare occurrences involving the disturbed child, or more typically the disturbed teacher. Due respect for the facts of life, however, suggests that prospective teachers today not only need to be taught more realistic propositions about the nature and purposes of democratic discipline, but also require adequately supervised, down-to-earth experience in coping with classroom discipline.

46. CORRECTIVE MEASURES, PUNISHMENT, AND DISCIPLINE

HENRY H. BATCHELDER

Following is material for a series of bulletins on classroom disciplines that has been used for faculty discussions in a number of secondary schools. Some have used them for posting or faculty circulation only. Some teachers have used sections for classroom discussions, debates, compositions, student paper editorials and articles, etc. The reader may find still other methods of using them.

Basically, these ideas came from a book whose title and author's name

Henry H. Batchelder, "Corrective Measures, Punishment, and Discipline," Journal of Secondary Education, *XXXIX, No. 2 (February 1964), 86–93. Reprinted by permission.*

have long escaped me. They have been refined, changed, added to, and modernized by teachers, students, articles, lectures, institutes, discussions, and practice. The author regrets his inability to give credits (or ask permission) to the originators of these ideas or to those who have contributed corrections and/or refinements.

If, perchance, a reader recognizes some of this, be thankful that it is here published and will be profitably used again by some of the readers of our journal—that it will help teachers and children of our schools.

Bulletin #1

Simple Control

By simple control is meant: a look at an offender, a shake of the head, a frown signifying disapproval, waiting for attention before continuing the instruction, a mild reproof, posing a question to a pupil whose attention has wandered, switching seats of offenders, movement of the teacher about the room to trouble centers, and laughing off minor infractions, etc.

ADVANTAGES

1. Simplicity
2. Allows instruction to proceed
3. Avoids unpleasant scenes
4. Has few harmful effects on the personality

DISADVANTAGES

1. Attacks surface behavior only
2. May be ineffective
3. Depends largely on the personality of the teacher

Much of the success in the use of simple control measures rests upon the tacitly implied dissatisfaction on the part of the teacher. Most adolescents comply quickly with methods of simple control, since they are unaware of the exact nature of what the teacher is thinking. This system rests upon the authority of the teacher and/or on approval and disapproval, but may be found expedient in maintaining order in the classroom for instructional purposes for the general welfare of the group.

If this appeal to simple authority is coupled with genuine understanding on the part of the teacher, and if it is employed to teach the pupil that his behavior is unacceptable to the social welfare of the group, then these measures may be justified and very valuable. In difficult, unruly classes, however, simple measures of control may be ineffective (at times).

Bulletin #2

Individual Conferences with Pupils

The individual conference between the pupil and the teacher is, by far, the most desirable single major corrective measure to be employed by the teacher. A serious and frank talk would appear to be the logical first step in the understanding of behavior problems.

ADVANTAGES

1. The individual conference provides an opportunity for a private talk between the teacher (as a guidance person) and the pupil who has exhibited a behavior problem.
2. It affords the teacher an opportunity to obtain further information.
3. It provides the pupil with an opportunity to express himself and to air his problems.

DISADVANTAGES

1. Some teachers find difficulty in carrying on an interview or a conference with an offender because of (*a*) lack of knowledge, (*b*) lack of time, (*c*) lack of interest, (*d*) lack of understanding of adolescent problems, (*e*) feeling of moral indignation at the offender's actions, and (*f*) some difficulty in achieving rapport between teacher and pupil.

All of us have had some study in the use of interview techniques. Conferences are helpful techniques, if they are designed to understand the causes of misbehavior, to learn the problems the pupil faces, and to interpret school or class regulations to the pupil as desirable for individual and group welfare.

Note: There is little or no relationship to effective value because some of these methods seem to have more itemized numbers of disadvantages or advantages. For instance, *one advantage* may outweigh ten disadvantages or vice versa.

Bulletin #3

Home-School Cooperation and Coaction

This measure of correction recognizes the fact that the behavior problems are rooted in the home environment as well as in the school environment. Genuine cooperation between home and school through conferences, home visits, and social contacts can achieve remarkable results, provided both parties are willing to understand the pupil's behavior in terms of causes and are sincere about wanting to help the pupil in his adjustment problems.

ADVANTAGES

1. Opportunity for establishing rapport between the home and the school.

2. Parent and teacher may supply each other with valuable information.

3. Provides opportunity for concerted attack upon the causes of misbehavior.

4. Visits to the home provide an opportunity to see the pupil in his home environment.

DISADVANTAGES

1. Some teachers are not trained to conduct interviews with adults nor to make home visits. A few teachers do not desire to make the effort.

2. Some teachers do not understand some causes of behavior themselves. It is then difficult to carefully interpret pupil behavior to parents.

3. It is difficult to get the parents into the school or the teacher into the home. Some teachers cannot seem to realize how valuable this type of visit can be.

Home-school cooperation can produce fruitful information and lead to correction of misbehavior. The method of handling the conferences or visits is important. Teachers must usually avoid "summoning" a parent to school. Parents readily resent this authoritarian display. The teacher-parent conference is certainly not an occasion for the teacher to "lay down the law" to the parent. This antagonizes, creates ill will, destroys good public relations, and defeats the purposes of the conference as an attempt to solve the youth's problems.

Bulletin #4

Restitution and Reparation

Restitution of things taken and reparation for things damaged or destroyed willfully are generally conceded effective and fair forms of punishment.

ADVANTAGES

1. Associates the punishment in a natural way with the offense.

2. Teaches the child that damages done through willful action on his part must be rectified.

3. Can be administered justly, fairly, impartially, and unemotionally.

DISADVANTAGES

1. Pupils and parents may not have the money to pay for damages.

2. Children may obtain the money too readily from parents (or steal it), thus destroying the educative values of the punishment.

To be effective, this form of punishment must educate the immature pupil to realize that what he destroys affects the welfare of the entire group. It teaches him that he must make amends. The teacher's responsibility lies in explaining to him the reasons for the punishment and in following through to see that restoration is made. If the pupil is financially unable to pay expenses of reparation, the school should find a way by which he may work out the damages and pay off his debt. Where parents are too free with money, the school should solicit their cooperation to make the punishment educative by permitting the pupil to work out his own debt to society.

Bulletin #5

A. Loss of Privilege

The loss of privileges, particularly those of a social nature, is generally a well-accepted method of punishment in the interest and training of the pupil.

ADVANTAGES

1. This form of punishment enables the child to feel that, if his behavior destroys the group's effectiveness, society will disapprove of that action by not associating with him.

2. This measure corresponds to the type used to a large extent in the home.

DISADVANTAGES

1. This measure of control may, if wrongly used, deny the child the very thing that he may need most, social participation.

When "loss of privilege" is applied, it should follow as a natural, logical form of correction with no sort of retributory attitude on the part of the teacher. Care must be exercised not to apply this sanction too long. Ways must be made available so that, after the child has had time to examine his conduct with the help of the teacher, he can restore himself to full privileges. This is one method of teaching the child the relationship of duties to privileges.

B. Rewards and Prizes

ADVANTAGES

1. It is a positive method.

DISADVANTAGES

1. Rewards may become ends in themselves instead of means to good conduct.

2. Rewards may not be made available to all students on an equal basis.

3. Marks (for citizenship as well as for scholarship) are sometimes used as rewards.

4. Tangible rewards such as money and material prizes appeal to greed.

Note: The use of rewards is justified if the rewards are available (and obtainable) to all and if they appeal to higher motives such as group welfare, citizenship and service. Praise from the group, recognition of useful service by the school paper and the local press, privileges, the use of students in assisting others, certification cards and plaques for achievement, the use of honor rolls, and the use of honor study halls under student leadership may be suitable types of the use of this method.

Bulletin #6

Detention after School

Advantages

1. Substitutes for more harsh forms of punishment.

2. Deterrent for those pupils who have something to do after school.

3. Easily administered.

4. Students can do constructive work while detained.

5. Teacher and student can repair damaged rapport.

6. Teacher can investigate causative factors and have helpful conferences.

Disadvantages

1. The pupil can readily sense that he is detaining the teacher at the same time.

2. It prevents the pupil from getting recreation and exercise outside after school.

3. It prevents the teacher from getting recreation and exercise outside after school.

4. It makes unnecessary demands on the teacher's time.

5. Parents may need the child at home. This system can alienate the parents.

6. The pupil may work after school. The home may need the income from his work. This situation may increase parental antagonism.

7. After-school appointments with the dentist, doctor, music teacher, or tutor cause conflicts.

8. Conflicts arise with other school activities, particularly with sports, clubs, and extracurricular activities. Frequently, this system causes friction among faculty members who want the pupil for some purpose after school.

9. It becomes a problem of what to have the pupil do during detention.

a. If he does nothing but sit, there is no worthwhile learning taking place. He may sit nursing his resentment.

b. If he does homework, he is learning further to detest school, since his homework becomes punishment.

c. If he does homework, he may take the attitude that this is an opportunity to get his homework done so he will not have to do it later. This destroys the punishment effect of detention.

d. If he does tasks other than homework, the punishment is no longer associated with the behavior in the class where he caused the trouble.

10. This type of control is often used for all types of offenders, and makes little or no distinction in fitting the measure of correction to the offense and to the offender.

Bulletin #7

Dismissal from Class and Isolation

Advantages

1. This gets rid of the troublemaker or silences him.

2. It has some effectiveness since it bars a pupil from association with his group.

3. It "saves the day"—for the other students.

4. It tells the administrator or other staff member that this child needs attention and/or correction.

DISADVANTAGES

1. Dismissal from class.

a. Bars a pupil from necessary instruction.

b. Creates a scene; can be humiliating to the offender.

c. The pupil gets considerable attention and may become a hero to the class.

d. It may be exactly what the pupil wants, relief from the "boredom" of classroom work.

2. Sending a pupil elsewhere in the building.

a. The teacher, in sending a pupil elsewhere in the building, may be shifting his burden to another faculty member.

3. Sending pupils to the "office."

a. Bars the pupil from instruction.

b. Transfers the teacher's problem to other authority (this may or may not be good).

c. Consumes some one else's time.

4. Isolation.

a. May not be harmful when the pupil is isolated in the same classroom; bars a pupil from instruction when he is sent out to an "isolation" room.

b. Other supervision is required if the pupil is isolated in a room other than the classroom.

Note: The practice of sending pupils to an "office" may be justified in severe cases. But we all frown upon a *large number* of cases being sent anywhere. The teacher may be shirking his responsibilities and creating a "bogeyman" in the principal and/or counselor and/or vice-principal.

Bulletin #8

A. Punishing the Group for the Offenses of One Person

ADVANTAGES

1. It may be expedient in arousing group disapproval toward the offender.

DISADVANTAGES

1. It may align the group against the teacher.

2. It may create a hostile group teaching climate.

Note: This procedure is condemned by all educational authorities. This applies whether or *not* the teacher can identify the offender.

B. Extra Tasks

ADVANTAGES

1. There are few worthwhile advantages.

DISADVANTAGES

1. Punishment bears little connection with the behavior.

2. It creates added distaste for school work and destroys incentive to learn.

C. Enforced Apologies

ADVANTAGES

1. It is often for teacher satisfaction only.

2. If the pupil can be shown how his actions are undesirable and if he can be induced to apologize with sincerity, this method may be useful.

DISADVANTAGES

1. It stirs up resentment on the part of the pupil and of the group.

2. It embarrasses the pupil.

3. It teaches the pupil to be hypocriti-

cal, if he gives an apology without meaning it.

Bulletin #9

Lowering the Marks

(Citizenship and/or scholarship.) This is quite different from giving low marks that have been earned. It means lowering marks already given!

ADVANTAGES

1. It satisfies the teacher's need for surface order or revenge.

DISADVANTAGES

1. It does not treat causes of behavior.
2. This is a misuse of marks, which are for indications of citizenship and scholarship achievement only.

The teacher who uses marks as a major disciplinary device is often considered a weak teacher.

Further undesirable practices most educators do not sanction for regular use are personal indignities and tortures, threats, humiliation before others, ridicule, satiation or saturation by repetition of the offense *ad nauseam*, fines, and nagging, scolding, tongue lashings, and diatribes.

Questionable is the practice of demerits. Though they may be effective in maintaining order, they do not attack causes of behavior. They entail unnecessary bookkeeping for already burdened teachers. Such time could be better employed in counseling and inservice study and work.

Fixed penalties for offenses should not be set. Some pupils may be willing to "pay the price" if they know the penalty attached to the offense. Fixed penalties cannot anticipate the many types of behavior that will arise.

Bulletin #10

Corporal Punishment

(Including: grabbing, shaking, punching, holding, slapping, hitting, standing in the corner, *forcing of the will*, etc.)

ADVANTAGES

1. Dramatic!
2. Associates punishment with pain.
3. Relieves the teacher's need.

DISADVANTAGES

1. Humiliates pupil.
2. Ineffective with some pupils, who may not dread it at all.
3. May create personal battle between the pupil and the teacher. Pupil may act in self-defense.
4. Deepens resentment and hostility of the pupil, creates a further hatred for school, arouses hostility toward all authority.
5. May alienate parents.
6. This measure of control is controlled by law.

Corporal punishment is based on the psychology of fear. It is often administered by the punisher in a state of anger. Corporal punishment may arouse the entire group against the teacher, thus augmenting the troubles.

Corporal punishment should be used by school administrators only after every other avenue is exhausted. In applying it the following precautions must be taken:

1. The pupil must be guilty of some major offense (proven, not suspected).
2. The teacher must know the laws regarding corporal punishment.
3. Obtain the parents' consent first.

4. Administer in private with one adult witness.

5. Do not be brutal. Do not leave scars or bruises.

6. Do not strike the face, ears, or head.

7. Do not administer in a rage or anger.

8. Record the offense and the punishment. Report is filed in the office of the superintendent of schools.

Teachers may find it just as useful to inform the parents of the child's misbehavior. Parents, in some cases, will administer the corporal punishment themselves. This too, must be done with caution, since parents, at times, can be brutal. Generally speaking, corporal punishment should not be used with adolescents or older students.

Bulletin #11

A. Suspension from School

Those who recommend suspension do so with the reservation that it is an extreme form of punishment.

ADVANTAGES

1. Removes the offender from the situation.

2. Allows the pupil time for reflection and time for parental and/or other corrective measures and study of the case.

(Pupils should have home assignments and should remain at home during the school day.)

DISADVANTAGES

1. Bars the pupil from instruction and causes him to fall behind in his work.

2. Does not treat the causes of behavior.

3. May be exactly what the pupil wants, reprieve from the scholastic setting.

4. Involves parents, who may resent this extreme action.

Suspension may be justified only in very unusual circumstances. Though action may start with the teacher, the principal and the board of education are the only authorities to suspend a pupil from school. Pupils who are suspended must be permitted the opportunity to make up the work they have missed. Suspension should be concluded as soon as the pupil is aware of the seriousness of his action.

B. Expulsion from School

Expulsion is considered desirable only as the very last measure which a board of education can take. It is reserved for those cases of erratic behavior for which there is no hope for improvement under school conditions. The welfare of the group, or others, has to be seriously endangered to justify expulsion.

ADVANTAGES

1. Empowers the school to get rid of extreme cases such as mentally deranged youths, severe delinquents, homosexuals, etc.

DISADVANTAGES

1. Removes the pupil from a normal setting.

Expulsion is generally regulated by state law. The principal, superintendent, and the board of education must be the final authorities for expulsion. In expelling a student who is within the compulsory age limits of education, provision should be made for other instruction, such as committal to an institution. Expulsion arouses public interest, but if it is justifiable, public sympathy will support the administration.

Bulletin #12

General Consideration and Summary

1. Corrective measures should be based upon understanding of the student and sound guidance procedures.
2. The purpose of any correctional device is the improvement of the adjustment of the individual or of the group.
3. Measures must be taken for the welfare of the individual and for the welfare of the group. A measure applied to an individual must be destructive neither of the individual's personality nor of the group climate. In case a choice has to be made between the welfare of the individual and the welfare of the group, the welfare of the group must take precedence.
4. In using punishment, the simple measures should be used before resorting to the more severe ones.
5. Punishment should usually be administered impersonally, objectively, unemotionally, and privately.
6. The corrective measure should fit the offender and the offense. Intent of the offender should affect the choice of the corrective measure.
7. All sources of idleness and lack of interest and preventive measures should be exhausted prior to using corrective measures.
8. Punishment has to be certain. Certainty acts as a deterrent to future would-be offenders.
9. Fixed penalties *should not be established.* They cannot anticipate all forms of misconduct. They may encourage pupils to "pay the price." They erroneously assume that all offenses of the same type are actually the same and that the same corrective measures should be applied.
10. Punishment should be exercised swiftly, though at times a short delay may be effective to enable the pupil to consider actions.
11. Teachers must remember that most offenses are *not* personally directed against them, though *it may seem* so on the surface.
12. Desirable corrective measures are simple classroom control, individual conferences, cooperation with parents, restitution and reparation, loss of privileges, and the use of rewards.
14. Undesirable or questionable measures are detention after school, dismissal from class, sending to the office, punishing the group, extra tasks, enforced apologies, lowering the marks, personal indignities, threats and warnings, humiliation, sarcasm and ridicule, satiation, nagging, scolding, and *demerits.*
14. Corporal punishment, suspension, and expulsion are to be used in extreme situations only, and then with appropriate precautions and care by the school administrators.

47. FORCE FIELD ANALYSIS

SALLIE E. TANCIL

Mike (that isn't his real name) is a sixth grader in our school, and like many another schoolchild today he is the center of a daily drama.

Mike enters the office holding a note. He hands me the paper with a look that is a mixture of defeat and defiance, and I read the note with resignation. "Mike has upset the class again by being involved in everything but his assignment. I'll talk to you about this situation after dismissal."

I ask questions and Mike answers, "Yes, ma'am," or "No, ma'am." He wants to do better but doesn't know how, and I don't seem to be able to help. He finally returns to his room, temporarily subdued.

The players in the drama—Mike, his teacher, and I—seemed to be trapped in our roles, unable to help Mike reorganize his behavior style and become a productive learner. Because of this, I decided to try a social science experiment, to apply action research to the problem of Mike's behavior.

The next time he was sent to the office, I held out a 12-inch ruler to him. "Grab hold, Mike," I said, "and pull hard." He did, and as he pulled on his end, I pulled on mine.

"These are opposing forces, Mike," I said. "They are pulling against each other and keeping the ruler in pretty much the same spot. That's what happens with you in class; some forces are driving you toward success and others are driving you away from success. These forces keep canceling each other out, and your behavior stays pretty much the same."

I was introducing the idea of force-field analysis, developed by the social psychologist, Kurt Lewin, and used by the NTL Institute for Applied Behavioral Science in training for problem solving. Lewin describes a situation as an equilibrium main-

Sallie E. Tancil, "Force Field Analysis," Today's Education-NEA Journal, *LVII, No. 3 (1968), 22–23. Reprinted with permission from the author and publisher.*

tained by opposing forces—driving and restraining, for and against, away from and toward the goal. Lewin's theory is that a situation changes when restraining forces are reduced or driving forces increased. Force-field analysis is a way of diagraming a situation so that you can see what the forces are.

After I told Mike about force-field analysis, we diagramed his classroom behavior on a large sheet of newsprint taped to the office wall. It took about 10 minutes of questions and answers to achieve a sheet that looked like this:

Mike's goal: Do better in school

Helping Forces →	← Holding Back Forces
I can do most of the work. I like to help my sister with her fourth grade work. I like school sometimes. I'm near the top of my class in ability.	I don't like history. Some boys in my room are always calling me names. Sometimes things go bad at home and I don't want to come to school. My mother gets mad when I mess the house doing homework. I don't have many friends.

This session with Mike was encouraging. He and I made a start toward understanding his problems. I was eager to share what I had learned about him with his mother and his teacher, but I decided to ask both of them to do a force-field analysis first and then bring them together to compare the analysis.

The teacher's analysis added these previously undisclosed data to the picture:

Helping Forces →	← Restraining Forces
Mike wants the class to know he can do the work. He likes to bring and share his encyclopedia. He wants to feel important.	He gets bossy, argumentative, and disruptive. Sometimes he is preoccupied with home life, which he says is "messy." He is only erratically motivated to work.

Mike's mother added a few more details:

Helping Forces →	← Restraining Forces
I want to help him and myself. He makes friends easily. I help him with his work when he brings it home.	He is the scapegoat when things go wrong at home. His home life is not stimulating. He doesn't seem to care about school or people. He is firm about what he will and will not do.

When the four of us met, the three different force-field views of Mike were on the wall, side by side. We read them independently, made sure each of us understood every item, and spent a few minutes silently contemplating how we might alter the balance of forces. Mike was then excused.

It didn't take the rest of us long to come up with action possibilities. The teacher felt that she could work toward strengthening several helping forces. She could recognize Mike's ability, meet his need for approval, and capitalize on his willingness to help others by using him as a helper in class.

Mike's mother was impressed by the boy's concern about his home life. She felt she could watch her tendency to blame him when things went wrong and could make the family aware of his ability and his needs.

The teacher, the mother, and I planned to check with each other once a week to see how our strategy for change was working out.

The next day I told Mike about what his mother and teacher were planning to do to help him. He said he was glad his mother knew he didn't do all the things she blamed him for. The suggestion that his teacher might let him help teach others in the class appealed to him.

By studying his force field, Mike learned that adults really want to help him. He decided that he would work to curb his tendency to be impudent.

"It won't be too bad coming to school every day," he said with a shy smile. "I guess they really like me."

I felt that force-field analysis had been a successful tool in working on Mike's problem.

48. DIAGNOSING A CLASSROOM PROBLEM

DOROTHY J. MIEL / STANLEY JACOBSON

When a doctor asks his patient "What hurts?" he is beginning his diagnosis of a problem. Once he knows all the symptoms, he can decide which ones are important and which can be relieved. He understands the problem and can determine what actions to take.

Dorothy J. Miel and Stanley Jacobson, "Diagnosing a Classroom Problem," TODAY'S EDUCATION-NEA JOURNAL, *LVII, No. 9 (1968), 79–80. Reprinted with permission from the authors and publisher.*

Diagnosis is also an important step in solving classroom problems. A class may be facing a specific problem: The same few students are always the ones to raise their hands, or a clash has developed between subgroups in the room. Or perhaps the students want to work on one of the kinds of projects mentioned in last month's

Interaction Briefs; for example, how to improve the classroom climate, how to make lunchtime more relaxing, how to learn most about a specific subject. Once the problem or idea has been clearly stated, the next step is diagnosis—finding out why the present situation is as it is. Through problem diagnosis, students can move from creative thinking toward creative action, and also learn to be more effective problem solvers.

An interesting method of diagnosing a problem that children as young as third graders can engage in is called force-field analysis. [See "Force-Field Analysis" in the March 1968 Journal and *Handbook of Staff Development*, pp. 105–111. NTL Institute.]* It is an approach developed by social psychologist Kurt Lewin, who saw a problem as a state of affairs kept constant by equal pushes in both directions—"an equilibrium maintained by a balance of driving and restraining forces," to use Lewin's language. To Lewin, changing a problem situation was a matter of altering the balance in this field of forces. Force-field analysis, a way of diagraming this view of a problem, has proved to be a widely useful technique.

Let us say the goal is to "improve our relationships in this class" and the problem being focused on is the divisive influence of a small clique. The situation would be diagramed this way:

Goal: To Improve Our Relationships →

Problem Situation: A Small Group Keep to Themselves

Forces for Improvement →	← Forces Against Improvement

* Article 47 in this chapter.

In the left column would be listed all the facts, attitudes, feelings, and so on that push toward making the small group more a part of the class. In the right column would be listed everything that tends to make the small group more tightly knit and exclusive. After the lists are made, the class can determine which positive forces can be strengthened and which negative ones can be decreased.

To use force-field analysis in the classroom, have the class select a problem and state both the goal and the problem situation. Draw the diagram at the top of the chalkboard, explain it, then ask the group to start naming forces to go in either column. The beginning lists might look like this:

Forces for Improvement →	← Forces Against Improvement
Others Feel Left Out →	← People in the Small Group Like One Another
Interest in the Small Group Interferes with Attention to Classwork →	← It's Natural to Have Special Friends
We Should All Be Friends →	← The Class Is Too Big

Given time and encouragement, pupils should be able to come up with a number of enlightening ideas. Some factors—class size for example—will be difficult, if not impossible, to do anything about; but the group can work on a number of the ideas.

Some factors will lend themselves to a force-field analysis of their own. For example, if "people feel left out" is taken as a problem statement, the group can list all the forces in the classroom that push toward and against feeling "left out." Other listed items might lend themselves to committee work. In the illustrated problem, a committee might work on "how we can keep interest in the small group from interfering with classwork." The class may produce creative action steps which will improve relationships without requiring authoritative decisions by the teacher.

With experience, force-field analysis becomes a way of looking at a problem situation that brings greater breadth and more innovative ideas to the consideration of solutions.

49. THE RIPPLE EFFECT IN DISCIPLINE

JACOB S. KOUNIN / PAUL V. GUMP

Discipline is a serious concern to many teachers, especially beginners. The teacher who seeks help in discipline is likely to get advice that draws heavily on lore. The counsel may carry the name of a respected authority or the prestige of a widely accepted educational philosophy.

But how much advice on classroom discipline, even advice offered under such auspices, meets the test of experimentation? How many widely accepted beliefs and practices have been upheld by careful research?

In Detroit, we are studying classroom management (1). In one phase of our study, we are paying special attention to the "ripple effect," or the influence that control techniques have—not on the children who are being disciplined—but on the other children who are watching and listening.

Briefly, the problem may be put in this way: While the teacher is correcting Sally, what effect is the disciplinary measure having on Ruth, who is sitting nearby, taking in what is happening?

Answers were sought in the kindergartens of twenty-six representative Detroit schools. In the study reported here, fifty-one undergraduates served as observers. The students began their observations on the first days of the new school year.

Jacob S. Kounin and Paul V. Gump, "The Ripple Effect in Discipline," ELEMENTARY SCHOOL JOURNAL, *LIX, No. 3 (1962), 158–62.*

The observers were carefully instructed on their assignment. They were to note any incident in which a kindergartner watched the teacher correct another child for misbehavior. They were to report in detail on three phases of each incident: the behavior of the watching child immediately before the incident, the behavior of the teacher and the child who was being corrected during the incident, and the behavior of the watching child for two minutes after the incident.

Four hundred and six such incidents were analyzed. In our analysis, we classified the control technique itself, the behavior of the watching child before the incident, and the behavior of the watching child after the incident.

The Control Technique

Three dimensions of the control techniques used by the teachers were measured: clarity, firmness, and roughness.

Clarity involved the teacher's directions to the children. How clearly did the directions define the misbehavior the teacher wanted to bring to an end?

A teacher might say: "Tommy, stop it!" Or "Tommy, you can't do that!" Or "Tommy, that will do!" However emphatically uttered, these directions did not make it clear what Tommy was to stop doing.

A teacher who wanted to make sure that a pupil understood what was expected of him might use one of several approaches. The teacher might give directions that defined the pupil's misbehavior: "Tommy, don't take the blocks away from Johnny while he's using them." Or the teacher might give the child an acceptable standard of behavior: "Tommy, in kindergarten we ask for things. We don't grab." Or the teacher might tell Tommy how to stop the misbehavior: "Tommy, put those blocks down and look at the picture books."

Firmness involved how much "I-mean-it" the teacher packed into the disciplinary technique. How did the teachers say "I mean it"?

By touching or guiding the child. By speaking emphatically. By walking close to the child. Or by following through, that is, by focusing steadily on the misbehaving child until he conformed. If the teacher brushed over the trouble lightly, the correction conveyed little firmness.

Roughness described techniques in which the teacher expressed hostility or exasperation. If the teacher touched the child, the touch had more pressure than was necessary. If the teacher gave the child a warning look, the look was angry rather than serious. The samples in the study showed no extremely harsh techniques. No child, for example, was shaken or spanked.

The Children's Reactions

The children who watched while a classmate was being corrected responded in various ways, which we classified in five categories. Sometimes boys and girls showed no reaction. They simply went about their business, making no observable response to the episode. If the children happened to be drawing when a classmate was admonished, they simply continued with their drawing.

At other times, children reacted sharply to the correction of a classmate. They lost interest in what they had been doing and became worried, confused, and restless. This type of reaction was classified under "behavior disruption."

At still other times, children responded with a special effort to be good. They stopped a misbehavior of their own, sat up taller, paid closer attention to the lesson, or tried in some other way to show that they were not misbehaving. These reactions were grouped under "conformance."

Sometimes the correction had no deterrent effect whatsoever. Even though a child had just seen a classmate corrected for misbehaving, he launched some mischief of his own. This response was classified as "nonconformance."

At times, children in the audience vacillated between conformance and nonconformance. During the two minutes after the teacher had corrected a classmate, they both conformed and misbehaved.

We related the children's reactions to the teacher's control techniques (2). When the teachers made it very clear what they expected of a child, the children in the audience responded with increased conformance and decreased nonconformance. When the teachers did not make it clear what they expected of the child they were correcting, the effect on the young observers was reversed, that is, they responded with less conformance and more nonconformance. The probability level (3) for this difference, by the chi-square test, was .01.

The clarity of the teachers' directions was plainly related to the responses of the children in the audience, but the firmness of the teachers' technique, the researchers found, only tended to be related to the reactions of these children. In other words, the knowledge that a control technique was firm or lacking in firmness did not enable us to predict how a watching child would react.

Finally, we found a relation between the roughness of the control technique and the response of the watching child. Roughness did not lead to increased conformance and decreased nonconformance. Instead, rough techniques were followed by an increase in behavior disruption. Severe techniques did not make for "better" behavior in the watching child. Severe techniques simply upset him.

Our study recognized that control techniques alone do not determine how a watching child reacts. Other influences are also at work.

The Impact of the Setting

We investigated three possibilities. First of all, we asked: "What was the watching child doing just before the incident?" Our next concern: Was the watching child psychologically close to the child who was being corrected? Was the child in the audience watching his misbehaving classmate with considerable interest? Finally, how long had the watching child been in kindergarten?

Children who were themselves misbehaving—or even innocently related to misbehavior—were much more responsive as they watched the teachers' efforts to control than were the children who were free of any connection with misbehavior. Children who at the moment were free of misbehavior were quite likely to show no reaction. Children who were misbehaving showed more conformance, more nonconformance, and markedly more vacillation between conformance and nonconformance (probability level .001).

It was instructive to compare the effects of clarity and firmness on the various groups. The effects already noted for clarity were obtained regardless of whether or not the watching child was associated with misbehavior. However, firmness affected only groups that had some connection with misbehavior. In these groups, high firmness increased conformance and decreased nonconformance (probability level .05).

The length of time the children had been in kindergarten, we found, affected their reactions. On the first day the children were highly sensitive to control techniques. They showed some outward reaction to 55 per cent of all control incidents. On the next three days they reacted outwardly to only 34 per cent of the incidents (probability level .001).

Among Our Findings

To the extent that we can generalize on cause and effect, the study indicates that the reaction of watching children to a teacher's control of a misbehaving child is related to at least three factors.

First, the newness of the situation. On the first day in kindergarten, watching children showed the strongest responses.

Second, the behavior of the watching children. Pupils who were themselves misbehaving or interested in children who were misbehaving were more likely to show the strongest reactions; the particular response was most likely to be vacillation.

Third, the disciplinary technique itself, that is, the clarity, the firmness, and the roughness of the technique.

When the teacher made it clear what behavior she objected to or what behavior she expected, the watching children responded with increased conformance and decreased nonconformance.

If the teacher's behavior conveyed firmness, the watching children sometimes responded with increased conformance and decreased nonconformance. This reaction occurrred if the watching children had been misbehaving or interested in a child who was misbehaving.

If the teacher used rough techniques, the children showed behavior disruption but not conformance or nonconformance.

It should be kept in mind that clarity in the teacher's directions led to greater conformance and less nonconformance in a new and unstructured situation. When children are new to kindergarten or to the teacher, they may be especially sensitive to his directions and desires. As the child feels more at home in kindergarten and more at ease with the teacher, we would expect clarity to be less important. Several studies are now in progress to check this expectation.

Fact and Lore

What meaning does the study have for teachers of children who are just beginning kindergarten? It is clear that a ripple effect does exist. What a teacher does to control children's behavior affects the children who watch as well as the children who are corrected.

The teacher who is interested in

controlling ripple effects can generally do so best by giving clear instructions to the child rather than by exerting pressure on him. However, some intensity or firmness is effective if the children who are watching are themselves inclined to "deviancy."

The study does not support the notion that the teacher must "bear down" on the first day or "make an example" of a child. Such steps are not necessary to induce conformity in children who are entering kindergarten. Nor does the study support the contention that roughness and anger are simply firmness intensified. Firmness and roughness are different qualities. Witness the different effects they have on watching children.

Notes

1. The research is sponsored by the Department of Educational Psychology, College of Education, Wayne State University. Financial support has been provided by the National Institute of Mental Health, National Institutes of Health, Public Health Service, Grant 1066.

2. The inter-coder reliability on a 24-item control technique code was 78 per cent agreement; on a 34-item audience reaction code, 83 per cent. Since the former was collapsed to three dimensions and the latter to five categories, the functional reliability would be even higher. To avoid possible bias, different teams coded the control techniques used by teachers and the reactions of the watching children.

3. Probability levels refer to the probability that the differences obtained could be due to chance. For example, a probability level of .01 means that the difference obtained would occur by chance less than one time in a hundred.

50. THE DYNAMICS OF LEARNING

NATHANIEL CANTOR

Mr. Robin was called to a conference with me. He had failed to hand in several previous assignments. He came 45 minutes late for the appointment. Another time was arranged and he was 10 minutes late.

Robin: What did you want to see me about?

I: I thought we might discuss your work in relation to the class. (Robin remained silent.) How do you feel about the quality of work you are doing?

Robin: I'm very much interested in the course as you can tell by my discussions in class.

I: Apparently your interest doesn't extend to handing in the written assignments.

Robin: Oh, those. The reason for that is simple. I don't like to hand in papers written in my sloppy handwriting, I prefer typing them.

I: Yes, I find it much easier to read. But I've received no typewritten papers.

Robin: I want to do good papers and haven't got 'round to complete them.

I: I believe they were all due weeks ago.

Robin: Well, you wouldn't want me just to hand in a paper for the sake of being on time if I haven't anything to say?

I: It may be that if you have nothing to say, the course isn't giving you enough, and you should resign from it. That sometimes happens.

Robin: I don't want to do that, I'm getting lots out of the course.

I: What are you giving to it?

Robin: You mean the papers, again?

I: That is your responsibility.

Robin: I am interested in the course, but I carry three lab courses and am taking the course in

Nathaniel Cantor, THE DYNAMICS OF LEARNING *(Buffalo, N.Y.: Henry Stewart, Inc., 1946), pp. 169–73. Reprinted by permission.*

flying. The trips to and from the flying field take an awful lot of time, and I can't get around to writing the papers.

I: You mean typewriting the papers.

Robin: Well, that was the original reason I gave.

I: If you are too busy with other matters, I suppose the wise thing to do is to select what interests you most. If you haven't time to carry out the responsibility of this class, perhaps it's best that you drop it.

Robin: I don't want to drop out. (There was a half minute of silence.) Suppose I accept whatever penalty goes with not handing in papers?

I: It isn't a matter of penalty which should interest us, but whether you are doing the best kind of work of which you are capable.

Robin: Well, what do you want me to do?

I: That's up to you. What do you want to do?

Robin: What's the point of going through the motions and just handing in black scribbling on white paper—just to hand something in?

I: There isn't much point to that.

Robin: Well, I could do that like others are doing.

I: Perhaps some of the others who just hand in anything also aren't meeting their responsibility, doing their best work? I suppose, too, that what they do is irrelevant to our problem. (There was silence for about a minute.)

Robin: Will you do something for me, Dr. Cantor?

I: If I can.

Robin: I've been in a jam in my other work, too. I don't know what's the matter. I'm having trouble with my girl and my parents. Can you understand what I mean? (Tears started to appear.)

I: I appreciate something of the difficulties which must be involved. And in addition you have the problem of doing something about your work in criminology.

Robin: You're the only professor I feel like talking to.

I: What would you like me to do about helping you in your work in criminology?

Robin: Will you give me a week's time to think the whole matter over?

I: What is there to think about?

Robin: I want to decide what to do about the course.

I: Very well, suppose we meet a week from today at the same hour.

Robin: Thanks, I know it's my problem and I'll settle it.

Mr. Robin was not doing satisfactory work, he failed to hand in written assignments, and when he did participate in discussion I felt his remarks were perfunctory. He was late for both appointments. His first direct remark, "What did you want to see me about?" carried a defensive tone. His first defense for not handing in the assigned papers was his failure to typewrite them. The second justification was lack of time. (He gives himself away when I remark he meant "typewriting" instead of "writing" by stating, "Well, that was the original reason I gave.") The third reason was that writing papers is formal and worthless, "black scribbling on white paper." He was unwilling, as yet, to face the fact that he has tried to escape his responsibility. My criticism gave him something to think about and feel about. He could not continue in the same way. Some new direction had to be defined one way or another, and he had to discover it for himself.

He was, apparently, dissatisfied with his work not only in CS but in his other courses. My holding him to account led him into another attitude. He suddenly dropped his slightly belligerent attitude, and asked me to help him out of a jam.

He wanted to talk about the backgrounds of his difficulty. It was a temptation to which I almost yielded since I felt that he would be immensely relieved if he could express what was troubling him. But by talking *about* what led up to his poor work would have been another way of avoiding doing something about it. I could offer my help to him only insofar as his difficulty was reflected in the kind of work he did in the CS course. I am not a therapist. My function is to deal with a student's difficulty only insofar as his work in CS is involved. My firm stand gave Mr. Robin a chance to come to grips with one definite obstacle if he would.

Sooner or later, the movement initiated by my criticism must have led to a reorganization on Mr. Robin's part with reference to the course, or he would have to leave it. If he accepted and assimilated my difference, it meant he recognized the legitimacy of it, i.e., his positive self was criticizing his negative self (represented by my negative criticism).

Two days after this conference, Mr. Robin handed in, at the regular time, his reactions to a long chapter in the text:

"The chapter makes clear the extensive disorganization and lack of effective policy in the treatment of prisoners. The problems involved in treatment are complicated and far from being solved.—Impressions not completed."

The last three words were hastily added in pencil. I had observed his writing this brief paper in class. Mr. Robin was again asked to see me. An appointment was made. He did not appear. I subsequently learned that he resigned from the college, having also been in difficulties with his other courses. (Some of the administrative officers of the college had tried to help Mr. Robin and had not succeeded. I do not know whether I would have helped him if I had permitted him to discuss his personal affairs with me. I feel, however, that that is not my function. I could, perhaps, have suggested, but failed to, that Mr. Robin make an appointment with the school psychiatrist.)

51. CONTROL IN AN EDUCATIONAL ORGANIZATION

DONALD J. WILLOWER / RONALD G. JONES

The study[1] reported briefly here examined certain social processes in a single educational organization, a junior high school in a middle-sized city in Pennsylvania. The school had an enrollment of approximately 1600 students and a faculty of 72. Its administrative staff consisted of a principal, three guidance counselors, one of whom was half-time, and eight department heads. The principal was new to the school, having succeeded a long-term principal who retired shortly after the study began.

Our purposes were simple ones: to describe social behavior in an educational organization, and to apply and develop concepts which might be theoretically useful and lead to further research. The techniques used were basically observation and interview. Numerous observations were made at the school over a 14-month period beginning in April, 1962, and more than 60 interviews were conducted. Since the study was limited to a single organization, it should be clear that only very tentative generalizations can be made from it.

During the study, we were quite naturally confronted by a multitude of data provided by our observations of behavior in the faculty lounge, in faculty and administrative meetings, in classes, in the corridors, in the cafeteria and the assembly, and by the feelings, perceptions and opinions expressed by those we interviewed. A central task was to give clearer meaning, order, and some unity to these diverse data.

In their study of organizations and of societies, sociologists and anthropologists have often employed con-

The original paper is reprinted here by permission of the authors. An edited version appears as: "When Pupil Control Becomes an Institutional Theme," Phi Delta Kappan, *XLV, No. 2 (November 1963), 107–9.*

[1] The study was supported by a grant from the Research Fund of the College of Education, The Pennsylvania State University. We also owe a considerable debt to the administration and faculty of the school studied for their cooperation and assistance.

cepts which are integrative and which portray social systems as unified wholes rather than as fragmented and unrelated parts. We sought and found such an integrative theme in the school under study; it was clearly that of pupil control.[2] While there were certainly many matters which could not be particularly related to this concept, pupil control appeared to be a dominant motif within the school.

Selected Data

Faculty informal structure was characterized by a number of groupings. One such grouping was based on differences in age, number of years at the school, and certain attitudes. On the one hand, those teachers who had been teaching at the school for a number of years and who were older held generally conservative views. On the other hand, those teachers who had been teaching at the school for shorter periods of time, usually five years or less, and who were younger held more liberal and permissive views. Members of the older group placed great stress on pupil control and discipline, and did not hesitate to communicate their views to the younger teachers whom they often viewed as being lax and failing to maintain sufficient social distance between themselves and students. Younger teachers sometimes tried to win the approval of their more conservative colleagues by talking or acting "tough" with regard to students. These attempts met with mixed success, one teacher reporting that "no matter how strict you are, they still think you're soft on discipline."

A good deal of the "tough talk" regarding students occurred in the faculty lounges. There were separate lounges for men and women teachers in the school, and while data concerning the men's lounge were based on direct observation, information regarding the women teachers' lounge was based entirely upon interviews. Talk in the men's lounge was primarily concerned with students and sports. The sports talk focused on the national level and on the school's extensive athletic program. With regard to students, the following kinds of discussion predominated: boasting about the tough and uncompromising manner in which a particularly difficult discipline problem was handled, ridiculing students, especially their answers to teacher questions and tests, and more pointedly aggressive references to students who were considered to be hopelessly uncooperative. Interviews indicated that talk in the women's lounge followed a similar pattern except that sports were not much discussed. The term "gossiping" was used in several interviews to describe teacher behavior there. This included more talk about a student's family, particularly about brothers and sisters who had preceded him at the school, than occurred in the men's lounge.

Another type of teacher behavior of some interest occurred in the "circle meetings," which were held prior to each marking period. A circle consisted of those teachers of the four "solid subjects" teaching the same students; it also included guidance personnel, and the principal who was an ex officio member of every

2 Pupil control is a form of social control. Social control is the process by which social order is established and maintained. See Paul H. Landis, *Social Control* (Philadelphia: J. B. Lippincott Co., 1956), p. 4.

circle but did not attend every meeting. The formally stated purpose of the meetings was to better meet student needs by coordinating the work of teachers, counselors, and administrators with regard to the problems of students. However, the circle meetings actually were used to come to a united front in the grading of students, particularly in the assignment of failing grades. While a variety of data led to this conclusion, the following occurrence illustrated it rather well: A circle chairman had some difficulty setting a suitable meeting time for the circle and became quite anxious because "I don't want to be out on a limb with my F grades."

With regard to teacher-administrator relations, two points relative to the pupil control theme should be made. The first concerns the retired principal and occurred prior to the study but was mentioned frequently in interviews. During the last few years of his tenure, the principal was in poor health. The faculty, to use a term employed by one of the teachers, "carried" the principal; that is, they handled things themselves wherever possible so as not to add to his work load. Instead of sending the more serious discipline cases to the principal's office, the teachers handled them or, more often, these cases were sent to the guidance counselor. The counselor, then the only full-time guidance person at the school, clearly recognized the undesirability of mixing guidance and discipline, but all involved gave higher priority to the maintenance of the discipline function.

When the new principal took over, the greatest single concern of the faculty was that he might be weak on discipline. This was mentioned by teachers again and again during interviews. He had to win his spurs with the faculty by showing that he was a stern disciplinarian. In so doing, he separated guidance and discipline, took full responsibility for discipline on himself, and worked hard to show the faculty that he was not "soft." While he has generally succeeded, many teachers appear ready to change their opinions at the slightest provocation. Thus, in tallying up at the close of the school year, a number of teachers noted that the new principal had suspended fewer pupils over the year than had typically been the case with his predecessor. Also, a number of the women teachers were annoyed when the new principal moved into a somewhat less accessible office than had been occupied by the former principal. We were told the reason for their annoyance was that they could not get to him as easily when they had a discipline case to bring to his attention.

The theme of pupil control fits the general climate of the school as the writers developed a "feel" for it, and it fits the behavior, particularly of teachers, which we observed in the corridors, in the assembly, and in the cafeteria. A symbolic referent was the single roll of toilet tissue found in the boy's lavatories; it hung by padlocked chain from a post near the door.

A final observation does not seem to fit the theme of pupil control: The concept of social obligations[3] appeared to be particularly useful in explaining certain relationships, especially those between the faculty and the old principal. The following inci-

[3] Peter M. Blau, *Bureaucracy in Modern Society* (New York: Random House, Inc., 1956), pp. 72–73.

dent illustrates this: At a faculty meeting a teacher objected strongly to a proposal made by the principal. The teacher expected the support of most of the faculty since the proposal involved extra duty for teachers. However, he spoke alone in opposition; our interviewees stated that this happened because most of the teachers were obligated to the principal for favors done. The concept of social obligations applied less well to relationships between the faculty and the new principal probably because it takes time for a new system of social obligations to develop after an administrator enters upon a new position.

Discussion

On the basis of our observations and interviews, we are convinced that the theme of pupil control is an apt one in the school studied. We are less sure that the school is a representative one. One factor which makes us particularly cautious in this respect is that the school exists in an area of high unemployment and low income.[4] On the other hand, all who are familiar with schools know the stress placed on pupil control in most of them, and the Tom Sawyer attitude which many students have toward school is too well known to chronicle here.

On a more theoretical level, public schools can be viewed as an organizational type. Carlson[5] notes that in some service-type organizations, the organization controls the selection of its clients while in others, it does not; in some cases, clients can refuse to participate in the organization while in others, they cannot. These considerations lead to a four-category classification scheme. Public schools fall in the category of organizations which have no control over client selection and where clients have no choice concerning their participation. That control should be identified as central in such organizations does not seem surprising. Indeed, studies of other organizations of the same type, e.g., mental hospitals and prisons, focus on control as a major variable. While mental hospitals and prisons are, in Goffman's[6] terms, total institutions and public schools are not, studies of the former organizations can provide helpful leads in analyzing schools. The concept of displacement of goals has been used extensively in such studies where it has been observed that control goals frequently replace treatment or rehabilitative goals. The circle meetings in the present study provided an example of goal displacement, and the general emphasis on control goals in the school could hardly fail to lead to displacement of instructional goals at certain points.

Whether stress on pupil control is

4 Another feature which seemed unusual to us was that nearly one-fourth of the teachers had themselves attended the school as students and more than one-half had attended the local high school. We do not know how this compares with other schools but it does seem meaningful to the relationships between older and younger teachers. The question of what kind of person returns is also interesting.

5 Richard O. Carlson, "Environmental Constraints and Organizational Consequences: The Public School and Its Clients." Draft of a paper prepared for the 1964 Yearbook of the National Society for the Study of Education, 1962.

6 Erving Goffman, *Asylums* (Garden City, N. Y.: Doubleday & Company, Inc., 1961), especially pp. 3–124.

viewed as functional or dysfunctional depends upon one's perspective. In terms of the limitations faced by many schools—overcrowding, low teacher pay, student apathy—an emphasis on control could be seen as functional, enabling the school to make the best of a difficult situation. In terms of a broader view of what education might become and ought to be, such an emphasis is largely dysfunctional. A strong emphasis on control usually returns definite but short-range gains and may be self-defeating in the long run. Clearly, the teachers in the school under study insisted upon the shorter range objective.

New teachers are quickly exposed to informal norms as well as to more formal expectations in the process of socialization into the organization. New teachers and sometimes student teachers were frequently silent but interested listeners in the faculty lounge discussions described earlier. They learned that they had to be "tough on discipline" to get along; and they knew that they were restricted in the kinds of innovations they could employ in their classrooms, since the use of more permissive methods left them open to the charge of softness. This created a serious problem for the more idealistic new teachers. As one teacher put it: "These new teachers come out of college filled with ideas, then they meet opposition from the old-timers who have been going over the same problems in the same ways for years." Ideals need reinforcement. If that is lacking, it seems logical that the idealistic teacher will, in consequence, employ certain adaptive behaviors. Thus, he may go along, submerge his ideals and not act on them, he may engage in conflict with his colleagues, or he may leave the organization. In the event that the first of these adaptations is employed, energies might be directed toward some other facet of the organization's activity. In this connection, it should be recalled that we observed unusual commitment and activity on the part of the male teachers with regard to the school's athletic program.

The "scapegoating" of students observed in the faculty lounge also deserves comment. Blau and Scott[7] discuss the same kind of behavior on the part of staff members in a public employment agency. They point out that such behavior has several functions. It furnishes an escape valve for releasing aggressive feelings against clients in a relatively harmless form and it provides social approval from peers, which helps to relieve feelings of guilt for not having done a more effective job with clients. While such behavior led to the reduction of staff tensions and increased social support, it also legitimated inconsiderate treatment of clients. These points appear to apply to the teacher behavior observed in this study.

It seems obvious yet important to note that the study reported here points to the kinds of issues which lie at the core of educational administration—the individual and the organization, idealism and disillusion, stability and the difficulty of instituting innovation and change, short-run and long-range goals, and the purposes for which administrative leadership in education ought to be employed. While its limitations have been noted, this research, among other things, points to pupil control as an integrative concept of some

[7] Peter M. Blau and W. Richard Scott, *Formal Organizations* (San Francisco: Chandler Publishing Co., 1962), pp. 84–85.

value in studying educational organizations. We have only scratched the surface. Further studies which focus on pupil control in schools are needed. Such studies may reveal still other useful integrative concepts.

ACTIVITIES

1. Discipline behaviors may be seen as symptoms. Several articles in previous sections are directed toward teacher behaviors that may be seen as preventative in nature concerning discipline problems. [See Gage (Chapter 1), Flanders (Chapter 2), L. E. Raths (Chapter 7) and the articles in this chapter.] Discuss the ways these articles suggest teachers might prevent discipline problems from arising.

2. Examine the rules and regulations pertaining to discipline found in faculty bulletins or school regulations. Do the rules and regulations relate to preventative practices or corrective policies? Are the policies stated in terms of positive behaviors or negative behaviors?

3. Observe classroom teaching. Identify ways teachers control apparent misbehavior. Describe each technique they used and the effects it had on the child being disciplined and the other children in the classroom (ripple effect).

4. In his interview, Cantor seems unsympathetic to the needs of his student. Is Cantor's behavior exemplifying corrective discipline? preventative discipline? neither? What would you have done in Cantor's place? Explain your answer.

5. How would you define "democratic discipline"? What consequences would your interpretation have for you as a classroom teacher?

6. Are Batchelder's recommendations consistent with Ausubel's point of view?

7. Do the recommendations of Batchelder in any way conflict with the research findings of Kounin and Gump?

8. Recall several situations from your own school experience in which the teacher "disciplined" a student or group of students. Do you think your teacher would have agreed with Ausubel? With Batchelder? With Willower and Jones?

9. If it were safe to generalize the findings of Willower and Jones to the school in which you will teach, what statements might you make to other teachers, and to the principal, about how you maintain or expect to maintain classroom control?

MOTIVATING STUDENTS

CHAPTER NINE

Motivation is a man-made construct. It cannot be seen or touched. Rather than a concrete entity, the word "motivation" refers to an explanation that accounts for observed behavior. If teachers see students working hard toward the accomplishment of a goal, they might explain the enthusiasm of the students in terms of high motivation. On the other hand, if a bright student time after time receives low grades on tests, teachers might attribute the discrepancy of high intelligence-low achievement to a lack of motivation. While motivation is not real or observable in itself, there is no question that it is important to catch the interests of students. There is no pat answer showing teachers how to accomplish this goal, and there is no indication that such an answer will soon be forthcoming. Nevertheless, the articles that follow are intended to acquaint teachers with some of the usable research findings in the field of motivation.*

* *Note to the Reader*: Answer the first 15 questions in the activities section before reading the articles in this chapter.

52. MOTIVATION: THE EDUCATOR'S DILEMMA

WALTER B. WAETJEN

The typical curriculum developer, supervisor, and teacher is highly interested in what pupils do in the classroom and how well they do it. Their interest is along the lines of how well a student conjugates irregular verbs or the extent to which he understands the mitosis of cells. On the other hand, there are curriculum specialists and teachers who are not only interested in *what* pupils do, but *why* they do it. It becomes clear that there are two orders of consideration involved. The first order is that of behavior; the second order of consideration, however, is that of motivation. One is always tempted to make judgments as to which type of teacher or curriculum developer is the better one. Obviously, these two factors cannot be discreetly separated in practice, although we can for the moment separate them for the purposes of discussion.

When a teacher asks himself the question "What motivated this pupil's behavior?" he is asking to have identified one or more of three different things. The first of these is an environmental determinant which caused the behavior to occur. This could be the pressure of a parent to have his child learn, a provocative bulletin board display in the classroom, or a well presented demonstration by the teacher. Second, it may be an internal instinct: want, desire, aspiration, plan, motive, purpose, urge, feeling, wish, or drive, which precipitated the behavior. Third, it may be the goal which either attracted the learner or repelled him. Thus, we can see that when we raise questions about the motivation of pupils, we are not asking easy questions. The complexity of the questions has given rise to a number of theories of motivation. It is unfortunate that teachers and curriculum

Walter B. Waetjen, "Motivation: The Educator's Dilemma." The original paper is reprinted by permission of the author. The manuscript is a part of the PROCEEDINGS *(1965) of the Ohio Association for Supervision and Curriculum Development Research Institute.*

developers seem to subscribe to none. In order that this discourse not fall into the same trap, a theory of motivation will be presented; but prior to that we shall make explicit our use of the term "motivation."

For the purposes of this paper we shall define motivation as "... the process of arousing action, sustaining the activity in progress, and regulating the pattern of activity" (24). This definition makes it clear that there must be some mobilization of energy and there must be continuous flow of activity in order to assure attainment of the goal.

A Point of View about Motivation

In the process of growing up and experiencing, a child has many contacts with varied aspects of his environment. These "contacts" become incorporated into the cognitive structure, which is much like a private map the individual has of his world. It is the cognitive structure that the teacher tries to develop by teaching the curriculum content. When a teacher gives a demonstration, has youngsters work on projects, shows a film or gives a lecture, he is attempting to introduce information into the cognitive structure of the youngsters. It seems clear, then, that teachers must be knowledgeable about the functioning of the cognitive structure since this strikes at the heart of the dynamics of learning and motivation.

A person uses his cognitive map to make predictions from the past to the present situation. For example, a pupil uses his previous experience with teachers and classrooms to make predictions about the classroom which he has just entered. In so doing he assumes the present environment to be identical to or highly similar to what it was in the past. Ordinarily this is a good assumption and benefits the pupil since his expectancies permit him to make optimal use of both time and intellectual resources. What must be emphasized is that the pupil is actually making hypotheses about the stimuli he will be receiving. Sometimes the environment has changed in relatively important ways and hypotheses are not fulfilled.

It is entirely probable that the learner does not expect or anticipate that the present situation will be *identical* to those of the past. A young child may make such predictions from his cognitive structure, but with increased experience he would anticipate some difference. Thus, the anticipation of change is partially an *experiential matter*. The pupil faces the present situation, then, with two anticipations: (1) the environment will be, in the main, comparable to what it was in the past, and (2) there will be change in the environment. As experience accumulates, it is probable that the child savors the novelty of change in the environment and this becomes the basis for epistemic behavior.

It is not too uncommon to find teachers who assume that they are able to transmit curriculum content to the cognitive structure of a pupil. This assumption means that we can teach directly, that nothing intervenes between what the teacher teaches and what the learner learns. It is believed that if the teacher makes the curriculum content "interesting" by a few audiovisual devices or by introducing a note of excitement into his voice, the students will be motivated to learn. To make such assumptions means that we minimize strategic individual differences as factors in learning rather than maximize them.

If the material to be taught to youngsters is already similar to or contained in their existing cognitive structure, learning is not facilitated. This is portrayed in Fig. 1. It will be noted in Fig. 1 that the curriculum content and the instructional methods (indicated by the arrows) are designed to communicate to the youngster. In the event the curriculum content is already known to the youngster or is inconsequential to him, there is little behavior elicited from the learner himself. For the learner, such a situation is extremely lacking in and probably devoid of meaningful content. Instead of engaging in learning activity, it is more likely that nonproductive verbal behavior will increase, that motor activity of a random nature will increase, and that the person will become increasingly unable to give attention to specific ideas or tasks.

In this instance, there is practically 100 per cent match between what the teacher is attempting to teach and the preexisting content of the cognitive map. In such situations learning is not enhanced. As a matter of fact, that situation which we shall call the *100 per cent match situation* is indeed an enemy to learning. The type of behavior elicited from the learner is not learning behavior, but is random and nonproductive in nature.

Figure 2 portrays a different state of affairs in which there is for the most part a match between the curriculum content (including the instructional procedures) and the cognitive structure of the learners. Since there is a generous portion of match between these two elements, it means that the youngster is familiar with the material or the situation because they fit into his predictions. On the other hand, there is also some degree of "mismatch," meaning there are some elements of either the content or the instructional procedures which the learner does not know and did not predict. This is a dissonant situation which results in arousal of conflict with a consequent need for the learner to assimilate or articulate the unknown, incongruous, or unfamiliar material into his cognitive structure (5). To do this, he engages in exploratory behavior. Exploratory behavior, as it is being used here, means that the learner scans the classroom looking for new experiences and materials. Likewise, it means that the learner avoids the more familiar aspects of the classroom. There is an increase in the type of verbal activity which evokes information from other people. In this condition the learner is a *seeker* of knowledge. It would be improper to believe that all youngsters who are in the motivated condition engage in similar exploratory behaviors. We must recognize that the modes or strategies by which youngsters seek information and by which they process it into the cogni-

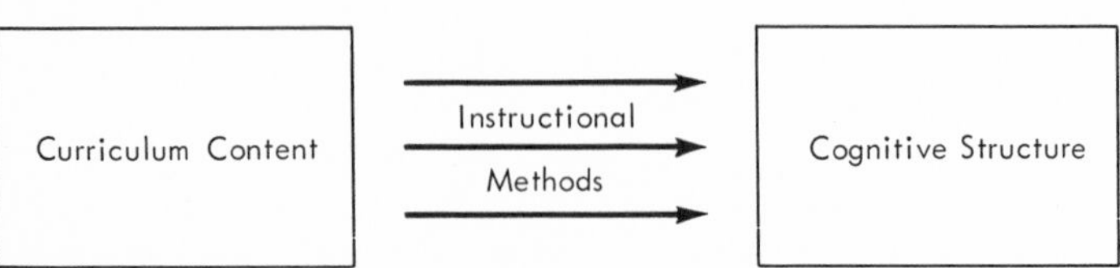

Figure 1.

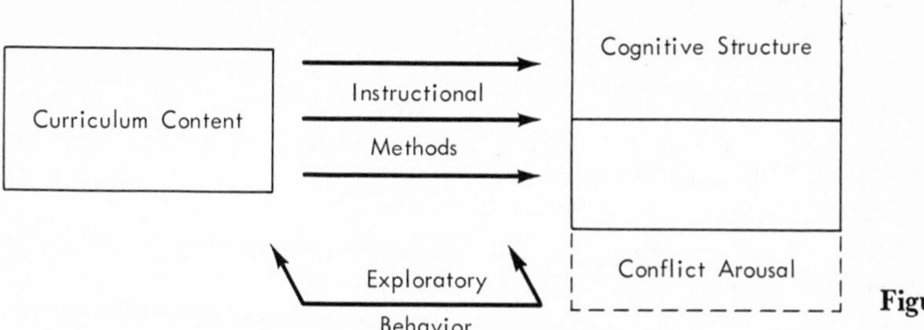

Figure 2.

tive structure are unique. We emphasize that this is an individual difference in learning.

In passing, we noted that verbal activity of the learner increased so as to cause him to evoke information from people. This is but another way of saying that a youngster engaging in exploratory behavior asks questions. It is altogether proper to speculate as to who asks questions in the typical classroom situation. The usual classroom situation is one in which teachers ask most of the questions. This is indeed a paradox for it should not be the teacher who is seeking knowledge by question asking. Herein lies one implication of this discussion: teachers can begin to reexamine the matter of *who* asks questions in the classroom and the *type* of questions asked.

Occasionally a teacher will attempt to get pupils to learn something by presenting them with a vast array of entirely new and different kinds of material. Literally, the learners are bombarded with new stimuli. The teacher is rather chagrined to find that the learners do not respond as anticipated and may even resist this seemingly rich learning environment. In this instance there is great mismatch between the learners' predictions and the material with which they came in contact. Figure 3 portrays the two things which eventuate when a great amount of mismatch

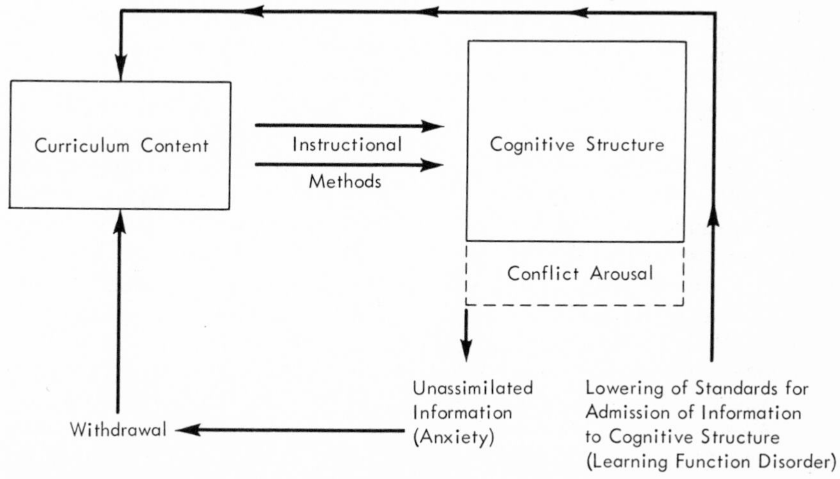

Figure 3.

occurs. In either case the information is unassimilated and usually is held in a context of anxiety. The learner is aware that he should be able to articulate the curriculum content with his present knowledge; but he is equally sensitive to the fact that he cannot do so and therefore he becomes anxious about the matter. To cope with this situation the learner may engage in a variety of withdrawing behaviors. He may withdraw from the conceptual material by being a gross dilettante in work production or by daydreaming to excess. On the other hand, he may physically withdraw by virtue of cutting classes or being a truant.

The second way of handling unassimilated information is more insidious and should cause teachers to be introspective. In this instance the learner abandons his usual strategies for admitting information to his cognitive domain. In abandoning these strategies he lowers his standards for admission of information into the cognitive structure. Instead of integrating simple facts into higher levels of organization the individual holds them at a lower level. This person can be thought of as having a learning disability, for good learning involves orchestrating simple acts or relatively simple ideas into higher and more complex acts or ideas. What is unfortunate about this type of learner is that he is often judged to be at least an adequate and maybe a good learner because he is able to retain facts even though he is not able to integrate them within the cognitive structure. When tests measure only the student's ability to retrieve data at the factual level, these students are erroneously perceived as progressing well even though they cannot be said to be effective learners. By lowering the standards for admission of information to their cognitive structure, they have at once put themselves in a position where they are functioning at a much lower level in their learning.

In summary, we have presented three conditions of learning based on the predictions that a pupil makes stemming from his cognitive structure. Condition One is when the classroom events entirely match the predictions the student has made (a consonant condition). Learning is not facilitated when there is this high degree of consonance. Condition Two is when the predictions of the learner are for the most part met but there is slight dissonance. Such a condition is highly favorable to learning, for the slight dissonance causes the learner to seek information (motivation) so as to reduce the conflict or dissonance. Condition Three is when there is great dissonance between the learner's predictions and the classroom events. Under such conditions the learner either withdraws from the situation, or he lowers the standards for admitting new material into the cognitive domain. Great dissonance, then, is the enemy of motivation and learning.

Although teachers tend to acknowledge motivating students to be one of their most important functions and they frequently complain about the lack of motivation in certain students or classes, the motive concept itself is generally invoked to explain or account for a pupil's behavior. Currently, little is known about the cues (from a child's behavior) which determine the basis for a teacher's judgments of motivation that underlie students' behavior. Also, there is precious little evidence as to how a teacher's subsequent behavior toward a learner is influenced by his perceptions of what causes or guides the learner's behavior. The main focus of an investigation by Johnson and others (9) was to discover how the characteristics and/or the behaviors of the student (the actor and his act) affect the teacher's perceptions of the locus of motivation, the attribution of characteristics by the teacher to the child, and the expressions of teacher's sentiment about the learner. In this experiment subjects attempted to teach an arithmetic unit (multiplying by 10's) to two fourth-grade boys, A and B (actually fictitious), who were situated in another room. After a subject had presented the concept, the student supposedly worked on problems that were based on the arithmetical concept. After a short period of time the experimentor returned with a previously prepared work sheet which was allegedly pupil A's work up to that time. At this time the subject was allowed to converse with B briefly by using a one-way intercom system. Later the experimentor returned with all of A's work and the rest of B's work on the task and the subject was permitted to talk briefly to A. The subjects were divided into 4 groups of 20 each.

The subjects were then given two "fictitious" cumulative record folders containing the personal history of A and B. They were asked to familiarize themselves with this material and then attempt to teach a second arithmetic unit (multiplying by 20's) after which the students again worked related problems. After a period of time the subjects were asked whose work they would like to see and they were allowed to talk with that student. Since the subjects were free to select either student A or B, these choices can be interpreted as expressions of sentiment. This choice was made again at the end of the task and the subjects communicated briefly with their choice. The experiment was designed to permit variation of B's performance on an initial task as well as it permitted variation of information concerning B's task, relevant characteristics from the accumulative record and also permitted variation of B's performance on the second task, that of multiplying by 20's. Throughout the experiment, A was constant on performance and on his characteristics as evidenced in the cumulative record.

The results on the perception of the locus of motivation are of particular interest since they suggest the manner in which these perceptions may be related to the problem of student motivation. A teacher's judgment that a student is internally motivated will tend to occur only when a student's performance is high or has improved and the perceived locus of motivation is internal. If the perceived locus is external, if the teacher sees himself as responsible for the student's good performance, the student will not be judged to be internally motivated. At the same time, judgments about lack of motivation also occur when performance is low and the perceived locus of motivation is internal. A large number of subjects perceived a positive external locus for B's good performance and few subjects perceived a negative external locus for B's poor performance. It is not surprising therefore that teachers should acknowledge that motivating students is an important problem. These findings suggest that students' motivation may be as much a perceptual problem involving the teacher as it is a psychological problem involving the learner.

It was noted that after the first

teaching task, the subjects in all four groups expressed positive sentiments that reflected trust of A, and negative sentiments reflecting distrust of B. It should be kept in mind that these expressions of sentiment came before the subjects supposedly had information from the cumulative record about the students. It should also be borne in mind that they had never seen the student but had only communicated with him through a one-way intercom system. It is equally interesting to note the kinds of characteristics that the subjects attributed to A and B following their first experience at teaching them on the first teaching task. For example, a significantly greater number of subjects attributed higher intelligence, higher achieving rate, more motivation, and more ambition to A and considered B to be least dependable, of lower social class, and most troublesome. What this seemingly adds up to is that these teachers vastly oversimplified what seemed to be involved in the motivation of A and B in the two learning tasks. It can be seen that even though the "teachers" had never seen A nor B, had only communicated with them through a one-way intercom system, and had seen their work sheets on only one learning task, they were prone to make many judgments about these students. Also, these teachers perceived themselves to be involved in B's good performance but did not see themselves as being involved in B's poor performance. In both cases, the locus for motivation was external but the teachers judged that it did not involve them.

Recently, research and theoretical formulations have tended to specify certain kinds of motives when human behavior is discussed. The following motives have been identified: achievement, power, affiliation, aggression, fear, dependency, and anxiety. It is usually conceded that almost all motives are learned. As such, one would assume that research on learned motives would be of a developmental or historical nature. Paradoxically, the research has tended to be of a cross-sectional nature. This state of affairs has led to great confusion and lack of any systematic clarification of learned motives.

It is generally conceded that motives are arranged in a hierarchy. Each individual has certain motives arranged in priority order and the priority order differs from one individual to another. It would follow that those motives high in the hierarchy would take precedence over those motives lower in the hierarchy. Recently, there has come to be another point of view (4) about the importance of a given motive. Specifically, this view holds that the master motive which underlies all other apparent motives is anxiety. This paper does not embrace such a point of view, but it does concede that anxiety may be present with other motives even if not generic to all of them.

Achievement Motivation

As early as 1950, McClelland (16) began a series of investigations designed to establish a procedure for measuring the achievement motive and also to determine some of the behavioral correlates of this motive. Two major assumptions underlie this research. One is that motivation may have some effects on fantasy or imagery. The other assumption is that motives can be brought into play by suitable conditions and that the degree of arousal can be varied by altering the conditions that cause the arousal. The first assumption gave rise to the basic methodology by which the achievement motive has been measured; namely, that of using a modified TAT technique.

The research having to do with achievement motivation indicates there are at least two components to the achievement motivation, doing things well and doing them alone. Rosen and D'Andrade (20) demonstrated that these two components are related to the degree of achievement training provided by parents to their youngsters and also the degree of independence training provided the youngsters. They concluded that the former component was somewhat the more important of the two. In essence they found that when parents provide high degree of achievement training as well as training in independence, the achievement motive tends to be rather high in youngsters. It should be pointed out that this experiment was conducted with ten-year-old elementary school boys. More recently, Mitchell (18) factor-analyzed the dimensions of the achievement motive. This investigation came about as the result of a larger study of the cultural and situational determinants of achievement motivation for a larger group of college students. The purpose of the study was to determine whether achievement motivation was a unitary construct with invariable meaning, or a complex of relatively independent dimensions. Twenty-nine different indices of achievement motivation were subjected to factor analysis. Ultimately, six factors were identified: academic motivation and efficiency (the only factor highly predictive of academic performance), wish-fulfillment motivation, nonacademic achievement motivation, self-satisfaction, external pressure to achieve, and imputed generalized motivation without attendant effort. What this seems to indicate is that the achievement motive is a rather complex psychological phenomenon which cannot be reduced to a simple construct for immediate application in the classroom.

Other studies have attempted to ascertain behavioral correlates of the achievement motive. For example, Atkinson (1) investigated the affect of individual differences in strength of achievement motive on risk-taking behavior. It was hypothesized that persons having high achievement motivation scores would prefer intermediate risk (or difficulty) to a greater extent than a person having low achievement motivation scores. The subjects for this study were sophomore-level psychology students at the University of Michigan. Achievement motivation was measured by the Test of Insight developed by French, which is a projective test consisting of single sentence descriptions of behavior which the subject is required to "explain." An example: "Tom always lets the other fellow win." An individual who is predominantly achievement oriented would be expected to see Tom's behavior as stemming from that motive and might say, "He's afraid that if he tried to win he would fail so he makes a big show of not trying." Each group of subjects was shown a shuffleboard arrangement consisting of a chalk circle one foot in diameter. Fifteen lines, 1 foot apart, were marked on the floor. The closest line was 1 foot away from the target; the farthest line was 15 feet away. The subjects were given ten practice shots and then told the "big game" would begin. They were told to try to get the highest possible score, the score being the sum of the distances of the hits, in five attempts, from any of the lines. The probability of success was written for each line beside them on the floor.

The results indicated that the high achievement motivation group took more shots from lines closer to the target than the low motivation group. On the first trial of test shots, 64 per cent of the high achievement motivation group shot from 2 feet to 6 feet, while only 39 per cent of the low achievement motivation group shot from this region. Five of the low achievement motivation group but none of the high achievement motivation group shot from the 15-foot line. Men who were high in achievement motivation showed a fairly strong preference for intermediate risk in a game requiring activity in which the outcome was contingent upon successful exercise of skill and a relative preference for intermediate risk in a game of chance where their own skill and confidence could not control the outcome. Men who were low in achievement motivation generally preferred extreme probability alternatives in the same games. It is good armchair sport to speculate as to whether or not these findings are related to pupil behaviors which teachers encounter frequently. For example, is it possible that the student who delays his studying until the night before an examination is engaging in a high risk activity, possibly indicating low achievement motivation? Is it equally possible that the student who postpones working on a long-term assignment, such as a term paper, until the evening before it is due, is also engaging in a high risk activity, again indicative of low achievement motivation?

Another behavior that appears related to achievement motivation is that of delay of gratification. Studies having to do with the relationship between delay of gratification, achievement motivation, and actual achievement are multitudinous. We shall select one of these studies because it seems to be typical of the relationship with which we are primarily concerned. The interesting part of this study is that it was done in a culture somewhat different from that of the United States. Mischel (17) tested the relationship between the need for achievement (achievement motivation) and patterns of preference for reinforcement with respect to delay of gratification. A total of 112 Trinidadian Negro children (68 boys and 44 girls) all in the age group 11–14 were tested in a government school. There were three measures of preference for reinforcement, of which one was a behavioral choice and the other two were questionnaire items. The behavioral measure consisted of a choice between immediate reinforcement or delayed reinforcement in the form of a small candy bar available immediately, or a much larger candy bar for which the subject must wait a week. The two questionnaire items were: (1) I would rather get $10.00 right now than have to wait a whole month and get $30.00 then; (2) I would rather wait to get a much larger gift much later rather than get a smaller one now. Need achievement was measured using the procedure developed by McClelland. The finding that is of particular importance to this discourse is that subjects showing greater preference for the delayed reinforcement had significantly higher need achievement scores than did subjects with lesser preference for delayed reinforcement. This seems to highlight the findings of other researches, namely that persons with high achievement motivation appear to be able to postpone immediate gratification for the sake of long-range goals.

The Affiliation Motive

The research on this motive has attempted to describe the degree to which people are motivated to affiliate or form relationships with other people and the degree to which they move away from affiliation. While not a great deal of research has been done on this motive, that which has been done deals in the main with adult subjects. This, of course, raises the question as to whether the dynamic is developmentally the same in youngsters, and whether the same instruments might be used to measure affiliation motivation with children as are used with adults.

French (7), using a projective test called the Test of Insight, measured achievement and affiliation motivation and the relationship of these motives to behavior in various situations. It will be recalled from an earlier discussion that the Test of Insight contains single sentence descriptions of behavior which the subject is required to "explain." The example was presented of a sentence which reads, "Tom always lets the other fellow win." An individual who is predominantly achievement oriented might be expected to reply, "He's afraid that if he tried to win he would fail so he makes a big show of not trying." A person who is primarily affiliation motivated might say, "He wants to make the other guy feel good." The first aspect of this study tested the hypothesis that groups of subjects with achievement motivation would give better task performances when they were given task-relevant feedback than when they were given feeling feedback; that is, feedback concerned with the interpersonal relations of the group members. All four subjects in any given group had either high achievement and low affiliation motivation scores or the reverse. They were given a task (a story reconstruction problem) to work on and at intervals their progress was discussed with them in either task-relevant terms or in terms of the friendliness of the group members. At the conclusion of the experimental period, each group was given a score based on the amount of work correctly done. The evidence made it clear that subjects with high achievement motivation scores working in a situation where achievement was stressed, and subjects with high affiliation motivation scores working in a situation where good performance was given an affiliation value, made significantly better scores than subjects for whom the inappropriate goal was stressed.

The final aspects of this study tested the hypothesis that the behavior of an individual who must make a work partner choice between a competent nonfriend and a less competent friend will be related to his relative levels of achievement motivation and affiliation motivation. The subjects with high achievement motivation should select the competent nonfriend; those with high affiliation motivation should choose the less competent friend, while those high in both aspects of motivation should show evidence of conflict. The subjects for the experiment were basic airmen. Members of the individual groups ranked each other according to friendship, had a sorting task explained to them as an important concept formation task, and then took the Test of Insight. On the basis of the friendship ratings, groups of four men were formed so that they contained three usual friends and a fourth man toward whom the others expressed indifference. The four worked individually on the sorting test, success on which was under the control of the experimenter. The nonfriend was made to succeed and the others to fail. The subjects were then told that they were to work on a similar task in pairs and were asked to write down their choice of a work partner. There were large differences in the distribution of choices from group to group and all in the predicted direction. That is, subjects with only high achievement motivation made more single choices of the successful subject but those with high scores in both achievement motivation and affiliation motivation made more double choices involving both a friend and a successful subject, while those with only high affiliation scores made more double friend choices.

Epistemic Motivation

In rather simple terms, epistemic motivation can be described as the drive individuals have to seek knowledge. For generations, teachers have described such knowledge-seeking pupils as "inquisitive" or "curious." We prefer to use the term curiosity not only because it has been used by those who research this motive but because its simplicity communicates well.

It is worth noting that the study of curiosity is in its relative infancy, but we are reassured by the fact that some of the investigations of curiosity have been done with school-age children in school situations. Typical of these studies is that done by Mittman and Terrell (19) who sought to determine the effects of three levels of curiosity on the selection by first- and second-grade children of size and form discrimination problems. Each of the 42 subjects was required to learn the size and form of a given object. With each trial he could then connect two successive dots on a dot drawing (either an elephant standing on its hind legs, or a dog begging). The subjects were randomly divided into three groups representing levels of curiosity: high curiosity, moderate curiosity, and low curiosity. For the low curiosity group the experimenter presented the completed dot drawing immediately following the instructions and just prior to the first trial in size and form discrimination. The completed drawing was shown to subjects of the moderate and high curiosity groups after the eighth and twenty-ninth correct responses, respectively, to the size and form discrimination. There was a significant difference in the number of errors committed by Ss of the high, moderate and low curiosity groups. The rank order of the three groups in terms of number of errors committed was low, moderate and high.

What is particularly noteworthy about the study cited above is that the Ss were not selected on the basis of some measures of curiosity. Instead, the environment was structured in such a way as to create uncertainty or curiosity in the children. This would suggest that we may create curiosity by the instructional procedures used.

The study suggests also that high curiosity enables a person to gain greater precision in his learning (fewer errors in size and form discrimination).

As we shall see, many investigations of curiosity, novelty, or uncertainty focus on the degree to which ambiguity is tolerable to the individual. This is reflected in the research done to determine the relation between qualitatively different types of environmental novelty and curiosity in children (23). The subjects were 44 first-grade children, half of whom were boys. Each of the subjects was seated before a mock TV set in which two film strips were placed. The strips contained sets of stimuli presented in different order for a variety of tasks. The mock TV set contained a response panel on which there were a button and a lever. Each time the subject pressed the button, a picture was repeated on the TV screen for 250 milliseconds. Pulling the lever permitted the subject to change to a new picture. The subjects were tested on three tasks: stimulus ambiguity (SA) in which one set of stimuli was patterned and the other random; perceptual conflict (PC) in which two sets of pictures of animals and birds were presented that were congruous or incongruous with their previous perceptions; and conceptual conflict (CC) in which six pictures were utilized which began with a circle and by progressive addition of details ended with a complete picture.

When the data were analyzed it was found that novel (incongruous, random) stimuli elicited significantly more responses than non-novel pictures ($P < -.001$). One could say on the basis of this finding that novelty generally evoked positive approach behavior. There was also a significant difference betwen the boys' and girls' performance. The girls were curious when confronted with an environment lacking in information necessary to complete a spatial or temporal pattern of events, but were relatively lacking in response when incongruous objects were presented them. In short, the girls were found to be more rigid and less curious than the boys. Apparently, rigidity and curiosity are negatively associated.

In the studies cited above, it was assumed that to a certain degree all of the subjects possessed curiosity, and an attempt was made to ascertain the impact of a modified environment upon curiosity. The studies to be discussed take a somewhat different theoretical position in the respect that groups of children are identified as having different degrees of curiosity motivation and their performance on certain types of tasks is assessed.

A recent experiment (15) hypothesized that children with high curiosity amass a larger store of general information than do children of the same intelligence who have low curiosity. The hypothesis was tested by selecting groups of fifth-grade children of high and low curiosity and comparing their scores on a test of general information. The curiosity groups were established on the basis of teacher and peer judgments of curiosity. Intelligence was statistically controlled. The groups were similar in age, popularity, and tested intelligence. A test of general information, consisting of items based on material in encyclopedias available to children, discriminated in favor of the high curiosity children.

A skeptic might raise the question as to whether children with high curiosity retain their knowledge after it has once been learned. Maw and

Maw (13) addressed themselves to such a question in a study using approximately 800 fifth-grade children as subjects. In this study, it was hypothesized that retention is due, at least in part, by the level of curiosity children have about their environment. Children high and low in curiosity were identified, using teacher and peer judgments. The children were given copies of a story which was a collection of strange but true facts, mostly about animal subjects. As far as the children were concerned the experience ended with the experimenter asking if they had liked the story and the one thing they liked best about it. Seven days later, a 40-item true-false test was given the pupils. Tests of significance showed that in every case the difference between the means of the groups was highly significant and always favored the high curiosity group.

The evidence from this study seems to indicate that children with a high level of curiosity either learn more in a given period of time or they retain more of what they experienced. Perhaps the high curiosity children savor the story in their thinking and the details of it are more available to consciousness at the time of testing. It matters little whether there was more learning or greater retention. What is important is that children of comparable intelligence, but differing in curiosity, performed differently in the learning situation.

The usual school is one in which learners take part in a variety of activities over a relatively short period of time. If one were to look for a common element in many of these school experiences he would discover reading to be that element. This would surprise no one since our schools employ the written word as a major means of communication and learning. It is, therefore, entirely proper to inquire as to whether curiosity has some influence on reading comprehension.

Using much the same procedure as in other studies, two groups were established to test the relationship between reading comprehension and high and low curiosity. The groups were matched on sex, race, popularity, and intelligence. A Foolish Sayings Test was developed containing 22 items designed to measure the child's ability to sense important aspects of sentences. Some of the items in the test were common absurdities while others were straightforward statements. When the test results were analyzed it was found that the difference between means of the groups was significant beyond the .05 level (12). This leads to the interpretation that children with high curiosity tend to comprehend the meaning of sentences more accurately than do low curiosity children of equal intelligence.

From these studies it might be deduced that children with a high degree of curiosity motivation move out from a familiar position and attempt to make contact with aspects of the environment that are novel. One might also deduce that children with low curiosity are prone to seek a balanced or homeostatic environment. Such was the basic position of a study (14) conducted to discover how varying degrees of curiosity in children affect their response to balanced and unbalanced stimuli. A group of high curiosity and a group of low curiosity fifth-grade students were established by using teacher judgments, peer judgments, and self-judgments of curiosity. Each child in each group was then administered a test which measured his acceptance of the unbalanced and unfamiliar. The test was a paper-and-pencil instrument consisting of 20 pairs of geometric figures. One figure in each pair was more symmetrical and/or presumably more familiar than the other to the children. Comparison of the test means of the two groups indicated there was a difference significant at the .02 level. The evidence lends support to the idea that children of high curiosity select unbalanced and unfamiliar aspects of their environment more frequently than do fifth-grade children having low curiosity.

Historically, educational research findings have had little impact on the educative process. One reason for this is that we are prone to discount the research because of its alleged sampling deficiencies, the inadequacy of the instruments used, or because it used subjects of one age group. With regard to the last criticism, the research on curiosity has dwelt mainly on the elementary-age child but there are a few studies done with high school or college students. For example, Berlyne (3) used two groups of college freshmen and two groups of high school juniors to investigate the relation between uncertainty and curiosity. A series of 28 quotations, each 1 to 2 sentences in length, was put into a test booklet and students were told that prominent men in English or American literature had made the statements. Three alleged authors were given for each of the quotations but in no case was the true author's name one of those. The subjects were told that 100 high school teachers had read the quotes and indicated which of the 3 names given was the name of the true author. Each quote, therefore, had three authors' names after it, each followed by a number indicating how many teachers had chosen it. Uncertainty was introduced by virtue of the evenness or unevenness of distribution of the numbers that followed each author's name. Some quotes were designated *hi-uncertainty quotations* because the distribution of teachers' choices was 34–33–33 (100 teachers); *medium uncertainty quotations* had a distribution of teacher choices that was 77–13–10; and, the *low uncertainty quotations* had a distribution of teacher choices that was 90–10. The quotations were read aloud, then the students were instructed to go back over the 28 quotations and mark the 12 whose true author they would most like to know. Then they were instructed to rank-order the twelve selections they had made. For all 135 students who participated in the experiment the mean curiosity score for even-distribution (uncertainty) items was 2.98, while the mean curiosity score for uneven distribution quotations was 2.56. The difference in these means was significant at the .01 level. This suggests that curiosity increases with evenness of distribution of alleged teachers' guesses. In turn, it suggests that when alternatives approach the level of equal-probability there is greater uncertainty as to the response that an individual will make.

The research on curiosity does not have immediate recommendations as to how the teacher may improve his instruction, but certain techniques used in the conduct of research sometimes suggest ways in which teaching might be altered so as to improve learning of students. One such suggestion emerges from a study (2) which sought to determine the effects of prequestioning on learning and curiosity. An experimental group of 24 high school biology students received a questionnaire about invertebrate animals prior to any other information about the animals. A control group did not receive the same fore-questionnaire. The 12 animals consisted of 8 familiar and 4 unfamiliar of which 2 of the latter were fictitious. Following this, both the experimental and control groups were given 120 word paragraphs describing the animals (information input). After the word paragraphs had been read a 48-item test was given each subject. The test was constructed in such a way that the subjects answered either that they were certain of the answer from previous knowledge or that they were surprised.

It was hypothesized that the experimental group would learn more effectively and would recall more answers than the control group, because their curiosity would be aroused by the fore-questionnaire. The findings support this hypothesis inasmuch as the experimental group made 32.41 correct responses on the posttest and the control group made 27.15 correct responses. The difference in these was significant at the .01 level of probability. Apparently, the prequestions did arouse curiosity and the surprising statements were more likely to be recalled as answers in the posttest than other statements. The prequestioning apparently "tuned" the organism by arousing curiosity which, in turn, predisposed it toward acquisition of information.

One might take the position that curiosity is an inherent human factor and, therefore, it should be manifest in varying degrees at all levels of intellectual ability. Conversely, one might argue that curiosity and intellectual ability are negatively correlated, and that low intelligence makes a person less sensitive to dissonant elements in his environment. The dissonant elements are the genesis of curiosity. Spitz and Hoats (23) contribute evidence that supports the latter point of view. Using a group of institutionalized high-grade retardates, a group of equal CA normals and a group of equal MA normals, they made comparisons as to "perceptual curiosity" of the subjects. The Ss were shown two patterns of a pair side by side for 3 seconds. One pattern of the pair was balanced and/or symmetrical or less irregular (LI), while the other pattern was more unbalanced and/or more irregular (MI). The subject was allowed after the 3-second viewing to press a button and to see for as long as he chose, either pattern of the pair. Thus, two scores were obtained, the pattern chosen and the length of time the chosen pattern was retained for viewing. There was a marked tendency for Ss to choose the less irregular over the more irregular patterns in all categories, even though there was variation among the groups. One of these variations was that normals, to a greater extent than the retardates, tended to look at complex stimuli relatively longer than at simpler stimuli.

Perhaps the findings of this study deviate with those of others because the methodology was different. Yet, it was not too different and, therefore, the study leads one to speculate as to why the retardates avoided the asymmetrical or uneven figures and apparently were more attracted to the redundant and balanced figures. It should be noted that balance rather than amount of information was the key factor in selection since each pattern of the pair contained the *same* amount of information but its arrangement was different. A brief excursion into the realm of "hunches" might suggest that the world of the retardate is one of relative chaos and complexity; his need therefore is to bring stability and balance into the picture. The work of Griffith, Spitz, and Lipman (8) on the difficulty of the retardate in neatly categorizing incoming information is related to the idea expressed above.

Attempts to Influence Motivation

Because of the very nature of the classroom setting, there is little question that teachers have impact on the motivation of learners. What impact they have is much less well known, but a variety of researches have attempted to ascertain this. One such study is that conducted by Kennedy and Willcut (10), who investigated the effects of praise and blame on a discrimination task under the variables of grade, intelligence, sex, race, social class, school, and examiner. The 720 subjects in the study were divided into 3 reward conditions: praise, blame, and no incentive; 4 grade levels: 2, 4, 7, and 10; three levels of intelligence: high, medium, and low; 2 sexes and 2 races. Thirty-two oddity-problems stimulus cards presented four patterns, one of which was different from the other three. The task was to identify the odd pattern as quickly as possible by depressing the correct key on a discrimination box. Subjects were administered the 32 stimulus cards followed by the experimental reward condition and then a second trial was given on the same stimulus cards. The same procedure was followed with the other two groups except that one group was given blame after the first trial and the third group received no incentive. The reaction time between the stimulus card appearing on the viewing screen and the depression of the key on the discrimination box was the criterion measure. The findings indicate that all subjects regardless of sex, race, grade level, or level of intelligence reacted to praise with decreased mean reaction time from trial one to trial two. Likewise, all subjects reacted to no incentive with decreased mean reaction time from trial one to trial two. Also, all subjects, regardless of sex, race, grade level, or level of intelligence responded to blame with increased mean reaction time on the second trial with some few exceptions. The results of this study indicate that the effects of praise and blame are quite obvious and quite consistent.

The impact of the teacher upon the motivation of youngsters became apparent in an investigation by Sechrest (21). Interviews were conducted with 128 kindergarten, first-, second-, and third-grade children about the experiences they were having in school. An attempt was made to gain knowledge about the motivational factors operating in the classroom and their effects on the children. The interviews were relatively structured and consisted of ten questions requiring an extensive reply by the child and ten additional questions on specific motivational procedures which could be answered "yes" or "no." Examples of the questions are "When you begin a new lesson at school, what kinds of things does your teacher do to get you started?" and "What does your teacher do that makes it fun to learn new things?" The results indicated that young children are able to report reasonably well the things that go on at school. It would appear that one of the most powerful motivating factors available to the teacher is her attention to the child, which she may give or withhold at will. Children are sensitive to the motivational devices such as stars and marks on their papers and also seem very likely to be affected very much by praise or reproof administered to other children. Verbal feedback, particularly of a positive nature, is apparently the most salient technique by which the teacher keeps the children motivated; but a substantial number of children mentioned that their teacher used nonvocal ways of giving them information about their performance. Interestingly enough, the use of nonverbal techniques apparently declined by the third grade. If this decline is general it would seem that teachers deny themselves a great means by which they can influence the motivation of students through nonverbal techniques.

To this point we have discussed the way in which a variety of motives have been measured by a variety of techniques. No matter the motive and no matter the technique of assessment, none of the studies dealt with the learner's perception of his motivation, which presumably could be an important factor in motivation and in learning. One study that considered this dimension was conducted by Fisher (6) in which eighth-grade students were separated into all-boy or all-girl classes for 1 hour per day for English instruction. A hypothesis of this study was that since boys would be removed from the unfair competition of the girls and since girls would be removed from the retarding effect of the boys, English achievement for both sexes would increase. It was also hypothesized that with increase in achievement, the pupils' perception of their motivation would become more positive. This was assessed by an instrument devised by one of the investigators which measured one's self-concept as a learner. One of the four components of this scale is the youngster's perception of his motivation. He responded on a Likert type-scaling to such items as "I am usually eager to go to class," "I do only the work I have to do and don't to extra work," and "I do things without being told several times." On a comparison of premeasures and postmeasures for both boys and girls no significant differences were found on the motivation index of this scale. This was not surprising for in only one out of five dimensions of English achievement was there any gain and that was by girls. It should be noted that teachers were not instructed to change their teaching style in this experiment. This study would seem to suggest that grouping alone without some type of different teacher intervention has little impact upon pupil's perception of their motivation and also upon pupil achievement.

Much earlier in this discourse it was mentioned that most motives are learned. But the question of when a motive is learned in relation to a certain task is considerably less clear. Many teachers believe that a youngster must be motivated *before* he learns. They are much less aware of the fact that motivation may be acquired *while* learning. That is, the youngster not only learns the curriculum content at a given moment but at the same instant he is acquiring or learning something about his own motivational pattern. This would seem to be exemplified in the study conducted by Kolodner (11) which compared the self-concepts of nonachieving readers and achieving readers in order to test the relationship between self-concept and reading disabilities in children. The sample consisted of 15 boys in grades 4, 5, and 6 with average or higher than average IQ, and a matched comparison group of 15 boys who demonstrated ability to read at what the school called a "normal level." The Self-Concept As a Learner scale (SCAL) was used to measure the boys' image of self as a learner. The four components of this test are: motivation, task orientation, problem solving or intellectual ability, and class membership. On all four components of this test there was found to be a significant difference at the 1 per cent level between the self-concepts of nonachieving and achieving readers. This study did not determine if an initial low concept interferes with learning ability or if the self-concept falls after a child has had difficulty with reading. Nevertheless, it gives some evidence that youngsters are achieving at levels commensurate with their estimate of their motivation and apparently are behaving consistently with that estimation.

In summary, this paper has presented various aspects of motivation. Also presented was a cognitive dissonance theory of motivation. Implicitly the position was taken that the research cited was related to the cognitive dissonance theory.

References

1. Atkinson, J. W., "The Achievement Motive, Goal Seeking and Probability Preferences," *Journal of Abnormal & Social Psychology*, LX, No. 1 (1960).

2. Berlyne, D. E., "An Experimental Study of Human Curiosity," *British Journal of Psychology*, XLII, No. 3 (1951).

3. ——, "Uncertainty and Epistemic Curiosity," *ibid.*, LIII, No. 1 (1962).

4. Cofer, C. N. and M. H. Appley, *Motivation: Theory and Research.* New York: John Wiley & Sons, Inc., 1964.

5. Festinger, L., *A Theory of Cognitive Dissonance.* Stanford, Calif.: Stanford University Press, 1957.

6. Fisher, J. K., "An Investigation of the Relationship Between Separation by Sex of Eighth-Grade Students and English Achievement and Self-Concept." Unpublished doctoral dissertation, University of Maryland, 1964.

7. French, Eliz., "Some Laboratory Studies of the Role of Motivation in Behavior." Air Force Human Engineering, Personnel, and Training Research. *National Academy of Sciences*, Publication 516, 1958.

8. Griffith, B. C., H. H. Spitz, and R. S. Lipman, "Verbal Mediation and Concept Formations in Retarded and Normal Subjects," *Journal of Experimental Psychology*, LVIII (1959), 247–51.

9. Johnson, Thos., Rhoda Feigenbaum, and Marcia Weiby, "Some Determinants and Consequences of the Teacher's Perception of Causation." Unpublished manuscript, University of Wisconsin, 1963.

10. Kennedy, W. A. and H. C. Willcutt, "Motivation of School Children." Unpublished research report, Florida State University, 1964.

11. Kolodner, F. K., "The Self-Concept of Nonachieving Readers." Unpublished Master of Arts thesis, University of Maryland, 1964.

12. Maw, Wallace H. and Ethel W. Maw, "Children's Curiosity as an Aspect of Reading Comprehension," *The Reading Teacher*, XV, No. 4 (1962), 236–40.

13. ——, "Information Recognition by

Children with High and Low Curiosity," *Educational Research Bulletin*, XL, No. 8 (November 1961).

14. ——, "Nonhomeostatic Experiences as Stimuli of Children with High Curiosity," *California Journal of Educational Research*, XII, No. 2 (March 1961).

15. ——, "Relationship Between Curiosity and Scores on a Test of General Information," *Association for Research in Growth Relationships*, I (1960), 27–32.

16. McClelland, D. C., *et al., The Achievement Motive.* New York: Appleton-Century-Crofts, 1953.

17. Mischel, W., "Delay of Gratification, Need for Achievement, and Acquiescence in Another Culture," *Journal of Abnormal & Social Psychology*, LXII (1961).

18. Mitchell, J. V., "An Analysis of the Factorial Dimensions of the Achievement Motivation Construct," *Journal of Educational Psychology*, LII, No. 4 (1961).

19. Mittman, L. R. and Glenn Terrell, "An Experimental Study of Curiosity in Children." Unpublished paper read at Society for Research and Child Development, April 1963.

20. Rosen, B. C. and R. D'Andrade, "The Psychosocial Origins of Achievement Motivation," *Sociometry*, XXII (1959).

21. Sechrest, L. B., "The Motivation in School of Young Children: Some Interview Data," *Journal of Experimental Education*, XXX, No. 4 (1962), 327–35.

22. Smock, Charles D. and B. G. Holt, "Children's Reactions to Novelty: An Experimental Study of Curiosity Motivation," *Child Development*, XXXIII (1962), 631–42.

23. Spitz, H. H. and D. L. Hoats, "Experiments on Perceptual Curiosity Behavior in Mental Retardates." Final report on NIMH M-4533. Bordentown, N. J.: E. R. Johnstone Training and Research Center, 1961.

24. Young, P. T., *Motivation and Emotion; a Survey of the Determinants of Human and Animal Activity.* New York: John Wiley & Sons, Inc., 1961, p. 24.

53. A DESCRIPTIVE APPROACH TO CLASSROOM MOTIVATION

EVAN R. KEISLAR

In developing a useful conceptual structure for education, the topic of motivation appears to require a central position. And yet motivational terms are exceedingly difficult to clarify; in fact, in psychology itself the status of the word "motivation" is very unclear. Richard Littman[1] has given a definition for motivation which appears to comprise no more than what investigators have at one time or another included under this term; the definition, as Littman himself points out, unfortunately encompasses just about everything which psychologists study.

In this report it is proposed that, for certain kinds of problems in the classroom, motivation be discussed without recourse to the usual constructs such as "motive" or "interest." Some motivational phenomena might be treated profitably in purely descriptive terms, that is, with words which refer only to observable events and their mathematical relations. As an illustration of the application of this purely descriptive approach to motivation a series of experiments is briefly reviewed. This attack upon problems of motivation is to be evaluated in terms of its usefulness in providing hypotheses for the control of student behavior, a process important for teacher and experimenter alike. When the utility of other motivational words becomes more clearly established, this descriptive approach could at such times becomes easily enriched.

Motivation as Stimulus Control

Motivation is usually assessed in education by noting the kind and amount of behavior of the learner. When we say that a student is motivated, we

Evan R. Keislar, "A Descriptive Approach to Classroom Motivation," Journal of Teacher Education, *XI, No. 2 (June 1960), 310–15. Reprinted by permission.*

[1] Richard A. Littman, "Motives, History, and Causes," in M. R. Jones (ed.), *Nebraska Symposium on Motivation* (Lincoln, Nebraska: University of Nebraska Press, 1958), pp. 114–68.

generally mean that he is or probably will be active. Pupils who read a good deal are said to be "interested" in reading, those who are aggressive have a "need" for aggression, students who study many hours a week have a strong achievement "motive," and persons who answer a set of items in certain ways have a particular vocational "interest." If motivational terms such as interest, motive, desire, goal, level of aspiration are inferred entirely from behavior, they have little use in attempts to produce such behavior. Such circularity of reasoning is found, for example, when it is said, "You can tell that Bill is interested in reading, since he spends so much time at it! His interest in reading is what makes him read so much."

As descriptions of observable behavior, these motivational terms possess considerable value. In the first place they are useful in predicting other behavior. On the basis of correlational data we may be able to predict, better than chance at least, that a student with a particular interest score on some test will engage in certain other kinds of activities, or that a child who says he is interested in tractors will read books about tractors. Secondly, such information about the "motives" of students can be used to supply parameters in the statement of relationships dealing with control; this description of prior behavior is therefore useful in the same way that data are about the student's age, intelligence, and socioeconomic status.

But when we infer, on the basis of observations alone, some internal motivational state, the usefulness of such language in education may well be questioned. Even from a practical point of view, a word like "interest" often adds little to the teacher's effectiveness. For example, it isn't very helpful for a teacher to make the hypothesis, "If I arouse my pupils' interest in arithmetic they will do their problems regularly," if such interest can be identified only by the way the pupils act. Since it is still necessary to clarify what must be done to "arouse" the interest, she might just as well formulate a hypothesis which suggests what she must do to get pupils to do their problems; she does not need to use the word "interest" at all.

Motivational terms will have far greater utility for education when they refer to antecedent as well as consequent conditions. In other words, we must identify the conditions which have to occur before the child is active or "motivated." The establishment of these conditions will then permit control of student behavior for teacher and experimenter alike; the conditions are then said to have "stimulus control."[2]

In the series of investigations being reported there was an attempt to distinguish "motivating" stimuli from other kinds of stimuli. Incentives, or "motivating" stimuli, control broad classes of behavior. General instructions may be regarded as stimuli which control behavior classes of intermediate breadth while cues are stimuli which control very narrow classes. While this concept of "breadth of class of behavior" is admittedly imprecise, it suggests that on occasion teachers might be helped by viewing their presentation in terms of incentives, instructions, and cues. This classification system may have "engineering" value in some school

[2] B. F. Skinner, *Science and Human Behavior* (New York: The Macmillan Company, 1953).

situations; in many others it may be quite adequate simply to describe the situations students face without regard to these categories.

Loosely speaking, an incentive may be regarded as a "promise" of a reinforcement. A grade of "A," social approval, or money are not incentives for a student; these are the reinforcements. The situations which "promise" these things are the incentives. Although a stimulus may become both an incentive and a reinforcement, when we refer to it as an incentive we are emphasizing its property of arousing a broad class of behavior subsequently. (Which particular responses in this class will be emitted depend upon the other stimuli, the instructions, and the cues which are present.) When we refer to a stimulus as a reinforcement we are talking about its usefulness in strengthening behavior which has just previously occurred. Parenthetically, it should be noted that the term "incentive" is here used with about the same functions as the term "drive-arousing stimulus" proposed by Dollard and Miller.[3]

Development of Stimulus Control of Problem-Solving Behavior

While it is valuable to continue normative studies of our pupils to find out what stimuli are effective incentives for them, it is even more important to find out how new incentives are developed. An attempt was made to conceptualize one such process in Experiment I. The hypothesis for this experiment was that if a neutral stimulus (a bell and light combination) is present when the child is reinforced for solving a variety of problems but is not present when he is not reinforced, then this stimulus will gain control of the problem-solving behavior; it will become an incentive.

Twenty-two second-grade children were tested individually. When presented with a picture card, each child moved a knob along any of three grooves. Moving the knob in the correct groove was reinforced with marbles to be exchanged later for trinkets. For each of three different cards, the children learned to give the correct response a variable number of times only when a bell and light were presented with the card; responses to the card alone were never reinforced.

On the test, in which no responses were reinforced, each child was shown a new card for just one trial. Half the children were presented with the bell and light (the incentive) in addition; the other half were given no such stimulus pattern. The number of responses each child gave before stopping was then recorded. Ten of the group with the incentive present and one of the group without the incentive were above the median ($p < .01$). Since the children were clearly more active in this new problem when the incentive was present than in its absence, we may conclude that, under these conditions, by associating a neutral stimulus with reinforcement in a variety of problems, its presence in a new task will bring about problem-solving activity.

This descriptive approach to motivation may have some utility in suggesting hypotheses for researcher and teacher. For the researcher it means that particular attention must be

[3] J. Dollard and N. E. Miller, *Personality and Psychotherapy* (New York: McGraw-Hill Book Company, 1950).

given to the prior reinforcements his subjects have had with the stimuli present during the experiment. In Hurlock's classic study,[4] for example, pupils who had been praised for several days were found to do better on an arithmetic test than pupils who had been reproved. That this may reflect nothing about a general change of skill in arithmetic may easily be tested by changing the incentives (but not the instructions or cues); if, after the experiment, the same type of test had been given by the local Kiwanis club with a promise of bicycles for superior performance, both groups might have done equally well.

Many school children appear inactive in school situations although they act differently on the playground or in the shop. Instead of saying that these children are "disinterested" or "nonmotivated," it may be more helpful to the teacher to say that the school setting is no incentive for such children. She might act upon a hypothesis which states that if such children are provided with a wealth of appropriately administered reinforcements in the classroom setting, they will participate actively in school.

Stimulus Control and the Energizing Function of Drive

It will be objected that the illustration of "motivating stimulus" given in the previous experiment was inadequate, that the bell and light merely informed the child when it would be worth his effort, or that the "real motivators" were somewhere inside the child. But we do not yet have any way of determining the "real motivators." If these motive states are inferred entirely from behavior, they have little value for control. In the field of primary motivation such as hunger, the energizing function of drive is a respectable intervening variable, anchored between data on antecedent conditions such as hours of deprivation and data on consequent conditions like eating behavior. But even here Estes[5] has proposed a stimulus-response theory of drive which places the energizing function in a position subordinate to that of stimulus. When we come to secondary or learned motivation, the energizing function of drives is even more confused. In very few instances have we a way of using secondary drive as a true intervening variable. Most of the time it is simply a construct which offers no value for the purposes of control of behavior. By regarding the stimuli as the "motivators" we can move ahead with our research in certain areas of education without waiting for psychologists of motivation to clarify the nature of secondary drives.

Learning Sets

A central "motivational" problem in education is that of getting students to change their behavior as a result of being presented with information or a pattern of stimuli. For example, when students are given a lecture, shown a film, presented with printed material, or provided with a demonstration, it is hoped that they will learn (i.e., change their behavior) as

4 Elizabeth Hurlock, "An Evaluation of Certain Incentives Used in School Work," *Journal of Educational Psychology*, XVI (1925), 145–59.

5 W. K. Estes, "Stimulus-Response Theory of Drive," in M. R. Jones, *op. cit.* pp. 35–68.

a result. This "motivational" problem has been frequently stated as one of teaching students to "pay attention," to "study hard," to "concentrate," or to "remember." With a descriptive approach to motivation, the above problem is regarded as one of developing stimulus control of a learning set. "Motivating students to study or to pay attention" is thus looked upon as a matter of presenting stimuli which control the appropriate learning sets.

A learning set was defined in this study as the relationship between a pattern of stimuli, which is not contingent upon the subject's responses, and a change in operant behavior. The distinctive feature of a learning set, as used in this study, is that learning results from sheer exposure to stimuli; there is apparently no three-term contingency (stimulus, response, and reinforcement) recognized generally as essential for operant learning. It is true that one can observe an orientation of sense receptors to the information; the student, for example, stops doing other things and looks directly at the material. But every teacher is familiar with the danger of assuming that students learn just because they appear attentive. The teacher (or experimenter) usually observes neither the response students ultimately learn to make nor the reinforcements contingent upon such responses. While one may explain such learning by assuming that students reinforce themselves for their covert responses or by discussing the phenomena in terms of some form of cognitive activity, the pressing problem, at the operational or practical level, is to find out under what conditions a set to learn is acquired and displayed. The position taken in this study is that a stimulus can acquire control of a learning set in exactly the same fashion as stimuli which control problem-solving behavior.

Development of Stimulus Control of a Learning Set

The general hypothesis of Experiments II and III was that a learning set (this relationship) is brought under the control of a stimulus through a reinforcement program. For example, if students exhibit this set in a variety of situations where a common distinctive stimulus is present and if they are reinforced for the appropriate learning in each case, this stimulus will acquire control of the learning set. In other words, students will learn if this stimulus is present, or, this stimulus will act as an incentive and will "motivate" them to learn. On the other hand, if subjects learn in a variety of situations where a distinctive stimulus is present but are not reinforced for this learning, this stimulus will lose control of the learning set; subjects will not learn when this stimulus is present, or, in this situation they will remain "apathetic" or "nonmotivated."

In Experiment II, 22 second-grade children (not those used in Experiment I, of course) were tested individually. Each subject was shown, through a window in a panel board, a series of 48 "information" cards, each of which presented pictures and colors to be associated. After each information card was exposed, there followed randomly either a blank card or a set of question cards, one question card for each pair presented in the information card. If the pupil indicated the correct color he received a marble from the automatic dispenser.

For half the subjects a green light was turned on when the information card was exposed, if the pupil was to be questioned on this card; a white light with black stripes was on when no questions, just the blank card, were to follow. The functions of these two lights were reversed for the other half of the subjects.

Information Card 49 was presented with a "test" light and Information Card 50 with a "no-test" light but three questions followed each information card, one question for each pair on the card. To counterbalance item difficulty these two cards and their three questions were interchanged for half the group. Fourteen children learned more when the "test" light was on; two children learned more when the "no-test" light was on. This difference, when tested by the Wilcoxon matched-pairs signed-ranks method, is significant at the .01 level. It may be concluded that these children learned more from information accompanied by a light previously associated with a test than they did from information presented with a light with no such association. Assuming that the test provided opportunities for reinforcement, the principles of operant conditioning appear to apply to the development of stimulus control of a learning set.

Effect of Knowledge of Results upon a Learning Set

In Experiment III an attempt was made to assess the effect of giving knowledge of results upon the learning set. Knowledge of results usually includes both positive and negative reinforcements. The material, apparatus, and general procedure were identical with the previous experiment, but the experimental and control conditions both involved test questions; pupils were given questions following each information card. When one light (the "KR" light) was turned on with the information card, pupils were given marbles for each right answer to the test question on this information. When the other light (the "No-KR" light) was on with the information card, pupils were never informed in any way as to whether their answers were right or wrong.

The criterion consisted of the nine questions on the last three information cards for each light condition. The pupils obtained a score of 6.3 when the "KR" light was on, and 4.8 when the "No-KR" light was on. This difference is significant at the .05 level. (Using the last half of the cards, seven under each light condition, the difference was proportionately about the same but was significant at the .01 level.) It has been well known that knowledge of results is an important factor in the acquisition of specific behavior. But the findings of Experiment III point up the fact that knowledge of results can also strengthen a learning set.

Shaping of a Learning Set

In the previous two experiments, the emphasis was placed upon the development of stimulus control of a learning set. Although this set to learn may have been altered, the relationship between the stimuli presented on the information card and the kind of change of behavior was not deliberately modified. This relationship was brought under the control of one stimulus and not another. In other words, pupils were taught *when* to learn.

In Experiment IV an attempt was made to alter the relationship, to modify what students learned. Students were reinforced for learning certain kinds of things from the information and not other kinds. This process of shaping a learning set may be regarded as analogous to response differentiation. In this experiment, therefore, students were taught *what* to learn.

What most high school and college students learn from their study in a course is less likely to be influenced by the stated objectives of the course, objectives which are often expressed in "high-sounding and broad" terms. Students are far more likely to learn those things for which they get reinforced on course examinations. The learning sets of students are shaped largely by the kind of reinforcements teachers actually provide. The specific hypothesis of Experiment IV was that pupils would learn better (1) the kind of information from a paragraph for which they had been previously tested than they would (2) the kind for which they had not been previously tested. Forty sixth- and seventh-grade children were tested individually. Each was presented with 22 paragraphs of pseudohistorical information containing a date, a name, and a place as well as three reasons for this event. Immediately after each paragraph was exposed, one half of the group was tested on the date, name, and place; the other half was tested on the reasons. Correct answers were immediately reinforced.

On Paragraph No. 23 both groups were asked questions on both kinds of material (order of presentation of the two sets of test items being counterbalanced). The mean score (1.5) made by the group on the questions about the information of the type on which they had previously been tested was higher, at the .05 level, than the mean score (1.0) on the questions of the other kind. It was concluded that, at this level of confidence, the learning set of these pupils in reading these paragraphs was altered by a program of differential reinforcement; the two groups of pupils had acquired different learning sets for this situation.

When students are shown the same film, given the same lecture, or taken on the same field trip, different students learn different things. This is often "explained" by saying that students differ in their "interests" and therefore "pay attention" to different things. But such language is of little value in making education more effective; it merely describes the phenomena we observe. It is far more fruitful, for purposes of controlling what students learn, to suggest that such learning sets have been shaped differently by virtue of different reinforcement histories. With appropriate reinforcement programs such learning sets might be altered and improved to make the students' educational experiences more effective.

Conclusion

This discussion of motivation has emphasized the stimuli in the presence of which the child is active or learns. But it has also stressed the fact that such stimuli function as they do because of prior reinforcements. The crucial aspects of motivation are therefore to be found in the systems of reinforcements which a school provides for pupils. Such a discussion of reinforcements already has been extensively presented by other writers, notably B. F. Skinner,[6] with implications for education. The descriptive approach presented in this paper may, however, bring many research problems in education more clearly within the framework of reinforcement theory.

[6] *Op. cit.*

ACTIVITIES

Pre-Test

1. Students will probably perform at a higher level in class if the teacher stresses:

a. achievement of each student
b. interpersonal relations of class members

2. Which of the following groups would probably retain information the longest:

a. curious children
b. very bright children
c. children with average intelligence
d. children who do not feel threatened by their physical or social environment

3. Which of the following most probably would motivate students to work harder at assigned tasks:

a. praise only
b. judicious mixing of praise and criticism
c. criticism only
d. comments which indicate neither praise nor blame on the part of the teacher

4. A person's motives are:

a. inherent
b. learned
c. determined by his physical environment
d. impossible to determine

5. An operational definition of motivation would most clearly be associated with:

a. how a person does something
b. if a person does something
c. why a person does something
d. when a person does something

6. When a teacher is interested in motivating his students, he must be primarily concerned with:

a. getting a person started on the assigned task
b. keeping a person working on the assigned task
c. having a person perform the assigned task to the maximum of his ability
d. providing a task which can be completed by his students

7-10. If you were planning a research project for your classroom to test student motivation, which of the following would you consider (mark "a") as plausible hypotheses; which would you *not* consider (mark "b") as hypotheses worthy of testing:

7. If I arouse my pupils' interest in my subject they will complete their homework assignments regularly.

8. Children who are active in sports or other extra-curricular activities, but who perform poorly in my class, are not motivated in my class.

9. If stimuli related to both the students and the subject to be learned are presented, then the subject will be learned more thoroughly than if such stimuli does not precede the teaching of the subject.

10. If reinforcements are presented at specified periods while a subject is being taught, then students will learn that subject more thoroughly than if such reinforcement is not presented.

11. Which of the following pre-conditions would you hypothesize as being the more effective stimulant to action:

a. need
b. satisfaction

12. Once a person has begun performing a task, which of the following conditions will more likely motivate him to continue:

a. constancy
b. variety

13. Which group is more likely to avoid strange or fear-invoking situations:

a. children who have been roughly treated
b. children who have been accustomed to an emotionally warm environment

14. Which of the following is more apt to reduce a person's facility for processing information into his cognitive structure:

a. external stimulus which is emotionally threatening, anxiety arousing
b. presentation of material which is intellectually incongruous or unique

15. Which of the following most probably will be stimulated to explore a subject:

a. a person who knows nothing about it
b. a person who has limited knowledge about it
c. a person who has much knowledge of it

END OF PRE-TEST

16. The questions in the pre-test above were intended to serve as a motivating device after the advice of Waetjen's article. To what extent did this device work for you?

Suggested Answers for Pre-Test

1. b	6. d	11. a
2. a	7. b	12. a
3. a and d	8. a	13. b
4. b	9. a	14. b
5. c	10. a	15. b

17. Observe several teachers beginning their lessons. Identify ways these teachers attempted to establish learning sets in their students.

18. Is there a relationship between who asks questions in a classroom and who is motivated to learn the curriculum content? What implications does your answer have for you as a teacher?

19. What is the relationship between Waetjen's description of what is transpiring in Fig. 3 and J. Raths' description of the rationale behind ad-

vanced organizers? Herrick's organizing center? Bruner's discussion of discovery?

20. What implication for motivating students in the classroom can you see in the findings of Waimon ("Feedback in the Classroom," found in Chapter 2)?